CW01081007

CARDIGAN

RA

Llangeitho

Howell
Harris

Pantycelyn

Trefeca

BRECKNOCK

GLAMORGAN

MONMOUTH

David
Jones

sea

Newport

Llan-gan

Cardiff

South Wales

# *The*
# CALVINISTIC METHODIST FATHERS OF WALES

---

## VOLUME ONE

Gyda llawer iawn o ddiolch
am bob help a chefnogaeth.

John Aaron

Mehefin 2008.

A statue of Daniel Rowland, Llangeitho

# *The*
# CALVINISTIC METHODIST
# FATHERS OF WALES

## VOLUME ONE

## JOHN MORGAN JONES
## AND WILLIAM MORGAN

### *Translated by* JOHN AARON

## THE BANNER OF TRUTH TRUST

THE BANNER OF TRUTH TRUST
3 Murrayfield Road, Edinburgh EH12 6EL, UK
P.O. Box 621, Carlisle, PA 17013, USA

*

Originally published in Welsh as
*Y Tadau Methodistaidd,* vol. 1, 1890
First Banner of Truth edition 2008

© John Aaron 2008

ISBN-13: 978 0 85151 942 5

*

Typeset in 10.5 / 13 pt Adobe Caslon
at the Banner of Truth Trust
Printed in the U.S.A. by
Versa Press, Inc.,
East Peoria, IL

# CONTENTS

# Illustrations

Illustrations from the original Welsh edition have been inserted between pp. 108–9, 356–7, and 651–2.

# TRANSLATOR'S PREFACE

Some might question whether there is any point in translating and publishing a work that was written over a hundred years ago and has never been reprinted since. Surely if there was any benefit or blessing to be found in the book for preachers, historians or believers interested in the history of the Christian Church, it would have been often reprinted since it first saw the light of day.

To think in this way is to forget the spiritual and intellectual condition of Wales during the last hundred years. Already, in 1890, when the first volume of *Y Tadau Methodistaidd* (*The [Calvinistic] Methodist Fathers [of Wales]*) was published, most Welsh ministers were liberal in their theology, and over the next thirty years or so they taught their congregations to question the authority of the Bible, to rationalize away the supernatural nature of Christianity, and to find in man himself the cause of all religious impressions and spiritual beliefs. As a consequence, the reaction of the professional clergy and academics of the land to the Welsh Revival of 1904 was mixed to say the least. Similarly, a book that described in detail God's dealings in the past with his appointed servants (the vast majority of them of little ecclesiastical standing and education), his irresistible power accompanying the preached word, his sudden entrance into the hearts of countless Welsh men and women, his changing of the morals and culture of a nation in a relatively short period – such a book held no attraction for most of the religious leaders of the day. The academics, if they gave any attention at all to the Methodist Revival in Wales, preferred to explain it in social, economic and cultural terms. The best known twentieth-century general history of modern Wales, published in 1950, is *The History of Modern Wales*, by David Williams, Professor of Welsh History at Aberystwyth University. It is a book of 300 pages, but deals with a hundred years or so of Methodist activity in about 14 pages of comment. He suggests that the reasons for the success of the movement are many: 'the appeal of novelty', 'the great release of energy' due to the formation of a new denomination, 'the great organisational ability of Thomas Charles', and so on. The fruit of the Revival is judged to be mixed:

The moral fibre of the people was stiffened, and they became more law-abiding. But they lost that carefree joyousness ... They became obsessed with the thoughts of death and of the fires of hell ... the people's concerns with the world to come, while it may have saved the country from social disturbance and anarchy, rendered them apathetic to the need for reform.

There were to be no twentieth-century reprints therefore of *Y Tadau Methodistaidd*. Nevertheless, the considerations which encouraged the authors, John Morgan Jones and William Morgan, in their labours are still valid today.

*Firstly*, in the Scriptures God's people are called upon often to remember, study and learn from God's glorious actions in the past. Not to do so is to deprive him of the praise and thanksgiving due to his name and to deprive ourselves of much comfort and encouragement.

You shall remember well what the LORD your God did to Pharaoh and to all Egypt: the great trials which your eyes saw, the signs and the wonders, the mighty hand and the outstretched arm, by which the LORD your God brought you out (*Deut.* 7:18–19).

I will remember the years of the right hand of the Most High. I will remember the works of the LORD; surely I will remember your wonders of old. I will also meditate on all your work, and talk of your deeds. Your way, O God, is in the sanctuary; who is so great a God as our God?' (*Psa.* 77:10–13).

The Methodist Revival in Wales provides one of the most remarkable examples in church history of what the prophet Isaiah describes as a nation being born at once, Zion travailing and bringing forth her children (*Isa.* 66:7–9). The accounts of such revivals, wherever they occur and in whatever period of history, should be essential reading for Christians.

*Secondly*, the experiences related by the men and women caught up in these periods of refreshing from the right hand of the Lord provide unique lessons for his people today.

As a consequence of the awakenings through which the Welsh Methodists passed, their sense of God's reality, power and love had a profound effect on so many aspects of their Christian life. In areas such as conviction, assurance, love, joy, witness and, especially, preaching, their testimony so often was of having learnt more in a few days of revival than in all the preceding years of their Christian profession. It is true that their experiences were *in essence* the same as those of every believer in every age, yet *in intensity* they far surpassed that which is generally the case today. To read their words in journals, diaries and letters is to be particularly struck by their continual awareness of the ministry of the Holy Spirit in his Church. For no one is this more relevant than for God's ministers and preachers.

In this context, Iain H. Murray has recorded for us the response of Dr Martyn Lloyd-Jones to this book:

> For sheer stimulus and enjoyment there were no volumes which he prized more highly than *Y Tadau Methodistaidd* which relate (in Welsh) the lives of the fathers of Welsh Calvinistic Methodism. They were constantly in his hands in the early years (*David Martyn Lloyd-Jones, The First Forty Years*, Edinburgh: Banner of Truth, 1982, p. 156).

And more than one minister has written of how Lloyd-Jones, at ministers' conferences, would explain that what kept him from identifying completely with the theological tradition of Princeton – though he had great admiration for such men as the Alexanders, the Hodges, B. B. Warfield and Gresham Machen – was his knowledge of the theological tradition of his own land, with its emphasis on the awakening work of the Holy Spirit as demonstrated in the ministries of preachers such as Howell Harris, Daniel Rowland, William Williams and John Elias.

A *third reason* might be added for studying this and similar periods in church history, though it would not have been so apparent in the authors' day. Men and women of the secular, unbelieving Wales of today – typical of so many of the countries of the western world – might not find any relevance in the spiritual experiences of men and women in past centuries. In particular they might not accept the validity of testimonies to the supernatural activities of the Holy Spirit as he fell upon congregations of thousands with a power of conviction that was overwhelming, and drew from the hearts of hundreds the age-old cry, 'What must I do to be saved?' But there are other peoples in the world – in Eastern Europe, in Africa, in South America, in China and Asia – who, even in our days, are familiar with such occurrences. Their lands and races might not possess that length of history of spiritual revivals and visitations; they might be finding it hard to comprehend the nature of the religious revolution occurring around them. For them therefore to have available the detailed narration of the progress of a nation-wide awakening as found in these volumes might be of profound help in understanding their own present experiences.

*Lastly,* as we in the West consider the growth of Christianity in the developing world and note that much of their present experiences mirror events that once occurred in the histories of our own lands, might not the reminder of what is possible for the people of God at any time and in any country provoke in us that necessary spiritual jealousy that results in prevailing prayer.

> I have set watchmen on your walls, O Jerusalem, who shall never hold their peace day or night. You who make mention of the LORD, do not keep silent, and give him no rest till he establishes and till he makes Jerusalem a praise in the earth (*Isa.* 62:6–7).

\* \* \* \*

JOHN MORGAN JONES[1] (1838–1921) was a minister with the Calvinistic Methodists of Wales for over fifty years. He was born at Llanddewibrefi, Cardiganshire (the village where Daniel Rowland was converted), educated at Trefeca College (where Howell Harris once presided) and ordained in 1870. A contemporary described his ministry as follows:

> There are some perhaps who are more popular among the ordinary people, but there is no one with a purer gospel or who understands it better. He does not depend on voice or gesture. He has no silver trumpet or triple harp, but he has a speech live enough to cause excitement among the bones.

He served churches in Dowlais, Ystalyfera, Treforest and, for 37 years, in Pembroke Terrace, Cardiff. For the last fourteen years of his life he was the superintendent of his denomination's 'Forward Movement', an organization formed to evangelize and build churches for the new masses of industrial workers that had moved into south-east Wales at the close of the nineteenth century. He published various commentaries and biographies in Welsh and innumerable articles. Much of his work had to do with contending against the rising tide of higher criticism. He wrote, in 1885:

> It is a grief to the feelings of godly men who have ventured their eternity on the old book's truth and who mean to draw comfort from its assurances when walking along the valley of the shadow of death, to see the Bible being cross-examined backwards and forwards as a witness in court; and its answers here being compared with answers elsewhere, to see if they are consistent; and not only are the evidences of the Bible compared with each other they are also compared with the historical facts chronicled by pagan authors, and if the critics consider that there is some apparent discrepancy to be seen between them, they jump immediately to the conclusion that the scripture errs. This

---

[1] Much of this information on John Morgan Jones is taken from J. Gwynfor Jones, 'The Revd. John Morgan Jones, Pembroke Terrace, Cardiff (1838–1921): Aspects of his contribution to the Christian ministry' (*Journal of the Historical Society of the Presbyterian Church of Wales*, 26–27, 2002–3, pp. 90–121.)

spirit shows a great lack of due respect, but doubtless it in the end turns out to be of advantage to God's Word ... since the Bible is truth all examination will only show more clearly the strength of its foundations.

Through his biographical labours he realized that much of the early history of his denomination would soon be lost if it were not gathered together and published. Together therefore with his friend, William Morgan, he set about researching what was to become the two volumes of *Y Tadau Methodistaidd*. In his own words:

> There was an immense amount of facts relating to Methodism ... hidden in valuable manuscripts and rare English books, but principally lying in Trefeca, not having been studied or read. With great diligence we set about to collect these ... and chiefly we read through the diary of Howell Harris, written by himself, a work which, as far as we can gather, has not been read by anyone before.

The book was produced privately; the first volume appeared in 1895 and the second in 1897. A third volume was intended, bringing the period considered up to the 1859 Revival, but the authors' finances were not sufficient for the task.

Because of his awareness of the importance of the Trefeca letters and journals, John Morgan Jones served as chairman of the committee formed in 1909 to facilitate their publication, and this committee led in turn to the formation of the Calvinistic Methodist Historical Society in 1914. He served as chairman of its committee from 1915 until his death in 1921. He was twice appointed Moderator of the General Assembly of his denomination – in 1897 and 1920. The only other men to have received that privilege were the Rev. Lewis Edwards, Bala, and the Rev. Owen Thomas, Liverpool.

John Morgan Jones's co-author, WILLIAM MORGAN, J.P., of Pant, Dowlais, was the son of a Calvinistic Methodist minister, the Rev. David Morgan of Pant. It is not known exactly how the two men shared the labour of writing, but it is certain that John Morgan Jones was by far the major contributor. A contemporary, Daniel Davies of Ton, Monmouthshire, wrote:

> Mr Morgan has limited himself only to the photographic department in the second volume, leaving all the work of writing completely to the Rev. John Morgan Jones.

Both men were interested in photography and obtained their own pictures for most of the scenic photographs. William Morgan also edited and published a volume on William Williams, Pantycelyn, in 1890.

1. The text has not been abridged in any way, in translation, apart from a few small omissions. On no more than two or three occasions an anecdote that did not add anything new to the discussion has been omitted, so as to avoid repetition. Similarly, a few stanzas of verse scattered here and there throughout the work have been left out as they did not provide any new information. More importantly:

i.      Three pages of the original work have been omitted from Vol. 1, Chapter 1. At this point the authors were addressing some late nineteenth-century controversies over the interpretation of denominational statistics. The discussion does not contribute in any way to our knowledge of the Methodist Fathers (see p. 20 and the footnote on p. 28).

ii.     These same controversies are raised again in a nine-page Appendix to the first volume; this also has been omitted.

iii.    Two sections have been excised from the chapter on William Williams, Pantycelyn (Vol. 1, Chapter 7). A brief description of the comments of some later Welsh poets on his poetic abilities has been left out, and a quotation from an article on his theology (see pp. 242–5) by the Calvinistic Methodist theologian, the Rev. Lewis Edwards (1809–87), has been cut short by about four pages. In the omitted section Edwards attempts, with little success, to prove that Williams believed that faith in Christ precedes regeneration by the Holy Spirit. The section is again more of a comment on late nineteenth-century disagreements in Wales than on those of the eighteenth century.

2. As mentioned above, John Morgan Jones and William Morgan were themselves responsible for most of the photographs in the original volumes. In weighing up whether to reproduce these or to obtain new photographs, it was recognized that many of the sites portrayed are no longer in existence. The resulting mixture of new and old photographs would be something of a mismatch. It was decided therefore to retain the originals although occasionally this has meant that a picture is not of the best quality. Similarly, some of the photographs of the Fathers are the only known portraits in existence and are therefore reproduced although not of the best quality.

3. A Timeline has been provided (see pp. xv–xix) so that an overview of the period under consideration may be obtained. Also, some notes on the

pronunciation of Welsh place names are given on pp. xxi–xxv for those with an interest in this area.

* * * * *

I am very grateful to the Revs. Iain Murray and Jonathan Watson of the Banner of Truth Trust for their encouragement and help in bringing this translation to publication.

My thanks are due also to Mr Dafydd Ifans of the National Library of Wales for advice with respect to the photographs.

I received much help from the Rev. Eifion Evans of Cross Hands, Carmarthenshire. In order to write the chapters on Howell Harris and on the early general history of the Calvinistic Methodist movement, John Morgan Jones had researched the Trefeca records thoroughly. Most of Harris's writings are in English. A considerable part of Chapters 5, 8, 9, 11, 12, 13, 14, 15, 16 and 17 in Volume 1 is made up of translations into Welsh of quotations from Howell Harris's letters, journal and diary, from other letters, and from the minutes of various Associations. From his own extensive knowledge of these records and of the relevant printed literature, Eifion Evans provided me with references for those quotations that have been published in some form or another (often correcting the printed forms from his own transcriptions). Furthermore, he researched the records in the National Library of Wales and made original transcriptions of material that had not previously been published. It is he therefore that must be thanked for the fact that we are able to hear so much of Howell Harris's own voice in these chapters.

I have added footnotes to all these references received from Eifion Evans. Other quotations whose sources could not be discovered I translated back into English from John Morgan Jones's Welsh renderings. These doubly translated portions may be identified in that they do not carry any footnotes.

I am grateful also to Mrs Ann Rhys of Porth-y-rhyd, Carmarthenshire, for painting the endpapers for the two volumes.

My final and most grateful thanks are to my wife, Jenny, without whose faithful and sacrificial support and encouragement this work would not have been begun, let alone completed.

JOHN AARON
Swansea
January 2008

| BIRTHS | DEATHS | EVENTS |
|---|---|---|
| 1683 Griffith Jones, Llanddowror | | 1699 Formation of the S.P.C.K. (Society for Promoting Christian Knowledge) |
| 1702 Edmund Jones, Pontypool | | |
| 1703 John Wesley | | |
| 1704 John Harris, St Kennox | | |
| 1707 Charles Wesley | | |
|      Selina, Countess of Huntingdon | | |
| 1711? Morgan John Lewis | | |
| 1713 Daniel Rowland | | |
| 1714 Howell Harris | | |
|      George Whitefield | | |
| 1716? Howell Davies | | |
|      Morgan Rhys, Llanfynydd | | |
| 1717 William Williams, Pantycelyn | | |
|      David Williams, Llysworney | | |
| 1719 Richard Tibbott | | |
|      William Edwards, 'the Builder' | | |
|      Lewis Evan, Llanllugan | | |
| 1721 Herbert Jenkins | | |
| 1722 John Harries, Ambleston | | |
| 1723 Peter Williams | | |
|      John Evans, Bala | | |
|      William Thomas, Pyle | | |
| 1729? William Davies, Neath | | 1730? Griffith Jones establishes his first circulating school |

| | |
|---|---|
| 1734/5 | Conversion of Daniel Rowland |
| 1735 | Conversion of Howell Harris |
| | Conversion of George Whitefield |
| 1738 | Conversion of Charles Wesley |
| | Conversion of John Wesley |
| 1740 | Howell Harris's first preaching tour in north Wales |
| 1741 | Separation between Whitefield and the Wesleys |
| 1743 | The first Calvinistic Methodist Association at Watford, Caerphilly |
| 1749 | Publication of William Williams's first hymn book, *Alleluia* |
| 1750 | 'The Disruption' between Howell Harris and his brethren |
| 1752 | The commencement of Howell Harris's 'Family' at Trefeca |

| | | | |
|---|---|---|---|
| 1731 | Thomas Foulkes, Machynlleth | | |
| 1733 | Thomas Gray | | |
| 1735 | David Jones, Llan-gan | | |
| 1737? | John Evans, Cil-y-cwm | | |
| 1741 | William Lloyd, Caeo | | |
| 1744 | Dafydd Morris, Twr-gwyn | | |
| 1745 | Robert Jones, Rhoslan | | |
| 1746 | Siencyn Thomas, Pen-hydd | | |
| 1747 | John Williams, Lledrod | | |
| | Robert Dafydd, Brynengan | | |
| 1749 | Nathaniel Rowland | 1749 | James Beaumont |
| 1750 | Edward Coslet | | |
| | Howell Howells, Tre-hill | | |
| 1752 | Dafydd Cadwaladr, Bala | | |
| 1753 | John Roberts, Llangwm | | |
| | Christopher Bassett | | |
| 1754 | John Williams, Pantycelyn | | |
| 1755 | Thomas Charles, Bala | | |
| 1756 | Thomas Jones, Denbigh | | |
| | David Griffiths, Nevern | | |
| | Simon Lloyd, Bala | | |

| 1761 | Publication of William Williams's hymn book *The Sea of Glass* |
| 1762–4 | The Llangeitho Revival |
| 1763 | Daniel Rowland expelled from his curacies |
| | Howell Harris reconciled with his brethren |
| 1768 | The opening of the Countess of Huntingdon's College at Trefeca |
| 1770 | Peter Williams's *Bible Commentary* published |
| 1785 | Thomas Charles recommences the circulating schools |
| 1787? | Thomas Charles establishes his first Sunday Schools |

| 1761 | Griffith Jones, Llan-ddowror |
| 1763 | John Harris, St Kennox |
| 1766 | Milbourn Bloom |
| 1769 | Howell Davies |
| 1770 | George Whitefield |
| 1771 | Morgan John Lewis |
| 1772 | Herbert Jenkins |
| 1773 | Howell Harris |
| 1779 | Morgan Rhys, Llan-fynydd |
| 1784 | John Richard, Llansamlet |
| | Christopher Bassett |
| | John Evans, Cil-y-cwm |
| 1787? | William Davies, Neath |
| | Charles Wesley |
| 1788 | John Harries, Ambleston |

| 1759 | Evan Richardson, Caernarvon |
| 1762 | David Charles, Carmarthen |
| | Robert Roberts, Clynnog |
| 1766 | Christmas Evans |
| 1769 | Ebenezer Morris |
| 1771 | William Lloyd, Caernarvon |
| 1774 | John Elias |
| 1778 | William Howells, Long Acre |
| 1780 | Michael Roberts |
| | Robert Saunderson, Bala |
| 1781 | Ebenezer Richard, Tregaron |
| 1783 | Thomas Richard, Fishguard |
| 1784 | William Roberts, Amlwch |

| 1792 | The Countess of Huntingdon's College is removed to Cheshunt, Hertfordshire |
| 1799 | The publication of *The Spiritual Treasury* by Thomas Charles and Thomas Jones |
| 1800 | The first Wesleyan Methodist missionaries arrive in Wales |
| 1804 | Formation of the British and Foreign Bible Society |
| 1805 | Thomas Charles publishes his *Bible Dictionary* |
| 1807 | Thomas Charles publishes his *Catechism* |
| 1810–40 | Period of the theological debates over the nature and extent of the atonement |
| 1811 | The first ordination of ministers by the Calvinistic Methodists |
| 1823 | Publication of the Calvinistic Methodists' *Confession of Faith* |

| 1789 | William Edwards, 'the Builder' |
| 1790 | Daniel Rowland |
| 1791 | William Williams, Pantycelyn |
|      | John Wesley |
|      | Selina, Countess of Huntingdon |
| 1792 | Dafydd Morris, Twr-gwyn |
|      | Lewis Evan, Llanllugan |
|      | David Williams, Llysworney |
| 1793 | Edmund Jones, Pontypool |
| 1796 | Peter Williams |
| 1798 | Richard Tibbott |
| 1802 | Robert Roberts, Clynnog |
|      | Thomas Foulkes, Machynlleth |
| 1807 | Siencyn Thomas, Pen-hydd |
| 1808 | William Lloyd, Caeo |
| 1810 | David Jones, Llan-gan |
|      | Thomas Gray |
| 1811 | William Thomas, Pyle |
| 1814 | Thomas Charles, Bala |
|      | Thomas Coke |
| 1817 | John Evans, Bala |
| 1820 | Thomas Jones, Denbigh |
| 1824 | Evan Richardson, Caernarvon |
| 1825 | Ebenezer Morris |
| 1828 | Edward Coslet |
|      | John Williams, Pantycelyn |

| 1796 | John Jones, Tal-y-sarn |
| 1798 | Henry Rees |

| 1831 | John Williams, Lledrod |
| | Nathaniel Rowland |
| 1832 | William Howells, Long Acre |
| 1834 | John Roberts, Llangwm |
| | Dafydd Cadwaladr, Bala |
| | David Charles, Carmarthen |
| | David Griffiths, Nevern |
| | Robert Dafydd, Brynengan |
| 1836 | Simon Lloyd, Bala |
| 1837 | Ebenezer Richard, Tregaron |
| 1838 | Christmas Evans |
| 1841 | John Elias |
| | William Lloyd, Caernarvon |
| 1842 | Howell Howells, Tre-hill |
| 1849 | Michael Roberts |
| 1856 | Thomas Richard, Fishguard |
| 1857 | John Jones, Tal-y-sarn |
| 1863 | Robert Saunderson, Bala |
| 1864 | William Roberts, Amlwch |
| 1869 | Henry Rees |

# WELSH PLACE NAMES

## 1. MEANINGS

The following gives the meaning of some of the words often found in Welsh place names:

| | |
|---|---|
| aber | the mouth of a river. Often followed by the name of the river, e.g. *Aberteifi* – the mouth of the River Teifi. |
| afon | river |
| allt | hillside, wood |
| bach | small |
| bae | bay |
| banc | bank, hillock |
| bedd | grave |
| betws | chapel-of-ease |
| blaen(au) | head, end, summit |
| bro | region, vale |
| bron | breast (of hill) |
| bryn | hill |
| bwlch | mountain pass |
| bychan | small |
| cae | field |
| caer | fort, castle |
| capel | chapel |
| carn, carnedd | cairn, heap, mound |
| carreg | stone |
| cas, castell | castle |
| cefn | ridge |
| cei | quay |
| celli (gelli) | grove |
| cil | covert, nook |

| | |
|---|---|
| cilfach | creek |
| clawdd | ditch, embankment |
| clogwyn | cliff, crag |
| coed | wood |
| coch | red |
| cors | bog |
| craig | rock |
| crib | ridge |
| croes | cross |
| crug | hillock, cairn |
| cwm | valley |
| dinas | city |
| dôl | meadow, dale |
| du | black |
| dŵr | water |
| dyffryn | valley |
| eglwys | church |
| esgair | ridge |
| ffin | boundary, edge |
| ffordd | road |
| ffos | ditch, dyke |
| ffynnon | well |
| glan | shore, bank |
| glas | blue |
| glyn | valley, glen |
| gwaun | meadow, moor |
| gwern | marsh, bog |
| gwyn | white |
| gwyrdd | green |
| hafod | summer dwelling |
| hen | old |
| hendre(f) | winter dwelling |
| hir | long |
| isaf | lower |
| llan | church. Often followed by the name of the associated Celtic saint, e.g. *Llandeilo* – the church of St Teilo. |
| llwyn | grove, bush |
| llyn | lake |
| llys | court |
| mawr | large |

| maen | stone |
| maes | field, square |
| melin | mill |
| moel | bare (hilltop) |
| môr | sea |
| morfa | sea-marsh, fen |
| mynydd | mountain |
| nant | stream |
| newydd | new |
| ogof | cave |
| pant | valley, hollow |
| parc | field, park |
| pen | head, end, top |
| pentre(f) | village |
| plas | mansion, palace |
| pont | bridge |
| porth | port, harbour |
| pwll | pool |
| rhiw | hill |
| rhos | moor, plain |
| rhyd | ford |
| sain(t) | saint |
| sarn | causeway |
| tal | front, end |
| tir | land |
| tomen | mound, earthworks |
| traeth | beach |
| tre(f) | town |
| troed | foot |
| twˆr | tower |
| tŷ | house |
| uchaf | upper |
| ynys | island |
| ystrad | vale |

## 2. Pronunciation

The following is adapted, with permission, from: Heini Gruffudd, *Welsh Talk* (Y Lolfa, Talybont: 2000).

Welsh is much easier to pronounce than English as most letters have just one sound. Almost all consonants have only one sound, while some vowels vary slightly.

Welsh has seven vowel letters: a, e, i, o, u, w, y.

It also has eight combination letters, each combination representing one sound: ch, dd, ff, ng, ll, ph, rh, th.

The stress on Welsh words is almost always on the last syllable but one, e.g. Dín/bych, Llan/dý/sul, Llan/géi/tho, Tre/fé/ca, Rhos/llann/erch/rú/gog, Pant/y/cél/yn, etc.

## THE WELSH ALPHABET

| Letter | English Sound | Welsh Example |
| --- | --- | --- |
| a | a (short, as in gala) | aber |
| | ah (long, as in park) | plas |
| b | b | bryn |
| c | k | capel |
| ch | ch (as in loch) | cilfach |
| d | d | dinas |
| dd | th (voiced, as in that) | mynydd |
| e | e (short, as in went) | pen |
| | eh (long, as in café) | hen |
| | ee (after 'a' and 'o', as in week) | cae, coed |
| f | v | hafod |
| ff | ff (as in off) | ffordd |
| g | g (hard, as in game) | glyn |
| ng | usually ng (as in wing) | Llanfihangel |
| | sometimes n-g (as in angry) | Bangor |
| h | h | hen |
| i | i (short, as in pin) | rhiw |
| | ee (long, as in week) | hir |
| l | l | melin |
| ll | ll (as 'l' but blow voicelessly) | llan |
| m | m | môr |
| n | n | nant |
| o | o (short, as in gone) | cors |
| | o (long, as in fore) | ffos |
| p | p | pont |

| | | |
|---|---|---|
| ph | ff | Caerphilly |
| r | r (trilled) | croes |
| rh | rh (trilled with an 'h') | rhos |
| s | s (as in **s**oon) | maes |
| t | t | tir |
| u | i (short, as in p**i**n) | Llundain |
| | usually ee (long, as in we**e**k) | du |
| w | oo (short, as in p**u**ll) | bwlch |
| | oo (long, as in f**oo**l) | twr |
| y | i (short, as in p**i**n) | bryn |
| | uh (as in f**u**n) | ffynnon |
| | ee (long, as in we**e**k) | rhyd |

# ABBREVIATIONS

The following abbreviations are used in the notes:

CH      *The Journal of the Historical Society of the Presbyterian Church of Wales.* CH followed by a number is used for the first sixty volumes (up to 1976); CH followed by a year, e.g. CH, 1980, is used for later volumes.

CH, MS   *Manuscript Supplements* of this *Journal,* issued in two series, (i) and (ii).

CMHO   D. E. Jenkins, *Calvinistic Methodist Holy Orders* (Caernarvon, 1911).

HHRS   Tom Beynon, *Howell Harris, Reformer and Soldier* (Caernarvon, 1958).

HHVL   Tom Beynon, *Howell Harris's Visits to London* (Aberystwyth, 1960).

HHVP   Tom Beynon, *Howell Harris's Visits to Pembrokeshire* (Aberystwyth, 1966).

HJH   Hugh J. Hughes, *Life of Howell Harris* (London, 1892).

STL, vol. 1   Gomer M. Roberts, *Selected Trevecka Letters* (1742–1747) (Caernarvon, 1956).

STL, vol. 2   Gomer M. Roberts, *Selected Trevecka Letters* (1747–1794) (Caernarvon, 1962).

# I

# THE MORAL CONDITION OF WALES AT THE BEGINNING OF METHODISM

## THE LOW MORAL SITUATION OF BRITAIN AT THE BEGINNING OF METHODISM[1]

Since Christianity was first preached in this island it is doubtful whether spiritual religion has ever been at a lower ebb than at the time when Methodism began. The Puritans, with their simplicity of life and of personal and domestic habits, their repugnance of all pomp, show, and pride, their intense seriousness, and their deep familiarity with the Word of the Lord, had all passed into the grave. A new age, of completely different spirit, practices and morals, had replaced them; one which was given over to all types of play and all kinds of licentiousness. The transformation can be explained in part as the natural reaction to the spirit of Puritanism, which was, perhaps, too strict; in part by the influence of the corrupt court of Charles II, in which virtue and every kind of seriousness was mocked, and immorality was boasted of; but mainly as the natural corruption of the human heart which is only evil continually. There was no lack of able men at this time. This was the age of Handel, the composer; Pope, the poet; Daniel Defoe, the novelist; and Samuel Johnson, the writer. It was about this time that Butler wrote his *Analogy*, a book for which no unbeliever, even up to the present day, has provided an answer. Within the Established Church there were men of ability such as Sherlock, Waterland, and Secker. Amongst the Nonconformists were Isaac Watts, Nathaniel Lardner, and the godly Philip Doddridge. But as has been said, greatness does not always give birth to goodness. And this age, for all the able and distinguished men it contained, was notable for its immorality. One able writer has written:

> Never has a century risen on Christian England so void of soul and faith as that which opened with Queen Anne, and which reached its misty noon beneath the second George – a dewless night succeeded by a sunless dawn. There was no freshness in the past, and no promise in the future. The Puritans were buried

and the Methodists were not born. The philosopher of the age was Bolingbroke, the moralist was Addison, the minstrel was Pope, and the preacher Atterbury. The world had the idle, discontented look of the morning after some mad holiday.[2]

This description is supported by the testimony of those who lived during these times. The Bishop of Lichfield, in a sermon before the Society for the Reformation of Manners in 1724, said:

The Lord's day is now the devil's market day. More lewdness, more drunkenness, more quarrels and murders, more sin is contrived and committed on this day than on all the other days of the week together. Strong liquors are become the epidemic distemper of this great city. More of the common people die of consumptions, fevers, dropsies, colics, palsies, and apoplexies, contracted by the immoderate use of brandies and distilled waters, than of all other distempers besides, arising from other causes. Sin, in general, is grown so hardened and rampant, as that immoralities are defended, yea, justified on principle. Obscene, wanton, and profane books find so good a market as to encourage the trade of publishing them. Every kind of sin has found a writer to teach and vindicate it, and a bookseller and hawker to divulge and spread it.[3]

At this time, the drinking of gin had become a general mania. In London, one house in six was a drinking parlour. On their sign-boards, inn-keepers promised to make a man drunk for a penny, and would provide straw for him to lie on until he had recovered his senses. Extravagance was the order of the day. Not one family in ten sought to pay its way. The grand question was how to eat better, to drink more, and to be clothed more fashionably than the neighbours. Every night the public gardens would be lit up by innumerable lanterns, and there would gather, dressed up in silk and purple and with masks over their faces, thieves, wastrels, gamblers, and prostitutes, together with the rich and the nobility of highest rank, together engaged in indecent conversation and slanderous lies. All classes were infected by this disease. Clerks, apprentices, servant-girls and cooks, would dress themselves up as gorgeously as their masters and mistresses.

To maintain all this prodigality required money, of course; and all ways of obtaining it, honest or dishonest, were considered legitimate. Stealing was accepted as gentlemanly, and gambling was a duty. Ladies would lay wagers in their homes, while their men would gamble out of the house. The sound of dice would be heard thrown into wheelbarrows used for carrying apples, salmon or cabbages, as well as on the tables of the gentry. Money had to be obtained, and it did not matter by what means. The *Weekly Miscellany* for 1732 stated that the people 'were engulfed in voluptuousness, wholly given to pleasure, that any zeal for godliness was thought as odd upon a man as would the antiquated dress of his great grandfather.' Atheistic clubs were formed with the express purpose of making the people a pagan nation. There was no price on virtue, and religion and godliness were despised. 'It was publicly avowed that vice was profitable to the state, . . . and that polygamy, concubinage, and even sodomy were not sinful.' The words of the prophet Isaiah could be applied to the nation, 'Ah sinful nation, a people laden with iniquity, a seed of evil doers; children that are corrupters; the whole head is sick, and the whole heart faint; from the sole of the foot even unto the head, there is no soundness in it, but wounds, bruises, and putrifying sores.'

At last, the governing authorities took fright at the general level of corruption and immorality. A House of Lords committee was appointed, 'to inquire into the causes of the present excessive immorality and corruption'. In its report, the committee stated that many men of evil character had lately gathered themselves into a club called the Blasters, and were using all means to draw the youth of the nation to join them; that the members of this club professed to be worshippers of the devil, and that they prayed to him and drank his health; that they used such blasphemous language against the majesty and sacred name of God, and spoke with such filthy and presumptuous expressions, as had never before been heard, and which the committee could only pass by in silence in that they were too dreadful to be repeated. It reported further that religion and everything sacred had lately been greatly neglected; and that there was more neglecting of divine service, publicly and privately, and greater disrespect of the Sabbath, than had ever been known in England; that idleness, luxury, gambling, and use of liquors, had increased alarmingly. It advised that bishops in their visitations of the clergy should charge them to warn their people and encourage them to attend divine service, and that young men in the universities be taught carefully the rudiments of religion and morality.

In 1744, the High Jurors of Middlesex presented the following complaint to a Sessions judge:

> The people are sliding into luxuriousness, extravagance, and idleness; in this way, families are being ruined and the nation dishonoured; and unless some authority puts an end to such behaviour, they feared it would lead to the destruction of the nation.

Wickedness was rapidly undoing the very foundations of society. Having thrown virtue and religion overboard, the people had no strength for anything. Their lusts threatened to become their graves; national and social destruction stared them in the face; and they appeared as if ready to sink eternally under the ruins of that morality which they had so effectively undermined. At the same time, the few godly individuals that remained in the nation trembled and raised their eyes to God, crying out, 'O Lord, how long! how long!'

It is natural to ask, 'What of the clergymen of the Church of England?' Were they not watching upon the walls according to the serious vows that they took at their ordination? Were they not attempting to staunch the flow in accordance with their office? No, unfortunately. 'As with the people, so with the priest,' was the state of things then, as in almost every other age. Very many of the clergy led immoral lives, and were almost as ignorant as moles of the doctrines of the gospel which they undertook to preach. They could challenge the champions of their parishes in their ability to drink beer and spirits; they could compete with the best, when sat in the chair by the fire of a long winter's night, in reciting comic or bawdy verse; they were authorities on the sports and various games played; but they were nearly all completely ignorant of the gospel of God and much more familiar with the life and works of Alexander the Great and Julius Caesar than in the history of the Lord Jesus Christ. In case anyone thinks this is exaggeration, we quote the words of Bishop Burnet in 1713:

> Our ember weeks are the burden and grief of my life. The much greater part of those who come to be ordained are ignorant to a degree not to be apprehended by those who are not obliged to know it. The easiest part of knowledge is that to which they are the greatest strangers; I mean the plainest parts of the Scriptures. They can give no account, or at least a very imperfect one, of the contents even of the gospels, or of the catechism itself.[4]

A dark picture indeed, is it not? And it must be remembered that it was drawn by a bishop. It must be acknowledged, in all fairness, that there was one group of clergymen at the time who lived moral lives, and amongst whom there were able and learned men. These, on the whole, were the High-Churchmen. But they were blemished by two faults. The first was their prejudice against Nonconformists:

> They held that none were ministers of Christ except those who had been episcopally ordained; and hence they held that all sacraments administered by Dissenters were invalid, and all Dissenting churches in a state of sin and damnation.[5]

Secondly, they were political hot-heads:

> Many of them, in heart at least, were Jacobites, and, while promising allegiance, regarded King George as a usurper and branded those of their brethren who differed from them with open opprobrium. Endless were the pamphlets published and fierce were the feuds of those who ought to have dwelt together in unity. The foulest sins were made sinless by intemperate

zeal for the Pretender, and the fairest virtues were besmeared in those who showed a friendly feeling for Dissenters. A man might be drunken and quarrelsome all the week, but if on Sunday he bowed to the altar and cursed King William he was esteemed a saint. He might cheat everybody, and pay nobody, but if he drank health to the royal orphan, hated King George, and abhorred the Whigs, his want of probity was a peccadillo scarce worth noticing. On the other hand, a man might be learned, diligent, devout, and useful, but if he opposed the Pretender and Popery, or if he thought the Dissenters should not be damned, he was at once set down as heterodox, and, according to his importance, became a target for the poisoned shafts of high church malice.[6]

Things were little better amongst the Dissenters. They grumbled that they were losing their young people, that a general indifference and a wintry coldness were pervading their congregations and that spiritual religion was notably low. They complained that many of their ministers were negligent and immoral, and that their sermons, which were read, showed more familiarity with classical authors than with the Word of God. The country had reached a grievous state, and Tyerman stated that it was only the rise and progress of Methodism that saved Britain from a temporal and social disaster. Macaulay judged similarly.

## THE WELSH SITUATION OF NECESSITY VERY SIMILAR

We have enlarged upon, and detailed, the religious and moral condition of England because the same factors, more or less, were at work in Wales, and did in fact produce the same effects. The influence of England on the Principality was greater, if anything, than it is now. It must be remembered that Welsh periodical literature had not yet made an appearance. The *Amserau* [*The Times*], Wales's first fortnightly paper, would not be brought out until another hundred years had passed, and the first monthly periodical in Welsh not for another fifty years. All the literature that was read and that reflected the thought of the age, came from England, and its influence was as a diseased wind, affecting every fair and beautiful flower it touched upon. It is true that the number of those who could read was small, but because of their social status they could, like the leaven of the parable, make bitter everything with which they came into contact. It must be also be remembered that there were very few schools in Wales, and the young people were sent for their education to large towns in England, with those who could afford it sending their sons to Oxford. As might be expected, they returned having been corrupted and having swallowed the atheistic views of the places where they stayed. Such a description is overwhelmingly supported by contemporary testimonies. These state that true religion had almost disappeared from the land; that immorality in its ugliest forms filled the country; and that the most extreme ignorance and most credulous superstitions flourished amongst the people. The numbers of Bibles were small, those able to read them were less. The winter nights were spent in narrating witches' tales of ghosts, apparitions, corpse-candles, and similar things.

## A WINTER'S NIGHT IN A WELSH FARMHOUSE

In order to provide the reader with some idea of the low state of the land, and of the superstition that was rife, we would describe an imaginary visit to a well-to-do farmhouse, one winter's night, where a happy company have gathered. Though cold outside, it is warm in the house, for a fire of peat and wood burns on the hearth. There are no candles lit as the glow of the fire provides sufficient light, and the flames are reflected in the pewter plates on the dresser. The old people sit inside the wide old-fashioned chimney, the younger folk sit further away, and they occupy themselves in the liveliest of fashions with the reciting of old and new stories and legends. One of them starts to relate an episode that took place on a neighbouring farm: One morning, the previous week, the wife of the house had found an old, ugly, yellow-skinned hag at her door, and the following conversation had taken place:

'The blessing of heaven be on you! Will you be so good as to give a cup of barley as alms to an old woman?'

'I am very sorry, we are quite out of barley. The boys will have to go to thresh in the barn before we'll have any more of it.'

'Do you refuse a cup of barley?'

'I have to refuse today, I have none at hand.'

'Long before sunset, you will regret being so close-fisted.'

The old woman departed in anger, murmuring threats, and the wife returned to her kitchen. There, the maid was preparing to churn the cream. She soon began her work, and she churned away for long hours but without any sign of the cream changing to butter. It dawned on her mistress that the old hag's curse was the reason for this failure. She hurried to her husband who was in the yard, saying,

'Go straight away, take the fastest horse from the stable, ride after the old woman who came to the door. She has charmed the milk. Bring her back by fair means or foul.'

Away goes the husband and he overtakes the old woman. He persuades her to return with him. She mutters a few words under her breath, and a few minutes' churning is sufficient to fill the churn with butter.

The appropriate comments on such a tale were made. Some of the company expressed their surprise, and yet it was no great surprise in that such events occurred all too often.

After a brief pause another took up a tale and spoke of Dafydd, Pant-y-ddafad, drinking in the village inn about a month before. The night was dark and stormy, the wind whistled down the chimney like some mocking demon, and the rain descended like a flood so that it was a danger to life and limb to leave the building. Dafydd sat glumly by the fire, wondering how he would get home to Pant-y-ddafad, two miles away on the other side of the Teifi. At his elbow was an old woman, wrapped in a red shawl, carding wool according to the old Welsh way. Dafydd emptied his pint, called for another, and after taking a deep draught extended it to the old woman so that she might drink. Soon, he pours out his sad story,

'It is an awful night. I do not know how on earth I am to get home.'

'Take heart. You will get home safely,' said the old woman with the wool-cards.

'Do you think the wind will drop, and the storm clear up?'

'Drop or not, you will be no worse.'

The farmer drank more pints, sharing them with the old carder, but there was not the least indication of any lessening of the storm. At last he rose, wrapped himself in his greatcoat and said that he would go, whatever the outcome. He closed the door behind him, took one step out into the stormy darkness, and with the next step he was at the door of his house, without having even got wet. She who drank from his pints had paid him back for his kindness by carrying him in a minute, over two miles of road, and across the Teifi, in some unimaginable way. This story evoked more reactions of surprise. To be carried miraculously in the air by an enchantress was a much more unusual event.

The third narrator has the story of a man caught in a ghostly funeral, and he is listened to with great interest. He says that the local parish tax-collector, when returning on the highway to his home late one night, suddenly found himself in the middle of a crowd of men. These stepped on his feet and pushed him sideways, until he found himself half-fallen into the hedge. He soon realized that a funeral was passing. The crowd became thicker, and soon the coffin appeared and he recognized those who were carrying the bier. Slowly the procession thinned and the funeral passed. But in amongst the stragglers, the tax-gatherer recognized a farmer who was in arrears with his tax, and he thought that this would be a good opportunity to save himself some miles of walking by making sure of his money that night. He ran after him and called his name. But the farmer would not answer. He continued walking as sober as a saint, not turning to the right hand or to the left, and without taking a bit of notice of the tax-collector's shouts. On getting tired, the latter realized that he was in a ghost's funeral; that it was spirits that generally marched in such gatherings, and that spirits never paid any taxes. He turned on his heels and went home disappointed.

We only have room to relate one more of the stories narrated and that one, like many of the tales repeated in those days, concerned a clergyman. It was said that the Rev. Thomas Jones, the vicar of one of the adjoining parishes, was a very learned man who could read Latin, and who possessed a book full of demons, and was strongly suspected of holding communion with the Evil One. The conjuring book would be kept chained and locked at all times. But the maid, full of curiosity, like many of her class, had found the book left half-open by her master and testified that it was covered throughout with unearthly pictures and with writings in red ink. On one occasion, Mr Jones decided to undo the lock and open the book. As soon as the covers were opened, a horde of devils rushed out, and demanded work to do. The great danger in releasing demons from a book is failing to find sufficient work for them to do, for if this is the case they will physically take up the man who released them and carry him down with them to the pit.

Fortunately, Mr Jones remembered Lake Aeddwen, a deep and wide lake, and he commanded the demons to go there and to throw out the water until the lake was empty. Off they went immediately; Mr Jones broke out in floods of sweat, feeling that he had been granted a great deliverance. But he possessed much courage and ventured to open another page. As he did so, another horde of demons emerged, demanding work, just like the first. The old clergyman was not lacking in cunning, and he sent this horde to the same lake to pour back the water emptied by the first contingent. How long the two armies spent throwing water back and forth the narrator did not say, nor did he record which of the two were the stronger, nor whether they returned to the book eventually, for the old vicar locked it up and returned it to its cupboard as soon as possible. And such was the fright he received that he did not venture on such mischief ever again.

As time passed the excitement increased and the stories became more terrifying. Now and again, the jug of home-brewed beer would be passed round and the stories would flow all the freer. They would not break up until midnight and by then the younger element would be completely overcome by fear. Cold thrills would pass through their bodies and their hair would be standing on end. On the way home they would imagine that every thorn bush was an apparition and that the glow-worm's gleam in the hedgerow was a corpse-candle.

This was the intellectual nourishment given to the youth of Wales a hundred and fifty years ago. These are the superstitious tales which they imbibed with their mothers' milk, and which were firmly believed by them. They knew nothing of God, apart from knowing his name. They had no idea of their own spiritual nature nor of the duties required of them. Of these great things they were almost as ignorant as the pagans of India. And their immorality was as great as their ignorance. The whole land was corrupt, with no difference between nobility and common people, clergy or laity. The pulpit possessed nothing that could affect the situation. Indeed, it was not often that the Saviour's name would be referred to from it, and no mention at all was made of man's sinfulness or of the work of the Holy Spirit. Sports were indulged in every Sunday, when the youth of the region would show their prowess in wrestling, jumping, running and kicking a football, while the old would stand and watch. The day would end with everyone gathering at the inn, where the night would be spent in drunkenness, and often in cruel animal fights. On Saturday nights, especially in the summer, meetings were held to sing carols, to sing with the harp, to dance, and to perform anterliwtiau [interludes[7]]. In these pastimes, the nobility of an area would mix with the common people. These activities had such an influence on the spirit of Mr Thomas Charles of Bala that throughout his life it was a pain to him to remain in a room where a harp was being played.

## DR REES'S CHARGE AGAINST THE METHODIST FATHERS

The Rev. Thomas Rees, D.D., Swansea, accused the Methodist Fathers of depicting the situation at the time in colours that were too dark. He suggests that they did so consciously, in order to minimize the labours of the Dissenters before them, and to exaggerate the revival produced by their own labours. Such a presumptuous and unfounded remark should never have been made. The Methodist Fathers would have been the last to over-rate their own work. Indeed, they had no idea of the greatness of the revolution that they were the means of effecting. It is ourselves, having the hindsight of a hundred and fifty years, who can understand how beneficial was their labours and ministry. Dr Rees bases his accusation on a few pages that he came across in London, and on a letter from the Rev. Edmund Jones, Pont-y-pool. We will consider these pages again, but it is clear that Edmund Jones, and Thomas Rees also, have misunderstood some lines in William Williams's elegy to Howell Harris. When Williams described Wales, at the time when Harris emerged from Trefeca full of zeal and passion, he wrote as follows:

| | |
|---|---|
| When the land lay dark and lifeless, | Pan oedd Cymru gynt yn gorwedd |
| In its long and deadly sleep, | Mewn rhyw dywyll, farwol hun, |
| When no bishop, priest or elder | Heb na Phresbyter' na 'Ffeirad, |
| Faithfully his watch did keep. | Nac un Esgob ar ddihun. |

He was not trying to deny that there were important exceptions. He wrote as a poet, and he did not intend his words to be taken completely literally. According to Dr Rees, 'Williams does not in any way moderate his statement that everyone in Wales was asleep when Methodism began.' This is a mistake. There are phrases in the elegy itself that show that the lines above were not intended to be pressed to their extreme meaning. Half way through the poem are found the lines:

| | |
|---|---|
| Griffith Jones, by now awakened, | Griffith Jones pryd hyn oedd ddeffro |
| Was proclaiming gospel fare, | Yn cyhoeddi Efengyl gras, |
| Loud his cries from many a pulpit | Hyd cyrhaeddai'r swn o'r pwlpud |
| Or, if need be, in th' open air. | Neu, os rhaid, o'r fynwent las. |

And before the elegy ends, more than just Griffith Jones are found to be awake. There were:

| | |
|---|---|
| Rowland, Harris, a few others, | Rowland, Harris, a rhyw ychydig |
| Here in Wales preached, line on line, | Yma yng Nghymru yn seinio maes, |
| Now from Sinai, now from Zion, | Weithiau o Sinai, weithiau o Sion, |
| The mysteries of grace divine. | Hen ddirgelion dwyfol ras. |

As a description of the general state of the country, Williams's words were true. A deathly sleep had overcome even those who were appointed to be watchmen. He did not wish to deny the exceptions, indeed, he refers to them, but he complains that they were only 'a few others.' Other lines in the elegy must be understood in the light of the whole. This is the golden rule when expounding Scripture, and if things were done otherwise, as by Dr Rees and Edmund Jones when they criticized the words of Williams, Pantycelyn, the Bible could be made to teach the most destructive errors. Furthermore, Edmund Jones wrote his letter when under the influence of angry feelings towards the Methodists. This is easily understood from his tone. He says:

Mr William Williams, the Methodist clergyman, in his 'Elegy for Mr Howell Harris,' plainly saith and plainly sings that neither priest nor presbyter was awake when Mr Howell Harris came out to exhort. A shameless intruth printed; for there were some clergymen awake before him, as Mr Griffith Jones, of Llanddowror; Mr Thomas Jones, of Cwm-iou; and many Dissenting ministers, as Mr John Thomas, in Caernarvonshire; Mr Williams, of Tredustan, and Mr Morgan, of Llanavan, in Brecknockshire; Mr Vavasor Griffiths, in Radnorshire; Mr Palmer, of Henllan, and Mr W. Morrice, in Pembrokeshire; Mr Phillip Pugh, in Cardiganshire; Mr James Davies, of Merthyr, in Glamorganshire; and it was I that brought Mr Harris to exhort in Monmouthshire. It is a wonder how that a man should say such a thing who himself was born of and educated among Dissenters. If the Methodists will not give over hard censuring as they do, God will by degrees desert them, and then they will become weak, and of little use.[8]

These are angry words and it is not difficult to account for the feelings of the author. Howell Harris had rebuked Edmund Jones for his proselytizing zeal and his work in forming Independent churches from Harris's own converts. The rebuke was notably gentle and mild – this is acknowledged by Dr Rees (a 'mild remonstrance'[9]) – but it appears to have embittered Edmund Jones's feelings and made him angry against the Methodists.

## DR REES'S ACCUSATIONS UNFOUNDED

But it is not necessary to depend on the writings of the Methodists as to the state of the country at this time. Their testimony is confirmed by others. No one knew more of the moral and spiritual condition of Wales at this time than the Rev. Griffith Jones, Llanddowror. No one had better opportunity than he to observe the situation. He was also a notably moderate man, careful in his choice of words. He wrote:

It has been found in several places, that where sixty or eighty young and old people came to these schools, not above three or four of them could say the Lord's Prayer, and they, too, in a very imperfect and unintelligible manner, not knowing so much as who their Father in heaven is, nor able to give a much better account of the easiest and more common articles of the Christian religion than those to whom you kindly extend your charity to instruct in the Indies. The complaints that profaneness, lewdness, violence and theft fill the land and are on the increase, are not without foundation.

These are strong words, and it is no wonder that the good man asked mournfully, 'What can a few private efforts effect?' He continued:

It must be that a black cloud of storm hovers above our heads, threatening destruction upon all who are at ease in Zion.

And again:

You will wonder at the foolish and shameful, if not blasphemous views that many of the poor cling to with respect to God, Christ, and the sacraments. They know nothing about baptism, other than that they have been baptized and made good Christians, soon after their birth; nor about the Lord's Supper, except that it is bread and wine, which some of them intend to receive when they are about to die. They hardly know more of the attributes of God, or the offices of our Saviour, or the covenant of grace, or the conditions of salvation, or of their own spiritual condition and their duties towards God and men, than if they had not been born into a Christian country. Such is the ignorance that has overcome our land, that in many parts of it the remains of its old paganism, together with the remains of a more recent Papistry, still prevail in the ideas, phrases and habits of life of the poor. No wonder therefore that such a flood of immorality and wickedness, such as jealousy, malice, lying, dishonesty, swearing, drunkenness, lewdness, and blasphemy, together with every kind of corruption and disorder have flowed from it. The only distinction made by many between the Lord's Day and other days is that it gives them more leisure to give themselves up to their lusts and filthiness.

We could easily quote other sentences, equally strong, from his writings, but these are sufficient. It would be difficult to draw a blacker picture. We see the country covered by the gloomy shadow of ignorance; ignorance of God, of Christ, and of religion, without any understanding of the way of salvation of the gospel and full of Roman Catholic ideas and practices. The rich and the poor were sinking into the most abominable immoralities. Griffith Jones knew what he wrote about, because he had journeyed through much of Wales on his preaching itineraries. It must be remembered also that he lived in the south, where some have stated that Dissent had greatly improved the religion of the common people; that he was raised as a young man amongst Dissenters, and that the churches where he served were within a few miles of Carmarthen town, where was a Dissenting academy. The testimony of such a man is worth a thousand conclusions drawn from doubtful sources.

As proof of the superstition of the generality of people, even in the south, and of the strength of Roman Catholic beliefs and practices among them, take the following quotations from a book written by Erasmus Saunders, D.D., and published in 1721, that is about fifteen years before the rise of Methodism. The book's title is *A View of the State of Religion in the Diocese of St David's about the Beginning of the Eighteenth Century*. The author's purpose in these quotations is to show that the Welsh have a natural religious instinct, and in passing, and almost unwillingly, he refers to their superstitions:

They cross themselves, as the first Christians were used to do, on many occasions, with a short ejaculation that through the Cross of Christ they might be safe or saved. In most mountainous parts, where old customs and simplicity are most prevailing, there we shall observe that when the people come to church, they go immediately to the graves of their friends and there, kneeling, offer up their prayers to God . . . [10]

The author does not say what they pray for, but it is quite certain, from the words of Mr Johnes and others, that this was prayer on behalf of the dead, that they might be freed from purgatory, for the form of prayer most often used was, 'May he have heaven.' But to return to Dr Saunders's description:

. . . but especially at the feast of the Nativity of our Lord; for they then come to church about cock-crowing, and bring either candles or torches with them, which they set to burn every one, one or more upon the grave of his departed friend, and then set themselves to sing their carols, and continue so to do, to welcome the approaching festival, until prayer-time.

But with these innocent good old customs, they have also learned some of the Roman superstitious practices in the later ages, such as many times in their ejaculations to invocate, not only the Deity, but also the holy Virgin and other saints; for Mair *wen*, Iago, Teilo Mawr, Celer, Celynog, and others, are often thus remembered, as if they had hardly yet forgotten the use of praying to them . . . In many parts of North Wales they continue in effect still to pay for obits, by giving oblations to the ministers at the burial of their friends, as they were formerly taught to do to pray them out of purgatory, without which useful perquisites the poor curates in many places would be very hard pushed to get their livelihoods.

And thus it is the Christian religion labours to keep ground here. Superstition and religion, error and truth, are so very oddly mixed, that it should in charity be concluded to be rather the misfortune of many that they are misled. For the generality are, I am afraid, more obliged, if not to their natural probity, to their religious observance of those ancient customs, or to the instruction that they get from their carols, or the Vicar of Llandovery's poems, than to any benefit received from the catechizing and preaching of a regular ministry. So that if we have not yet unlearned the errors of our Popish ancestors, it is because the doctrines of the Reformation, begun about two hundred years ago in England, have not effectually reached us, nor is it likely that they ever will without a fit and learned clergy. [11]

Other evidences may be presented as to the increase of Sunday sports-playing and other practices disrespectful of the Sabbath in the south as well as the north. We will confine ourselves to the testimony of the Rev. John Thomas, an Independent preacher, minister at Rhayader and two other chapels in Radnorshire. He published an autobiography in 1767, and we quote from the translation provided by the Rev. William Williams, Swansea, in his excellent book, *Welsh Calvinistic Methodism*:

I remember on one Sabbath afternoon going near the church of my native parish, where there were many playing quoits, and great numbers, like a fair, looking on. In my childish way I began to speak to them of the state of their souls; they laughed, and seemed to regard me as a madman; and yet, whether it was in consequence of my words, or because of being threatened by others, or because of being pricked in their own consciences, on being thus reproved by a child, several of them ceased from their play in the churchyard. But they would afterwards go to out-of-the-way corners, where I made it my business to follow them, and to speak to them of the evil of thus profaning the Lord's Day. Sometimes I would threaten to call the churchwardens, but I knew that that would have been in vain, for they, regardless of their oath, would not come out of the taverns, though I went to those places to seek them. O ye perjurers, where are your oaths?[12]

The author continued:

He began to preach in his twentieth year, travelled about for that purpose, and met with rough treatment in several places in South Wales. At Mynydd Ty'n-croes, near Colwinstone, in the Vale of Glamorgan, while preaching in the open air, he was pelted with rotten eggs until his sides were sore and his clothes in a most filthy condition. His head was not touched, for a woman held a hat to protect it; and at Llangatwg, Breconshire, a squire of the village, the clergyman, and the sexton came out from the public-house, with the landlord, to oppose him. The first of these collared him and gave him a blow upon the cheek, and then they all returned to the place from which they had come. At Crickhowell, the 'howlings of the mob caused terror to his flesh,' and they smashed the window of the house in which he was preaching. 'I was by the church of Ystrad, in Glamorganshire, at one time when games were going on, and I stood to speak by the churchyard wall. Then the ballplayers and dancers left their work, and came to the other side of the wall to hear, fiddlers and all. Then the clergyman, who was there with them, having lost his company, said to the fiddlers, 'If you expect to be paid, go on with your work, and you that are talking, go away from the churchyard. It is consecrated ground.'[13]

These descriptions, together with many others which could have been included and which were written quite independently of each other, and with the sole intention of presenting historical facts, prove that the state of Wales at this time was completely as described by Williams, Pantycelyn, and Thomas Charles, Bala; that is, full of ungodliness, near pagan ignorance, and Roman Catholic superstition; the common people without any real knowledge of God, nor any real respect for the Sabbath, but given up to sports, drunkenness, and every other type of corruption. These testimonies are confirmed, if any further confirmation were needed, by the cruel persecutions suffered by the early Methodists when going about to preach the gospel. It may be seen that these attacks were not at all confined to north Wales, though it is there that they were fiercest and were continued longest; they occurred also in the south. Surely, if large areas of the south had been almost fully possessed by the Nonconformists, as Dr Rees maintains, such malicious attacks, upon men who were itinerating with the single aim of bringing the world to Christ, would have been quite impossible.

## THE ESTABLISHED CHURCH

In order to understand clearly the religious condition of Wales at this time, we must describe the state of religion in the Established Church, and amongst the Nonconformists. As for the Established Church, its own historians acknowledge that its religion was in a very deteriorated condition. Dr Erasmus Saunders states that a large number of churches:

> ... had either been converted into barns or stables, or only served for the habitations of owls and jackdaws ... The use for which they were intended is almost forgotten, unless it be as at Llan-y-bri, where I am informed the impropriator or his tenant has let the church to the neighbouring dissenters, who are free to rent it for the desirable opportunity of turning a church into a conventicle[14] ... In some places we have churches without chancels; in others we have but some piece of a church, that is, one end, or a side aisle that is remaining, and in some parishes even none at all ... In some not only the bells are taken away, but the towers are demolished, and in many others there are scarce any seats, except here and there a few ill-contrived and broken stools and benches. Their little windows are without glass, and darkened with boards, mats, or lattices, their roofs decaying, tottering, and leaky; their walls green, mouldy, and nauseous, and very often without wash or plaster; and their floors ridged up with noisome graves, without any pavement, and only covered with a few rushes.[15]

It is easy to see that no one cared for these places, nor attended them for worship. The parsonages and vicarages also were but poor cottages; the clergy, though so poor, could yet not live in them, so that they were rented out to anyone who would take them. They often fell to the sexton, who, in order somehow to keep body and soul together, would be given the privilege of selling beer next to the cemetery.

The clergy were not much better than the people. The Welsh bishoprics were all in the hands of Englishmen who were not the least concerned over the fate of the country. Nor did they intend to remain long in their impoverished dioceses; they remained only until they were promoted to a richer see. They would appoint their sons, brothers, nephews, or friends, to Welsh livings, even though these, as Englishmen, were unable to read or preach in the language of the natives. At the beginning of the eighteenth century, nearly the whole of Radnorshire was Welsh-speaking, and there exists an interesting correspondence between the parishioners of Glascwm, a parish lying in the middle of the county, and the Bishop of St David's, concerning a clergyman newly appointed over them. Previously, the lessons had been read in both Welsh and English alternately, so also the prayers, and the sermons were in Welsh and in English on alternate Sundays. But as for the new clergyman, he conducted everything in English. The parishioners requested that the Bishop require him to conduct the service bilingually, or to employ an able minister that could do this for him. It seems that the new vicar, on being told by the Bishop, sought to do this for them. But within a few months, the parishioners sent a new complaint to St David's, that the vicar was undertaking himself to read the service in Welsh, and that no one understood a word he said, as he was not Welsh himself and had not learnt the language. This took place in 1743. The English bishops and clerics had purposed to suppress the Welsh language completely. The Churchman and poet, the Rev. Evan Evans (*Ieuan Brydydd Hir*) wrote in a letter dated 23 June, 1766, to his friend Richard Morris:

> As for us in this Episcopate (St Asaph), the Bishop may do what he wishes without hindrance, in that, like another Pope, he has promoted three or four of his nephews to the best places, where native Welshmen used previously to minister, and the curates under them are not allowed to read the lessons in Welsh. And recently I also heard it said that two other Englishmen in Montgomeryshire, in the churches of Castell and Aberhafesb read only in English throughout the year, although less than half the parishioners understand a word that they say. I heard that the people of Anglesey wish to banish the arrant Englishman who was made Parson of Trefdraeth back to his own country.

No wonder that Evan Evans added:

> God bring us better times, and frustrate their extravagance, lest they destroy men's souls eternally!

Very few of the Church of England parsons could preach in the language of the people, not even those of them who were themselves Welsh. The majority were men of ignorance, having no learning and not possessing any qualification for their sacred office in terms of ability, character, fluency of speech, but only a talent for gaining the favour of someone of influence amongst the patrons of church livings. As in every age of religious decline, the clergy were drawn from the dregs of society. According to Dr Erasmus Saunders:

It is not to be doubted but that the ordaining of persons that are themselves contemptible has an apparent tendency to derive contempt on their profession; and it is so when any little A. B. C. D-arian schoolmaster, a gentleman's butler, a mountebank, and what not, shall be so cheaply admitted to commence clerks, on the prevailing merit of some potent impropriator's recommendation, who may be solicitous for a cheap chaplain, or so to pack off a useless servant.[16]

These possessed a smattering of Welsh; enough to socialize with their fellow drinkers in the taverns but not enough to use in the pulpit. The Rev. G. O. Jones states that they would read English books when trying to prepare for the Sabbath, but having cobbled together some kind of sermon, when they came to the pulpit to deliver it, it was such a babble of dissonant, inaccurate gibberish that none could understand a word of it.[17] This is a similar accusation to that made against the clergy of his day by John Penry, the Welsh martyr, that they were deficient in religious vocabulary and theological terms, and unable therefore to make themselves understood from the pulpit, though they were able to maintain a conversation on the high-road or around the hearth.

Worst of all, they were not men of character. Many of them, indeed, lived openly ungodly lives. They were unable to counsel the immoral or rebuke the wicked because they themselves were corrupt. Griffith Jones declared:

It cannot be concealed that many lewd wastrels acknowledged that the true reason for their infidelity and carnal life was their low opinion of the clergy; who, as they believed, had no greater faith in Christianity than they themselves, for otherwise they would preach and live better.

The same man, in a letter of his on catechizing, attacks mercilessly,

. . . the lazy rectors and vicars who lead careless lives and spend their time in keeping company and in drunkenness throughout the taverns, instead of sticking to their books and fulfilling their duty.

When the ministers of the Word were themselves living in ungodly extravagance, and showing clearly in their lives that they did not believe nor had any respect for the truth, to which they had vowed allegiance at their ordination, it is no wonder that those outside, both gentry and common people, took it for granted that Christianity was false and religion but a myth, and turned their backs on the means of grace, giving themselves to riotous living.

Dr Erasmus Saunders acknowledged that in many churches, preaching, catechizing, and administering of the sacraments would take place only rarely, if at all; and that in others, the prayers would only be read in part, and perhaps only once a month, or once a quarter. He blames the low salaries of the curates for this. They were forced to serve two or three churches, and these often far from each other, for some ten to twelve pounds a year and he asks, in anger, that if this was how matters stood, what order or regularity could be expected?

Forced they are (now they are ordained) to submit to any terms, they must starve or even be contented with the meanest salaries, and yet trudge and labour for it as long as they are able; and having so little time and so many places to attend upon, how precipitately and as if out of breath are they obliged to read the prayers, or to shorten and abridge them! What time have either they or their congregations to compose themselves while thus forced to a kind of perpetual motion, or like hasty itinerants to hurry about from place to place? There is no time fixed for going to church, so it be on Sundays, so the poor man must begin at any time, with as many as be at hand, sooner or later as he can perform his round. He then abruptly huddles over as many prayers as may be in half an hour's time, and then returns again to his road, fasting (for how earnestly so ever his appetite may call for it, it is seldom that he has time, or that the impropriator's farmer can afford to give him dinner) till he has despatched his circuit, or that weariness or darkness obliges him to rest, or perhaps for the want of a little refreshment at home, to go where he ought not, where it's odds but he will again meet with many of his congregation, who when their short service is over are too apt to think themselves at liberty to spend the remaining part of the day at an ale-house or at some pastime or diversion as they are disposed.[18]

These testimonies, which are all taken from Anglican authors, and could be greatly added to, prove that the Established Church was completely unable to withstand the corruption which was entering as a flood, and to maintain religion and morality. With unhealthy, dirty and ruined buildings; with apathetic, rushed, religious services on the Sundays, without prior warning as to the times of service; and with immoral clergy, held in contempt by the common people, more familiar with an armchair and the happy company of the tavern than with God's Word, and so deficient in their own mother-tongue that they could not preach and be understood, it was impossible that any spiritual good could be done. Too often the clergy were the sources of corruption. They were at the van of all ungodliness and extravagance; they mixed with wastrels on the Sundays, taking the chief part in the licentious sports and their private lives were often shameful. What wonder therefore that religion was blasphemed?

## NONCONFORMITY

It is not an easy task to discover an accurate evaluation of the number and strength of the Nonconformists of the day and of the influence they possessed in the land. By the 'Nonconformists' we mean the Presbyterians, Independents and Baptists, though the Quakers also were strong in some parts of Wales. We would not wish to diminish in any way the praise due to the Nonconformist Fathers, nor minimize the success that followed their labours. They were courageous men, and full of faith. They laboured untiringly for the sake of the gospel under extreme difficulties, and they did not count their lives dear when proclaiming the truth of God to their countrymen. The privations that they endured could almost be compared to those of the Apostle Paul. They were oppressed by unjust laws and by merciless state officials; they were hunted as partridges along mountain ridges; they were familiar with imprisonments, famine and nakedness. The names of Walter Cradoc, Vavasor Powell, Stephen Hughes, Hugh Owen of Bron-y-clydwr, and other fellow-labourers equally as famous, will always be remembered in Wales. Their histories read as a romance. If the low estate of the land when they emerged, is taken into account, and the obstacles against which they had to contend, all must conclude that they accomplished a great work. They were the means of gathering together congregations and of forming churches in many different parts of the country, many of which remain to this day. It is true that the churches were small, and that they met in private houses to hear the gospel preached, but if they could not frustrate and drive back the sinful flood that had swept over the land, they could bear a witness for God in the midst of it, so as to trouble some consciences.

The Rev. Thomas Rees in his *History of Protestant Nonconformity in Wales* argues that the Principality, and south Wales in particular, had been evangelized to a considerable extent before the rising of Methodism by the labours of the famous men mentioned above, and their successors, and that the Methodists Reformers merely entered into their labours and reaped that which was sown by them. In this, we believe that he has been led astray by his denominational zeal. One proof given by him is that the first congregations of Howell Harris and Daniel Rowland were gathered from those neighbourhoods where Dissenting chapels already existed. The suggestion is that these people had previously been members in Dissenting chapels. This is completely contrary to Harris's testimony. When he rebuked Edmund Jones, Pont-y-pool, in a notably tender and evangelical manner, for forming Dissenting churches at Defynnog and other places, without first conferring with either himself or Daniel Rowland, he says:

> As to the manner of effecting it, you know it was such as gave us a just cause of offence; as you did not send to Mr Griffith Jones, Mr Rowland, or myself, that we might have weighed, reasoned calmly, and spend some time in prayer together about it; as it was the first step of this kind in Wales, and as most

of the people had been called through our ministry. I know, if you will put yourself in our place, that you will see it was not quite right, any more than it would be for me, if I was to come and take your people secretly from you, though they sent for me.[19]

This quotation, to which Edmund Jones answered not a word, proves that it was not from the Dissenting chapels already in existence, that the first societies of Howell Harris and Daniel Rowland were formed, but from ungodly men converted by the preaching of these two men. In the same way, the church at Groes-wen, in the letter they sent to the Association in 1746, when asking if some of their assisting preachers might be ordained, acknowledged that their members were the spiritual children of the Methodist ministers. What is shown by the establishment of Methodist societies in the neighbourhoods of old Dissenting churches is that those churches at the time were few in number, that they were declining quickly, and without much influence upon the neighbourhood about them.

Dr Rees acknowledges that the spiritual condition of north Wales was completely equivalent to the description provided by Mr Thomas Charles in the *Trysorfa Ysbrydol* [*Spiritual Treasury*] when giving an account of the state of the Principality. Mr Charles's reputation was such that no one could accuse him of misrepresentation. But Dr Rees claims that Gwynedd alone is being described and that the conditions in the south were very different. But he has forgotten that Mr Charles was raised in the south and lived there until reaching manhood, apart from the time spent at Oxford. He was therefore fully acquainted with the state of religion throughout Wales. If the condition of the south had been very different from that of the north it is quite certain that a man of Mr Charles's fairness, carefulness and moderation, would have called attention to it when portraying the general picture.[20]

Two further general points concerning the Nonconformists need to be mentioned. Firstly, *in the period between the beginning of the eighteenth century and the rise of Methodism, the strength of Dissent in Wales had declined sharply because of bitter controversies in the churches.* In the original Dissenting churches, Congregationalists, Presbyterians, Baptists and Paedobaptists were found side by side. For some time, no great weight was attached to these differences; the great issue was the securing of the preaching of the essential truths of the gospel in their purity, and the cruel persecutions suffered tended to unite every congregation, notwithstanding the differences of opinion existing between individuals. But after the passing of the Toleration Act in 1689 with the consequent ending of the persecution, more attention was given to their differing opinions and the churches experienced much agitation as a result.

One argument was that between the Presbyterians and the Independents concerning the governance of the Church. This caused much trouble and divided at least two of the churches of the land. Perhaps the largest and most influential Dissenting church in Wales towards the end of the seventeenth century was the church at Wrexham, founded by Walter Cradoc. The famous Morgan Llwyd of Gwynedd had ministered there for a season with great success. But the argument between Dr Daniel Williams, who was born in Wrexham, and Dr Crisp, on church governance, disturbed their peace. In the end, after years of painful quarrelling, both in the congregation and in the press, the Presbyterians withdrew and established their own cause. The members remaining gradually changed their views on baptism, and became Baptists. A similar controversy occurred at Henllan Church, Carmarthenshire. The minister, the Rev. David Owen, together with the majority of the members tended to Presbyterianism, but the deacons were firmly for Independency. The argument continued from 1707 to 1710. Many appeals were made to other congregations and ministers in an effort to reconcile the two parties but every attempt was in vain. In the year 1710, the Congregationalists departed and formed the Independent Church at Rhydyceisiaid. Within about ten years, the Presbyterians at Henllan changed their minds. They dismissed their minister, the Rev. Jeremiah Owen, and appointed in his place Mr Henry Palmer, one of the deacons who had been arguing for Independency. Although, as far as we know, it is only in these two churches mentioned that this controversy resulted in division, it is certain that the same issue caused much trouble and quarrelling in many other churches.

Another controversy, proceeded with in a very unchristian spirit, was on baptism. It began about the end of the seventeenth century, soon after the passing of the Toleration Act. There is an account of a public debate on the matter occurring in 1692 in a place called Penylan, on the slopes of the Frenni Fawr in Pembrokeshire. The Rev. John Thomas of Llwyn-y-grawys argued for Paedobaptism, and the Rev. Jenkin Jones, Rhydwilym, for believers' baptism. Instead of ending strife, this debate only served to stir it up. It continued in the press in a very bitter spirit. The Rev. Samuel Jones, Brynllywarch, came out in support of the Independents, while the Baptists had to send for help from London. The result was a complete separation; the two parties divided, forming churches of their own views. But we may be certain that this did not occur without painful disturbances in the various congregations, which weakened them and was the cause of a considerable decline in their religion.

But of all the arguments, that which brought about most quarrelling and resulted in the most grievous consequences was the 'Great Arminian Controversy'. Arminian views began to leaven the Dissenting churches of Wales about the beginning of the eighteenth century. They were advanced by Mr Thomas Perrot, a tutor in the Dissenting Academy at Carmarthen; or, at least, the large majority of students who studied under him left the Academy as confirmed Arminians. This Arminianism was of a low tone and completely unevangelical; a truer name for it would be Pelagianism. It bordered on Arianism, and it very soon developed into Unitarianism. It is the reason why so many churches, belonging to the Independents and to the Presbyterians in Cardiganshire, Carmarthenshire and Glamorganshire, that were once orthodox are now completely Socinian. The new heresy was the cause of much argument and great disturbance in the Dissenting churches.

The different parties sought to overcome one another in every possible way. If the Calvinistic party was the stronger, they would choose a man of their own views to pastor the church. In a little while, perhaps, the Arminians would be the greater numerically, they would dismiss the Calvinistic minister and appoint an Arminian in his place. Sometimes there would be two ministers, one a Calvinist, the other an Arminian, both pastoring the same people – not because of the multiplicity of members, but only in order to satisfy the differing views present. What their method of preaching was, we do not know. Did they preach on alternate Sundays, or on alternate services? But the appointed work of the one was the demolishing of the work of the other.

An example of this occurred in the church of Cwm-y-glo, near Merthyr Tydfil, which met on the site of possibly the very first Dissenting chapel built in Wales. At the beginning of the century the minister was the Rev. Roger Williams, an Arminian who preached his views boldly, to the great satisfaction of one class of his hearers. But the Calvinists became uneasy. It appears also that they grew in number, and they insisted on the appointing of Mr James Davies, a man from Llanwrtyd, as a co-pastor. This occurred sometime between 1720 and 1725. When Roger Williams died and only James Davies was left to minister to the cause, the Arminians grumbled, and Sion Llewellyn, a member of the church and a rhymester, expressed their unease in the form of a ballad. Within two years, in 1732, the Arminian party succeeded in ordaining Richard Rees, a young man from amongst themselves who had been under the tutelage of Mr Perrot at Carmarthen, as co-pastor with James Davies. Sion Llewellyn again produced a ballad, this time expressing the satisfaction of his party with the ministry of Richard Rees:

| | |
|---|---|
| For the gospel's further progress | Er cynhaliaeth mawr i'n crefydd, |
| God sent Mr Rees to teach us; | Duw gododd Mr Rees i fynydd; |
| An able man, of gifts and learning, | Gwr llawn deall, dysg a doniau, |
| Gracious, fervent, and forebearing. | Llariaidd, gwresog ei rasusau. |
| Hear him, on the anvil striking, | Mi glywn y gwr yn rhoi ergydion, |
| See him gather nails for building; | Ac yn dechrau hela hoelion; |
| By the Spirit's oil anointed, | 'Nôl eu hiro yn olew'r Ysbryd, |
| These will pierce all hearts appointed. | Fe gerddai'r hoelion hynny'n hyfryd. |

Matters continued in this way at Cwm-y-glo for another fourteen years. The Arminian preacher driving in his choice nails and seeking to maintain them in the minds of his congregation, in one service; and the Calvinistic preacher at the next service attempting to remove them and replace them with his own different nails. No peace or success could ever flourish here. It is no surprise to read therefore that the Arminian party left in 1747 and settled at Cefncoedycymer. This gradually became an Unitarian church. Within another four years, those members at Cwm-y-glo who lived the other side of the mountain, withdrew and formed a church at Aberdare. This also became Socinian. In 1750, by which time the original church had moved from Cwm-y-glo to Ynysgau, Samuel Davies, the son of James Davies, was ordained as co-pastor with his father. Samuel had also been taught at Carmarthen and, like all the students there at this time, had adopted an Arminian creed. Therefore, at Ynysgau, father and son would be found preaching opposing views, and leading different parties within the church. But the Calvinists complained that James Davies accepted from his son what he would never have accepted from Richard Rees, his previous co-pastor. Many further changes occurred in the Ynysgau pulpit. At times it would be Calvinistic, at other times Arminian, if not Unitarian even. But we are glad to record that it was the evangelical party that overcame in the end, and that the church is presently as strong in the faith as any church in Wales.

A similar situation arose in the churches of Cefn-arthen and Pentrety-gwyn in Carmarthenshire, where William Williams's parents were members. There were here three ministers in the years 1731 and 1732, namely, David Williams and John Williams, the sons or relatives of Roger Williams, Cwm-y-glo, and D. Thomas. The first two were zealous Arminians, but the third a Calvinist, appointed by the Calvinistic wing of the church to counteract the influence of the others. Matters became too uncomfortable for the two parties to remain together so that in 1730, D.Thomas delivered his farewell sermon and with his fellow Calvinists, established a cause at Ty-yn-y-pentan. These two churches remained separate for many years but the Rev. Morgan Jones, Tygwyn, succeeded eventually in reuniting them.

Though there was no separation because of the Arminian Controversy in many churches, there were fervent arguments throughout all the congregations, and a bitter spirit arose to the great detriment of spiritual religion, and the great enfeeblement of Dissent. Under these conditions, progress was impossible. Churches that tolerated two ministers preaching against each other, each calling the other a heretic, and containing two parties, one being angered when the other was satisfied, must of necessity have been in a woefully low condition. It is no wonder that the Dissenting churches were feeble and powerless when the Methodist Connexion made its appearance.

The second point to be considered is that the Nonconformists, at the time of the Methodist awakening, were characterized by formality, apathy, and painful coldness. The ministers had lost the pioneering spirit of the Fathers. They no more itinerated in their efforts to evangelize the land and to draw the people to Christ. They were satisfied with pastoring the small flock that remained, seeking only to keep those from wandering. The little life that was in them was manifested mostly in controversy rather than in any efforts to do good. We readily admit that there were some worthy exceptions in their midst, but these were very few. This coldness of religion was no doubt due in part to the consequences of the Arminian heresy, which froze the atmosphere like an iceberg, even for those who had not drawn too near to it. The cold formality was accompanied by an indifference to discipline. This had gone so far that some zealous ministers were half desiring a separation. In a letter from the Rev. Edmund Jones, an Independent minister in Pont-y-pool, to Howell Harris, dated 7 August, 1741, are found the following words:

> I wish some of the sound Dissenting ministers separated from the erroneous and loose Dissenters; but perhaps it will come to that. Both the ministers of Penmaen deny that there is any need of discipline among them, and call my attempts of discipline by the opprobrious names of rigid, punctilious, and novel customs; upbraid my friendship with the Methodists, whom they call my new friends, but tell me that I had as well or better, or to that purpose, have accorded with my old friends, etc. Thus these men refuse to be reformed – the more is the pity.[21]

It seems that Howell Harris preached particularly severely against the lukewarmness of the Dissenters, and this is referred to in the same letter of Edmund Jones's:

> I am glad Mr Whitefield hath borne his honest and bold testimony against the lukewarmness and worldiness of Dissenters, and against the loose walking and levity of some of their ministers. There was the greatest need in the world of it; but Mr Whitefield doth it in a prudent, though yet honest manner; and had you dear brother, done this with less passion and intemperance of spirit, and with more prudence and distinction, observing a regard to their persons, you might have done much good; but as it was I fear it did but little good. It is my presumption upon your honesty and self-denial makes me venture to tell you this much; but I see our own much greater fault. We should have borne our just reproof, and be humble, and confess our great degeneracy before God and man, and strive to reform. . . . and while you exclaim so much against the lukewarmness of our Dissenters, do not neglect warning of the spiritual pride and intemperate spirit of the Baptist Dissenters, which are yet worse, though accompanied with the zeal which the other lukewarm Dissenters want.[22]

To some of the ministers, the zeal and passion of Howell Harris and Daniel Rowland were an offence. According to Dr Rees, they would use expressions that would pain the refined taste of the Nonconformists. He quotes a Thomas Morgan, who went to hear Daniel Rowland preaching near Carmarthen:

> Went this afternoon to Clyngwyn (near Carmarthen), to hear Mr D. Rowland. Ben. Thomas prayed before him; then he preached from Hosea 2:14. He did not much confine himself to his text, but was very earnest, endeavouring to win the affections. I think I found some efficacy attending his work, though he had some very weak expressions.

The same man heard Rowland preach at Caerphilly, and wrote:

> Went to Caerphilly, where I met many of my old acquaintances. On my way home I heard Mr Rowland at Pen-y-groes-wen, from Judges 5:23. His sermon was practical, but not critical; for he said several things which I think he would not have said, had he well considered the matter before hand.[23]

Dr Rees describes this Thomas Morgan as 'one of the most unprejudiced of the Nonconformists'. Such begrudging faint praise for one who is generally acknowledged to be probably the best preacher that Wales has ever seen would seem to suggest that the critic's spirit was cold within him, and that he attached more importance to form than to the saving of souls.

The Rev. John Thomas, to whom we have already referred, bears testimony to the awful coldness that predominated amongst the Dissenters at this time. He began his spiritual life with the Methodists but in 1761 joined the Independents or, as he called them, the Dissenters. With reference to this, he commented:

> There were several who from time to time advised me to go to the Academy, that I might have a little more human learning ... I saw that the Dissenters were in their discipline according to the Word of God, and nearer the Apostolic order of the New Testament than the Methodists; but I loved the life and zeal of the Methodists, and feared the lukewarmness of the Dissenters, lest, if I joined them, I should become lukewarm as they were; but some of them said to me that if I would come among them, I might be the means of warming them.

He decided upon seeking admission to the Academy at Abergavenny:

> ... and I mentioned this purpose to the Rev. Daniel Rowland, who said nothing against me ... I arrived at Abergavenny about the end of 1761, and when I came to set about learning Latin books, and saw so much ungodliness in the congregation, I felt that it had become a change of climate with me, and fearing that I would lose ground in my spirit, I retired daily at noon to the plantations by the side of the river Usk to pray, where I often found it very sweet ... During the four years that I stayed at the Academy I preached frequently here and at other places, and in the holidays I would go through several of the counties of Wales, especially Cardiganshire, preaching with the Methodists and the Dissenters, when I got a little of the fire of Llangeitho to keep my soul from freezing in the region of Abergavenny. Mr Rowland was very kind to me, and would sometimes ask me to preach at Llangeitho ... The most earnest and experimental of the Dissenters loved me, but the lukewarm and formal regarded me as too much of a Methodist, especially when I had help from Heaven to preach; but when I was dry and dead, and spoke only from my own understanding, they would say that I was like a Dissenter.'[24]

Such comments, of which there are no reasons whatever to doubt the accuracy, prove that Nonconformity was at a very low ebb at the beginning of Methodism; the ministers amongst them were formal, critical and cold, and laid no great weight upon the the main doctrines of evangelical religion; their churches were small and declining rapidly, the members divided into different parties which were bitter towards each other. Arminianism, which tended to Arianism, was entering in as a rising tide and, in all probability, had it not been for the Methodist Awakening, most of Wales today would be Unitarian. In the whole of Gwynedd, the Nonconformists had six churches, all relatively small. They were stronger in the south, but here also they were declining. A. J. Johnes says of them :

These Dissenters exhausted their strength by controversies amongst themselves on the rite of baptism; on which subject a difference of opinion had long existed amongst them, though persecution had prevented them from making it a ground of disunion. Till the breaking out of Methodism, their cause continued to decline.[25]

He adds:

Properly speaking, the history of Methodism is the history of Dissent in Wales.[26]

## THE NEW ELEMENTS INTRODUCED BY METHODISM

When news of the awakening produced by the powerful preaching of Harris and Rowland spread abroad, the Dissenters rejoiced greatly; they began to hope for salvation from the very jaws of death, as it were. In 1736, the Rev. Lewis Rees preached at the Dissenting Chapel at Pwllheli. He found the small flock there notably discouraged. They complained that their numbers were decreasing, the old people dying, no new faces seeking religion, and that the cause would soon come to an end, in all probability. Mr Rees advised them to be encouraged, declaring that the dawn had already arisen in the south, that Howell Harris was a remarkable man, that he was going about to preach and warn, and that wonderful effects accompanied his efforts. Soon, Lewis Rees requested and received a promise from Howell Harris that he would visit Gwynedd. The same feelings were shared by Edmund Jones, Pont-y-pool; David Williams, Watford; Henry Davies, Blaen-gwrach, and others. They saw in the Methodists a new regiment arising to fight God's battles in the land, and though they had been guilty of staying their hands and were on the point of giving up, the effect of the springing up of this brave new regiment was to fill them with a new spirit. It may be said that Methodism introduced the following elements:

1. A bold forward spirit, which dared to oppose untruth and extravagance in a determined and public manner.

2. A clear proclamation of evangelical truths from warm, passionate hearts. In particular, the necessity of regeneration and of the work of the Holy Spirit were emphasized.

3. The ministry of unordained men, if they possessed preaching skills.

4. A loving care for the converted, particularly by means of the societies.

We do not wish to claim for the Methodist Connexion the credit of being the only instruments in the Lord's hands for the evangelizing of Wales. We know better than that. It is true that it was on Daniel Rowland that the heavenly fire fell first at this time of revival; it was the Methodists who went about as Samson's foxes, lighting a beacon that is still with us today. But, true though this is, the fire soon kindled in the other Nonconforming denominations that were already on the field. They also partook abundantly of the same heavenly influences. But it was the spirit of Methodism, first felt at Llangeitho and Trefeca, that quickened them. And that spirit pervaded them, and all their works, to this very day. Indeed, we may look upon present day Welsh Nonconformists, in the ardour of their zeal and commitment, in their audacity to oppose wickedness in all its forms, in the evangelical nature of their ministry, and in the great emphasis placed by their preachers upon the essential elements of our religion, as well as in their care of converts, as the children of Daniel Rowland and Howell Harris, rather than as successors of that primitive Dissent. At the same time, every Christian acknowledges that the efforts of the Methodist Fathers, together with the labours of the able preachers that followed them almost without a break, from then until now, form a brilliant and glorious chapter in the history of religion in Wales.

[1] The basis of much in these opening paragraphs is L. Tyerman, *The Life and Times of John Wesley* (London, 1890), vol. 1, chapter 3.

[2] *North British Review* (1847).

[3] Quoted in L. Tyerman, *Wesley*, vol. 1, p. 62.

[4] Ibid., p. 64.    [5] Ibid.    [6] Ibid., pp. 64-5.

[7] These were humorous or satirical dramatic presentations, often performed in the open air.

[8] Diary entry in 1773, quoted in Thomas Rees, *A History of Protestant Nonconformity in Wales* (London, 1861), p. 306.    [9] Ibid., p. 383.

[10] Erasmus Saunders, *A View of the State of Religion in the Diocese of St David's about the Beginning of the 18th Century* (London, 1721), p. 35.    [11] Ibid.

[12] William Williams, *Welsh Calvinistic Methodism* (1884; republished Bryntirion Press, 1998), pp.42-3.

[13] Ibid., pp. 43-4.

[14] Saunders, *Religion in St David's*, p. 23.

[15] Ibid., p. 17.

[16] Saunders, *Religion in St David's*, p. 60.

[17] *Welch Piety*.

[18] Saunders, *Religion in St David's*, p. 24.

[19] Thomas Rees, *Nonconformity in Wales*, p. 383.

[20] At this point, the authors take a few pages to discuss various statistical evidences on the numbers of Nonconformists in early eighteenth-century Wales. The discussion had more to do with the denominational politics of the late nineteenth century than with the history of the Methodist Fathers and is therefore omitted in this translation.

[21] HJH, pp. 180-1.    [22] Ibid.

[23] Thomas Rees, *Nonconformity in Wales*, p. 394.

[24] William Williams, *Welsh Calvinistic Methodism*, pp. 47-8.

[25] Arthur James Johnes, *An Essay on the Causes which have produced Dissent from the Established Church in the Principality of Wales* (London, 1831), p. 8.

[26] Ibid., p. 9.

# 2

# GRIFFITH JONES, LLANDDOWROR

## HIS BIRTH AND UPBRINGING

*W*ales has never been blessed with a greater benefactor than the venerable Griffith Jones. The country has never known a purer and more selfless patriot and no more excellent man has ever breathed its air. It is very appropriate that he is called the Morning Star of the Revival. He was on the field of battle long before Rowland or Harris; he gave himself, in all the energy and liveliness of his nature, to the great work of enlightening and evangelizing his nation; he never faltered in this work, for all the many oppositions that he encountered, until he closed his eyes in death. And even as he died, the condition of his country weighed heavily upon him, and he made provisions in his will for continuing the good work that he had begun. The Welsh nation will be in his debt for as long as it survives.

He was born in the year 1684, in the parish of Cilrhedyn, on the boundary between Carmarthenshire and Pembrokeshire. His parents were both religious and were members with the Dissenters. Dr Rees believed that they attended at Henllan, where John Thomas, Llwyn-y-grawys; David Lewis, Cynwyl; and other popular ministers often came to preach, and that it was there that Griffith Jones received his first religious impressions, together with his commitment to Calvinistic doctrines. His constitution was not strong; as a child he was troubled with asthma so that he could not walk across a room without pain and difficulty, but he strengthened as he grew and succeeded to some extent in throwing off the weakness.

His father died when he was young so that the responsibility for his upbringing fell entirely upon his mother. Mr Charles says that he was of a religious nature from birth. His mental alertness and desire for education were evident from a very early age. Because he expressed a desire to enter the ministry, his mother arranged that he be given every possible educational advantage and once he had received all that the local schools could offer he went to Carmarthen, either to the Dissenting Academy there, or

to the Grammar School. It is recorded that he was ordained a deacon of
the Established Church by Bishop Bull, in September, 1708, and accepted
into full orders in September 1709, by the same man. What made him
throw in his lot with the Established Church, having been raised amongst
the Dissenters, is not known, but it was certainly not for financial gain,
for his whole life demonstrated that he was a strong and conscientious
Churchman. It is probable that his first curacy was at Cilrhedyn, his
native parish.

## HIS FAME AS A PREACHER

He very soon began preaching with much power and solemnity. Mr Charles
states that Griffith Jones's understanding of the doctrines of the gospel and
the order of salvation was not clear initially, and that only gradually did
the divine illumination enter his soul in all its glory. Mr Charles gathered
this from Mr Jones's letters to Madam Bevan, but these same early letters
reveal much deep thought and seriousness. He devoted himself to the study
of theology and as he was a man of powerful abilities, with a sharp mind
and good memory, he soon became familiar with the writings of the more
eminent English and foreign theologians.

'By divine aid,' said Thomas Charles, 'and with God's blessing upon his
hard work, he quickly grew in grace and in the knowledge of God, and
of the Saviour Jesus Christ.' He obtained the curacy of Laugharne parish
and there demonstrated such progress in fluency and ministerial skills
that his eloquent and evangelical sermons caused considerable excitement
in his own parish and in those adjoining. He married Miss Phillips, the
daughter of Sir Erasmus Phillips, Picton Castle. His wife was known for
her godliness and it is possible that it was through his ministry that she
was converted, but she was weak in health and they do not seem to have
had any children.

Two years after receiving full orders, he was appointed Rector of Llandeilo Abercywyn and, in 1716, Vicar of Llanddowror, by his brother-in-
law, Sir John Phillips, the patron of the living. Sir John Phillips was a man
of considerable nobility, and Thomas Charles argues, after having studied
his letters, that religion and godliness were the source of this nobility. This
conclusion is confirmed by many facts. Whenever he was in London, Sir
John would seek the company of Whitefield and the two Wesleys. There
are many references to him in their journals as a gentleman of evident
religion, and like them he, at one time, attended the Moravian Society at
Fetter Lane. As well as ministering at Llandeilo and Llanddowror, Griffith
Jones visited Llan-llwch Church fairly often. It was under his ministry
there that Miss Bridget Vaughan, the heiress of the Derllys estate, and

known now throughout Wales by the name of 'Madam Bevan', was con-victed. This lady was a friend to him throughout his life; she supported him in his labours in every way, and her purse was always ready when any need arose.

Griffith Jones's fame as a preacher spread through the land and the people came in their thousands to hear him. His eloquence and the power that accompanied his ministry were known even in Scotland. He was invited to preach before Queen Anne. Our authority for these statements is a stanza in the elegy to him written by William Williams, Pantycelyn, which states:

| | |
|---|---|
| Scotland's people heard him gladly, | Fe gadd Scotland oer ei wrando, |
| Far away in northern lands, | Draw yn eitha'r Gogledd dir, |
| There the gospel thundered loudly | Yn dadseinio maes yn uchel |
| As he shared redemption's plans; | Bynciau'r iachawdwriaeth bur; |
| Hosts received the words of mercy | Cadd myrddiynau deimlo geiriau |
| From the lips of this good man, | Hedd, o'i enau'n llawer man; |
| She heard also his entreaty, | Clywodd hithau rym ei ddoniau |
| Noblest majesty, Queen Anne. | Frenhinol ardderchocaf Anne. |

He came to the attention of the Society for the Propagating of the Gospel in foreign parts, the S.P.G., as an appropriate person to send as a missionary to India. There are letters in existence that show that he was pursued by them with considerable importunity. At last, he consented. We do not know what it was that frustrated this purpose. It may have been love of his fellow-countrymen and compassion for their low condition that overcame it. But Providence had its hand in the matter – there was great work prepared for Griffith Jones in his native land.

## HE BEGINS TO PREACH OUTSIDE HIS PARISH

Mr Charles gives the following description of him as a preacher:

His texts and style of speaking were admirably suited to the conditions of his hearers; often sharp, often fiery and awakening; always doctrinal, prac-tical, and moral; keeping away from both Antinomian licentiousness and comfortless and barren legalism. To see him ascending to the pulpit was a solemn and impressive sight. He would read the prayers with great seriousness, and the lessons slowly and with understanding. When preaching he would begin carefully, dividing his matter systematically and with much clarity, in a friendly manner almost as a conversation. But as he was gripped by his mes-sage, his spirit would kindle and warm, his expressions would become lively and authoritative until his hearers were completely mastered. His physical appearance was respectable, his voice clear and musical, his reasonings strong, his illustrations excellent, and his counsels and warnings severe and holding the conscience. His whole soul was in the work and he felt within himself all the appropriate responses to the truths he preached. To sum him up in one phrase is to describe him as endued with power from on high, and as such, he fulfilled God's sacred ministry with appropriate propriety and comeliness, in much authority, and great usefulness.

This is a very lively description. We can imagine the man of God slowly climbing the pulpit stairs with serious steps and with the solemnity of eternity upon his countenance. After reading the lessons and prayers clearly, he takes up his text and lays down his headings. He speaks slowly to begin with but his heart is soon warmed by the truths he pronounces; his spirit flames up; he is now as an angel flying in the midst of heaven, having the everlasting gospel. He pours forth streams of sacred eloquence upon the great congregation that has gathered to hear him, and they are silenced in his presence, quite overcome by his authority. No wonder that his fame spread abroad. There had probably not been such preaching heard within the churches of Wales for some centuries, if ever. Invitations came from adjoining parishes for him to visit them, and he believed, as with Paul and the call from Macedonia, that these constituted a summons from above, and he obeyed them to the utmost of his ability.

Often the churches would be too small to contain the congregations; he would then preach in the cemetery, with one of the memorial stones of the dead as a pulpit under him, and the sky as a roof over his head. This is how Williams's elegy describes him:

| | |
|---|---|
| Out he went, in zeal and glory, | Allan 'r aeth yn llawn o ddoniau, |
| Out to preach the Gospel tale, | I bregethu'r 'fengyl wir, |
| And to spread salvation's story | Ac i daenu iachawdwriaeth |
| Throughout Wales o'er hill and dale; | Olau, helaeth 'r hyd y tir; |
| Thousands gathered for his sermons, | Myrdd yn cludo idd ei wrando, |
| Filled each church, from wall to wall, | Llenwi'r llannau mawr, yn llawn, |
| Cemeteries he used as churches | Gwneud eglwysydd o'r mynwentydd |
| So that all might hear the call. | Cyn ei glywed ef yn iawn. |

The other reason why he preached outside, as well as the smallness of the churches, was the envy and anger of many of the clergy. They were thoroughly angered by his visits to their parishes without their permission. They wished to frustrate him because of their jealousy of his abilities and popularity. They would therefore lock the church doors against him and take home the keys with them. But they still could not keep his voice from being heard. Griffith Jones longed to preach, and the people longed to hear him, and therefore, in Williams's words, 'Cemeteries he used as churches.'

He gradually extended his journeys to the neighbouring counties and then to the whole of the south. It was under his ministry during such a preaching itinerary that Daniel Rowland was brought under conviction at Llanddewibrefi Church, and if he had done no more throughout his life than been the instrument for the conversion of Daniel Rowland, he would have performed excellent service to religion. As it was mainly during the Easter and Whitsun holidays that the Welsh used to hold their gluttonous gatherings and ungodly sports, he would arrange his journeys at these times, in order to preach down such corrupt practices, and it is said that there would hardly be a sermon without someone being saved. His congregations would often be made up of the worst ruffians and wastrels of the district, gathered to him out of curiosity, but he would not hesitate to denounce their bad habits. Mr Charles described their attitude as they listened. At first, they were wild and animal-like, but gradually, as Mr Jones preached, they were seen to become solemn. The tears began to flow in streams down their cheeks. Soon, they wept openly, and cried out, 'What shall we do to be saved?' He would proceed to explain to them the way of salvation, preaching sometimes for over three hours.

## THE CIRCULATING SCHOOLS

But for all his fame as an evangelist, Griffith Jones is perhaps even more famous as an educator and by means of his Circulating Charity Schools a new era dawned in Wales. It is often repeated that he modelled his plan on the system of schools set up by Thomas Gouge. But there was no similarity between the two approaches. Thomas Gouge's schools were English schools, Jones's were Welsh, and their only purpose was to teach how to read. The nearest comparable system that we know of, was the charitable endowment of John Jones, the Dean of Bangor, except that the latter was on a much smaller scale. In his will, dated 10 March 1719, the Dean left a sum of fifty pounds for the Rector of Llandegfan, Anglesey, and for his successors after him, to administer to the poor. The interest on the sum was to be used:

> . . . to teach ten of the children of the poor of the parish to read clearly the Bible and the Book of Common Prayer in Welsh; and also to teach them the principles of the Christian religion according to the Catechism of the Church of England.

Dean Jones left an equivalent sum for the same purpose to the parishes of Llanfair-yn-neubwll, Llanffinau, Llanfihangel-yn-Nhywyn, Llanfihangel Ysgeifiog, Rhoscolyn, and Pentraeth, all in Anglesey. He also left a hundred pounds to the Rector of Llanllechid, Arfon, that the interest might be used to teach twelve children of the poor of the parish:

> To read Welsh perfectly and to teach them the Catechism of the Church of
> England in Welsh so that they may not only recite it but by clear and godly
> explanation may understand it; and also that they may be able to read clearly
> the Bible and the Book of Common Prayer; and if possible to teach them a
> little writing and arithmetic.

He left the same sum of a hundred pounds for the same purpose to the
parishes of Cyffyn, Aber, and Bangor, in Caernarvonshire. To the parishes
of Llanddecwyn and Llanfihangel-y-traethau, in Merionethshire, the
philanthropic Dean bequeathed fifty pounds for the purposes noted. This
is the only example known to us of someone before Griffith Jones's time,
attempting to teach Welsh in the day schools. Not that Griffith Jones was
following the Dean's example. There is no evidence at all that he knew of
the attempts. The Circulating Schools was an idea that built up in his own
mind gradually, as a possible method of meeting the awful ignorance of
the land at the time.

The history given by Mr Charles of the commencement of the schools
is as follows:

> On the Saturday before the administration of the sacrament of the Lord's
> Supper, Mr Griffith Jones would have a kind of preparatory meeting. He
> would read the appropriate service and lessons, and would then ask if any-
> one in the congregation had not understood any particular verses. He would
> then explain these as clearly as he could, at the level of the congregation's
> understanding.

But he found that those most in need of such teaching were reluctant
to attend, particularly men who had grown old in ignorance. He therefore
announced that bread would be distributed to the poor on these monthly
Saturdays, bought by the monies contributed at communions. When they
came forward to receive the bread, he would ask them to stand in rows
and would ask simple questions of them, but in a kindly way so as not to
confuse or shame them.

For all his kindliness there was much of the wisdom of serpents in him,
and in order that his questions might not be left without answers, he
would make sure of drilling some well, beforehand, so that their answers
could encourage others. In this way, he began to realize the extent of the
ignorance of the gospel in the land, even of its most basic truths, and he
realized also the impossibility of improving the country without some
method of teaching the people to read God's Word.

He started a school in his own village to teach both children and adults
to read Welsh. The school was maintained in part by communion money,

but almost certainly a large contribution came from his own pocket. The school succeeded not only beyond his expectations but beyond his fondest hopes. As well as children, older men and aged people came, who wept aloud, partly in sorrow at their ignorance and partly in joy at the privilege being offered them. Even the blind would attend, in order to hear the Word of God being read and in order to memorize it. This led to the establishing of other schools further afield. The first school at Llanddowror was opened in 1730, some six years before the beginning of Methodism. In 1737 was published the first issue of *Welch Piety*, which gave a summary of the circumstances that led to the planning of the schools, the reasons for them, and answers to any objections against them. Within fifteen years, the number of schools had increased to 116, containing 5685 scholars receiving education. Griffith Jones's finances, even with the help he received from Madam Bevan, could never maintain so many schools. He was supported by many of the gentry, mainly from England, so that the work did not suffer from lack of means.

Griffith Jones's method was to employ a number of effective teachers and to disperse them through different parts of the country, according to the need. He was glad if a request came from the vicar of the parish, but if not invited in this way he would not hesitate to respond to an invitation from a number of parishioners. Usually the school remained in the neighbourhood for three months. It was considered that a man or child of average ability could learn to read the Bible reasonably well in this time, and the school would then move on in its circuit. Sometimes, if the need arose, a school could remain in the same place for six months, or even a year. In the schools, the scholars would be taught to read the Bible in Welsh; instructed in the Catechism of the Church of England; taught to sing the Psalms; and every means would be used to civilize them and make them religious. Not only children but mature and old people were taught, and on average about two-thirds of the scholars were adults. So that as many as possible could attend, the schools were open in the evening as well as in the day; and if, because of circumstances, someone could not attend in the day or the evening, it was expected that the teacher would visit them and provide lessons for them in their homes. There has never been a more flexible and convenient method of education than Griffith Jones's schools. They were adapted to every age of scholar and to all circumstances, and any who could not read the holy Scriptures were completely without excuse. After some years, the schoolmasters would return to a particular neighbourhood so as to teach the next generation of children. The following is a summary of the rules of the schools, as found in *Welch Piety*:

1. The schoolmasters must be sober, loving godliness, members of the Church of England, and faithful to the King and the government.

2. As well as teaching the scholars to spell and to read the books apportioned to them, they must also, twice a day, instruct them in the Catechism of the Church of England; and teach them to respond to the clergyman respectfully, capably, and devotionally, in the Church service.

3. The masters and scholars must be present at school early in the day, and attend consistently every Sabbath at public worship; then, on the following Monday, that the scholars be questioned in detail concerning the chapters read, the text, and the headings of the sermon heard in the Church the previous day.

4. The masters must produce, every quarter, a detailed account of the scholars; their names, ages, and the periods during which they had attended the school.

In order to ensure that these rules were kept, and that the schoolmasters were faithfully fulfilling their duties, the schools in each neighbourhood were, when at all possible, placed under the supervision of the local clergyman, who was to send in a report on the master's conduct and on the success of his efforts during the term. *Welch Piety* contains many examples of these reports and they all bear the highest testimony to the energies and godliness of the teachers, together with the great transformation wrought by them upon the morals of the youth and their behaviour in God's house. Griffith Jones had great difficulty finding suitable schoolmasters that were religious, of blameless life and able to teach. Dr Rees says that he was forced to recruit most of them from the Dissenters, in that very few from the Established Church possessed the necessary qualifications. There is not the slightest evidence for this. The rules of the schools state positively that all teachers had to be members of the Church of England, and Griffith Jones himself wrote in the 1745 issue of *Welch Piety* that for the first fifteen years of the schools this rule had been kept without exception. Before a Dissenter would be employed by Griffith Jones he had first to abstain completely from his Nonconformity and become a communicant in the Church. Griffith Jones overcame the problem of finding suitably qualified teachers by establishing a kind of Normal school at Llanddowror, with himself as Superintendent, where he prepared the teachers. Others were trained for the ministry here.

## THE CLERGY OPPOSE HIM

This good work was not suffered to proceed without opposition. The bishops were not at all sympathetic to the schools, though they did not dare to forbid them completely. Perhaps the main reason for their opposition was the fact that the schools were in Welsh. They had no sympathy with anything Welsh. They did not understand Welsh themselves and believed that the sooner the language was swept off the face of the earth, the better. It was no wonder therefore that they resented these schools that aimed to teach the common people to read the language. Griffith Jones's defence against this feeling is eloquent and unanswerable. He said that to establish English charity schools for a people that understood nothing but Welsh was as foolish as preaching an English sermon to a Welsh congregation that knew no other language than their mother-tongue. 'Should we', he asked, 'be more zealous for the propagation of the English language than for the salvation of our people?' He argued that it was impossible for many of the poor, particularly those who were old, to learn English, but that it was not right because of that to leave them to fall into eternal destruction. To set up English schools for them, he said, would be like establishing French Charity schools for the poor of England. 'It is folly,' he wrote, 'according to reason and to the nature of things, to attempt to teach people the principles of religion by the means of any language other than that which they speak.' Griffith Jones was a true philosopher. He understood clearly that it is only by means of what is known that one can discover what is unknown, and he was arguing the principles of the Society for the Utilization of the Welsh Language, one hundred and fifty years before that society was formed. Not that we believe he was motivated in any particular way by love of language, but he understood that Welsh was the only means by which the people could be informed of the things pertaining to their peace.

Though Mr Jones was a moderate man and took great care in his choice of words, his spirit at times was stirred up by the opposition of the bishops and nobility, and he could use strong and solemn language:

If Jesus Christ was on earth presently, and if he asked the question, 'Have ye never read?' many thousands of the poor would have to answer, 'No, Lord; we were never taught how to read; our parents could never afford the expense of sending us to school; and our spiritual leaders would not help; and when efforts were made to educate us without charge, some of our betters, who had authority in the parish, would not allow it.

This is strong enough, but we do not remember ever having read anything as scorching as the following:

If anyone were, not merely to be careless of, but to frustrate this charitable design (of teaching the people to read the Welsh Bible) it would be well for him to consider whether it would be an unspeakable pleasure or unendurable pain to him, on that great day of account, to have poor, ignorant, lost souls pointing at him, and saying, 'There's the man; the cruel, unmerciful man, the enemy of God and betrayer of our souls, who obstructed our salvation, and kept us out of the kingdom of heaven. He is therefore guilty of our blood; he is the cause of our damnation, in that he opposed the means offered to lead us to the knowledge of Christ the Saviour.

Griffith Jones realized that he was using strong language, and drawing a terrifying picture, so he defended himself by saying:

Perhaps some feel that I am shaming magistrates, ministers and bishops. I am far from shaming any, apart from those to whom shame belongs.

As if to say, 'Let no one wear the cap unless it fits.' He then added:

You know that I was born a Welshman, and that I have not yet unlearnt honesty, nor the unpoliteness of my mother-tongue, nor yet mastered the oily smoothness of the English tongue, which is now so refined as often to merge upon flattery.

Yet, in spite of such words, the antipathy of the bishops and the jealousy of the lazy and drunken clergy, persisted. In 1752, a scurrilous anonymous pamphlet was printed that mocked him and sought to increase prejudice against him. The title of the essay was, *Some Account of the Welsh Charity Schools, and of the Rise and Progress of Methodism in Wales through the means of them, under the sole Management and Direction of Griffith Jones, Clerk, Rector of Llanddowror, in Carmarthenshire; in a Short History of the Life of that Clergyman, as a Clergyman.* The author was the Rev. John Evans, the rector of Eglwys Gymyn, close to Llanddowror, an immoral man, and an inveterate enemy of Griffith Jones and the Revival.

John Evans had been encouraged in this work by the Bishop of St David's. The Bishop had no hesitation in using secretly the worst of instruments to blacken a man that he dared not accuse publicly. Nothing more obscene than this pamphlet can be imagined; its language is coarse, and in places too crude to print; enmity and malice is evident in every line. The following are some of its accusations:

1. That he had distributed 24,000 copies of Matthew Henry's Catechism in Welsh in his schools, from 1730 to 1738, when it was generally believed that he was using the catechism of the Church of England.

2. That he maintained that there were many of the precious lambs of Christ among the various denominations.

3. That his parents were Nonconformists and that he himself 'was never rightly reconciled to the Established Church, its rubrics, canons, homilies and clergy'.

4. That he spent some time, while rector at Llanddowror, studying Hebrew under Mr Perrot, tutor of the Presbyterian Academy at Carmarthen.

5. That nine-tenths of his communicants at Llanddowror were Dissenters, who would not enter any parish church but his.

6. That he secretly corresponded with the Methodists, and that all the teachers of his schools were either Dissenters or Methodists.

7. That in his exposition of the Church Catechism he explains away the precious doctrine of baptismal regeneration, and insists that neither baptism nor any other thing can make anyone a Christian, without saving faith in Christ.

8. That he and his friend [Madam Bevan, probably] had been at much expense and trouble to put down all wakes, sports, etc., to the no small lessening of Christian love and charity, and of all good neighbourliness to which they very much contributed, with very little or no ill consequences attending.

9. That he had been brought up to the trade of a turner of wooden dishes, and that he exercised that trade for his pleasure and diversion at Llanddowror since he was rector there.

10. That he was paid for preaching the length and breadth of the country, and that he expected half a crown to be slipped into his pocket at the end of every sermon, whilst he himself would not pay anything to those who served in his place at Llanddowror.

11. That he made changes in the Litany and omitted large sections of the Service, in order to have time for his own prayers and sermons.

The pamphlet contains a host of other similar accusations. Griffith Jones is described in the roughest and filthiest language as a foul hypocrite, a cruel oppressor, a matchless liar, and his followers are classed as thieves, lazy creatures, prostitutes and ignorant hot-heads. Very sensibly, Griffith Jones took no notice of this publication; he continued with his work as if he had never heard the scorning and insults of his opponents. We do not know if anyone took notice of it up until 1776, when the Rev. Evan Evans (*Ieuan Brydydd Hir*) referred to it in the introduction to his first book of sermons, where he said that:

. . . many conscientious ministers of the gospel have suffered cruelly during the last years under lordly and oppressive bishops. If this is doubted, I refer them to the writings of the late godly and truly reverend Mr Griffith Jones, of Llanddowror, who suffered all the scurrility of bribed clergymen, paid by the bishops to blacken him, though he, by the particular grace of God, had no spot or wrinkle upon him, except for that which malice and lunacy chose to throw.

## THE SPREAD OF THE SCHOOLS THROUGHOUT WALES

But in the face of all opposition, the schools flourished and increased. Griffith Jones never faltered in his efforts on their behalf. He argued for them in *Welch Piety*, year after year, setting forth proofs of the good work done through them, and publishing favourable reports of them received from all over the country. And on the other side, there was the insatiable longing of the common people to learn to read. The blind, the lame, the disabled, and the old, came to the schools and wept for joy for the privilege. The schools spread all over the Principality. They would be planted on the loneliest of hillsides and in the most isolated of valleys, so that all might have the opportunity to read the Scriptures. The following is a summary prepared by Mr Jones for the year 1760, the year before his death:

| COUNTIES | SCHOOLS | SCHOLARS |
|---|---|---|
| Breconshire | 4 | 196 |
| Cardiganshire | 20 | 1153 |
| Carmarthenshire | 54 | 2410 |
| Glamorganshire | 25 | 872 |
| Monmouthshire | 2 | 61 |
| Pembrokeshire | 23 | 837 |
| Anglesey | 25 | 1023 |
| Caernarvonshire | 27 | 981 |
| Merionethshire | 15 | 508 |
| Denbighshire | 8 | 307 |
| Montgomeryshire | 12 | 339 |

It is difficult to find an explanation as to why Radnorshire and Flintshire are not included in this table. Some attribute it to the fierce enmity of the clergy against the Revival; but we have no evidence that this was worse in these two counties than in other parts of Wales. Perhaps the knowledge of English was stronger in these counties; Radnorshire certainly was Anglicizing quickly at this time and was not therefore perhaps in such need of the Welsh schools as the other counties. During the thirty years continuation of the Circulating Schools, it is said that over 150,000 were taught to read God's Word. The ages involved varied from six years to over seventy. Only on 'that day' will the full extent of the good work produced by these means be known.

## GRIFFITH JONES'S LITERATURE WORK

After having created readers, Griffith Jones realized that necessity was placed upon him to provide them with books, and his efforts in this direction were fully equal to his efforts as a preacher and educator. In particular, the country lacked Bibles. To answer this need, he appealed to men of goodwill towards the Saviour's cause, in both Wales and England. After receiving much support he succeeded in persuading the Society for the Propagation of Christian Knowledge to print a new edition of the Welsh Bible. This was published in 1746 with a print run of 15,000 copies. Its editor was Richard Morris, brother of Llewellyn Morris (*Llewellyn Ddu*) of Anglesey. He worked at the Naval Office in London and was a learned scholar. As well as the Bible, it contained the Book of Common Prayer, the Apocrypha, the metrical Psalms, and an Index. The Bibles were sold at a low price, so that the common people could buy them. If there were those too poor to buy, they were given them freely. No wonder therefore that the stock of 15,000 copies was soon exhausted. In 1752, the same Society, again at Griffith Jones's instigation, printed another edition, also under the editorship of Richard Morris. This again involved 15,000 copies and was similar to the first except that the Apocrypha was omitted. Alongside his efforts for the provision of Bibles, Griffith Jones composed very many books and translated others of a doctrinal or devotional nature. The following list demonstrates the extent of his labours in this direction. [All but those in Sections 2 and 3 were, of course, in Welsh]:

1. TRANSLATIONS AND REPRINTINGS

1712     *Ecclesiastical Oddities*
1722     *The Whole Duty of Man, etc.*
1743     *Summary of the Metrical Psalms, etc.* 164 pages
1749     *A Selection of the Poetry of the Chief Poet of Wales*
         [This 'Chief Poet' was Vicar Rees Pritchard, Llandovery].
1758     *Poetical Gleanings*, namely 46 Songs of the work of Mr Rees Pritchard, 92 pages

2. ENGLISH REPORTS ON THE CIRCULATING SCHOOLS, THAT IS, ISSUES OF *WELCH PIETY*

1737     From 1734 to 1737.
1740–54   Fifteen issues, the total being 824 pages.
1755–60   Eight or nine issues.

3. OTHER ENGLISH BOOKS

1741     *An Address to the Charitable and Well Disposed*, 20 pages.
1745     *A Letter to a Clergyman*, 90 pages.
1747 (?) *Twenty Arguments for Infant Baptism*

1750   *Instruction to a Young Christian.* An explanation of the Church of England Catechism in the form of questions and answers (bilingual; price 4d).

17(?)   *The Christian Covenant, or the Baptismal Vow, as stated in our Church Catechism, Scripturally explained by Questions and Answers.* (2nd ed., 1762; 3rd ed., 1770).

17(?)   *The Christian Faith, or the Apostles' Creed, spiritually explained by Questions and Answers.* (2nd ed., 1762).

17(?)   *Platform of Christianity, being an Explanation of the 39 Articles of the Church of England.*

## 4. DEVOTIONAL BOOKS

1730   *Two Forms of Prayer,* 48 pp. (2nd ed., 1762).

1738   *A Call to the Throne of Grace,* 148 pp. (2nd ed., 1750).

1740   *A Directory for the Throne of Grace;* second part of the *Call to the Throne of Grace,* 140 pp.

17(?)   *An Exhortation to Worship God.*

## 5. CATECHISMS

1737   *Free Advice to the Illiterate, or a small book in the form of queries and answers.*

1741   *Instruction for a Saving Knowledge of the Principles and Duties of Religion, being Scriptural Questions and Answers together with the Doctrine contained in the Catechism of the Church. Essential to be learnt by Young and Old.* In 5 parts, totalling 612 pp.

1748   *A Mirror of Theology, or an Instruction in Saving Knowledge* (Probably a second edition of the previous book, under another name.)

1749   *A Letter concerning the Duty of Catechizing Children and Ignorant People,* 48 pp.

1749   *A Suitable Instruction in Saving Knowledge,* 330 pp. (An abridgement of the 1741 *Instruction*).

1752   *A Brief Commentary on the Church Catechism.* In 5 parts, 170 pp. (An abridgement of the previous book. It was also published in 1762, 1766, and 1778; and in separate parts since then by the S.P.C.K.)

Griffith Jones began as an author in a very small way. He started as a translator and continued as an abridger, and it is thought that he made changes to *The Whole Duty of Man* in order to make it more evangelical and Calvinistic. Of all his books, the Catechisms are the most well-known, and most useful. He was nearly sixty years old when he wrote the Instruction, which, as is shown, is a large work of 612 pages. Its basis is the catechism of the Church of England, and in it he explains clearly and in some detail the basic Christian doctrines. He deals fully with the material, providing proof-texts from Scripture for each answer, and dividing the answers into as many as ten or twelve heads, each head taking up to a page of explanation. It had a wide distribution. It is said that as many as 12,000 of the first part have been printed. In an advertisement for the book he stated that he did not expect any to memorize such a long catechism but that it was provided to be read thoughtfully and often; for two or three questions to be read on a Sunday night, or during the week, to the whole family, and for them to answer in their own words. But such was the desire for knowledge filling the minds of the youth of the country, that he later added that some promising young people had memorized the whole of it. He thought it necessary, however, to cut it down it so that it might be more suitable for the majority, and so, in 1749, the abridgement was published at about half the size. But in another three years he abridged the abridgement, calling it a *Brief Commentary on the Church's Catechism*.

It is this shortest Catechism that is most well-known. This was the book that Mr Charles took as a model when writing his *Hyfforddwr* [*Instructor*], though in clarity, order, and content, Charles's book was a great improvement on its predecessor. In his introduction to the *Summary*, the first form of the *Instructor*, Mr Charles states, 'I was bold enough to take many of the Questions and Answers from Mr G. Jones's excellent *Commentary*.' While holding Mr Jones in the greatest respect as a theologian, Mr Charles did not view him so highly as an author because he was not sufficiently clear and concise. He said:

> As a writer he had many skills but was prone to be diffuse, overfull and verbose, with his sentences confusing and overlong. He always manifests extensive knowledge of that on which he writes, and expresses his mind in most excellent and appropriate phrases and language. His later essays are much better than his first productions as far as order of composition, carefulness of expression and correctness of language are concerned. He always writes scripturally, seriously, and impressively, as one wishing to be of profit to the souls of men. In all, he appears a good theologian, of abundant gifts and knowledge, and of fervent love to the work of the gospel.

The truth is that Mr Charles far excelled him in writing concisely and clearly, and in elegance of style, but by his writings Mr Jones did a great service to the Welsh nation. The final judgment alone will reveal its full extent. Through these books a new era dawned on the country, which before had been greatly deprived of popular religious literature. His catechisms in particular were distributed from one end of the Principality to the other; you could hardly have found a hillside cottage that did not contain one. He received much support for his publications from the Society for the Propagation of Christian Knowledge. This enabled him to sell them cheaply and to give them freely to those too poor to buy.

## HIS CONNECTIONS WITH THE METHODISTS

Griffith Jones lived for twenty-five years after the commencement of the Methodist Revival, but he did not throw in his lot publicly with the Reformers. It is not known for certain why he refrained in this way. Williams, Pantycelyn, attributes it to the darkness of his upbringing, and to his lack of faith:

| | |
|---|---|
| But because his days were clouded | Ond am fod ei fore'n dywyll, |
| And his faith was small and bound, | Ac nad oedd ei ffydd ond gwan, |
| He would not agree to preaching | Fe arswydodd fynd i'r meysydd, |
| Save on consecrated ground. | Ac i'r lleoedd nad oedd llan. |

Perhaps what Williams said of him is true in his early days, but there is no sign whatsoever of lack of courage or faith in the life of the Evangelist of Llanddowror in later days. It is probably the case that there were elements of the Revival to which he could not bring himself to be reconciled. Howell Harris says in one of his letters, written, it seems, in 1743, that Griffith Jones in *Welch Piety* administered a mild rebuke to the Methodists, but that he did not do so without reason, for there was much disorder among them. There is room to believe also that he did not agree with the excitement and shouting that accompanied the powerful preaching of Daniel Rowland, and also that someone had carried lies to him concerning Rowland's behaviour and his attitude to Jones. In a letter to Rowland, Howell Harris tells him that he has had to defend him before Griffith Jones, and to tell Jones that he had never heard Rowland express criticism of him, but on the contrary, that the latter always spoke respectfully of him and of his work, and that Rowland had always used his Catechism and encouraged the people to buy it.

Probably, Griffith Jones believed that he could do more for the Saviour by not joining publicly with the Methodists, in that this would create a prejudice against his schools and against his books. And in this, he might well have been correct. Notwithstanding, it is clear that he sympathized deeply with the Revival and wished it God's blessing. Howell Davies was a pupil of his, brought up at his feet in the school at Llanddowror. Jones felt a deep interest in him, and on the day of Davies's ordination he made a public appeal to his congregation that they pray for him. Certainly Howell Davies would never have gone into the high roads and fields of Pembrokeshire, nor united publicly with Rowland and Harris, without having sought his old teacher's advice. There are frequent references also to Griffith Jones in Howell Harris's letters. The following are a few:

I had the privilege of conversing for some hours with the dear and valuable Mr Griffith Jones. He increases remarkably. The more I am with him the more I see his value.

Mr Davies and I had about five or six hours of converse with the Rev. G. Jones a fortnight yesterday. He is full of zeal, and approaches closer, closer on hearing the cries of the lambs. He has now in the press a commentary on the Articles.

A fortnight tomorrow I hope to hear the old battling soldier, Mr Griffith Jones, who has been prospered in the smiting of Satan's strongholds for over thirty years, and who still continues, and is remarkably blessed in his ministry.

Harris recorded that towards the end of 1742 he visited Llanddowror, and stayed there for a communion Sunday:

My Lord did shine on me sweetly indeed as He always does under this ministry. At the sacrament had such a sight of Christ, solid and calm, scriptural and rational as I never had before. With the dear Mr Jones toward Llanddowror, sweet conversation to 9, very edifying discourse indeed. He was exceeding loving, and showed his catholic spirit, truly loving the cause of Christ (I said all of the state of the Church, Moravian, Wesleys and us). I prayed in the family. Discoursed with him and had very great light in many things, to past 1, he showing me many things I never saw so clear.

It is easy to see the nature of Harris's feelings towards Griffith Jones, and his fellow-labourers probably all felt the same.

Nor does it appear that Jones did confine himself only to a ministry within the Church. He preached in the chapels of the Countess of Huntingdon at Bath and Bristol. When that 'elect lady' visited Wales in 1748, she was met at Bristol by Howell Harris, Daniel Rowland, Howell Davies and Griffith Jones, who were an escort to her throughout her journey through the Principality. They travelled slowly, and for more than fifteen days two of the preachers would preach each day at whatever town or village they were passing through. When we consider Jones's eminent preaching skills, and the respect in which others held him, we can be sure that he was not allowed to remain dumb on these occasions.

In Cardiganshire they were joined by Philip Pugh, Llwynpiod, and after further long travel they reached Trefeca, where Williams, Pantycelyn; Thomas Jones, Cwm-iou; Thomas Lewis, Brecon; Lewis Rees, and others, joined them. At Trefeca, three or four of them would preach each day in the open-air to the large concourse that would gather to hear the gospel. On one occasion, Griffith Jones had a very powerful open-air service, when preaching on the words from Isaiah, 'What shall I cry?' Such powerful influences accompanied the message that many were convicted and cried out in a most heartbreaking way. When the meeting was over, the Countess asked some of them why they had cried out. They answered that they had been so convinced of their miserable state and their guilty condition before God that they feared that he would never have mercy upon them. This history proves that Griffith Jones would sometimes preach at unconsecrated places, and that he occasionally co-operated with the Reformers, although he was not joined to them.

It is evident that Griffith Jones's work in distributing Bibles, Catechisms and other religious books, and his work through the schools in teaching people to read, all of which was carried out for twenty-five years alongside the efforts of the Methodist Fathers, must have proved an immense support to the Revival. Apart from his labours, it is doubtful whether Harris's zeal and Rowland and Davies's preaching would have left any permanent effect on the land. If we began to analyse the influences of the various instruments raised up by God to evangelize Wales at this time, it might well be that we would conclude that the significance of the Evangelist and Educator of Llanddowror was the greatest and the most widespread of them all. The common people, after having experience of reading, were eager to exercise this newly-obtained gift. In the long winter nights, instead of trading ghost stories, the sons and daughters in the farmhouses and cottages would read aloud the Word of God as best they could; and the old people listened, with tears rolling down their cheeks, as they heard such glorious news. They would meet to recite the Catechism together, and the valleys and villages would be full of the sounds of those reading it aloud as they sought to memorize it. Before the quiet influence of Scriptural education the hobgoblins and spectres vanished from the land and no further place was found for them. Mr Johnes very correctly traces the beginnings of Methodism back to Mr Jones, although, perhaps, the latter did not intend anything of the sort. The same author made the following comment:

> A few pious ministers are the weakness and not the strength of an establishment, when the majority of its ministers are sunk in indifference to their ministerial duties! The zeal of the few only serves to cast into darker shade

the apathy of the many; and, by raising the moral sentiments of the people, to make them more sensitively intolerant of the abuses that surround them.

## HIS DEATH

Griffith Jones died on 8 April 1761, when 78 years old, in the house of Madam Bevan. His wife had died some little time before. He died gloriously, not trusting in any of his works, but full of faith in his Saviour. To a friend who called to see him, he confessed his sickness and barrenness. His friend answered that he should not speak in such a way, as he had accomplished so much during his life and that the Lord had made so much use of him. The sick man was bent over in his bed, his elbows leaning on his knees, but he straightened up and looking his friend in the eye, asked him, 'What! Are you taking the enemy's side?' To another friend, he said:

> I must bear testimony to the goodness of God. I am now free from the asthma that so attacked me when I was young; I am not blind as I was for three weeks as a baby with the smallpox; and I am not a poor blind beggar seeking food from door to door. How wonderful is the goodness of God, in that I feel no pain, and look likely to go to the grave in comfort. How wonderful is the mercy of God, that I can see clearly that which Christ did and suffered for me, and that I do not have the slightest doubt of my possession of my Almighty Saviour. Glory be to God! His consolations fill my soul!

Mr Charles states that his funeral was very sorrowful, with great numbers of the poor testifying by their wet cheeks and salt tears of their love and sorrow on losing such an excellent man.

Though we have made every effort, we have failed to discover a picture of Griffith Jones. It is said that no such picture exists. In his will Griffith Jones left all his money, about £7,000, to Madam Bevan, in a trust, to be used for maintaining the Circulating Schools. She lived for another eighteen years, until 1778, and throughout her life she superintended the schools. She bequeathed a further £3,000 to the trust. Her executor, however, Lady Stepney, tried to gain possession of the money for herself. As a result, the schools were closed and the case was referred to Chancery. There the money remained until 1808, by which time it had accumulated to £30,000. Arrangements were then made to reopen the schools but on a completely different plan from that of Griffith Jones and Madam Bevan. They all became associated with the Church of England, and only church-goers were accepted as pupils. They became of little use therefore to the people of Wales. We will leave Griffith Jones and his glorious story by quoting further from the elegy written for him by William Williams, Pantycelyn:

See the Bibles, in great numbers,
Thirty thousand, when all told,
Printed, published, and made use of,
All through his arrangements bold;
Two editions, pure revisions,
Pearls and treasures held in store,
Scriptures found throughout the nation,
And the cottages of the poor.

Providence, in all its myst'ry
For our blessing takes the lead,
Knows no purpose printing Bibles
If there's no one that can read;
Raises schools, as if from nowhere,
From the Severn to the shore,
Midst the lambs, the joyful shepherds
O'er the glorious Scriptures pour.

Soon their total was three thousand,
Schools throughout the length of Wales,
Six score thousand scholars learning,
Men and women, boys and girls;
From Rheidol's banks to Severn's meadows,
See the light go shining forth,
Passing o'er Plynlimon's shoulder
To illuminate the north.

Hardly a parish or a district
Had to wait so very long
For a school that would soon teach them
How to read their mother tongue.

Here's the man who, striding forwards,
E'er the sun had shed one light,
Sowed his seed, beheld it ripening,
Saw the mighty harvest bright;
After him came reapers many,
O, how fruitful is the field!
Now the threshers and the riddlers
Winnow joyfully the yield.

Griffith Jones was once his title,
Now a newer name he bears,

Dacw'r Beiblau teg a hyfryd,
Ddeg-ar-hugain filoedd llawn,
Wedi'u trefnu i ddod allan,
Trwy ei ddwylo'n rhyfedd iawn;
Dau argraffiad, glân ddiwygiad,
Llawn ac uchel bris i'r gwan;
Mewn cabanau fe geir Beiblau
Nawr gan dlodion ymhob man.

Hi, Ragluniaeth ddyrys, helaeth,
Wna bobpeth yn gytsain llawn,
D'wed nad gwiw argraffu Beiblau
Heb eu darllen hwy yn iawn;
Daeth yn union ag ysgolion,
O Werddon fôr i Hafren draw;
Rhwng y defaid mae'r bugeiliaid
Nawr a'r 'Sgrythur yn eu llaw.

Tair o filoedd o ysgolion
Gawd yng Nghymru faith a mwy,
Chwech ugain mil o ysgolheigion
Fu, a rhagor, ynddynt hwy;
Y goleuni ga'dd ei enyn
O Rheidol wyllt i Hafren hir,
Tros Bumlumon faith yn union
T'wynnodd ar y Gogledd dir.

Braidd ca'dd plwyf nac ardal ddianc
Heb gael iddo gynnig rhad,
O fanteision ddysgai'n union
Iddynt ddarllen iaith eu gwlad.

Dyma'r gwr a dorodd allan
Ronyn bach cyn torri'r wawr;
Hâd fe heuodd, fe eginodd,
Fe ddaeth yn gynhaeaf mawr;
Daeth o'i ôl fedelwyr lawer,
Braf, mor ffrwythlawn y mae'r yd!
Nawr mae'r wyntyll gref a'r gogr
Yn ei nithio'r hyd y byd.

Griffith Jones gynt oedd ei enw,
Enw newydd sy arno'n awr,

| | |
|---|---|
| Writ in letters none can cipher, | Mewn llyth'rennau na ddeallir |
| Who earth's fleshly garb still wears; | Ei 'sgrifennu ar y llawr; |
| Sing, rejoice, stay there in glory, | Cân, bydd lawen, aros yna, |
| If our God, from heaven on high, | Os yw Duw, o entrych ne'. |
| Sees fresh need of books and teachers, | Yn gweld eisiau prints, a dysgu, |
| Another Griffith he'll supply. | Fe fyn rywun yn dy le. |

Williams's prophecy came true. God raised a worthy successor to Griffith Jones in the Rev. Thomas Charles of Bala, of blessed memory.

# 3

# THE METHODIST REVIVAL
# IN ENGLAND

## WELSH METHODISM WAS NOT A BRANCH OF
## ENGLISH METHODISM

*T*here was no visible and external link between the beginnings of the Methodist Revival in Wales and the Revival in England. No spark from the fire begun at Oxford was carried with the breeze to Llangeitho and Trefeca, kindling the hearts of Daniel Rowland and Howell Harris, as some have maintained in their ignorance. God's fire descended on Wales directly from heaven, and Rowland and Harris had been labouring for nearly two years and had produced remarkable results by their ministries before they heard of events the other side of the Severn. But attention must be paid to the English Reformers because of the close union that existed for a long time between them and the Welsh Fathers. It was from them that the Connexion received its name. Many of them came often on preaching journeys throughout the Principality, and the ministries of the two Wesleys and, particularly, of Whitefield, were notably blessed.

At one period, the followers of Whitefield and Cennick in England, and those of Rowland and Harris in Wales, were looked upon as forming one connexion. Whitefield was the Moderator of the first Association at Watford, and he contributed as much as Rowland and Harris in giving form to the Revival. He was present in many subsequent Associations, and when present was always in the chair. He was looked upon as one of the leaders. Harris, Rowland, and others of the Welsh preachers, would go to England, and to the Tabernacle in London, remaining there for weeks, sometimes, to minister. When they could, they attended Associations in England, and took part in them. It was probably language difficulties and the inconvenience of travelling that caused the Welsh Reformers to separate gradually from their brethren on the other side of Offa's Dyke.

The commencement of English Methodism may be traced back to the meetings arranged by a number of young men at Oxford, for reading the Greek New Testament together. This occurred in November 1729. It is difficult to assess the numbers of the members of this 'Holy Club', as it was called, as these varied over time. Certainly the following were members: John Wesley, Charles Wesley, his brother, Robert Kirkham, William Morgan, George Whitefield, John Clayton, Thomas Broughton, Benjamin Ingham, James Hervey, John Gambold, Charles Kinchin, William Smith, and others. Not all of these remained. There were heated arguments and considerable bitterness of spirit amongst them at times. Some went in one direction and others in another, but they were all serious men, full of the desire to serve the Saviour. Some remained in the Established Church and served as clergymen, others joined the Moravian Church and held high office within it, others again formed new religious connexions and became head over them. But, as Tyerman comments:

> The reader is challenged to produce a band of godly friends, whose lives and labours have, upon the whole, issued in such an amount of blessing to mankind as that which has resulted from the lives and labours of the students who in 1735 were known as 'Oxford Methodists'.[1]

Their lives were as those rivers that flowed out of Eden, springing up from the same source, yet taking different directions and making the lands through which they flowed green and fertile. Such also were the 'Holy Club' members, and it is a pleasure for any historian with religious sympathies to trace their various influences.

The life and soul of the Holy Club was undoubtedly John Wesley. Often, the beginnings of this movement are attributed to him but this is not correct. This honour belongs to Charles Wesley and William Morgan, and it took place when John had left Oxford to serve as curate to his father. When he eventually returned and found a movement closely akin to his own spirit he threw in his lot with them with all the enthusiasm of his nature, and very soon the leadership of the group fell quite naturally into his hands. He had been raised under the strictest discipline. Though his father was the vicar of Epworth, and an excellent man, it was his mother who was the stronger character, notable for her determined good sense and personal godliness. Her influence upon John was to remain with him throughout his life. He himself was a man of almost inexhaustible energy and liveliness. He possessed a strong, inflexible will, the eyes of a hawk for perceiving any opportunity, and great efficiency in taking advantage of it. Has there ever been a better organizer? He would have been incomparable as a general had he pursued a military career; a second Wellington or Napoleon. He was not a profound philosopher, and his discernment of biblical truths in their mutual consistency was not acute. He wavered much in his theological views: at one time a High-Churchman; then tending to the Moravians and greatly influenced by them; but for the latter part of his life he was a type of Arminian evangelical. He laboured unceasingly; he travelled and preached without stop throughout a long life; and he lived to see the Wesleyan Connexion, which he founded, spread its branches throughout the known world. Charles Wesley, his brother, was the hymn-writer of the movement, but John also wrote many excellent hymns that are still sung. Charles was a kind, cheerful man, less able than his brother, and throughout his life he was a kind of lieutenant to the more determined John, assisting him with his arrangements and carrying out his plans.

The preacher of the English Revival was George Whitefield. He did not join the 'Holy Club' until some years after its formation. Because of the poverty of his background he was only a servitor at the University, maintaining himself there by the income he received while acting as a servant to the sons of the nobility and the rich. He therefore looked up to the Wesley brothers, the sons of a clergyman. Though he was of religious temperament and had begun praying and singing Psalms daily by himself, he was too shy to join the Methodists. But by some providential circumstance he became acquainted with Charles Wesley and soon threw in his lot with them.

Whitefield was a man overflowing with good nature; he could not abide controversy and argument, though was often forced into them; and was much more peaceable and mild than John Wesley. Of all the English Reformers, none could compare with him for the brilliance of his pulpit skills; his eloquence affected the learned and unlearned equally; he would melt the colliers of Bristol and the London mob, and at the same time charm and overcome the atheist Hume, who did not believe a word of the doctrine he preached. And he was pre-eminently a preacher. He himself believed he had been called primarily to preach the gospel. He was not deficient in organizational skills, though he could not be compared in this respect to his friend John Wesley, and as mentioned, he would often chair the Association in Wales. But he disregarded organization, believing that others were more qualified than himself, and stated positively that his qualifications were for the convicting of the ungodly. Wesleyanism in England therefore took advantage of his labours. If he had sought to form his own connexion and give himself to it, he would have had many followers in England and America. He also travelled much. He had great affection for Wales, and his wife was Welsh, coming from near Abergavenny. He crossed the Atlantic seven times, and was in America when he died. He was the means of converting thousands of sinners. His followers in England are known as the Countess of Huntingdon's Connexion.

The only one of the 'Holy Club' who is known to be a Welshman was John Gambold. Most probably William Morgan was also Welsh, though he was born in Dublin. It is known that many Welsh families emigrated to Ireland at the time of the Whig Revolution. John Gambold was born in Puncheston, Pembrokeshire, on 8 April 1711, and his father was a clergyman of the Church of England. He also was a servitor at Oxford because of the poverty of his background. He was a cheerful, lively character, fond of poetry, and it is said that he spent much time with the writings of the main English poets and dramatists. Two years after arriving at Oxford, his father died, and the circumstances of the death, together with his father's death-bed counsels and warnings, sobered him, and caused him to seek the salvation of his soul as his main purpose in life. For a long time he was under conviction, unable to see the way of salvation. He was in deep depression for two years, and the Lord, in order to break his pride, made his life bitter to him. 'I had no one,' he said, 'to whom I could unburden myself, no one who cared for my soul. They were all comfortable, and they could not understand why I was so sad.' God led him to the Wesleys however, and he united with the despised Methodists. He was ordained by the Bishop of Oxford in September, 1733, and as soon as he was eligible for a living, was appointed vicar of Stanton-Harcourt, not far from Oxford. He spent the next seven years in relative solitude in this rural village, meditating on deep philosophical and theological questions, and preaching far above the level of his simple parishioners. But as with John Wesley, he came under the influence of the Moravians and changed his views on certain aspects of the gospel. He threw his philosophizing to the winds and became a simple believer in Jesus Christ. In 1742, he left the Anglican Church and joined with the Moravians, spending the rest of his life, twenty-nine years, amongst them. They soon made him a bishop. About two years before his death, he came, because of ill-health, to pastor the Moravian Church at Haverfordwest, Pembrokeshire, in the hope that the air of his native land would benefit him. But his health slowly deteriorated. He died in September, 1771, and was buried in the cemetery of the Moravian Church, Haverfordwest.

John Gambold was a man of wide learning and an excellent scholar. He wrote many books, mainly of an apologetic nature for Moravian principles; published two sermons; but was mainly known for his hymns. He edited the first book of hymns published by the Moravians in England, and it is thought that many of the hymns contained in it were by him. He was notable for his spirituality and gentleness of character. While John Wesley had failed to endure the autocratic and vehement nature of the Church's leader, Count von Zinzendorf, Gambold served the Church peaceably and fraternally throughout those twenty-nine years. At the same time, he was not without backbone. He could sacrifice everything for the sake of principle. When he left the Established Church all he could expect was poverty. There were only 72 Moravians at that time in the whole of London. He grieved over the direction taken by the two Wesleys, and his friendship with them ended; indeed, he said to John that he had a shame of being in his company. Yet, John Wesley respected him greatly, and a little before he died said that Gambold was one of the wisest and most prudent men in England. Wales may be proud of Bishop Gambold.

Our comments on the other 'Holy Club' members must be short. Benjamin Ingham was the descendant of one of the ministers of the Church of England ejected in 1662 for failure to conform. When twenty-two years old, he joined the Methodists in Oxford. He also entered the Moravian Church and remained in its communion when the Wesleys departed from them. He laboured mainly in Yorkshire. He was a powerful preacher; the people came in their thousands to hear him; many were saved by his ministry, and he established Moravian churches throughout the land. At the end of his life he withdrew from the Moravians and formed a connexion of his own. Because of internal rifts, this had almost disappeared by the time of his death and the few churches remaining joined with the Scottish Independents. James Hervey, another of the 'Holy Club', remained in the Established Church. He was a man of much culture, a stylish writer, and by means of his writings did much to strengthen the hold of evangelical religion upon the upper classes. John Clayton also remained with the Church of England and continued a ritualistic High-Churchman throughout his life.

We have noted that Methodism began with a group of young men reading their Greek New Testaments. But the group soon became a religious society. They began to pray together and to plan together how to help their fellow-men. They decided to abstain from the luxuries of life, eating only that which was necessary to sustain life. They would not drink tea or beer, nor, to a large extent, eat meat, so that they would have more to contribute to the poor. This was not an easy task for some. One of them, writing with remarkable zest to John Wesley, described how he had enjoyed a plate of veal and bacon with the contents of a newly-tapped barrel of cider. They drew up detailed rules to be kept daily and weekly. They were to spend two hours a day in prayer; to pray while going to church and when coming from church; to pray apart at the same time for an hour, three days in the week, so as to maintain their communion together. They were also to rise early every day and to spend an hour every day speaking to men directly of religious things; to do their best to frustrate evil; as much as was in them, to persuade men to attend public worship. These were clearly young men with an intense desire to do good. They were gripped by a profound seriousness. They warned their immoral fellow-students as to their souls' danger; they visited the poor of the city, and thundered against sin; they contributed all they could to various charities, and they visited workhouses and prisons, counselling all to seek eternal life. John Gambold says that they used to meet every evening, usually in John Wesley's room, in order to review their activities during the day, and to arrange the next day's programme. They also helped in a school that had been established by John Wesley and its matron supported by him. He was also the main provider of clothes for the children. The following story reveals the nature of their charity:

> One cold winter's day, a young girl, whom the Methodists kept at school, called on [John Wesley] in a state nearly frozen, to whom he said, 'You seem half-starved; have you nothing to wear but that linen gown?' The poor girl said, 'Sir, this is all I have.' Wesley put his hand in his pocket, but found it nearly empty. The walls of his chamber however were hung with pictures, and these now became his accusers. 'It struck me,' says he, 'will thy Master say, "Well done, good and faithful steward?" Thou hast adorned thy walls with the money that might have screened this poor creature from the cold! O Justice! O Mercy! Are not these pictures the blood of this poor maid?' To say the least, this story shows the intense conscientiousness of the man, and his dread of spending anything upon himself that might have been spent more properly upon the poor.[2]

In addition, they received communion weekly, and walked in procession together to Christ Church for this purpose. When we remember how ungodly Oxford was at this time, the way in which evil was considered fashionable and atheism professed publicly by many, it is easy to understand how Wesley and his company immediately became the centre of attention. They were referred to publicly. They were mocked in every way. The reservoir of the English language was exhausted in the quest for words of sufficient contempt to be used upon them. They were called the 'Holy Club', the 'Godly Club', and lastly, 'Methodists', a reference to an ancient Roman sect of physicians who were notably methodical in their prescriptions. This last name stuck to them. But the small fraternity did not allow themselves to be troubled by the contempt of the University; they proceeded according to the principles of their consciences. They adopted the name given to them in jest, and it gradually became a name of honour.

It must be acknowledged, however, that the Methodists at this time were almost wholly ignorant of some of the most basic truths of evangelical religion. They knew nothing of justification by faith or of the work of the Holy Spirit. The truth is that the movement at the start was completely devotional and sacramentarian, as fully so as the Tractarian movement begun in the same city by Pusey and Newman, a hundred years later. No Pharisee was ever as careful and detailed over the rituals and phylacteries of his religion as were the Oxford Methodists over the vestments, forms and rites of the Church of England. They believed in the Real Presence of Christ in the sacrament, and considered Holy Communion a sacrifice. They carefully kept all the saints' festival days. They sanctified both the Saturday and the Sunday; the first as the Sabbath, and the second as the Lord's Day. They fasted often. Throughout Lent they would not eat meat, except on Saturdays and Sundays, and they fasted every Wednesday and Friday, not eating anything until after three in the afternoon. They believed in penance and in the confessional. They slipped into the Roman Catholic error of requiring that water be added to the sacramental wine, in that water as well as blood flowed from the Saviour's wounds when he was pierced by the soldier's spear. John Clayton wrote to John Wesley in some concern over the rightness of communicating when no water had been mixed in the wine. They were full of the doctrine of apostolic succession.

Such was John Wesley's abhorrence of everything outside of the Established Church, and his contempt of Nonconformity, that he refused communion to John Martin Bolzius, one of the godliest men of the period, because he had not been baptized by a clergyman of the Church of England. It is no wonder that in later years he was ashamed of his bigotry. When he was in Savannah, he was considered a Roman Catholic. His biographer describes him as a Puseyite, a hundred years before Pusey. He considered seriously the possibility of founding a sacramentarian and High-Church society, which would carefully maintain all the half-Papistical rites which have the slightest foundation in the rubric, and would keep the saints' days and holidays and everything else associated with extreme ritualism.

But the Lord had different intentions for the Methodists. As they were thoroughly serious and acting according to the light that they possessed, the Lord led them about to cause them to understand, and finally brought them to the clear light of the gospel. This occurred for John Wesley at the beginning of the year 1738, through the instrumentality of Peter Bohler, a minister with the Moravians. He himself judged that up until this time he had been an unbeliever. Peter Bohler explained to him the nature of faith, and its consequences:

'My brother, my brother,' said Bohler, 'that philosophy of yours must be purged away.' And purged away it was. Wesley thought that, being without faith, he ought to leave off preaching. But Bohler replied, 'By no means. Preach faith till you have it; and then, because you have it, you will preach it.' And on the 6th of March, he began to preach accordingly.[3]

From then on, he was a believer, leaning on the Saviour for acceptance, and crying with Paul, 'That I may . . . be found in him, not having mine own righteousness, which is of the law.' Before long, most of his Methodist friends were brought to the same gospel liberty as himself. Indeed, it is doubtful whether Whitefield was ever a ritualist at any time.

Oxford Methodism may be considered as continuing from 1729 to 1735. In this latter year the fraternity parted and was never re-formed. John Wesley crossed the Atlantic to the colony of Georgia with the intention of evangelizing the Indians, and remained there for two years; Charles his brother, and Benjamin Ingham, went with him. Whitefield had left Oxford earlier because of a breakdown in health. John Clayton had settled in Manchester, and John Gambold was in Stanton Harcourt. Those few that remained were weak and leaderless. So, the University returned to its old corruptions with no one to disturb its peace, and when Howell Harris went up, in the November of 1735, he heard nothing of a 'Holy Club', and found wickedness being given such latitude that his spirit was stirred within him. At exactly the time of John Wesley's return from Georgia, Whitefield was on a ship setting sail for the same place. In 1740, Wesley published a sermon entitled 'Free Grace', based on Romans 8:32, in which he attacked the Calvinistic doctrine of the election of grace. Together with the sermon was a hymn by his brother Charles, teaching universal redemption. Whitefield heard of the sermon before its publication and wrote immediately to his friend appealing to him not to print, in that this would lead to controversy and division. He wrote:

Dear, honoured sir, if you have any regard for the peace of the Church, keep in your sermon on predestination.

In another letter, he appeals:

If possible, I am ten thousand times more convinced of the doctrine of election, and the final perseverance of those that are truly in Christ, than when I saw you last. You think otherwise. Why then should we dispute, when there is no probability of convincing? Will it not, in the end, destroy brotherly love, and insensibly take from us that cordial union and sweetness of soul, which I pray God may always subsist between us? How glad would the enemies of the Lord be to see us divided! How many would rejoice, should I join and make a party against you! How would the cause of our common Master suffer by our raising disputes about particular points of doctrine! Honoured sir, let us offer salvation freely to all by the blood of Jesus . . . [4]

Whitefield was greatly troubled because of the possibility of division. On 7 June, the same year, he wrote to James Hutton:

For Christ's sake, desire dear brother Wesley to avoid disputing with me. I think I had rather die, than to see a division between us; and yet how can we walk together, if we oppose each other? [5]

Howell Harris, in Wales, was similarly troubled and he also wrote a strong letter to Wesley. He said:

Letters have . . . informed me, that . . . you turned a brother out of the society, and charged all to beware of him, purely because he held the doctrine of election. My dear brother, do not act in the stiff, uncharitable spirit which you condemn in others. If you exclude him from the society and from the fraternity of the Methodists, for such a cause, you must exclude brother Whitefield, brother Seward, and myself. I hope I shall contend with my last breath and blood, that it is owing to special, distinguishing, and irresistible grace, that those that are saved are saved. O that you would not touch on this subject till God enlighten you! My dear brother, being a public person, you grieve God's people by your opposition to electing love; and many poor souls believe your doctrine simply because you hold it . . . The more I write, the more I love you. I am sure you are one of God's elect, and, that you act honestly according to the light you have. [6]

It may be seen that Harris, like Whitefield, is full of concern as he writes, but that a strong personal affection towards Wesley permeates every sentence. It was only because they felt duty bound to affirm what they judged to be the truth of God that they wrote in this way. But their efforts were in vain. Wesley had made up his mind, and not the influence of friend or foe could make him change it. He published the sermon and stated in the introduction:

Nothing but the strongest conviction, not only that what is here advanced is 'the truth as it is in Jesus', but also that I am indispensably obliged to declare this truth to all the world, could have induced me to oppose the sentiments of those whom I esteem for their works' sake. [7]

All accept that John Wesley was conscientious in his behaviour. But would it not have been wise on his part to have listened to his brothers, and not discussed publicly the points upon which he and they differed? Describing the free grace of the Calvinists in his sermon, he argued that:

> Free grace in all is not free for all, but only for those whom God hath ordained to life. The greater part of mankind God hath ordained to death; and it is not free for them. Them God hateth; and therefore, before they were born, decreed they should die eternally. And this he absolutely decreed, because it was his sovereign will. Accordingly, they are born for this, to be destroyed body and soul in hell.
>
> ... [It is a doctrine that] renders all preaching vain; for preaching is needless to them that are elected; for they, whether with it or without it, will infallibly be saved. And it is useless to them that are not elected; for they, whether with preaching or without, will infallibly be damned.[8]

It is seen that Wesley misrepresents his opponents' views dreadfully; he holds them responsible for conclusions which he himself drew, and which they would have rejected absolutely. His theology was very one-sided, and was, as Harris tells him in one of his letters, the fruit of his upbringing rather than of the careful study of God's Word.

But the lot had fallen. The Methodists divided into two camps. The Welsh Methodists held as one body to Calvinistic doctrines; the division brought about no rending in their own ranks, nor any great controversy in the churches. Indeed, it does not appear that Wesley made any attempt to propagate his particular views in the Principality. Very probably it was the great respect that he had for his brethren in Wales, Howell Harris particularly, that was the reason for this. As would be expected, Charles Wesley followed his brother, but Cennick remained with Whitefield. John Wesley moved to Kingswood, Bristol, at the beginning of 1742, and threw John Cennick and over fifty other members out of the society. In the middle of this confusion, Whitefield returned from America and immediately published a reply to Wesley's sermon on free grace. He soon began printing a newspaper called *Weekly History*, the first ever Methodist periodical, in order to counteract the views of the two Wesleys. Its editor was a Welshman, John Lewis from Builth Wells. As might have been expected, the division increased. Whitefield was refused leave to preach in many chapels that he himself had established. But his spiritual energy and the brilliance of his talents were such that he could not be stopped from gathering congregations. Very soon, chapels were raised for him in many parts of the country, and the Tabernacle was built at Moorfields, London, where thousands gathered. Vast numbers were brought to eternal life. At the same time John Wesley pursued his plans. He established the particular societies; he gave permission for laymen to preach, and arranged that they visit the members regularly in their homes; and he printed tokens, signed by himself, admitting the bearers to the communion table. Charles Wesley was the first to administer communion at a site that was not consecrated. 1741 can be taken as the year in which the Wesleyanism that we know today began.

Many attempts were made to reconcile and reunite Wesley and Whitefield. Very often Howell Harris was the main mover behind these attempts. He remained on friendly terms with both, and loved them deeply. Wesley often praises his passion, love, and greatness of heart. The attempts were not successful as far as any visible union and co-operation were concerned. The two men were too far apart, and too conscientious to sacrifice what each considered to be the truth for the sake of friendship. But they did succeed in reconciling them. The two men met; each believed that the other was sincere in his desire to save souls and to extend the kingdom of the Mediator; they agreed to differ, and they remained friends to the grave. Whitefield said later of Wesley, 'Mr Wesley I think is wrong in some things . . . yet I believe that [he] will shine bright in glory.' Again, in a letter to Wesley in 1742, he wrote:

> Yesterday morning I had your kind letter . . . In answer to the first part of it, I say, 'Let old things pass away, and all things become new.' I can heartily say 'Amen' to the latter part of it. 'Let the King live forever, and let controversy die.' It has died with me long ago.

Whitefield possessed a genial, loving nature. He could not bear coldness between old friends, and John Wesley felt the same. It is not our intention to follow the labours and successes of the two branches of Methodism further. The Welsh Methodists from now on were involved only with Whitefield and his followers, a group of which continued as the Countess of Huntingdon's Connexion. The two Wesleys often visited Wales to preach. We will consider these matters again in later chapters.

---

[1] Tyerman, *Life and Times of John Wesley*, vol. 1, p. 68.
[2] Ibid., p. 71.
[3] Ibid., p. 179.
[4] Ibid., pp. 313–4.
[5] Ibid., p. 315.
[6] Ibid.
[7] Ibid., p. 318.
[8] Ibid., pp. 318–9.

# 4

# DANIEL ROWLAND, LLANGEITHO

## HIS BIRTH AND UPBRINGING

On top of a hill overlooking the beautiful valley of Aeron, about a mile and a half below Llangeitho and on the west side of the river, stands the rather ordinary-looking farmhouse of Pant-y-beudy. This is where Daniel Rowland was born, in the year 1713. His parents were Daniel and Jennet Rowland. The father was a clergyman in the Established Church, holding the livings of Llancwnlle and Llangeitho, and without any outstanding characteristics to distinguish him from the other clergymen of the county. Daniel was their second son, but he greatly excelled his older brother, John, in ability; though John also would be raised to become a clergyman. Very little of Daniel's youth is known, but tradition has it that he was a lively boy, full of vivacity and high spirits, the leader in any kind of game or mischief. Amongst his peers, he was the natural leader. Whatever the activity, fishing for trout in the River Aeron, chasing foxes along the slopes of the forested valley, or battling with a football, Daniel would be at the front. He excelled in school as much as at play; he drank in his studies as a behemoth drinks water.

Though he possessed no religious tendencies of any kind, he was educated with the intention of following a career as a minister in the Established Church, being sent to the grammar school at Hereford to complete his education. When he was eighteen, he was called home from the school on the death of his father, and he does not seem to have returned there. But he was a sufficiently good scholar for his bishop to ordain him in 1733, when he was only twenty years old, that is, before he had reached the legal age requirement. For some reason that is now unknown, he was ordained in London on the basis of recommendatory letters from the Bishop of St David's. He walked all the way to London for the ceremony. This fact emphasizes both the poverty of his circumstances and his firmness of mind. It seems that his brother John had been given the livings of Llancwnlle and Llangeitho on the death of their father, and he soon obtained that of Llanddewibrefi also. Daniel Rowland was appointed curate to his very unremarkable brother. He never rose higher than curate throughout his career in the Church, and never received more than ten pounds a year in acknowledgement of his labours.

These were days of darkness in Wales. The clergymen used to gallop through the lessons and prayers in the churches without the least degree of solemnity of spirit, and at the close of the service would join their parishioners to drink beer in the nearby inn, or in games and contests in the field. There is no reason to believe that Daniel Rowland was any different; we might rather conclude, from his energetic nature, that he was at the forefront of the dissolute sports, the ungodliness and prodigality. But he was not left long in this state. He had been predestined by God to be one of the chief instruments in the evangelization and spiritual elevation of Wales.

## ROWLAND'S CONVERSION AT LLANDDEWIBREFI CHURCH

There are two differing traditions of the circumstances that led to Rowland's conversion, but they are not difficult to harmonize. According to one tradition, he was jealous of the large congregations that gathered to hear the Rev. Philip Pugh, the Presbyterian minister of Llwynpiod, whilst he himself was preaching to the bare walls at Llangeitho. On inquiry, he found that this man's ministry was effective in quickening the conscience by his denouncing of the sins of his hearers and his descriptions of their wretchedness and danger. Rowland decided to follow the same plan. He began to thunder terribly against wickedness and to portray the wretchedness of the ungodly in the world to come in the most dramatic and horrific way. He would therefore choose those texts that best fitted his plan, 'The wicked shall be turned into hell,' 'These shall go away into everlasting punishment,' 'The great day of his wrath is come.' The plan succeeded beyond his expectations. The church became too small to hold the congregation. People gathered from all over the neighbourhood to hear him, and were deeply frightened by the terrifying ministry of the eloquent, young clergyman. It is said that over a hundred men were brought under deep conviction, before the preacher himself felt anything of the influence of the truth. But gradually, the truths that he was proclaiming with such power began to prick his own conscience.

According to the second tradition, which is related by the Rev. John Owen, Thrussington, the Rev. Griffith Jones, Llanddowror, made one of his preaching visits to Llanddewibrefi Church. There were so many in the congregation that there was not room for them all to sit and Rowland, along with some hundreds of others, had to stand throughout the service. He stood directly facing the preacher, and his appearance and attitude was arrogant, scornful and full of mockery. It was clear that he felt only contempt for the man in the pulpit and for the people who had gathered to hear him. His appearance caught the attention of Griffith Jones; so much so that he referred to him publicly, and broke out into solemn prayer on his behalf. The prayer struck Rowland's heart like an arrow. His face fell, his knees trembled, and the proud creature was transformed into a helpless sinner before God. He travelled home amongst his companions, in deep silence, his eyes cast downwards towards the ground, a solemn look on his face.

The two stories are not in any way inconsistent. It may well be that his convictions began through the truths which he himself was preaching, though it was the ministry of Griffith Jones that was to overcome him fully. It is not impossible that his conscience smote him even as he stood proud and upright before the preacher at Llanddewibrefi Church. Perhaps it was that very agitation, and his efforts to overcome it, that caused him to appear so much more scornful and challenging than was really the case. Here was the last throw of his corrupt nature against the strength of the truth, and it is easy to believe that it was a hard and stubborn battle. However, he returned home a new creature. Because of the view he had had of his own nature and of his insincere motives in preaching, he felt very sad on the way home and full of hopelessness, and decided never to ascend into a pulpit again. The people around him kept talking of the wonderful sermon that they had heard and testifying that they had never heard its like before. Their words felt like lead in his heart, and his spirit failed within him, strengthening his resolve never to preach again. But one farmer amongst them who was mounted next to Rowland, placed his hand on the young curate's shoulder, saying, 'Well, well, you can praise today's sermon as much as you like, It did nothing much for me. I have cause to thank God for the little curate of Llangeitho.' The farmer's words had a powerful effect on the curate's timid thoughts. He decided not to give up the ministry, saying to himself, 'Who knows but that the Lord will make some use even of a poor creature like me.' How significant is a word in season!

## HIS FIERY PREACHING DRAWS MANY TO LLANGEITHO

As a result of this great change that took place in Llanddewibrefi Church, Rowland's ministry became more passionate. The content of his preaching was the law; the law in its spirituality; in the detail of its commandments;

and in the terror of its threatenings. He himself had been in the awful darkness where God is, his heart had been melted like wax before the divine presence, and he stood now on Sinai's heights proclaiming destruction to a guilty world. According to the Rev. John Hughes:

> His ministry was of awful lightning and thunders. His hearers felt as if the ground was shaking beneath them because of the power of the threats which he proclaimed. He shot forth lightning bolts and his hearers were overcome. His preaching was now accompanied by remarkable effects. His words would fall upon the careless attenders as a sudden terror; they were awakened as by the roar of a thunderclap. The hundreds, and thousands, which sometimes came to hear him were possessed by an immense fear, and many of them fell as if dead. Horror and fright could be seen portrayed on the faces of the vast gatherings; their consciences were overcome by the sharp arrows; their tears flowed like rivers down their cheeks, as showers of rain after great thunder.[1]

As he ministered in this way, threatening the ungodly, it is said that there was no harshness in his voice, no severity in his countenance, but the very opposite – a most melting tenderness, as if his own heart was breaking because of the awful condition of his congregation.

| | |
|---|---|
| Rowland's name was Boanerges, | Boanerges oedd ei enw, |
| Son of thunder, flaming true, | Mab y daran danllyd gref, |
| Shaking heaven and earth together, | Sydd yn siglo yn ddychrynllyd |
| With a voice both strong and new; | Holl golofnau dae'r a nef; |
| 'Come! Awake!,' his voice in echo | 'Dewch, dihunwch,' oedd yr adsain, |
| Calls to all, 'Our town's ablaze. | 'Y mae'n dinas ni ar dân;' |
| Flee this moment without turning, | Ffowch oddi yma mewn munudyn |
| God to ashes all will raze.'[2] | Ynte ewch yn ulw mân.' |

Though Daniel Rowland's ministry at this time was so powerful, and the influences accompanying his preaching so intense, it does not appear that his grasp of the essential doctrines of the gospel was in any way firm. He had swallowed some of the erroneous views of William Law. He also hardly understood that salvation was wholly of grace. He preached, rather, as if it was partly by grace and partly by works. Because of this, some of those attached to the Llwynpiod congregation complained to Mr Pugh, their pastor, hoping he would visit Rowland and deal with him because of his errors and endeavour to place him on the right lines. But the venerable old minister had a better understanding of human nature. 'Leave him alone,' he said, 'he is an instrument whom the Lord is raising to do some great work in the land. He will reform in time. He is yet a child; his heavenly Father will teach him better.' Here is an answer worthy of an apostle. Dr Lewis Edwards's comment on this was, 'I do not know of anything in the whole history of Daniel Rowland that shows more moral greatness than these words from the Dissenting minister of Llwynpiod.'

## HE BEGINS TO PREACH OUTSIDE HIS OWN PARISH

We aim to pursue the guidance of divine providence in the life of Daniel Rowland. He did not take a step without the direction of God's finger. He was brought to preach outside the boundaries of his own parish in the following way. A woman who lived in the neighbourhood of Ystrad-ffin in Carmarthenshire had a sister who lived at Llangeitho. On a visit to this sister, she heard her mentioning the remarkable preaching of Rowland and the strange effects that accompanied it, so that the nickname for him amongst the thoughtless of the area was 'the angry clergyman' ('y ffeiriad crac'). She decided to go to hear him. She then left on the Monday without a word to her sister about the sermon or the preacher. The following Sunday however she returned to her sister again. The latter was frightened, thinking that some tragic event had occurred, and asked her fearfully:

'What has happened? Has anything happened to your husband or children?'

'No,' replied the woman, ' everything with the family is well.'

'Why did you come here today, then?'

'I don't rightly know,' was the answer. 'Something which your angry clergyman said has so lodged in  my mind that I can't find any rest, day or night.'

She went again to hear Rowland, and kept coming every Sunday, though she had over twenty miles of rough mountainous paths to journey. She eventually approached him and asked:

'Sir, if what you preach is true, there are many people in my neighbourhood in a very miserable state. For the sake of those many precious souls that are hastening to perdition in their ignorance, come over to preach to them.'

Rowland was struck by her words, and after thinking for a while he answered, in his characteristically sudden way, 'I will come, if I can get the permission of the vicar.' This permission was granted, and Rowland preached at Ystrad-ffin, and continued to do so regularly for some years. Many were converted through this ministry. It is to this that Williams refers in another stanza of his elegy:

| | |
|---|---|
| Sounding o'er the hills of Dewi, | Daeth y swn dros fryniau Dewi, |
| Hear his voice, a flaming stream, | Megis fflam yn llosgi llin, |
| Echoing round the rocks of Towy, | Nes dadseinio creigiau Towi, |
| And the church at Ystrad-ffin. | A hen gapel Ystrad-ffin. |

It is doubtful whether the Church of England was making use of the chapel at Ystrad-ffin at this time. It had been shut for some time without any services being held there, and this was probably still the case when Rowland first went there.

One event worth recording occurred during his first sermon in the Towy Valley. An ungodly gentleman living in the neighbourhood used to spend his Sundays hunting with his dogs. He heard that Rowland was to preach at the chapel, and that he was a madman and said strange things. He and some friends came to hear the preaching, hoping for entertainment or possibly even to cause a disturbance. He stood on a bench in front of the preacher and in opposition to him. He hoped to confuse God's minister. Rowland understood his intention, but it only resulted in making him bolder for the Lord. His text was, 'It is a fearful thing to fall into the hands of the living God.' He began to thunder terribly, his eyes flashed in holy zeal for God, his expressions fell with such power and influence that his listeners became pale with fear. Soon, the terrors of judgment got hold of the ungodly gentleman; his proud countenance fell and his face became white; his knees shook like those of Belshazzar when he saw the fingers of a man's hand writing on the plaster of the wall; and he fainted in a heap on the floor. There he stayed until the end of the sermon, trembling and weeping. At the end of the service, he went up to Rowland and confessed his sin and malice in coming to hear him. He humbly asked his pardon, and requested that he return home with him for a meal and stay the night. The man was saved; he attended at Llangeitho once a month throughout his life, and his good character and consistent devotion were undoubted testimonies to the reality of his religion.

This is how Daniel Rowland was led to minister outside his own parish. It is interesting also to notice how he was brought to preach in places that were not consecrated. It must be remembered that Ystrad-ffin Chapel was a church building and had in the past been formally consecrated by a bishop for the purpose of holy worship. It seems that a number of ungodly youth from the neighbourhood of Llangeitho had so hardened themselves in wickedness, that not even Rowland's fame could bring them to hear the gospel. They spent their Sundays on top of a hill opposite the village and gave their time to all kinds of ungodly sports and contests. This was a considerable grief to Rowland. He tried his best to put a stop to their activities but every attempt proved unsuccessful. At last, he decided to go there to preach. He climbed to the top of the hill one Sunday, his brave spirit full of holy boldness. The wicked company failed to withstand the sharpness and power of his doctrine, and they quickly scattered. In this way that nest of ungodliness was demolished. Having begun to rebuke wicked men outside the walls of the church by attacking them on their own ground, and having experienced such success and blessing in the attempt, it was natural for him to proceed to preach wherever he found an open door, with no thought as to whether the place was consecrated by a bishop or not. Within a few years, he had visited very many areas in Wales, proclaiming the gospel with great success.

It is said that he was also led quite independently of Howell Harris, indeed, without even having heard of him, to form experience meetings or societies. This occurred as follows. He asked one of the parishioners at Llancwnlle to visit those who attended the church there and to invite them to a meeting to be held on a particular night in a house called Gelli-Dywyll, near Bwlchdiwyrgam, a lonely and narrow valley leading from the Aeron valley. Those invited gathered together by the appointed time, but they could not imagine why their curate had called them together. They feared that he would rebuke them for sins that he had discerned in them. But their fears were soon dispelled when they realized that Rowland wished to question them on the nature and purpose of the Lord's Supper, and to teach them more of the sacred sacraments. They spent much of the evening in this pleasant work, being built up and strengthened in the truth. These meetings were kept up for some time in this house. It belonged to a tailor, and was convenient because of its distance from any other dwellings. Eventually the meeting-place was moved to one of Rowland's barns. At first they met only occasionally, as opportunity afforded, sometimes on a Sunday; on other times during the week, in the day or evening; or sometimes again after a sermon, when a preacher came on a visit. Gradually however, they developed into a weekly meeting, and the fraternity that gathered was called a 'seiat', 'religious society', or 'band'. They never met in the church in case they offended some of the Church folk. It will be seen that the spiritual needs of those convicted had led Rowland and Harris quite independently to establish specific groups where they might nurture the flock and keep them from error. By now, of course, these societies are an important element in the spiritual life of the nation.

## THE FIRST MEETING OF ROWLAND AND HARRIS

Historians vary in their opinions as to which of Harris and Rowland was the first to emerge in the Revival. The Rev. John Hughes, Liverpool, states that it appears evident that Harris was first on the field by a short period,[3] but Mr Hughes does not give any reason for his assumption and from what he writes later in his book, he is clearly in some confusion over the matter. The Rev. Hugh J. Hughes, Cefncoedcymer, suggests that Harris was undoubtedly the pioneer, both as regards time and boldness and fearlessness of spirit, but he also fails to present any evidence. Howell Harris's own words are:

> As for the other minister, and great man of God, Mr Daniel Rowland, he was awakened about the same time as myself, in another part of Wales, namely in Cardiganshire, where, by reason of there being but little correspondence between that county and Breconshire, he went on gradually growing in gifts and power without knowing anything of me, or myself knowing anything of him; until by providence, in the year 1737, I came to hear him in Defynnog Church, in the upper part of our county.[4]

Williams, Pantycelyn, often suggests that Daniel Rowland was first in the work of the Revival, and it must be remembered that Williams was a close friend to both men, and contemporary with them. He was moreover, not only a fine poet and an incomparable hymn-writer, but also an excellent historian. We do not attach much weight to his words in his elegy to Rowland:

| | |
|---|---|
| When gross darkness covered Britain, | Pan oedd tywyll nos trwy Frydain, |
| With no sign of dawning light, | Heb un argoel codi gwawr, |
| And a deep sleep from the Almighty | A thrwmgwsg oddiwrth yr Arglwydd |
| Held the people in their night; | Wedi goruwch guddio'r llawr; |
| Daniel blasted on the trumpet . . . | Daniel chwythodd yn yr utgorn . . . |

Clearly, no conclusions may be drawn from these words. Williams used identical expressions when writing of Howell Harris:

| | |
|---|---|
| When the land lay dark and lifeless, | Pan oedd Cymru gynt yn gorwedd |
| In its long and deadly sleep, | Mewn rhyw dywyll, farwol hun, |
| When no bishop, priest or elder | Heb na Phresbyter' na 'Ffeirad, |
| Faithfully his watch did keep; | Nac un Esgob ar ddihun; |
| In the all-prevailing darkness | Yn y cyfnos tywyll, pygddu, |
| From Trefeca, burning bright, | Fe ddaeth dyn fel mewn twym ias, |
| Came a man of fierce passion, | Yn llawn gwreichion golau, tanllyd, |
| Blazing fiery sparks of light. | O Drefeca fach i maes. |

These quotations clearly do not decide the matter. The words are almost interchangeable. But there is one line in Rowland's elegy that appears to turn the scales firmly in his favour:

| | |
|---|---|
| Rowland first broke out in power, | Rowland startodd allan gyntaf, |
| Through the years, he kept his place, | A'i le gadwodd yntau'n lân; |
| And no man, however lively, | Ac nis cafodd, er gwisgied, |
| Overtook him in the race. | Ungwr gynnig gam o'i flaen. |

But even here, according to the Rev. Lewis Edwards:

> There is a danger of being too hasty, because it is not certain that this is a reference to Howell Harris. Yet, if Harris had 'broken out' first, it is not very probable that Williams would have forgotten the fact when he came to write the elegy, and this would certainly have stopped him from using such strong words about Rowland.[5]

All the evidence suggests that Rowland began his ministry of warning sinners just as early, if not earlier, than Harris. Harris came under conviction in 1735. In the October of that year he went to Oxford. But he had previously begun the work of exhorting his compatriots. He came home at about Christmas time and did not return. He recommenced the work early in 1736. The following year, 1737, Daniel Rowland is preaching at Defynnog Church, some forty miles, as the crow flies, from his home; and in the same year he went on a journey through Carmarthenshire. It is not probable that he journeyed through other counties before having spent some considerable time in the districts around his home, and before noting evident signs of blessing upon his efforts. Joshua Thomas, the Baptist historian, and another contemporary of Rowland's, says of him:

> I remember hearing him about 1737 in Carmarthenshire. There was a great many hearing him, and I heard some of the Dissenters discussing the sermon on the way home. I remember that some of what they said was, 'We have never heard any one like him from the Church of England except Griffith Jones. There has not been in our time such a light amongst Church people.[6]

It must be remembered that Daniel Rowland was only a young man at this time, just beginning his work, and with his preaching skills not yet having developed. The comparison being made with Griffith Jones is therefore all the more remarkable.

It may not be possible to prove without any shadow of doubt that Rowland had priority but this is of no great importance. What was important was the meeting between himself and Harris at Defynnog in 1737. Their joint histories for the next fifteen years make up the history of Welsh Methodism over that period. In the letter already quoted, where he describes the meeting, Harris goes on to say:

> . . . upon hearing the sermon and seeing the gifts given him, and the amazing power and authority with which he spoke, and the effects it had upon the people, I was made thankful, and my heart burned with love to God and to him. Here began my acquaintance with him, and to all eternity it shall not end.

Harris returned with Rowland to Llangeitho, and 'on hearing more of his doctrine and character, I grew more in love with him.' Daniel Rowland could not itinerate to the same extent as many of his friends because of the churches under his care, yet he still succeeded in traversing most of Wales many times, as Williams, Pantycelyn, testifies:

None of all of Gwalia's counties,
Hardly a parish in the land,
But that Rowland there has travelled,
There the gospel flame has fanned;
Over mountains, through the rivers,
Ferried over many a tide,
From St David's cross to Ludlow,
From Holyhead to Severnside.

Nid oes un o siroedd Cymru,
Braidd un plwyf sy'n berchen crêd,
Na bu Rowland yn eu teithio
Ar eu hyd ac ar eu lled;
Dros fynyddau, drwy afonydd,
Ac aberoedd gweitha' sydd,
O Dyddewi i Lanandras,
O Gaergybi i Gaerdydd.

## ROWLAND'S MINISTRY BECOMES MORE EVANGELICAL

As we have noted, he preached the law at first. But, writes Dr Lewis Edwards:

> Not the law as a summary of commandments, but the law as a revelation of the holiness of God. Rowland had seen God, and felt that he had received a message from him, and he therefore spoke as one having authority . . . The people soon realized that a fountain of invincible life was flowing forth from Llangeitho. Gradually, through his labours and that of others, the sound spread throughout Wales; and on those who believed its witness, its effects were rather like those in our day when the news came of the discovery of gold in Australia.[7]

How long his ministry continued in this thundering, terrible strain, is not known, but he had travelled through much of the Principality before its tone changed. According to Williams's elegy:

Five Welsh counties heard the thunder,
And with awesome, fearful dread
Fell with slaughter and with terror
On the ground in heaps, as dead;[8]
Wounds were taken, grievous woundings,
Wounds no mortal man could cure,
But the potent balm of Calv'ry,
Jesu's blood, is medicine sure.

Pump o siroedd pennaf Cymru,
Glywsant y tarannau mawr,
A chwympasant gan y dychryn,
Megis celaneddau i lawr;
Clwyfau gaed, a chlwyfau dyfnion,
Ac fe fethwyd cael iachâd,
Nes gael eli o Galfaria,
Dwyfol ddwr a dwyfol waed.

For about five years, it is thought, he was a Son of Thunder and a bringer of terror. In 1739, he published one of his sermons. Its title was 'Spiritual Milk' and its text, 1 Peter 2:2, and though it has awakening and fiery elements to it, yet it is very evangelical and comforting in tone. It is said that it was Mr Pugh of Llwynpiod who was instrumental in effecting this change in him.

'Dear Mr Rowland,' he said, 'preach the gospel to the people. Apply the balm of Gilead to their spiritual wounds, and show them the necessity of faith in the crucified Saviour.'

'I fear that I do not have that faith, in its full active strength, myself,' was the reply.

'Preach it until you feel you have it,' answered Mr Pugh, 'If you continue to preach the law in this way you will kill half the population of the county! You thunder forth the threatenings of the law, and preach so fearfully, that no one can stand before you.'

I cannot think of a more interesting scene: a Dissenting minister, without jealousy or prejudice, advising a young clergyman of the Established Church; one who has displaced him in the popularity of the neighbourhood, and had stolen his congregation to a large extent. Rowland, on the other hand, was sufficiently humble and simple of heart to receive the loving advice in the same spirit as that in which it was given, and to act upon it. From now on, he became a Son of Consolation. According to Williams, Pantycelyn, again:

| | |
|---|---|
| He declared the law's strong terror | Nôl pregethu'r ddeddf dymhestlog, |
| For some years with great alarm; | Rai blynyddau yn y blaen, |
| Many wounds were thus inflicted, | A rhoi llawer yn friwedig, |
| Then he sang with gospel charm; | 'Nawr, cyfnewid wnaeth ei gân; |
| He proclaimed divine salvation, | Fe gyhoeddodd iachawdwriaeth |
| Full, complete, sufficient, free, | Gyflawn, hollol, berffaith, llawn, |
| Through the death of the Messiah | Trwy farwolaeth y Messiah |
| Once forever on the Tree.[9] | Ar Galfaria un prynhawn. |

With this change in the tone of his ministry, the effects upon his hearers changed also. Previously they fainted with fear, so frightened were they by the terror of the Judge, and their souls melted within them as wax. The effect after this was no less remarkable, nor any less powerful, but now they broke out in rejoicing and in song. This was the beginning of the rejoicing for which Llangeitho was to become famous. It seems that Rowland himself at the beginning was unhappy with the praising and jumping; he feared that it was not completely pure, that it could give occasion to the flesh, and cause the enemy to blaspheme. He tried therefore to stop it and demanded that the people maintain control of their feelings. But it would have been easier to keep water from boiling when the fire is burning under it. When the congregation had been pressed to the very edge of despair, and had seen the jaws of hell opening before them to swallow them up, then to see the Lord Jesus in all his glory as an all-sufficient Saviour on their behalf was more than could be contained.

Their feelings broke through all restraints and they had to praise for such a salvation. It is said that Rowland was hardly reconciled to the phenomenon throughout his life. But he defended the rejoicers in comparison to the lukewarm English:

> You English blame us, the Welsh, and speak against us and say, 'Jumpers, jumpers.' But we, the Welsh, have something also to allege against you, and we most justly say of you, 'Sleepers, sleepers.'

It may be that not all the agitation, the crying out, and the shouts of praise, were fully free of the flesh in all; that not all the feeling, as it flowed over the edge of the vessel, was the product of the Spirit of God; and it is not unlikely that some ungodly men were carried away by the influences, and joined in the singing. Yet, after all, it must be realized that the light had shone so suddenly into the minds of the people, and they had felt the relief of escape from the wrath of God which had been pressing as mountains upon their consciences; and that in thousands, the rejoicing, though extreme and of unusual form, was yet as pure and spiritual as any godly feeling may be on earth. Many of those who had rejoiced at Llangeitho proved, by their godly lives, their sufferings for their faith, and their commitment to serve the Lord Jesus in the face of all opposition, that they had been born again to eternal life.

The effects that followed Daniel Rowland's ministry were now remarkable. In a letter that he sent to George Whitefield on 1 March, 1743, Howell Harris wrote:

> I was last Sunday at the ordinance with Brother Rowland, where I saw, felt and heard such things as I can't send on paper any idea of. The power that continues with him is uncommon. Such crying out and heart-breaking groans, silent weeping and holy joy, and shouts of rejoicing I never saw. Their 'Amens' and cryings 'Glory in the highest', etc., would enflame your soul was you there. 'Tis very common when he preaches for scores to fall down by the power of the word, pierced and wounded, or overcome by the love of God and sights of the beauty and excellence of Jesus, and lie on the ground. Nature being so overcome by the sights and enjoyments given to their heaven-borne souls, that it can't bear. The spirit almost bursting the house of clay to go to its native home . . . His congregation, I believe, consists of above two thousand, whereof a great part are brought to glorious liberty and walk solidly in clear light in the continual enjoyment of God, without a moment's darkness.[10]

Again and again, in almost all his letters at this time Harris refers to the glorious influences accompanying Rowland's ministry. He repeats continually that these influences are indescribable. In a letter from Llangeitho to his brother, written at the end of 1742, he says:

Today, I heard dear Bro. Rowland, and such a sight my eyes have never seen.
I can't send you any idea of it. There was such light and power in the congregation that cannot be expressed. The people went in their thousands from one
parish church to the other, three miles apart [from Llangeitho to Llancwnlle,
most probably] singing and rejoicing in God. And after partaking of the Lord's
Supper they returned the same distance in order to hear me in the night. I was
empowered to speak with a strength that I do not often have, to about two
thousand on the highway, till about eight at night. Some of the carnal professors, who had built upon the sand, come daily under conviction. The lambs
grow, and many walk in glorious liberty. The fire of God's love finds a place in
many hearts. They hold societies every night, and such is the influence they feel
while at prayer, they are often struck by an aweful silence; at other times the
voice of the one praying is drowned by the cries of broken hearts.

This is typical of all of Harris's letters at this time. He cannot hold back
from expressing his great wonder at the powers accompanying his friend's
ministry. When he later hears Williams, Pantycelyn, and Howell Davies,
preach in Pembrokeshire, the highest praise that he can bestow upon them
is to say that they had partaken abundantly of the fire of Llangeitho. And it
was not only at home that Rowland was so blessed, but wherever he went.
He wrote to Harris in London on 20 October 1742:

The last week I have been in Carmarthenshire and Glamorgan, and brave
opportunities indeed they were; whole congregations were under concern, and
such crying out that my voice could not be heard. Some persons of quality did
entertain me with uncommon respect. O what am I, that my ears and eyes
should hear and see such things![11]

In another letter to one of his hearers who was in London, Rowland
wrote:

Religion flourishes now in our parts. Thousands flock to the Word, and while
under the Word great part of them are under such agonies as is enough to
melt the hardest heart. Some make it their business to chide them, and now
they themselves are overcome by the power of God. They cannot but cry out,
'What shall I do? etc.' You would all wonder at what we daily see and hear. For
my part I can say I never had such power as I have now every day.[12]

The result of this powerful ministry and its accompanying effects was
to draw large numbers to Llangeitho from every part of the country. The
small, nondescript, rural village became the Jerusalem of Wales.

## HIS ITINERATING MINISTRY CONTINUES

Perhaps Rowland did not travel as much as Harris and Williams, Pantycelyn, who were itinerant preachers, but he ministered regularly in the

three churches where he had been appointed curate: Llangeitho, Llancwnlle and Llanddewibrefi. At the same time, it is certain that he travelled much, throughout the Principality. He preached monthly at Ystrad-ffin, Twr-gwyn, Waunifor, Abergorlech and Llanlluan. Unfortunately we have very little account of his journeys because his papers were all lost. After Rowland's death, all his literary remains were gathered by his son, Nathaniel Rowland, and were sent to the Countess of Huntingdon, who intended to find an appropriate person who would write a biography. Before this was arranged the Countess died, and all the valuable material sent to her was lost.

The Rev. John Evans of Bala mentioned in an article a visit by Rowland to Llanuwchllyn in 1740. He asked permission of the clergyman and wardens to preach in the church, and it was given. It seems that the clergyman, like Gallio of old, cared for none of these things. He was not concerned who preached, nor what was preached. He and Rowland discussed the rebirth and the old clergyman acknowledged that he knew nothing of the subject. 'What?' said the Reformer, 'Are you a master in Israel, and you do not know these things?' Rowland Lloyd, the Rector of Llangower, near Bala, was in the village at the time, and when he heard that one of the Methodists had had permission to preach in the parish church he was greatly annoyed. He rose up in great affront and hastened to the church. The service had already commenced and he immediately caused a disturbance. Rowland at the time was reading the chapter in Deuteronomy on the curses, chapter 28.

'What?' said Lloyd, 'Is Stephen, Glanllyn, accursed?' (This was a nobleman who lived nearby.)

'Yes,' was Rowland's answer, 'If the man is an ungodly man.'

This served only to increase the disturbance. Some old woman began ringing the bell noisily, and what with the blustering of the Llangower rector and the peal of the bell, Daniel Rowland, to the great disappointment of the congregation, was obliged to leave without preaching.

Rowland returned to Llanuwchllyn later. This time he preached from the mounting-block of Felindre, a farm on the boundary of the Llangower and Llanuwchllyn parishes. The date is not known. His text was, 'Behold, he cometh leaping upon the mountains, skipping upon the hills' (*Song of Sol.* 2:8). We have no account of the effect of the sermon, except that the people were so ignorant that they looked up to the hills around them, expecting someone remarkable to make his appearance.

He visited the north also in 1742. In a letter he sent to Howell Harris in that year he said that he had lately been on a journey to

Montgomeryshire and that, either on the way there or while returning, he had preached in many churches and farmhouses in Breconshire, and that a Mr Phillips of Builth Wells had committed him to the Bishop's Court for speaking in an inn there. He added that Brother W. Williams (Williams, Pantycelyn, no doubt) had been referred to the same court for preaching in a parish where he was not resident. Rowland asked Harris, who was in London at the time, to confer with the brethren in the capital as to how he should behave in such circumstances. It is more than probable that Rowland in the following year, 1743, travelled through Caernarvonshire as far as Anglesey, though there is no record of this in his biography, nor in *Methodistiaeth Cymru*.[13] In a letter from Evan Williams, an exhorter, written in 1742, it is said:

> Mr M__ H___s has been last week in Anglesey and it is wonderful how the work progresses there. Bro. Rowland intends to go there within a month.

That he carried out his intention is certain because a letter written by a Thomas Bowen, another exhorter probably, contains the postscript:

> Bro. Richards and Bro. R___s have been in Anglesey. Now Bro. Richards is travelling in south Wales.

The 'Bro. R___s' is almost certainly Daniel Rowland. His name was sometimes written 'Rowland' and sometimes 'Rowlands', by others and by himself. The remainder of Evan Williams's letter is so interesting that we must record it:

> Bro. Beaumont was greatly blessed to the town, particularly in silencing the persecutors. But the Bishop's Court happened to meet soon after, and the Chancellor preached against the Methodists and against Mr Whitefield, so that the minds of many were turned again. Many were called to account in the court as to why they allowed the societies to meet in their homes. Some thought it best to pay the fines, as they were weak, so that they might go free. After examining them, they were told that they were people who intended good but that they should attempt to keep Rowland and Harris within their bounds. The Chancellor said that he would seal a warrant to apprehend Rowland the next time.

The old exhorter's letter explains how the Methodists were persecuted at this time by the Church authorities. Evan Williams, the author of the letter, was a native of Ystradgynlais. He had been brought under conviction when reading John Bunyan's *Come and Welcome to Jesus Christ*, and he soon began exhorting with the Methodists. For a time, he was one of Griffith Jones's schoolmasters and was sent by him to Caernarvonshire to keep a school. This was in 1742. He was dreadfully persecuted there and was in danger of his life, so that he fled back to Griffith Jones. The town to which he refers in his letter was probably Carmarthen. He ended his days with the Independents.

There is a reference to a visit undertaken before 1745 by Daniel Rowland to the Lleyn Peninsula, Caernarvonshire, in an old 'anterliwt'.[14] Whether it was the 1743 journey, or another in the following year, we do not know. The following is the title-page of the anterliwt:

> The Interlude of Morgan the Sieve-maker on the Cradockians, or, The Scourge of the Methodists, in three Acts. By William Roberts, of Llannor in Lleyn. Shrewsbury; published by R. Lathrop for the Author, 1745.

This was one of the most popular interludes opposing the Methodists. It was played at fairs and gatherings, to the great amusement of the mob of low taste, and with the approval of the nobility and clergy of the neighbourhood. As well as putting lying words into the mouths of the different Methodist characters, the language is foul and obscene in many places, so much so that we would not dare to quote many of the lines. 'Chwitffild', as Whitefield is called, is portrayed as saying to Howell Harris:

| | |
|---|---|
| What use is a job to a pauper, | Pa beth a dâl trâd i ddyn truan, |
| Hard work and continuous bother, | A rhoi'r mawr anhunedd arno fo'i hunan |
| To send many ruffians a'roaring to heaven, | I yrru dynion anonest i'r ne' |
| Unless he gets paid for his labour? | Dan rorio, oni cheiff ynte'r arian? |
| | |
| I gave a good sauce to the Saxons, | Mi rois i sos go dda i'r Saeson, |
| I've left them in utter confusions, | Mae yno bob bedlem yn abl boddion; |
| If you make a go of bewildering the Welsh, | Ped feit tithe'n medru gyrru'r Cymry o'u co', |
| We'll filch all the Bishops' possessions. | Nyni a 'sguben holl eiddo'r Esgobion. |
| | |
| The King, he'll agree, that's for certain, | Ac a gaem ferdid y Brenin ar fyrder |
| To build a huge bonfire mountain | A'r Parlament i wneud ffwrn saith mwy ei phoethder, |
| That's seven times as hot as Nebuch'nezzar's of old, | Na ffwrnas Nebucodonosor sur, |
| To burn all the clergy in Britain. | I losgi gwyr Eglwys Loeger. |

We are informed at the bottom of the page that the last verse contains 'words expressed by Mr Dan. Rowland in Lleyn and by Tho. Jones, of Porth Dinllaen'. The interlude is some sixty pages long and is, throughout, full of caricatures of the aims of the Methodists and of the doctrines they preached. But our present purpose in quoting from it, is to show that Rowland had visited Lleyn before 1745.

There is also an account of a journey by Rowland through parts of Caernarvonshire and Anglesey in 1747, and fortunately much of the history of the journey is available. At Penmorfa, near Porthmadog, he was severely threatened, being assured that if he preached his bones would be broken so small that they might be placed in a bag. He ignored the threats. He continued to Lleyn, where he met with some kind friends. A request was made for him to have the church at Llanmellteyrn, in that he was an ordained clergyman, but it was refused. He preached from the mounting-block at the cemetery gate. His text was Jeremiah 30:21, ' "Who is this that engaged his heart to approach unto me?" saith the Lord.' In his sermon, he proved that none but Jesus had so fully committed his heart to that degree of perfection required by God. He then depicted Justice displaying beforehand to Jesus the sufferings he would have to undergo, if he was to proceed with paying the debt of sinners.

'Know,' said Justice, 'that though you come to your own, yet you will have only an animal's home to lodge, a manger for a crib, and swaddling clothes to wear.'
But instead of retreating, the Saviour answered,
'I am content with that treatment, for my elect's sake.'
'If you face a world that is under the curse, you will have no place to lay down your head; yes, you will be the target for the worst anger and malice of men, those very men who are being sustained by yourself, every moment of their lives.'
'O, my pure Law, I am content with that!'
'You will also sweat drops of blood on a cold night, and will have them spit on your face, and crown you with thorns; and your disciples, after having seen so many of your miracles and heard so much of your heavenly doctrine, will leave you in your direst hour; yes, one of them will sell you; another will deny you, blaspheming and swearing that he never knew you.'
'Though this is so hard,' said Jesus Christ, 'yet will I not turn back. No change of heart will be mine.'

As a result, Justice and the Law testify together:

'O Thou, the object of the praises of all the angels of heaven, and the true delight of the Jehovah Father, if you venture upon this incomparable surety-ship, all the powers of hell will attack you, and the unmitigated wrath of your heavenly Father will fall upon your sacred body and soul upon the cross; yes, if all is to be said, you will have to suffer the shedding of your last drop of blood.'

Now, who can think, without amazement and wonder, of that glorious Surety committing himself, in the face of such storms, to undertake such a burden, and in the face of all shout out, 'Content!'

He could not proceed with his sermon because one great victorious shout of weeping and thanksgiving burst forth, like the alabaster box of old, filling the place with its perfume. Many were never to forget this occasion for the rest of their lives.

Rowland visited the north many times after this. It is said that he traversed most of Wales once a year for a considerable span of his life. He ministered much in London and preached often in the chapels of the Countess of Huntingdon at Bristol, Bath, and other places.

## HE SUFFERS PERSECUTION AND IS EXCOMMUNICATED FROM THE CHURCH OF ENGLAND

Like most of the Reformers, Rowland was much persecuted and maltreated. Often, the parish priest or local nobleman would pay a number of ruffians to attack him when he sought to speak. In a letter to Whitefield dated 14 February 1743, Howell Harris wrote:

> I saw Bro. Williams on his return from Bro. Rowland, he informed me that while he and Rowland discoursed at the seaside in Cardiganshire, ruffians with guns and staves beat them unmercifully, but they escaped through the care of the Good Shepherd without much hurt; only Bro. Rowland had one wound on his head. They were set on by a gentleman of the neighbourhood. But no wonder the enemy rages, where he sees his kingdom so set upon.[15]

He was often in danger of his life. The worship was disturbed at times, and he and his hearers had to flee from the ferocity of their persecutors under a rain of mud and stones, until they had escaped out of their reach to some quiet corner, and there, in peace, they enjoyed such a comfort and blessing that more than compensated for all the abuse and oppression.

He was attacked viciously on one occasion at Aberystwyth by some half-drunk creature who swore that he would shoot him. He aimed the gun at him, and pulled the trigger, but the gun did not fire. Having failed in this, he beat Rowland dreadfully with the butt of the gun. There is an account of another evil attempt to destroy him and his hearers. It was understood that he was to preach in the open air, and one vicious man prepared a great amount of gunpowder under the spot where he and his congregation were to gather, and with a thin line of powder from the store to some distance away, where it ended in a pile of straw. The aim was to fire the straw and blow up the preacher and his hearers. Providentially, someone arrived at the scene before the service began and discovered the plot. In almost every place, he was in danger of abuse unless he stopped his work. Howell Harris wrote to Whitefield on 1 March 1743:

Brother Rowland had a little interruption a fortnight ago by some drunkards, but God fills his soul sweetly.[16]

The Reformers conferred many times to decide whether to summon to the courts those who mistreated them, but they never did so. Instead they made their persecutors the special objects of their prayers. But Rowland saw no harm in using a little cunning at times in order to escape from their enemies. On one occasion when he was preaching in a town in the north, he heard that a crowd of ruffians had decided that he would not be allowed to enter the place. The mob marched from the town to welcome him. When he realized from the noise that they were near, he placed his hat on his head in the most fashionable way, and quickened his horse to a gallop. 'Here he comes,' said some. 'No, that's not him,' said others, 'The Methodists never ride like that.' When he came up to them, he said, 'Children of the devil, what brought you out so early?' This decided the matter, 'He has used the devil's name,' they said and he was allowed to pass in peace.

Daniel Rowland continued his work in the face of the most determined opposition from the Church authorities. The English bishops and the majority of the clergymen not only opposed the disorderliness of his conduct, as they viewed it, but the Calvinistic doctrine that he taught was also hated by them. The Church of England, and nearly all its clergy, had been corrupted by the Arminian heresy. He preached a salvation wholly of grace, with all the righteousnesses of man as but filthy rags. He exalted Christ as the only Saviour, and faith in him as the only means of justification before God. Because of this, only persecution and scorn awaited him in the Church. The first step was to refuse him permission for the use of the chapel at Ystrad-ffin. In a letter dated 1742, to Mrs James of Abergavenny, who afterwards became the wife of Mr White-field, he wrote:

I am suffered to be no more at Ystrad-ffin. I preached them my farewell sermon from Acts 20:32. It reached their hearts. I believe such crying out was not heard in any funeral in the memory of man. May the Lord hear their cry and send them an able and powerful minister, who will dispense them the word of truth as it is in Jesus. Now I am to settle at Llanddewibrefi, which is a large church as will contain several thousands of people. Several of my communicants at Ystrad-ffin will join there at the next month's end at Abergwesyn.[17]

The word 'settle' is in italics in that Rowland had had a clear hint that he would not now be allowed to itinerate as previously. For all his popularity and gifts, no promotion was ever offered to him by the Church. He was left throughout the years as a curate serving three churches, on ten pounds a year. In 1760, his brother John Rowland, who held the living, died; he drowned when bathing at Aberystwyth. The living was not offered to Rowland. That he was a Methodist was an insuperable barrier. It was offered instead to his eldest son, who then held it throughout his life. Daniel Rowland therefore served as curate to his own son. Complaints against him were made continually to the bishop, and he was frequently summoned to appear before him. Sometimes he was severely rebuked and released only after being threatened. Other times, the bishop sought to restrain him with fair words. William John, an exhorter, wrote to Howell Harris in 1743, on one of these occasions:

> The Bishop refused to ordain Mr Williams [Pantycelyn]. The Rev. Mr Rowland was with the Bishop on Monday who conducted himself kindly towards him and with much respect.

At last, he was given to understand that he was not to minister outside his parish nor preach in unconsecrated places. If he did so he would not be tolerated further. He answered quietly that the circumstances of the land, in his view, were such as called out for an itinerating ministry, and that he thought that his work had received the acknowledgement of heaven and he therefore could not desist, whatever might be the consequences. As a result his dismissal from office was quickly proceeded with. There are some clergymen presently who argue that Rowland was never dismissed, and they base their argument on the fact that there is no reference to such a dismissal in the records of the Bishop's court at St David's. But they forget that there was no need for a legal case in order to turn him out; he was only a curate. The Bishop could take his licence from him at will, not only without any trial in his court but without even a record of the act in his books. And this is precisely what Bishop Squire did.

Daniel Rowland was evicted in the year 1763. Two differing traditions relate to the circumstances. The Rev. John Owen stated in his biography that it was done publicly on a Sunday in Llanddewibrefi. He had been told the story by a godly old man who lived in the village and who remembered the occasion well. Two clergymen came to the church when Rowland was ascending the stairs to the pulpit. One of the two was the Rev. Mr Davies, the brother of Captain Davies, Llanfechan; the other is not known. A letter was handed to Rowland in the pulpit. After reading it, he turned to the immense congregation that had gathered and told them that he was not allowed to preach. He descended from the pulpit and left the church, followed by the people, many of them weeping bitterly. This is the report followed by the Rev. Edward Morgan, the vicar of Syston, in his biography, except that he adds that the congregation after leaving the church pressed Rowland to preach to them, which he did from the cemetery wall.

But the Rev. John Hughes, Liverpool, obtained a different account from David Davies, Dolau-bach, who was an elder at Llangeitho and an able man. According to his account:

> At Christmas, 1763, he was turned out by the officers of the Bishop. I believe that there is a mistake in the account provided by the Rev. J. Owen, when he says that it took place at Llanddewibrefi. The history that was told me emphasized that it was at Llangeitho and Llancwnlle that he was ministering at the time. I was talking to an old man called John Jenkins who, when a boy of fifteen, went with his parents to Llancwnlle to hear Rowland one Sunday, and that the two officers came from the Bishop to turn him out, and that Rowland had started the service before they arrived. The people kept the two men at the door until Rowland had finished preaching, then someone went to him to inform him of their presence and purpose. He descended from the pulpit immediately and came to them at the door, inquiring what was their message. They informed him. 'Oh,' said Rowland, 'his lordship need not have concerned himself with sending you to me. As far as I am concerned I shall never come within these walls again. If you wish, we will leave them to the bats and owls. The people are ready to come with me.' The old man testified that he was present at the time, seeing and hearing all this, and that these were the true circumstances of the event. And all over a certain age, can also remember that nearly all of the parish churches of this area were almost completely deserted for a very long time after throwing out Daniel Rowland.

The two reports are not necessarily inconsistent. It is not impossible that Rowland was refused permission to preach in the morning at Llanddewi-brefi, and that he rode the six miles or so to Llancwnlle by the evening service, where the events narrated by the godly old elder from Dolau-bach took place. But that he was turned out is certain. No Churchman or Dissenter doubted the matter for more than a hundred years after the event. The Rev. Howell Davies mentioned publicly in Llangeitho Chapel that the results of the turning out had proved a bitter experience to the Bishop., that he was in much pain of soul because of it when on his death-bed, and cried out, 'I fought the fight,' (was it the fight against the Methodists that he meant?) 'I have finished my course, but I lost my soul, and I am now forever ruined!' And he died under the most awful pangs of conscience. This, without any other proof, would be sufficient testimony that the doors of the Church were closed against Rowland, because he and Howell Davies were the closest of friends throughout their lives and were moreover related, after Nathaniel, Rowland's second son, married Davies's daughter. The circumstances of Rowland's eviction must therefore have been completely familiar to Howell Davies. Rowland could see the storm coming and had prepared to leave the Church of England. Dr Lewis Edwards writes:

> It is interesting to read how the observant old elder of Dolau-bach succeeded in obtaining proofs that Rowland was a willing Dissenter. There is no sounder reasoning in Euclid. But though Rowland had made his plans for leaving, the Established Church pulled down upon its own head the shame for throwing him out. If there was any sin of schism associated with this event, it must be that it was the Bishop who evicted him who was guilty of it. And we cannot but think that that guilt still abides upon the Church from which he was excommunicated.[18]

## LLANGEITHO BECOMES THE JERUSALEM OF WALES

Daniel Rowland was now a free man. No bishop could interfere in his work from now on, nor could the jealous clerics of various Welsh parishes send in their complaints against him. He was free to preach the everlasting gospel by whatever means and in whatever place he so desired, without anyone being able to call him to account. Preparations had already been made to build a large chapel for him, the other side of the River Aeron, on the edge of Gwynfil village (often misnamed Llangeitho village in ignorance). The building was now proceeded with, in all haste.

After its completion, it was called 'The New Chapel'. It was about 45 feet long, the same in width, and without a gallery. The pulpit was opposite the door at the far end of the building, with an entrance to it from the back, so that the preacher would not have to push through the congregation. This is where Rowland now ministered until the day of his death. The barn on Rowland's land, which was used for the society meetings, had long been changed into a kind of chapel and was where the unordained exhorters used to preach. This old barn was a poor, bare building, its walls of mud and clay and its roof a mixture of straw and reeds, and it measured only ten yards by six. The barn had become too small. It was changed into a dwelling place, and a small chapel had been built in 1760, some three years before Rowland's eviction. This also had mud walls and a thatched roof. Both of these buildings were called 'The Society House'. Rowland would often be present in the meetings in these buildings, either in an experience meeting, or listening to the exhorters, but he would make his way there secretly, so that his enemies might have no occasion to complain of him to his bishop. Edward Morgan, Vicar of

Syston, states that he was considerably straitened in circumstances after being evicted, that he had nothing with which to support his wife and children, and that the Methodists at the time had no system at all to maintain their preachers. As proof of this, Morgan relates that Rowland, soon after his dismissal, walked on foot to Llanddowror seeking counsel from Griffith Jones and that he had no food for the journey except a small cake and the water he obtained from the streams on the way. This story cannot be true. Rowland was evicted in 1763, as far as is known, and Griffith Jones had died two years before. Furthermore Daniel Rowland had married into one of the best families of the neighbourhood and Mrs Rowland was considered to have sufficient means of her own. The Rev. John Hughes suggests:

> It is fair to say that Rowland received more from the Methodists than it is said he received as a curate. It appears that some thousands would receive communion at Llangeitho every month, before and after his eviction, and it was usual for the communicants to contribute what they could after the service. Many of them certainly were very poor, but a considerable number were able and willing to contribute generously. What the total sum might have been is impossible to say, and unnecessary to ask. This labourer was fully worthy of his reward whatever it might have been. The communion money that was contributed in the various other places as well as Llangeitho would have produced a considerable total.

At the same time, there is no evidence that at any period in his life was he rich, nor that the amassing of money was one of his aims at any time.

The new chapel now became a gathering point for thousands. They came there from all over the Principality and this remained the case for the remainder of Rowland's life, and for many years after his death. The whole population, for an area of some fifteen miles, would attend every communion Sunday, once a month, together with crowds from the furthest extremities in the north and in the south. Every house for many miles around would be full of strangers. Often there would be more than 5,000 present. Rowland would make sure that he was at home on a communion Sunday. He would preach a preparatory sermon on the Saturday before, at eleven in the morning, and usually one of the visiting preachers or of the exhorters would preach at three in the afternoon. He would usually be assisted at the table by two or three other ministers, and sometimes by seven or eight. It is said that the assembly at Llangeitho on these occasions would be like an enormous fair. The roads and streets would be full of people, but without any of the bustle and tumult of a fair. Instead, the solemnity of eternity would rest upon the multitude. No levity or joking would be heard – the young and thoughtless, those who had been drawn by the crowd or had come to satisfy their curiosity, would feel a solemnity taking hold upon them. The fields would be full of the horses of the visitors, and some hundreds of animals would be tethered together in lines alongside the hedgerows. Rowland's ejection became a great spur to the work. He was freed from his chains, his ministry became more powerful, and the crowds that came to hear him increased.

We have drawn attention to the powers that accompanied his ministry. Very rarely did he preach without gaining a complete mastery over his hearers. Throughout his career he was clothed with power from on high, and with the unction of the Lord. But on occasions there broke out what was called 'revival'. This 'revival' was a descending of the divine fire in greater intensity than usual, transforming the whole throng into a flame. The wicked would shake like aspen leaves, the mouths of the godly would be filled with singing and praising. We are perfectly satisfied that these 'revivals' came from God directly. The fruit that ensued proves this undeniably. It is useless to criticize them in a wordly spirit; the flesh has no right to sit in judgment over the work of the Holy Spirit.

There are accounts of very many of these revivals breaking out at Llangeitho. One began shortly before Rowland was thrown out of the Church. He was at that part of the service where the Litany is read. When uttering the words, 'By thine agony and bloody sweat, by thy cross and passion, by thy precious death and burial, by thy glorious resurrection and ascension, and by the coming of the Holy Ghost, Good Lord, deliver us,' a strange influence fell on his spirit; his tone was most melting; his voice shook with feeling; the whole congregation was struck by the same influence; they too saw him whom they had pierced, and they mourned for him as one mourns for his only son; but soon the mourning turned into unspeakable glory. This revival spread through large areas of the region. Another revival broke out at Llangeitho in 1762, after the publication of a collection of William Williams's hymns entitled, *'Caniadau y Rhai sydd ar y Môr o Wydr'* [*'The Songs of Those who are on the Sea of Glass'*]. In singing these glorious hymns, which are so full of exalted and evangelical views, the believers' souls were filled with worship, and the rejoicing spread throughout the surrounding areas. But the greatest revival occurred soon after Rowland's ejection, almost as if the Lord was expressing publicly his pleasure in the courage and self-denial of his servant. It is called 'the Great Revival', because it spread through most of south Wales and large parts of north Wales, and was the means of bringing thousands to the feet of the

Saviour. Nathaniel Rowland remembered the revival beginning during a sermon from his father. His account is as follows:

> The entire chapel seemed as if it was filled with some supernatural element, and the whole assembly was seized with extraordinary emotions, hundreds of them, with tears streaming down their faces, some evidently from excess of sorrow, others from overflowing of joy; some broken and contrite with penitence, and others rejoicing in hope of glory.

Nathaniel Rowland related further that this light began to shine in the service when Daniel Rowland referred to the verse from Matthew's Gospel, 'I thank Thee, O Father, Lord of heaven and earth, because Thou hast hid these things from the wise and prudent, and hast revealed them unto babes; even so, Father, for so it seemed good in Thy sight.' A thunderbolt, striking in the midst of the congregation, seemed to spark from the words; hundreds were blinded by the brightness of the light; the effect was so direct, powerful and overcoming, that it is pointless to try to describe it. It is said that this revival did much to dispel the depressed and disconsolate feelings that had resulted from the sad disruption that took place between Rowland and Howell Harris. The effects that accompanied these revivals were incredible. Some fell in a faint; others broke into groaning and crying from terror and agony of mind, as if the Judge was at the door; whilst others were heard breaking out in praise and rejoicing at having been saved from the jaws of death. During these days, many would often return to their homes from Llangeitho, some on foot and others on horseback, men and women, boys and girls, singing and rejoicing, so that their noise would be carried far by the breeze. This is how Williams describes them:

| | |
|---|---|
| All the hordes are homewards journeying, | Mae'r torfeydd yn dychwel adref, |
| In a glorious frame of mind, | Mewn rhyw ysbryd llawen fryd, |
| Having parted with their burdens, | Wedi taflu lawr eu beichiau, |
| Left their guilty loads behind; | Oedd yn drymion iawn o hyd; |
| Miles of highway full of singing, | Y ffyrdd mawr yn frith o werin, |
| Praises to the Lamb abound, | Swn caniadau'r nefol Oen, |
| Till the barren rocks and valleys | Nes mae'r creigiau oer a'r cymoedd |
| Echo with the joyful sound. | Yn adseinio'r hyfryd dôn. |

Daniel Rowland was not left without earthly honour, for all the prejudice of the Bishop of St David's and of the clergy. About the time of his eviction he was made Chaplain to the Duke of Leinster, 'one of His Majesty's most honourable Privy Council in the Kingdom of Ireland'. It is not known what services were required of him in this office, but it probably provided substantial help for supporting himself and his family. Rowland was also offered the living of Newport, Pembrokeshire, by the philanthropist, John Thornton. Mr Thornton came to know of him through a woman from the Llangeitho district who, like many Cardiganshire women in those days, would go to London in the summer months to weed gardens. She was employed by Thornton and would attend every Sunday at the church of William Romaine and much appreciated his ministry. She wished also to hear him during the week and went to her employer to ask him whether she could leave her work a little earlier, promising to rise earlier the following morning to make up the lost time. He asked,

'Do you like Mr Romaine's sermons?'

'Oh yes, Sir,' she replied, 'They remind me of Wales, because we have there a preacher without equal.'

This led the gentleman to inquire into Rowland's history, and gradually he became one of his closest friends. One result of the friendship was this offer of the Newport living but when the Llangeitho people heard of it, they were filled with sadness. They gathered in crowds about his house, begging him not to leave them. They argued that he was their father and that they would have no one to break the bread of life for them if he were to leave. Rowland was overcome by their petitions and decided to remain where he was and to trust to Providence. When he sent his answer and the reasons for it to London by the hand of his son, Mr Thornton replied:

I had a high opinion of your father before, but I have now a still higher opinion of him, though he declines to accept my offer. The reasons he assigns are highly creditable to him. It is not a usual thing with me to allow other people to go to my pocket, but tell your father, that he is welcome to do so whenever he pleases.

It is said that Rowland, before this, refused a living in north Wales for the same reasons.

## LEADING THE METHODIST CONNEXION

We will refer later to the unhappy division between Rowland and Harris and the disruption that this caused in the Connexion. After the Disruption, Rowland was considered the leader. The care of all the churches was upon him; he, together with his close friend, Williams, Pantycelyn, was considered responsible for maintaining the purity both of doctrine and discipline. He did not seek to excuse himself from the burdens placed upon him, and indeed they were no small burdens. It does not appear that the Arminian heresy caused him much trouble; the ministry of the Welsh Reformers was thoroughly Calvinistic from the beginning. But gradually, some of the exhorters went to the opposite extreme. One of

them swallowed the Sandemanian error, namely that the faith that justifies is merely bare assent to the truth of the gospel. This heresy had caused
much damage to the churches in England, and a Mr John Popkin, a very
popular preacher, began teaching the same views amongst the Methodists.
This man was the cause of much grief to Rowland. At last, he was brought
before the Association, his ministry was terminated, and they were not
troubled by him any further. After his expulsion he travelled about, even
reaching Caernarvonshire, in an endeavour to propagate his principles
but his attempt to win followers was completely unsuccessful. (Sandemanianism would have found no home at all in Wales had it not been for
J. R. Jones, one of the leading ministers of the Baptists, who was drawn to
it. His subsequent ministry proved very damaging to the Baptist cause in
the north.) Many Methodists however were attracted to the Antinomian
heresy and led loose lives, making God's grace an occasion for the flesh.
One of these was a man called David Jones, a very gifted preacher, who
was popular in the north and the south and was moreover a nephew of
Daniel Rowland's. David Jones became so proud and so intolerably selfish,
that he did not hesitate to oppose Rowland and Williams publicly in an
Association. When they emphasized the necessity for repentance and holy
living, he would say, 'How blind and legalistic you are. You do not seem
to have understood the gospel.' Many were inclined to follow him, and it
was feared that the whole country would go after him, At last, Rowland
decided that this man had either to give up his Antinomian views or be
expelled from the Connexion. Jones was too stiff-necked to submit and was
therefore excommunicated. In his folly, he thought that he could become
the founder of a new religious party. But when he journeyed about after his
expulsion, seeking to gain followers, very few joined him, and even these
left after a short time. In the end, he was deserted by all and was left as
salt that has lost its savour.

   Rowland's courage in disciplining Popkin and Jones was of great profit to
others who had shown the same tendencies. They returned to the simplicity
of the gospel, asking forgiveness for the trouble they had caused. Rowland
himself was of a notably forgiving spirit, though there is an account of one
popular preacher who had travelled considerably in north Wales teaching
Antinomian views, being placed under what was to him a very severe discipline. He was required to return to those societies previously visited and
retract his errors, acknowledging his fault and mistake. This he carried out
willingly. Williams refers to this in his elegy to Rowland:

| | |
|---|---|
| Many men went after by-paths, | Ac fe wibiodd amryw ddynion, |
| Left and right, they went astray, | Rhai ar aswy, rhai ar dde; |

| | |
|---|---|
| Heaven's decree ensured that Rowland | Ond fe gadwodd arfaeth nefol |
| Never swerved or fell away; | Rowland onest yn ei le; |
| And whenever any wandered | A phwy bynnag gyfeiliornai |
| From the paths of truth and grace, | O wiw lwybrau dwyfol ras, |
| He'd expose their wayward thinking, | Fe ddatguddiai'u cyfeiliornad, |
| So that others might be safe. | Hyd nes gwelai pawb hwy'n gas. |

We had occasion to converse with many old people from the Llangeitho neighbourhood who remembered Rowland well, in particular, David Jones, the godly old elder from Dolau-bach. They described him as a relatively short man, quick of foot and lively in his actions. Dr Owen Thomas states that the portrait of him by R. Bowyer, painted a little before his death and shown a month after his funeral – with its high, broad forehead, arched brows, piercing eyes, Roman nose, wide mouth and thin lips, and a look of determination – was very accurate. During a visit to Llandeilo, while on a preaching journey to south Wales in 1837 on behalf of the Temperance Movement, Thomas recognized Rowland's daughter from this portrait, though at the time he did not realize that Rowland had had a daughter, let alone one that was still alive. The portrait, it seems, had only been painted after considerable difficulty. 'I am only a lump of clay myself,' Rowland had complained. And while the artist was at his work, he would repeat time and again, 'Oh! Oh! Painting a portrait of a poor old sinner!'

Like many famous orators, he was prone to nervousness. When he saw the thousands streaming over the nearby hillsides and gathering in the narrow Aeron Valley to hear him, he would often tremble with fear and be terrified of having to face them in the chapel. He would often say to himself out loud, 'The Lord have mercy upon me, a contemptible worm, sinful dust and ashes.' He would spend many weeks in painful anxiety over the Sunday sermon to be delivered. When Sunday morning arrived, he would tell his old servant that he feared he could not preach, but the latter was to say, later:

> Once we got him to the pulpit, we knew that everything would be all right; he would gain strength gradually; his words would be as flashes of lightning darting through the congregations inside the chapel and outside, for there would usually be more people outside than in, and the effects upon them would be remarkable.

He would sometimes feel a strengthening of his spirit on seeing the crowds and hearing their singing. There was a well about two miles to the north of Llangeitho where the travellers would gather by the hundreds to eat their bread and cheese, and to drink the water. After their strength was revived, they would sing a hymn and then, often, would descend the slopes of the valley, still singing. In the meantime, he would be walking quickly along the banks of the river with an anxious mind. But on hearing the noise, he would suddenly lift up his head with a smile, and say, 'Here they come, bringing heaven with them.'

## ROWLAND AS A PREACHER

All the elements of a true preacher met in Daniel Rowland. He had the very best of voices – penetrating and clear – easily able to reach the furthest limits of a crowd of twenty thousand. Some say that he did not shout, though he generally spoke with great energy. But the old folk of Llangeitho said otherwise, and one who was his maid testified that he had to change his shirt after every service because of how much he would have sweated.

His voice could portray every kind of feeling, and when expressing the tender truths of the gospel the sweetness of his tones would be over-powering. His wonderful familiarity with his Bible meant that he had a quiver of the best arrows at his elbow continually. His memory would never fail when he wished to quote a verse from Scripture, the verse would invariably be at hand, and invariably it would be the most relevant verse for the context. He possessed a strong and daring imagination that would create in living images before his mind's eye the circumstances he was describing. When preaching once at Llancwnlle on the sufferings of the Saviour, he felt as if the Lord Jesus in all his wounds and stripes, was personally before him, and he cried out, 'O, pale face! O, empty veins! O, smitten back!' until the impression upon himself and the congregation was almost overwhelming.

His emotions were fiery and strong. One that knew him said that he had as much animal spirits as half a dozen men. With a mind that was notably quick and clear, and an understanding fertile of ideas, the overall result was that the strength of his feelings lent wings to his words and caused them to be full of fire. And he drew inspiration from the presence of the congregation. To find himself standing before a vast gathering would quicken him throughout, and that excitement would not confuse him but would stimulate every instinct he possessed, so that his mind would become quicker, his understanding more fertile, and the warmth of his spirit more heated than at any other time. It may be that it was when in the pulpit, under the influence of that inspiration which he drew from his hearers, that he discovered the brightest of those pearls that fell from his lips. And to crown all, he was owned of the Holy Spirit in an extraordinary way, almost throughout his preaching career. When the divine influences fell upon him he would be as a great volcano, pouring forth from his lips streams of fiery liquid, so that no flesh could stand before him.

His sermons were usually short, of half an hour or forty minutes duration at most, but on some occasions he would forget himself completely and preach for three or four hours. There is an account of one particular occasion when he and his hearers were so caught up in delight that they lost all sense of time. It was only on seeing the rays of the sun shining in through the west window of the church, an indication that the day was drawing to its end, that they realized how long the service had been. His spiritual sensitivity was particularly acute. Once, in an Association, the services had been hard. A clergyman had preached a lifeless sermon at ten on the morning of the main day and Rowland was to speak after him. He felt that he could not preach without first warming the climate somehow. He called on the godly old exhorter, Dafydd Hugh, Pwll-y-march, who was noted for his short and powerful prayers, to turn to prayer for a minute, 'Only a minute,' he said. The old exhorter immediately addressed the throne:

> Lord Jesus, for the sake of thy blood and passion, hear me. Thy servants have been winnowing here, yesterday afternoon and this morning. But in vain. Not the slightest breeze has blown upon us the whole time. The Wind, Lord! The Wind, gracious Lord! For the winds are in thy hands, Lord, now as ever. Amen.

A wave of emotion passed through the crowds. A balmy air blew over them, cheering and quickening all, and the man of God preached with invincible power and influence.

Comments are sometimes made suggesting that Rowland's power lay entirely in his oratory and that his sermons, apart from himself, were fairly ordinary compositions. This is a complete mistake. His published sermons are now before us and they are truly excellent, full of matter, and woven throughout by biblical quotations. They are Puritanical in nature and notably Scriptural, and full of the most arresting and charming illustrations. Certainly, the fluency and spiritual life of the preacher would add much to their effectiveness, but even on their own it would be difficult to find anything to match them in any language. Take the following example from 'Good News to the Gentiles.' He refers to the wise men going to Jerusalem rather than to Bethlehem to look for Jesus:

> They came, not indeed by the direction of the star, but by the guidance of their own reasoning. They thought that as Jerusalem was the capital city of the land and the place of kings, that they would be sure to hear there of the birth of Christ. They followed, I say, the reasoning of men, and therefore they found not Jesus. He cannot be found but by his own light and directions. Reason indeed is a good gift and of royal origin, but, since the fall, it is like

Mephibosheth, lame in both its feet. That person would never have come to
David, had he not been carried in some way or another; therefore, it was good
that David came to him. Thus it is with reason; it desires to die the death of
the righteous; it sees in some measure what is good, and commends it, but
it does not follow it, except it be drawn: 'No man can come to me, except
the Father which hath sent me draw him.' As long as they followed the star,
they did well. When they left the star and followed their own reason, they
did badly. Let the blind man follow his guide, though he lead him through
thorns and briers, through valleys and over mountains. He must trust to the
eyes of others, not having sight himself. We are all blind by nature, and out
of compassion towards us Christ sent the Comforter to lead us.

Or take the following quotation from the same sermon, and full of
similar pearls:

It is sad to think what little value some see in Jesus Christ; they will not come
from the house next door to view his face. How far will some travel to market
when the necessities of life are wanting? The souls of many have long suffered
without being satisfied. I long to argue on behalf of your souls, and to plead
that they might have a bit of bread, at the very least, once a week. If they were
to have only that, I would expect them to get stronger and to look out for
more. The wise men came more miles than you will take steps.

OBJECTION: If you could show him to us, we would be very glad to come.

You may see him, and more gloriously than ever the wise men saw him. We
show Christ to you in the gospel; not to the eyes of the flesh, but to the soul;
not lying in a manger, nor praying on a hillside, nor bleeding in the garden,
nor dying on the cross, but sitting on his throne, glorious in the heavens. If
someone entered an elegant room, full of beautiful pictures, but with the
curtains drawn, they would not be able to see anything, but if someone were
to open the curtains, all would be revealed. So is Christ's appearance in the
gospel but some have a veil, a cover, over their eyes so that they cannot see.
O! pray for a tearing of the veil, a taking away of the cover; then you will see
the excellence of the Lord Jesus in his congregations.

We could continue almost indefinitely adding similar examples of
Rowland's high degree of understanding, but we must be satisfied with
one more example. It is from a sermon on 'Christ All in All'. The content
of the sermon is the appropriateness of the Lord Jesus, as the anointed of
the Father, to be a Saviour:

He was not weak, but sufficient for the work of redemption. In Isaiah 3:7, it is
said, 'I will not be a healer; for in my house is neither bread nor clothing: make
me not a ruler of the people.' It is right that princes should be wealthy; beg-
gars would only swallow up the possessions of their subjects. Christ could not
answer as the man in Isaiah, because he is suitably endowed with all necessary

graces and gifts for the work to which he was appointed; Psalm 89:19. We see then that our help is not laid upon a weak man, one that would faint under the load; no, not at all, but upon a strong, yea, an almighty man, who would fulfil his task. Just as Samson arose at midnight and carried the gates of Gaza to a high hill some miles from the city, so also Jesus, the mighty, rose from the grave, and carried the gates of hell and of death, and ascended to heaven. Therefore it is said, 'He is able also to save them to the uttermost that come unto God by him, seeing he ever liveth to make intercession for them.' We do not come to one who is weak, as to the high-priest of old, but to a strong man, chosen from the people. Behold, the comfort of every weak believer: that the Lord is able to complete the work he has begun. The comfort of the leper was, 'If thou wilt, thou canst make me clean.' Soul, you have a God in whom it pays to trust; he is as full of desire to save you as he is of power to do so. In that he is almighty, let us rest and trust in his ability. Let men run to and fro, whithersoever they wish, to seek aid; no one can help them but him. In whatever difficulty we find ourselves, let us lean on him. He could keep Noah in an ark of wood, and he could keep Moses in a basket of reeds, 'He sendeth ambassadors by the sea, even in vessels of bulrushes upon the waters,' (Isaiah 18:2). He will save by means, without means, in opposition to means, and over and above means.

It is impossible to read the above without a sense of the excellence of the content. At the same time, it must be admitted that the strength of feeling and the warmth of spirit of the preacher would contribute greatly to their power.

Many of Rowland's most telling phrases, expressed in public or in private, have been kept in the memories of our old people. He said once to a slanderer:

You say that we must reveal and exhibit sins; that as they are too prevalent in the church, they should not be hidden. Take care, man. Who are you? I think I know your family, and your elder brother, namely Ham, Noah's son. His two brothers wished to hide their father's nakedness, but he did not wish so. What reward did they receive for their work of hiding? The blessing of God and of their father. What did your brother receive? A curse from God and from his father. I do not doubt that your reward will be no different.

In order to pre-empt a too harsh discipline, he once said:

The discipline of the gospel is like a golden comb, pulling and gathering all together, for profit and protection, and not like a fork that throws afar and scatters.

It is doubtful whether God, since the days of the apostles, ever raised such a preacher as Daniel Rowland, possessing such gifts for the work of the pulpit. The clear judgment of all who heard him, some of them being men of great learning, was that they had never heard anyone else gifted to such a degree. He was as Saul in their eyes, higher, head and shoulders, than all others. In a letter from which we have already quoted, Howell Harris says of him:

> The Lord is with him in such a way that I believe the dragon trembles at his progress. Though I have now had the privilege of hearing and reading the work of many of God's eminent men, I do not know, as far as I can judge, that I know of anyone so blessed with so many gifts and power; such discerning light into the spirit of the Scriptures, to portray the mystery of the godliness and glory of Christ. And though he is often accused of errors, yet the eternal Spirit has led him into all truth, and kept him from falling into any error, so that his ministry, I believe, is one of the greatest blessings that God's Church enjoys in this region.

Harris wrote like this after having heard most of the leading preachers of England and Wales, including Griffith Jones, Whitefield, the two Wesleys, and many of the other famous names raised in those notable times, but in his opinion none were as gifted as Rowland.

The judgment of Mr Charles of Bala was the same, and it is known how prudent and moderate he was in all his expressions. He wrote in the *Trysorfa* [*Treasury*] as follows:

> There was loftiness, and grandeur, and every other excellency in the endowments of Daniel Rowland – profound thoughts, strength and sweetness of voice, clearness and lively energy in proclaiming the deep things of God to the astonishment and effectual arousing of his hearers.

Again, in an article he wrote entitled, *A Conversation between Scrutator and Senex, Senex* declares:

> This man's ministry, as you know, was most glorious; excelling all others in its majesty and authority.

And again, in the same article:

> The gifts of Mr Rowland, and the power that accompanied his ministry, were such that no hearers in the present age can form any adequate idea of them. There is no one who has not heard him, that can imagine anything equal to what they were. I often compared him in my mind to that Tachmonite who was one of David's mighty men; he was the chief of the three, and though many others were very great yet they attained not unto the first three. Oh! how wonderful the authority and light that accompanied his ministry, and how wonderful the effects on the hearers! The multitudes, having heard a sermon or two from him, would go their long and tedious journeys with great gladness, praising God for his unspeakable gifts received at Llangeitho.

When attempting to describe Rowland to an English friend, Thomas Charles wrote:

> Rowland preached repentance, until the people repented; he preached faith until men believed. He portrayed sin as so abhorrent that all hated it; and Christ so glorious as to cause all to choose him.

In a letter written by him in 1780, to Sally Jones, who afterwards became his wife, Charles commented:

> I think with you, that not only Bala bach but Wales itself is a highly-favoured country. That aged herald of the King of Glory, D. Rowland, is and will be, an eternal honour to it. I seldom can speak of him in moderate terms. I love him dearly, and honour him as my father in Christ; and not without reason; for to him under God I am indebted for whatever light I have into, and experience I have of, the glorious salvation through Christ.

It would be difficult to find stronger words, and when it is remembered that they come from Mr Charles, they must clearly be taken at their full value.

Mr David Jones of Llan-gan bears the same witness. In a letter of his to the Countess of Huntingdon, dated 'Bridgend, 14 May, 1773,' he says:

> We would have been very pleased to have seen you at our Association. It truly was a very excellent day. The Lord Jesus fulfilled his promise to his servants, 'Lo, I am with you.' Great power from above accompanied the word preached. Many returned to their homes rejoicing. And who would not rejoice at seeing the Prince of our salvation himself making his appearance on the battlefield, and assuring the hearts of his poor people that he would have the victory for them and in them? I trust that the careless were pricked in their hearts. Mr Rowland preached the second sermon in the morning, from Acts 9:4, 'And he fell to the earth, and heard a voice saying unto him, Saul, Saul, why persecutest thou me?' Mr William Williams preached before him. We had two sermons in the afternoon also. The first from Mr William Lloyd of Caeo, an unordained preacher, and the second from Mr Peter Williams. Some of the people made our small town echo with their, 'Gogoniant i Fab Dafydd,' 'Hosanna drwy'r nefoedd, Hosanna hefyd drwy'r ddaear,' 'Amen, Amen.'[19] There are enough within your reach to translate the Welsh words to you. Mr Rowland preached the next day in a small town, some twelve miles west from us, where he had a truly sweet service. He spoke wonderfully on Abraham lifting up his eyes and looking, Genesis 22:13. I never before heard such a sermon. He is most certainly the greatest preacher in Europe. May the Lord acknowledge him more and more. That little town also was echoing its 'Gogoniant.' Continue, glorious Jesus, to ride prosperously through our land. Fill our cold hearts with thy love, and we will then praise thee from coast to coast.

The venerable Rev. David Griffiths of Nevern held Rowland in the highest regard:

> This great preacher, in his public ministrations resembles the gradual swellings and bursting of the waves of the ocean, when the wind agitates the bosom of the deep. The overwhelming power of the mighty influences of the Spirit in his ministry came on gradually, in manner like a wave of the sea, increasing more and more. He commenced his address calmly, but as he advanced, both his matter and his manner increased in interest. His congregation, which was always of immense numbers, would look fixedly upon him, their eyes shining like stars as they gazed with pleasure upon him as he proceeded so excellently. Their thoughts and feelings would be carried along with him in the most sweet and powerful way, being quickened to a high degree of spiritual excitement. Then, at length, his eloquence attained its climax, and then his preaching under divine influence would most nobly break forth like the rising swell of the sea, and would overwhelm the great concourse of people in an astonishing manner.
>
> The intensity of their feelings found relief in the same moment in a simultaneous burst of hallelujahs and ascriptions of praise to the most high God. The preacher would then pause for a short interval, until the people had enjoyed the feast; indeed, he would not have been heard had he continued. It was necessary also for their enthusiasm to pass, in order that they apply themselves with profit to the remainder of the sermon. They therefore sought to restrain their feelings, and to quieten down, being anxious to enjoy the repast prepared for them by the wonderful ambassador of heaven, who had been so signally gifted.

He would then commence another paragraph of his sermon, reading it slowly and quietly, rising gradually, like another wave of the sea, to a glorious height of thought and feeling, which are indeed the true and natural effects of evangelical truths and of the influence of the Spirit. Under the tutelage of the Spirit of God, these produce such effects in the hearts of the hearers. They hang by his lips. They watch every one of his actions, knowing from his matter and attitude that there is a break approaching. His voice, his countenance, and his discourse, gradually altering wonderfully as he continued. When his evangelical and extraordinary eloquence arrived at its climax, it was most glorious, it went forth like the bursting of another wave. And the great mass of the people would again be overpowered by their feelings, and again burst into loud Hosannas to the Son of David.

The tone, voice, and bearing of this great man would at such times be indescribably wonderful and effective. All the muscles of his face spoke, his countenance would shine with brightness as the sun in its strength.

As proof of the strength of Rowland's influence and of the way in which travellers from the furthermost corners of the Principality would forget their weariness under the delights of his ministry, Dr Owen Thomas relates the following account which he obtained from the venerable old preacher, John Williams, Dolwyddelan, 'who,' he says, 'was not in any way a weak, thoughtless man, ready to give himself up to every breeze blowing upon the feelings'. John Williams said that he remembered walking all the way from Dolwyddelan to Llangeitho once [more than sixty miles], and that he was so tired after the journey that he ought to have gone to bed rather than to chapel. He went however to hear Rowland. His text was Isaiah 25:6, 'And in this mountain shall the LORD of hosts make unto all the people a feast of fat things, a feast of wines on the lees, of fat things full of marrow, of wines on the lees well refined':

> You never heard such a thing in your life. He began to tap the barrels of the covenant of grace, and to let out the wine well refined, and to give to the people to drink. It flowed over the chapel. I also drank, and became, as I may say, quite drunk. And there I was, and scores of others, in an ecstasy of delight, praising God, having forgotten all fatigue and bodily wants.

It would be a mistake to omit Christmas Evans's description of Rowland. Christmas, like Rowland, had been born and raised in Cardiganshire, and was twenty-four years old when the older man died. He had opportunity, no doubt, to hear him many times therefore. This is the eloquent old Baptist's testimony:

> His doctrine was Calvinistic in every sense of the word; his mode of speaking was axiomatic, in sentences, neat, accurate and pregnant with sense. His mode was his own, inimitable. I seem to see him now, dressed in his black gown, opening the little door that led from the outside to the pulpit, and making his appearance to the multitude. His whole countenance was clothed with a majesty that betokened sense, eloquence and authority. His forehead was high; his eyes were keen and piercing; his nose was Roman or aquiline; his lips comely, and his chin projecting and rising a little; and his voice was sonorous and high-toned.
>
> Some preacher would usually read and pray, according to what I have heard, before Rowland rose up to preach. He then very frequently gave out to sing the following stanza from Edmund Prys's *Psalms* [Psalm 27:4]:

| | |
|---|---|
| I've made to God this one request, | Un arch a erchais ar Dduw Naf, |
| To this I still adhere, | A hynny a archaf eto, |
| That I may in his house be blest, | Cael dod i dy fy Arglwydd glân, |
| And have my dwelling there. | A bod a'm trigfan ynddo. |

One stanza only was given out at a time in those days of remarkable power-ful influences. After singing the stanza with great fervour but without much doubling of it before the sermon, lest the heavenly ointment should overflow the vessels too soon, Rowland would stand up and read his text clearly in the hearing of all. The whole assembly was all ears, as if it was to hear some evangelical oracle, and the eyes of all were fixed on him. He had some stir-ring thought, as a small ointment-box, before proceeding to the main mes-sage of the sermon. This he opened, and the odours of its ointments spread throughout the whole congregation, preparing them to expect the opening of other boxes, one after the other . . . After thus rousing the congregation by some striking thought, he divided his text, and began with the first division, bending his head downwards a little, as if to glance at the notes he had on a slip of paper.

I saw his notes on the text, 'Repent, etc.' They were very short:

(1) The meaning of Repentance is a change of mind, concerning God, con-cerning man, concerning the law and the gospel, concerning sin and holiness, concerning the evil of the heart and life, concerning the merit of man and the merit of Christ, and concerning the ability of man, concerning heaven and earth, and hell below.

(2) God, in his grace, calls men to repent. Listen to the ministry of John the Baptist, of Christ, of Peter on the Day of Pentecost, and of Paul in Pisidia.

(3) God, in his grace, provides repentance through Jesus Christ. He is the golden pipe through whom flow all the streams of grace and glory. Remember Peter's word, that God gives repentance and forgiveness of sins, coming, by blessing, from the great womb of heaven's predestination, and as two twins they follow each other inseparably – or as two ropes pulling the ship of salva-tion through the dangerous shallows, through the effects of the intercession of Christ, drawing sinners to himself.

We now come to that part of this description that is most difficult, because we cannot make a dumb image speak or a dead man live. After glancing thus at the paper, more as a matter of form than anything else, Rowland began to speak with a clear, free utterance. I would compare him to the blacksmith placing the iron in the fire, and telling his bellows-man to blow more, or less; always keeping his eye on the iron in the fire while he speaks of shoeing, of hardening the ploughshare and coulter. The fire flames higher and higher, and the sparks of the blaze fly up. He then seizes the iron, brought to a molten and flexible temper, brings it to the anvil and the great sledge and the hammer strike it so that the sparks fly throughout the forge. So also would Rowland gradually grow warm and intense as he handled his matter. Then, at last, his voice would rise and become authoritative, and resound through the whole chapel. The effects on the people would be remarkable. You would see nothing but smiles, and the tears flowing down the faces of the people, accompanied with exclamations throughout the assembly. All this arose from the flame of his voice and the grandeur of his matter. His own animation arose from the glory of the sublime thoughts that he delivered, in the powers of the Holy Spirit. This would be the difference between himself and Whitefield. When Whitefield would be at his most passionate and in the sweetest tone of voice, it is then that his content could become weaker; whereas it was his matter that would fire Rowland's eloquence, and his voice was at its most exalted when his matter was at its most sublime. When this first flame of heavenly devotion under the first head, had become tranquil, he would look hurriedly at his notes, and then began the second time to melt and render supple the minds of the people, until he brought them again into the same heavenly temper. And this he did, as some say, six or seven times in the same sermon. He would usually have little to say by way of conclusions or application at the close of the sermon, in that he would have applied and pressed the glorious truths of the gospel throughout. He would end with a few striking and powerful comments; then, he would pray briefly and sweetly, and pronounce the benediction. Covered in perspiration, he would hurry from the pulpit and through the little door as quickly as when he entered. If there was no communion afterwards, the great congregation would be left in a most heavenly frame, enjoying the brightness of their Lord's countenance, and all in a way that cannot be described on paper.

The face and voice of Rowland underwent changes and emotions . . . until there was a sort of vehement flame transforming and driving away the earthly, dead and careless spirit, and the people drew nigh to Christ and to Moses and Elias in the cloud, as it were, and eternity and its realities rushed into their minds! He was a star of the greatest magnitude and surely there has not been his equal in Wales since the days of the apostles. I drew the above portrait of this prince of preachers out of respect to his memory, and indeed, I cannot think of Rowland and his associates but with respect.

We could provide a host of other witnesses testifying to Daniel Rowland's greatness but will be satisfied with this last description provided by Dr Owen Thomas from his *Life of John Jones, Talsarn:*

He would begin speaking rather quietly, but very quickly, so much so that it could be hard to follow him. For many minutes he would appear nervous, without complete confidence in himself. But gradually this would disappear and he would become fully self-possessed. He now spoke more slowly, but louder and more powerfully, becoming heated as he progressed, and the whole congregation would be quickened with him so that a thrill of gentle feeling would spread through the crowd. He has now finished with his first point; he lowers his voice; gives himself a sideways shake ; and then proceeds with the second head. Again, he begins rather slowly and measuredly, but he soon quickens and speaks with power and unusual fluency. His eyes pierce throughout the chapel; his voice rises; his feelings are aflame; his warmth has now been caught by the people; tears begin to flow over their cheeks;

the warm 'Amens' fall from their lips; and they and the preacher are in happy possession of one another. He ends his second point. He descends gradually again to the quiet and measured tones which he seems to consider necessary for every recommencement. And we remember a comment made by more than one of his old hearers that he never spoke better than when descending from the heights of feeling to which he and the assembly had been raised, to that moderation which gave him the best position from which to begin again. He was never observed to *fall* from the heights, but to *descend tenderly* and *gently*, still possessing all the power with which to reascend again.

So now he rises again, bringing his congregation with him, to higher, more intense and overcoming levels of affection. The 'Amens' are now louder and more numerous. Shouts of 'Diolch,' 'Bendigedig,' and 'Gogoniant',[20] are heard from every corner of the chapel, and the whole concourse in the warmest of frames is rejoicing in salvation. But the preacher slows, and descends again, gentler and more beautifully even than before, and provides a few seconds of rest for the people to settle with him. But he has not finished. He begins again, and ascends, *higher*, HIGHER, HIGHER. He is now a wonderful sight. His eyes are aflame; his voice is breaking; his countenance shines; his whole body appears inspired; the great soul pours forth the most sublime truths in one stream of living eloquence. These fire the whole congregation, and raise them to wondrous levels of praise and worship. The voice of the preacher is now lost in the shouts and singing of the crowd. He comes to an end, in what manner only he himself knows; and he leaves the assembly to its rejoicing for some hours. He takes a little food, rests on his bed for a couple of hours, and through sleep recovers somewhat of the nervous energy lost during the hour in the chapel.

Daniel Rowland excelled as a preacher but he was also a notably able organizer, and a safe and wise leader. After the Disruption it was he who would chair the Associations whenever he was present. He spoke little himself as a rule; he would listen to others for a while, walking up and down along the room; he would then put a stop to the discussion, saying, 'That's enough talk,' and would give his own views on the matter, clearly and concisely and, almost invariably, his directions would be followed. As a leader he displayed a determined will, accompanied by a notably kind spirit. It is certain, for example, that he disagreed with the views of Peter Williams. He could hardly do otherwise in the light of the position he took with regard to Harris's opinions, but he was far from condoning the attacks made upon the old commentator. Peter Williams knew this well enough, and he refers to Rowland's gentleness in the elegy he composed to him:

| | |
|---|---|
| Rowland, I will ne'er forget thee, | O, mrawd Rowland, ni'th anghofiaf, |
| Nor thy frequent reprimands; | Ti roddaist i mi lawer sen; |

| Yet, in every storm and trouble, | Ymhob tywydd, ymhob dirmyg, |
|---|---|
| Who but thee would heal my wounds. | Pwy ond ti orchuddiai 'mhen. |

He had great sympathy for young men and a discerning eye to know them. He never felt anything like jealousy when a new, young preacher would rise in popularity. Griffiths, Nevern, was greatly gifted. When Rowland first heard him preach, he approached him after the sermon, his eyes shining with joy, saying,

My dear son, you have struck the vein, the golden vein of the ministry; be careful to keep to it, and to give all the praise to God.

It is said that he hesitated at first as regards permitting the liberty of the pulpits to Roberts, Clynnog. It is difficult now to arrive at any reason for this. But when Roberts made his first visit to Llangeitho, Rowland arrived secretly at the chapel, keeping himself from view. He was greatly pleased by the bright talents of the fiery seraph from the north. At the close, he went up to him with great friendliness, congratulating him on the successful service and after some conversation, he said,

'Would you take a word of advice from an old white-haired man?'

'Yes, with the greatest willingness,' was the reply.

'You know that the shopkeepers have small compartments in their counters in which they place all that they receive; whatever it might be, whether gold, silver or brass, they place it all in these compartments. Dear brother, may you do the same. Whatever you receive, place it in the treasury. Do not pocket even a farthing of the Master's money.'

His ability to understand the hearts of the young men, and his sympathies towards them in their hopes and ambitions were great advantages to him as a leader.

For all his great popularity and the immense respect in which he was held, God kept him from arrogance. In the midst of it all his heart was truly humble. Many stories are related as proof of this. He often journeyed on foot, and when announced to preach at one particular neighbourhood, a good woman who lived at a farmhouse called Bryn-y-brain, sent her servant with a horse to meet him. Somehow the servant mistook the road, or the preacher arrived on a different route from that expected, so that Rowland reached the place on foot and very weary. The woman was very sorry, and expressed her disappointment many times. He answered:

'Nel *fach*, I have never considered myself worthy that anyone should come to meet me, not even for a hundred yards.'

There is an account of a widow called Mrs Griffiths, Glanyrafonddu, who, for her love for him and for the great profit that she received from his ministry, left him a carriage in her will. He used this for his journeys in the last years of his life. In a particular village where he used to preach, no one would receive him into their homes except for one very poor woman. When this woman saw him arrive at the village in the carriage for the first time, she began to worry and to feel that her house and board were no longer worthy of such a great man. She expressed her worries to him, and received the answer,

'Please, be quiet; I see that you are in more danger of receiving harm from my carriage than ever I am of being harmed by your home and bed.'

## ROWLAND'S LITERARY WORK, HIS LATTER YEARS, AND DEATH

It would be inexcusable of us not to mention the books that are attributed to Daniel Rowland, either as author or as translator. In 1739, he published a translation of a sermon, entitled *Llaeth Ysbrydol; o gasgliad Eglwyswr* [*Spiritual Milk; from the collection of a Churchman*], written by the Puritan, Henry Smith. It is based on 1 Peter 2:2.

Soon after establishing the experience meetings or societies in 1742, he published with others a book with the title-page, *Sail, Dibenion, a Rheolau'r Societies neu'r Cyfarfodydd Neilltuol a ddechreusant ymgynull yn ddiweddar yng Nghymru. At y rhai y chwanegwyd rhai hymnau i'w canu yn y cyfarfodydd. Gan wyr o Eglwys Loegr* [*The Basis, Purposes, and Rules of the Societies or Private Meetings which have lately started coming together in Wales. To which is added some hymns to be sung in the meetings. By gentlemen of the Church of England*]. There is no name on the title-page, but Howell Harris's name is by the first hymn, Morgan Jones's by the second, Daniel Rowland's by the third, and Herbert Jenkins's by the fourth. It is thought that Daniel Rowland was mainly responsible for its composition.

In the following year, was published a translation of Ralph Erskine's essay, *Law-death, Gospel-life: or the Death of Legal Righteousness, the Life of Gospel Holiness*. The translation was by John Morgan but six of Rowland's hymns were added to it.

In 1744, he published *Hymnau Duwiol, i'w canu mewn Cymdeithasau crefyddol* [*Godly Hymns, to be sung in Religious meetings*]. It is interesting to note that it was in this same year that William Williams published his first part of *Alleluja*. Rowland's next publication arose from his controversy with Howell Harris. The book was called *Ymddiddan rhwng Methodist Uniongred ac un Camsyniol* [*Dialogue between an Orthodox and an Erroneous Methodist*].[21] The date of the first edition is not known. A second edition came out in 1750, and a third is dated 'Carmarthen, 1792.' In 1759, he translated an essay depicting the horrors of war, *Aceldama, or the Field of Blood*. He next published a sermon, preached in 1761 and entitled, *Llais y Durtur. Gwahoddiad grasol Crist ar bechaduriaid* [*The Voice of the Turtle-dove. The gracious Invitation of Christ to sinners*]. Then, in 1762, another sermon, from Revelation 3:20, 'Behold, I stand at the door, and knock, etc.'

According to Mr Morris Davies, the publisher and editor of the first editions of Rowland's sermons was a Thomas Davies from near Haverfordwest, Pembrokeshire. He suggests that Davies was one of the exhorters that laboured with the Methodists and that as a publisher he was a hard-working, lively and careful worker. The author does not seem to have received any financial gain from the sale of his sermons. He gave copies of them to the publisher, and he, at the end of a list of subscribers, thanks Rowland publicly for them. He says that the demand to print them was so great that the author, in the midst of his labours, had no time to read them after having written them, before handing them over for printing.

The following year, 1763, was a notable one in Rowland's history – the year of his eviction from the Established Church. During the year, he published *Pymtheg Araeth, ar Amryw Destunau* [*Fifteen Discourses, on Various Topics*]. The book contains a preface by Peter Williams. It is thought that Rowland produced the translation of *The Crook in the Lot*, by Thomas Boston, which appeared in 1769.

In 1772, he published three sermons, and within the same year, another five sermons, to which were added various hymns. In 1772, he contributed a short Foreword to a translation of Bunyan's *Holy War*. In the same year, Thomas Davies published eight sermons of his in English, with the comment on the title-page that they were preached on practical subjects in the 'New Chapel, Llangeitho'. By this 'New Chapel' was meant the chapel built for Rowland after he had been turned out. John Davies, Rector of Sharnecote, Wiltshire, was the translator. Three more English sermons, translated by the same man, were brought out in the following year.

In 1776, he published *Ychydig Hymnau yn ychwaneg* [*A few more Hymns*]. The last publication from his hand was *Llwyddiant wrth Orsedd Gras* [*Success at the Throne of Grace*], a sermon on Jude, verse 20, preached at Llangeitho in 1782. When one considers his many journeys, and the extent of his labours in the ministry of the gospel, it is remarkable that he wrote as much. On the whole his Welsh is accurate and strong, and his style clear and concise.

For all the excellence of Rowland's preaching and for all the glorious nature of the work accomplished by him, he did not escape being accused of faults and defects, not even after his death. Dr Thomas Rees, in his

*History of Nonconformity in Wales* (1861) stated that he was far from being unblemished as a preacher, and suggests, on the evidence of the diary of Thomas Morgan, a little-known Independent minister, that he could be weak in the content of his sermons:

> 23 February, 1744. Went this afternoon to Clyngwyn (near Carmarthen), to hear Mr D. Rowland. Ben. Thomas prayed before him; then he preached from Hosea 2:14. He did not much confine himself to his text, but was very earnest, endeavouring to win the affections. I think I found some efficacy attending his work, though he had some very weak expressions.

> 24 May, 1744. Went to Caerphilly, where I met many of my old acquaintances. On my way home I heard Mr Rowland at Pen-y-groes-wen, from Judges 5:23. His sermon was practical, but not critical; for he said several things that I think he would not have said, had he well considered the matter before hand.

It would be difficult to find a better example of damning with faint praise. Dr Rees comments:

> Even Harris and the clergy [and Rowland is included amongst the 'clergy', without doubt] would say many things in their unpremeditated discourses, which offended the refined taste of the Nonconformists, and furnished the irreligious of all classes with subjects for profane jesting.

Certainly Rowland, when his whole nature was aroused and his congregation raised to great excitement, would use strong expressions. It was perfectly legitimate for him to do so; the situation justified such words. But the response of some Nonconformists, if indeed that was the case, in taking offence at such expressions, was proof, not of lack of taste in Rowland, but of their own narrowness of spirit and affectation. The unanimous agreement of those who both heard the Reformer of Llangeitho and were men of some discernment, was that he was excellent in both content and taste. According to Christmas Evans:

> Rowland's voice, countenance, and appearance used to change exceedingly in the pulpit, and he seemed to be greatly excited; but there was nothing low or disagreeable in him; all was becoming, dignified, and excellent.

That is the testimony of a Nonconformist, and one of the pillars of the Welsh pulpit. Again, consider those words, already quoted, from Thomas Charles of Bala, a man of the purest taste:

> There was loftiness, and grandeur, and every other excellency in the endowments of Daniel Rowland – profound thoughts, strength and sweetness of voice, clearness and lively energy in proclaiming the deep things of God to the astonishment and effectual arousing of his hearers.

To every unprejudiced man, such testimonials must constitute sufficient evidence for the purity of taste and excellence of content of Daniel Rowland's preaching.

He was also accused of narrowness of spirit towards the Nonconformists, and of blind allegiance to the Established Church. His whole history proves otherwise. Throughout his life he never forgot his debt to Mr Pugh, the Independent minister of Llwynpiod. It is certain that Howell Harris's commitment to the Church was much greater than Rowland's. It was because of Rowland's definite encouragement, as we shall show later, that many churches in Glamorganshire and Monmouthshire that were associated with the Methodists, ordained ministers amongst them according to the Nonconformist pattern. Thomas Gray, Mr Pugh's successor at Llwynpiod, wished to join the Methodists, mainly because of his great love for Mr Rowland. But Rowland's response to him was:

> You had better continue working that side of the hill; I will continue on this side. Perhaps we will meet one day, as we dig to undermine Satan's kingdom.

As can be seen, he was generous in his attitude towards Nonconformists and Churchmen alike, and completely free from a proselytizing spirit.

But the most libellous accusation directed against Daniel Rowland appeared in the *Quarterly Review* of September 1849, nearly sixty years after his death. It was written by the Vicar of Meifod and suggested that Rowland was a heavy drinker, that he often preached his sermons under the influence of drink, and indeed that the extraordinary influence of his preaching could be traced to the effects of drink. The relevant passage reads:

> One fatal circumstance that has come to our knowledge, though not written in the chronicles of Methodism, would alone prevent us from styling Rowland an Apostle. His wife proved unworthy of his affection, and he drank deep consolation at a source that undoubtedly contributed to give his preaching its peculiar energy. Yet we would not mention otherwise than with regret a fact that touches the consistency of his conduct rather than the sincerity of his principles.

This shameful accusation was based on the testimony of William Williams, a drunken curate of worthless character, who was the son of *Sion Sgubor* [22] (John Williams), an old servant of Rowland's. Fortunately, these libels against his character were made early enough for them to be investigated and proved false, so that the shame fell upon those who maintained them.

The Rev. John Griffiths, Rector of Aberdare at the time, but after-wards Rector of Merthyr, took a leading part in the matter. With the help of Mr David Jones, the godly old elder of Dolau-bach, he gathered evidence from those old enough to remember Rowland, one of whom was an eighty-five year old man who had been in his service for seven years. They all testified unanimously that there was no shadow of truth in the suggestions; that they were malicious libels. The Rev. T. Edwardes, rector of Llangeitho, whom we knew well, said that as an inhabitant of the parish for sixty years, never having lived outside it, he had received many communicants who had also been communicants under Rowland, one of them an old man of eighty-eight, who had all testified not only that Rowland did not drink to excess but that he was particularly moderate. Rector Griffiths also collected evidence from notable Churchmen raised in the Llangeitho neighbourhood, who stated that they had never heard of such accusations until reading of them in the *Quarterly Review*. Among these were Canon Jones, Tredegar; Canon Jenkins, Dowlais; and the Rev. David Parry, Llywel. We feel that we are considerably indebted to the late Rector Griffiths for the pains he took to clear the character of this man of God. Not only was Rowland free from immoderation himself, but he would unhesitatingly condemn this failing in others. A clergyman from the Llangeitho neighbourhood desired once to be sent as a missionary to a particular place, but Rowland had no confidence in his purity of life. He turned to him and said:

> I remember a time, Sir, when we received a very poor welcome and living, as we journeyed over hills and mountains on our ponies with only bread and cheese in our pockets, and nothing to drink except for the water of the streams, and if we had a mouthful of butter-milk in some of the cottages we considered that a great favour. But now, Sir, they have their tea and their brandy, and unless I mistake, you have had too much of this brandy.

One who could speak out so strongly on this subject would have to be of irreproachable character himself.

Rowland's days approached their end. His health deteriorated sig-nificantly during the last year of his life, but he continued to preach at Llangeitho. On Friday, 15 October 1790, he was taken ill, and he entered his eternal rest on the next day, being seventy-seven years old. Thousands had gathered at Llangeitho on that Saturday for the preparatory sermon. Rowland was expected to direct them, as usual. But in the middle of the service the news of his death arrived, which excited such feelings of grief that the service could not be continued. He was buried in Llangeitho cemetery near the chapel's east window. Lately [1883], a fine statue of him was placed outside Gwynfil Chapel, on the site of the original chapel built for him by his people, a site made sacred by him to all who love the Lord Jesus. Carved on the base of the statue are words proclaimed spontaneously by Rowland during a sermon at a time of revival:

O Nefoedd! Nefoedd! Nefoedd! Buasai dy gonglau yn ddigon gwag oni bai fod Sion yn magu plant iti ar y ddaear.

[O Heaven! Heaven! Heaven! Your mansions would be empty enough if Zion did not nurture children for you on earth!]

We cannot refrain from quoting more of the fine elegy written for him by his old friend, Williams, Pantycelyn:

There's no need to honour Rowland,
With a hymn, or marble shrine;
T'would be vain to paint his picture,
Sketch his face in shade and line;
His own life was his memorial,
He himself carved out his fame,
And the golden lists of heaven
Evermore proclaim his name.

Nid rhaid canu dim amdano,
Nid rhaid marble ar ei fedd;
Ofer tynnu dim o'i bictiwr
Ar bapyrun sâl ei wedd;
Gwnaeth ei farwnad yn ei fywyd,
Rhodd ei farble yn ei le,
Fe sgrifennodd arno'i enw
A llyth'rennau pur y ne'.

And this name was Boanerges,
Son of thunder, flaming, true;
Shaking heaven and earth together
With a voice both strong and new;
'Come! Awake!' his voice in echo
Calls to all, 'Our town's ablaze.
Flee this moment without turning;
God to ashes all will raze.'*

Boanerges oedd ei enw,
Mab y daran danllyd, gref,
Sydd yn siglo yn ddychrynllyd
Holl golofnau dae'r a nef;
'Dewch, dihunwch,' oedd yr adsain,
'Y mae'n dinas ni ar dân;
Ffowch oddi yma mewn munudyn,
Ynte ewch yn ulw mân.'

At Llangeitho, forth he thundered
Judgment on all sinful hearts,
And the crowds drew round about him,
Gathered from the furthest parts;
Terror, shock, amazement, held them,
As they stood there, great and small,
Every creature pale and trembling;
The fear of God upon them all.

Yn Llangeitho fe ddechreuodd
Waeddi distryw'r anwir fyd,
Miloedd ffôdd o'r Dê a'r Gogledd,
Yn un dyrfa yno ynghyd;
Arswyd, syndod, dychryn ddaliodd
Yr holl werin fawr a mân,
Nid oedd gwedd wynebpryd un-gwr,
Fel y gwelwyd ef o'r blaen.

Hearts were pounding, bodies trembling,
As if death itself had come,
And processing through the concourse,
Had possessed them everyone.

Gliniau'n grynu gan y daran,
Fel be buasai angau'i hun,
Wedi cymryd llawn berchnogaeth
Ar y dyrfa bob yr un;

'How to save our souls eternal?'
Was the one concerted shout,
You who wish to know of Daniel,
This is how he started out.

Five Welsh counties heard the thunder,
And with awesome, fearful dread,
Fell with slaughter and with terror
On the ground in heaps, as dead;*
Wounds were taken, grievous woundings,
Wounds no mortal man could cure,
But the potent balm of Calv'ry,
Jesu's blood, is medicine sure.

Make a visit to Llangeitho,
Come and see the wondrous sight,
See the numbers that have gathered,
Thousands waiting, left and right;
And each heart is hungering, hungering,
With a longing to be fed;
Hear them shout as home they journey:
'O! The taste of heavenly bread!'

See him, Daniel, boldly preaching,
In the fire, and smoke, and cloud;
Here, a thousand voices praising,
Hallelujahs echo round;
There, the blind, the lame, the ungodly,
See them, deep in anguish, pray,
Every wordly thought struck from them
By the sight of Judgment Day.

Christ Himself on Calv'ry's mountain,
Clearing books in Heaven's store;
Paying all of sin's demerit,
Healing thus transgression's sore.
All who hear are now rejoicing,
All are full and satisfied;
On the heavenly manna feeding,
From the dawn 'till day has died.*[23]

'Beth a wnawn am safio'n henaid?'
Oedd yr unrhyw gydsain lêf;
Chwi sy' am wybod hanes Daniel,
Dyma fel dechreuodd ef.

Pump o siroedd pennaf Cymru,
Glywsant y tarannau mawr,
A chwympasant gan y dychryn,
Megis celaneddau i lawr;
Clwyfau gaed, a chlwyfau dyfnion,
Ac fe fethwyd cael iachâd,
Nes gael eli o Galfaria,
Dwyfol ddwr a dwyfol waed.

Deuwch drosodd i Langeitho,
Gwelwch yno ôl ei law,
Miloedd meithion yno'n disgwyl,
Llu oddiyma, llu o draw;
A'r holl dorf yn 'mofyn ymborth
Amryw'n dweud, 'Pa fodd y cawn?'
Pawb yn ffrostio wrth fynd adref,
Iddo gael ei wneud yn llawn.

Gwelwch Daniel yn pregethu
Yn y tarth, y mwg, a'r tân,
Mil ar unwaith yn moliannu,
Haleliwia yw y gân;
Nes bai torf o rai annuwiol
Mewn rhyw syndod dwfn, a mud,
Ac yn methu rhoi ei meddwl
Ar un peth, ond diwedd byd.

Crist ei hunan ar Galfaria
Yn clirio holl hen lyfrau'r nef,
Ac yn talu'n llwyr bob hatling
O'r holl ddyled ganddo ef;
Mae'r gwrandawyr oll yn llawen,
Oll yn hyfryd, oll yn llawn,
Wedi bwyta'r bara nefol,
O lâs fore hyd brynhawn.

[1] *Methodistiaeth Cymru*, vol. 1 (Wrexham, 1851), pp. 69–70.
[2] Taken from William Williams's elegy to Daniel Rowland. The stanza is quoted from the translation by Eifion Evans in *Daniel Rowland and the Great Evangelical Awakening in Wales* (Edinburgh: Banner of Truth, 1985), p. 41.

[3] *Methodistiaeth Cymru,* vol. 1, p. 66.

[4] HJH, p. 46-7.

[5] Lewis Edwards, *Traethodau Llenyddol* [*Literary Essays*] (Wrexham, c. 1865) p. 481.

[6] Joshua Thomas, *Hanes y Bedyddwyr* [*The History of the Baptists*] (Pontypridd, 1885), p. 60.

[7] *Traethodau Llenyddol,* pp. 482–3.

[8] The first four lines are translated by Eifion Evans, *Daniel Rowland,* p. 41.

[9] Translated by Eifion Evans, *Daniel Rowland,* pp. 43–4.

[10] STL, Vol. 1, pp. 81–2.

[11] Eifion Evans, *Daniel Rowland,* p. 202.

[12] Ibid., pp. 199-200.

[13] *Methodistiaith Cymru* [*Welsh Methodism*] (Wrexham: 1851–6) written by John Hughes (1796–1860) is a three volume history of the Welsh Calvinistic Methodists. 'A remarkable work for the time at which it was written, and indispensable even today in spite of its shortcomings.' (R. T. Jenkins)

[14] See p. 9 and note 7 on p. 28.

[15] HJH, p. 231.

[16] STL, vol. 1, p. 83.

[17] Eifion Evans, *Daniel Rowland,* p. 153.

[18] *Traethodau Llenyddol,* p. 489.

[19] 'Glory to the Son of David,' 'Hosanna in the highest, Hosanna also upon earth,' 'Amen, Amen.'

[20] 'Thanks,' 'Blessed be His name,' and 'Glory.'

[21] See pp. 570–4.

[22] *John of the Barn.*

[23] The stanzas or parts of a stanza marked with * are taken from the translation by Eifion Evans, *Daniel Rowland,* pp. 41, 172.

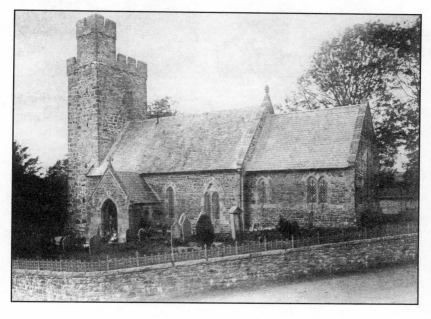

Top: Llanddowror
Bottom: Llanddowror Church

ENGLISH METHODISTS WHO LABOURED IN WALES
1. JOHN WESLEY    2. CHARLES WESLEY    3. THE COUNTESS OF HUNTINGDON
4. GEORGE WHITEFIELD    5. JOHN FLETCHER (FIRST PRINCIPAL OF TREFECA
COLLEGE)    6. JOSEPH BENSON (SECOND PRINCIPAL OF TREFECA COLLEGE)

THE HOLY CLUB:
TOP: JOHN CLAYTON (LEFT); THOMAS BROUGHTON (RIGHT)
MIDDLE: JAMES HERVEY
BOTTOM: BENJAMIN INGHAM (LEFT); JOHN GAMBOLD (RIGHT)

TOP: PANT-Y-BEUDY, DANIEL ROWLAND'S BIRTHPLACE
MIDDLE: PORTRAITS OF DANIEL ROWLAND, LLANGEITHO. LEFT - PRINTED BY
R. BOWYER, LONDON, 1790; RIGHT - FROM *THE GOSPEL MAGAZINE*, 1778.
BOTTOM: LLANGEITHO

# 5

# HOWELL HARRIS

## HIS BIRTH AND UPBRINGING

*N*o darkness obscures the history of Howell Harris for, unlike all the other Methodist Fathers, he wrote an autobiography; one which reveals not only the facts of his life but also his thoughts and experiences. The autobiography was edited and published with additions after his death by 'those who were witnesses from the beginning.' These were members of the 'family' at Trefeca, over whom he ruled and amongst whom he went in and out for twenty-three years. Furthermore, he kept a journal in which, on every evening, he noted in detail all that had happened to him during that day, commenting in particular on the state of his mind and on the temptations of heart and mind by which he had been assailed. He was also a writer of innumerable letters of which a vast number have survived. By means therefore of Harris's own writings and the witness of the family that he gathered about him, who knew all his movements and motives, the fullest light possible illuminates his character and work. No one can deny that he was a remarkable man. He appeared like an Elijah, bold in countenance, with God's Word burning as a fire within him, and thundering with all the passion of his nature against the wickedness of the faithless and perverse generation to which he had been sent.

Howell Harris's family were from Llandeilo, Carmarthenshire. They moved to Breconshire about the year 1700. Harris's parents, Howell and Susannah, owned Trefeca Fach (Little Trefeca), the cottage in which they lived. They were by no means rich. The father could not afford to give his children any better education than was received generally by the children of the neighbouring farmers. Howell was born in 1714 and was therefore a year younger than his friend and fellow-reformer, Daniel Rowland, and three years older than his son in the faith, William Williams, Pantycelyn. He was the youngest of three brothers. It would be difficult to find three brothers more different from each other, but each of them eventually became famous in his particular occupation. The eldest, Joseph, by effort and perseverance, progressed from village blacksmith to Assay-master at the Royal Mint, London. It was his responsibility to ensure that the coins of the realm were without blemish and of full weight. Because of his scientific achievements he became familiar with many of the main scholars of the day. He had worked with Halley, the Astronomer Royal, in testing navigational instruments, and wrote some influential works. Some of these were: *A Treatise on Navigation*, 1730; *The Description and Uses of the Celestial Globe and Orrery*, 1729; *An Essay Upon Money and Coins*, 1757; and (posthumously) *A Treatise upon Optics*, 1775. He became wealthy, and married the daughter of Thomas Jones, Tredustan, a neighbour of his father's. He died in his accommodation at the Tower of London, some nine years before the death of his brother, Howell.

Thomas, the second brother, settled as a tailor in London and with the help of an influential acquaintance obtained the contract for supplying uniforms to the army. He made a large fortune and after retiring from business, bought the Tregunter estate, near Trefeca. He served as High Sheriff for Breconshire in 1768, and died in 1782. Joseph and Thomas had little sympathy for the Methodism of their brother. There are many letters surviving, written by Howell Harris to his brothers in London, warning them seriously of the dangers of being overcome by longings for wealth and for the pleasures of this world. There is also in the Trefeca Collection a letter from Joseph, where he complains to Howell of his folly in burying himself in obscurity amongst the Methodists, whereas he might, by taking a change of direction, gain fame, honour and wealth, and rise to the level of the highest nobility in Wales. How blind were these brothers! Howell Harris's name shines today as a star in history's firmament whereas their names would have been lost but for their relationship to him.

We know little of Harris's childhood, but he seems to have been at a good school and was intended for the ministry of the Established Church. Fulfilling this intention was a heavy burden on the family finances. Joseph, writing when his brother was about fifteen years old, sought to be excused from helping in the matter. His funds were low after having recently published a book. He promised to help as soon as the book began to pay. Howell wrote in his *Autobiography*:

> My parents kept me at school till I was eighteen years old; I made a considerable progress in learning. My father then dying, I was so far discouraged as not to entertain any thoughts of appearing in the world in a public capacity, and therefore undertook to keep a country school.[1]

There must be some mistake here because on his father's gravestone in the cemetery of Talgarth Church, the date of his death is recorded as 9 March 1730, when Howell was only a little over sixteen. His father's death was an occasion of a severe trial for Howell. He had no hope now of becoming a clergyman and had to take work as a schoolmaster in order to gain a living. He suggests that he was given to some religious thoughts before this time but had now no serious friend with whom he could talk. His sense of liberty became an avenue for corruption and he was carried away by the ways of the world, by pride and youthful lusts. His personal vanity may be realized from a list of expenses recorded by him at the beginning of 1732. He says that he spent money on dancing, a wig, a razor, gloves, a hunting whip, and many other worthless things. Yet for all his commitment to pleasure, he had no rest. 'Some instinct of conviction' would often overcome him, and he wrote down a list of his failings as a witness against himself. He began these confessions when he was about seventeen years of age, and they are still to be found in the Trefeca Collection. They show not only that his conscience was not completely hardened but also that he was an excellent scholar. They reveal a regular handwriting, good grammar, and very many Latin abbreviations.

After keeping school for about two years, his prospects brightened. He became acquainted with men of local influence who promised to support him in his pursuit of holy orders, and Joseph also by now was able to do something for him:

> But while I was thus about entering more publicly on the stage of life, and while all my corruptions grew stronger and stronger in me, and many provi-dences seemed to concur to raise me in this world; the Lord was pleased to glorify his free grace in awakening me to a sense of the miserable state I was, and had been in, though I knew it not.[2]

An event was to occur which would change the whole course of his life.

## HIS CONVICTION AT TALGARTH CHURCH

The history of Howell Harris's conversion deserves to be told in detail. On 30 March 1735, the Sunday before Easter, when he was twenty-one years old, he went as usual to Talgarth Church. The vicar, the Rev. Price Davies, announced that Holy Communion would be administered there the fol-lowing Sunday and read the warning from the Book of Common Prayer for those who neglect to attend the ordinance. Not being satisfied with reading the warning only, he continued by proving that it was the duty of all to attend, and to answer the usual objections of those who neglected the duty.

> Our parish minister was using arguments to prove the necessity of receiving the Sacrament, and in answering objections which people make against going to

it, viz. *our not being fit*, etc. I resolved to go to the Lord's Table the following Sunday, being Easter-day. And by his saying, 'If you are not fit to come to the Lord's Table, you are not fit to come to Church, you are not fit to live, nor fit to die', I was convinced, and resolved to leave my outward vanities; for as yet, I knew and saw but very little of my inward corruption; and as a step to prepare myself (as I thought it). I was immediately in going home reconciled to a neighbour I had some difference with; acknowledging my own fault, and forgiving his. But knowing nothing of the wedding-garment, being yet an utter stranger to all inward religion, and the misery of my state by nature; and consequently knowing nothing truly of the Lord Jesus, but only what I learned from reading, and in notions; I had advanced no farther than forming a resolution to lead a new life, though I knew not where to begin or what to do.[3]

On the following Sunday Harris was at the church. At the close of the service he went forward with the others that wished to receive communion, falling on his knees before the altar. But as he recited with the vicar, the general confession

'We acknowledge and bewail our manifold sins and wickedness, Which we from time to time most grievously have committed, By thought, word, and deed, Against the Divine Majesty, Provoking most justly thy wrath and indignation against us. We do earnestly repent, And are heartily sorry for these our misdoings; The remembrance of them is grievous unto us; The burden of them is intolerable':

I began to reflect within me, to search whether this was my case, and soon found my confession was only words, and could not find any inward grief at the remembrance of them, nor indeed was their burden a heavy load to me; I was then convinced it ought to be so, and finding it was not, I saw I was going to the Lord's Table with a lie in my mouth; this, and a sense of the solemnity of the sacred feast struck me, so that I was inclined to withdraw; till my mind was quietened, by having determined to lead a new life.[4]

For some time afterwards, he tried to keep to his resolution. He gave himself to prayer, and tried to settle his meditations upon God. But by the end of a fortnight he found that he had lost all his convictions. On 20 April, he came across a book that renewed the sense of guilt within, and later the same day this conviction was strengthened:

I found again the same evening a book written by Bryan Duppa, on the Commandments, which made my convictions somewhat deeper; the more I read, the greater did the spiritual light shine in my mind, by showing me the extent of the Law of God, calling me to account, not only for the outward gross sins, but for our looks, aims, and ends, in all we think, say, or do; then I saw plainly and clearly, that if I was to be judged by that Law, I was undone forever.[5]

For more than a month the storm raged over him. His conscience was roaring like a she-bear within him, and he trying to quieten it by prayer, fasting, and punishing his body. He felt that he was sold under sin; that he was carnal; and that he could not believe nor grieve sufficiently for his wickedness any more than he could fly up into the sky. Hell had opened its jaws to receive him, and he had no knowledge of the voice of the Saviour. But when at prayer, one day, he felt a desire to give himself as he was to the Lord Jesus, leaving all the consequences completely in his hands. Against this, however, the legal spirit within him resisted; he felt that if he gave himself to the Lord he would lose his liberty and not be in charge of himself. After a hard struggle, he was made willing to bid farewell to all temporal things and to choose Christ as his eternal portion:

I believe I was then effectually called to be a follower of the Lamb . . . [6]

## FINDING PEACE IN CHRIST

He had not yet received full liberty. He went to Communion on Whit Sunday, weary and heavy-laden under the weight of his sins, but:

. . . having read in a book, that if we would go to the sacrament, simply believing in the Lord Jesus Christ, we should receive forgiveness of all our sins; and so it was to me; I was convinced by the Holy Ghost, that Christ died for me, and that all my sins were laid on him; I was now acquitted at the bar of Justice, and in my conscience. [7]

During this time of conviction, he had been tormented by atheistic thoughts, but he could now write:

. . . those sore trials that I bore from atheistical thoughts, that made my life a burden to me . . . but at the sacrament, by viewing my God on the cross, I was delivered from these temptations; now, the world and all thoughts of human applause and preferment were quite vanished from my sight; the spiritual world, and eternity began (though as yet but faintly) to appear. [8]

Harris was now a new man and a free man. His chains had been dashed in pieces; he had been acquitted by his Judge. As a result, peace flowed into his conscience like a river; his feet hardly touched the ground as he went home; he could leap and dance just like the lame man at the gate Beautiful after he was healed. On leaving the church, he said to his companions, with a voice full of rejoicing, 'My sins have been forgiven!' They looked at him in stunned amazement, not understanding his meaning in that they knew nothing of his experience of conviction. He proceeded on to the next group, telling them also, 'My sins have been forgiven!' This was as much to him as if he had seen heaven. He had never heard anyone else say anything similar before, but the joy of his heart was such that he could not restrain himself, and he longed for his neighbours to rejoice with him at his release. From now on, we find him communing often with God and being given frequent assurances of God's favour:

> June 18th, 1735, being in secret prayer, I felt suddenly my heart melting within me like wax before the fire with love to God my Saviour; and also felt not only love and peace, but a longing to be dissolved, and to be with Christ; then was a cry in my inmost soul, which I was totally unacquainted with before, 'Abba Father! Abba Father!' I could not help calling God my Father; I knew that I was his child, and that he loved me and heard me. My soul being filled and satiated, crying, ''Tis enough, I am satisfied. Give me strength, and I will follow thee through fire and water.'[9]

We are tempted to continue to quote from the autobiography but we must resist the temptation. He was still not yet completely free from snares. He had many confrontations with the enemy after this. He continued with the school, expecting a call at any time from a close relative for him to go up to Oxford. One day, he lost his temper with a child, and immediately the enemy rushed at him, declaring that he had fallen from grace and had forfeited his right in Christ. After being in an agony of soul for a while, God sent comfort to him from Malachi 3:6, 'For I am the LORD, I change not.'

> That such a word was scriptural I knew not, and how to apply it to myself was at a great loss; till light broke in upon my soul, to show me that my salvation did not depend on my own faithfulness, but on the faithfulness of Jesus Christ; therefore, though I change, yet because he changeth not, I was secure.[10]

From now on, Howell Harris sought to live for Jesus. He withdrew from his old acquaintances; he decided to reject all offers of wordly promotion; he sold everything he possessed and gave the money to the poor. Amongst other things, he thought that much of the clothes he used to wear were too costly for a Christian and conformed too much to the fashion of the world, he therefore sold these also. He did not worry over his future, but ventured all on God's promise.

## BEGINNING TO EXHORT

The spiritual condition of his fellow-men now began to weigh heavily upon him. He saw that they were travelling along the broad way, and that there was no one warning them solemnly of their danger. He could not stop speaking to them of spiritual matters, but the result was that some despised him, and others pitied him. One set would try to terrify him, while another sought to advise him. They viewed him as a fanatic.

I did not even think at that time that the Lord would use me as a blessing for others; for I did not see the least likelihood of that, but rather the opposite.

But God's Word burned within Harris and he continued counselling all whom he met. He spoke mainly of death, judgment and eternity, together with the necessity of prayer and receiving the sacrament. His opinions were unclear, his understanding of the doctrines of the gospel was very limited, but he did not hide under a bushel the little light that he possessed. He began to hold family worship in his mother's house, and on Sunday mornings, before the church service, a number of neighbours would come to hear him read the lessons and Psalms. He said:

I could not rest day nor night, without doing something for my God and Saviour; nor could I go with satisfaction to sleep, if I had not done something for his glory that day. Time was so precious, that I knew not how to improve it entirely to the glory of God, and the good of others.[11]

He gave himself to reading and to prayer when on his own, and he began to counsel those who came to hear him read every Sunday afternoon. By now, on his own confession, he had become an object of local derision. Some scorned him and others threatened him with violence, 'but,' he says, 'I was carried as on wings through all my trials.'

His brother Joseph, who was now in London, did not know what to do with him nor with his letters, and he half suggested that depression had taken hold of him. In order that Howell be freed from this, he tried to stir up wordly ambition in him and encouraged him to hasten to Oxford. Howell answered:

Don't think me to be so melancholy as you imagine, I enjoy a treasure of joy which indeed I can't know how to communicate. (Grief is almost a stranger).[12]

Nor was he blinded by the brilliant prospects held before him:

Let those that love to see and to be seen to make a complete outside, though the inward part be not so perfect, lay hold of those illusions of Madam Fortune . . . Allow me so much seriousness as sincerely to deal honestly and justly with my soul.[13]

Harris could not see the way clear before him, but he says that he had no fear of not earning a living. He had hopes that he was intended to do some good, and that he did not consider any trouble or pain too much in preparation for that. He no longer intended to apply for holy orders:

You see that I am unshaken in my resolution and therefore don't dissuade me, but direct me in this road; never study to make me a public man for (if I'll be allowed to judge of myself) I assure you I think I was never designed for it.[14]

Clearly, he was not a good judge of himself or his strengths, and had no idea of the work to which he was to be called.

## OXFORD

At the beginning of November, 1735, he went up to Oxford, registering as a student in St Mary's Hall under his tutor Mr Hart. His friends and brother hoped that University would educate him out of what they considered his fanaticism. And if any place or institution possessed the power to undo a young man's religion and to cause him to lose all spiritual seriousness, Oxford, at this time, was that place. John Wesley wrote that the city was full of:

Men who retain something of outward decency, and nothing else; who seriously idle away the whole day, and repeatedly revel until midnight, and if not drunken themselves, yet encouraging and applauding those that are so; who have no more of the form than the power of godliness.[15]

Into the middle of these, Harris was thrown, and he felt almost as if he had been thrown into hell. The immorality of the place frightened him, and he spent most of his time there in private prayer or at the public service. It must be remembered that the Oxford Methodists had by this time been scattered; John and Charles Wesley, together with Benjamin Ingham, were on the Atlantic, bound for Georgia and intending to evangelize the Indians; Whitefield had returned ill to Gloucester; John Clayton had settled at Manchester; and John Gambold, the Welshman from Pembrokeshire, was at Stanton Harcourt. There was hardly anyone therefore at the University attempting to stem the tide of corruption that carried all before it. Harris depended upon friends and especially upon his brother, Joseph, for support while at the University. A letter to him from Joseph Harris, at this time, proves this:

You'll find in this box an old suit of mine which my brother has altered for you, with two pairs of breeches belonging to it, also my old leather breeches. These may do you a good deal of service for common wear either in the country or at Oxford.[16]

His earthly prospects were now very bright, were he to proceed to take orders. A situation as a teacher over a large school was promised him, and some nobleman had offered a church living worth £140 a year. But Harris wrote:

The Lord Jesus had now got possession of my heart; so that notwithstanding the promising prospect before me, it had no great effect upon me . . . when I saw the irregularities and immoralities which surrounded me there, I became soon weary of the place.[17]

He could not remain the necessary period in Oxford. Throwing aside all the bright prospects, he returned home, committing his way to the Lord.

## HIS EXHORTING STIRS UP OPPOSITION

Howell Harris left Oxford at the end of 1735 and never returned there. As soon as he arrived home, he began to go about exhorting, doing so with intense zeal. He went from door to door in his own parish and adjoining parishes, warning his neighbours to flee from the wrath to come; he hailed the people whom he met on the roads. When he saw a farm-hand ploughing a field, he would push through the hedge to get to him and would walk with him, up and down the field, in order to impress upon him the importance of escaping from hell. His activities soon disturbed the whole neighbourhood. The homes where he exhorted became too small to hold the numbers that gathered to hear him. He says in his *Autobiography*:

The word was attended with such power, that many on the spot cried out to God for pardon of their sins – and such as lived in malice, confessed their sins, making peace with each other, etc., and appeared in concern about their eternal state. Family worship was set up in many houses, and the churches, as far as I had gone, were crowded, and likewise the Lord's table.[18]

The leaven had been introduced into the dough, and the bread was beginning to rise.

Harris did not confer with flesh and blood to discover if what he was doing was perfectly regular. He did not consider that he was preaching, and did not aim at being a preacher; nor was he following any plan, except that of seeing his fellow-men in danger of destruction, in great ignorance and danger, and feeling that woe was upon him if he did not warn them. He without doubt is the father of that lay-ministry which has been so blessed to Wales, but he himself did not plan to introduce any such novelty. It was the desire to save immortal souls that burned so fiercely in his spirit. He wrote:

It was now high time for the enemy to make a stand in another manner; therefore he not only influenced the populace to revile me, and persecute me, but caused the Magistrates and Clergy to bestir themselves.[19]

In February, 1736, he received a letter from Mr Price Davies, the vicar of Talgarth:

Sir,

When first I was informed that you took upon you to instruct your neighbours at Trefeca on a particular occasion – I mean of the nature of the Sacrament – and enforce their duty, by reading a chapter of that excellent book, '*The Whole Duty of Man*', I thought it proceeded from a pious and charitable disposition. But since you are advanced as far as to have your public lectures from house to house, and even within the limits of the Church, it is full time to let you know the sin and penalty you incur by so doing. The office you have freely under-taken belongs not to the laity any farther than privately in their own families; and if you will be pleased to take your Bible in hand, you will there find the heavy judgments which God indicted upon the sacrilege and impiety of those who audaciously presumed to invade the office ministerial. If you will consult the histories of this and other nations, you will see the dismal and lamentable effects of a factious zeal, and a puritanical sanctity: for it is an easy matter to seduce ignorant and illiterate people, and by cunning insinuations from house to house, induce them to embrace what tenets you please.

I have yet one heavy crime to lay to your charge, which is this: that after you have expatiated, upon a Sunday, upon the '*Whole Duty of Man*' to your auditors, which, in my opinion is wrote in so plain and intelligible a manner that it is incapable of paraphrase, unless it be to obscure and confound the author's meaning, you concluded with a long extempore prayer, with repeti-tions, tautologies, etc. Pray consider how odiously this savours of fanaticism and hypocrisy. What I have already said will, I hope, dissuade you for the future from such practices. But if the admonition of your minister will not prevail, I will acquaint your brother of it; and if you will persist in your way, I must acquaint my diocesan of it, which will prove an unmoveable obstruc-tion to your ever getting into Holy Orders; for your continuance in it will give me, as well as others, just reason to incude that your intellectuals are not sound.

I am your well-wisher, and assured humble servant,                    P. Davies[20]

It was not any enmity of evangelical religion that agitated Mr Davies, nor complete indifference as to the spiritual state of the country; it is evi-dent that he was a deeply serious man; but he wrote according to the light within him. To him, and others like him, regularity was the great issue. It was good to save souls, but only if that were done regularly, by means of a minister who had received a bishop's ordination. He considered the inter-ference of laymen in the work an unforgivable sin. He could not see that the salvation of the world was a greater matter than that of office. It may be that he also feared that if laymen could go about exhorting it would be the end of the clerical office.

The vicar's letter did not cause Harris to change direction. Some of those who regularly came to hear him became troubled by their vicar's letter and by the persecution of the common people. But they were willing to meet in secret even when they feared doing so in public. Gradually, the storm blew over and in the following spring he restarted his door-to-door visitation. By now he had encountered many of the local Dissenters. There was a Dissenting church at Tredustan, across the valley from Trefeca, in which, though it was weak and frail, some remains of true religion lingered like a smoking flax, and he received a warm welcome in the homes of these believers. For his livelihood, he established a day school at Trefeca, which he soon moved to Talgarth Church. Though he had visited the Rev. Griffith Jones at Llanddowror, mentioning his purpose and asking for advice, it does not appear that this was one of Griffith Jones's schools, but rather a personal venture of his own. But he was in constant correspondence with the godly clergyman of Llanddowror. He described his successes to him with enthusiasm, and he received from him gifts of books and every support. The school was of considerable help to the revival:

> By this means, great many young persons had laid hold of this opportunity, and came to be farther instructed in the way of salvation.[21]

## ESTABLISHING SOCIETIES

Another opportunity arose for him to warn his neighbours on the state of their souls. A man from the neighbourhood used to go about teaching the young people to sing Psalms.

> There was no objection made, any more than to assemblies met to cock-fighting, dancing, etc.[22]

He writes thus, with no humour intended, seemingly unconscious of the picture the words give of the state of the country. After the singing teacher had finished his musical tuition, the Reformer would stand up and give a word of counsel and by this means many more came under conviction. This led to the formation of societies:

> I began in imitation of the Societies which Dr Woodward gave an account of, in a little treatise he wrote on that head. There being as yet no other societies of the kind in England or Wales. The English Methodists not being as yet heard of, though the Lord was now, as I found afterward, working on some of them in Oxford and elsewhere.[23]

The Dr Woodward mentioned was a member of the Established Church. He had established his societies according to a plan and rules set out by the

Archbishop of Canterbury. The purpose was to gather together those who sought to live a holy life and who agreed to form a fellowship, to which they would all be responsible and in which they would abide by specific rules. They were not very dissimilar to the present guilds found in the Church of England. The societies established by Dr Woodward were in London only, and though they had once been strong they had by now declined into a low and lifeless condition. In truth, there was very little similarity between Harris's societies and those of Dr Woodward. The purpose of Woodward's groups was discipline. Their governing spirit was legalistic – they mainly required obedience to a set of external rules and ordinances. The purpose of Harris's groups was to help each other on the way to heaven. They provided opportunities for those who had been convicted to share their experiences, and to pour out their hearts, the one to the other, so that they might comfort and help each other. They were thoroughly evangelical in tone, paying attention mainly to the spiritual and subjective. Essentially, Harris's idea was completely novel. He was certainly correct in saying that no similar groups existed at the time in England or Wales. It was not for another three years that John Wesley formed his first societies. The Rev. James Hervey, one of the Oxford Methodists, had formed a religious fellowship in Bideford in 1739:

> The society at Bideford was by no means in contradistinction to the Established Church, but, in dutiful conformity to her.[24]

He wrote that the following advantages were to be derived from such societies:

> 1. Because we are ignorant and short-sighted, and oftentimes unable to discern the things that are excellent. But God is pleased to reveal to one what is concealed from another; so that, in a multitude of counsellors, there is wisdom.

> 2. Because we are lovers and admirers of ourselves, unwilling to see our own errors, and, therefore, unlikely to amend them. Whereas, our friends will, with a meek and impartial spirit, show us our faults.

> 3. Because we are weak and irresolute; easily shaken from the most laudable purposes, and apt to let go our integrity upon any opposition. But a band of friends, who are like-minded, inspires us with courage and constancy.

> 4. Because we are slothful and lukewarm in religious duties. How often have I gone into the company of my dear friends, listless and spiritless; yet, when I came home, I have found myself quite another person, vigorous and active, sanguine and zealously affected in good matters.[25]

However, Hervey failed to keep his Bideford society on these lines. Those who attended did not feel they could maintain religious conversation in a way that contributed to their being built up, nor were they spiritual enough to examine each the other as to the state of their souls. Therefore, instead of sharing their experiences, they would read a devotional book. But that which Mr Hervey failed to establish became in Wales a meeting of the greatest importance, and part of the religious life of the country. In the societies introduced by Howell Harris and Daniel Rowland, each not knowing of the other's work, the ignorant were taught more clearly in the principles of the gospel, the newly-converted were shown how they must walk in order to avoid the snares of the enemy, those in danger of losing their zeal were warned, those troubled by fears were comforted, and the saints of God fellowshipped with one another in Jesus Christ. Nothing contributed more to deepen the spiritual life of the country than the societies.

## EXTENDING HIS BORDERS

Up until now, the sphere of Harris's ministry had been Talgarth and the surrounding neighbourhoods. But soon matters changed:

> But, however, the beginning of the following summer, in 1737, a certain gentleman in Radnorshire sent for me to discourse at his house; this stirred the curiosity of some of the better sort of people to come and hear me; whilst others in conversing with me, had their prejudices much removed; and others were convinced. I had reason to believe the Lord would be pleased to bless my labours; though I still continued to keep school, yet I went out every night to such places where I was sent for, and did the same on Holy-days, and on the Sabbath – until, at last, about the latter end of this year, I was turned out of my school; which conduced to enlarge my sphere.
>
> After this I readily complied with every invitation, and went wherever I was sent for, by day and night; discoursing generally three or four, and sometimes, five or six times a day, to crowded auditories. Now I was loaded with all manner of calumnies, from all quarters; the Magistrates threatened me, the clergy preached against me, branding me with the character of a false prophet, and deceiver, etc., the Mob was active, laying in wait with intentions of mischief; yet during all this I was carried, as on the wings of an eagle, triumphantly above all – I took no particular texts, but discoursed freely as the Lord gave me utterance. The gift I had received was as yet to convince the conscience of sin.[26]

It is difficult for us in our day and age to form an opinion of the warmth and power of the ministry of Howell Harris. As far as compositional style, and depth and height of thought, were concerned, they could not be compared to those of Griffith Jones, or, particularly, those of Daniel Rowland. For some years, he made no attempt to deliver sermons on texts. He would give unpremeditated addresses, of no particular structure, thundering against sin. He said:

> As to the subject of my discourse, it was given unto me in an extraordinary manner, without the least premeditation, it was not the fruit of my memory; for, naturally, my memory was bad, therefore it was the effect of the immediate strong impulse which I felt in my soul. I was not able to rest; consequently, necessity was laid on my spirit to go and awaken souls.[27]

He had been specially prepared, by nature and by the depth of his own convictions, for warning the ungodly. His figure was majestic and drew the attention immediately; his voice was strong and clear; his eyes flamed; the solemnity of eternity was settled upon his countenance; and his speech was of overpowering authority. He went to the races and to the fairs, to the saint-days' celebrations and other licentious meetings of the times, warning the people to flee for refuge. His words fell as balls of fire on the careless multitudes. After securing a congregation, the preacher would stand up, and as he opened his mouth a tempest of thunder and lightning would fall upon the heads of his listeners. They were shaken above hell until some grew pale and some shouted out. It was not rare for a crowd of two thousand to stand in the rain listening to him speak. Some would be convicted, and others would attempt to stifle conscience by persecuting the preacher. It would be useless to try to account by human reasoning for the influence that accompanied the words; he had a message to deliver from God to men, and he would so deliver it with such passion that carried all before him. It is appropriate to include William Williams's description of Harris:

In the all prevailing darkness,
From Trefeca, burning bright,
Came a man of fierce passion,
Blazing fiery sparks of light.

In the thundercloud he sojourned,
Midst the storm-clouds, far above,
(Only bruised and broken spirits
Know the King of Heaven's love);
From the skies he sent forth lightning,
Fearful, powerful bolts from high,
Piercing hearts, convicting sinners,
Making them afraid to die.

Vain the attempt to avoid the summons,
Such the authority of heaven;

Yn y cyfnos tywyll pygddu,
Fe ddaeth dyn fel mewn twym ias,
Yn llawn gwreichion goleu, tanllyd,
O Drefeca Fach i ma's.

Yn y daran roedd e'n aros,
Yn y cwmwl roedd ei le,
(Ysbryd briw, drylliedig, gwresog,
Sy'n cael cwnsel Brenin Ne');
Ac yn saethu oddiyno allan
Fellt ofnadwy fawr eu rhyw,
At y dorf aneirif, dywyll,
Yn eu pechod oedd yn byw.

Gorfu gwrando ei eiriau geirwon,
Cadarn yw awdurdod nen;

If the sinner hardens to it,
Heavier still the burden given;
Blow upon blow rains down upon them,
Till their hearts, made willing now,
Fall in faith before the Saviour,
Now at last by grace brought low.

At such times, great hordes of sinners
First received a thirst for grace,
Which, while breath remains, their spirits
Still with joy, will e'er embrace;
All his words, severe and solemn,
Though not studied beforehand,
Had been given by the Spirit
To fit the case of every man.

Os gwrthw'nebu wna pechadur,
Trymach cwymp hi ar ei ben;
Dilyn ergyd a wnaeth ergyd,
Nes gwneud torf yn foddlon dod
At yr Iesu mewn cadwynau,
Fyth i ddilyn ôl ei droed.

Gwerin fawr o blant pleserau
Y pryd hwnnw gafodd flas,
Ag na â tra fyddo anadl
O'u hysbrydoedd ddim i maes.
Roedd ei eiriau dwys, sylweddol,
Heb eu stydio mlaen llaw'r un,
Wedi eu ffitio gan yr Ysbryd
I gyflyrau pob rhyw ddyn.

## TWO IMPORTANT EVENTS

Two important events in the life of Howell Harris and in the Revival took place in the summer of 1737. The first was his meeting, for the first time, with Daniel Rowland at Defynnog. Though the two men had for some time broken out of the common path in their warning of the ungodly, they yet knew nothing of each other. This fact only emphasizes the boldness and courage of their behaviour. In the name of Christ, Harris went out to the villages and mountainous valleys of Breconshire and Radnorshire, believing, as Elijah of old, that he was the only witness for the Saviour. But Rowland had been invited to Defynnog Church by the vicar of the parish. Harris, also present, most probably, at the invitation of the vicar, arrived to meet him. On experiencing Rowland's seraphic preaching gifts and the power with which he declared the glorious truths of the gospel, his soul embraced the apostle of Llangeitho and he journeyed with him to Cardiganshire, before returning home. If, humanly speaking, Methodism is considered as springing up from two separate and independent sources, it was here at Defynnog that the two streams joined and became a river.

The second important event was the conversion of Mr Marmaduke Gwynne, one of the foremost of the Breconshire nobility, who lived at Garth, in the north of the county. Harris was due to preach in the neighbourhood. Mr Gwynne had heard much against this preacher, that he was a rebel against the King, an agitator of the people, rousing them to rise up against the civil authorities. He felt that it was his duty as a justice of the peace to apprehend this villain and deliver him up to prison. But he was a just man, and said to his wife, 'I will listen to him before arresting him.' He went to the meeting, with the Riot Act in his pocket in order to break up the gathering and scatter the hearers at the least indication of rebellion. But Harris never mentioned any current issues; he declared God's threatenings against the ungodly; he pleaded with his hearers to flee from the wrath to come; he rebuked them for their shameful sins, and immoral lives. He appeared to Mr Gwynne as God's angel, a messenger from another world. Instead of apprehending the preacher, he himself was apprehended, and brought in bonds to Christ. At the end of the meeting, he approached the preacher and, confessing his evil intentions, asked his forgiveness. He then pressed him to stay at his house. It was terrible for Mrs Gwynne, herself a member of one of the noblest families, to see her husband return accompanied by the rebellious preacher, and paying him as much respect as if he had been a bishop. She rather thought that her husband had lost his senses. But the daughter, Miss Sarah Gwynne, was soon converted as well as the father. Mrs Gwynne was for some time hostile to the Revival but she eventually was saved, and the whole family became Methodists. Later, Sarah Gwynne married Charles Wesley. Mr Gwynne used all his influence to help Howell Harris; he defended him continually, and his influence and example moderated the persecution and brought about a more favourable public opinion of the Methodists.

## MONMOUTHSHIRE AND GLAMORGANSHIRE

By the spring of 1738, societies had been formed in nearly every neighbourhood in Breconshire; in many places in Radnorshire; and in some places in Herefordshire. This was achieved despite the persecution of clergy and nobility and the riots of the mobs. There was not a locality in these three counties that Harris had not visited many times. He sometimes preached in the meeting-houses of the Dissenters, but mainly in the open-air. He often visited Llangeitho also, not only to enjoy the ministry of Daniel Rowland but also to confer with him on the progress of the work. His journal for 1737 shows that he was at Llanddowror at least twice during that year, visiting Griffith Jones, whom he respected as a father. Almost certainly he would have preached along the way in parts of Cardiganshire and Carmarthenshire, as he made these journeys. As a result of these efforts, together with those of Daniel Rowland, signs of revival began to be seen in many counties. The people crowded to places of worship; very few attended the dissolute local gatherings, and immorality began to be ashamed of itself. Stories of his ministry and the unction attending it began to be repeated in Monmouthshire and Glamorganshire. Some of the

Dissenting ministers in these counties began to believe that a dawn of hope was beginning to break in Wales, and they decided to invite him to their region, trusting that his visit would be the means of awakening some of their feeble causes that were wilting and ready to die.

The first to invite Howell Harris was the Rev. Edmund Jones, Ponty-pool. Mr Jones was the son of poor parents who were members of the Independent Church of Pen-maen. He had never had the advantages of an education. It does not seem that he had great preaching gifts but he was full of zeal and work. He had succeeded in gathering a congregation and forming a small church in the Pontypool neighbourhood, but it was a weak and stuttering cause. They did not have a meeting-house but met in various homes in the area. The whole valley, together with the adjoining valley, from Blaenau Gwent southwards, was ungodly and without religion. Mr Jones decided that he would attempt to get Howell Harris to preach to them. In the spring of 1738, he journeyed on foot to Trefeca with the sole purpose of inviting him, and on returning he brought Harris with him. The Reformer's visit produced much agitation in the minds of the Mynydd-dislwyn and Bedwellty clergy, and one of them wrote to him:

> Mr Harris, I am surprised at the liberty you take of coming to my curacies of Mynyddislwyn and Bedwellty. You must recede, or else yourself, and the person or persons that hath invited and sent for you, must expect that just resentment due for such unlawful practices. Yours, David Perrot.[28]

This letter is dated, '17 March 1738'. Harris paid no attention to Mr Perrot's threats. He continued thundering powerfully against the bad habits of the inhabitants of the locality, and fear and terror fell upon many of them. We do not have a list of the places he visited but extraordinary influ-ences accompanied his ministry, and such was the authority of his speech that even the most arrogant were terrified, and the kingdom of darkness was shaken to its foundation. The visit produced a thorough revolution in the moral situation of the neighbourhood. Take the events in the locality of Mynyddislwyn for an example. Near to the parish church was a mound known as *Twmpath Tudur* [Tudor's Mound]. Harris stood upon this mound amidst the hundreds of games-players that had gathered to hear. It is said that they understood little of the content of what was preached, but they realized that the preacher was proclaiming terrible curses against their immoralities, and was threatening those who indulged in the sports and pleasures, with the lake of fire. His solemnity struck them in the depths of their hearts. They imagined that the ground beneath them was shaking, and that hell was going to open up beneath them and swallow them alive. This one sermon put paid to the licentious habits of the neighbourhood and rendered all their sports distasteful to them. An old man told the late Rev. Thomas Evans, Risca:

> I never afterwards enjoyed football, though previously I was one of the best at it. When I went to play, I used to think, especially if it was after sunset, that the devil himself was playing with us.

The general opinion held by the people in the locality was that the man who came to preach at *Twmpath Tudur* had spoiled the sports. The same result occurred in other places, though we do not have such detailed accounts of them. Edmund Jones wrote that many were saved at this time in the Blaenau Gwent and Ebbw regions; some of them joined the Church of England, others the Baptists and the Independents. It must be remembered that these were rural areas in that time, inhabited by farmers and their labourers and of little population. Says Edmund Jones:

> This was a happy time in the Ebbw Fawr Valley, such as was not seen, I believe, before or afterwards, One could believe that the whole valley was turning to God. Out of thirty-seven houses there were but seven, if that, to which the Word of God had not come. Those who had turned to religion far outnumbered the others.

Harris's ministry at this time was blessed to many who afterwards became preachers themselves, amongst whom were Philip David, who was a minister with the Independents at Pen-maen for nearly fifty years; Thomas Lewis, who was appointed superintendent of the Methodist causes of east Monmouthshire; John Powell, a native of Breconshire, who was raised in a tavern; and Morgan John Lewis, the first minister of New Inn, to whom we will refer later. Soon, there were societies formed in Goytre, Glasgoed, Mynyddislwyn, Llangattock, Trefethin, St. Bride's, Llangattock-nigh-Usk, Llanfihangel, and Llanhilleth. Whether they were established on this visit, or during another journey through Monmouthshire in the October of the same year, we do not know. Howell Harris was received as an ambassador from heaven by the Dissenting ministers that preached Calvinistic doctrine; and his arrival was as life from the dead for many of the failing causes in their care.

Very soon, Edmund Jones was building a meeting-house in Pontypool and the numbers of Dissenting churches in the area greatly increased. But as for those men who tended to Arminianism, and they were the majority at the time, they did all they could to frustrate the revival and to oppose Harris. Their complaint against him was that he was not ordained and therefore had no right to preach. These formal Nonconformists placed as much weight on ordination as did the Church of England clergymen. Edmund Jones commented, in a letter to Harris:

I cannot but observe that they are our best men who are favourable to you, and that they are for the most part dry and inexperienced Arminians, that are against you – at least, who are bitter.[29]

He says also that the evangelical Dissenters viewed him as a man called to the ministry, though not in the usual way. Harris called? This is as certain as that the Apostles were called by the Saviour. It is undeniably proved by the unction that accompanied his preaching, and by the hundreds that were being converted by it. If Paul could appeal to the believers amongst the Corinthians and say, 'The seal of mine apostleship are ye in the Lord', Harris also could refer to many hundreds throughout the land who were living witnesses of his divine calling. The Arminian ministers had personal reasons for opposing the Reformer. One reason was the Calvinistic doctrine which he preached, and preached so unapologetically: mankind lost in sin; the heart desperately wicked; all the efforts of man to attain to the standards of the righteous law of heaven, completely in vain; the obedience and atonement of the Lord Jesus the only ground of salvation; and all the praise belonging to the sovereign grace of God. These were the truths he proclaimed. His creed can be summed up in a phrase he used once, in prayer, 'I am hell, but Thou art heaven.' Against these doctrines, the unevangelical Arminians recoiled violently. Furthermore, Harris thundered terribly against the coldness, sleepiness, and worldliness that had overcome the Dissenting churches, as well as against the lukewarm and legalistic preaching of the ministers. He scourged them mercilessly and called upon them, in the Lord's name, to awake, before they were overtaken by judgment. Edmund Jones believed that he was too severe:

> I am glad Mr Whitefield hath borne his honest and bold testimony against the lukewarmness and wordliness of Dissenters, and against the loose walking and levity of some of their ministers. There was the greatest need in the world of it; but Mr Whitefield doth it in a prudent, though yet home manner; and had you, dear brother, done this with less passion and intemperance of spirit, and with more prudence and distinction, observing a regard for their persons, you might have done much good; but as it was, I fear it did but little good. It is my presumption upon your honesty and self-denial makes me venture to tell you this much; but I see our own much greater fault.[30]

We will not attempt to judge whether Edmund Jones was correct. Certainly Harris was very warm in spirit and particularly severe in his uncovering of evils, particularly evils in the context of the service of God, and it is very clear that his boldness aroused much opposition from the unevangelical ministers. Nevertheless, God's hand was upon him and he did not fear what man could do to him.

Another Dissenting minister who invited Howell Harris to his neighbourhood was the Rev. David Williams, the minister of the Presbyterian churches at Watford and Cardiff. He wrote to Harris telling him that he had announced him to preach at Eglwysilan parish for two days, on the Wednesday after Whit Sunday at Bwlch-y-cwm, and the Thursday at Maesdiofal, and that a great gathering was expected. Harris went faithfully to his appointment. It seems that he passed through Monmouthshire on the way, for Mr Williams promised to meet him on the Tuesday night at Bedwellty and to bring him back to stay at his own house. We do not know if he preached in other places in Glamorganshire at this time. Probably he did; we would not expect him to travel here all the way from Talgarth solely for two days' work. The same influence followed on his ministry here as in Monmouthshire, and it was no temporary influence, soon disappearing. It was rather like yeast in the flour, changing the whole nature of the dough. In a letter sent to Trefeca some time after this, the Rev. David Williams wrote:

> The two days' service with us has been attended with marvellous success. The churches and meetings are crowded, Sabbath-breaking goes down; it is looked upon as a very abominable thing; dancing has been much interrupted, profane swearing and cock-fighting are exclaimed against. But you do not imagine that the devil is mute and still; no, he speaks and acts, but I think there seems to be more against him than for him in this part of the country. Your friends are more numerous than your adversaries; you are preached against in some places, but it turns to the reproach of them who attempt it . . . I hope that as soon as God shall restore you to health and strength, you will come to the places above mentioned; whether it be harvest time or any other time, I think it will not make much difference, because people are so eager of hearing you. I . . . had four or five places fixed upon to propose to you, that wanted your service.[31]

This letter is dated 12 June 1738. The reference to bad health suggests that Harris's unceasing efforts in travelling and preaching was beginning to affect him, for all the great strength of his constitution. Within a month, David Williams wrote to Harris again, asking for another visit:

> The last week of this instant [i.e. July], or the first beginning of the next, will be very convenient. The places in view, besides those that have been disappointed, are Llanedeyrn (from St Nicholas there), thence to Machen, or Bassaleg, either of the two, as those concerned shall think most convenient; thence to our parish . . . I should have told you that you are expected from our parish to Gelligaer. The curate who called the other night at our house, is for promoting it all he can; though he may act a little behind the curtains, being now about to receive priest's orders.[32]

The letter ends with the writer's assurances that Harris 'need not be so shy of conversing with the Dissenters' in that region, compared to other places, because prejudice was falling away quickly. The places mentioned as being disappointed in their hope of a visit from Harris were Aberdare, Llanwynno, Llantrisant, and St. Nicholas, in Glamorganshire. In these towns, large congregations had gathered, and their disappointment was great when it was understood that ill health had prevented the preacher.

About the same time that Harris first visited the Caerphilly area, he preached in the western part of Glamorganshire. This was as a result of an importunate invitation from the Rev. Henry Davies of Blaen-gwrach, the pastor of a Dissenting congregation in the Neath Valley. He was on friendly terms with the Methodists throughout his life. He was present at the first Association at Watford and in many other Associations, and was a thoroughly God-fearing man. After his death, his congregation became Unitarian. It seems that Harris's illness had prevented him from visiting this area in June, as he had intended, and that thousands had been disappointed here also because of this. In a letter to him, dated 28 July, 1738, Henry Davies says:

> That serious, zealous, and pious man, Mr William Thomas, clergyman at Llantwit-juxta-Neath, is very desirous to see and to have your company. He came purposely to hear you at the [Neath] Abbey, but was disappointed, and many thousands more. He was reproved by a bitter clergyman who lives at Neath. The clergy are divided one against another in our parts. A captain of the cock matches, who heard you at Bettws, promises never to follow that wicked game any longer, and another dux omnium malorum, near the sea side, did cut off the heads of his cocks when he went home after hearing you. I have seen him last Lord's day, and he appears a serious hearer. He did invite me to his house. The praise is due to God alone . . . I believe the devil has lost some skilful soldiers, who have listed themselves to be faithful soldiers under the great captain, our Lord Jesus . . . Oh pray that there would be more cannons sent to batter down the towers of Satan.[33]

About this same time, Harris received similar invitations from the Rev. John Davies, a minister of Cwm-y-glo, near Merthyr Tydfil, and from the Rev. Vavasor Griffiths of Radnorshire.

Harris's journal for the latter part of 1738 has not been found, but there is reason to believe that in accordance with the requests of these Dissenting ministers, he journeyed through extensive areas of Glamorganshire and Monmouthshire in the August and September of 1738, and that his ministry met with much success. The Rev. David Williams wrote to him on 17 October of that year:

The bearer [of this letter] has been very wild. But has reformed exceedingly. Since he heard you last in our parish he frequents every meeting about, both upon week-nights as well as Lord's Day. Meetings here are crowded. There be sixteen that have bespoke communion next time at Cardiff... We have a Welsh School going up.[34]

Two months later, he writes again:

Things have a comfortable aspect here at present. Praying societies go up everywhere. Seventeen have been admitted to communion last time; more have been proposed. We have a large Welsh School, in which praying is come to be fashionable, and have a mind to put another up.[35]

Mr Williams ends by requesting another visit about Christmas time, though it was not expected that Harris should preach in the open-air at that season. We have included these last two letters, not only for their interest but to prove that Harris made successful visits to these two counties in the early autumn of 1738. If he had not been able to agree to the earlier pressing requests there would surely have been a more disappointed tone running through these letters. But instead, they are full of praise because of success. Many churches were established in Glamorganshire before the end of 1738 as the fruit of his labours, including Cardiff, St. Fagans, Whitchurch, Pen-tyrch, Aberthin, Llantrisant, Tonyrefail, and Llanwynno. Many families, considered to be of the gentry in the area, were also won to the ranks of the Methodists. Squire Jones, of Fonmon Castle, was convicted when listening to Howell Harris preaching at Aberthaw. Mr Jones had gone there together with some other gentry, a drawn sword in his hand, with the intention of frustrating the meeting. The speaker was not in any way intimidated by him, he rather asked the people to divide and make way for the party and he himself turned to English so that they could understand. The squire's horse got stuck in the mud so that it could not move, and the rider was therefore forced unwillingly to listen to God's Word. But an arrow shot home. He removed his hat, to show respect; he opened his heart to receive the gospel; and he returned to his castle with the preacher by his side. He raised a pulpit in his house for the benefit of speakers, and his mansion immediately became a home for the Reformers when on their journeys. Preaching took place there regularly throughout the Squire's life and for years afterwards. This is where Whitefield stayed when in the vicinity.

Another of the gentry who was won at this time was Thomas Price of Watford, near Caerphilly. He is mentioned by Williams, Pantycelyn, in his elegy to Grace Williams, as 'Price the Justice'. He also became a preacher. Many others were brought under the influence of the gospel and became preachers, or, as they were then called, 'exhorters'. Amongst these were Thomas Williams; William Edwards, the builder of the famous bridge at Pontypridd; and John Belcher. Of these, Belcher was the most greatly gifted. He was sent on his own to the north in the hope of evangelizing the land, and old John Evans of Bala said of him that he was 'a brave man, of robust abilities, and a good preacher'.

As we mentioned, Howell Harris was not following any kind of plan at the beginning. He did not consider that he had been called to be a preacher, indeed, he believed firmly that he was not. It was an internal necessity that drove him to warn men of their spiritual misery. But as he saw the remarkable impressions that accompanied his efforts, and the divine unction upon his words, he came gradually to appreciate that to proclaim Christ Jesus, the Saviour, was to be the supreme occupation of his life. This appreciation rekindled in him the desire for ordination. During October, 1737, he wrote in his journal:

Aberedw, Sunday the 30th. Sacrament. Rose after seven. Dull as usual. A desire today to be convinced of my mistaken views. After eight, went towards Honddu Valley chapel; on the way meditated on the sacrament, feeling overburdened by fears. In the chapel dull for a while; then desiring to be a light for the world, and being in great inward tribulation, fearing being ordained in that it will keep me from going about. But I was enlightened to see that if God called me he would keep the door open for me, putting it in men's hearts to allow me in to their churches.

This quotation sheds much light on Harris's thinking at this time. After much concern of mind, he had decided to seek ordination; his intention in so doing was not to obtain a good living, nor for the opportunity to evangelize within the limited confines of a parish, but in order to regularize his own position in the work, that he might no longer have to go about preaching without authority or episcopal ordination. He made his decision in the assurance that the churches of the land would be thrown open to him as a consequence.

The phrase 'desiring to be a light for the world' is very significant; it shows that he would not accept ordination if it would mean that he would have to give up his itinerating. It is certain that he carried out his resolution and applied to the Bishop for ordination. Whitefield says that he applied twice, and there is later evidence of a third application. But the irregularity of his behaviour, and the fact that he was one of the despised Methodists, were insurmountable barriers to his being ordained. The Bishop refused him on the ground that he was too young, 'Though,' said Whitefield, 'he was at the time twenty-two years of age, and in possession of every qualification for holy orders.' But though his application was refused, Harris did not give up his exhorting.

At one time it seems as if he was in great anxiety over his behaviour and considered himself to be unacceptably irregular. On the one hand, he saw the revival fire spreading abroad through his instrumentality, precious souls being saved, the fields white unto harvest, the immorality of the common people melting away under the influence of the gospel, and providence continually opening new doors for him. On the other hand, he knew of no other unordained person going about to exhort other than himself. The Dissenters were as fully opposed to a lay-ministry as was the Church. Even John Wesley, as late as the year 1742, about seven years after Harris had begun his work, was considerably agitated on hearing that Thomas Maxfield, a layman, had begun preaching, and had rushed back to London to stop him. But Wesley's anger was moderated by advice from his mother:

> John, take care what you do with respect to that young man, for he is as surely called of God to preach, as you are.[36]

Nor did Harris wish to join the Dissenters in order to regularize his activities. Their formality, controversies, and particularly their spiritual coldness was unendurable to him, though he had great respect for the evangelical men amongst them, and co-operated heartily with them. Among all this, his mind was very troubled, and the frequent accusations of the clergy and the unevangelical Nonconformists only made matters worse. But he would continue his work, whatever happened. At the end of 1738, he received an encouraging letter from Whitefield:

> Go on my dear Brother, go on, be strong in the Lord, and in the power of his might . . . There have been, and will be, many adversaries; yet be not afraid, He that sent you will assist, comfort, and protect you, and make you more than conqueror, through his great love . . . My dear Brother, I love you, in the bowels of Jesus Christ, and wish you may be the spiritual father of thousands, and shine as the sun in the firmament; in the kingdom of your heavenly father. My hearty love to Mr Jones; Oh how shall I joy to meet you, at the judgment seat of Christ.[37]

This letter is interesting in that it represents the very first correspondence between the Welsh Reformers and the English Methodists. Its contents cheered Harris's spirit greatly; it was to him as cold waters to a thirsty soul; it strengthened him in his belief that he was under the influence of the Holy Spirit. No doubt the impression made by the letter was all the greater because it came from a man who had received a bishop's ordination, and possessed a unique fame as a minister. He soon replied with a loving letter giving a brief account of the revival in Wales. Having received it, Whitefield commented:

> Mr Howell Harris, and I, are correspondents, blessed be God! May I follow him, as he does Jesus Christ. How he outstrips me![38]

This was the beginning of a correspondence that developed into the closest of friendships and which continued all their lives. Mr Whitefield's letter settled Harris's doubts considerably, but he said that he was not completely freed from them until he was summoned to the presence of a man of some authority to give an account of his behaviour, and the words of Revelation 3:8 came with power into his soul, 'Behold, I have set before thee an open door, and no man can shut it.' He firmly believed that the words had been sent to him as a direct message from the Holy Spirit and he did not doubt again.

## EXTRACTS FROM HIS JOURNALS

Howell Harris's energy and activity were unceasing and at the beginning of 1739 he undertook another journey through Glamorganshire and Monmouthshire. We will quote something of the history of the journey as he described it in his journal. To give the journal in full would be out of the question. There would be no end to the volumes required, for Harris wrote continually. He recorded not only the events that occurred but also his meditations and thoughts.

Collene, near Trefeurig, Sunday, 9 January 1739.
Woke early. Rose after eight. Dull in family worship, but feeling a desire to be on my own, holding fellowship with God. Lifeless also while at family prayers. About ten, went to Llanharry Church; and thought on the way over what I would speak; but afterwards had thoughts that God had made me for his own glory. Felt indifferent as to what would become of me, as long as I am helped to glorify God. O Lord, wilt thou not allow me this? I do not ask for anything else in life. If it were granted I would be the happiest man in the world. The deep desire of my soul is to be nothing in my own sight, and to live for God. But Oh! When I speak, I generally cannot discern from where the words flow. Do they come from grace and love towards God, or from the habit of speaking? Reached Llanharry Church after eleven (closer to twelve). Felt sleepy at first; then I was filled inwardly with pity for the souls of those around me. After three, I went out, saw the blind people polluting the Lord's Day everywhere, in their ignorance, and was filled with compassion for them. I was drawn out to pray, 'O Lord, send faithful men to thy vineyard! O Lord, art thou not a God of mercy? O, was it not thy love that first sent thy Son to

the world? O, dost thou not still remain a God of love? O, dost thou not see thy poor creatures ignorant of thee in every place? Send labourers!'

After this, I was overtaken by a restless and displeased spirit, until I was humbled on perceiving how little of the divine nature was in me. I feared going to speak tonight, as I had been filled with unloving thoughts towards dear friends, particularly Mr Edmund Jones. Self came in, asking what I would say tonight, in that he [Edmund Jones, no doubt] would be present. Went amongst the people at six, when Mr Henry Davies was praying, and I was brought to feel my unworthiness more, and to wish that another would take my work in hand. O, I have forfeited every favour; I am upheld only by this, that God can sustain me, and that he does not provide the support for my sake, but for the sake of his Son. There are two things, which, if we could but perceive them, would change us greatly: a view of ourselves; and a view of God in all his attributes.

I was helped to overcome the slavish, self-seeking thought of seeking to please men. I soon obtained an open door; I showed in a most powerful and terrible manner how the godly will enjoy in love, and the ungodly in terror, and with more conviction than ever, and with no respect of persons. I showed what hell is made of, and of the way parents bring up their children . . .

I had much liberty in prayer at the end. I was very weak in my body for lack of food, but I prayed for strength, and I was aided. Afterwards, having enjoyed fellowship with friends, to fulfil my joy, I received a letter from Mr Whitefield. And on seeing that he was one with me in spirit; which I have proven often in my own spirit towards him, though without any hope of seeing him down in Wales nor of hearing from him, I was amazed at the goodness of God.

It appears from these lines, in which Howell Harris opens his heart to us, that Edmund Jones, Pontypool, had begun to show that proselytizing spirit, and the tendency to turn the labours of the Reformer to the advantage of his own denomination, for which a gentle rebuke was administered to him later. In his tenderness of conscience, Harris blamed himself for indulging such a thought; but it soon became clear that the suggestive thought that he had put out of his mind, was based on fact. It is seen also that Harris received Whitefield's letter at Collene, Glamorganshire, on the ninth of January, whereas the latter was dated the 20th of December of the previous year. It must be remembered that postal arrangements in those days were very imperfect, and probably the letter was first delivered to Trefeca, before being sent on to Mr Harris.

Trefeurig, Monday, 10 January, 1739. Woke often, could have risen but was careless. Rose about eight. I hope to be brought to complete victory over the flesh. Private prayer; lifeless, lifeless; but I was given a determination to wait.

On seeing that news of me had spread over England, and how ready my heart is to swell, and how superficial I am, I was brought to cry with anxiety of soul, 'O Lord, I fear that all this tends to my destruction, because of the pride of my own heart. How slippery is the place where I stand! Thankfully I did not go about in order to gain a name. O that I might be obscure! But Lord, I commit all to thee. I am willing to go if thou dost send me, whatever may happen to me. Thou canst pull down all the pride of my heart, and keep me humble. O Lord, have mercy on the world. Extend the lives of Mr Whitefield, Mr Griffith Jones, Mr Edmund Jones, and all thy faithful ones. If the Baptists are falling into error place them in the right way. Let not this [baptism] be a cause of division amongst us. O that we might all be one. I fear controversies and their consequences upon the young chicks. I praise thee for so many faithful ones. Thou dost know, O Lord, how unfit I am to go about publicly: how little time I have to read; and how little ability I have to spend and to continue. O, I would like to be active, but as I cannot, I commit myself to thee; enlighten me; and lead me into all truth. Let me have more light on thy Word. If I am one of thy children, let me feel more of an interest in thy cause. Help me today to be bold for thee, and save me from this monster, self.

On Monday, he left Trefeurig, and crossed the mountain past Tonyrefail, reaching Cymer in the Rhondda Valley by mid-day.

Cymer. Discoursing on the way. But flashes only belong to me; it does not spring from love. I see self always laughing because of the weaknesses of my fellow-creatures. O, what am I, that I might be in the same world as God's saints? But if I am made some day to be something for Christ, it will be to the eternal praise of free grace. On the way, heard of one of the Methodists, a sea captain, exhorting soldiers. My heart was filled with joy for hours because of it. I had a deep longing and weeping in my soul for the Spirit of God. O that I might have thy Spirit, Lord; without him what can I do with thy societies? At Cymer after one. Began by saying, are not those in prison glad when they hear of one who will release them? And the sick on hearing of a physician? But we are dead, dead in sin. Warned that they keep from dancing and all playing. Christ draws sinners to himself by conviction. The Word (in conviction) is like a fire, a hammer, a light, a sword, like fuller's soap. I referred to the Jews being pricked in their hearts and to Nebuchadnezzar. The marks of conviction are the washing of the heart, the drawing of the heart away from all things and to him, our being drawn away from trusting upon ourselves. Found some delight and pleasure in the work; some degree of love to souls and pity for them; together with longing for God. God gave us fine weather.

After this I was convicted by Mr Henry Davies of my ingratitude to the Lord for the help he was giving, and that I was therefore forfeiting all; and, O, the little love there is in my soul.

On Tuesday morning, 11 January, he again spoke at Cymer, then travelled for four miles along the Rhondda Valley, reaching Ynysangharad, near Pontypridd. On Wednesday, he crossed over the mountain to Parc in Eglwysilan parish; and in the afternoon of the same day he was at a place called Tyn-y-coed. His journal continues:

We had a delightful gentleness, and a spirit of love towards the young people; and I hope some of them were brought to Christ. After one, I discoursed till about four. Again today the weather was fine; not often is it like this at this time of year. I hope that God is with us. I was given what to say; I had not premeditated it as I had thought to speak on something else. Afterwards, to Llanbradach Fach, and on the way, was attacked by a Baptist, who tried to pick a quarrel with me. I felt within me a revulsion of argumentation, because of the fear of the consequences. I cannot say why I feel more of a spirit against these than against any, except the Papists. I fear that there are fanatics amongst them who, unless God sees fit to humble them, will damage the Church of Christ. But I am loth to take up the cudgels against them, not for fear of the argument, because I am clear on the matter, but for fear of pulling down the glorious work of the revival. I see the marks of a hypocrite often on these fanatics. For one thing, all their conversation is directed to this one thing [baptism] and very little towards Christ. Secondly, their warmest love is directed only towards those of the same opinion as themselves, but that of a godly man is directed towards all members of Christ's Church. Thirdly, all they clearly long for is to make proselytes for themselves, and the desire of the godly is to bring converts to Christ.

From 7 until 11, an extraordinary delightful meeting; I never experienced one so sweet. I was given the words to speak; but I did not experience enough in my spirit. Very good prospects tonight.

Llanbradach Fach, Thursday, 13 January. Woke early and rose at nine. Had help by looking at the cross. I hope that his death mortifies sin in me. At ten, secret prayer, and was humbled by a sense of God's majesty, so that I could not look up. 'O Lord, for Christ's sake, and not for the sake of my tears and poor prayers (for I am wretched, like the worst worm that crawls upon thy world, seeking self and sin), will it not please thee to keep us from controversy, because of their results? At least, Lord, I pray that thou wilt keep me out of their arguments, and send another to control them. But if thou dost send me I am willing to do whatever is thy will.' Then my soul was granted such a view of God's goodness, that I was drawn out in praising – 'O Lord, surely I should praise thee continually for what thou hast done for me? Wilt thou receive my praise? Keep me low, for I am all sin. Here is my prayer; have mercy on me; I throw all upon thee. I trust in thee that when I go to Cardiff, thou wilt give me what to say for thy glory.

He is next at Werndomen, a farmhouse near Cardiff, on Friday, 14 January. Here again, the Baptists are disturbing him. He writes:

> O Lord, I go today to discourse; what shall I do and say? Wilt thou keep me from fanatics who torture my soul? If thou dost wish, Lord, that I change my views, let me see thy will; and if thou dost lead them to me, guard me that I be correct. O, may we know love and unity. I know that I do not wish to reason, if thou wilt grant me to be kept from it. O, I would not strive, unless thou dost send me to it.

After this, we know nothing of him until Wednesday, 19 January, when he was at Gwrhay, near Mynyddislwyn. Whether part of the journal is lost, or he discontinued it for a while, we do not know. We can only speculate also where he spent the intervening time, but more than likely he went to Cardiff, as he had intended. On the Thursday, he was at Llanhilleth, near Pontypool; on Friday at Blaenau Gwent; and on the following Sunday, 23 January, at Llanbedr (the Llanbedr near Crickhowell, more than likely), not far from his own home.

It may be seen that he was travelling across country, from the west of Glamorganshire to the furthest east of Monmouthshire, and that the Revs. Edmund Jones, Pontypool, and Henry Davies, were with him for some of the journey. Whether this was Henry Davies, Blaen-gwrach, or Henry Davies, the Dissenting minister of Llantrisant, is uncertain, but it was probably the latter.

It is impossible to read the journal without feeling that Harris's whole heart was on saving his fellow Welshmen. He lived in the spiritual world; there is hardly any reference to worldly circumstances. His relationship with God, and the great work which he was undertaking, had swallowed up his soul. Though he complained about the Baptists, it is clear that he feels no bitterness of spirit towards them. Rather, he feared that giving too much prominence to the doctrine of baptism at that time, and being taken up in controversy over it, would prove an obstacle to the revival. He was quite willing to co-operate with the Baptists, if they would be willing to forget their favourite topic, and give themselves to proclaiming Christ as a Saviour for sinners. By means of his journal we may look into the depths of his heart; the very furthest reaches of his soul are disclosed. He tends to reveal more of his weaknesses than of his strengths, and we see how unsophisticated he was, how humble, and how desirous of keeping self down, and to give all the praise to God.

As far as we can gather from the notes given, his sermons were rather scattered in structure. They do not reveal any great depth of thought, and he never dealt with profound theological topics. But every sentence was accompanied by an arrow, aimed straight at a sinner's heart, and he would throw his whole soul into the work of pulling the bowstring, so that it is no wonder that men by their scores and hundreds were being wounded.

Come, hear him now describing
Man's heart, polluted, vile,
And searching out the evils
That lie there all the while;
Revealing to the godly
Great depths, before unseen,
And opening up sin's darkest rooms
Where light had never been.

Come, listen to him plumbing
The depths of sovereign grace!
Revealing the Messiah
In all his wondrous ways;
And comforting the afflicted
Under conviction's sway,
So that they rise rejoicing,
All terrors passed away.

Dewch, gwrandewch ef yn pregethu,
Calon ddrwg, lygredig dyn,
Ac yn olrhain troion anial,
A dichellion sy yno ynglyn;
Dod i'r golau â dirgelion
I rai duwiol oedd yn nghudd,
Agor hen stafelloedd tywyll,
Angau glas, i oleu'r dydd.

Dewch, gwrandwch ef yn agoryd
Dyfnder iachawdwriaeth gras,
Gosod allan y Messiah
Yn y lliw hyfryta maes;
Ac yn dodi'r cystuddiedig,
Ag sy'n ofni ei ras a'i rym
Fel i chwerthin i orfoledd,
Ac i 'mado heb ofni dim.

## MEETING WHITEFIELD AT CARDIFF

According to the journal, Harris seems to have spent the February of 1739 visiting different places in Breconshire, Radnorshire, and the north-west of Glamorganshire. He may have been kept from his intention to visit the north by a letter from Mr Whitefield promising to come to Wales. The two men had become very close, though they had never yet met. Whitefield left Bristol on 6 March. An interesting fact in his history is that it was only a fortnight or so previously that he had preached in the open-air for the very first time. All the churches of Bristol had been closed against him, and he had gone out to the colliers of Kingswood and preached before them. From now on, he would preach wherever he was given opportunity, never asking whether a bishop had consecrated the ground with salt, or not. Though it was early in the year and the weather cold, thousands had gathered to hear him in Bristol. On one occasion when he preached from a bowling green, he says that about eight thousand people had been present. He had also recently met the venerable Griffith Jones, Llanddowror, at Bath, from whom he had obtained the news of Wales, the news of Howell Harris in particular, and of all the various obstacles to the spread of the gospel in the Principality. Mr Whitefield felt his heart warming to the old soldier, and was convicted that he was only a very inexperienced soldier still.

Accompanied by his friend William Seward, he arrived at the New Passage on Monday afternoon, 6 March. They there met with the Rev. Nathaniel Well, the vicar of Cardiff, who was so opposed to the Methodists that he would not cross in the same boat as the two evangelists. But because of stormy weather they were forced to wait for twelve hours, and Mr Well had nothing better to do than to spend the time playing cards. He also complained that during the crossing of the Severn, the two men were singing hymns so loudly that the man at the rudder could not hear the instructions from the lookout, so that he had to ask them to stop. According to a letter written by William Seward:

> We are now going to meet our brother Howell Harris at Cardiff. The minister of which place, being here, will not even go over in the passage-boat with us. He says our brother shall not have the church; so I hope the fields will be white at Cardiff, as well as at Bristol. There is also a society there who long for our coming.[39]

This suggests that Howell Harris had already established a Methodist society in Cardiff. The two men arrived at Cardiff about eleven o'clock on the Wednesday. Whitefield immediately began to exhort the people at their inn, while Seward went to look for somewhere to preach. He managed to obtain the use of the town hall, and Whitefield preached from the judge's chair to a congregation of four hundred. Most of them listened attentively, but some mocked. As he regained his seat, he saw Howell Harris. Harris had travelled down through the Taff Valley, having stayed the previous night at Eglwysilan, probably at David Williams's house. According to Harris:

> The first question that he asked me was, 'Do you know that your sins are forgiven you?'[40]

Harris could hardly find a reply, so sudden had been the question. According to Whitefield:

> When I first saw him, my heart was knit closely to him. I wanted to catch some of his fire, and gave him the right hand of fellowship with my whole heart . . . we spent the remainder of the evening in taking sweet counsel together, and telling one another what God had done for our souls . . . we took an account of the several societies, and we agreed on such measures as seemed most conducive to promote the common interest of our Lord.[41]

This is a good example of the way the Reformers used to meet and confer with one another, and it was these informal conferences that developed gradually into the formal structure of Monthly Meetings and Associations. The morning of Thursday, 9 March, was spent in prayer and conversation with the members of the Cardiff society. At ten, Whitefield preached in the town hall to a large congregation, with Harris sitting close by. While he spoke, some thoughtless creatures were dragging the body of a dead fox about outside and trying to get foxhounds to hunt it and so disturb the meeting. Afterwards, the two Reformers, together with two Dissenting ministers, went to a service held in the church. Whitefield wrote in his journal of Harris:

> A burning and shining light has he been in those parts, a barrier against profaneness and immorality, and an indefatigable promoter of the true Gospel of Jesus Christ. About three or four years God has inclined him to go about doing good. He is now about twenty-five years of age. Twice he has applied . . . for Holy Orders, but was refused, under a false pretence that he was not of age, though he was then twenty-two years and six months. About a month ago he offered himself again, but was put off. Upon this, he was, and is still resolved to go on in his work . . . For these three years . . . he has discoursed about twice every day for three or four hours together, not authoritatively as a minister, but as a private person, exhorting his Christian brethren. He has been, I think, in seven counties, and has made it his business to go to wakes, etc., to turn people from such lying vanities. Many alehouse people, fiddlers, harpers, etc., . . . sadly cry out against him for spoiling their business. He has been made the subject of numbers of sermons, has been threatened with public prosecutions, and had the constables sent to apprehend him. But God has blessed him with inflexible courage . . . and he still continues to go on from conquering to conquer. He is of a most catholic spirit, loves all who love our Lord Jesus Christ, and therefore he is styled by bigots, a Dissenter . . . Many call and own him as their spiritual father, and, I believe, would lay down their lives for his sake. He discourses generally in a field, but at other times in a house, from a wall, a table, or any thing else. He has established nearly thirty Societies in South Wales, and still his sphere of action is enlarged daily. He is full of faith, and the Holy Ghost.[42]

We have quoted extensively from Whitefield's *Journal* because it gives much of Harris's history, and also demonstrates the warmth of Whitefield's affection for him. Harris felt exactly the same towards Whitefield. He says that he loved Whitefield, because Whitefield loved the Lord Jesus. Harris also preached in Cardiff at this time, with much power and authority. On Friday they left Cardiff and travelled to Newport. Whitefield was allowed the pulpit in the church there. Large numbers from Pontypool and other places came to hear him, and the congregation was counted as over a thousand. Harris went with him to Bristol. He was there, and in Bath where Griffith Jones was ministering at the time, from the Saturday to the Wednesday, preaching to the colliers in the field and to the societies also. No doubt the passion of his spirit and the Welsh fire within him, amazed the English and impressed them greatly. Before his return, Mr Seward gave him a gift of a watch as a token of their affection.

On Thursday, 16 March, Harris spoke at Whitchurch, some three miles from Cardiff; on Friday, at Pontypool; on Saturday, at Llanfihangel in the same neighbourhood. In the following thirteen days he preached at Mynyddislwyn, Bassaleg, Pentre-bach, St Bride's, Cardiff, Ynysangharad, Eglwysilan, Llanwynno, Aberdare, Cwm-y-glo, and Vaenor. On Thursday, 30 March, he was at Cantref, on the lower slopes of the Brecon Beacons, within a day's journey from home. Most probably he arrived at Trefeca the next day, after a journey of between three weeks and a month.

But there was no rest for the servant of the Lord. He had less than a week at home before he met with Whitefield on his second visit to Wales on 5 April, at Usk in Monmouthshire. The church was refused them there, and Whitefield preached from a table under the shade of a large tree, with Harris preaching in Welsh after him. The two men were followed to Pontypool by an escort of about fifty men. Here they obtained a church, but as there was not sufficient room for the crowd that had gathered they again preached in the open air. In the company of about thirty men on horseback, they continued to Abergavenny. Whitefield compared them to Joshua and his army taking possession of the land of Canaan. They had a congregation of about two thousand in the open air and, whilst preaching, did not spare the gentry who had come to mock. They had expected some rioting at Abergavenny, but no one dared open their mouths against them. From there they progressed to Cwm-iou, to the godly clergyman, Mr Jones. Their hearers were again too many for the church and they spoke in the cemetery. This was all the work of one day. On 6 April, they reached Caerleon in the company of about sixty horsemen. According to Whitefield, this was, 'A town famous for having thirty British kings buried in it, and producing three noble Christian martyrs.'[43] A pulpit had been raised in the open air here, when Howell Harris had last visited, and they both now preached from it. Thousands had gathered to hear them and again no one dared disturb the meeting, though they had beaten drums and shouted during Harris's previous visit. This proved to be a remarkable meeting. Whitefield wrote:

I prayed for him [Harris] by name, as I have in every place where I have preached in Wales. God forbid that I should be ashamed either of my Master or his servants. Many thousands were there from all parts to hear me, and God gave me such extraordinary assistance, that I was carried out beyond myself.[44]

He was probably referring to the fact that Harris was not ordained. The Gloucester Journal for 24 April 1730, attributes the huge numbers of the gatherings to Whitefield's attractive personality and also to the doctrine of the new birth which he preached. This emphasizes the fact that there was little mention of regeneration from the pulpits of the Church. From Caerleon they went to Trelech. The mounting-block outside the inn was the pulpit there. They were given use of the church at Chepstow, the last Welsh town which they visited on this journey, and on 9 April, they reached Gloucester.

In this city, all the churches were refused to Whitefield, one after another, though this was his native city. He took to the open air, with Harris at his side, and the gatherings frequently numbered three to four thousand. Whitefield's comments were:

> Cry out who will against this my forwardness, I cannot see my dear country-men and fellow Christians everywhere ready to perish through ignorance and unbelief, and not endeavour to convince them of both. Those who forbid me to speak to these poor baptized heathens that they may be saved, upon them I call to give a reason for their doing, a reason which may satisfy not man only, but God ... I am, and profess myself, a member of the Church of England ... I keep close to her Articles and Homilies, which, if my opposers did, we should not have so many dissenters from her. But it is most notorious, that for the iniquity of the priests the land mourns. We have preached and lived many sincere persons out of our communion. I have now conversed with several of the best of all denominations; many of them solemnly protest that they went from the Church, because they could not find food for their souls. They stayed among us till they were starved out.[45]

These are most solemn words, and we quote them because they became literally true of Wales. The Methodists, and the body of the nation with them, left the Established Church, not because of any strong views as to the relationship of Church and State, but because their souls were dying of hunger and thirst within it. There was a hunger for the gospel, and the Church was offering stones instead of bread. So the people went out into the fields, where the Word of God was being preached by faithful men. Howell Harris was one of the most loyal members of the Church of England, he never tired of stating it, but the immorality of life and indifference of the clergy forced him into being in the vanguard of a movement that emptied the churches up and down the land.

## HIS FIRST VISIT TO LONDON

Harris accompanied Whitefield to London. They preached in various places on the way and the fire and determined boldness of the Welshman proved of great benefit. In the neighbourhood of Bristol, Whitefield was frustrated in preaching by the antics and mocking of an actor, paid to silence him, and he was forced to give up. Harris jumped into the pulpit, and took as a text, 'The great day of his wrath is come; and who shall be able to stand.'

> The actor said, 'I am able.' 'What!' said Harris, with piercing eyes, bold countenance, and strong voice – 'What, such a poor contemptible worm as thou art!' Upon which the wretched man fell down – a peculiar awe and tremor having seized him, from which, it is said, he never recovered.[46]

The Reformers reached London on 25 April, and Harris stayed there until the beginning of June. While in the capital, he accompanied Whitefield frequently to the religious fellowship of the Moravians in Fetter Lane. Many good and godly men were members of this society, and amongst them many of the nobility, such as the Earl and Countess of Huntingdon; Sir John Phillips, the Welshman from Pembrokeshire, and brother-in-law to Griffith Jones; etc. Harris would have had fellowship after his own heart. The society was agitated at this time over the issue of lay preaching. Charles Wesley wrote in his journal:

> An argument arose as to the right of laymen to preach; many were zealous for it; but Mr Whitefield and I stood firmly against it.

Gradually, however, Whitefield moderated his views. In a letter to John Wesley, dated 25 June, 1739, he wrote:

> I suspend my judgment of Brother Watkins and Cennick's behaviour till I am better acquainted with the circumstances of their proceeding. I think there is a great difference between them and Howell Harris. He has offered himself thrice for holy orders; him therefore and our friends at Cambridge I shall encourage.[47]

Harris had placed the societies that he had established in Wales in the hands of faithful men who were to superintend them and send information as to their state to him in London. Amongst these were James Roberts; David Williams, Watford; Edmund Jones; and Henry Davies. James Roberts wrote to him on 17 April 1739, in a rather teasing letter:

> Dear Howell,
> Let me be a moment or two a little cheerful with you. You are a sort of Superintendent or Lord Archbishop in several counties; it is proper, therefore, your poor chaplain, who has obeyed your commands and written the letter of which a copy is herewith sent you, should inform you of his discharge of duty.[48]

The 'letter' was an exhortation to the societies at Longtown, Llandefa-then, Crugcadarn, and Gwendwr. Mr Edmund Jones wrote a letter to him on 21 May, 1739, from which we quote:

> I have been about your societies as a watch, to see both how they did, and whether the devil was attempting to mischief them or no; and I can say, blessed be God, I found all well . . . I have not had so much of God's presence in any journey I have made these several years. But especially was it well with me at Maesyronnen; whilst praying at Gwenddwr; during the Lord's Day at Tredustan, and Monday at Grwynefechan . . . The warrant against you is come to nothing. Counsellor Gwynne would not meddle with any of it, nor any of the Justices except the clergy Justices, and Price Davies was observed especially to be your adversary; but they were discouraged and seemed to be ashamed of it. Parson James, of Llanhamlwch, who was active against you, narrowly escaped drowning some time ago, which deserves notice. I desired the young people of the societies to pray especially for those gentlemen who stood for you.[49]

These letters reveal many interesting points:

1. That the Churchmen, especially the parsons, were again full of wrath against Howell Harris and eager to punish him if they could.

2. That the nobility were beginning to favour the revival, at least in some neighbourhoods.

3. That Harris had already established a number of societies that were quite independent of the Dissenting churches of the land and that, at this point, the Dissenting ministers were not envious of the situation.

## RETURNING TO WALES

In June, Harris bade farewell to his London friends and returned to Trefeca. After only a night's rest at his mother's home he set out for Abergavenny. The brethren's fellowship there was so sweet that he could not return home until late, and he then stayed up writing until one. The next day, he preached twice at Hay, Breconshire, and on the next, he faced an ungodly crowd at Longford, Herefordshire. When at the edge of the gathering he heard a man swear, he rebuked him severely. The rumour that Howell Harris had arrived passed through the whole town and soon a crowd of about two thousand stood around him. Later, he would write in his journal:

> The Lord gave me strength to attack the devil in his own country, he set my face like a flint, filling me with what to say. Especially, when I saw some of the gentlemen and ladies coming to hear, I was made stronger and stronger to reduce their pride.

He appealed also to the magistrates, and to the clergyman of the parish, asking them what sort of account they would give of their charge, as they supported swearing and drunkenness. Some of the gentry laughed. 'Pull the ranter down', said another. 'But my time had not yet come', wrote Harris. After preaching in many other places, he arrived at Pontypool, where he spoke on the courage of Daniel and the three youths, and of how the Lord stood by his people in the day of battle. But by now a spirit of persecution had arisen in Pontypool. A justice of the peace interrupted his sermon before one gathering by reading the Riot Act and instructing them to disperse within an hour's time. Harris promised that they would do so, but he asked the magistrate whether he was in the habit of reading the Act at the various sports and at the cock-fights. A constable was called to arrest him. Harris wished to go to the prison, but he was persuaded to provide a surety that he would appear before the Monmouth Assize. The following discussion took place between him and the magistrate:

> Harris: I did not expect that the son of Captain Hanbury would be the first to attack a congregation of peaceful Protestants, because he was a kind man.
>
> Magistrate: I receive my orders from above.
>
> Harris: Do you mean from heaven?
>
> Magistrate: No, I do not mean that.
>
> I then told him that I thought, if his majesty knew how loyal and harmless we were, he would not like him the better for suppressing us. Thus I parted with him, leaving some arrows in his conscience, by telling him that he must soon give an account of himself at an awful tribunal, but that I would pray for him, and he thanked me.[50]

This was in the middle of June, and the Assize at Monmouth was not until August. In the meantime Harris went to Bristol, and preached there to a Welsh congregation. There also he met with John Wesley for the first time. It seems that there was some prejudice in his mind against John Wesley because of the latter's rejection of the doctrines of election and perseverance in grace. It is possible that this prejudice had been confirmed by the influence of William Seward who had fallen out with Charles Wesley. Mr Wesley preached from Isaiah 45:22, 'Look unto me, and be ye saved, all the ends of the earth: for I am God, and there is none else.' He proclaimed the great truth of justification by faith so distinctly and clearly, together with the necessity, the privilege, and duty, of looking to Jesus for justification and strength; and such heavenly influence was felt in the meeting, that all of Harris's prejudice melted away, and though he disagreed with Wesley in later times, he never doubted that John Wesley was a minister of Christ. He visited him afterwards at the house where he lodged, and when he made himself known, Wesley fell on his knees to pray for him and for Griffith Jones and for Wales. The two remained friends all their lives.

After travelling through much of Wales, Harris returned to Monmouth for the Assize. He felt anxious and low in spirit. He knew that he had neither money nor friends to support a legal case and he feared that the persecution was an indication that he was not called to exhort and, just as the clergy were claiming, that he was running without being sent. But on arriving in the town, his heart was cheered. The Lord had put it into the hearts of many good men from London, Gloucester, and parts of Wales, to come to take up his cause. In the face of this general support and, no doubt, with the conviction that the law was against them, the justices allowed the case to fall, and Harris could leave with no fine or imprisonment. The event proved of great benefit to the revival. It was seen that it could not be put down by legal means. It produced a significant cheerfulness in Harris's heart also. His fears were removed and he was convinced that it was the Lord's will for him to itinerate and exhort sinners. No one rejoiced with him more than Whitefield. He wrote from Philadelphia:

> I congratulate you on your success in Monmouth. Within twelve months, if God wills, I would like to make use again of your field-pulpits. Our principles agree as one face answers another in a mirror.

Most of Howell Harris's labours in 1738 and 1739 were in Glamorganshire and Monmouthshire. We have already mentioned the effects of his ministry in Monmouthshire and East Glamorgan, and it seems that the same influences followed him to West Glamorgan. He was an instrument for awakening the land from one end to another. He ventured to the ungodly parish-wakes and fairs, striking fear into the hearts of the revellers. His name became a terror to the sportsmen, and he established a large number of societies. All this he did with hardly any human aid; he himself, together with God's presence, produced the revolution. He received very little help from the clergy or from the Dissenting ministers. We can refer to only a few of his exploits.

An account is given of a sermon at a fair in Crug-glas, near Swansea. The bustle of the fair was immense, the noise was enough to deafen all ears, and the fights were bloody and cruel. An ordinary man would have been overcome by fear, but the circumstances only quickened Harris's zeal. He stood up in the midst of the tumult with his countenance so fierce as to appear the very embodiment of the terrors of Sinai. He threw one look of scorn over the playing field and began to pray. Gradually, the solemnity of his face, his far-reaching voice, and the importunity of his prayer, gained attention. The tumult quietened as if oil had been poured on troubled waters. The players became ashamed and gripped by fear; they fled from the scene as if pursued by a horde of demons. When the harpist realized that he had been deserted, he also laid aside his instrument and was quiet. Present at the time was an ungodly creature known as 'Rog of Cadle' [Roger Rogers of Llansamlet]. It seems that an arrow lodged in his conscience but he did not leave his wicked ways. He knew that he was on a wrong road but he would not forsake it. It was said that he had spent all his money on his lusts, and did not now know how to continue. He imagined that the one whom he served so energetically should give him help, so he addressed the evil one:

> Well, I have been a faithful servant to you; let me see what kind of master you are; put some money in my hat.

He then placed his hat on the ground and left it for a while. Returning to it and finding it empty, he began to complain to the devil, saying, 'I see that you are a hard master after all.' What means were used to bring him to himself is not known. He went, one Sunday morning, to fetch hunting dogs ready for the Monday. It may be that he recalled Howell Harris's words while on the way. Whatever the means, he returned without the dogs and went to his bed, in unimaginable torments of guilt. He had been caught by a heavenly summons, and was chastized as with scorpions. He referred to this later in a song:

| | |
|---|---|
| When on my bed a-lying, | Pan oeddwn yn fy ngwely, |
| Upon a time, | Un prynhawn, |
| With all my thoughts on sinning, | Heb feddwl dim ond pechu, |
| Upon a time, | Un prynhawn, |
| There came his fiery arrow, | Fe ddaeth ei danllyd saethau, |
| The law with all its sorrow, | Y ddeddf a'i dychryniadau, |
| And cut me to the marrow, | I'm torri i lawr yn ddiau, |
| Upon a time, | Un prynhawn, |
| Despairing of tomorrow, | A gado'm holl bleserau, |
| Upon a time. | Un prynhawn. |

His conviction was severe. He would go to the seashore, lift up a handful of sand and begin to count the grains. 'I will come to an end of this task sometime,' he said, 'but as for eternity, that can never be counted.' He enquired of his old friends, but they knew nothing of any way of escape, they were all miserable comforters. He met with an old bailiff in Swansea and in the agony of his soul asked him, 'Do you know something of Jesus Christ?' The bailiff looked in amazement at him and went off without a word. But at last, wine and oil were poured into the wounds of 'Rog of Cadle', and the means blessed to that end was the ministry of the Rev. Lewis Rees of Llanbryn-mair, who had recently become the pastor at Mynydd-bach Chapel, Swansea.

We have included this story as typical of the experience of so many at this time. Another of the strong cedars that were cut down in 1739 was William Thomas of Pyle, when he was only a youth of sixteen years of age. He was convicted when hearing Harris preach at a place called Chware-lau Calch [Lime Quarries], near Neath, but he remained in this state for nearly four years afterwards before committing himself fully to the Lord Jesus. He subsequently became a well-known exhorter and a man of great usefulness.

An old man, called John Morgan, used to relate of Howell Harris coming to Waun-gron, not far from Gopa, on the border between Glamorganshire and Carmarthenshire. A parish-wake was being held there. The service had already begun by the time John Morgan, on his way to the revelries, arrived. When he was about a quarter of a mile away, the voice of the preacher was heard. 'It came with such authority,' he said, 'that I felt it passing into my bones on the spot.' He was converted, and many others, there and then. The respected old minister, Hopkin Bevan from Hirwaun, described Howell Harris coming once to Crug-glas. A man who was half-drunk approached him, encouraged by some wastrels, with a gun in his hand, and tried to shoot him. He tried a second and a third time, but the gun would not fire. 'Turn the muzzle in another direction,' commanded Harris. The man did so, and the gun fired. Soon afterwards, this man was found burnt to death in a lime-kiln where he had fallen in his drunkenness.

At about this time, or soon afterwards, and as a result of Howell Harris's labours in West Glamorgan, societies were formed at Palleg, near Ystrad-gynlais; Creunant, near Neath; Gopa, not far from Swansea; Neath; Hafod; Cnapllwyd; Llansamlet; and Dyffryn, near Margam.

In the beginning of December, he visited Pembrokeshire. This was prob-ably his first visit to the county. We do not have an account of the journey so do not know how far he travelled nor where he evangelized, but he refers to the visit in a letter to 'a sister in Momouthshire'. The letter is dated 30 November, 1739. He wrote:

> I am now in my way to Pembrokeshire, I lost my way on the hills last night – but the Lord remembered his covenant.[51]

We do not imagine that he stayed there long on this occasion. There was no end to his journeying at this time. He visited Cardiganshire, in the neighbourhood of Penmorfa; from there he went to Llanarth, and to Lampeter; he crossed Mynydd Mawr and preached at a small farmhouse amongst the reeds, called Brynare, near to the source of the River Towy. Within a week he was at Hereford, proceeding from there to Gloucester, through parts of Monmouthshire. His constitution must have been of iron and his zeal all-consuming.

## THE FIRST VISIT TO THE NORTH, AS FAR AS BALA

At the beginning of 1740 he set out for his first journey to the north. Mr John Evans, Bala, gives the date as 1739 and *Methodistiaeth Cymru* states that Harris's journal agrees with this date, but they are both mistaken. The journal, together with all the letters that Harris wrote during the journey, to Mrs James of Abergavenny, to Miss Anne Williams of Skreen, and to others, show that it took place during February, 1740. It is easy to explain how they were mistaken. Howell Harris followed the old church calendar. From January to 25 March he would date his letters with both old and new years so that his letter from Builth, his first on this journey, is dated 'Builth, Feb. 1, 1739-40.' He went on the invitation of Mr Lewis Rees, the Dissenting minister of Llanbryn-mair, who had come over the wild mountains with the one object of securing his promise.

As Mr Rees was the means of introducing Methodism to north Wales, it might be interesting to give a little of his history. He was born at Glynllwydrew in the Neath Valley, Glamorganshire, in the year 1710, and so was some years older than Harris and Rowland. His parents were members of the Nonconformist Church at Blaen-gwrach, under the care of the godly and unprejudiced Henry Davies. He was converted when very young. His intellectual powers and other abilities, his gift in prayer particularly, caused his parents to raise him with a view to the ministry. He had abundant educational advantages; he attended Joseph Simons's grammar school at Swansea; he was under Mr Rees Price at Bridgend; and lastly with the Rev. Vavasor Griffiths in Radnorshire. The latter said that he was a good enough scholar already and so encouraged him to take up the ministry immediately. At this time, the Rev. Edmund Jones passed by, having been on a journey to the north. He depicted the sad state of that part of the country, and he pressed Lewis Rees to take pastoral charge of the small flock at Llanbryn-mair, promising to return with him in order to introduce him to the people. Before arriving at their destination they lost their way and spent some hours wandering around the neighbourhood of

Coedfron. In this awkward situation, they talked much together of the things of the gospel and greatly enjoyed one another's fellowship. Their wanderings suddenly ceased when they came upon Llanbryn-mair at two o'clock in the morning. This was in 1734, about a year before the beginning of the Methodist revival and about six years before Howell Harris's first journey to Gwynedd. At this time the spiritual state of north Wales was lamentable. The gospel was preached in its purity in only very few places. The small church at Llanbryn-mair was in decline; the number of the faithful at Bala, where a cause had been established by the Rev. Hugh Owen, Bronclydwr, was very small; and the flock at Pwllheli were about to give up in despair. Mr Rees gave himself to preaching. He went to Pwllheli as often as he could, and to Bala once a quarter. He continued in the face of much discomfort and danger. The roads were long, mountainous and only barely passable. The weather was often cold and stormy and the inhabitants of Dinas Mawddwy and Llanymawddwy, the villages through which he had to pass, were determined to kill him, once they had understood his purpose.

Once, when he was preaching at Bala, a man called Meurig Davies, from the upper part of the mountainous parish of Llanuwchllyn, happened to be one of his hearers and was much pleased with the preacher and the sermon. He desired Mr Rees to come to his house to preach. He promised to go, and the time was fixed. On the appointed day he went, and found many of the neighbours assembled there, but all, both men and women, according to the custom of the country at that time, busily employed in knitting stockings. He took a Bible, and read a chapter, expecting the people would lay aside their work and attend to the Word of God; but they went on still with their work. He then endeavoured to explain some part of the chapter; but nothing prevailed with the hearers to lay aside their stockings. At last he thought he would attempt to pray, though he could have but little hopes that the congregation would join him. The last thing he observed, before engaging in prayer, was, the fingers of all the people busily employed with their knitting-needles; but though he had no encouragement from them to begin his prayer, he was abundantly assisted by the Spirit of God. He soon began to hear the groans and sighs of all around him, and perceived that there was much weeping among them. When he had finished his prayer, he learnt, with pleasure, that his hearers had been brought under such concern for the salvation of their souls, that (like the woman of Samaria, who left her water-pot) they had quite forgotten their employment, and had let their stockings, knitting-needles and all, fall to the ground. He now found his hearers in a suitable frame to attend to what he had to say, and experienced great comfort and enlargement in preaching to them. That sermon was made the power of God unto the salvation of many.[52]

After this, Morgan, Meurig's brother, who was a very strong man and well-known as a great wrestler, was very kind to him. He would accompany him through Llanymawddwy with a strong ash cudgel in his hand and if anyone sought to harm the preacher, he would shake the cudgel and say, 'Once I have seen the preacher home, I will come and talk with you.'

On many occasions a warrant was obtained to arrest Lewis Rees for going about to preach. Once, he was brought before Chancellor Owen, who was also the vicar of Llanor and Dyneio. When this gentleman realized that Rees had a licence to preach and that he could not send him to prison, he became incensed. He took hold of his sword, threatening to kill him, and in his rage cut the preacher's coat in shreds with his sword. At another time, Mr Rees was passing through Llanymawddwy and met with the parish clergyman, to whom he complained of the behaviour of his parishioners. The following conversation occurred:

'Where are you from?' asked the clergyman.

'I am from Llanbryn-mair, sir,' answered Lewis Rees, mildly.

'What brought you to Llanbryn-mair?

'The Dissenting congregation was without a minister. At their request I came to them, firstly on probation, and both sides being satisfied, I was appointed pastor over them.'

'How,' said his reverence, 'can you, being a Presbyterian, expect to be tolerated in this country? Go to Scotland. That is the Presbyterians' country.'

'I hope, sir,' said Mr Rees, 'that you act from a higher principle in religion than a regard to the custom of the country in which you happen to live; else, if you were to change your country you would change your religion: if you were to go to Scotland you would turn Presbyterian; if to Italy, a Roman Catholic.'[53]

The force of his reasoning, and the mildness of his answers, struck the cleric, and by his influence over his parishioners Mr Rees was not inconvenienced further from then on. Lewis Rees did immense good in the north. His spirit was quite free of prejudice and he continued to welcome the Methodists throughout his time at Llanbryn-mair. After labouring there for twenty-five years, he moved to Mynydd-bach, near Swansea. He died on 21 March 1800, at ninety years of age.

We must return to Howell Harris's journey to the north. It seems that before setting out he was undecided whether to go north, or to

Pembrokeshire. Very probably it was the importunity of Lewis Rees, together with the element of danger involved, that made him decide for Gwynedd. It seems that the gentry of Montgomeryshire had bound themselves with an oath that they would imprison any Methodist that would venture into their jurisdiction. This came to Harris's ears, and the boldness of his spirit and his zeal for his Saviour produced a fierce determination to brave the storm. On 1 February, he was at Builth, well on his way north. We will quote portions of his journal and of his letters so as to provide his history and to reveal his state of mind:

> When I came here [Builth] I found them singing, and a young gentleman was drawing a dead cat about in order to create disturbance, but was disappointed, the dogs would not hunt. I hope we had great power among us. I learn very sweet things here of Mr Gwynne; pray for him much.[54]

> Rhayader (8 miles from Builth) Feb. 3, 1739–40. My body is much tired having been enabled to labour hard, and 'tis now near four in the morning but there is something within that when 'tis put to actions, that makes us almost indefatigable ... Yesterday, I was enabled to discourse twice and travail 10 miles and write many letters, and today, 6 miles, I discoursed twice and 2 family duties [i.e. family worship] and write 6 letters. Tonight, I had the agreeable news that I am really to be taken in Montgomeryshire. I know that you'll rejoice and pray and praise God for me. They had a meeting there on that occasion and hitherto I find the Lord strengthening me in the inward man. The Lord did set 1 Peter 3:11 to 15 on the mind of a dear friend with me here, and he came and told me of them before I heard the news. The Lord cover my head in the day of battle. Tomorrow, I am going to Cwmteuddwr to the feast [of St Bride, patron saint of Llansanffraid Cwmteuddwr], and tomorrow night to part of Montgomeryshire. The Lord has given me many victories over Satan.[55]

> Llanbister (4 miles from Rhayader), Feb. 5, 1739–40. Yesterday was a glorious day and I was at a great feast. I chose to oppose the Devil on his own ground, and so I discoursed within a few yards to a public house where the diversion was to be. At first I was strongest, but at length, discoursing on Zaccheus' conversion, I endeavoured to draw them by love, but I had lost my authority. It was dead and dry till near the end. The Lord did lift up my voice like a trumpet and enabled me to declare home about the Lord's enemies. I never tasted more power. I believe some were cut through and many wept and one fainted. Others felt a great trembling, and all had an awe upon them. Afterwards, there being a burying, I went to Church and when we came out, I was afraid the Devil would bring them to the snare. I told them I would discourse in the town of Rhayader, a quarter of a mile away. And there they came, I believe almost all, except some few in the house, and I was helped to

discourse with less thundering and with more consolation . . . From there I
went to a place called The Lodge, in Llandinam, Montgomeryshire, where I
was enabled to discourse with power, last night and today. I met no opposition
again and many had a sweet opportunity. Many are kept from coming to hear
by a report passing for truth that I correspond with the King of Spain really,
and that there is £40 for taking me. Tomorrow, I expect to be taken, but if I
am I shall write immediately from my new lodging.[56]

Howell Harris had now planted his feet in Gwynedd and preached
at Llandinam. This was the first Methodist sermon in north Wales. The
above account shows the folly of some of the stories spread abroad about
him.

Llanbryn-mair, Saturday night, Feb. 9, 1739–40. Hitherto has the Lord stood
by me giving me more and more visible success. Satan seems to be chained. I
was in daily expectation of chains but had no opposition . . . Yesterday, I met
Mr Lewis Rees, and I never had such power in all my travails as I had last
night discoursing to about a thousand in Llanwnnog parish . . . you might hear
hearts broken to pieces. Such groans and tears, crying out, I seldom heard the
like. Many hearts I hope opened to Jesus Christ. I was almost carried out of
myself. O praise God for me . . . next Monday, I am going to Merionethshire
. . . Poor North Wales, they live here like brutes, knowing nothing.[57]

On his journey he passed through Llanidloes. He does not mention
the town in his letters but it is said in *Drych yr Amseroedd*[58] [*A Mirror of
the Times*] that he was allowed to preach in silence with no one disturbing
him. There was more persecution in later years at Llanidloes than in any
other Welsh town. He also preached at Trefeglwys, and it is said that this
was the occasion of the conversion of Lewis Evan, Llanllugan, a young
man of twenty-one years of age. Lewis Evan was a weaver; after his conversion he gave himself to the reading of the Bible and soon afterwards
took it about with him to read from house to house. He began gradually
to insert his own exhortation and to close with prayer, and became an
exhorter without knowing it, and without knowing either that any others
were acting in this way. It was a strange thing for the neighbourhood for
a young weaver to go about exhorting and his behaviour caused much
disturbance.

Howell Harris does not mention preaching at Llanbryn-mair in his letters, but he must have done so, and it is said that it was from outside an inn
called *The Wynnstay*. The news of him that had spread over the neighbourhood was that he was a man who had received a vision, and who travelled
about proclaiming what he had seen and heard. Among the crowd who
came to hear him here were three brothers, William, Edward and Richard

Howell, together with another man called Richard Humphrey. In order to hear more conveniently, they climbed on top of a small house nearby. The man of God began to preach and to point out the sins of the day, in his own severe and solemn way. They imagined that the preacher must know of them, and was pointing them out. They were forced by their consciences to descend from the roof, like Zaccheus of old from the sycamore tree, with the arrows of conviction having pierced all four men. This was the beginning of Methodism in Llanbryn-mair. After having said that he would delay going into Pembrokeshire because God had a work for him in Gwynedd, Harris continued the account in his letters:

Merionethshire, near Bala, Tuesday, Feb. 12, 1739-40. Yesterday, the Lord did me the honour of being once more taken prisoner in his work in Cemais parish in Montgomeryshire, by one Wynne, a Justice, who with another Justice and another gentleman with the minister, came upon us having sent their spies before; and the constable came to me and apprehended me. I have not yet had the honour of going to Montgomery in chains; they took cognisance of the facts, and oaths, and names, and intending to see if the law could reach me, telling they would do the utmost to fine me at £20; the man of the house £20; and the hearers 5 shillings a piece. They complained that I was breaking the Conventicle Act. I said that they could not prosecute me on that Act, that it was an Act for the Dissenters, while I was a Conformist of the established Church. 'We will be advised by the best lawyers,' they said, 'and if there is a law to be found, you will suffer its full severity.' I told them till they showed the law was against me, I should go about willing to suffer whatever they thought fit to inflict on me. The Lord filled me with courage and did not forsake me. Many tears were shed by the congregation and many had engaged to go to Montgomery. I returned with some dozens that had come with me to the place I was taken in, and discoursed with them about standing in time of tempest, etc. Today, I came twelve miles here. I discoursed twice on the way.[59]

I did alight in a little cottage via where I wrote this, and saw in an old woman, love to God's Word and to Christ and great simplicity and tender affections. I am afraid to follow my own will in anything, I rejoice at knowing that I am the servant of another, and there is great peace in submitting to God in all things. I felt my heart warm to the old woman – she said that God would draw to us if we drew near to him. She was very grateful and saw herself as all sin, she had a strong love to Christ, I found my heart open to give to her three shillings out of love to Christ and two shillings to the man of the house. I found a greater delight to be in her house than in a palace. I did eat a little hard oaten thick cake and cheese, then went on to Meurig David, Gweirglodd Gilfach.

From thence, towards Llanymawddwy, I was hooted along as I went by. The children and others, crying and running after me, 'Down with the Rumps, etc.' Satan roared and was very bitter. I felt no disturbance in my soul, but I prayed for them, and pitied them – though not so much as I would have liked. And I could not get myself back to that sweet state of mind which I had before.

When I came near the Church, there was a crowd of grown persons and boys met together. As soon as I, and the man with me, came into sight they hallooed, 'Down with the Rumps, etc.,' and got the dogs together to run at us. When I saw them, I felt my soul perfectly willing – so also have I felt along all the way – I had great encouragement to continue, I discoursed without fear, and had liberty of thought. When I came there, a woman (called, as I found, a gentlewoman) asked me what I wanted here, a damned devil, and with that got some wire and a clod of earth (stones being fast by frost) and threw it at me, but I saw here more of Satan's malice than I received of hurt.

They cried after me when I was gone, but while I went by, the Lord chained them and stopped their mouths.

Afterwards, I came to Llanuwchllyn Church (a little town by Bala Pool), in all about twelve miles. Something like fear came upon me on hearing I was approaching the town but by determined thought I was quietened. My meditations were too light, and O how little of God is in my thoughts! I had some sweetness of soul on seeing God's goodness in giving things to me, and I found myself praying, 'O Lord, do not let me sin in will or thought.'

Afterwards, my head aching, almost starving, I came there at almost five. There I was ashamed, here had been a very great congregation and were gone away. I discoursed to six, on St. Paul's conversion. Was enabled here to evangelize with power and many wept. Answering all doubts and objections and calling all to Christ. I had sweet liberty to discourse to broken hearts, persuaded hearts.

I was then given grace to pray to God's Spirit, that I might sing and pray, and love and speak, and live in that spirit, and O, how necessary this is!

Afterwards, I went to the house. There a spirit of lightness came on them. O, how soon is the word taken from the heart. Eating, etc., to near eight. Then the Lord opened a door for me to discourse to them and they gave ear. Many wept. I had a door (it being in a public house) opened to read and explain Romans 12, and to sing and to pray. They seemed to be loving, harmless people here. Was helped to be faithful. Writing a letter to past ten; in private to past eleven, crying with some concern on reading Acts 2:17, 18. 'O, give me of thy Spirit; O, give me of thy Spirit, that I might praise and honour thee.

O God, can I be happy while thy glorious Majesty is dishonoured by myself and others? Dear Lord, why do I place such little worth on thy love? I thank thee for the knowledge of thyself which thou hast given to others. O God, when will I come to know and love thee? O what wonder that thou shouldst perform so many wonders for me, and I yet without love for thee!'[60]

Llanuwchllyn (near Bala), Merionethshire, Wednesday, Feb. 13. Awoke early. Up at eight. I am still far from God, and yet unhappy without him. I went to secret prayer, and prayed long in words, from the head and from the understanding, but not from the heart. I could not find sincere desires to do good. But at last, while waiting there, and afraid to follow my own will without God, the Lord enabled my soul to cry, 'O Lord, I am here, far from thee, and in a strange land. Let me have thee as my portion; I renounce all other things. Give them to whomsoever thou willest, but let me belong to thee. O Trinity, I give myself to thee.' From nine until ten, I discoursed to some hundreds of people. I began by showing from Romans 7 – as I did the previous night when discoursing on St. Paul's conversion – that when God's grace comes to the heart, we are drawn:

1. To see the corruption of our nature; how body and soul are wholly polluted; our unreadiness to do good, and our readiness to do evil. (I showed this from their own experiences.)
2. To see that the sense of this impossibility to do good is a pain and a great grief to the soul.
3. They cannot be quiet without seeking relief. 'Who shall deliver me from the body of this death?'
4. As we see from Romans 8:2, when the soul looks diligently for escape Christ reveals himself, to liberate the soul from guilt and corruption of sin and the chains of darkness.

And here, I had great light to show:

1. That we are under the law while we remain under ourselves. I was granted to understand more of the law than ever before; I showed how God cannot forgive the trespassing of his law until he obtains satisfaction for his righteousness. 'Would you not condemn, and consider unjust, that judge who pardoned a lawbreaker of obvious guilt, without requiring any recompense for the law?'

2. That God cannot look upon us until our natures are changed, and we cannot delight in him. Could a man and wife agree, if one loved what the other hated? So we cannot be one with God if we love lust, pride, avarice, drunkenness, darkness; which things God hates; and while we cannot love the holiness and purity which God loves. Therefore, either God must lose his attributes of righteousness and purity, or we must be delivered from the guilt and nature of sin, before we can stand before him.

3. That the darkness must be removed from our eyes; that we might see death in ourselves, and life in Christ; darkness in us, and light in Christ; filthiness in us, and purity in him; weakness in ourselves, and power in him. But we must feel how wretched we are before we will go to him, and he must be united to us by a living faith, or there will be no more benefit to us to hear of justification by faith and the misery of those without Christ, than if we were to listen to a physician when ill, but not take his medicines. I was given power, and when I came to this place I saw that many were feeling to the quick, and I was able to preach sweetly. A delightful shower came upon us as I told them that I could not deceive them. I then told them of the great privileges of those who accept Christ. Those who possess Christ possess all things; and those who do not have him, have nothing. General exhortations. Praising God. False hopes are vanity. When God is teaching and providing strength, to work is sweet, and it is easy. As we feel the first Adam in us, so also we must feel the second Adam. In secret prayer, I found that the desire of my soul was to be faithful, and to glorify the name of him who sent me. May God perform his will in me. And O, how can I be happy, while people dishonour and forget God.

Writing to near twelve, and then to Bala, five miles. Could not get my soul to meditate on any matter on the road, only light thoughts – this is what I would always be except for grace.

Came there before two, and discoursed to near four to some hundreds. While I discoursed many laughed at each other, and there was a gun shot twice at my side.

I overheard one damn himself, if he knew I was a Presbyterian, I should not discourse. I told them I was of the Church. (I discoursed in the street by the Hall, it was like to discourse on the cock-pit). I began on the Catechism, the Baptismal Vow, the two duties to God and man, and the Sacrament Office. I had yet no great authority, but tender to bring them in, if I could. Many gave no ear, others wept. Discoursed on Luke 19:12. Had authority to speak to them of their sins. Was given great light, as in the house before coming out, of clearer knowledge; and showed the evil of sin as it is sin against the goodness of God, to the conviction of many, I hope. I fear that no great good was done here, but I had strength to be faithful.

Afterwards, in private, eating, etc., to five. Then I discoursed to six. [Showing] how the Lord carries on the work gradually, step by step. I sought to assist their minds to see their wretchedness; I showed how Satan and the world conspire against us when we begin to change within and without, and how the soul may obtain strength to withstand them; and I recited to them the history of my own conversion. I had sweetness, and strength to be faithful. And I cried in secret, 'O Lord, let me always feel thee in me, and give me strength to be faithful to thee, dear Lord.'

Afterwards, parted in great love. Toward Talar-ddu, five miles. I had a view on the way of the misery of those who die without Christ, but could not press it closer upon my soul. I see that I am but sin, dead and all dark; I have only sin and wretchedness; I can do nothing but forget God all the time; I know nothing, except what is given me.

I had a deep concern set on me for mother, to plead for her with pity and concern. O Lord, snatch her from misery. O that I may see her changed. O give her thy Spirit, and kill her unbelief; set her free; reveal thy dear Son in her. Let me see clear signs of a change in her, and in my own poor soul. O Lord, enlighten my mind; and hear me for my brethren's sakes. Will they be allowed to continue in their sins, and in rebellion against thee? Remember #, who is part of my soul.[61] And do not call me to eternity while dead in my sins.

I had a view of the awful condition I would have been in to all eternity, and the thought of how righteous God would be in doing this caused me to humble myself in the dust before him. And then, I was shown the tenderness of God towards me in comparison to others. Could I not have trained to be a soldier, and been left to myself, or been a persecutor? O, what am I, that I am loved by thousands? Woe is me if I do not glorify God. O Lord, I fear sin. Make me one who is led on by love. Draw my whole love to thee, and do not let me rest until I know for certain that I belong to thee, and thou dost belong to me more and more fully. And O, let this remain with me to feel fresh love, and a desire to glorify God.

Arrived at Llanuwchllyn, and stayed there till eight; I then turned towards home, and # was much in my thoughts. O Lord, give me an assurance that thou art a God to me, and that I am thine in all things.

I was somewhat low in spirit on seeing that Christ is light and life and purity, and on seeing how little of each of these is in me. I fear that he is not in me – but yet there are degrees, and who is it who raises my thoughts? O that I might be forever thankful.

On the way, had clearer views of the greatness of God. This majesty was before my eyes the whole time: 'Which alone spreadeth out the heavens.' I was in amazement at the thought that he would consider dust; and at seeing the wonder of his eternal love in sending his Son, I lost myself in admiration. O draw me completely to love thee.

Before arriving at Llanuwchllyn, I was weary, body and spirit, and my natural strength was failing. I discoursed on the excellency of faith:

1. As it is the key to unlock God's treasures of grace in Providence.
2. As it is the hand of the soul to receive from God.
3. As it is the foot to run after God when he is withdrawing, and to follow him when he is drawing us.
4. As it is the eye to see Christ, and every grace treasured up in him.
5. As it is the ear to hear Christ's voice in everything.
6. As it is the voice and tongue of the soul.
7. As it is the soul's seed.
8. As it digests spiritual food.

I tried to show the power of Christ's love, but I had to leave off. Went to bed about midnight.[62]

Talar-ddu in Llanuwchllyn Parish, Merioneth. Thursday, Feb. 14. Up before seven; having dreamed last night. Had some desires set in me that God would go with me and give me holy meditations on the way today (having on their computation sixteen miles), so that I might see that my fellowship is with the Father, and with the Son. I desired well, but do not feel sufficient emptiness in my soul to receive God. Surely no one ever had such a nature that found it so hard to turn to God, and to believe the Bible and delight in it. I then came to read the Bible, but little of it with my heart; but he had compassion upon me and follows me with his love. No one possessed more of Satan than myself, no one is so hard to affect, but the nature of grace is wondrous – the grace that made hypocrisy into honesty and integrity, that made the greatest hate into love, the grace that made the greatest pride into humility, the grace that made the greatest lust into purity, the grace that raised me from the dunghill to honour. O that I might praise it forever!

Having eaten and prayed in family before eight, came toward Machynlleth, sixteen miles. As soon as I was outside, my soul was given importunity and cries, and intreaty for poor north Wales, 'O Lord, give them knowledge. O have mercy upon them. Dost thou not see the thick darkness that is amongst them everywhere? O dear Lord, do not refuse my entreaty; send knowledge to them by some means or other.'

I could not bear to be refused but was made to continue with much importunity. After some sleepiness, I prayed again, but I am far from God. Then I thought of my visit to Machynlleth today, and I cried, 'If I knew, Lord, that I was going to dishonour thee, I can say, by grace, that I would not go. There is enough dishonouring of thee without me dishonouring thee also. Do not allow me to be amongst those who are against thee. Though I gave way to idle thoughts, and though these dried up my soul, O give thyself to me, and then let me be what thou wilt, feeling my soul weaned from all else, and being able to think for a while of the perfections of God. Put thy nature in me, I fear nothing but sin. Let there be no will in me but thine; teach me to glorify thee in everything.

I came to Dinas Mawddwy (a town eight miles from Machynlleth). They seemed to be a little more tender here, and said they would be glad to hear me. Then I resolved to discourse there. Went to discourse to some few of them that came together. Some laughed. All had their hats on. Others went by and took no notice, and others cried, 'I hear enough in church.' (This is a dreadful place. They owned that on the Sabbath there are many hundreds dancing, playing at tennis, swearing, and all rioting, etc. So it is in Mawddwy churchyard, etc.) I had no authority, nor fixed on one place, but discoursed in general about Dives, judgment, eternity, common sins, etc., but no authority. I left off when I saw some running up, thinking they were come to disturb, but

I found they were coming to hear. I discoursed a little again, and had some tenderness, but very little. I had no effect upon them, my spirit was brought low. I was willing for them to trample me underfoot, but I had compassion upon them, and some anxiety for God's cause. I had a spirit of compassion to pray, feeling low and very humble.

From thence at half past twelve, towards Machynlleth. I had again, as before, a spirit to beg for north Wales. I met a poor young man that was well disposed and we had sweet discourse together. I felt I loved him, and was enabled to exhort him. He had God's fear in him but was ignorant of Christ.

The little boys ran after me today to halloo. This week, until now, Satan has had some time of liberty. I was deserted and low in my spirit. I grieved as I heard them taking God's name in vain, and cried, 'O Lord, how long wilt thou suffer us? Stand for thyself, for thine own house. Gird up thy loins, Lord, defend thy glory. Dost thou not see that the clergymen are against thee? Dost thou not see that the leaders are rising up against thee? O God, be with me. Let everything that grieves thee, grieve me; and everything that delights thee, delight me. My strength was renewed, but I was still weak. I felt some communion with God, but I was too careless in my meditations.

Came to Machynlleth a quarter past three. Did alight at the Excise Office. There I was met by an old gentleman drunk, who seized me, despising me, and asking impertinent questions, etc., but had no commotion, etc. I heard the language of hell – men damning themselves, etc. – about my ears, and the mob gathered themselves to play at foot ball. Having a little refreshed myself, I went out intending to go to a common just by. The Lord had prepared three or four friends to be here to guard me, who had got a place for me in another house, in a little door that opened from an upper room above stairs. I stood within, looking to the street. I did not, as I ought in a place of such danger, seek the Lord, but went to begin on our covenant vow in Baptism, but they were so enraged they would not hear. A minister (Mr Griffiths of Penegoes, a Dissenter's son from Cardiganshire) and an attorney, Lewis Hughes, and a gentleman, Mr Thomas Owens, seemed to be set on fire of hell by Satan. They enraged so that one could see fury in every face. The mob enraged and did fling stones, earth and old bones, etc., at me, but the Lord did not suffer one to touch me. I have cause for shame for my carelessness in not seeking the Lord, and especially for not exercising faith. I was weak and could have no words, but at last they eased a little, and then I had a little authority. I spake a little of the great mortality among them, many throwing at me, and the minister and attorney roaring, threatening the constables on me if I would not give over, and one stirring up the mob. I felt that God had not called me here, or that I had transgressed. I was afraid that I had been proud, but here, my pride has been pulled down. I had help to tell them to look to it, that great men would not stand in the judgment in their position.

When I continued to discourse, the attorney, in great fierceness and violence ran up, with his mouth filled with oaths, damning terribly, and came to the room where I was, seemingly to drag me down. I spake to him fair, and asked him how unreasonable it is to be thus passionate, without a reason. I was obliged to give over, none could hear. Then the gentleman came up from without the door, in the greatest violence, and shot a pistol out among us, and roared. Then I went downstairs, seeing I was in danger. I went with five friends to a private room. They came about the window and roared again. I saw I was now in hell, fighting with beasts in Ephesus. I went out, intending to go away, but in the crowd I found my life in danger, expecting to be stabbed privately. In the crowd I had already had two private kicks, and made a public laughing stock. They, in ridicule, calling me, 'Parson, etc.' Death appeared many ways.

I had a private room again from a friend and we bolted the door. They so roared without that I expected to see death when I would come out. I strove here to seek God, but was deserted. I see now, on the trial faith is weak. I desired they would not murder us, then we opened the door and went among them, and the Lord saved my life and inclined them to suffer me to go, when I said I was going away.

When I asked for peace in the King's name, one said I should not have any hurt, another said, when they were trampling me, to all purpose, to consider he is a fellow creature, etc. I then took horse, and went the back way, but was obliged to come through the upper end of the town again in any way, and there they were all to meet me again. One ran toward me through the field, taking up two clods. I desired he would not kill me, but he cast one at me and that failed. The other he cast just by my head. Then I went through the middle of them and the stones were flung after me, but the Lord saved me and none touched me. One man ran with a staff, level with me, to strike after me with renewed fury, but the Lord enabled the horse (though before tired) to gallop, and so I escaped. But my friend was on foot among them, and I did not feel love drawing me back to save him, though I could have done nothing. But the Lord saved him and all the rest. When I came to them, my friends, three or four called after us, but I was suspicious of them. At last, I stayed for them, and I think they were some come to take me in my words, asking me about my living, and what makes me go about, etc. When I went to private, the Book opened on 2 Timothy 4:17, 18.[63]

I tried to seek the Lord, but he had withdrawn; I could not find him, but I could cry, 'Lord, I will not go from here unless thou look upon me,' O how comfortless we are unless the Lord come of himself. His withdrawal from me caused me to look to myself, and I saw that everything was wrong:

1. I had not had a clear call to come here.
2. I did not conduct myself, I am afraid, for God's honour; and I see that I will not, unless God upholds me every second, and unless I am taught of God. But I was encouraged to think that I had done, if not what I should have done, at least what came to my mind to do.
3. I did not expect sufficient from God, and I broke the commandment, 'Fear

not them which kill the body.' But I yielded to carnal fear, I spoke gently to God's enemies, I saw myself full of self-love, taking more care for my life than for God's cause, and concern for his honour did not fill my heart.

All these things came to my mind; but as I waited for God, he remembered mercy; though I was for so long as hard as a stone, without love, hard and cold, with my heart boiling over with bitter thoughts about God. I had help to lay the whole matter before God, and to plead with him, feeling some of the guilt that so hardened me. I could not leave off – I expected, I hoped on seeing the gentleness of Christ – and my soul was in chains. At last, I was released, and I was enabled to cry with some concern, on remembering that I had fallen in Adam, and lost his image; 'Will thine image never more be seen upon me? O dear, glorious Lord! Is it not enough for thee what Christ did for me? Turn away from me the face of justice, and look upon me in mercy in Christ. O look upon his blood!'

My mind was freed to pray over all these things, but I could not find importunity. 'O Lord, dear Lord, I long to be with thee. O how long must it be before I may come! O, I long, I long. Take me, gain the victory over me completely. I am sure there is no devil in hell who deserved hell more than me, but thou hast mercy – wash me in the blood of Christ, seal me as thy child.'

I then recovered my soul, to utter sweet words of love and gratitude. I then went to my brethren. We prayed and sang about seven. After this, I went to my friend's house and was there till ten, then to bed.

I learnt from today:

1. How the Lord is angered, and how he shows his patience in my suffering.

2. How much rebellion there is in Satan, when so much agitation is seen in men, notwithstanding all restraints – conscience, human laws, hope, shame, etc.

3. That I must always be thankful for such restraints for the privilege of speaking and living for God.

4. How I am when deserted, so ready to look down. How good for me that he always keeps hold of me, otherwise I would very soon lose my hold on him.

5. How strong is Satan's rage against me; and all this must be his rage, for there was nothing else to incite the people against me. They calling me a Pretender, and the author of this disturbance, and if they had led me out they intended in mock to have carried me in a chair about the town.

He then notes his thoughts and prayers until he slept, a little before one o'clock in the morning.

Rhiwgriafol Farm, near Penegoes Parish, Montgomeryshire, Friday, Feb, 15, 1740. Body tired, having travelled yesterday twenty miles, I lay to near nine. Dreamt that I did receive the Sacrament with the Dissenters and the memory remained sweet in my soul. O, how lacking in energy I am; and when

I am down, how can I arise? And faith, grounded on the promises, gave me strength to wait for an answer, because God has promised, and Christ is in heaven. I argued thus, as on the previous evening.

Afterwards, I exhorted to near eleven. I had some help while in prayer. And it was sweet to exhort on laying the foundation deep, and of the unreasonableness of persecution. Many verses came to my mind saying that we shall suffer persecution here. I was helped to speak, I hope, without respect of persons, and with tenderness.

From here he went to Talerddig, and it was night in his soul as he travelled. He could no more believe than he could fly, but he succeeded in praying. He preached on Peter's fall, quoting verses from his beloved Letter to the Romans. He evangelized and there was 'much weeping'. In the middle of writing his account of the sermon, he notes:

I find so much wickedness in my heart that I cannot share it all with my brother, Lewis Rees. When one asked me where to go to receive communion, I could not tell her to go to him, because I would like to have societies in our own church; but when I see that God does not will this, I submit. I cannot go one step before his Spirit.

After anticipating that his faith would be tested; much enjoying the preaching; mentioning a 'carnal clergyman'; he proceeded to Cwmcarne, where he discoursed powerfully on the activity of Satan and other matters. When in prayer, Lewis Rees was given much light, but Howell Harris was still dark. Yet, he still felt something supporting him.

I spent some time organizing where to go next week. I felt a strong desire to go home; I had a longing to pray that I might return and see my mother and #. But I was persuaded, against my feelings, to take another route, out of compassion for souls.

We hope that readers are not wearying of the journal. We quote it so extensively as it sheds a strong light on the condition of the country and the circumstances surrounding the Reformer's efforts to evangelize his compatriots; but particularly because it illustrates the nature of his experiences, the low spirits that often assailed him, his longings for God, and his warring against unbelief and the corruptions of his heart. It might be thought that after so much weariness and persecution he would be longing for rest, but his comments next day at Llanbryn-mair are involved with arranging new engagements. He writes:

I propose to preach in this county until Tuesday. On Friday night, I intend, if God wills it, to sleep in the home of my dear mother, and to preach there on Sunday morning.

He then arranged to meet with friends at Dol-y-gaer on Saturday night and to continue then to Cwm-iou, in the mountains between Abergavenny and Talgarth, in order to hear the evangelical clergyman Thomas Jones. He would preach in the afternoon, near Cwm-iou, and return to Abergavenny to sleep. Then he proposed to speak on Monday at Llandeilo, near Abergavenny, and on Monday night at Goetre, near Pontypool; on Tuesday at William Powell's school, and Tuesday night at Transh; on Wednesday, at Llanafan, near to the home of an old man who was anxious to meet him; and at Brooks on Wednesday night. From there, he would go to Llangynidr on Thursday morning, and arrive back at Trefeca in the evening. He intended to preach at Trefeca on the Friday morning, spend the Sunday in the Brecon area hearing the Rev. Thomas Lewis, a young clergyman who was a good preacher, and then to set out from Brecon on a long journey through Pembrokeshire. His spiritual zeal seems almost to lift him above the exigencies of the body, nor did he count his own life dear if he could but fulfil some service for Christ his Saviour. At the same time, he was anxious over the condition of Montgomeryshire, 'I fear that this county is under a curse; I find that most, if not all the gentry are enemies.'

## FURTHER JOURNEYS, AS DESCRIBED IN HIS JOURNALS

In the next few weeks Howell Harris carried out all his prearranged plans. He started for Pembrokeshire on a Monday morning in March 1740, preaching three times during the day. A fair was in progress at Trecastle; he preached at its centre, with authority. Satan tried to frustrate him by setting up one to ask him questions, another to ring a bell, and a third again to make various noises. But they were all unsuccessful. After his sermon was over, they arranged a dance in the cemetery. His spirit would not allow him to leave while a dance was in progress; he strode in amongst them and so thundered the curses of the divine law in their hearing that they all fled. Throughout the following week he travelled about ten miles, and preached three times, every day, until, on the Saturday night, he arrived at the home of Mr Griffith Jones at Llanddowror. He spent the Sunday with him and Madam Bevan and, according to his journal, their fellowship was a sweet feast to his soul. On Monday, he was at Llwyndrysi, in the parish of Llangan, Carmarthenshire, and on Tuesday he arrived in Pembrokeshire.

At this time, Pembrokeshire was in the same condition of immorality, ignorance and superstition as the rest of the Welsh counties, if not indeed, more superstitious. It is said that the inhabitants went to church on Easter morning in their stockinged feet, for fear of disturbing the ground. On Christmas Day they would arise before dawn to look at the rosemary bush and to swear that it was in bloom; but somehow the blooms would never remain to the break of day. They believed that spirits would be in the church on New Year's Eve announcing the names of all those in the parish who would die in the coming year. A few brave individuals would listen under the chancel window. On their own they would hear the names listed, but whenever they took a companion the voices failed. On May Day there would be much excitement about 'wearing the beech'; crowds would gather together, and the end would always be drunkenness and fights. Even the earth suffered through the ignorance of its inhabitants.

Agriculture could hardly be said to exist in the county; the land received little or no cultivating. A little wheat seed would be thrown here and there, on clearings that were easiest to plough; but there would be no hedge or ditch around them and in the summer it would be the work of the inhabitants to watch over them and drive off animals. Even the land was indebted to the revival. Some Independent and Baptist churches had been planted in the county in the previous century and baptism, it seems, had been a bone of contention and a source of bitterness amongst them ever since the great public debate of the topic on the slopes of the Frenni Fawr in 1692. Harris's journal is full of references to the arguments over the issue, and it clearly grieved his heart. We will follow his course through the county with the help of his journal and letters.

Trefhowell, Llanfrynach Parish, Pembrokeshire, Tuesday: The first thing he did after rising from his bed was to pray for John Powell, a local Baptist minister probably, in whom he believed a good work had begun, but whom he feared would be led astray and do harm. He then asked that he might be heard on behalf of the Baptists generally, amongst whom he was confident there were many of God's people, but he doubted whether their condemning spirit was from God. 'Sweeten them mildly with thy love',[64] he prayed, 'that they may be a pure people for thee.' He next prayed for the Methodists, that they might be kept from heresies; and then for all ministers of the Word. He acknowledged that he was completely out of order and unique in his position, but yet obtaining an open door to minister. 'Perform, O Lord, thy will towards me. Do not let me go in my own strength or in my own understanding.'

He was pressed to speak on a controversial topic, baptism no doubt, but he would not, because of the love that filled his heart. Instead, he attacked corruption, as it manifested itself in the forms of pride, drunkenness, lust and avarice.

In the afternoon of the same day, Harris travelled to Maenclochog, and on the road his spirit was affected by a conversation on Enoch Francis, a late minister amongst the Baptists. He grieved over the loss to the Baptists resulting from his death and prayed that Satan would gain no inroads amongst them, now that Mr Francis had been removed. Enoch Francis was an excellent preacher who had a firm hold on evangelical truth. It was his influence predominantly that had kept the Baptist Churches in Wales from Arminianism, as had occurred to many of the Presbyterian churches. On arriving at Maenclochog, nobody was waiting for him; they had not heard of his coming. But within an hour a congregation of many hundreds was gathered, and he preached for three hours. Before beginning he had a fierce encounter with Satan, but the Lord gave him victory over the enemy, enabling him to cry, 'Satan, do your worst! In Jesus's name, I challenge you! I will pull down your kingdom and will make bare your deceits.' In the first half of his sermon he thundered against the evil of the heart; he then turned to show that this was the reason why they should come to Christ. 'At this,' he wrote, 'many wept bitterly; and great power manifested itself amongst us from then to the end.' Before leaving, he encouraged believers not to enter into controversy and fight one against another, but to unite in their efforts against the enemy.

Howell Harris met here with the Rev. John Powell, for whom he had prayed in the morning, 'and I was enabled to rejoice heartily at his success.' In the evening, he departed for Haverfordwest, preaching at the roadside on the way. On arriving, he heard that a certain M— P— was preaching against the baptism of infants, and felt his spirit stirred by a desire to take up argument against him. But on reconsidering, he broke out in prayer, asking the Lord to rule his heart and spirit. He heard also that if he went to St David's he would be taken into custody, for a Justice Vaughan had signed a warrant to that purpose; 'All I heard,' he wrote, 'worked sweetly on my soul to draw me more out of self to Christ.'[65]

On Wednesday he was at Haverfordwest. As he communed with God in the morning, he thought:

> I am asking for help only in order to be faithful to my Lord; the fact that I am trampled underfoot is in no way painful; I fear nothing except that I through my work might dishonour thee.

Harris hoped that the Lord would use John Powell to awaken the county, and that he himself would be enabled to do everything possible to strengthen Powell's hands. He preached to many hundreds, his own estimate being two thousand. On the same day he preached in English for nearly two hours. The sermon's theme was that religion involves power, as illustrated in the conversions of Zaccheus and Paul. He experienced great power whilst preaching:

> The Lord filled my mouth with words; my voice was raised up; my spirit was made strong; I hope that authority accompanied, and that I was enabled to look up to God.

He preached again in Welsh on the same theme. Both services gave him much pleasure, but particularly the Welsh one. Afterwards, he conferred with friends as to the route to take through the other parts of the county.

He was still at Haverfordwest on Thursday, visiting the Rev. Evan Davies,[66] who had been listening to him. Their fellowship was so sweet that Harris cried out, 'Glory!'

> I had a long conversation with him on various matters. He called sanctification the condition of salvation; I acknowledged that there could be no salvation without it, but that I was not willing to call it a condition, in case people were sent to look for it in themselves and not in Christ, thinking that they will not be received unless they possess it. We are justified for Christ's sake, and are saved through seeing the great love of God in giving his Son. We talked of feeling, and the means of proving its genuineness by the change it effects upon our souls and lives; of the necessity of faith before works; of the danger of morality without principle; of the danger of being deficient in poverty of spirit, causing us to despair of ourselves, and to draw us out of ourselves to Christ; and the means by which we are justified in God's sight through Christ, and not because of our repentance and good works.

Harris felt that he had strong reasons for seeking a deeper understanding of the Scriptures. 'We parted sweetly,' he wrote. As he left Haverfordwest he heard such dreadful news of the moral state of the county – that drunkenness, prostitution, swearing, and similar evils were prevalent – that he did not know what he could do.

On Friday, Harris was at a place called Loveston, about seven miles from Haverfordwest. Here again he referred to the Baptists, and it seems as if his feelings towards them had undergone a complete change:

> I had strong feelings when praying for John Powell. It was once that I could not love the Baptists, nor rejoice in their success; but now, all the chains have been shattered; I feel love towards them, and pleasure in their success; and great is the heaven I enjoy in this.

He preached here again, both in Welsh and in English, on the Fall that we experienced in Adam, and on the love of Christ. He hoped that many were convicted in heart during the service. He went from there to the house of a Quaker in Llanddewi parish. 'While I am still this side of eternity,' he wrote, 'let me never offend one of thy children, of any party or denomination.' He preached here on the power of godliness, from the words, 'Thy kingdom come.' He lodged at the house of the Quaker, and it seems that the fellowship the two enjoyed was particularly sweet. Harris hoped that he would never speak harshly of these people again.

On Saturday, Harris was at Bullhook, near Clarbeston. He spoke with much authority on the necessity of grounding our hope on the blood of Christ, and the meeting continued for over two hours. 'O that God would have pity on this county,' he says, 'I am leaving the place in order to study, following the advice of my friends, as it appears that this is the will of God.' It is seen that the possibility of seeking episcopal ordination is still in his mind. From here, he goes to a place that he does not name and where a crowd of at least three thousand had gathered. He had great power when praying, and then preached on, 'Thy kingdom come,' comparing and contrasting the two kingdoms. He was at Wolf's Castle on the Sunday, where he spoke on justification. He preached in the afternoon also but without much authority. Many thousands then gathered to hear him at a place called Trecomau. On the Monday, he was at Trecadwgan, in the parish of Whitchurch. He was very tired while praying but the Lord strengthened him to some extent. He then saw a letter against the Baptists written by a minister of the Established Church, and he complained that it did not savour of the spirit of Christ. At ten he set out for Tygwyn, where he met a Baptist minister called Thomas Williams, who asked him what proof he had for baptizing infants. Harris referred him to 1 Corinthians 7:14, 'For the unbelieving husband is sanctified by the wife, and the unbelieving wife is sanctified by the husband: else were your children unclean.' Mr Williams had no answer other than to say that he could not see infant baptism in the verses. 'I was in a hurry,' wrote Harris, 'and could not stay; but I saw that they were blind, and imagined it a duty from God to defend one truth, without considering that in doing this they were harming other truths. I told him he did right in obeying his light honestly, and so did I in mine.'

On the Tuesday, he was at Hendre Einion, St David's. He wrote that he realized that God had already used him for much good in Pembrokeshire, and that a Captain Davies and his wife, had joined them. He prayed, 'O Lord, have compassion on this county. I am willing to be led by thee with respect to my actions in the future, whether I should go about or not. Enable me to bear up, body and soul.' He preached to many thousands on the misery of those without Christ, on the new creature, and on the faith that justifies and lays hold of the Saviour. All that he says of the meeting is that there was power, and that the truth searched all hearts. In *Method-istiaeth Cymru* a fuller description is given by Mr T. Rees, Trepuet. He says that Harris preached at the Cross in the middle of the road. The meeting had been previously advertised and a large gathering had collected. The preacher very directly and unsparingly denounced the immoral behaviour of the people, and every word from his lips flashed and flamed so thunderously into the consciences of his hearers that they feared that the Day of Judgment had come upon them. So powerful were the effects that brave and strong men fell as dead upon the road, fainting in fright and terror. It was a service that would never be forgotten by those present.

The predominant emotion that Harris's preaching produced was terror. As he mentioned himself, his main theme was the misery of those without Christ and the pronouncement of doom upon idlers and frequenters of the games and revels. As a result, these traditional pastimes that had reigned supreme for centuries were overthrown, nor have they yet been able to raise their heads again. The influence produced by Harris's preaching is found in the experience of a fifteen-year-old youth, the son of man called Sion Griffith. He came quite thoughtlessly to the meeting only because he was curious. But an arrow entered his heart and for all his efforts he could not shake free of it. His turmoil increased. The agony of his heart bordered on insanity, until at last he determined to put an end to himself by throwing himself into the sea, in that to continue to live would only multiply his sins and increase his punishment. But while walking towards the cliffs, the words, 'Son, be of good cheer; thy sins be forgiven thee,' came forcibly into his mind. Such was the light that shone upon him that he fell to the ground. Having recovered, he sought to convince himself that the word was not for him, but the attempt was in vain, and before rising to his feet he had committed himself to the Saviour's care. Everything that he saw around him seemed to be clothed in a new light. No doubt he was typical of many others.

At about eleven on the same day, Harris travelled to Tre-fin. On the way, his spirit grieved because God was dishonoured in the land and the Sabbaths were polluted. He noted that good work was continuing by means of the revival, as long as it would not be frustrated by its own supporters through party-spirit. At Tre-fin, he conferred with dear friends who wished to ask how to come to Christ, and the Lord helped him to be faithful. By the time he went outside, there were some thousands waiting for him. He had much power in prayer, and then spoke for three hours from John 15:1, showing the necessity of finding ourselves in Christ. 'I hope it was a glorious day,' he wrote. This refers, perhaps, to the sermon at St David's as well as to the one at Tre-fin. At the house afterwards, someone came to him wishing to argue over baptism. He refused to discuss the matter, emphasizing instead the necessity of having Christ within us.

He was at Trefhowell near the sea coast, in the parish of Llanwnda, on the Monday. From there he proceeded to Fishguard, where he preached in English and in Welsh to many thousands. Many of the gentry of the locality had come to listen and he hoped that through a spirit of love and prudence he had been able to reach them. In Welsh, he had preached on the conversion of Paul and the meeting had been of great effect. 'I was enabled,' he wrote, 'to thunder in a terrible way concerning hell.' Before ending, however, he referred to the love of Christ. Many were convicted under the word. He complained that John Powell was agitating over baptism, and that on the previous Monday he had called the doctrine of infant baptism, heretical, hellish, cursed and devilish. 'O,' he groaned, 'how I long for peace and love.'

On Thursday, at Nevern, about a mile from Newport, Harris felt constrained to preach on, 'Prove the spirits.' He was asked to accompany a man called 'Pastor Thomas', a Baptist minister, most probably. Harris thought:

> I believe that it is to God's glory that I go; not in order to debate with the Baptists, but to try to avert the storm and for all to prove themselves. Certainly, God is dishonoured and souls are being destroyed by this controversy.

He continued towards Glyn Meredydd. 'I believe,' he wrote, 'that I belong to thee. Thou art my King and my Master.' As he sang, the sufferings, death and love of the Lord Jesus were so real in his mind's eye that a flame of love was kindled in his soul. We find him next at a place called Dygoed. On the Saturday he was at Bwlch-y-clawdd in Maenclochog parish; on Sunday at Rhydhir, Llanddewi Velfrey; and on Monday he left Pembrokeshire, arriving at a place called Gwenallt.

This journey to Pembrokeshire occurred in 1740; the letters and journal prove this without doubt. It is clear that the visit stirred up much excitement. When congregations of many thousands were addressed, in a county of such small population, it is clear that the body of people from some miles' radius had gathered together. Quite certainly also, the services, or at least some of them, were of amazing power and force. His hearers bent before his words as a field of wheat before a tempest. The Baptists sought debates on baptism; his soul abhorred strife, and would not enter into discussion with them. He had no great objection to the doctrine of believers' baptism, but he believed it was being made too much of, and to the detriment of other more important issues. But what grieved him most was that the arguing was inimical to any religious spirit, and an insuperable obstacle to the revival. There is no doubt that this intense itinerary by Harris, of more than a fortnight's continual preaching, made an indelible impression upon Pembrokeshire and was an excellent preparation for the faithful labours of Howell Davies in later years.

## THE DEATH OF WILLIAM SEWARD

In September of 1740, he accompanied William Seward on a long journey through parts of Monmouthshire, Herefordshire, and Breconshire. Seward was from a distinguished social background. He had been convicted as early as 1728. He became acquainted with the two Wesleys but chose to side with Whitefield and accompanied him to America in 1739. He was also with Whitefield when the latter first visited Wales. He was a thorough Calvinist in doctrine and after a disagreement with Charles Wesley, he crossed the Severn estuary and met up with Howell Harris at Cowbridge. They preached in many places and eventually reached Newport. There they were set upon. Harris's clothes were torn, his wig stolen, and he was forced to stand bareheaded in the rain. 'How sweet,' he wrote, 'to bear the reproach of Christ.' Stones, rotten apples and mud were thrown at them. Harris's friends tried to get him to stop but he did not feel free to do so until the Lord had gained the victory over Satan. From there they passed on to Caerleon. When Seward was praying, with great sweetness, all was quiet, but when Harris stood up to speak, much turmoil broke out. The people howled at him. They threw dung, eggs, and cherry stones at them. Seward was struck over the eye and the bruise swelled up so that he could not see. 'Better to suffer this rather than hell,' he said.

At Monmouth, a horse race was being held and both common people and gentry had gathered together. Harris began to speak near the town hall, where many of the gentry and their wives were having dinner. He thundered fearfully against dances, licentious meetings, prostitution, and drunkenness. His words were too painful for the ears of the gentlemen and they sent someone to beat a drum so that his voice would be drowned. The mob began to throw stones, apples and mud. But Christ's servants continued onward, conquering and to conquer. They proceeded through parts of Gloucestershire, and then returned to Trefeca. On 22 October, they went to Hay-on-Wye where they were violently attacked. Harris escaped without injury, but someone struck poor Seward on the forehead with a stone so that he died within a few days. He was the first Methodist martyr.

## A SECOND JOURNEY TO NORTH WALES

About the beginning of the year 1741, Harris visited the north for the second time. This was at the invitation of Robert Griffiths of Bryn Foyno, who pressed him to come because so many had been convicted by his ministry on his previous visit to Llanuwchllyn. He set off, full of faith, despite the wrath of his enemies and the threats of the clergy. The news of his arrival spread like lightning through the land, and extensive preparations were made to prevent him from preaching and to belittle him. As he approached Bala, the parish clergyman met him on the shores of the lake. He warned him that if he wished to escape with his life he should not enter the town. Harris answered that it was his sense of duty that drove him on, that he could not turn back, and that his only purpose was to proclaim the way of salvation to the people, having no wish to offend any. The parson became angry and lifting his stick, threatened to beat him. Harris answered him mildly and was suffered to continue. By the time he reached Bala, where a few followers were waiting for him, he found the town full of excitement. The people had gathered together and were swearing that they would kill him. Leading them on was the clergyman. He had prepared a barrel of beer, placing it conveniently on the mounting-block near the tavern, in order to increase the rage of the mob with drink.

Harris began to preach at the roadside to the people, but the clergyman bellowed out that all who loved the Church should come to defend it. A host of those who had drunk heaviest came forward in their shirtsleeves and with cudgels in their hands. It was as if hell had been let loose. It was judged useless to continue the service in the street and they adjourned to a private house in the middle of the town. Here Harris tried to speak on the words, 'Saul, Saul, why persecutest thou me?' In the meantime, the barrel of beer having been finished, the parson exhorted the mob to attack the house. Harris was only allowed a few minutes to talk. The windows were smashed and some of the rioters forced their way in, roaring like wild animals. But the minister of Christ possessed his soul in patience, he felt no fear and he continued speaking without a pause. When on the pleading of his friends, he eventually stopped, he felt as if the Lord had deserted him. Though he was silenced, he was not left in peace. The rioters had determined to get him out. Some climbed on the roof, threatening to bring the house down. Others pushed their way in through the shattered windows. He was forced to leave the building along with some of his hearers, like sheep thrown to the wolves. His friends did their best for him but they could not defend him. The malicious mob, both male and female, fell upon him in the cruellest way. The women flung the dung of the street at him and the men beat him with their fists and staves, until his blood flowed freely. He was pulled out of the town and towards the lake. At one point he fell and was for a time trampled underfoot, so that he thought he would surely lose his life. He was dragged about by the cloth around his neck and would have choked had not the cloth become loose. But the Lord intervened for him in a way that was almost miraculous, and he escaped from their grasp.

Jenkin Morgan, one of Griffith Jones's teachers, had come to hear him, and he also fell into the mob's hands and his life endangered. On succeeding in mounting his horse and attempting to escape he was pulled down by the rioters. An attempt was made to throw him and his horse over the edge of a rock and into the lake. His foot caught in his stirrup and he was for a while dragged about. In the mercy of Providence, he also escaped. It is certain that God's manifest judgment overcame the ringleaders of this scandalous outrage. After the rioters had dispersed, the believers gathered in the darkness at the house, where they attempted to clean and dress their wounds. Harris encouraged his fellow-sufferers to cleave to the Saviour and to rejoice at being counted worthy to suffer shame for his name. Harris himself was full of determination. 'This was the first blood that I had lost for Christ,' he said, 'though I had been threatened often.' The only thing that distressed him was that he had been persuaded to stop preaching. He knew that for him death was but the door to happiness.

## HIS FIRST PREACHING IN CAERNARVONSHIRE

Having been so mistreated at Bala, it is natural to conclude that he turned his back on the north and returned home, but he pressed on. Luther, in his determination to proceed to Worms even if it contained as many demons as there were tiles on the roofs, was in no way more courageous for God than was Howell Harris as he now confronted Gwynedd. On Saturday night, he arrived at Pwllheli, but no one there knew who he was:

On Sunday morning I enquired for the best preaching in the Church, and was recommended to hear a certain chancellor, at the distance of a few miles . . . He had heard of my coming to North Wales, and had determined that very day to forewarn the people, lest I should lead them astray. First he pretended to point me out as the minister of the devil, an enemy to God, to the Church, and to all mankind. He described me as being, in several respects, worse than the devil, since he could only act here by such instruments as I was. So he went on, and made a repetition of my being the devil's minister, a deluder, a false prophet! And after he had painted me worse than any monster heretic, or the devil himself, he showed that it was a duty incumbent upon the people out of love to God and his Church, as well as out of love to the country, to join unanimously against such a man, who carried with him a destructive poison, that would not only injure their persons and estates, but destroy their souls forever! It was not known, during the service, that I was present; but on my speaking to the chancellor, as he came out of the church, on the subject of the Welsh schools, and expressing my dislike of so intemperate a sermon, I was concluded to be the person publicly exposed. On this supposition the people set themselves in array, intending to take my horse from me, that they might pelt me with stones. But though many stones were thrown at me, the Lord saved me from any considerable harm, and kept them from laying violent hands on me. I was, however, in much danger all the week, and often thought I should not return from that journey.[67]

It seems that the Chancellor mentioned, the Rev. John Owen, who was also vicar of Llannor and Dyneio, was a surly man, ever wrathful against the Methodists. It is said that he was a very able man, a fluent orator, who had considerable influence over the surrounding neighbourhoods. In order to frustrate the revival he arranged, together with his fellow-clerics, to meet every Wednesday at Dyneio, near Pwllheli, to preach against what they called the destructive heresies that were spreading over the land. Various clergymen would take their turn to preach and their texts would be, 'Beware of false prophets'; 'Having a form of godliness, but denying the power thereof'; 'For of this sort are they which creep into houses, and lead captive silly women laden with sins'; etc. It does not appear however that this slanderous ministry in any way hindered the advance of the revival. This Chancellor had a talented sexton who was also a considerable scholar. This was the man who composed the Interlude entitled *Anterliwt Morgan y Gogrwr*,[68] which we have already mentioned. In this lewd song (which however demonstrates some considerable ability), Howell Harris is described as addressing Whitefield with the following words:

> If you'd be so kind, Mr Holiness,
> As to give me a touch of your genius,
> I believe that I could, with no learning or lore,
> Cheat hundreds or more in their foolishness.

> I can shout and weep tears a-plenty,
> Look solemn, though my mind might be empty;
> Without any qualms I'll hypocrisy preach,
> And teach the poor gullible daily.

> For boldness in speech I'm exemplary,
> Teach as Scripture the most trivial ribaldry;
> Turn God's pure Word – so holy and clean,
> And make it to mean quite the contrary.

So many in Wales I've enraptured,
They follow me, though they've been plundered;
They'll ask my advice, they'll bask in my smiles,
And travel for miles, to be pilfered.

Ped faech chi mor dda'ch tuedd, Mr Sancteiddiol,
A rhoi i minne beth o'ch awdurdod nefol,
Rwy'n tybied y gwnawn heb ronyn dawn dysg,
Waith odiaeth yn mysg ynfydion.

Mi medra grio ac wylo'n greulon,
Mewn golwg, heb ddim ar y ngalon;
A phregethu rhagrith heb ronyn rhith rhaid,
I dwyllo trueiniaid tlodion.

Mi fedraf, pan fynwyf, roi pres ar f'wyneb,
A dweud mai Gair Duw a fydd pob gwiriondeb,
A throi'r Ysgrythyr, loew bur wledd,
Gwaith anial wledd, i'r gwrthwyneb.

Mae gennyf ddigon wedi eu hudo yn y Deheudir,
A ddaw ar fy lledol fel ped fawn i garn lleidr,
I 'mofyn am ryw gyngor gwan
Mewn hylldod wedi can' milltir.

And this is how Harris commands Jenkin Morgan:

Go on, as the prophet Elias,
I'll be Simon Magus, or Judas;
We'll gather them round, and continue to bray,
While there's any remaining to pay us.

Dos di 'mlaen yn rhith y proffwyd Elias,
Mi ddeuaf finnau'n swydd Simon Magus, neu Suddas,
Ni a fynwn arian am gadw nad,
Os bydd dim yn y wlad neu'r deyrnas.

We cannot follow the *Interlude* further. It must be acknowledged that it is an accomplished piece, but its greatest creativity is the pack of lies it contains that seeks to pour scorn and shame upon those who faced every kind of danger for no other reason than the desire to save souls. The sexton succeeded in pleasing his master at least. A meeting of the local nobility to read the Interlude was arranged at Bodfel mansion, and so satisfactory did they find it that they immediately subscribed fifty guineas to the sexton in recognition of the service he had performed for the Church. It was not long however before he met with judgment. When returning after having his work printed, he called at a mill, near Bala, for a rest. Some men who happened to be there at the time asked him what he was carrying. He answered that it was an interlude against the Cradocs.[69] But these men were sympathetic to the revival. 'What did they ever do to you?' they asked him. 'Where is the rope? We will hang him immediately.' The rogue was terrified and ran from them. Soon after, he and the Chancellor quarrelled bitterly. The latter thought the sexton had tried to throw the bell on his back to kill him. He rushed upon him like a bear and a bloody battle took place, as a result of which the sexton was dismissed. He died miserably in poverty.

According to Drych yr Amseroedd, Howell Harris first preached in Caernarvonshire at Glasfryn Fawr, the home of Mr William Pritchard. Glasfryn Fawr stands in the parish of Llangybi, near Pwllheli. William Pritchard had been converted when listening to a Dissenter called Francis Evans conducting family worship. He had sent to Griffith Jones for a schoolmaster to keep school and to preach. In answer to his request, Jenkin Morgan had come to the north and his school was held at Glasfryn Fawr. All this aroused the wrath of Chancellor Owen against William Pritchard and he had summoned him to the Bishop's Court. When Harris began his sermon at the house, the Chancellor, with a crowd of wastrels at his heels, rushed upon him. Harris stopped preaching and began to pray. The cleric tried to stop any from hearing by placing his hands over Harris's lips. At this Harris stood up and said:

'What is this? Would you stop a man praying to God? I will be a witness against you at the Day of Judgment.'

'I will be a witness against you, you foul wretch,' was the answer, 'for going about the country deceiving people.'

He then called upon one of his faithful followers to come forward and take hold of Harris. But he had been frightened on hearing of the Day of Judgment and refused, saying:

'Would you hear these men? I do not know which of you is the most foolish. Neither of you would dare say a word on that Day.'

William Pritchard was a strong and brave man. He pushed the Chancellor and his men over the threshold and closed the door on them. Peace having been restored, Harris sought to preach again but he had no liberty, he had become too agitated by the excitement. He concluded by warning the people to keep away from ungodly spiritual shepherds. In time, Chancellor Owen died, under evident circumstances of judgment.

Harris proceeded to a place called Ty'n Llanfihangel, near Rhydyclafdy. An enormous crowd gathered, having heard that he was a man who saw visions. Amongst them was a gentleman who intended to shoot the preacher. But because Harris was late arriving, he grew impatient and went home to his dinner. Straight after his departure, Harris arrived. He preached in the open air and was given extraordinary power in speaking. His words fell as fire upon the consciences of his hearers. Directing his remarks to ungodly people who attended the churches, he said:

> You are used to praying, 'Thy kingdom come.' What if it were to appear now, in great power and glory, in flaming fire and with thousands of angels? Would you not cry out, 'O Lord, I am not ready! Let thy coming be delayed!'

A divine power accompanied the words; strong men failed to stand before them. They fell as if dead upon the ground, and as they returned to their homes, they groaned and wept along the way, as if the Day of the Lord was at hand. This was a truly remarkable service. One of the congregation said that Harris preached on this occasion until Lleyn trembled, adding, 'And it has never yet recovered.'

The next day, he preached at Towyn, near Tudweiliog, again with extraordinary unction. This was the day that John Griffith Ellis was convicted, who afterwards became a preacher and was said to excel all his contemporaries in some respects. One remarkable sermon of his at a Bala Association is mentioned. His text was, 'Awake, O sword, against my Shepherd,' and such a notable outpouring occurred, like a cloudburst, that he and many of his hearers fainted under its influence. At this same sermon from Harris, one of the daughters of Tyddynmawr was converted, who afterwards became the wife of Jenkin Morgan. Tyddynmawr was hereafter to be 'a lodging place for wayfarers', and a refuge for many a weary pilgrim when the winds of persecution were at their strongest.

Harris appears to have preached twice again in Caernarvonshire on this journey: at Rhydolion and at Porth Dinllaen. He returned home through Barmouth and Machynlleth. He had a difficult time when crossing Traethmawr. He was attacked by a mob of persecutors in whom 'the spirit of murder was to be seen in their eyes', but he escaped from their clutches and found refuge in the home of a Dissenting minister. He was in danger also at Machynlleth, but received a warm welcome from Lewis Rees at Llanbryn-mair, and his soul was greatly encouraged by seeing small societies established in various places.

## UNCEASING LABOURS AND JOURNEYINGS

It would be folly to attempt to provide even a summary of all of Harris's journeys during these years. He itinerated in Wiltshire, Gloucestershire,

Herefordshire and Shropshire. He visited Bristol, Bath and London, spending much time in the last named city. He travelled from one part of the principality to another, as if he were an angel without a body – through rivers and over rough mountains – warning sinners. In the summer of 1742, he was in London for four months, evangelizing the English at Moorfields and at Lambeth. It is said that he often preached in Welsh at Lambeth for the benefit of his countrymen. He refers in his journal to one occasion in particular, when he preached at three o'clock in the afternoon to a crowd of Welsh people, from the words, 'Simon son of Jonah, lovest thou me?' While he was in the capital, the care of all the churches weighed upon him but still his brethren in Wales felt his absence greatly and they pressed him continually to return. Daniel Rowland wrote to him:

> Don't you hear all the brethren in Wales crying out loudly, Help! Help! Help! Help! Brother Harris. Thou bold Champion, where art thou? What! In London now, in the Day of Battle! What! has not London champions enough to fight for her? . . . Good Lord, pity poor Wales. Send our dear brother among us with thy power, and in the fulness of thy blessing: and let the devil tremble before him. Amen, Amen.[70]

As an example of his great labours and of the unceasing nature of his journeying, we are tempted to include his account for part of November and December, 1742. On Monday, 11 November, he left London in a coach at six in the morning, to return to Wales. His final meeting with the society in the capital was notably tender. The coach was fairly empty and he had opportunity to talk to the coachman concerning his soul, and with a young woman travelling with them, and he hoped that the conversations were not in vain. On Friday, he was at Reading, feeling heavy and weak because of lack of sleep. He sought the Lord, and found access to him. He wondered at the nature of the covenant by which the Lord safeguards his own glory and also saves the sinner, beyond the reach of corruption. He prayed for the Church in London, for the Church in Wales, and for all ministers and exhorters. He travelled through Wiltshire on Saturday, passing through Bath, and arriving at Bristol by evening. He rose on the Sunday at eight, and went immediately to preach, together with Brother Humphrey with whom he shared sweet fellowship. He felt his heart cleave to his fellow-preacher because of the faithful testimony he bore against Arians and Unitarian ministers. When preaching he was given much liberty, and though he had only just risen from sleep, he was full of energy and liveliness. He preached again from ten until twelve, from 1 Thessalonians 4:14, and he judged that his ministry had been profitable.

On Monday, 15 November, he left Bristol for Wales before six in the morning, reaching the Passage about nine. He had to stay here for the rest of the day because it was impossible to cross the channel. But the time was too precious in his judgment to waste. After regaining strength by a meal, he wrote in his journal until twelve then went out to preach to those who, like himself, were waiting for the boat. The Lord gave him the words and he prayed that he might be made the salt of the earth. After dinner he was attacked by an old temptation, but what it was he does not say, and God gave him deliverance. He failed to cross on the Tuesday also, because of the storm, but took advantage of the opportunity to exhort and the Lord opened the ears of the people to hear. He spoke of his conversion, of the day of judgment, of the account we must give for all our talents, of the way he was brought to see that he could not be justified by works, of the merit of Christ, of faith, what it is, and what it is not, and of obedience and love as the fruits of faith. In the afternoon he exhorted a second time. At about eight in the evening they were able to cross over. The winds were stormy and the waves high. He thought that death perhaps was imminent but was given strength to trust.

On Thursday he was at Redwick, Monmouthshire, and arrived at Watford, near Caerphilly, on Thursday night – his home from home when travelling in these parts. How many times he preached he does not say, but certainly he would not have crossed so many miles over country without compelling souls to Christ. It seems also that some deep anxiety concerning the revival was weighing upon him at this time. Time and again he repeats that he himself was not to blame, but that his heart was on the point of breaking because of it. What the cause of this anxiety was, we can only speculate. It could well have been some lying story, slandering his character, which was being spread abroad. On Saturday night, he dreamed that the Bishop of Oxford was preaching in the street and saying that all should know the love of Christ spread abroad in their hearts, as it was in his. This filled Harris's soul with pleasure.

On Sunday, 21 November, he was at Llandeilo, near Abergavenny, where he complained of physical weakness. He saw and felt that he loved God as clearly as he saw his sin. He poured out all his anxieties to Brother Price. Afterwards, he went to Cwm-iou to hear the Rev. Thomas Jones. After dinner he journeyed to the society at Longtown but lost his way in the mountains and it was nearly seven before he arrived. He had one notable visit from the Lord during the journey. Yet the trouble, whatever it was, still weighed upon his spirit. He feared that the worst would occur and that awful consequences would result, so that the work would be destroyed. It then dawned upon his mind that the work did not depend on him, nor on his name, but that it was God's. On Monday, he was at Clydach, where a lovely breeze from the Spirit of the Lord played upon him. He felt that he had no desire but for the glory of God, nor any fear, except the fear of dishonouring him. He said that he had never had such a visitation before. Brother Price was with him on the journey and each was made a great blessing to the other. He said that he was happy, eternally happy.

Harris arrived at Trefeca on Monday night. Many of the dear sheep had come to welcome him, to whom he opened his heart on many matters, particularly his marriage. He stayed in Trefeca on Tuesday and went to Erwood, not far from Builth Wells, on Wednesday; to Dol-y-felin on Thursday; and Llansanffraid, Montgomeryshire, on Sunday. Here he preached on the words, 'I am the resurrection and the life,' and had much liberty of expression. He hoped that many had been liberated. He was at Erwood again on Monday, and his meditations were upon Miss Ann Williams. He says that his prayers with respect to her were almost answered and that she was almost persuaded. Previously she had feared the crosses and trials and his own rough temper, but now Jesus had given him a heart of tenderness. He was very powerful when preaching. He had a day and night that he would long remember; the people were as a flame of love and they had been enlightened, fed and awakened. The fire had come down, and they tasted much sweetness. He reached Trefeca on Monday night. On Tuesday, he was at John Price's house in Merthyr Cynog, some fifteen miles away, and the text of his sermon was, 'For me to live is Christ.' On Wednesday, he was at Cantref, at the foot of the Brecon Beacons; Thursday, at Beiliau; and Friday, at Llanwrtyd, where he felt that God was with him. On Saturday, he was at Llwynyceiliog, near Caeo. Here he felt that he was the blackest sinner on the face of the earth. He arrived at Llan-crwys, at the lower reaches of Cwm-twrch, about twelve, and reached Llangeitho late the same day. He says that he was expected there, and in prayer he pleaded fervently on behalf of the sheep, and that he might be delivered from the hellish nature within him. 'O wonderful love,' he prayed, 'that I am not in hell, having tempted God so much.'

On Sunday, 5 December, he went to the church at Llangeitho early in the morning, where dear Rowland preached from the words, ' Because I am a man of unclean lips,' and Harris's soul was deeply disturbed by the severity of the message. He felt that he was the greatest wretch in the world. In the afternoon he went to Llancwnlle, one of the churches served by Rowland and as he listened to the word being read, he had a view of the glory of Christ as a friend of publicans and sinners. He was made thankful on hearing Rowland preach. He then received the sacrament and saw himself as the poorest, worst, most blind of all. 'I am in need of life,' he said, 'and light, and strength, and righteousness.' It seems that the fellowship between him and the apostle of Llangeitho along the way, was most sweet. Harris wrote:

> Christ will not condemn me, though I deserve it, for that is his will. Then light broke in upon me. Rowland is mine. More than ever before, I saw that Christ was mine, and therefore all things are mine.

In the evening, Howell Harris preached in the open air near Llangeitho to a congregation of two thousand, until eight o'clock. His theme was the day of Pentecost, and the Spirit of the Lord as a fire. The service was one of much power. As he spoke of the fire, the fire came down and all broke out in great rejoicing. At the end, he prayed for the bishops; for the Church in general; for many of the Reformers by name; for the societies in Glamorganshire; and for his own departure overseas. This last prayer suggests that he had it in mind to follow Whitefield and journey to America. In the house, he and Rowland, together with the leading brethren in the revival, conversed until three in the morning on the need to set up some degree of organization over the work. Clearly the good work was proceeding satisfactorily. Before going to bed he planned his next journeys, and it was four o'clock before he rested.

On Monday, he set out for Mynydd Bach and reached Llanddewi Aberarth by the seashore. He was given much power here to exhort on the need to bear fruit, and to speak against pride and idleness. He then preached the gospel to those who had been wounded. On Tuesday, he was at a place called Gwndwn, near Llangrannog. His text here was, 'For this purpose the Son of God was manifested, that he might destroy the works of the devil.' He had a powerful service. His voice was raised as a trumpet, and he says he was at his most influential when inviting to Christ. After this, he wrote to the leading exhorters and his comments were full of zeal, showing them the way in which the work was progressing on all sides and encouraging them to zeal, life and fire. Then after singing and praying, they sat at table. After supper, Harris spoke again to the family, exhorting them to love, tenderness and kindness to all.

He went to Llangrannog on Wednesday and felt much pleasure in praying, and in speaking from the words, 'How then can I do this great wickedness, and sin against God?' By one, he came to Twr-gwyn, and spoke from Matthew 12:43, saying:

> I am determined not to leave this benighted Church; I will stand in the breach and will cry from her walls; I cannot give up the ministry nor the people.

The service was not as effective as the one at Llangrannog. At six the same day, he preached at Newcastle Emlyn. He here again declared his determination never to leave the Church of England. He does not seem to have chosen a text but preached from many verses that answered his purpose. He spoke with considerable unction. On going to a house, he heard that opposition was being prepared against him. As he listened, his soul was filled with strength; he felt that he could withstand all persecution. He wrote that the young man he intended to have as an assistant (either John Belcher or James Ingram, most probably) was with him on this journey, and he went to much trouble to counsel and direct him, and prayed much that he might have faith. On Thursday, he was at Blaenporth, where his text again was, 'How then can I do this great wickedness?' He longed that he might have a thousand lives to be given to Jesus. From here he went to Cardigan and had sweet fellowship with heaven along the way. He felt great strength when praying and preaching; he had never had such power in evangelizing. He prayed earnestly for his companion, 'O Lord, equip him to assist me; make him strong to go through difficulties, obedient, humble, and loyal. I now hope that nothing but death will separate us.'

On Friday Harris left Cardigan, having traversed the county from Llangeitho southwards, and arrived at Dygoed in Pembrokeshire. He had great opposition from Satan, who stood at his right hand, but when praying he was drawn within the veil in a way that he had not experienced previously, and he preached from the words, 'As ye have therefore received Christ Jesus the Lord, so walk ye in him.' Pembrokeshire seemed to him to be in a wretched state. 'I know of only very few in this county,' he wrote, 'who have been awakened to see that they are condemned in Adam.' He spoke until about eight. From then until eleven he was with young converts, forming them into societies and instructing them in church discipline. He showed them the nature of the Spirit's activities – that he was sometimes praise, another time sorrow; that he instructed, guided, quickened, and strengthened. He described the responsibilities of members of a society and that they should not refer publicly to the sins of ministers of the gospel without having first sorrowed because of them. He mentioned the societies in London, and how the great work was proceeding throughout the world. He prayed with power and went to sleep about one, feeling happy in the Lord. He preached again on Saturday morning at Dygoed, on, 'Abide in me.' By Saturday night, he had arrived at Ty'r Yet, near Newport. He preached about ten on Sunday morning on self-denial. He had much light and some strength, but he was dry. By one he was at Llys-y-frân. On the way there he had been counselling the lambs who, he hoped, were deeply convicted of the sinfulness of self. An immense congregation had gathered at Llys-y-frân. He estimated it at five thousand, but he was very dry and dark at the beginning. 'I had no strength,' he wrote. But gradually the Lord had mercy upon him; he was drawn out of himself while praying, and he was helped to preach on the Seed of the Woman bruising the serpent's head. He preached in Welsh and in English and referred to the first covenant, the way in which it was broken, the curse that resulted, and that by it we were all as condemned as demons. He then turned to describe the nature of the new covenant:

> Had great power and sweetness as I generally have on this subject when led to it of God. I hope that many were saved and converted; it was truly sweet here; but I was very pointed and severe in the first part, so that flesh could not stand before me, showing that they could not keep their hearts settled in God for five minutes of themselves, even if they were to be given ten thousand worlds for it, nor could they look on him whom they have pierced.

In a private conversation that followed, he found that some blamed him for not giving room in his preaching to morality, and for placing moral and immoral men on the same footing as far as their conditions were concerned. He saw that he needed wisdom from Christ as well as strength; he felt ready, if he had said anything amiss, to withdraw his words or to explain them, and he then went to Jesus to seek wisdom. He had great pleasure in prayer at family worship, and was made deeply serious particularly when praying for the elderly. He wrote in his journal until about twelve. He then mentioned that the anxiety to which he had often referred was a thorn in his flesh still. Had it been allowed to occur, he could not have borne it, he would have sunk under it. He had been 'agreeably surprised by the bitter cries of three little female lambs crying together and weeping before the throne':

> How beautiful are broken hearts, particularly those of the young; how splendid is the sight; no lightness or disputes, or dry talk, but on their knees pleading their misery earnestly with the friend of sinners. I never heard such harmonious music, like little pigeons exactly.[71]

On Monday, Harris was at a place called Treinar. The state of the Church of England pressed heavily upon his mind; he had been sorrowing, weeping, and interceding on its behalf. By twelve, he was at Newcastle Emlyn, and preached until after two on, 'Looking unto Jesus.' At the beginning he was dry but gradually he found liberty and he was drawn out in great love. He attributed his dryness at the start to the pride of his heart, for which God was obliged to keep him captive that he might learn to be humble. He had much pleasure and light. He showed also that if there was darkness in the Church of England, there was deadness amongst the Independents:

> Therefore, let us grieve together, and not leave the one or the other, nor weaken one another's hands; the Spirit of God does not desire the destruction of denominations or men, but that all the churches might be filled with God.

Harris next proceeded to Fishgate, about five miles away. He was happy on the way, yet not as close to his Saviour as he would have desired to be. Though it was mid-December, he wrote that he was obliged to preach out in the open air at every place because of the numbers of those who gathered to hear him. He had much delight in praying, and then preached on, 'For me to live is Christ.' He was dry here again at the beginning, but his Lord returned to him before long. He was given great vigour when compelling the people to Christ. He then went to the society, where a roomful had gathered. He had power here also, he hoped, to kindle their hearts. He told them that their chief need was fire. He described the Church and Nonconformity as dead. He counselled them to accept all whose spirits were quickened; yet, none were to be encouraged to exhort other than those whose words God was using to quicken others.

On Tuesday, Harris went to Fishguard. The Lord was very close to him in his bedroom. He felt much affection for his companion; he viewed him as having been given to himself by God, and he prayed for him:

> O Lord, he is thy servant; give him all wisdom, all zeal, all humility, and all power of faith, to glorify thy name. Thou dost know that it was for thy glory that I desired to have him.

He prayed, with much solemnity, for the lambs, particularly for those whom God had given to him. He felt such closeness to them that he did not know how to leave them. He wondered why the High and Lofty One who inhabits eternity, should make use of one like him, and he was humbled to the dust by such knowledge. He asked the Lord to bless his labours, and the labours of all the brethren, and that there might be no division amongst them. He seems to have heard that there was a disinclination amongst the clergy to allow Methodists to receive communion in the churches, and he prayed for these clergy that even if they had not been called to preach, they might be kept from opposing and from stopping the people to come to the ordinance. He preached from Colossians 1:12, 13. On the whole, he felt pleasure in the work. He passed on to Long House, near Tre-fin, where he spoke from Acts 2:4, 'And they were all filled with the Holy Ghost.' He had much light, sweetness and power. On Wednesday, he went to St David's. He preached until past three o'clock, and felt an infinite compassion filling his soul as he looked upon the concourse that had gathered. He had much liberty in prayer and a strange power accompanied the ministry. He preached there again in the evening, when he warned the people not to put more trust in baptism than in the blood of Christ, and he had more pleasure than ever in speaking of the wounds of Christ. On Thursday, he was at Wolf's Castle, and at Haverfordwest on Friday. He went to Prendergast Church in the morning, attending a private society until twelve. He then preached with tremendous power until nearly two. He went from there to a place called Fenton. Here he was in captivity to begin with, and struggling in prayer, but at last he found relief when preaching. He proceeded to St Kennox, where he spoke on the songs of Simeon and Mary, and was drawn out remarkably. He hoped to meet there with Brother Howell Davies but was disappointed. He prayed for him however.

On Saturday, Harris went to Llwyndyrys. To his great joy, Howell Davies arrived to see him. He wrote in his journal on the Sunday:

> Having parted last night with the dear and lovely Howell Davies, having agreed with him in everything (Satan having strove to work divisions), told him of the order of the Church in London, and of the great work in every place. Had wisdom to lay things out clearly.[72]

He said that he was eager for the revival to proceed, even if he had no hand in it; willing for it to go forward as God saw fit, and through whomsoever He appointed. He was willing not to go to the ministers' meeting in case he should cause them embarrassment. He then prayed:

> O Lord Jesus, when will I be allowed to come home! O, how I long to come home to thee! There, my Father, my Brother, I will never sin!

He proceeded to Llanddowror, and to the church at Llandeilo where the Rev. Griffith Jones preached in the afternoon, and a lovely breeze swept through his soul. Mr Jones – 'the valuable Mr Jones,' as Harris called him – preached on the resurrection of Lazarus.

Harris left Llanddowror on Monday and was at Cilgarw, near Carmarthen, on Tuesday; at Llan-non on Wednesday; at Llansamlet, near Swansea, on Thursday; and Llanddeusant, Carmarthenshire, on Friday. On the Saturday, which was Christmas Day, he was at Llan-ddew, near Brecon, at the five o'clock Christmas morning service, where the Rev. Thomas Lewis ministered. From there, he hurried on to Trefeca so that he could receive communion at Talgarth Church as was his custom. On the way there he heard that his friends had been prevented from taking communion at the church. He received the news quietly. His mind was full of perfect peace:

> Not because of dullness but because of faith, in that I see Christ in all things. I felt a willingness to leave the Church, and sufficient strength to suffer it; but I did not feel I could leave my friends to be thrown out without leaving with them.

He visited the vicar, the Rev. Price Davies, to enquire and complain. The latter said that he had sufficient reason for deciding that the Methodists were not to receive of the sacrament.

'Do you forbid me from coming to the ordinance?' asked Howell Harris.

'Yes, certainly,' replied the Vicar.

The Reformer's heart was filled with a deep peace as he heard the answer; he trusted in God's words that all things work together for good to those who love him:

> I saw that great good was sure to follow on this. The work is of God. I am willing to follow. My soul was filled with pity and love for the clergyman and the people.

He hoped, though he had been turned out, that God would come to save the poor people. He was willing to be scorned and to see only few secede with them.

This was before he had gone to the church. In the service, as he heard the Litany being read and the lessons, he had great pleasure. He felt that the verses were particularly apt. The vicar preached against those who attended religious services outside the parish church. He called them Schismatics, and said that they wounded the Body of Christ, and pierced his sacred side as surely as the soldier who had pierced him with a spear. Harris felt deep compassion towards him, seeing that he spoke according to the light that was in him. But the Reformer had to leave without the privilege of commemorating the death of the Saviour. On the way back to Trefeca he decided to place the matter before the Bishop, and if he also were to support the vicar's actions there would be nothing to do but to turn his back on the Church, notwithstanding all his love for it.

He arrived home about one. Peace like a river flowed into his spirit. He wrote letters and recorded his feelings in his journal until after three, and then preached to a large congregation from Isaiah 40, 'Comfort ye, comfort ye, my people.' He had unusual power to turn their eyes to Christ; he hoped that many had met with the Lord that afternoon. He referred to the clergy's work of closing the doors to the privileges of the house and said that he accepted that the question as to who was the true prophet for God could be decided in the last judgment. This is where he experienced the most power during the sermon, and he wondered at the strength of love that filled the lambs. Though he had not slept the previous night and had been in six public and private meetings during the day, he set out that evening for Sancily, a fairly large farmhouse in the Usk valley, between Talybont and Brecon. He had therefore travelled a total distance of thirty miles during the day. Though it was so late, he preached at a place called Tygwyn. His text was, 'Look unto me, and be ye saved, all the ends of the earth.' At the beginning he was very lifeless; no influence attended his words. But he was released and had remarkable strength, love and light to look at Christ.

On the Sunday morning Harris was at Sancily, and he thought again of the possibility of going overseas. He felt Anne Williams and Wales very close to his heart, but he was enabled to commit them to the Lord Jesus. The Orphanage House built in Georgia by Whitefield and the churches in the other side of the ocean, weighed upon his mind and he longed to visit and see them. He believed that Jesus could carry on his work in this country without himself. He went to Llan-ddew Church, where the Rev. Thomas Lewis preached. There he had profit for his soul. He had a twofold purpose in going to Llan-ddew. He could receive the sacrament forbidden him at Talgarth and could also confer with Thomas Lewis in the light of this new confusing development. His heart melted as wax within him as he approached the table. His spirit was drawn very closely to Jesus and the fellowship was sweet. He felt that Jesus remained faithful, even as he was being thrown out of the parish church. As he looked at the elements, he saw more than ever of the mystery of the union between the divine and the human in the person of the Son.

Harris went from Llan-ddew to Merthyr Cynog. He heard how the work was advancing in every place and he resolved to remain with the lambs. He arrived there about four. 'Look unto me,' was his text and he enjoyed much power while praying and addressing the crowd. In the evening he went to a place called Alltmawr and preached there until after nine, on Zechariah 12:10, 'And I will pour upon the house of David, and upon the inhabitants of Jerusalem, the spirit of grace and of supplications: and they shall look upon me whom they have pierced,' and he felt the smile of heaven upon him. He stayed down until after eleven o'clock, counselling the lambs. On Monday, he went to Llanddewi'r-cwm and exhorted the people to look to Christ. He travelled then to Llamgammarch where he met with dear Mr Gwynne. His text was, 'Behold the Lamb of God,' and he was given much power. After sweet fellowship with Mr Gwynne, he traced his steps towards Dol-y-felin. On the way it was well with his soul. He saw sin as it is against Jesus, and he therefore feared before it; similarly he feared before his wisdom, his will, his reason, and his own righteousness. He saw Christ glorious and himself terrible, so that he prayed, 'O, save me from myself!' He preached from Hebrews 12:1, 2, with much conviction. Afterwards he went towards Builth Wells. His connection with Miss Anne Williams of Skreen was weighing heavily upon him. At the same time, he felt ready to give her up and never to see her again, if that would be of more advantage to Christ's lambs. He had heavenly union and much freedom of faith in the company of the saints at Builth. He saw that the light of Christ caused them to scorn the old covenant. He preached here again from, 'Look unto me,' and had much liberty and sweetness in the work.

On his way to his next stop, at Hirgwm, he made a broad survey of his labours since beginning to go out with the gospel. He had delivered between six and seven thousand sermons, had noted events and his thoughts in his journal and written innumerable letters. In addition, he had counselled the societies. He had a notable meeting at Hirgwm. When praying, a remarkable influence descended upon his spirit. He saw all his sins accounted to Christ:

> I saw him overcoming death and hell, and doing so for me, more clearly than ever before. Then, when preaching from, 'Behold the Lamb of God,' I was terrible, more overcoming than ever; I had such a spirit and authority that could not be stood against. I cried out to the revellers, condemning their language, cutting off everything before me and referring to the old world, to Sodom, and to the sin against the Holy Ghost.

It seems that the meeting, which he described in great detail, was an immensely solemn one. He answered the objections of the ungodly, condemned prayerless families and those that raised their children to participate in the games, and said that if God's Word was true the whole land was on its way to hell. 'I had little for the lambs, but I never had such authority before.' It must truly have been an awful place. The lightning of Sinai would have lit up for the people their lost condition, and the thunders of the Almighty would have roared in their hearing, until their faces were white as a sheet and their knees trembling together. He was at Hirgwm again on Wednesday; from there he went to Cefn-llys in Radnorshire; Thursday, he was at Cefn-brith, not far from Cefn-llys. He was next at Gore, and on the way, read Vavasor Powell's book describing the condition of Wales in 1641. He preached here from Isaiah 45:22. At the start, he was very dry, no influence and hardly able to find words. But he suddenly turned to the law, and immediately great power came as he showed them that they loved, feared, trusted and wondered at everything but God. On Friday, the last day of 1742, he was at Rhiw; and on Saturday, the first day of the new year, he was at Skreen, visiting Miss Ann Williams.

These references from his journal shed much light on his history, on the revival, on the difficulties that he met with, and on the nature of his own thoughts. But our main reason for including them was to give a better idea of the greatness of his labours and his indefatigable energies.

After returning from the seven-week long journey, he wrote a letter to a friend, Samuel Church of Deptford, London, summarizing his labours:

> Having travelled since this day seven weeks (the time I left London) near seven hundred computed miles, above a thousand measured, and discoursed about one hundred and twenty times, and often in the open air (no house being able to contain the congregations) through great winds, rain, and frost, and yet I am no worse in body than when in London. 'Tis sweet to be on full stretch for God.[73]

In another letter,[74] to a Thomas Boddinton, he wrote:

> If you would take a turn with me, for two or three months, seeing my labours and tribulations, I am sure you would not wonder so much that I have not sent to you before now. 'Tis now about 9 weeks since I began to go round South and North Wales, and this week I came home from my last journey round North Wales. I have now visited in that time 13 counties and travelled mostly 150 miles every week, and discoursed twice every day, and sometimes three or four times a day; and this last journey I have not taken off my clothes for seven nights, and travelled from one morning to the next evening without any rest above 100 miles. Discoursing at 12 or 2 in the morning on the mountains, being obliged to meet at that time by reason of persecution.[75]

Howell Harris's labours were truly almost unbelievable. The wonder is that his constitution, strong as it was, did not give way under such a burden of work. After a wearying journey, and many sermons before riotous mobs, with the whole neighbourhood in turmoil and agitation about him, he would stay down until two or three in the morning, praying, striving hard against the corruption of his heart, and writing, so that he had hardly any time to rest. He, above everyone, was the pioneer, breaking the ice for the gospel. He often thought that his end was near but he felt no sorrow at such times, his soul, rather, was stirred at the prospect of going to his Saviour.

As an example of his suffering for the cause of the gospel, consider the following. One night, a Mrs Rumsey of Tynywlad, near Crickhowell, heard a weak voice outside her door about two o'clock in the morning. She recognized the voice as being that of Howell Harris. She hastened to open to him and in the candlelight he presented an awful sight. On returning from Monmouthshire he had been attacked and badly beaten, his body was covered in blood and wounds and bruises. Thirteen wounds were counted on his head, and it was a wonder that he had not been killed. He had every possible care in the farmhouse, and he departed the next morning happy in spirit, considering it a privilege to suffer shame for Christ.

At another time, in June, 1741, he and John Cennick were in Swindon on their way to London. Cennick described what happened:

> We found a large company assembled in the grove with whom I sang and prayed but was hindered from preaching by a great mob who made a noise and played in the midst of the people and then with guns, fired over our heads, holding the muzzles of their pieces so near our faces that we were both black as tinkers with the powder. We were not affrighted but opened our breasts and told them we were ready to lay down our lives for our doctrine and had nothing against it if their guns were levelled at our hearts. Then they got the dust out of the highway and covered us all over, and then played an engine upon us, which they filled out of the stinking ditches, till we were just like men in the pillory, but as they played upon Brother Harris, I spoke to the congregation, and when they turned their engine upon me, he preached, and thus continued till they had spoiled the engine . . . This persecution was carried on by Mr Gothard, a leading gentleman of that place, who lent the mob his guns, halbert, and engine, and bid them use us as bad as they could only not to kill us, and himself sat on horseback the whole time laughing to see us so treated. After we had left the town, they dressed up two images and called one Cennick and the other Harris and then burnt them.[76]

No doubt this is what they would have done to the preachers themselves, if they had not been frightened of doing so. This was not a rare occurrence; they met with similar reactions almost daily.

As a preacher, Howell Harris was a John the Baptist. His work was mainly the hard, rough preparatory work. As far as ministerial skills were concerned, he could not be compared with Daniel Rowland. In his early years there would be very little order in his remarks, he would not usually take a text but would speak on whatever was given him at the time. He would pour out whatever was uppermost in his own heart, without much arrangement, but with such an edge and authority that none could withstand it. At the same time, there was a character in his ministry that made him unique above all the preachers of the times. Williams refers to it in his elegy:

| But for all the skills of others | Ond yng nghanol myrdd ohonynt |
| We still miss thy gift divine. | Mae rhyw eisiau o dy ddawn. |

Dr Owen Thomas writes:

> We have only to look at his picture to realize immediately that he was no
> ordinary man. The long face, and especially that long jaw, the aquiline nose,
> the heavy brows, the wide, though high, forehead, the wide, open mouth, the
> piercing eyes, and that determined countenance, testify that he possessed strong
> natural abilities, and particularly that there was no fear in his make-up.

The intensity of his convictions also, the awful agony of soul which
he had passed through, the closeness to eternity in which he lived,
sharpened his speech and put an edge to his words. The Rev. John Hughes
wrote:

> God gave him a commandment, 'Cry aloud, spare not, lift up thy voice like
> a trumpet, and show my people their transgression, and the house of Jacob
> their sins.' The voice said, 'Cry!' and he obeyed: 'All flesh is grass, and all the
> goodliness thereof is as the flower of the field.' His face was set like a flint.
> He cried out before men of careless hearts until their faces blanched.

Harris was chiefly a preacher to the careless and indifferent populace. Had
his language been less rough, his speech more tender, and his matter more
philosophical, he would not have been that appropriate instrument for the
work that God had prepared for him. John Wesley referred in his journal
to the power of his ministry. On Monday, 22 January, 1750, he wrote:

> I prayed in the morning at the Foundry, and Howell Harris preached – a
> powerful orator, by nature as well as by grace – but he is not in any way
> indebted to art or learning.

Harris himself often mentioned his deficiency in knowledge and his
failure to find time to read as obstacles in his path with respect to his
ministry. But he was best suited for the condition of his country as he was.
In unsparing commitment to work, in long and dangerous journeys, in
intense conscientiousness before the Lord Jesus, in holy boldness before
scorn and persecution, and in the deepest feeling for the value of souls that
were carelessly rushing to destruction, not one of the Reformers could be
compared to Howell Harris.

He could almost have used Paul's words: 'I laboured more abundantly
than they all,' and he is very appropriately called 'the Luther of Wales'.
His organizational ability also was almost as great as his gifts as a speaker.
His was a great, indeed the greatest, contribution to the formation of the
constitution of the Methodists at the first, and his image is clearly seen
upon the Connexion even to this day. We leave the history of Howell
Harris at this point, but will return to it again.

[1] *A Brief Account of the Life of Howell Harris, Esq.* (Trefeca, 1791), p. 9. [2] Ibid., p. 10.

[3] Ibid., pp. 10-11. [4] Ibid., p. 11. [5] Ibid., p. 12. [6] Ibid., p. 13.

[7] Ibid., pp. 13-14. [8] Ibid., p. 14. [9] Ibid., pp. 15-16.

[10] Ibid., pp. 16-17. [11] Ibid., p. 21 [12] CH, MS (i), p. 53. [13] Ibid., p. 54.

[14] Ibid.

[15] Luke Tyerman, *The Oxford Methodists* (London, 1873), p. 18.

[16] CH, MS (i), p. 67. [17] *Brief Account*, p. 22. [18] Ibid.

[19] Ibid., pp. 22-3. [20] CH, MS (i), pp. 69-70.

[21] *Brief Account*, p. 23. [22] Ibid. [23] Ibid., p. 24.

[24] Tyerman, *Oxford Methodists*, p. 227. [25] Ibid., p. 210.

[26] *Brief Account*, pp. 24-5. [27] Ibid., p. 27.

[28] Thomas Rees, *History of Protestant Nonconformity in Wales*, p. 366.

[29] Ibid., p. 369. [30] Ibid., pp. 369-70. [31] Ibid., p. 371. [32] Ibid., p. 372.

[33] Ibid., p. 374. [34] HJH, p. 56. [35] Ibid.

[36] Tyerman, *Life of John Wesley*, vol. 1, p. 369.

[37] *Brief Account*, pp. 110-11.

[38] *A Select Collection of Letters of the Late Reverend George Whitefield*, vol. 1 (London, 1772), p. 47.

[39] Luke Tyerman, *The Life of the Rev. George Whitefield*, vol. 1 (London, 1890), p. 187.

[40] CH, MS (ii), p. 145.

[41] *George Whitefield's Journal* (London: Banner of Truth, 1960), pp. 229-30.

[42] Ibid., p. 229. [43] Ibid., p. 246. [44] Ibid.

[45] Ibid., pp. 249-50.

[46] Edward Morgan, *The Life and Times of Howel Harris, Esq.* (Holywell, 1852), p. 90.

[47] Tyerman, *Life of John Wesley*, vol. 1, p. 277.

[48] HJH, p. 90. [49] Ibid., pp. 90-1.

[50] Edward Morgan, *Life of Howel Harris*, p. 39.

[51] *Brief Account*, p. 116. According to Harris's Itinerary the date should be 1738.

[52] Thomas Rees, *History of Protestant Nonconformity in Wales*, pp. 442-3. [53] Ibid., p. 444.

[54] CH, MS (i), p. 257. Letter to Mrs Elizabeth James, Abergavenny. [55] Ibid., p. 264.

[56] Ibid., pp. 274-5. [57] Ibid., pp. 279, 280, 281.

[58] Robert Jones, *Drych yr Amseroedd* (Trefriw, 1820). This was an early account of the Methodist revival in north Wales, written by Robert Jones of Rhos-lan (1745–1829).

[59] CH, MS (i), p. 286. [60] Ibid., pp. 422-3.

[61] Harris used '#' to refer to Ann Williams of Skreen, who afterwards became his wife.

[62] CH, MS (i), pp. 423, 424, in part. [63] Ibid., pp. 425-6, in part.

[64] HHVP, p. 24. [65] Ibid., p. 25.

[66] Evan Davies (1694?–1770), was a minister with the Independents, and tutor at Haverfordwest Academy. John Morgan Jones mistook him for Howell Davies, the Methodist clergyman, and some of his later comments in this paragraph have therefore been omitted.

[67] Edward Morgan, *The Life and Times of Howel Harris, Esq.*, pp. 65-6. [68] See p. 76.

[69] The Methodists were often called Cradocs or Cradockians, after Walter Cradoc (1610?–59), the seventeenth-century Welsh Puritan.

[70] *Account of the Progress of the Gospel*, vol. 2, no. 1, pp. 5-6.

[71] HHVP, p. 79. [72] Ibid., p. 81.

[73] HJH, pp. 216-7.

[74] John Morgan Jones has misplaced this letter; it was written in 1748 and describes a completely different journey to north Wales. The circumstances described however would be typical of all these early visits to the north.

[75] STL, vol. 2, pp. 20-21.

[76] *The Awakening in Wiltshire* (Moravian Archives, Bristol), pp. 2-3.

# 6

# HOWELL DAVIES

## HIS EARLY ASSOCIATIONS WITH THE METHODISTS

The Rev. Howell Davies, The Apostle of Pembrokeshire, is the Calvinistic Methodist Father of whose history we know least. It is not known where he was born; what were the names, occupations and social standing of his parents; nor what was the history of his early years. He appears as Melchizedek of old, 'without father, without mother, without descent'. We come across him first, at the school of the Rev. Griffith Jones, Llanddowror, as suddenly as if he descended there from a cloud. At the end of the elegy composed to him by Williams, Pantycelyn, it is stated that he died in 1770 when 55 years old. He would therefore have been born in 1717, and would have been the same age as William Williams; three years younger than Howell Harris; and four years younger than Daniel Rowland. It would appear that he was born somewhere in Monmouthshire. The evidence for this is an account written by Lorenz Thorstan Nyberg, the first minister of the Moravian Church at Haverfordwest. He ministered in that town from 24 June 1763 to 23 August 1768, and would have been closely acquainted with Mr Davies in that the latter at that time was the most respected minister of the town and occupied the highest social position.

There is a tradition that Howell Davies was a member of an honourable family and had from his youth displayed considerable intellectual abilities and a firm desire for learning. At Griffith Jones' school he made swift progress, becoming a fine scholar in Greek and Latin, and being decidedly inclined towards the ministry of the Established Church. His health as a child was frail but he gained strength to a considerable extent on reaching adulthood, though he never possessed anything like the strong constitutions of his fellow labourers, Daniel Rowland, Howell Harris and William Williams. It is also said that he was naturally of a serious disposition and that he was brought under the authority of the truth under the ministry of his teacher, Griffith Jones. It is probable therefore that he never knew the agonies and afflictions felt by Rowland

and Harris. He never lay trembling at the foot of Sinai listening to the
thunder; he was never left suspended above the fearful abyss. His experience was rather:

| | |
|---|---|
| Quietly and most mysteriously | Fe'm denodd i yn ddirgel iawn, |
| He drew me to himself. | A distaw ar ei ol. |

Whatever the nature of his conversion, Howell Davies' religion was
beyond question. From this time onwards he became more decided in his
mind with regards to the ministry of the gospel and no doubt he received
every encouragement from his teacher. He was Griffith Jones' favourite
pupil, and on the day of his ordination the venerable clergyman appealed
to the congregation at Llanddowror to raise their prayers to heaven on
his behalf. And indeed their prayer was answered abundantly. Davies was
placed as curate at Llys Brân, or Llys-y-frân as it is commonly called.
Strangely enough, no account of his ordination as deacon is to be found
in the books for the St David's diocese. The Rev. E. Meyler has researched
diligently but has concluded that the registration was completely overlooked. This only demonstrates how careless and untidy was the recording
of church registers in those days, and that no real conclusion can be drawn
from their lack of testimony on any matter. Neither is there any reference
to him in the Llys-y-frân register. Mr Meyler found that the page relating
to this period had been torn out of the book. It is quite possible that this
was done by one of the curates that succeeded him, so that nothing of any
connection with the infamous Methodists be left preserved in such a sacred
volume. But that he was a curate at Llys-y-frân is certain. It is confirmed
by the testimony of many who heard him preaching there and received
much spiritual good from him.

Howell Davies began his ministry about the beginning of the year
1740, and he proceeded at once to thunder forth against the ungodliness
of the region with such vigour that the local ne'er-do-wells trembled at
his presence. The quiet hamlet, lying as if in sleep in the Pembrokeshire
hinterland, almost immediately became a meeting place for an immense
congregation. The church was too small to contain them, the heavenly
rains descended in glorious showers as at Llangeitho, and many were
turned to the Lord.

As his ministry commenced in 1740, the comment in *Methodistiaeth Cymru* that Davies was amongst the foremost workers in the Methodist revival
both in time and in reputation is incorrect. Daniel Rowland and Howell
Harris had already been labouring in the harvest for nearly five years.
Five years is not a long time, but in a period of awakening, as it was then
in Wales, when events follow quickly upon one another and deep and

long-lasting impressions are made in a short time, five years is an extensive period. Rowland and Harris had travelled through large areas of south Wales and some regions in north Wales, before Davies brought his sickle to the field. But he was of equal standing to the other two both in his ministerial gifts and in his fame. It is true also that he began his labours quite independently of them. He did not start as an assistant but was a pioneer, and it is perfectly appropriate that he is called 'the Father of Methodism in Pembrokeshire'. To place him on a lower rung would be inexcusable. When he met with Howell Harris at Haverfordwest in the spring of 1740, it is probable that he was already ordained and already drawing the crowds to Llys-y-frân. Harris refers to him in his journal with much respect.

Howell Davies did not minister long at Llys-y-frân. His time there was less than eight months at most. His fiery, awakening preaching became unbearable to some of his sleepy parishioners and they succeeded in driving him away. We find him being ordained priest by Dr Nicholas Claggett, Bishop of St David's, on 3 August 1740, and assigned to the curacy of Llanddowror and Llandeilo Abercywyn under the Rev. Griffith Jones. But the nature of his ministry did not change. He did not cease from warning the ungodly, nor did heaven's blessings cease to flow by his instrumentality. From this time forward he was considered one of the Methodists, and a leader in their midst. No doubt one of Howell Harris's intentions when visiting Pembrokeshire in December 1742, a fortnight or so before the Association at Watford, was to agree with his friend in the gospel the arrangements that had to be discussed. And we find that both were in complete agreement.

Although Howell Davies' ecclesiastical connections were in Carmarthenshire, his main ministerial labours were in Pembrokeshire. He travelled the county from one end to the other, preaching in farmhouses and in the open air because the churches were shut to him, and forming many societies. Though the visits of Howell Harris and Daniel Rowland produced much excitement and brought about unusual blessing, yet it was the labours of Howell Davies that evangelized the county and subdued it under the gospel. It appears that his preaching was notable also for its sweetness. Harris continually refers to him in his letters as excelling in power and charm. In a letter to Whitefield, written from Milford about the end of 1743, he states:

> These last two Sundays I have heard the two most vehement trumpets in the land, namely Brother Rowland and Brother Davies. The light, ability and heavenly wisdom for wounding and healing, and for revealing the Lord Jesus Christ, was such that it is beyond the power of words to convey it.

In a letter from Fishguard, Pembrokeshire, to his brother in London, he writes:

> The news that I have received of the effects accompanying the ministry of Brother Howell Davies is remarkable; particularly so amongst the English (half of this part of the county is English). An unusual power resides here, so that frequently when they pray for a blessing before a meal, the spirit of prayer will fall upon many of them, one after another, so that they are kept before the throne of grace for up to three hours. Many when singing are so charmed by the love of Christ that they swoon away.

In March 1743 he writes to the Tabernacle church in London:

> Last Sunday I was at another of Brother Davies's churches in this county and we received a greater day of glory than even the previous Sunday. I believe the congregation was between ten and twelve thousand. Language cannot express the blessing upon Brother Rowland in Cardiganshire and Brother Howell Davies here.

We could quote many similar references that are scattered throughout Howell Harris's letters, and which reveal the heights attained under the ministry of the Apostle of Pembrokeshire and the blessing of God upon his words.

He was not present at the first Association at Watford. A possible reason for this is that he had perhaps expressed his mind fully to Harris on the various issues to be discussed and did not consider the long journey necessary. His poor health generally explains his many absences from the Associations over the years, together with the fact that he confined his labours to a fairly limited field. As far as the arrangements made in that first Association for the various counties is concerned, the whole of Pembrokeshire was committed to Howell Davies' care, and he, when present, was to preside over the Monthly Associations of the county. We do find that he was present in many of the earlier Associations and Monthly Meetings. He was at the Monthly Association at Longhouse, 1 May 1743; at Trefeca Association, 29 and 30 June 1743; and at the Quarterly Association also at Trefeca in 1744. We find him presiding at the Pembrokeshire Monthly Association at Llangwm, when John Sparks, George and William Gambold, were applicants for the office of exhorter. The two Gambold brothers were natives of Puncheston, though living at the time in Haverfordwest, and brothers to John Gambold, the Moravian bishop, who had once been a leading member of the 'Holy Club' at Oxford. In the minutes for that Association is found:

> We approve and accept George Gambold to the office of exhorter, for him to go about as much as he can, and also to care for his grandmother.

We find a reference here also to the placement of William Edwards (well-known later as William Edwards, Rhydygele) under the supervision of Mr Davies, the Moderator, to be accepted for communion and to be kept under probation before being considered as an exhorter. Permission was also granted to John Sparks to exercise his preaching gifts under Davies' superintendence.

Howell Davies also presided at the Haverfordwest Monthly Association, 28 January 1745, even though Howell Harris was present in his role as General Superintendent. Many of the private exhorters were also present on this occasion and three of the public exhorters, namely John Harris (to be mentioned later), William Richard and Thomas Meyler. It is evident therefore that Howell Davies shouldered heavy responsibilities in the ordering of the affairs of the revival in Pembrokeshire.

## HAVERFORDWEST, PRENDERGAST AND PARKE

The town of Haverfordwest was the centre for his labours and Prendergast (or Prengast as the locals call it) Church was where he preached most frequently. It is difficult to ascertain his exact relationship with this church. He is sometimes called 'Rector of Prendergast' but it does not appear that he was either rector or curate here. The church register is still available in complete form, dating back to the days of Oliver Cromwell, but it contains nothing to show that Howell Davies had any connection with it whatsoever. Yet, without doubt, he regularly preached and administered the sacraments here for many years in the period before the Methodists possessed any chapels in this part of Pembrokeshire.

Haverfordwest is the centre of the county. The people of the surrounding countryside meet there for the markets and fairs; in particular, the people of Llys-y-frân would regularly pass through the Prendergast area of the town. And so, because of the power and charm of its preacher, the church became the regular destination of many. Immense congregations gathered. Prendergast was second only to Llangeitho in its size of congregation, and the nature of the powerful influences that descended upon the two places was very similar.

Howell Davies also preached and administered the sacraments at St Daniel in Castlemartin and at Mounton near Narberth, both places being in the English region of the county. The sum of his communicants in all three churches was over two thousand. The buildings would be filled and emptied two or three times on Communion Sundays, such were the numbers of applicants eagerly desiring to commemorate the death of the cross.

About 1744 Howell Davies began considering marriage. He clearly had some anxieties over the step for he asked advice of Howell Harris. His letter, and Harris's reply to it, have both been published. Harris was in the right frame of mind to sympathize with him, for he also was on the point of getting married. His reply was very serious in tone. He noted that Davies' position was such a public one and his cause of such supreme importance, that great care was needed not to confuse one's feelings with the guidance of God. He has nothing against the lady and calls her 'the dear sister C—', which shows that he knew of her as a godly young woman. He ends with the request that he might meet with her at Capel Ifan so that he might more fully understand her state of mind. The resulting meeting was favourable and Howell Davies became a married man.

His wife deserves our attention. Her maiden name was Catherine Poyer and she was the daughter of John Poyer, Esq., a gentleman descended from the Normans and a member of one of the noblest families of Pembrokeshire. One member of the family, another John Poyer, was in charge of Pembroke castle during the Civil War and it appears that he conducted its defence against Cromwell's forces with much bravery and ability. Catherine Poyer grew up in the fine mansion of the Parke estate, the home of her mother's parents, Griffith and Catherine Twyning. It was here that she was first convicted spiritually, probably under Howell Davies' ministry, although a sincere religion of some sort was practised in the Twyning household. A relative, another Griffith Twyning, was vicar at Walton, a parish adjoining Llys-y-frân, in 1747, and it may be that he was Howell Davies' successor in the Llys-y-frân curacy. This man's daughter, a Mrs. Scourfield who lived at Pwllhook, was a member with the Methodists at the time that the Rev. David Jones, Llan-gan, was in Pembrokeshire. There is some reason to believe that Howell Harris and Daniel Rowland, as well as Howell Davies, often visited Parke on their travels and it is possible that Catherine had received abundantly of the spirit of the revival.

Both grandparents had died before her marriage and she was the sole beneficiary of their estate. Immediately on marrying, therefore, Howell Davies became a rich man. But sudden wealth brought about no change in the extent of his labours for the gospel. He continued with the same commitment and zeal as before, and clearly received every encouragement to do so from his wife.

But the happiness at Parke was short-lived. Death entered the stately house and bore Catherine away. She died at the birth of her first child, a daughter, and before the little girl was two years old she also was carried to her grave and Mr Davies was left alone.

He eventually remarried, his second wife being Miss Luce Phillips, daughter of Mr Hugh Phillips, a wealthy gentleman from the same neighbourhood. As all of Hugh Phillips's other children died without heirs, his wealth eventually passed on to Howell Davies. Mrs Davies was noted for her beauty, her good sense and her godliness; she was also a fine singer. Mr Davies also was an excellent singer and this gift remains in the Parke family to this day. As a result of these marriages Howell Davies was the owner of two fine houses, the Parke, and his wife's home at Prendergast. He would live at both houses, according to his convenience. His life was not free from sorrows. His only son, Howell, born in 1749, died when only seven months old. On the other hand, a daughter, Margaret, became the wife of the Rev. Nathaniel Rowland, and it is their descendants who still live today at Parke.

Howell Davies continued with his labours, and heaven continued to bless these labours. The revival spread throughout Pembrokeshire and especially throughout the central region around Haverfordwest. In 1748, he moved his society to another building in order to accommodate all of the Haverfordwest flock. The building was called The Tabernacle, after Whitefield's Tabernacle at Moorfields, London. The assistant to Davies at The Tabernacle was the exhorter John Sparks mentioned in the Llangwm minutes. John Sparks had been born in Haverfordwest in 1726. He experienced powerful convictions when young and had begun taking part in the religious services held by his parents in their home. He was a good preacher and an eminently godly man. When Rowland and Harris separated, Sparks sided with the latter. We read of him preaching often at Harris's Associations and it is said that he ministered with unusual unction. In 1751, however, he left the Methodists and joined the Moravian Church.

## BUILDING CHAPELS

A strong cause had been established by Howell Davies at Woodstock. A chapel was built here in 1754 and opened in the following year with a sermon from Whitefield. The preacher also administered the sacrament of the Lord's Supper that day, and it is believed that this was the first time for the ordinance to be observed in Wales in any building not consecrated by a priest, or registered as a Nonconformist place of worship. The occasion reveals Howell Davies's boldness and independence of thought and proves that he had freed himself of the fetters of the Established Church considerably sooner than most of his fellow Reformers. It is also true however that Whitefield and Howell Harris, together with the Methodists in England, had agreed as early as 1743 to administer communion in the societies if and when this privilege was refused them in their parish churches, and this decision had been made known by letter to Howell Davies. The ordinances of baptism and the Lord's Supper were administered regularly at Woodstock for fifty-six years before the Ordination of 1811. Therefore, in one sense, Woodstock is the mother church of the whole Connexion. When serving the table Mr Davies would use the Service of the Church, but he would often deviate from it, speaking of the Saviour's sufferings with a power and a sweetness that would overcome the gathered congregation.

Davies was also instrumental in opening a place of worship in north Pembrokeshire. The building was called Capel Newydd (New Chapel). A religious society had been established at Cerrig Gwynion nearby as early as 1743. For the convenience of its members this gradually divided into two, one cause meeting at Llechryd and the other in a farmhouse called Hen Barciau, in the Clydau parish. Howell Davies preached often at both places. As he was a priest in orders he was allowed to preach at Llechryd Church but the size of the congregation often forced him to preach in the cemetery outside. The farmhouse at Hen Barciau, also, soon became much too small for the meetings but for some time it proved impossible to obtain land to build a place of worship. Eventually, land was obtained from Stephen Colby, Esq., a captain in the Navy whose wife was sympathetic towards the Methodists. Howell Davies chose the site. While passing over the hill from Llechryd to Hen Barciau he threw his whip in amongst the scattered gorse bushes, telling his friends, 'Here's the place for the chapel.'

The building was opened in 1763 and Mr Davies preached from the words, 'Gad, a troop shall overcome him: but he shall overcome at the last.' The ordinances were administered at Capel Newydd from the beginning and it was well-known as the only place in the area where the sacraments were distributed amongst the Methodists. Great crowds gathered on Communion Sundays and, as at Woodstock, it remained the main meeting place for the believers of the area until the Methodists ordained their own ministers. Howell Davies would usually serve the table. In his absence, Daniel Rowland; or his son, Nathaniel Rowland; or Jones, Llan-gan; Davies, Neath; or Williams, Lledrod; would administer. It is said that, after the Disruption period, Howell Harris preached there many times. It was at Capel Newydd, when Daniel Rowland was preaching from Hebrews 4:15, that the deepest impressions were made upon Mr Charles of Bala; impressions whose effects upon him were never to be erased. Here also Jones, Llan-gan, preached his last sermon, as he was returning home from taking services at Llangeitho, in August 1810.

## HOWELL DAVIES AS A PREACHER

Howell Davies never suffered the degree of persecution that befell others of the Fathers. His high social standing and the support of the Rev. Griffith Jones, proved a considerable protection. But he did not escape completely from the storms. In a letter to him, dated 13 September 1743, Howell Harris wrote:

> I should have been glad to know how it has been with you in the Bishop's Court. Perhaps it might have been in my power to speak to some body here [London] for direction how to act but I believe they will do nothing, especially if they shall understand that you know that their court has indeed no power at all and that you are resolved to the Civil Law and dispute the authority of their Court and to bring the course of their black doings to light. This I think to be our duty in the defensive but if we have our liberty let us thankfully and humbly use it.[1]

We do not know what became of the trouble in the Bishop's Court but it is quite certain that Christ's minister pursued his way without turning aside to the left or the right, esteeming the persecution a privilege in that he suffered for his Saviour's sake.

Howell Davies was predominantly the apostle of Pembrokeshire. His apostleship was directed as fully towards the English-speaking area of the county as towards the Welsh, and he preached in each language according to the need. He was a rain cloud appointed for Pembrokeshire. The gracious showers descended heavily on all parts of the county wherever he preached. It was granted to him to see a harvest ripening and bearing forth much fruit – a whole region subdued to the gospel of Christ to a considerable extent. Though he was more domesticated than many of his fellow-labourers, he still travelled much throughout south and north Wales and to many of the English cities. He was many times in London; he visited Bath and Bristol in turn, together with other towns where the English Methodists preached. He was of the party that met with the Countess of Huntingdon at Bristol in 1748 at the beginning of her visit to the Principality and acted as her escort during the tour. John Evans of Bala mentions that he often visited that town. 'He was a kind and gentle man, and a most engaging preacher,' was his opinion of Davies.

Howell Davies was present at the very first Association held at Bala. He wrote to Howell Harris:

> Since we departed from the Conference I have travelled through Glamorganshire, which proved a glorious time for many. For myself I long to return there soon again, for doubtless God is with them. As far as my entering north Wales is concerned, I believe it will be too painful for me, for I am still weak

and unhealthy; however I am determined to attempt it, even if I should die on the way.

It was no small thing in those days for an ailing man like Howell Davies to undertake such a journey to the north. The roads were bad and mountainous; the lodgings poor and scarce. The friends of the gospel were generally of poor circumstances and few in number; the places of worship were deficient: cold, and few and far between. The prejudice of the day against the Methodists was as cruel as the grave; the people were rebellious and unfeeling; and the gentry and clergy full of spite and watchful for every opportunity to persecute and scourge those whom they considered the troublers of nations. No wonder that Mr Davies feared as he contemplated the venture. But he was resolved to proceed even though the journey might result in his death. William Williams, in the magnificent elegy that he composed for him, referred to the extent of his labours and itineraries.

They tell us how he journeyed,
When his health was still preserved,
When Monmouth, Denbigh, Gwynedd,
Merioneth, Flint, he served;
How he proclaimed the gospel,
In his fluent, lively way,
From Presteigne to St David's,
Holyhead to Cardiff bay.

Dwedent i ni fel y teithiodd,
Pan oedd yn ei iechyd gynt,
Mynwy, Dinbych a Chaernarfon,
Môn, Meirionydd, a Sir Fflint;
Fel cyhoeddodd yr efengyl,
Gydag yspryd bywiog, rhydd,
O Lanandras i Dyddewi,
O Gaergybi i Gaerdydd.

'Mongst London's hordes he laboured,
Proclaiming words of light,
As he preached the Kingdom message,
From morning until night;
Cold, bustling Bristol also,
Received the Word with joy,
As he, throughout all weathers,
Continued on his way.

Dwedent i ni fel y chwysodd,
Fry yn Llundain, boblog iawn,
Wrth bregethu Gair y Deyrnas,
Weithiau foreu, weithiau nawn;
Bryste hithau, oer, derfysglyd,
Glywodd swn ei 'fengyl gref;
Tide a thonau, llif a storom,
Gurodd ganwaith arno ef.

It is clear that he did his utmost to avoid publicity. Howell Harris wrote to him on 7 March, 1744:

You gave me some hopes of a letter – you should not let the fear of inserting it in *The Weekly History* withhold your pen, for I should not do it without your leave – I won't dictate to my brother but I'll simply and humbly give my opinion that according to the design of the paper I don't know why Brother Davies should refuse to give his name among the poor labourers there, and say what he has got to say of the progress of the gospel. I believe he has near as much if not more, as to its course in his own heart and by his ministry and under his observation if not more than most there – I am sure then he loves them and will willingly partake of their sufferings, and knows that he and they speak the same language, are led by the same Spirit, fight under the same Banner, and are accounted as one by their enemies. The fear of praise should not keep us from speaking what we know any more than the desire of praise should encourage us to speak. My brother knows that it is the Lord who accomplishes all.[2]

After gently rebuking him in this way for his shyness and for his fear of publicity, Harris goes on to press Davies to attend the forthcoming Association, doing so in a manner that reveals how much he valued his presence:

I know my dearest brother will not be offended at my intreating him not to refuse coming to meet the brethren at Abergavenny on Wednesday, 28th instant . . . it can be so contrived that all the time in going and coming may be filled up with preaching through Breconshire and Monmouth. I am the more pressing because it appears that the importance of this does not affect my brother's heart to the degree it should. . . . Let us now the more associate and unite that our enemies may be convinced we are indeed earnest so that if they go to destroy one it won't do unless they do the whole. . . The dogs always drive the sheep closer to one another.[3]

It seems that Howell Davies was the instrument in the conversion of Mr Bateman, the vicar of Great St Bartholomew in London, who was later considered one of the most evangelical ministers in the capital. Mr Bateman was in possession of a small living in Pembrokeshire. On one occasion, whilst on a visit to this parish, he was appointed to preach at one of Mr Davies' churches. At the time Mr Bateman was unregenerate and his sermon was full of slanderous accusations against the Methodists. He warned his hearers for the sake of their souls to keep away from them. After the sermon, he was overcome by a depression for which he could give no account. He could not sleep or eat, nor could he enjoy the company of his irreligious friends as before. He went to hear Howell Davies in the very church where he had previously mocked him and his followers. He felt the word 'as a spear piercing his heart'. His sins now overcame him, he felt as if he were buried in them over his head; they were a burden too heavy to bear. It was a whole month before his soul found peace. But after this experience he himself became a blessing to many in Wales and London.

Undoubtedly, Howell Davies was a most powerful preacher. The older believers accounted him second only to Rowland himself. Wherever he preached, in farmhouse or barn, or in large Bristol or London buildings, he gained the attention of his hearers immediately. He would read or recite a verse or a hymn and then lead the singing himself with his clear, musical voice and the whole congregation would join with him in praise of the God of the whole earth. In the introductory prayer he would be notably importunate, approaching the Divine Presence and drawing heaven into the place. Then, in his importunity before the throne, he would present the same request over and over again, as if he could not leave go of it. His congregation would be thoroughly softened and affected before he began his sermon, and a certain heavenliness about his person would ensure a favourable reception and seemed to draw out both love and reverence towards him simultaneously.

He would read his text clearly with an attractive, musical voice. For a while he spoke slowly, expounding the verse and its context. But soon, it could be sensed that his soul was stirred within him. He would raise his voice like a silver trumpet and the congregation to its very furthest reaches would stand confounded before him. He would hurl the severest darts at his hearers and every sentence would wound. The place by now would be truly dreadful. Hundreds would groan and sigh. The granite rock had become a pool of water. Tears would be flowing freely and there would not be one dry cheek in the crowd. All at once the preacher would change key. Laying aside the thundering he would direct the tearful listeners to that Saviour who can save them to the uttermost. The sighs would stop and the groans cease and in their place would be heard shouts of 'Gogoniant!' and 'Diolch iddo!'[4] The whole vast crowd, from one end to another, would be glorying together. The tears would flow again, but they would now be tears of joy, and the preacher would conclude, leaving his congregation in the heavenliest of frames.

> Come see this great preacher with glory displaying
> The doctrine of heaven, the rainbow of blood,
> Thus spanning with ease the eternal horizons,
> The oceans dividing poor sinners from God.
>
> Fel hynny y rhodiai y pennaf areithydd,
> Dros nef yr athrawiaeth, y bwa o waed,
> A roed i rychwantu y bythol wybrennydd,
> Yr eigion rhwng daear a nefoedd a gaed.

Together with the dignity of his personal appearance and his superb oratory, one of his hearers noted the unique way he had of moving his right hand and bringing it to rest in his left hand in a most effective gesture. He would draw the most vivid pictures in his sermons. In particular, when portraying the Saviour's crucifixion his descriptions were so moving and powerful that every eye would be fixed upon him. It is said that when he preached at Llechryd on a Sunday morning, the congregation would sometimes remain behind, praising and rejoicing, until nightfall. He himself would leave during the afternoon but on reaching the hill known as Craig Cilfowyr would stop and look back down on the rejoicing crowd with amazement and thankfulness. On one occasion he and Howell Harris were together at Llechryd. Howell Davies preached inside the cemetery and the other Howell outside. One of them had been under the influence of a bishop's hands, and the other had not. The unordained Howell Harris had therefore no right to preach on consecrated ground!

In the sad separation between Rowland and Harris, Howell Davies, together with Williams, Pantycelyn, and the majority of the Methodist clergy, sided with Rowland. It was due to his great influence that this storm passed over Pembrokeshire leaving it relatively unscathed compared to other regions of the country. As Cardiganshire and Pembrokeshire share so many miles of border, the fields of labour of Howell Davies and Rowland touched over a large area, and without doubt the two of them embraced every opportunity for co-operation and conference. It does not appear either that any occasion of coldness or envy arose between them at any time. Although Howell Davies possessed the gentlest of temperaments, kindly and liberal, he would yet oppose every departure from the faith and every irregularity of life with boldness. Williams described him in his elegy:

| | |
|---|---|
| We have heard how he confounded | Clywsom fel y gwrthwynebodd |
| All who wrest the eternal Word; | Ef heresiau diried ryw; |
| How his sermons ever thundered | Mellt a tharan oedd ei eiriau |
| 'Gainst the enemies of God; | I elynion 'fengyl Duw; |
| Orthodox in all his teaching, | Cywir yn ei egwyddorion, |
| Faithful, honest, truest friend; | Syml, gonest yn ei ffydd; |
| Kind and generous in his giving, | Elusengar yn ei fywyd, |
| Ever useful to the end. | Llwyr ddefnyddiol yn ei ddydd. |

Neither his popularity as a preacher nor the riches which came his way produced in him the slightest degree of spiritual pride, for he remained particularly humble all his life. He preferred to consider himself as of the same rank as the lowest. On a communion Sunday he would often walk to Woodstock – a rough road of about fifteen miles. One reason for this was in order to place himself in the same position as the majority of his congregation who would make their way to the church from distances of up to twenty miles away. But he did so also in order to enjoy fellowship along the way with the faithful pilgrims, whose hearts were full of warmth and whose experiences were lively and spiritual. There is no doubt that the heavenly feast was enjoyed in part before ever reaching the chapel, and that the fellowship was an excellent preparation for the sermon and the sacrament. Williams calls him 'the shepherd of four large churches'. As mentioned previously, these were Capel Newydd; Woodstock; St Daniel, Castlemartin; and Moulton, Narberth.

## HIS DEATH AND FUNERAL

Howell Davies's days came to an end whilst he was still in the midst of his labours and usefulness. He was only a little above middle age. Very many more years of activity might have been expected from him. But his immense labours had worn down the little strength present in his frail constitution. He was buried on 13 January 1770, when only fifty-three years old. He had died at his mansion at Parke. Elizabeth, his second wife, had predeceased him by ten years. Their graves, together with that of their only son, Howell, are in Prendergast cemetery. The day of Howell Davies's funeral was a dark day for the Methodists of Pembrokeshire and none felt it more keenly than themselves. Though Parke is some twenty miles from Haverfordwest, the congregation that gathered for the funeral was enormous. As well as those who walked the whole distance, crowds also arrived from the various preaching stations where he had ministered. They met the funeral party at a crossroads in order to pay their respects, and as the coffin passed by they wailed loudly. By the time Haverfordwest was reached the concourse was immense, extending for up to a mile along the road. So greatly was his loss felt, and so strong the emotions of all, that the ministering clergy failed to read the funeral service. It was therefore amidst showers of bitter tears and signs of a grief of an extent seldom experienced, that Howell Davies was laid in the ground. He was the first of the Methodist Fathers to be taken. He left behind in Pembrokeshire a thriving cause. His own communicants numbered nearly three thousand, and the other Methodists of the county were very numerous.

[1] STL, vol. 1, p. 105.
[2] ibid., pp. 133–4.
[3] ibid.
[4] 'Glory!' and 'Thank Him!'

# 7

# WILLIAM WILLIAMS OF PANTYCELYN

## OPENING REMARKS

*W*illiams of Pantycelyn is the foremost literary figure of the Methodist Connexion in Wales and, it may well be, its greatest figure. In his day he enriched the literature of his country more than any other contemporary. And in one important branch of literature, that of sacred poetry and hymns, it is generally acknowledged that he stands head and shoulders above all. It is difficult to conceive of any greater honour for a man than that he should have provided the foremost medium of praise to the Almighty for a whole nation. Williams presently holds this honour, and will in all probability retain it for as long as the Welsh nation continues to use its mother-tongue.

Williams was a unique personality, gifted with unique qualifications for the work he carried out. He contributed much in general to the work of the revival and laboured as diligently as any in seeking its advance. It is true that he was not of those few who were abroad very early at the dawning of the awakening. This was the privilege of Daniel Rowland and Howell Harris. But he was up with the sun; he laboured in the field from early on; and he continued until evening, enduring the heat and burden of the day. He outlived the first three Methodist Fathers, and he survived them in more than one sense. We must acknowledge that even these giants, Daniel Rowland, Howell Harris and Howell Davies, are considered to be spent forces by this present generation – possessing influence today only within the religious organization they founded or through their history and example. But Williams remains a present and abiding influence amongst us, as if having escaped the cold hand of death entirely. It is the poet who lives longer than any. Indeed, he is immortal.

We will endeavour to portray Williams's many-sided character to the best of our ability. We will present him as a reformer, an author, and a poet. But we must first provide a brief account of his life.

Though Williams's writings were extensive, he left his compatriots in complete ignorance of his own personal history. Probably very many autobiographical references are to be found in his literary works, especially in *Theomemphus* and the *Elegies*. But these are too vague and imprecise to be of any historical use. Some fewer specific references occur, and these are important. As far as we know, the only surviving comments by Williams of an autographical nature are found in a brief paragraph in the middle of a long letter which he wrote to the Rev. Thomas Charles, some three years before he died. These are:

> My days are drawing to an end, my course is nearly run: I have had a long life. I am now 73 years old. My strength would yet be pretty good, were it not for the affliction my Heavenly Father has laid upon me. I have been preaching for the last 43 years,[1] and have travelled on an average between forty and fifty miles every week during that time. I had four or five long journeys last spring through the counties of south Wales. Each was about a fortnight's space, and I travelled each time about two hundred miles. I intended going through North Wales, but these long journeys have, together with my complaint, so weakened me that I have no hope of mending.

This constitutes the length and breadth of William Williams's Auto-biography, and is very typical of him. The only reference is to his work as an evangelist, there is not the least mention of his literary achievements.

Furthermore, very little was written about Williams by his contemp-oraries. No doubt his secondary role was to some extent responsible for this. He was after all merely Daniel Rowland's assistant! This was the office he was appointed to by the Watford Association and certainly, no-one ever had a better assistant. The comment of the Rev. David Griffiths, Nevern, was very apt: 'Rowland could rule the whole world, if he could have Williams, Pantycelyn, at his elbow.' No doubt Rowland and Harris were the heroes of that age. It was of them that all spoke and wrote, and Williams, like all others, was in their shadow, especially at the beginning of the revival.

## THOMAS CHARLES'S BIOGRAPHY OF
## WILLIAM WILLIAMS

It was not until twenty-two years after his death that any attempt was made to write a biography. The first to do so was none other than the Rev. Thomas Charles of Bala. He was perfectly qualified for the work. He had known William Williams; he was very aware of his labours as an evangelist and was a great admirer of his literary works. This *Life* appeared, not as a separate volume, but in the periodical edited by Thomas Charles at the time, namely the old *Trysorfa* [*The Spiritual Treasury*]. It was published in January 1813. Nobody, as far as we know, has noted the fact that it was at the request of the Rev. John Williams, the son of the poet, who was living at the time at Pantycelyn, that the life was written. In a letter that John Williams wrote to his brother, the Rev. William Williams of Truro, Cornwall, he refers to the death of Thomas Charles, saying:

> The loss to the whole of Wales was great, and especially to the Methodist body. He was eminently useful in so many different ways. He published many excellent books. It was he who, at my request, wrote the *Life* of our father. I provided him with a skeleton and he filled it out. I sent the materials and he built the edifice.[2]

This biography in the *Treasury* is really only a short essay of about a dozen pages. It contains however all that a spiritual man like Thomas Charles believed was appropriate to record, briefly and concisely, concerning Williams. He left out of the essay any interesting narratives about his subject. At least he left out all but one, and that single exception was included, we presume, not so much because of its humour as because it reveals the sensitive conscience of the hymn writer.[3]

No doubt Mr Charles knew dozens of such stories but as they were not profitable for doctrine, reproof, correction or instruction in righteousness he laid them aside, keeping only to what was edifying and appropriate. Later historians have been busy collecting all such tales and as it is the case that a good story will last a long time, many of them have survived, and are deemed by now to be essential to the history of William Williams. They are the delicacies which our more zestful age loves to consume.

## HIS EARLY LIFE

Williams was born in 1717 in a farmhouse called Cefncoed in the parish of Llanfair-ar-y-bryn, near Llandovery, Carmarthenshire. He lived here until his marriage. His father was John Williams, an honest and responsible farmer and a deacon at the Independent church of Cefnarthen nearby. John was the owner of Cefncoed. His wife's maiden name was Dorothy Lewis, and her father was the owner of Pantycelyn farm. The two houses were within a few miles of each other, and William Williams became the owner of one through his father and of the other through his mother. His love for his mother was proverbial. It is said that he wrote a verse of praise on the window of a house where he stayed during a preaching journey, to the little girl of the house whose name was the same as his mother's:

| | |
|---|---|
| As your name is Dorothea, | Dorothea yw dy enw, |
| And this means you are *God's gift,* | Ystyr hyn yw *Rhodd dy Dduw,* |
| According to that sweet description | Ac yn ôl yr enw hyfryd |
| May your whole life long be lived; | Yn y bywyd bo it fyw; |
| A gift your mind, a gift your talents, | Rhodd yw'th ddysg, a rhodd yw'th ddoniau, |
| The fairness of your face, the same; | A rhodd yw'th fod yn ferch fach lân; |
| 'Tis the gift of gifts will keep you | Rhodd y rhoddion ydyw hyny |
| Safe from Hell's eternal flame. | I'th gadw di rhag uffern dàn. |

There was an unusual age difference – thirty-three years – between Williams's mother and father. The following story is told of their courtship:

> It is said that John Williams had befriended a lady who lived some distance from his home, and on his visits to her his journey would take him past Pantycelyn. On one of these occasions he was passing Pantycelyn's door and met the daughter of the house, Dorothy Lewis. The young girl evidently thought this too good an opportunity to miss in amusing herself at the expense of the 'old fellow'.
>
> 'You are travelling far to find yourself a wife, Uncle John,' she said. 'It appears to me that you could find one a good deal nearer home!'
>
> 'It may well be that it will turn out so in the end,' was the reply. And certainly, in the event, so it proved.[4]

It is often said that John Williams died when his son was still young and that therefore the responsibility of raising him fell solely upon the mother. This is a considerable mistake, and it is difficult to understand how it ever arose. John Williams died on 1 April 1742, when William was twenty-five years old. The father lived another four years after his son's conversion under the preaching of Howell Harris. He was alive during the two years in which Williams was preparing for ordination in the Established Church, and during the following two years when his son was curate over Llanwrtyd and Abergwesyn churches.

If the mistaken story arose out of an attempt to explain why the son of a prominent deacon with the Independents became a priest, it is completely insufficient and contrary to the truth. It is true that the father was an old man for he was eighty-six years of age when he died. He had lost his sight, being blind for the last six years of his life. But he was in full possession of understanding to the last and a man of much ability. As proof of his strength and energy it is sufficient to mention that, two years before his death, he led the Calvinistic party of the Cefnarthen Church in their separation from that church, in order to worship apart from the Arminian element which formed the majority of the congregation at that time. William Williams no doubt profited from the counsels of both mother and father when deciding to join the Church of England, and his change of denomination was not contrary to their wishes.

When Williams married at thirty-two years of age he moved from Cefncoed to Pantycelyn, taking his widowed mother with him. She lived until she was ninety-five, dying only seven years before her son. Williams and his wife were members with the Methodists at Cil-y-cwm but it seems that the mother remained with the Independents throughout her life. This is confirmed by the old Society Book of Cil-y-cwm where the members and their families are registered. We find there, *'William Williams, Pantycelyn'; 'Mary, the wife'; 'Mary, the maid'*; but not *'Dorothy, the mother.'* During these years, Pantycelyn was the home of representatives of three denominations – the Methodists, the Independents, and the Established Church.

The period of William Williams's life for which least is known is his youth. The only certain knowledge that we have of him at this time is that he grew up without receiving any significant religious conviction. We have his own testimony for this, as we shall see later. The question as to whether he passed these years in indifference and insensibility, or in active immorality and ungodliness, is one that cannot be answered. He was given the great advantage of being raised in a Christian home. It is said of his father that as well as being a 'ruling elder' (the most responsible position amongst the deacons) of Cefnarthen Church, he was also 'a kind-hearted, honest Christian of integrity, who, free from any fears, obtained an entrance from this wilderness into a better land'.[5] Such was his father's character according to those who knew him best. And it is certain that his mother was of identical quality. But though his upbringing was religious and the influence of the home healthy and happy, Williams grew up with a careless and disregarding attitude.

It may perhaps be useful to consider the moral and religious nature of the neighbourhood in which he lived at the time. This is a fairly easy matter to determine. Llandovery lay as deeply in immorality and sin as any other locality in Wales. The place was notorious for its ungodliness and wickedness. A hundred years earlier Vicar Rhys Prichard had delivered his curses upon the town, and there is ample evidence at hand testifying that it had not improved a jot in the meantime. The following is a sample of the old Vicar's warnings to Llandovery town:

'Mene, Tekel,' O Llandovery!      'Mene Tecel,' tre' Llan'ddyfri!
God has weighed you in your misery;    Pwysodd Duw di yn dy fryntni;
Naught but dross in you he found,     Ni cha'dd ynot ond y sorod,
Now beware his wrath profound!     Gochel weithian rhag ei ddyrnod!

| | |
|---|---|
| You've been warned so many times, | Cefaist rhybudd lawer pryd, |
| Oft have I reproved your crimes; | Nid yw cyngor 'mheuthun id'; |
| For excuses 'tis too late, | Nid oes lun it wneuthur esgus, |
| O! how awful your estate! | O! gwae ti, y dref anhapus! |
| | |
| I rose early at the cockcrow, | Bore godais gyda'r ceiliog, |
| Long I laboured to exhort you | Hir ddilynais, yn dy annog |
| Now to turn to God for mercy; | Droi at Dduw, oddiwrth dy fryntni, |
| Vainly I performed my duty. | Ond yr oedd yn ofer i mi. |
| | |
| I piped to you, to dance you would not, | Cenaist bibau, ond ni ddawnsiaist, |
| I sore complained, repent you could not; | Tost gwynfanais, nis galeraist; |
| I used all means, both foul and fair, | Ceisiaist drwy deg, a thrwy hagar, |
| But you would only mock and swear. | Ni chawn gennyt ond y gwatwar. |

## THE NONCONFORMITY OF THE LOCALITY, AND THE CONTROVERSIES AT CEFNARTHEN CHURCH

The parishes of Llanfair-ar-y-bryn, Llandingad and Cil-y-cwm were in the blackest darkness at the beginning of the Methodist revival, with the clergy no more than blind watchmen. But what of the local Presbyterian churches? Were they not still standing bravely against the floods encompassing the land? No doubt that was the case to some extent, but not to the degree that they had done in earlier days. The extent of their influence was very largely curtailed because they were so torn by agitations and schisms, due mainly to doctrinal disagreements. There were two Nonconformist churches in the Llandovery area: the Baptist cause at Cil-y-cwm, and Cefnarthen Independent Church. The Cil-y-cwm church was small and rather insignificant, but that in Cefnarthen was numerous and of considerable fame. This is where Williams's parents were members and where he would have been taken during his youth. The reader must be given an outline of the history of this cause in order to appreciate the religious upbringing it provided. It was one of the oldest churches in Wales and had proved of immense service to religion in the Llandovery area in the Protectorate period and during the times of persecution after the restoration of Charles II. A full and most interesting history is given in *Hanes Eglwysi Annibynnol Cymru* [*The History of the Independent Churches of Wales*].[6] We must summarize it here.

Cefnarthen Church was begun by Mr Jenkin Jones, Llanddeti, as early, possibly, as 1642. Persecution scattered the congregation and imprisoned the pastor and many of the members. The cause was re-established about 1688 by Mr Rees Prytherch. He remained a faithful pastor until his death in 1699. His successor was Mr Roger Williams. The first two pastors were

Calvinistic in doctrine, and so also was Roger Williams at first, but in his later period he preached Arminianism and succeeded in propagating that doctrine amongst his members and congregation. He died in 1730, having been preaching here and at Cwm-y-glo, Merthyr Tydfil, for thirty-two years. There were two parties in the church when he died, with the Arminian group by now in the majority. In the period following, the church had three ministers. One party appointed two men of Arminian persuasion, and the other appointed a Calvinist. These three ministers pastored the church at one and the same time, not because the numbers involved required them, but solely in order to cater for their divided condition. Two different theologies were preached in the same chapel and from the same pulpit for seven years.

At last the church split up. The Arminians retained possession of the meeting-house and the Calvinists worshipped at a farmhouse called Clinypentan, which stands between Cefncoed and Pantycelyn. William Williams's father led the Calvinistic party out of the church. After the division, the Calvinists multiplied and the Arminians declined. A new chapel was built for the Calvinists on a patch of ground, now called Pentretygwyn, given to them by Williams and his mother. In time the two churches were reunited under the ministry of Mr Morgan Jones and Arminian doctrine was thoroughly purged from amongst them.

That is a brief history of Cefnarthen Church. It is seen that Williams was raised in one of the most turbulent churches of Wales; a church of more argument than religion. It is not that they were a people who agreed to disagree, but were those rather, so inflexible in their own opinions, that they were capable of maintaining a sustained warfare over many years. We do not know if Williams was a professing member of the church but it was there he attended for public worship up to the time of his departure to college as a young man of seventeen or eighteen years of age. It is probable that Roger Williams had become an Arminian before Williams was born. During his first years it would be immaterial to the young Williams what doctrines he heard. But before the end of Roger Williams's ministry the blue-eyed boy had perhaps some vague idea of that which he was hearing: that there was a difference, though he could not grasp what it was, between what his father believed and the messages of his pastor. It is not improbable that he overheard heated discussions between the two men.

He was thirteen years old when the minister died. It was a much more serious matter what teachings were proclaimed in his hearing during the next five years. This was the period in which his young mind would blossom, in which he would put away childish things as he became aware of approaching adulthood. It is to be regretted that the public ministry of Cefnarthen Church and the private teaching of the home did not reinforce each other at this crucial time. We fear that it was rather the case that the edification received at home was being undermined at the chapel. We know to our grief that there is nothing that so alienates the sympathies of the young from religion than experiences of arguments and quarrels, of whatever nature, within the church, and this was a period when doctrinal warfare was fierce at Cefnarthen. The Arminians had wrested control in the church and the struggle between them and the Calvinists was bitter. Would it not have been better for them to separate much earlier, in that all unity between them had in reality broken down entirely? This is possibly so; but perhaps their attachment to the famous old meeting-house made this impossible to them.

As was said, the two parties preached against one another from the same pulpit for seven years, and Williams attended the church for five of these seven years. It is to be regretted that he did not provide for us a history of these years, describing all he heard and saw. This could have shed light on so much that we do not now know. Did the parties preach in opposition during the same service, or at different times? If at different times, did the opposing parties frequent each other's services? Did Williams take part in these controversies or did he deprecate them and refuse to be involved? Such queries must now remain unanswered but we are sure of one thing, that these quarrels and arguments contributed nothing to his soul. They could hardly be considered a means of grace to him. If he was involved in them, then at the most they might have widened his sphere of knowledge and sharpened his mental faculties.

It may well be that the history of Cefnarthen Church was in the forefront of Williams's mind when he composed Theomemphus. We believe this to be the case, and that he was searching his memory rather than drawing upon his imagination when he portrayed those preachers who were seeking to undermine the influences of Boanerges and Evangelius upon his hero. If the following lines are read in the light of the above history of Cefnarthen we believe that the correspondence is very evident. This is how one of them, called *Arbitrius Liber*[7] by the poet, preaches justification by faith:

> 'Now listen, race of Adam,' declared the preacher bold,
> ''Twas love alone that placed you to walk this earth, of old;
> Good thoughts abound towards you e'er since the hills were laid,
> And from eternal ages, before one thing was made.

\*     'Your Maker is your Husband, your Husband through and through,
His goodwill is forever, for every creature too;
He wills the death of no one, he wills that all should live,
This is the Bible's message, its words this witness give.

\*     'How often Scriptures teaches, its promises declare,
That God's not out to damn us, but all the world to spare?
Woe be to such as limit God's mercy to the few
Whom God has fore-determined, before their faith he knew.

'How any reasonable person can make the awful claim
That God predestines people, some to the eternal flame?
This is a bitter insult to the character of God,
Whose mercy flows as widely as waters of the flood.

\*     'The words of God are clear, "Come, whosoever will,
Come without hesitation, though you be well or ill";
This call has no foundation, unless there's real choice,
Mere stones and vegetation can hear no living voice.

\*     'Man still is free and able, although he's gone astray,
The human will and reason's not yet defiled away;
The mind still governs reason, and this maintained its own
When sovereignty departed and man lost heaven's crown.

'Here is my message to you, the proclaiming of the true;
So as to do my duty I make it clear to you;
Reflect upon this teaching, commit to it all your might,
Fulfilling all your duties from morning until night.

'Stir up your many virtues, keep to them every day,
To honour every statute, this only is God's way;
To break the Law is damnation, this is His stated word,
Those who transgress one precept can but expect His sword.

'And further to all duties, there's none that can compare
With those most heavenly duties of charity and prayer;
These pearls of greatest beauty – faith, hopeful joy and love,
To death itself these virtues a mortal blow shall prove.

\*     'Part with each sin you know of, in thought as well as deed,
All jealousy and malice, give worldly bliss no heed;
Our duty's done by seeking, grace comes to us this way,
And then foul sin we'll conquer, with ease and joy each day.

---

\* The stanzas marked with an asterisk on this and the following pages are taken from translations by Eifion Evans in *Pursued by God* (Bridgend: Evangelical Press of Wales, 1996).

\*
> 'All that remains is simple, we now must do our best,
> The Word provides our witness that God will do the rest;
> He gives us grace for seeking; all we must do is call;
> As soon as we have sought him, God freely gives us all.'

Another example is *Orthocephalus*, an orthodox minister, but selfish, boastful and dry:

> 'So many false in teaching,' said he, 'are found abroad,
> How little understand they the doctrines of the Word;
> They have no form or reason, but carelessly proclaim
> A hotch-potch of confusion and doctrines false and vain.

> 'The Church of Rome, my brethren, so many years ago,
> Departed from the gospel entirely, as you know;
> The Greek Church too in darkness extends to Muscovy,
> Though scorning Rome's departures, no better off is she.

> 'The Coptics and Armenians throughout Egyptian lands
> Are far removed in error, O poor, unhappy bands;
> And here within our nation opinions may be heard
> Which contradict entirely the Gospel's saving word.

> 'The blind Arminian trusts to the ability of man,
> Experience should dissuade him, if nothing other can;
> Proud Socinus and Arius, the same false notion hold,
> That Jesus Christ the Saviour is not Almighty God.

> 'The wretched Antinomian presumptuously shouts out,
> "That I am sure of heaven, whether I sin or not;
> Before He first betrothed me God knew my every bent,
> My sins were all forgiven before I did repent."

> 'Of Calvin's many pupils some have beclouded sight
> And lost a proper balance by pressing to the right;
> Equating both election and preterition sore,
> Forgetting mercy's promise, which God in mercy swore.

> 'I can't agree with Baxter, that God acquits two ways,
> Nor Crisp, who, in his method, the Law's commands betrays,
> Nor Zinzendorf's ideas; I put aside all three;
> And Athanasius also will find no slave in me.

'The Articles of Cranmer: not all of them I hold,
Nor all of Calvin's precepts, Geneva's creed of old,
Though pure the Church of Scotland, 'tis not refined quite through;
I'll be no slavish follower of systems old or new.

    *

'These times are full of peril, false doctrines multiply,
False teachers and deceivers their own ideas ply;
A preacher's only able with learning on his side
To shepherd God's flock safely, and be their sure guide.

'I have stood, and I shall stand, nor will I fear ought,
Though floods of many waters on me their streams have poured;
I've fought in many a battle, but never fought for long,
As truth fought alongside me, mine soon the victory song.

    *

'My preaching's full of doctrine, no deviation here,
For this will make you happy, give life, and make secure;
No heresy or error, within this system's found,
That's either very blatant, or secret, underground.

    *

'Faith I maintain as foremost, and then good works are done,
The holiness I plead for, here Christ's the founding stone;
Whatever obligations that piety can scan,
They're emphasized with vigour in full salvation's plan.

'I ne'er omit one aspect of Scripture's holy truth,
And some that be forgotten, I strive to hold them forth;
In that rich box of treasures, God's covenant of grace,
Not one of all its jewels, its glories I'll not trace.

    *

'I Christ exalt through preaching, and man I cut to size,
And in his best achievements I show no merit lies;
And any hint of error is shunned both left and right,
And all my flock is gathered with care to realms of light.

    *

Though the wide world you travel, this is the only place
Where your soul will find teaching, and more of God's own face;
You will become bright Christians, of this you may be sure,
Doctrinal orthodoxy alone makes Christ's flock pure.'

And the following is the sermon of *Schematicus*. He was another orthodox preacher, but one who condemned all principles and doctrines other
than his own:

*
Schematicus, another, with zeal and fervent heat,
Dwelt much upon one tenet, to him like drink and meat;
Although his sermons sometimes touched on Christ's birth and cross,
That other tenet triumphed, all else seemed only dross.

Election was his idol, and thus it formed the core
Of faith, sanctification, repentance, and much more;
He traced out all its branches, connections weak and strong,
From one verse of the Bible, through sixty sermons long.

He authored many volumes, of many pages long,
With every tome detailing the same consistent song;
Whoever would not sing it, still lacked the heavenly cure,
Of this (his private judgment) Schematicus was sure.

His unremitting pushing at last provoked a war
Of bitter disputation, not known to us before;
One name opposed another, one reputation now
Might to the heavens be lauded, another buried low.

*
It set men's thoughts in turmoil, divisions followed fast,
The church split into parties, for union could not last;
Zeal for obscure issues, in those already blind,
One pulpit's favoured doctrine flayed by the other kind.

Division, party spirit, where once was unity,
Ten versus one, it may be, or five opposing three;
Assemblies mustered often, throughout the South and North,
To find the scriptural teaching, to set true doctrine forth.

Bad temper, agitation, ill will at every hand,
A lusting for new teachers, sought out throughout the land;
They preached, they wrote, they argued, all for their own pet theme,
They tore the Word to pieces, that once was without seam.

The Scriptures, Greek and Hebrew, each text was sieved and scanned,
"This one's a fine edition! That other should be banned!"
Old authors were examined, on each the sentence passed,
"A fine and godly writer! A heretic outcast!"

*
In this way many people who previously had been
Attentive to Boanerges, at Sinai's hill were seen;
With all this empty wrangling, they lost a contrite heart
Which pined with earnest longing, in Christ to have a part.

Some seek for water baptism, forgetting that which came
By means of heaven's showers, with tongues as if of flame;
They rage against the vestments, against the Common Prayer,
And lose a prayerful spirit, that grace beyond compare.

Long hair's a crucial issue, the locks must be cut short,
Better divide ten churches than lose this vital thought;
This voice insists on Bishops, that, on a Presbytery,
Some see the very devil in Independency.

The above description is practically a literal description of the state of affairs in Cefnarthen Church in the period when Williams as a youth was under its influence.

## LLWYNLLWYD ACADEMY

It appears that Williams did not have to leave home to receive his education, until his departure for Llwynllwyd Academy. No doubt it was at some neighbouring school, in Llandovery perhaps, that he spent those years. He was fully seventeen or even eighteen years old when he went to Llwynllwyd for we find that he had finished the normal three or four year course there by the time he was twenty-one. The name Llwynllwyd Academy is strange to our ears now. No such school now exists. It would be just as correct, and much more understandable, if we said that he went to Carmarthen Academy – where so many famous Welshmen have been educated.

This was indeed the institution where William Williams completed his education, but the Academy had at that time moved from Carmarthen town and was situated at Llwynllwyd, near Hay-on-Wye, Breconshire. The reason for this removal was as follows. On the death of Mr Thomas Perrot, the tutor at Carmarthen, in 1733, Mr Vavasor Griffiths, pastor of Maesgwyn, Radnorshire, was appointed in his place. Mr Griffiths refused to go to Carmarthen, judging that it would be better for the Academy to be in a rural area so that the students would not be open to the temptations of town life. The trustees of the Academy agreed and so the institution removed to the tutor. During the seven years in which it was under the care of the godly Mr Griffiths, the Academy was situated at three or four different places because there was no one particular building designated for it. While Williams was in attendance it was at Llwynllwyd farmhouse, the home of Mr David Price, the minister of the Independent church of Maesyronnen. Mr Charles stated that Mr Price was the tutor, but in this he was mistaken. And the Rev. J. Kilsby Jones is just as mistaken in believing that Llwynllwyd was the home of Vavasor Griffiths.

Vavasor Griffiths was one of the best scholars and godliest men of his day. It is said that he exercised greater strictness than was natural to him because the extreme mildness of Mr Perrot had been the occasion for many of the students to relapse into dangerous by-ways of belief and behaviour. Griffiths died three years after Williams had left the establishment. We have no information whatsoever of Williams's history while at the Academy, but we may conclude that he made good use of his opportunity. He lodged, most probably, at Llwynllwyd and attended Maesyronnen Church on Sundays. During this time he would have concentrated most on acquiring knowledge, particularly knowledge in those fields associated with a medical calling, because this was the direction that he intended to take. The Academy was an institution for preparing young men for the ministry, but he had obtained a place as a lay student. It is not known how long he spent here, but he finished his studies in 1738. As it was usual in those days, just as today, for college studies to take three to four years, he must have started there about the year 1734 or 1735.

William Williams's arrival at Llwynllwyd therefore must have coincided with Howell Harris's conversion, and it is a strange fact, difficult to account for, that he did not come into personal contact with the reformer from Trefeca during his time at the Academy. He must have heard a great deal about him. After his conviction, Harris came into rapid prominence as he immediately began exhorting his neighbours at Talgarth and agitating the surrounding countryside. Before the end of 1737 he had visited every locality in Breconshire establishing societies, and had also set up some in Radnorshire and Herefordshire. But it does not appear that he had preached at Glasbury, the nearest village to Llwynllwyd, at this time. Perhaps, because the academy was in the vicinity, he concluded he could leave the place to the godly and learned minister who was tutor there, and to the Rev. David Price, the respected minister of Maesyronnen. After this time however, in 1738, Vavasor Griffiths wrote to Harris, inviting him to Llwynllwyd and he, no doubt, accepted the invitation for the minutes of the first Association at Watford reveal that there was a Methodist church at Glasbury in 1743. But all this, most probably, was after Williams's departure from the place.

There can be no doubt that his powerful activities and the strange nature of his ministry was a great talking point in the academy, especially when we consider that most of the students were those with an eye on the ministry for themselves. Many, probably most, of them took the journey to Talgarth, about six miles away, with the sole intention of hearing Harris. We can only speculate why Williams did not go with them. Perhaps, like many of the Nonconformists of the period, he scorned the idea of an unordained man travelling around in order to preach. Or perhaps his desire for education was dominant and his interest in religion weak. What is certainly true is that while Howell Harris was disturbing the whole region, warning many to flee from the wrath to come, the young man from Pantycelyn was lost in his studies and quite indifferent to the state of his soul.

## HIS CONVERSION UNDER THE PREACHING OF HOWELL HARRIS

In 1738 it was time for him to leave the Academy, and his return home to his father's house involved a journey of more than thirty miles. His route took him through Talgarth and past the church cemetery. Harris was preaching in the cemetery as Williams passed by. He entered the grounds in order to listen for the first time to this man of whom he had heard so much – and conviction fell upon him as suddenly and as effectively as in Paul's case on the road to Damascus. As far as Williams was concerned the whole occasion was a matter of pure chance, but:

| | |
|---|---|
| That which is darkest chance to man | Yr hyn sy'n ddamwain ddall i ddyn |
| Is God's most bright design. | Sy'n olau arfaeth Duw. |

That chance morning meeting between William Williams and Howell Harris was an event of immense significance to the former, and immense significance also to the Church of Christ in Wales for as long as that Church continues to worship in the Welsh language.

The temptation to include the description by the late *Gwilym Hiraethog* (Dr William Rees) of Williams's conversion is too great to be withstood, although, as we shall see, it is far from being historically accurate:

One morning (on a Sunday, most probably) in the year 1738, the pealing of the parish bell in an isolated village in Breconshire invites the inhabitants to gather for the service. Among them is a young man of some twenty-one years of age. He is of medium height and graceful build and with more of a gentlemanly air about him than those around. He attracts more than the usual share of attention for he is either a stranger or newly returned to them after a considerable absence. Come and look at him! For there is something about his face and about the set of his eyes which makes you believe that there is more to this young man than to any other in the congregation, though you cannot tell exactly what marks him out. Unconsciously almost, your eyes return time and again to steal a fresh look at him.

The minister enters and the service begins. At this point, a middle-aged man, rather short in stature and with an air of great solemnity and seriousness, enters the place. All eyes in the building turn upon him. His appearance brings forth a completely different reaction in the congregation, revealed by the expressions on the faces and in the eyes. His very presence produces a kind of amazement and terror throughout. This strange attention and reaction arouses the curiosity of the young man referred to previously, and he asks, quietly and humbly, of the person next to him:

'Who is that strange man who is producing such an effect?'

'That man is Howell Harris.'

The thoughts and attention of the youngster are immediately concentrated. He has heard much of this man but never seen him before. Here is he who has troubled the whole world, who has seemed to drive men and devils to a frenzy, now present before his eyes! He studies him with a measure of fear and trembling.

The service ends. It has been conducted throughout in a dull, dead manner. The congregation is dismissed by the minister and he, with one or two of his parishioners, proceeds to the parsonage. But the congregation remain in the cemetery and others, from the village and the neighbouring countryside, join with them. In a little while, the middle-aged man whom we observed entering the church, climbs on to a gravestone, and every eye is fixed upon him. The young man in particular is intensely interested. Heaven's ambassador begins to deliver his charge. His voice is as strong thundering, or as the echoes of many waters. His words fall as fiery coals upon his audience. Their faces change colour as he proceeds from one sentence to the next. Are these, in the cemetery, the same hearers as those who were in the church? Yes, it is on the whole the same congregation, but there is a different preacher! This man speaks as one who has authority, and not as the scribes.

Something has now taken such hold of the minds and consciences of the listeners that the heart of the bravest amongst them is brought to fear, and the strongest of them begins to shake at the knees. It is as if heaven is showering fire and brimstone upon them. Some are filled with rage against the preacher and his doctrine, others almost faint under the pangs of conviction, others again cry out, 'What must we do?' The whole place is excitement and agitation. But where is the young man? There he is; his face white as a sheet, his whole body shaking in fear and dread. He is the very image of terror. He expects every moment to see the Son of Man coming on the clouds of heaven. A razor-sharp arrow driven by the bow of the preacher's doctrine has riven his heart. The two-edged sword has divided asunder soul and spirit. His view of himself is now quite different from what it ever was before. In a word, he is a new creature. He emerged from the cemetery that morning having been created anew.

We know by now that this stirring description does not exactly match the historical facts. It is so well expressed that there is a danger of forgetting that it was intended as a romantic picture, and as such it may mislead. *Hiraethog* took considerable poetic licence in writing it and the description is faulty in many details. Probably, if not certainly, Williams did not intend beforehand to hear Harris preach at Talgarth. Almost certainly also he was not present at the church service that morning, and even if he was, he would not have seen Harris there. Nor was it from on top of a gravestone that Harris preached, nor is the age of the preacher as given. He is described as 'a middle-aged man', whereas Harris was at this time only twenty-four. Again, the probability is that it was not a Sunday. Williams was journeying on his way home, and the old Presbyterians were rigorous in their maintenance of the Sabbath. And if it was old Rice Davies who was ministering, he certainly would not have run through the service in a 'dull, dead manner'. But the picture given is impressive for all its faults.

This is how Williams himself, in his elegy for Harris, describes his conversion:

> There's the place where first I saw you,
> All my life I'll ne'er forget,
> Before the church's portals standing,
> On the pathway firmly set;
> In a solemn, serious spirit,
> (God's demands brook no delay)
> Calling, urging, all your neighbours,
> Warning of the judgment day.

This verse contradicts the above description in at least two details. It is 'before the church's portals' that the poet 'first . . . saw' Harris, so he could not have seen him at the service. Nor is he preaching from the top of a gravestone but 'on the pathway firmly set' [or, as it is in the original Welsh, 'with no hillock underfoot'], which suggests that he was standing on level ground. There are three stanzas also from *A View of Christ's Kingdom* that appear to exclude the idea that Williams was eager to hear Howell Harris as he passed through Talgarth. In that poem Williams addresses his own soul:

> O soul! what preparations, what thought, what clear intent,
> Dwelt in you on that morning, when heaven's call was sent?
> That unexpected moment my foolish heart was drawn,
> By unexpected measures, my very life reborn.
>
> 'Twas God's decree in action, His pure and holy plan,
> All unbeknown, drew near me, His grace towards me ran;
> All things worked to their purpose, wheels within wheels went round;
> Saul sought his father's asses, but ended being crowned.

> Zaccheus little pondered, when climbing up the tree,
> That God's gift of salvation his house that day would see;
> And so with Paul and Peter, with Magdalen and more,
> I also, without seeking, found life for evermore.

We are sure that the poet's purpose in these lines is to demonstrate how little he himself contributed to the circumstances of his conversion, and how completely he was guided by divine Providence. All proceeded without any purpose, thought or preparation on his part. It happened at 'that unexpected moment' and 'by unexpected measures'. It was indeed a fulfilling of that prophecy: 'I am sought of them that asked not for me; I am found of them that sought me not.'

Was Williams only stricken that morning in Talgarth cemetery or were the healing ointments poured into his wounds at the same time? It may not be possible to answer that question. He himself tells us that he was caught from the summons from on high, but he does not state whether he then experienced the gospel's balm also. This is how he expresses it himself:

> \* This the morning, still remembered,
> That I first heard heaven's sound;
> By a summons straight from glory,
> With his voice, my heart was bound.
>
> After many a weary journey,
> Back and forth this world of ill;
> While I've breath left in my body,
> I will call him Father still.

It is the thunders of Sinai that is heard in these verses, and a similar ministry is found in the preaching of Boanerges where, it is believed, the poet is again describing his conversion:

> \*    Boanerges started preaching as if he stood between
> High heaven's brilliant splendour, and earth's dark ways, unclean;
> Some thousands, with Theomemphus, were straining all to hear,
> His knees with terror trembled, his heart was filled with fear.
>
> Far above Sinai's summit, above all peoples high,
> On clouds of speeding tempest, midst black and frowning sky,
> Where hosts of men could hear him, where echoed forth his voice,
> Thus seemed, in power and glory, the pulpit of his choice.
>
> \*    His words were claps of thunder, diverse and threatening all,
> Or like the final trumpet, sent forth the dead to call;
> Creating awful terror throughout the country round,
> Some thousands heard his preaching, and fainted at the sound.

If Harris was not preaching from Zion's hill on this occasion, we can be sure that Williams heard him from that summit at another time, and that it was by Harris's ministry that he experienced relief, or else he would hardly have acknowledged Harris as his spiritual father. His portrayal of Harris as an ambassador of peace is as follows:

> Come, listen to him plumbing
> The depths of sovereign grace!
> Revealing the Messiah
> In all his wondrous ways;
> And comforting the afflicted
> Under conviction's sway,
> So that they rise rejoicing,
> All terrors passed away.

Williams was to experience unusually powerful convictions. The arrows reached the very depths of his soul. But when the relieving balm was applied to his wounds, he was healed completely. Thereafter he was a new creature – fully regenerated – and a world to which he had previously been quite dead now became alive to him. This is the first time that he approached, with faith, the great truths of the gospel. A revelation of the spiritual and the eternal had been given him. His mind was sobered, his spirit was sanctified, his motives were raised and straightened, and he became acquainted with those whose hearts burned with zeal for the salvation of souls. He gave his own heart to the Saviour, trusted in him for salvation, and found himself possessed by fervent desires to bring others to Christ. He was brought to ask Saul's question, 'Lord, what wilt thou have me to do?' and his own heart testified that Jesus Christ required his life's service. He was determined not to be unfaithful to the heavenly vision, to turn his back forever upon the secular employment for which he had been trained, and to consecrate his life to the ministry of the Word. His new friends were Howell Harris, Daniel Rowland, and the exhorters who followed them, and he drank deeply of the spirit of the Methodist Revival.

## WILLIAMS JOINS AND LEAVES THE ESTABLISHED CHURCH

Until now, he had been brought up completely in Nonconformist and Dissenting circles, and no doubt he held to the principles and prejudices of these parties. It is true that he had not held strong convictions on religious matters but it must be expected that anti-Church feelings were natural to him. This supposition is strengthened by a phrase he uses when describing Harris, the instrument of his conversion and his father in Christ.

In the verse already quoted for another purpose, he writes:

> That unexpected moment my foolish heart was drawn,
> By unexpected measures, my very life reborn.

We do not know of any other reason for Harris to have been described as an unexpected measure other than the fact that he was a zealous Churchman, while Williams was a Nonconformist by upbringing, if not by principle also. This fact, together with the young age of the preacher, accounts, we believe, for the 'unexpectedness'. But the unexpected came to pass, and through it Williams came under the influence of Churchmen and was carried away, as if by a flood, from his early connections. Williams is often blamed for joining the Church of England, and this action of his cannot be viewed other than as a mistake, but he very soon corrected matters. Once he had come into contact with Rowland and Harris his entry into the established Church was completely natural and almost inevitable. They believed that the great need of the age was to get more men of ability and learning as clergy; men in whose hearts burned a love for the Saviour and a compassion for the state of the land. In Williams they saw a chosen vessel of God, and the best place for him in their opinion was the ministry of the Established Church. And while his new companions pressed him towards the Church, it does not appear there was any influence upon him in the opposite direction. There was nothing in the chapel where he was raised that could have induced him to consider the ministry with them. They possessed three ministers already, and two out of the three preached doctrines that he would have considered heretical. Unfortunately Williams had never experienced Nonconformity other than in its most unattractive mode. He had left Cefnarthen Church in the midst of its warfare when he departed for the Academy three or four years previously, and the battles were continuing to rage all the more fiercely on his return. Under the circumstances it is hardly surprising that he left them for the Church. The leaders of the Methodists, whom he was now ready to follow wherever they led, were found within her walls. To him the Methodist awakening was wonderful and glorious. Many years later he was to describe the beginnings of Methodism in glowing terms:

> But O! glorious morning! The Sun shone on Wales. God here raised instruments from the dust and set us with the princes of his people. The net was cast into the sea and it emerged with a multitude of fishes – great and small. Six counties in the south embraced the gospel very early on; the cockerel was heard crowing; the watchmen that had been sleeping awoke; preaching occurred every Sabbath in the churches; the Nonconformists were awakened; when they were mourned unto, some lamented; when they were piped unto, some danced.[8]

How he prepared for the bishop's examination is not known. He was a good and ready scholar, and he probably received the necessary preparatory help from some Churchman in the locality. This is how Thomas Charles describes his ordination:

He was ordained deacon of the Established Church in 1740 AD, by Nicholas Claggett, Bishop of St David's, to the curacies of Llanwrtyd and Llanddewi-Abergwesyn. He served as curate for three years, preaching to an immoral and ignorant people, but with little success. He used to relate with much humour how he was summoned to the Bishop's Court to answer charges of nineteen sins, of all of which he was guilty. Such things as failing to make the sign of the cross when baptizing, failing to read some parts of the service, and so on.

Thomas Charles continues:

It was the Rev. George Whitefield who encouraged him most strongly to leave the Church and to go out into the highways and fields. He ministered to his parishes from Cefncoed, a good twelve miles from Llanddewi-Abergwesyn. In those days he maintained family worship three times a day, and lived a simple and godly life. He never received full ordination, his bishop refusing to ordain him because of his irregularity in preaching in all places, not merely the churches of his parishes. After leaving the Established Church, or being thrown out, we do not know which,[9] he became known to the Rev. Daniel Rowland who, on occasions, would visit Ystrad-ffin Chapel, in Williams's parish, to preach.

There are many things in this passage that are not correct in detail. Most certainly, Williams was well acquainted with Daniel Rowland long before he left the Church of England. Indeed, he knew him before he ever became a member of that Church. Daniel Rowland preached at Ystrad-ffin from very early on. Harris and Rowland had begun their acquaintance the year before Williams was converted, and it is reasonable to believe that when Williams's friendship with Harris began it was not long before he was introduced to Rowland. The following are the first references to Williams that we find in the correspondence between the Welsh Methodists, as published in the Weekly History. Firstly, a letter from Daniel Rowland to Howell Harris, dated 20 October 1742:

I hear that Brother Williams has been taken to the Bishop's Court for not living in his parish.

Another reference towards the end of the same year appears in a letter from Harris to Brother H—t:

I left this morning together with Brother Williams, the curate of Llanwrtyd. He also has remarkable power. He burns with zeal and love.

In a letter from the exhorter, Evan Williams, dated 29 August 1743, it is said:

> I have just returned nearly twenty miles from listening to that notable man of God, Mr Rowland. His power on the Sabbath was wondrous, as also Mr Williams on the Saturday before and in the *seiat* ... Mr Williams wishes me to inform Brother Harris that the Bishop has refused him full ordination because he is a Methodist, although he has recommendatory letters from many clergymen and from his own parishioners. It was not well received that the parishioners were expressing their approval of him.

Lastly, Thomas Jones writes to Howell Harris on 30 August 1743:

> At one o'clock I was at Llangammarch, where a *seiat* had recently been established. By six at night I came to Bronydd where I met with the dear brother Williams. He refused to preach. After the service we had a sweet *seiat* with about twenty present.

The above references show that Williams was well-known to the early ministers and exhorters of the revival and was acknowledged as their co-worker whilst he was still in the Established Church. It does not appear that his association with the Church was any particular asset to the revival, nor to himself personally. Had he succeeded in becoming fully ordained within its order no doubt his own status and opportunities to do good would have become considerably greater. The Methodists of the period considered Church orders to be of great significance and they were eagerly sought after. Only those in orders could preach in the churches and in consecrated buildings, and they only had the right to administer the sacraments.

A priest was considered a man of unique honour; he was respected, homage was paid to him, and his authority was almost unlimited. Williams failed to obtain this status, and he failed only because of lack of patience and prudence. Instead of confining himself to his appointed area of work he engaged in activity further afield, following the example of Howell Harris. This incited the rage of the clergy against him and his path to the promotions and honours of his church was closed up with thorns. We have noted the charge against him of breaking as many as nineteen Church regulations during a period of three years. Thomas Charles called them small, unimportant sins, but they were considered presumptuous and atrocious acts by the Church authorities. He had to bear his punishment and the consequences of his actions and to remain an unordained man, for the remainder of his days. It appears that Williams himself put a great store on holy orders and felt deeply his deprivation. Thomas Charles comments:

[Williams] did not condone this irregularity in later life. He considered it rash behaviour on his part and judged that he could have been much more useful had he been more careful and patient. But God can fulfil His purposes through the rashness of men, and it may be that in his actual situation he was better positioned to accomplish God's wise ends.

In our judgment, this sentence by Mr Charles has been misunderstood and misinterpreted by modern writers. We confess that it is ambiguous, but it is not that difficult to understand. What was his 'irregularity' that Williams later could not condone? Not his becoming a member of the Established Church, as some argue; nor his departure from it, as others judge. Mr Charles defines the irregularity clearly enough, namely 'preaching in all places, not merely the churches of his parishes'.

Are we then saying that we believe that Williams repented of venturing out to preach in the highways and fields? Not at all! But on Mr Charles's testimony we are prepared to believe that he repented of not confining himself, during the period of his curacy, to his own parishes. By acting as he did he lost a position of respect among his brethren for the rest of his life, and the churches lost his service in the administration of the sacraments. This was much more of a disadvantage to him than perhaps we realize. We usually consider him as equal in status to Daniel Rowland, Howell Davies, William Davies of Neath, and others, but it was not so. He was only a preacher, while these others were ordained ministers, in possession of the privileges of their office.

Any of the Methodist clergy could take the place of Daniel Rowland at the Llangeitho Communion when there was need, but Williams did not dare do so, though he was present there most frequently. He assisted at the communion but he did not administer it. He fulfilled this secondary position at Llangeitho for nearly fifty years. He also preached once a month for thirty-five years at Llanlluan Chapel, where the sacraments were also administered. Every Communion Sunday therefore he had to give place to some ordained man who was very possibly of less ability and less qualified than himself. It is only natural to believe that Williams must often have felt pained at this secondary position, and it is perfectly believable that later on in years he acknowledged to Thomas Charles that he had acted impatiently and unwisely when a curate at Llanwrtyd. But for him to have expressed repentance for preaching in unconsecrated places, other than when under the particular circumstances of being a curate, is completely unbelievable. His words and actions throughout his life prove otherwise.[10]

## HIS APPOINTMENT AS ASSISTANT TO
## DANIEL ROWLAND

1743 was a notable year in the history of William Williams, the year in which the first Association of the Connexion was held. In that Association, meeting at Watford on 5 and 6 January, he was first introduced to George Whitefield. It may be that this was the occasion when the latter urged Williams to leave the Established Church and go out to the highways and open places. If it was so, it must have been during a private conversation for there is no reference to it in the minutes. The first notice of it is in the minutes of the second Association, also at Watford and held on 6 and 7 April, 1743. A decision was there made '*That the Rev. Mr Williams should leave his curacy and become assistant to the Rev. Mr Daniel Rowland.*' In addition, he was appointed Moderator of one of the five regions into which the country was divided, namely the counties of Radnorshire and Montgomeryshire, and the well-known Richard Tibbott was made superintendent under him. In a Monthly Meeting held at the home of Jeffrey Dafydd of Rhiwiau, Llanddeusant parish, Carmarthenshire, on 3 February, between the two Watford Associations, another heavy responsibility was laid upon his shoulders. Howell Harris, Daniel Rowland, William Williams, and two or three other exhorters were present. Mr Charles states:

> Although they were only few in number they were greatly honoured with the presence of the Lord. On the second day Howell Harris encouraged all who were present to compose a few verses by the next meeting, in order to see whether the Lord had given any of them the gift of poetry. This was done, and after they had all read their efforts it was agreed unanimously that Mr William Williams was the gifted man and he was exhorted by Harris and all the others to exercise his gift for the glory of God and the good of His Church.

## HIS LABOURS AS AN EVANGELIST AND PREACHER

We see then that Williams was appointed to serve as an evangelist and as a poet at about the same time. How did he fulfil these duties? Consider first his work as an evangelist. He was made the chief steward over the societies of Radnorshire and Breconshire, but as he was assistant to Daniel Rowland, upon whom was the responsibility for Cardiganshire and Carmarthenshire, a good deal of the care of the societies of these two counties also rested upon him. He carried out his work with a zeal and commitment that was hardly matched by any other except perhaps Howell Harris himself. He not only maintained a general care of his societies but made up also for any deficiencies in the exhorter set over each society, by visiting each one and writing reports for the Associations on their condition. We have examples of these in the histories of the Llangwyryfon, Lledrod, Rhydfendigaid, and other societies in Cardiganshire. The superintendence of these societies was entrusted to Morgan Hughes. For some reason or other he had failed to fulfil his duty and Williams had visited them. Two of the reports that he subsequently sent are preserved in the Williams manuscripts at Trefeca. The first is too long to insert here. It provides a detailed description of the five societies and ends:

I visit them once every six weeks, and conduct a church meeting, so that I know their thoughts and condition. I feel a love and commitment towards them and so also do they to myself. They maintain a loving respect for their private exhorter, and they appreciate being examined by him and by myself. I notice that according to the spirit of the exhorter, be he zealous, cheerful and faithful, or lukewarm, etc., so also will be the spirit of the people under his care.

Another brief report by him on the same societies, dated 29 June 1745, reads:

I have no particular news from them, other than that which you previously received. They continue to adhere diligently to the Lord. The majority of them increase in knowledge of him. Both they and myself are in some difficulty in that they lack private exhorters to visit them weekly. Those whom they wish to receive, cannot come; and those who can come, they will not receive. But I hope that this shall be accomplished.

To follow the journeys and labours of Williams for the next fifty years is impossible. They are not recorded other than in the Lamb's book of life. This is how the author of *Methodistiaeth Cymru* describes him:

That old sweet singer, Williams Pantycelyn, in his old age, when 73 years old and nearing the end of his life, used to say:

'My days are drawing to an end, my course is nearly run: I have had a long life. I am now 73 years of age. . . . I have been preaching for the last 43 years,[11] and have travelled on an average between forty and fifty miles every week during that time. I had four or five long journeys last spring through the counties of south Wales. Each was about a fortnight's space, and I travelled each time about two hundred miles.'

Some idea of his journeys can be gained by considering that he travelled sufficient miles to encircle the world four times – not far less than 100,000 miles! We can hardly imagine the measure of this man's usefulness to benighted Wales. How many sermons did he preach? How many church meetings did he lead? How many public meetings did he attend? And when we recall the liveliness of his spirit, the seraphic warmth of his thoughts and his constant dependence on God for his blessing, how much goodness was wrought by him? What is certain is that from this cloud, over a period of forty-three years, many showers of blessing rained upon the barren ground of the Principality. Indeed, he being dead, yet speaketh through his lively hymns and poetic works. With these he is still today building up and comforting God's children in all their thousands throughout Wales, in many English cities, and indeed in far off Western lands. I have no doubt that his poetry will continue in its savour and usefulness for ages yet to come.

It has been suggested by some that Williams was only an ordinary preacher and that his talents lay in other directions. This was not how his contemporaries judged him. They held his preaching in high esteem and allocated him the foremost positions in the preaching festivals of the Associations. He would often preach before Daniel Rowland. It is true he could not compete with Rowland as a preacher, and it is possible that he was not so popular as Howell Harris, but there were certainly no others who excelled him. Harris, speaking of his preaching skills, testified that he had 'amazing ability'. The following is Thomas Charles's view of him as a preacher:

> His oratorical powers were great, his sermons evangelical, experiential and sweet; searching and examining false teachings and experiences and discriminating in detail between true and false spirits. His imagination was strong, his eyes sharp and piercing, and heaven's influences lay heavily upon his spirit when ministering publicly and when conversing with men in the private meetings on the state of their souls.

He depended heavily on the heavenly breezes when preaching, and it is said that he commented to his friend, the Rev. Peter Williams, 'You, Peter, can preach when the Holy Spirit is in France; but I cannot do a thing unless He is at my elbow.' The Rev. Thomas Jones, Denbigh, praised him as a theologian and preacher. After describing Daniel Rowland, he continues:

| | |
|---|---|
| Williams also, more's the pity, | Ond ai rhaid i Williams hefyd, |
| After him was summoned shortly, | Ar ei ol yn fuan ddiengyd? |
| (God delivers warnings often | Oedd un ddyrnod ddim yn ddigon, |
| To return his wandering children!) | I geryddu plant afradlon? |
| Two strong leaders, learned, able, | Dau arweinydd eon mawrddysg |
| Leaving us still in the battle; | Yn ein gado yn y terfysg! |

Happy now, as they bow! O! how
  bright their portion!
We remaining in affliction
In this world of tribulation.

Llon eu gwedd, y'nt mewn hedd,
  tudraw i'r bedd llychllyd;
Gweiniaid yn yr helbul dybryd
Ar ei hol yng ngwlad yr adfyd.

Rare the gifts to Williams given,
Blessings from the stores of heaven;
Sound in doctrine, full of learning,
Principled in all his dealing,
Knowing how to note and search
All the ailments of the church;
Strong and weak, to him seek,
  meekly he, sustaining,
Gives direction to the straying,
Comfort offers to the grieving.

Doniau ar ei ben ei hunan
Oedd gan Williams, fywiog, wiwlan;
Medrus, manwl mewn athrawiaeth'
Egwyddorion a disgyblaeth;
Ca'dd ei ddysgu i drin yn gymwys
Bob rhyw gyflwr yn yr eglwys;
Cryf a gwan, ym mhob man,
  a wyddan' lle teithiai
Llwybr ceimion a ddangosai,
Cysur, maeth i'r gwan a roddai.

Solid as a theologian,
Safe and sure as an historian,
He set forth sweet gospel blessings
Satisfying mind and feelings;
Preaching, to all hearts' contentment,
The wounds of Christ, the full atonement.
Full and free! Come and see! Christ,
  He has provided
A sacrifice by God appointed
For all who are of sin convicted.

Cadarn ydoedd fel Duwinydd;
Nid anfuddiol fel Hanesydd;
I'r serchiadau ac i'r deall
Taflai ffrwythau'r Ganaan ddiball;
At y galon, Balm o Gilead,
Clwyfau'r Oen, a'r cyflawn bryniad,
Llawn iachad, rhydd a rhad,
  i'r anfad a'r dinerth,
Yn yr unig ddwyfol Aberth,
A wnaeth IAWN am feiau anferth.

There is ample evidence that men of sound judgment like Thomas Charles and Thomas Jones did not consider William Williams an ordinary preacher. It would seem that this is a more recent opinion that has no historical foundation. How then did such a view arise? The answer is to be found in a comment made by the late Dr Lewis Edwards of Bala. When speaking on Williams as a theologian he said:

It is difficult for us to appreciate more than one excellence in any one person, and so, in his case, the brilliance of his poetry tends to hide from us his greatness as a theologian.

The poet casts the theologian into shadow, and the same fate has also befallen the preacher. Yet he possessed preaching gifts of the highest order. His oratorical abilities were many, his learning and knowledge extensive, his imagination strong, his spirit warm, and his readiness of speech unusually complete. A man in possession of all these could never be a common preacher. Williams was also a man of much humour and mirth but he does not seem to have made use of this dangerous gift in his ministry. He often gave it a good deal of rope in personal conversation, and sometimes in the societies, but never once in the pulpit.

However, though we believe that Williams was well respected in his day as a preacher, it is common knowledge that it was in the gatherings of the saints – in the societies – that his various gifts would be seen to best effect. It was here that his conversational abilities were most evident in operation. No one could compare to him for leading a *seiat*. It would be impossible to exaggerate the value of his service to the Connexion in this most important area. He had been endowed most notably and specifically with the gift for discerning spirits. He understood men, as if by instinct, and he was honest and upright in his dealings with all. He was known also for his ability to pacify strife and to reconcile the various contending parties that appear from time to time in the churches. He was often sent for in such circumstances, and was remarkably successful in restoring the peace and order that had been lost. There are many examples noted in church records of his services in this capacity. He was also most useful in the Quarterly Meetings and the Associations, particularly when a point of doctrine or a heresy troubling the churches was under consideration. His natural discernment and wide knowledge of religious doctrine marked him out amongst his brethren, and he made full use of those talents with which the great Head of the Church had entrusted him.

## HIS EARLY HYMNS, AND THE PUBLICATION OF *ALELUIA*

Let us turn to consider his writings. It is on these that Williams's fame is primarily based. On these his reputation stands, firm and secure. As we have seen, he was encouraged in 1743 by his brethren to exercise his poetic gifts, but it is clear that he was composing hymns long before this time, perhaps as early as his conversion in 1738. Recently, we noted an old school book of his, now in the possession of Mrs Jones, the wife of the Rev. Josiah Jones, Machynlleth, the great-granddaughter of the poet. Without doubt this is his first writing book. It is a handsome volume in good condition, with leather covers and a brass clasp. On the back cover is the only date that it contains, written in Williams's handwriting – 25 March 1745. It contains some six to eight hundred verses, written it would appear in his early years. Presumably the date was added after they had all been composed, and the author would then have been only twenty-eight years old. The contents clearly involve many years of work, so that the first parts must have been written very early on. Perhaps the first verses were composed soon after his conversion and are indicative of his state of mind at that first stage of his religious thought. They show that his experiences were pretty mixed. He begins by walking in darkness, praying for relief, beholding the light, increasing in assurance, and praying for perseverance in grace. He falls again into darkness, complains of persecution, has a view of the Mediator, finds cause again for confidence, and prays for assurance of hope. These hymns from Williams's juvenile period are appreciated mainly for the way they reveal to us his state of mind during what was a relatively dark period for him. We also find in them the beginning of the blossoming of his talent.

The fact that Williams published the first part of his *Aleluia* within a year of the time his brethren encouraged him to write, shows he was ready for the work and suggests that composing hymns was no novelty for him. This was Williams's first published work; it was printed by Felix Farley in Bristol. It came out in six parts: Part 1, about the beginning of 1744; a reprint of the same, at the end of the same year; Part 2, in 1745; Part 3, in the same year; Part 4, in 1746; Part 5, in 1747; and Part 6, about the end of the same year. It was thought until recently that the various parts were not published together in one volume until 1758, which is the publication now called the 'Third Edition'. It is presently agreed, however, that another edition was published by Felix Farley in 1749, and this is now referred to as the 'Second Edition'. The title of the work is *Aleluia, or a Collection of Hymns (mostly) of the work of the Rev. Mr William Williams*. The 'mostly' relates to hymns in Part 6 under the names of other authors. It appears that Williams set aside his pen for four years after publishing the sixth part of Aleluia towards the end of 1747, because he had an important matter in view, namely marriage. Mr Charles describes his marriage thus:

> When he was about thirty-two years of age, he married Mary Francis, a native of Llanfynydd, who afterwards lived at Llansawel. Miss Francis used to stay with the Rev. Griffith Jones, Llanddowror. She was a sensible, godly girl. The Lord's care of him was evident in this provision of a discreet, beautiful, wise, godly, kind and affectionate wife.

We might add that Miss Jones was an excellent singer who could therefore judge how singable his compositions were, before they were passed on to the printer. As she was an only child and the sole heiress of her father, she was also well blessed in the things of this life. Her father's name was Thomas Francis of Penlan. Through his own inheritance, and that obtained through his marriage, Williams was a moderately rich man. They had two sons and five daughters. Both sons entered the ministry of the Church of England. The younger, John, left the Church and joined the Methodists, but the elder, William, remained with the Established Church to the last.

## HIS PUBLISHED WORKS

Let us return to the published works of William Williams. It would be impossible within the limits of this chapter to go into detail on the chronology of his works. We refer the reader instead to the information provided in *Gweithiau* [*The Works of*] *William Williams, Pantycelyn* by the Rev. N. Cynhafal Jones, D.D., a book which will remain as a perpetual memorial to the bard, and an enduring testimony to the hard work and ability of its editor. The following is a list of Williams's hymn-books:

WELSH HYMNS:

1. *Aleluia*
2. *Caniadau y Rhai Sydd ar y Mor o Wydr*
   [*The Songs of Those upon the Sea of Glass*]
3. *Ffarwel Weledig* [*Farewell to Visible Things*]
4. *Gloria in Excelsis*
5. *Rhai Hymnau Newyddion* [*Some New Hymns*]

ENGLISH HYMNS:

6. *Gloria in Excelsis*
7. *Hosannah to the Son of David*

OTHER POETICAL WORKS:

8. *Golwg ar Deyrnas Grist* [*A View of Christ's Kingdom*]
9. *Caniadau Duwiol* [*Divine Songs*]
10. *Theomemphus*
11. *Myfyrdodau ar Angau* [*Reflections upon Death*]
12. *Tair-ar-ddeg-ar-hugain o Farwnadau* [*Thirty-three Elegies*]
13. *Llyfr Amrywioldeb* [*A Book of Miscellany*]
14. *Cerdd Newydd ar Briodas* [*A New Song on Marriage*]
15. *Gweddillion Awenyddol* [*Poetical Fragments*]

PROSE WORKS:

1. *Sicrwydd Ffydd* [*The Assurance of Faith*]
   (a translation of a sermon by Ebenezer Erskine)
2. *Pantheologia, neu Hanes Holl Grefyddau'r Byd*
   [*Pantheologia, or the History of the World's Religions*]
3. *Llythyr Martha Philopur* [*Martha Philopur's Letter*]
4. *Ateb Philo Evangelius* [*Philo Evangelius' Answer*]
5. *Hanes Llwyddiant yr Efengyl* [*The History of the Gospel's Success*]
6. *Crocodil Afon yr Aifft* [*The Crocodile of the Egyptian River*]
7. *Y Tri Wyr o Sodom* [*The Three Men of Sodom*]
8. *Aurora Borealis*

9. *Antinomiaeth* [*Antinomianism*]
10. *Drws y Society Profiad* [*The Door of the Experience Meeting*]
11. *Cyfarwyddwr Priodas* [*A Marriage Directory*]
12. *Hanes Troedigaeth y Parch. Thomas Goodwin*, D.D..
    [*The History of the Conversion of the Rev. Thomas Goodwin*, D.D.]
13. *Ymddiddan rhwng Philalethes ac Eusebes, mewn Perthynas i Wir Gristionogrwydd* [*A Conversation between Philalethes and Eusebes, in Relation to True Christianity*]

When we consider that Williams travelled on average some forty-five miles a week throughout his life, constantly preaching and leading societies, the literary work he accomplished seems little short of miraculous. His hymns number 916, with over four thousand verses. His two long poems, *Theomemphus* and *A View of Christ's Kingdom* each contain more than five thousand lines, and many of his other poems are lengthy compositions. His main prose work is the *Pantheologia*. Williams's genius is seen in all these works, the prose works revealing the same characteristics as the poems. His mind was wonderfully productive. His muse could sustain long flights on the wing. He aimed for the heights and long remained aloft without sinking. Others of our poets and hymn writers have reached the same heights as himself, but theirs were short flights, they could not sustain such standards. Williams's muse was as a strong eagle, rising rapidly, soaring effortlessly above, and then descending at will with no indication of fatigue. Or, to change the metaphor, we find in the compositions of our other national poets the wide rivers and beautiful lakes, but in Williams's works we view the ocean. He was indeed an unordained bard, just as Howell Harris was an unordained preacher. Williams's description of Harris the preacher could be applied to himself as a poet:

| | |
|---|---|
| Howell was not called to labour | Yntau, Howell, heb arddodiad |
| By the laying on of hands, | Dwylo dynion o un rhyw, |
| Nor ordained by any bishop, | Na chael cennad gan un esgob |
| Or other power in the land. | Ag sydd llawer llai na Duw. |

But they were both ordained directly, without mediation, by the Father of lights. Williams was soon acknowledged by the Welsh nation as a poet of the highest order, and he quickly became more acceptable and popular than any previous poet. His works were eagerly read and sung, and his books received a circulation greater than any before. The bardic fraternity were very slow to acknowledge him. He was not of their order and they therefore ignored and disdained him. But if he never won the admiration of his fellow poets, he achieved much more in winning the hearts and minds of the people. One of the first to praise him as a poet was Thomas Jones of Denbigh, who was also perhaps the first to describe him as the 'Sweet Singer of Wales'. Dewi Wyn of Eifion, one of the ablest of Welsh poets, said: '[He] could sit all night, on the coldest winter night and without a scrap of fire, reading Williams's works, and [his] body would be warmed to a hot sweat by the reading.'

During the last fifty years it has become fashionable to praise and admire Williams. All pay homage to him. He is the 'Sweetest Singer of Wales', 'The Nation's Chief-bard'. The wise and learned acknowledge their respect for him and all ranks appreciate the charm of his poetry. It has become apparent that the more his works are read, the more markedly do their excellencies stand out. Until the year 1867, Williams's work existed only in scattered fragments, rare volumes and pamphlets still in the form in which they were printed by the author. They were therefore out of the reach of the general public. In 1811, all his hymns were collected together and published, by his son, the Rev. John Williams, Pantycelyn, but the country had to wait for another fifty years and more before the complete works were published in 1867. The editor of this large volume was the late Rev. J. R. Kilsby Jones, a man of some literary eminence in our land, and one who admired the Poet of Pantycelyn beyond measure. This complete edition had a wide circulation and for the first time Williams's works became generally known. Lately, the country has been favoured by the appearance of a cheaper, more accurate and much improved edition by the Rev. N. Cynhafal Jones, D.D. so that all are now in a position to form their own judgment of the true worth and merit of his literary efforts.

We do not have the space to detail the great change effected by Williams in the hymnology of our country. It was nothing less than a revolution. The leaders of Methodism in Wales judged, as did their counterparts in England, that there was a great need of better hymns for their religious services than those in use at the time, and they were very eager for qualified persons to undertake the work. In England, the Spirit fell upon Charles Wesley and Toplady, and in Wales upon Williams, Morgan Rhys, and others. Mr Charles of Bala states very appropriately of Williams as a hymnist:

> His poetic gifts had been given to him naturally and abundantly by the Lord. He is often lifted up on the strongest of wings, which carry him to glorious heights. The great sacrifice of the cross is the main topic of all his writings, and while a love of that great subject abides in the hearts of Welshmen, his work will be most acceptable to them, especially his hymns. He soared on the breezes of heaven but made use of the nearest words lying to hand so that all he wrote was completely intelligible to the common people, who love his songs

greatly. His hymns produced an evident transformation of the form of religion among the Welsh. Some verses in his hymns are as glowing coals that warm the people, firing their emotions, as they are sung. They are often repeated, over and over, until all are shouting and jumping for joy. These strong effects are proof sufficient of the power that lies within these hymns.

A very clear proof of the thoroughness of that transformation wrought in the hymnology of our land by the Methodist Revival is found in the rarity of use today of any hymns written before that time. In the works of Williams and others of his period is felt the passionate warmth of the Revival and the sound of joy and singing.

It is evident that to compose and write poetry was as natural to Williams as breathing. He says so himself in some places. In his preface to *Theomemphus* – a composition of more than five thousand lines – he wrote:

> This book issued from my spirit like water from a spring or like a web from the spider's body. It is an original piece of work, there being no model for it, as far as I know, in English, Welsh, or Latin . . . It came to my mind as you find it, and in the belief that it may be profitable to others, I have printed it.[12]

The last stanza in the *Elegy to Grace Price* notes the fact that he composed that magnificent elegy in a few hours only. It contains forty-two stanzas and met with such approval that the poet made many scores of pounds of profit from it. Many of his hymns are evidently written extemporaneously. It is said that he was preaching once at Meidrym, Carmarthenshire, on a Sunday morning, and reading at the beginning of the service from John's Gospel, chapter 4. He continued reading until he arrived at verse 35, which states: 'Say not ye, There are yet four months, and then cometh harvest? behold I say unto you, Lift up your eyes, and look on the fields; for they are white already to harvest.' After reading the verse, he said, thoughtfully:

> 'Wait a bit. The thought in this text has not been put into verse before.'
> 'Wait a bit,' he said a second time, more to himself than to his congregation.
> 'It would go something like this, wouldn't it?'

> 'Do you not say assuredly that four months yet must come,
> Before it is expected to bring the harvest home?
> Lift up your eyes, take notice, says Jesus, heaven's King,
> For ripe and white already is the harvest we must bring.'

> 'Onid ydych chwi'n dywedyd fod eto bedwar mis,
> Ac yna daw'r cynhaeaf toreithiog gyda brys?
> Dyrchefwch chwi eich llygaid, medd Iesu, brenin nef,
> Cans gwynion ydyw'r meusydd lle mae ei wenith ef.'

And he then read on to the end of the chapter.

Many of his most popular hymns are extemporary productions, and some of these can be connected with particular localities. Almost certainly it was the romantic view of the River Tywi from the road that traverses the steep rocks between the Fannog and Soar Chapel, which suggested to Williams the thought in the following well-known verse:

| | |
|---|---|
| Strait the path on which I travel, | Cul yw'r llwybr i mi gerdded, |
| On either side lie dangers steep, | Is fy llaw mae dyfnder mawr, |
| And my heart within me fears | Ofn sydd arnaf yn fy nghalon |
| Lest I fall into the deep; | Rhag i'm traed i lithro i lawr; |
| In thine hand I'll keep my footing, | Yn dy law y gallaf sefyll, |
| In thine hand I will prevail, | Yn dy law y dof i'r lan, |
| In thine hand I will not falter, | Yn dy law byth ni ddiffygiaf, |
| Though I am so weak and frail. | Er nad ydwyf fi ond gwan. |

And there is an even greater local influence upon another of his hymns. The River Cothi, not far from Pumpsaint – a hamlet through which Williams would often journey – drops into a deep gorge called *Pwll Uffern Gothi* [Cothi's Hell Gorge], and a new road past this point was being laid in Williams's time. It was at this spot, it is said, that he wrote of:

| | |
|---|---|
| A new high road by Christ was made, | Ffordd newydd wnaed gan Iesu Grist |
| To bypass Hell it's path was laid; | I basio heibio uffern drist; |
| And he himself has paved the way | Wedi ei phalmantu ganddo ef |
| Out of the world and to the sky. | O ganol byd i ganol nef. |

But although these verses, and others like them, were suggested to his mind by natural scenes and were composed with relatively little effort, yet Williams himself emphasizes that his major works were not produced without much preparation and labour. He wrote of *A View of Christ's Kingdom*, his pre-eminent poetic work:

I did my best, when writing this little book, to read as many as I could of relevant texts, of an orthodox and sound nature if possible. And whenever I saw anything that was to the point, I took it up in my own mind and would then write down something of its substance in my own words, after having first meditated upon it myself and woven it in with my own thoughts. For this I can hardly be blamed. But it was to that book I cleaved most, namely, God's Book . . . I now release this work into the world, and may God be on its side! I am ashamed of it because it is clothed so poorly and yet takes upon itself to praise One who is so excellent . . . I hope that God will hide it from crafty men, the critics, who lay hold of truths merely to argue over them, rather than to build up . . . If anyone decides to look closely at the poetry, let me acknowledge that there is no lesson without its faults. And this has often discouraged me from putting it in print. The longer it remains on my hands, the more I revise it. But I am afraid of doing any more in case it loses its edge. Therefore, let it go as it is. What effect it will have, I do not know; but this I do know, that it cost me much pain and time in bringing it to birth.

His biographer states that he exerted himself to such an extent with his studies in preparing and composing this outstanding poem that it affected his health for the rest of his life.

## THE VIEWS OF GWILYM HIRAETHOG AND LEWIS EDWARDS

It is not an easy task to categorize Williams's genius and to point out the source of his power. Nevertheless, many scholars of eminence have commented on his works. *Gwilym Hiraethog* (Dr William Rees), after comparing Milton's *Paradise Lost* with Williams's *View of Christ's Kingdom*, and confessing his inability to decide which is the greater, wrote:

The certain proof of a true nobility of poetic faculty is the ability to charm every degree and class of society together – that the strongest intellects, the most polished minds, and also the simple peasantry, can enjoy and feast in common upon its works. The genius of Williams's hymns touches the human heart at its core, so that the feelings of the refined philosopher, and the feelings of the country shepherd, spring up together under the influence of its thrill. From the princes of learning and talent down to the insignificant widow in her lonely cottage, all together acknowledge its virtue. The sensitive ear of the scholar and the untaught ear of the lowest peasant join in their blessing upon it when 'they hear the words; for they are sweet'. Its accents bring forth the tear from the eye that sparkles with intelligence and fluency, together with the eye that is heaviest and most deficient in mental expression. There is a great difference between the nature of the satisfaction proved by the refined and cultured mind and that felt by the untaught mind, though the source of the satisfaction is the same. The hymns of Williams are sung for spiritual profit by hundreds of Christians throughout Wales, who may have hardly any discerning awareness of their innate excellence. One reason for the remarkable effectiveness of Williams's hymns is that they employ the most natural language of the simplest, undecorated form. They gain our natural sympathy without our knowing it. The fellowship of his songs melts the heart, and draws the tear from the eye, all unwittingly. Whether it is longing or doubt; fear, confidence, or joy, that is being expressed, we must join together in the experience because of the accuracy with which each emotion is portrayed in our minds. He never uses an obscurity of dialect, nor a deeper language than would be understood by an untaught labourer, and yet the most learned of teachers could not in any way improve the expression or imagery of so many of his hymns.[13]

The following remarks on Williams' abilities as a *poet*, have been made by Dr Lewis Edwards:

> The first prerequisite of poetry is *life*. This is what makes the songs of Homer so charming; they have little in them of what is now considered 'decorative', but they are all full of life . . . No one possesses more of this element than Williams. This is why one old pilgrim mentioned once in my hearing that 'the hymns of Williams are like *marbles*, while so many other, more regular, hymns fall like lumps of *clay*'. We cannot account for this life in the poet's soul, except to believe that his emotions were so much more strongly part of him than is generally the case – a feeling for the beauty of nature, a feeling for the troubles of humanity, in its majesty and misery, its joy and sadness, its love and hate, its virtue and vice.[14]

It would be easy to continue with further examples. We feel it more important presently to consider Dr Lewis Edwards' views of Williams as a theologian. He published an essay in *Yr Arweinydd* of 1878 on *The Theology of Williams, Pantycelyn*, and although it is long we do not feel that we can abridge it.[15] It begins with a sentence that we have already used for another purpose:

> It is generally acknowledged by those able to see past the form of words and to the underlying thought that Williams is a poet of the highest order, and that as a hymn writer in particular he excels in that intensity of feeling so necessary in true poetry. It is difficult for us to appreciate more than one excellence in any one person, and so, in his case, the brilliance of his poetry tends to hide from us his greatness as a theologian. For this reason I wish to take this opportunity to draw attention to his theological views.
>
> In the first place, it would be of advantage to all of us to be tutored carefully by Williams on the doctrine of the Person of the Mediator. In the controversy that arose against Howell Harris it was undoubtedly the hymns of Williams that were the predominant means that kept the Methodists from going to the opposite extreme. And, notwithstanding the great respect in which he was held, there were many then, as there still remain today, who could not whole-heartedly welcome such words as 'divine blood,' 'divine anguish,' 'divine wounds,' which are so common in his songs. Sometimes they are changed or omitted or, when they are used, it is on the understanding that they are to be taken as poetic exaggeration, and not as accurate theology. Now, my intention here is not to provide excuses for such words and others similar, but to show that they stand in no need of excuses. In all their finest detail they are perfectly consistent with the doctrine taught in the New Testament on the Person and work of the Lord Jesus Christ. It is said there that there were persons who killed the Prince of life, who crucified the Lord of glory. The Word was made flesh. He who was in the form of God, made himself of no reputation, humbled himself, and became obedient unto death, even the death of the cross.

It is important that we do not mix the two natures; but it is equally as important that we do not divide the Person. He sacrificed himself; not a part of himself, but himself. Therefore, it is he, in all the infinitudes of his person, not in part of it, who is the atonement. Consequently his blood, in the widest meaning possible, is divine blood, the blood of the Son of God himself.

A man's death is generally appropriated to the whole person, by saying that the man has died, and not part of the man. This illustration, though imperfect, shows the reasonableness of the statement that the blood of Christ is divine blood. But there was a closer union between the Person of the Son and his human nature than there is between the human soul and the human body. Furthermore, the divinity of his Person was operative in his death. To find some equivalent illustration, we have to think of a man dying voluntarily, committing himself as prey to death in order to save the lives of some of his fellow men. In such circumstances his death would not only be passive, but active; and his whole soul would be in the deed. So also it may be said of the Lord Jesus Christ, that his whole Person was made flesh; that his whole Person was made of no reputation; that his whole Person was operative in his dying, being obedient unto death, even the death of the cross.

In some hymns, Williams has even stronger phrases, and I see no reason to apologize for these either. The following is one complete verse, and part of another, taken from two hymns that are next to each other in his works:

| | |
|---|---|
| An open road now leads | Mae'r ffordd yn awr yn rhydd |
| From earth to heaven's bliss, | O'r ddae'r i entrych ne', |
| Since God himself came down | Er pan ddaeth fy Nuw |
| To suffer in my place; | I ddioddef yn fy lle; |
| The way to heaven is clear and free, | Mae'r nef, mae'r nef, o led y pen, |
| For God has suffered on the tree. | Can's hi ddioddefodd ar y pren. |
| | |
| May Calv'ry's name aloft be raised | Boed bryn y groes, boed Calfari |
| And far above all mountains praised | Yn uwch na'r bryniau mwya' eu bri, |
| For there God's precious blood was shed. | Am mai yma collwyd gwaed fy Nuw. |

The sooner the reader learns not to be frightened and offended by such strong words on the death of our Lord, the better. Instead let him familiarize himself with being sustained by such strong meat. Not that they are stronger than some of the phrases already quoted from the New Testament; this also is the language of the Church in general.

In that the poet of Pantycelyn held such wide views of the Person of the Saviour, and of the divinity of the blood, it is no surprise that he believed in the infinite virtue and worth of the atonement. What is surprising is that anybody ever doubted such an evident truth. It is not appropriate for us to belittle sin in any way, for although man by comparison is such a small creature, there is yet more evil in one sin than anyone can imagine. Nevertheless, when we consider that One so great that there could never be a greater, has humbled himself in such a way that there could never be a greater humiliation, every equivalence disappears from sight, and we are ready to avow, with Williams:

| | |
|---|---|
| Sin on one side, Love on the other, | Pechod yma, cariad acw, |
| Thus the fateful scales were weighed; | Fu yno yn y glorian fawr; |
| And, despite our mass of evil, | Ac er trymed oedd y pechod, |
| On Love's side the balance swayed, | Cariad bwysodd hyd y llawr, |
| 'It is finished!' | Y gair Gorphenwyd |
| Were the words that turned the scales. | Wnaeth i'r glorian bwysig droi. |

It appears that this is the form in which the stanza was first composed and published. Those responsible for changing it were not guilty of any great error.[16] But when individuals concern themselves with the detailed correction of others, it is only natural for us to be detailed in judging the correction; and, most certainly, Williams would hardly have been happy to say that love was weighed, for it is impossible to weigh infinity. Love was placed in the scales, not to be weighed, but to overweigh sin. In the same hymn this thought is expressed even more strongly, perhaps, in the following verse:

| | |
|---|---|
| Divine merit! What its measure | Haeddiant Duwdod, o'i gymharu |
| Next to Hell's immense display? | 'N erbyn uffern fawr o'r bron; |
| Just one drop of Jesus' lifeblood | Dafn gwaed sy'n ganmil rhagor |
| Carries greater weight than they; | Nag aflendid dudew hon: |
| By God's passion | Gw'radwyddiadau |
| A world's sin is borne away. | Duw rydd iawn am feiau'r byd. |

Another hymn contains these two excellent stanzas:

| | |
|---|---|
| If myriad worlds together, | Pe buasai fil o fydoedd |
| Could for this price be bought, | Yn cael eu prynu 'nghyd, |
| 'Twould still be far too costly, | Â'r cyfryw bris fuasent |
| 'Twould set his blood at nought; | Yn llawer iawn rhy ddrud: |
| No cherubim, no seraph, | 'Does angel fyth, na seraph, |
| No holy angel, could | Na cherub o un rhyw, |
| To a thousandth part imagine | I'r filfed ran all ddywedyd |
| How precious God's own blood. | Mor werthfawr gwaed fy Nuw. |

| | |
|---|---|
| O that I could this moment | O na allwn innau'r awrhon |
| Ascend to heaven above, | Ehedeg fyny fry, |
| And join the glorious choirs | A dysgu rhyw ganiadau |
| In hymns and songs of love; | Sydd gan y nefol lu; |
| Our praises then would sweetly | Fel byddai cytsain hyfryd |
| From earth to heaven span, | Rhwng dae'r a nef yn un, |
| Immortal songs proclaiming | Caniadau anfeidroldeb |
| The death of God as man. | Marwolaeth Duw yn ddyn. |

Many other verses teaching the same doctrine could be quoted, but this is unnecessary as they are already in the hands of most Welsh readers. I will therefore only add a single stanza from *A View of Christ's Kingdom* that was drawn to my attention by a wide-reading and discerning deacon from Merionethshire:

| | |
|---|---|
| Rest now, uneasy conscience, | Distawa, fy nghydwybod |
| Atonement has been made, | Anesmwyth, rowd ddim llai |
| And all that God required | Nag y mae Duw yn ei ofyn |
| For sin has now been paid; | O daliad am fy mai; |
| Satisfaction, and more over, | Boddlondeb, a mynd trosodd, |
| Prepared for heaven's wrath, | Rowd i anfeidrol lid; |
| Redemption, and more over, | A heddwch, a mynd trosodd, |
| For a repenting earth. | I edifeiriol fyd. |

## CONCLUDING REMARKS

We have, no doubt, given too much consideration to the literary worth and doctrinal consistency of Williams's hymns and of his other works, but we would not forget that their main pre-eminence lies elsewhere. To many a weary pilgrim they have been as cold waters to a thirsty soul. They have provided strength to the weak, and oil and wine to many a broken spirit. Many have been granted glimpses of a better land and of the King in all his beauty through these hymns. They have proved a means of grace to thousands in Wales, and we trust that they will continue in such ministry for ages to come.

We cannot leave Williams without noting some of the many anecdotes that are told of him. He was preaching once in Anglesey and his wife was travelling with him, as was often the case. They arrived at Llangefni. After the sermon they lodged at the Penybont inn. A local band of persecutors who were conspiring against him found out his whereabouts and congregated in a crowd outside the inn door. They had with them a fiddler. Williams and his wife at this time were in the parlour. They heard the sound of many men at the entrance and then the parlour door opened and in came the fiddler with a mob of ruffians behind him. When Williams saw him, he cried out: 'Come in, man.' The fiddler asked, with a show of mock courtesy, if they wished for a tune. 'We would,' was the reply, 'let us hear you playing.' 'What tune?' asked the fiddler. 'Any tune you like, man – Nancy Jig, or some other one.' The fiddler began, and Williams called on his wife, 'Now, Mali, sing:

> Fly abroad, thou mighty gospel,
> Win and conquer, never cease;
> May thy lasting wide dominion
> Multiply and still increase!

Sway Thy sceptre,
Saviour, all the world around.'

And they sang together until the mob's frenzy was dispelled, its members slipping away and not disturbing them further.

Williams used to relate another episode of persecution that he experienced in the north. He was preaching in Bala at an inn. At the beginning of the service the local squire arrived, together with a crowd of people, intent on doing him harm. He retreated from sight, and the innkeeper persuaded him to change his clothes and disguise himself. This he did, making his escape, for the persecutors did not recognize him as the preacher. But soon a storm arose in Williams's conscience over the appropriateness of his behaviour, and the Saviour's words came into his mind with striking force, 'Whosoever shall deny me before men, him will I also deny before my Father which is in heaven.' He had to return, put on his own clothes, and face the danger. He was immediately recognized and was attacked, but with the help of the inn-keeper he received no harm.

He was the first of the Methodists to attempt to preach in Caernarvon town. This was on returning from a journey to Anglesey when his wife was with him. As they crossed the straits near Talyfoel, Mrs Williams was, somehow or other, caught up in the skirts of the sail and thrown overboard. There was a strong suspicion that this had been done deliberately! However, she was saved from drowning, and they proceeded to Caernarvon. Williams soon realized that he could not risk preaching there, in that they were determined to stop him or even kill him. They hid themselves and departed secretly the next day. He was not able to stare persecution in the face as the heroic Howell Harris could do.

Williams would often compose in the depths of the night, when everyone else would be asleep. It is said that he would often, after going to bed, wake up his wife with a sudden shout, 'Mali, Mali. A candle! a candle! I've got to write.' Mali would promptly find him one, without grumbling, but he would not always receive the same attendance when on his journeys. Once, at Collenau, near Tonyrefail, the poet failed completely to wake up the maid, with the result that she was presented with the following, the next morning:

| I now am quite persuaded | 'R wy'nawr yn gweld yn eglur, |
| That if the church bells all, | 'Tai clychau mawr y Llan, |
| The axle of the windmill, | A rhôd y felin bapur, |
| And churns, both large and small, | A gyrdd y felin ban; |

| The saucepan and the cauldron, | A'r badell fawr a'r crochan |
|---|---|
| Came tumbling down the stair | Yn twmblo oddeutu'r ty, |
| And broke her bed in pieces, | A'r gwely'n torri dani, |
| All would not waken her. | Mae cysgu wnelai hi. |

Williams used to trade his books with a lady called Sali Stringol, who lived in Neath, Glamorganshire. His practice was to receive her payments for a previous trip on his arrival with new books. On one occasion, when on an itinerary, Sali did not come to meet him as expected, and the preacher began to worry whether he had lost his money. He wrote to her to complain and noted a particular date when he would be at Fforchonllwyn, Ystradgynlais, and would hope to meet her there, with the money. Sali took great offence, and when the time came, she walked the considerable distance and arrived in a bad temper. Williams was lodging with Mr Jones, the vicar. When Sali came to the house she was taken to the parlour where the poet, the vicar, and one or two others were seated. Williams greeted her warmly, inquiring how she was, but she was too angry to answer and just threw the money on the table and demanded a receipt. Williams saw that the good woman was offended. 'Yes, yes. Yes, of course,' he answered, with complete composure. 'Would you find me some paper, Mr Jones,' he asked, and having obtained some he sat down to write. Having finished, he passed the paper to the clergyman who burst out laughing, and when the latter read out its contents to the company, Sali laughed as much as anyone. Here is the receipt:

| Kind-hearted Sali Stringol, | 'Rwy'n rhyddhau Sali Stringol, |
|---|---|
| Be cleared by this, my vow, | Y wraig a'r natur fawr, |
| Of every debt you owe me | O bob rhyw ddyled imi |
| From Noah until now; | O Noah hyd yn awr; |
| I wish the best to Sali, | Dymunaf dda i Sali, |
| A Christian true is she, | A'i chrefydd gyda hi, |
| May she make peace with heaven, | A gwnaed hi hedd a'r nefoedd, |
| As she made peace with me. | Fel gwnaeth hi hedd â mi. |

Some time during the year 1788, Williams was preaching in Dyffryn chapel (Clwyd Valley) and, as was the custom at the time, leading a church meeting after the service. Two were present having remained behind for the first time to apply for membership: a carpenter in the locality, and a young girl. Williams conversed with them, in his usual manner, and having finished turned to the church and said, 'Let this girl remain with you, and nurture and care for her. But as for this man, he has no more religion than my stick.' And he threw his walking-stick to the floor. Subsequent events upheld his judgment.

A man called William Powell, a member of the Llansamlet Church, Swansea, had veered towards Sandemanianism, following Mr Popkin who had turned to that error before him. When he was on his death-bed the preacher from Pantycelyn visited him, and by what he said to comfort the invalid we can see that he had a good opinion of the man's faith, though he had departed a little from the narrow way.

'Wil, Wil,' he said, 'you kept looking for perfect saints for years. I can see that you are closer to them now than ever before.'

It was of this Mr Popkin that Williams referred when he said that there were four things that would make him a great preacher: Samson Thomas's periwig, Howell Davies's horse, Popkin's wealth, and Rowland's gifts.

It would appear that he was indifferent as to his personal appearance. There was no service too low for him to perform. He would travel the country on horseback usually, with a sack of books upon his saddle, and if the weather changed and caught him unprepared, he would borrow his wife's cloak or a coat from a friend without any thought as to whether such clothing was appropriate for a responsible and respectable man as himself. We hear of him once preaching in the parlour of a nobleman from Margam, Glamorganshire. His pulpit was a polished oak table and with the two-fold intention of avoiding damage to the table, and avoiding damage to himself through slipping on the shiny surface, he removed his boots and, in his stockinged feet, preached happily on the feast of fat things in Isaiah's prophecy.

Morgan Rhys, the famous hymn-writer, was born in the same Llandovery neighbourhood as Williams. At one time they were fellow members of the Cil-y-cwm church. It is a strange fact that two hymnists as notable as William Williams and Morgan Rhys were born in the same district and members of the same church. All agree to place Williams at the head of all Welsh hymn writers, and many people of good judgment, Hiraethog amongst them, would place Morgan Rhys next to him. They used to recite their hymns to one another. Morgan Rhys's productions could at times be verbose and a little exaggerated. Once, having listened to the reading of a new hymn pitched at a rather high level of spiritual experience, Williams said to his friend, 'Well, in that one, at any rate, you have got the experience of a good Christian and a half,' suggesting that perhaps the hymn was pitched a good deal above the reach of the majority of believers.

We must bring things to an end. It appears that Williams was blessed with a strong physical constitution and enjoyed good health, though he was at times very careless of it. He would often sit up writing until morning, and rarely went to bed before two in the morning. This would bring on occasional attacks of 'gravel' (kidney stones), and in his last years he was troubled by depression. He was so nervous at the end of his life that he would not go out at night on his own. He died on 11 January 1791, when seventy-four years old, in his armchair, where he had been placed while his bed was being made. His soul flew to that eternal rest of which he had sung so often, while they were engaged about his bed. He was buried with much respect in the cemetery of Llanfair-ar-y-bryn, and a sermon preached on the occasion at Pantycelyn by Mr Lloyd, Henllan, Caeo, to a large congregation that had gathered there to pay their last respects.

[1] This is a mistake. See note 11 below.

[2] Maurice Davies, *Coffadwriaeth y Parch. J. Williams, Pantycelyn* (Pontypool, 1830), p. 24.

[3] *Trysorfa*, vol. 2 (Bala, 1813), p. 449. The story concerns the occasion when he was persecuted at Bala. See p. 246 above.

[4] William Williams, Swansea, *Trysorfa* (1865), p. 123.

[5] Thomas Rees and John Thomas, *Hanes Eglwysi Annibynnol Cymru*, vol. 3 (Liverpool, 1873), p. 582–93.          [6] Ibid.

[7] 'Free Will'.

[8] From *Ateb Philo-Evangelius [Philo-Evangelius' Answer]*

[9] He left the Church of England of his own accord at the request of his brethren at the Watford Association. He was the first of the Fathers to do so.

[10] This suggestion is confirmed by a minute found in the Trefeca records of a decision taken at a Monthly Meeting at Longhouse, 8 June 1743, that is, two months after the decision for Williams to leave his curacy. The minute reads: 'That brother John Jones is to remain silent, in order to be ordained, until his ordination be accomplished.' This shows that the leadership (Daniel Rowland, Howell Davies and Howell Harris were present) had realized that it was better for the curates of Methodist tendencies to reconcile themselves to being unexceptionable followers temporarily, until they were ordained. They judged that the present labours of these curates were less important in the long run than the greater service they might contribute to the revival in the future. It may be that it was the bishop's refusal to ordain Williams that had opened their eyes to this. By this minute they were ensuring that John Jones did not fall into the same embarrassment as William Williams.

[11] This is a mistake. When Williams was 73 years old he had been preaching for 50 years not 43. A correct account is given in another letter from Williams to Thomas Charles published in *Yr Arweinydd*, vol. 5, p. 180. The letter is dated 1 January 1791. In it Williams states: 'Understand that, although I have recovered somewhat from the severe pain of which I suffered, I am but weak and frail still and very unable. I have very little hope of travelling much again, if at all, as I am 73 years old. Only consider the disappointment for a man who used to travel nearly three thousand miles every year for over 50 years, that he now scarcely travels more than four feet a day, namely from his bed to the fireplace.'

[12] Translated by Eifion Evans, *Pursued by God* (Bryntirion: Evangelical Press of Wales, 1996), p. 57.

[13] *Y Traethodydd*, Vol. iii, p. 160.

[14] Lewis Edwards, *Traethodau Llenyddol* (Wrexham, 1865), p. 157.

[15] Only the first part of the article is translated here.

[16] In later hymn books the second line reads: 'In the balance both were weighed'.

# 8

# THE FIRST EIGHT YEARS
# OF THE REVIVAL

## THE RAPID PROGRESS OF THE REVIVAL IN THE SOUTH

*T*he Methodist Revival began in 1735. The instruments by which it came into being were obscure and of little consequence, no one greater than a poor curate from a rural valley in Cardiganshire, whose salary was never more than ten pounds a year, and a young man from the slopes of the Brecon Beacons, whose bishop would not ordain him. A third young man from the heart of Pembrokeshire might be added to them. By the end of 1742, that is, before eight years had passed, they had set the whole of Wales aflame from Holyhead to Cardiff. As far as the south is concerned, it need hardly be said that the back of the work had been broken in this initial period. There was hardly a locality, however rural and remote its position, where these evangelists had not been preaching.

Howell Harris was the most energetic. It is impossible to convey the speed of his itineraries. He was in the saddle, or preaching the grace of the gospel to poor sinners from dawn until dusk. He not only preached in the cities and in the small hamlets of lonely valleys, but under the shade of a tree wherever a crowd might be gathered, whether there were houses nearby or not.

Stories relating to him are found in almost every neighbourhood. Many years ago, Mr Daniel Davies of Ton, Rhondda, was walking from Glanbran, Llandovery, towards the Sugar Loaf, the high mountain separating Carmarthenshire and Breconshire. On his journey he passed Aberwyddon cottage, the home of an old woman called Kitty Parry, who was born in 1775. As Mr Davies asked her about her memories of the locality, she pointed to a tree across the stream, and said, 'Howell Harris preached beneath that tree when a young man.' But there is no church or hamlet within miles of the spot. Similar traditions survive in all parts of the south. Rowland and Williams, Pantycelyn, also travelled much, and Howell Davies, too, undertook long itineraries.

As a result, religious societies had been established throughout the region, from Presteigne to St David's. At the time, these met in private houses. The numbers of members involved was not yet great but their zeal was extraordinary. Radnorshire was possessed from one end to the other. We often read of Howell Harris at Llanbister, and it appears that the rejoicing and praising that occurred there was similar to that at Llangeitho. James Ingram wrote to Howell Harris:

> The Lord blesses Brother William Evans amazingly indeed. There is fire kindled by him at Llanbister, of the same nature as at Llangeitho, and in as high a degree, in about eight or ten of the members of the society. Glory be to God. I was there lately, and my voice could hardly be heard by reason of their cries. Some, under deep convictions of their lost estate, said they were damned; others, for joy of the discovery of salvation by Jesus Christ, saying, 'Glory! Glory to God for Jesus Christ to all eternity.' This held with them for about four hours.[1]

The brother referred to is William Evans, the old exhorter from Nantmel. Societies were formed at Nantmel, Llanbister, Llandrindod Wells, Clyro, Aberedw, Diserth, Glascwm, Llansantffraed, and other places in Radnorshire. There were societies also throughout Monmouthshire, from Blaenau Gwent to Newport, and from the Rhymney river in the west to the Wye river in the east. We mention these two counties in particular because afterwards they were lost almost completely to Methodism. Other societies considered within the range of the Welsh Methodists were founded at Shrewsbury, Ludlow, Leominster, and within Gloucestershire, Wiltshire and Herefordshire. A little later, Thomas Jones, one of the superintendents, informs us that a society of some fifteen people had been formed in Hereford. Many of these were justified, and others 'seeking delightfully'. There were others also in the town who were eager to listen. As for Breconshire, Glamorganshire, Carmarthenshire, Cardiganshire and Pembrokeshire, these were thoroughly planted with societies, some large and others small.

It must be conceded that there was very little hold as yet upon the north. Although Howell Harris's visits had stirred up much excitement, it does not appear that he had been instrumental in establishing any societies. He wrote in his journal that it was as if the door to Gwynedd had been kept closed against him. The only exception was Montgomeryshire. This county was near at hand and he visited it frequently, particularly those parts that bordered on Breconshire and Radnorshire. We find that societies were formed at Llanbryn-mair, Builth Wells, Llanllugan, Mochdre, Llangurig and Llandinam. The cause at Llandinam was particularly flourishing, as is demonstrated by the report sent to the Trefeca Association of June 1743: 'There are here', writes the superintendent, 'about forty members and four private exhorters. Our dear Lord is here an Emmanuel. He brings forth his work excellently, despite many obstacles.' There was little difference between Montgomeryshire and the counties of the south as far as the labours and success of the Methodist preachers were concerned, but as for the rest of Gwynedd, very little impression was made. At the same time, it must be remembered that Lewis Rees was labouring with a degree of success at Llanbryn-mair, and that he visited parts of Merionethshire fairly frequently. Jenkin Morgan also, one of Griffith Jones's schoolteachers, was tolerated to preach a little in Caernarvonshire.

It was in this period that the spirit of persecution was overcome to a large degree. At the beginning of the revival many meetings were broken up by the unthinking peasantry, stirred up by clergy and gentry, and various public officers would threaten fines and imprisonments. But this stopped almost completely in the south during the first eight years. Not that we do not have examples of persecution after this time but they are rare, and more the result of accident than of premeditation. There were two reasons for this. The first was that in nearly every county men of influence had been won for the revival; men such as Marmaduke Gwynne; Price, the justice of the peace; Squire Jones of Fonmon; Howell Griffiths, Trefeurig, and others. For fear of such men, many of those who would have liked to disrupt, did not dare do so. And secondly, public opinion had turned strongly in favour of the Reformers. The people saw that their regular pastors were careless in their concern for the souls of their flocks and were, many of them, leading publicly immoral lives. They felt that Harris, Rowland, and their fellow-labourers, were serious men, longing to save others from destruction.

If the societies were small in number, the congregations that gathered to hear sermons were immense. A rumour that Harris or Rowland was to visit an area would stir up the whole region, and so many thousands would gather together to hear them that no building could contain them. Perhaps only a relatively small number might be saved, but very often the whole congregation would be so shaken and consciences so awakened that many more souls were won over to the truth. In such circumstances it was impossible to stir up persecution. Whitefield used to say that there were hundreds up and down the land who were willing to give their lives for Howell Harris. Many of these were immoral men, no doubt, drunkards who could not resist their lusts, but who at the same time were completely convinced that the Reformers were men of God.

## THE METHODIST REVIVAL AKIN TO THE REVIVAL IN NEW TESTAMENT TIMES

The Methodist Revival seems to us to bear remarkable comparison to the revival of the Apostolic era. For one thing, it broke the minor rules that were generally in use, and introduced new methods of operating. Methodism was new wine, and its activity so strong that the old skins were rent to pieces. It was life, and like all life it evolved its own form and fashion. Though the Reformers were faithful to the Church of England and were extremely reluctant to leave its communion, it must be acknowledged that they ran counter to all the traditions and rites of that Church. As examples, we could refer to their itinerant ministry, which was quite contrary to the parish organization of the Established Church; to their lay ministry which, by authorizing unordained men to itinerate, seemed to undermine episcopal ordination; to the gatherings in homes and in the open air, which was contrary to the regulations with respect to consecration; or to the formation of societies, in which relatively ignorant men would act as exhorters. These were all new forms of religious activity. They arose because of the spiritual energy and zeal of the Reformers and because of their desire to face up to the circumstances of the country at the time. They accepted that their methods were not regular but they argued that they were necessary because of the state of the land. Their main aim now was to save souls, and they were not concerned if any man-made rules were trodden underfoot in the pursuit of that aim, and as they marched forward they heard the crunching noise of traditions, around which so much moss had gathered over the years, being crushed under their feet.

The Methodist Revival furthermore tended to make use of every talent and gift within the Church to carry forward the work. There are many examples in Howell Harris's letters of his readiness to use female assistance, as was done by the Wesleyan Conference later, not for preaching the gospel but for superintending and counselling in the societies. In a letter to Mrs James of Abergavenny, who afterwards became Mrs Whitefield, he asked her to write to various societies in order to encourage and awaken them. He writes:

> Stir up all for God; let none that profess his name be negligent. Search them home, and pray don't, when you are writing, so much consider what you are now, Mrs James, and what will be the opinion of the world of you, as what you'll think of things when you are putting off this tabernacle and putting it on again to shine forever. Let nothing appear unfashionable, improper or

unbecoming, more. St Paul mentions some honourable women that helped him in his work. No doubt of it, the Holy Spirit may breathe with your letters to be useful to souls, as well as on other words.[2]

There is no doubt that he is here stirring Mrs James to a work that is more or less public in nature. She was indeed a notable woman whose memory deserves more attention than is normally given it. She provided never-ending hospitality to all the exhorters; she was full of the gentleness of wisdom, whilst at the same time completely fearless. After marrying Mr Whitefield they were once crossing the Atlantic on the way to Georgia, when their ship was threatened by an enemy. The ship was secured for battle and the guns brought forward. Whitefield confessed that he was a natural coward and was trembling with fear, but as for his wife, she was busily making cartridges and preparing for the conflict. On another occasion, a mob had gathered around Whitefield as he preached. Stones were thrown at him from all directions; as he was preparing to give up and flee, she pulled at his coat, commanding him with much authority, 'Now, George, play the man for your God.' Howell Harris judged that this excellent woman was fitted for the office of deaconess and he encouraged her to commit herself to the service of God's Son. Similar sentiments are found in his letters to 'A Sister from Monmouthshire' and to the 'Dear Sister, Paul'. We do not know what was the obstacle to using female labour in the work; perhaps some of the other Reformers doubted its appropriateness. Nevertheless, every possible contribution was pressed into Christ's service: the zeal and speaking gifts of the comparably ignorant; the wisdom and organizational abilities of the slow of speech and slow-tongued like Moses; no one in any society was to be idle, nor any gift to be overlooked.

## THE NONCONFORMISTS COOPERATE AT FIRST, BUT THEN WITHDRAW THEIR SUPPORT

Again, in its beginnings, the revival drew to itself everything of true religion and seriousness within the Principality. It recognized no sect or party. Members of various denominations, who used to view one another with considerable prejudice, worked together happily. To awaken the country, bring souls to the Saviour, and build them up in the truth, was the great objective. In comparison to this, denominationalism was nothing. On the one hand, many clergymen of the Established Church were contributing to the awakening. It is said that at least ten of these were acknowledged as Methodists at the time, and there is reason to believe that many others were secretly sympathetic. On the other hand, all the Nonconformist ministers that possessed any degree of spiritual seriousness, whatever might have been their doctrinal differences, welcomed the revival with open arms. Historical truthfulness and justice to their memory require that we acknowledge this. They received Daniel Rowland and Howell Harris as angels, they invited them to their neighbourhoods to preach and did everything within their power to support them in the work. They immediately recognized the revival as God's finger, as the breath of the four winds upon the dry bones, and great was their rejoicing at its coming.

This is true only of those who were orthodox. The Arminians opposed, but very soon the revival swept away all unevangelical Arminianism, just as a gust of wind blows away a valley-full of mist and fog, and it was no more seen in Wales other than in a few corners where it developed, according to its nature, into Arianism and Socinianism. The Baptists contributed to the work, as much as the Independents, and if they desired to give undue prominence to the topic of baptism, as far as the judgment of the Methodist Fathers was concerned, it was easy to forgive them, in that they also were eager to do that which they could for the gospel's sake. We wish to emphasize the fact that, at the first, all the serious ministers in Wales, almost without exception, from every denomination and party, welcomed the revival. They were amply rewarded from heaven. They were deeply baptized into the same spirit. They, also, were made as heavy rain clouds to pour the gracious rains upon the dry ground, and the revival spread beyond the bounds of Methodism. Its effects are still to be seen on every orthodox religious body in Wales today.

But this brotherly love and general cooperation lasted only a short time. Prejudice had not died, though it had fallen into a deep sleep for a season. We find that Edmund Jones, Pontypool, (the first man to invite Howell Harris into Monmouthshire and the man to whom Harris entrusted the societies of that part of the country) in the heat of his proselytizing zeal tried to form the converted into an Independent church without any discussion with those who were the instruments of their conversion. He did this in Brychgoed near Defynnog, in Neath, in a place in Wiltshire, and even in the neighbourhood of Trefeca. We have already referred to the letter that Harris sent to him as a result of these events – a courteous generous letter and catholic in spirit. But Edmund Jones took such offence at it that he would not cooperate any further. Tenderly, Harris rebuked him, because by his behaviour he was undermining the work of the Reformers and giving cause for their enemies to view them as sectarians. From the beginning they had stressed that they had no wish to form any new party, but now their opponents would consider them hypocrites, proclaiming their allegiance to the Established Church but at the same time raising up another sect in opposition to that Church. It was also introducing a new significant element of which there was no proof that it was pleasing to the Lord, in that it was in their previous condition that he had drawn near to them and blessed them. Harris explained also the instructions that he gave to all the converts with respect to hearing the Word, that they were to go:

> 1. Where the gospel is most purely preached; 2. Where their hearts are most preached to; 3. Where they find the Lord most powerfully working on their souls; 4. Where they are most pressed on, led on, fed, kept from drowsiness, and urged to grow up more and more to a conformity with God, and out of self and the spirit of the world.
>
> As to the ordinance, I advise all, for peace's sake, to abide to the utmost where they are, whether in church or meeting.[3]

Edmund Jones could not agree with these views, and Harris complains to him of his denominational zeal in many of his letters to him. Eventually, all cooperation between them came to an end. Edmund Jones was not present in the first Association at Watford.

David Williams, Pwll-y-pant, behaved in a similar fashion to Edmund Jones. Though he was the first to invite Harris to Glamorganshire, and thanked heaven for the marvellous effects produced by his ministry, he also by now had stumbled and was absent from the Watford meeting. There was also another reason for David Williams's defection. He had begun to lose his hold on evangelical doctrines. Gradually he lost the sympathy of the better wing of his denomination, and before his death he had embraced Pelagianism, if not Arianism. It seems that a low view of Howell Harris had become general in the majority of the Nonconformist ministers at this time. He said, with respect to them:

> At the first, they liked me greatly, as I exhorted the people to go to hear at any place where Christ was preached and where they would receive most good. And when they found that their chapels were overflowing because of this, I was for a time held in great respect by all parties, and not without encouragement to join with them.

But prejudice soon raised its ugly head. Harris thundered against the coldness, legalism and lack of discipline of the Nonconformists just as vociferously as he had previously done against the immorality and indifference of the Church of England. And his continuing allegiance to that Church was a stumbling block. The Nonconformists referred to the dissolute lives of the priests and people of the Church and to the determined opposition of those in authority within it to the revival. They argued that it was not right to encourage the converted to take communion with such as these; that it could not be a true Church when it tolerated such things; that to remain within it was to seek the living amongst the dead and that it was the duty of the Methodists to leave. When Harris and his brethren saw fit to disagree, they were viewed with suspicion and cooperation was refused.

Indeed, in some places the Nonconformists became persecutors, at least to the extent that this was within their power. In a letter from William Richards, an exhorter in Cardiganshire, to Howell Harris, dated 12 September 1742, is found the following:

> The society that I had at Blaenporth and Penbryn are joined to Mr Howell Davies at Llechryd, saving one who stole from us privately to the Baptists, and threw himself out of the society, and has not come to us since. I hope still he is a sweet soul, but is now miserably deluded by the Devil. The Lord keep us from self. The Devil has moved the Dissenters against us as the wind moves the trees of the grove. They wrest our words and actions, and draw what horrid consequences they can. Our dear Sister Betty Thomas is plagued much by them. They threaten to excommunicate her, if they have not already done so, because she receives the Methodists to her house, and she is the mother of I don't know how much mischief by them; and, besides, the worst of all is that she comes to our private society, and they know not what to make of that. They say it is a door opened for Popery, and a hundred such teasing blaspheming expressions.[4]

This letter shows that the Nonconformists in some areas had joined with the unbelieving and the persecuting to misrepresent the experience meetings by suggesting at times that they were similar to the Roman Catholic confessional, or, as implied by the word 'blasphemous', that sinful practices took place within them and that this was why they were conducted in private. The Rev. Thomas Rees, D.D., states that all involvement of the Nonconformists with the Methodist Revival ended after 1747, and that from then on the only ministers who associated with Howell Harris were the Rev. Henry Davies, Bryngwrach, and the Rev. Benjamin Thomas, and the latter eventually became a professed Methodist.[5]

## THE METHODISTS IN DANGER OF EXCOMMUNICATION FROM THE CHURCH OF ENGLAND

On the opposite side, the Church authorities did everything they could to hinder the Reformers. By hiding behind false excuses, the bishop refused to ordain Howell Harris and to receive Williams, Pantycelyn, into full orders. Howell Harris says also that a number of gifted young men of unquestioned qualification for the ministry, who had thrown in their lot with the

Methodists, had applied for Episcopal ordination and had been refused without even being examined. This discouraged others who had similar intentions from seeking ordination, in that they assumed their application would be in vain. As a result the cry was raised amongst the Methodists themselves for them to leave the Church. And when their leaders failed to respond to this, many of the exhorters took it upon themselves to leave and were subsequently ordained by the Nonconformists. They were followed by many hundreds of the people.

Howell Harris gives the following reasons for his behaviour: that the prophets of old did not encourage the godly to leave the Jewish Church, even though it had become so corrupt; that Jesus Christ himself worshipped in the temple and the synagogue as a member of the congregation of Israel, even though the priests were immoral and hypocritical; that the apostles, after the resurrection, did not turn their backs upon the synagogues until they were forced to leave; that the benefits of the sacraments did not depend at all on the godliness or otherwise of the officiating clergy but on the faith of the recipient; that their responsibility was not to leave that which was deficient but to reform it and to act within it as the salt of the earth; that many poor creatures, who were benefiting from them, were so prejudiced in favour of the Church that they would listen to no one from any other party; that it was in their present situation that the Lord had blessed them and that their duty therefore was not to take any irrevocable step until they had unambiguous proof that this was God's will.

We believe that it was this last point which was the main reason. Harris protested time and time again that it was not blind partisanship that kept him in. We often find him referring to 'this benighted Church'. It was the fear of moving without having the pillar going before that troubled the Reformers. Certainly, the possibility of being driven out by circumstances was often in Harris's mind at this time. When, during his journey through Pembrokeshire, he stated his decision not to leave the Church of England, he was expressing his feelings in the light of circumstances that were almost too much for him. Whitefield had sent a letter to the Reformers at the end of 1741, mentioning that a separation from the Church was certain to take place. The letter is so remarkable, coming as it does from a clergyman, that we would wish to quote it in full:

> Different persons have different gifts and graces. Some are called to awaken, others to establish and build up. Some have popular gifts fit for large auditories. Others move best in a more contracted sphere, and may be most useful in the private Societies. Those who are called out to act in a public manner, I think ought to give themselves wholly to the work, going out wirhout scrip

or purse. The Master will bear the cost. Others who can only serve privately, may mind their secular employ and give their leisure time to the service of the Church. Some of you are ministers of the Church of England, but if faithful I cannot think you will continue in it long. However, do not go out till you are cast out, and then, having been thrown out for Jesus' sake, be not afraid to preach in the fields.[6]

Then, after referring to various arrangements, he writes:

All this may be done without a formal separation from the established Church, which, I believe, God does not call for presently.

This was exactly the feeling of the Welsh Reformers with regard to the Church. They believed that separation lay before them, but they preferred to be excommunicated rather than to leave of themselves. They could then be sure that it was God's will for them to form a new group, for the idea of giving up the work never entered their heads.

At the time, the work of the clergy in Pembrokeshire, together with that of the Breconshire clergy, led by the vicar of Talgarth, in refusing the sacrament to those in membership with the Methodists, was bringing matters to a crisis. Mr Price Davies should not be blamed overmuch. He and his brethren were acting honestly according to their lights. It must be acknowledged that the attitude of the Methodists at the time was completely unorthodox and inconsistent. According to the Rev. David Lloyd, a Breconshire clergyman, in the very able debate which he conducted with Howell Harris:

You seem to complain that some persons are refused the sacrament. I hope no clergyman doth refuse it to anyone of his own parish without good reasons. I hope also you would not have any clergyman prostitute such a sacred thing, or give it to any that are not of his congregation or assembly – to any that divide and separate from him upon pretence of greater purity – to any that condemn our doctrine and our worship. Can you reckon those of our communion who never come to their parish to our assemblies but upon sacrament days, and then stay out until the communion service, and in the evening of that day go we know not where – to meeting houses, etc. Is our worship but administering the sacrament? Do you think that coming to church and receiving the sacrament once a month is sufficient to give one a name of a Church of England man? You have strange notions. Is not this making the sacrament a tool of the body and blood of Christ? Is not this making the sacrament a cloak for schism and hypocrisy? Is it not to deceive people to seem to be of the Established Church when at the same time they are for destroying it root and branch, and maintain doctrines of the wildest enthusiasm, I may say doctrines of devils, from which I pray God to deliver them?[7]

David Lloyd and Howell Harris were redoubtable debaters, approaching the task seriously, and each was worthy of the other's steel. In some matters – the right of an unordained man, under particular circumstances, to go about warning sinners to flee from the wrath to come, for example – Harris was undoubtedly the victor; but with respect to the inconsistency of the Methodists in expecting to receive the sacraments in the parish churches without darkening the doors at any other times, the Rev. David Lloyd had the upper hand. The truth is that, even at this early stage, the Methodists could not in all fairness be considered faithful members of the Church of England. The leaders clung to the Church, not wishing to leave without clear guidance, but the common people had no respect for her. They were only inside her walls at Communion Sundays, and even then they avoided the common service and the sermon, if there was one. They knew that the clergyman could not preach the gospel of Christ, but would only be babbling the wildest prattle, or cursing those people who went about exhorting without any authority from the bishop. So, they would stand outside the doors until the communion service would begin and then they would approach the altar to partake of the sacrament. It must be acknowledged that their behaviour was inconsistent. It was almost unseemly, and from one viewpoint it is not surprising that many of the clergy had decided to refuse them the sacrament.

The result of this inconsistency was that the Methodists were unacceptable to both Churchmen and Nonconformists. Howell Harris wrote, 'All parties seem to agree to oppose us.' It may well be that Rowland and Harris mistook the signs of the times and were looking for more definite indications than they had a right to expect. The Rev. Thomas Rees, D.D., says that, had they left the Established Church at this time, Wales would now be predominantly Methodist. At the same time, it is possible that that they knew of obstacles of which we, sitting in judgment upon them over a hundred and fifty years later, have no idea.

## FIRST ATTEMPTS AT ORGANIZATION

During the period from 1735 to the end of 1742 much had been done in the area of organization. Harris and Rowland had cooperated ever since their first meeting at Defynnog Church in the summer of 1737. Every opportunity for conferring and for planning how to proceed with the work had been taken. They had enquired of the English leaders of every party, so that the decisions that had been taken were to a large extent the fruit of mature judgment. Gradually, these conferences, which had occurred occasionally whenever any major issue arose, began to be arranged beforehand on a regular basis. On the front page of the Trefeca Minutes is a note written in Howell Harris's handwriting:

> The brethren in Wales did meet above two years – once a month, and once in two months in 1740 – before the date of this book [January 1743], and examined many of the exhorters and searched to know the place of each, but no outward settled agreement was formed till the date of this book, when Mr Whitefield was sent for, and it seemed to be the will of the Lord, by the united light of all the brethren, after freely waiting on the Lord and debating the whole matter – that superintendents and private exhorters should be ordered among the lay brethren, and Brother Harris should inspect them all, and the ordained ministers go about as far as they can, and the superintendents have such a district, and the private exhorters only inspect one or two societies and follow their ordinary calling, whilst some few seemed to be intended by their gifts and being under a blessing, etc., to be a help to the superintendents in a more general manner.[8]

This note is of the greatest importance. It shows that the regular meetings of the Reformers began about 1740 when they met once every two months. This became a monthly meeting in 1741 and continued so for the following year. The main point of discussion was the proving of the qualifications of the exhorters. In complete agreement with this is a letter from Mr Whitefield published in the *Evangelical Magazine* for 1826, dated Bristol, 28 December 1741, and addressed to the chairman of one of these meetings. In this letter, from which we have already quoted, he says that the matters to be discussed were of the utmost importance and that he is sorry that he cannot be present with them. He then expresses his views of many of the points that were to be raised. It is also clear from this note that these meetings carried no great authority; they were intended mainly for organizing and counselling. No permanent regulations were laid down, nor any authority claimed by which to impose them on other brethren. The establishing of an Association at the beginning of 1743 was a completely new step, and it was in order to emphasize its importance, and in order to gain the help of an able man, who agreed with them on every point of doctrine, that Whitefield was invited to be present and to chair the meeting. This is conformed by Harris's testimony contained in a brief account of his life. He writes:

> This summer (1740), as many are standing up to speak, in different places in Wales, some of the ministers thought that an effort should be made to organize matters so as to avoid disorder, and so that no unsuitable persons should undertake the work. Then, all who spoke in this way were encouraged to meet, to speak of their experience of the work of grace in their hearts, so that they

could recognize one another, and mainly so as to have unity and communion as brethren. Then to express their motivation, what it was that caused them to undertake the work, and what reasons each could give as proof that they were called to it, and then to commit matters to the judgment of the whole. Yet we did not consider that we were being called to form a denomination apart, nor did we take it upon ourselves to examine any, with a view of ordaining them to a ministry; we only considered that we were required to go this far, if we were to form ourselves into a society which cannot exist without some kind of rules.[9]

This reference sheds a great deal of light on the nature of the organizational meetings preceding the establishing of the Association. We see: (1) that all who went about exhorting were invited to them; (2) that their main purpose was to hear both the experiences of the exhorters and their motives for undertaking public work; and (3) that they did not claim any authority over the exhorters. They did not, on the one hand, give them permission to go about, nor, on the other, stop them doing so. All they did was to express their opinion and give advice, leaving it to the exhorters to act accordingly or otherwise. But by 1742, the Reformers realized that if the unsuitable were to be prevented from undertaking that for which they were not qualified, so that the revival and the gospel might be kept from disgrace then, in these planning meetings, they would have to take more responsibility into their hands. This was one of the main reasons for proceeding to establish the Association.

The exhorters referred to above were associated with Methodism from its beginnings. They existed, not as a result of any human decision, but because of a call from heaven. It is not too much to say that the office, if indeed it can be called an office, was instituted directly by the Spirit. One reason why the revival spread so rapidly and why it assumed such a permanent form was the sudden appearance, in all parts of the land, of these unordained men, able to counsel their fellow-believers. Without them the small societies would have died out from lack of care. Daniel Rowland, Howell Harris and the other leaders were as great clouds, full of rain. Wherever they went they poured forth their blessing upon the dry land, like thunderstorms breaking over a complete neighbourhood, but having watered the ground abundantly they continued on their way to provide similar blessing to other regions. But these various regions would have wilted for lack of water during the absence of the clouds had not the Lord raised the exhorters who, by God's grace, were as refreshing dew to the societies. Their rise occurred very simply. Because of their natural abilities and their deeper experience of the work of grace in the heart, they were called upon in their own society to read and pray publicly, and to give a word of exhortation from the passage read. Over a period of time, some of them developed considerable skill in this area; the word of exhortation became something similar to a sermon; their names became known to the neighbouring societies and they were invited to exhort and expound God's Word to them. Soon, almost without their realizing it, they were looked upon as forming some kind of separate office.

The exhorters did not leave their daily occupations, they received very little remuneration for the work, they suffered much scoffing and abuse at the hands of the wicked and the falsely religious, but their bows abode in strength through it all, by the hands of the mighty God of Jacob. They varied considerably in their social backgrounds, their breadth of knowledge, gift of speech and spiritual experience. Amongst them were some of very respectable station, of good upbringing and education and considered as belonging to the nobility, but who had chosen to suffer the reproach of Christ with the Methodists than to enjoy the pomp and respect of the world. Some were from the ranks of Griffith Jones's schoolmasters. It was a necessary qualification to be a schoolmaster that a man should have sufficient knowledge of the Scriptures. He had to address his pupils from the Word and catechize them. It was a small step therefore for them to proceed to address adults. We find many of the chief exhorters in this category.

Many others of them were of the poorest circumstances, not only lacking in education but also relatively ignorant of the doctrines of religion. But they had been given a view of the crucified Christ as an all-sufficient Saviour, his glory had shone in their souls with an overpowering intensity, their hearts were filled with an enduring love for him, and though they did not know that much about him they felt bound to express what they did know to all around them. As Ahimaaz of old, they were full of desire to run for the King, and if they had no clear tidings at the beginning, they soon found it before running very far. The woman of Samaria knew very little about Jesus, but after his words had touched her heart she left her water-pot at the side of the well in order to tell her fellow-citizens of the remarkable Person she had met. So also with the Methodist exhorters: they entered into the work as they were, and God sealed their labours with blessing.

The world loves to mock the work of lay ministers and to refer with contempt to their secular employment. As Dr South said of the Puritans: 'They could literally hit the nail on its head; they could construct a pulpit before climbing into it to preach from it.' To Dr South, the possession of such skill in joinery was sufficient to disqualify a man for the ministry. The author of *Methodistiaeth Cymru* comments: 'One method of mocking a good preacher, long ago, was to ask, "Is not this the carpenter?" But in God's sight, that Carpenter was held in the highest respect; he received from God the Father honour and glory.'

We do not doubt that the addresses of some of these Methodist exhorters were badly set out. It may be that their language was not the most exalted, their comparisons were homely, even rough at times, their gestures unnatural; and their delivery completely devoid of any oratorical grace. But they were full of zeal. They had experienced deep convictions themselves, and had as a result drunk deeply of the sweetness of the gospel. They knew what it was to have been wounded and to have been healed. If they had no educational qualifications, they had experiential qualifications, and God blessed their work. Very probably it was exactly these conditions that made them so suitable. They knew how to survive on the poorest of diets while on their journeys, they could endure the roughest weather without harming their constitutions, and as they dealt mostly with uncultured men and women, their deficiencies turned into advantages and enabled them to draw more closely to the people. And God raised from this class of men preachers who shook the country; men whose gifts and powers of oratory swept all before them and whose names are household words in Wales to this day. It is said that at the time of the first Association about forty exhorters existed throughout the land. It must be acknowledged that some men rushed into the work of exhorting having none of the appropriate gifts. These lusted after the celebrity and attention, like Simon Magus of old, and they travelled from society to society, causing more harm than good, so that they began to undermine the character of the revival. One of the main aims of the Association was to bring the exhorters to order, by encouraging those fit for the work and putting a stop to the unsuitable.

A second purpose, just as important, for the Association was the bringing of some uniformity to the societies. Previously these had been completely independent of each other; there was no unifying organizational connection among them. Their only connection in fact was that they all partook, to a greater or lesser degree, of the spirit of the revival, and that they held Rowland, Harris and Howell Davies in great respect, accounting them as their fathers in Christ. The obedience rendered to the instructions of their leaders was based on their personal allegiance to them. If any society departed from true doctrine, or tolerated wrongdoers amongst them, there was no power that could call them to account and to restore matters, other than the personal influence of one of the founding fathers. The necessity of uniting the societies by one authoritative constitution was soon appreciated, so that the revival's influence might be continued and that it might be kept from running to extremes. About the beginning of 1742, a series of rules were drawn up for the societies. But no attempt to unite them in one organization was made prior to the gathering at Watford. Such an important step was certainly not taken without much forethought and discussion and, just as certainly, it is to Howell Harris that the Calvinistic Methodists are indebted for the plan and outworking of the basis of their constitution. He, more than all the other Fathers, was the organizer. His fertile mind was forever planning and on this point he had conferred with many others outside Wales, as well as with his Welsh brethren.

One man with whom he had corresponded was Mr Oulton, a Baptist minister at Leominster. Mr Oulton was a truly godly man, full of the spirit of the revival, but a strong Baptist. In a letter to him Harris noted that it was hard for all to agree on those parts of the Bible which refer to church government, to the time and mode of baptism, and a few other similar externalities which are soon to come to an end. He thought that unity would be impossible until all agreed not to ask for any condition of membership beyond a saving knowledge of Jesus Christ and a lively faith productive of a sanctified life and proving its existence by its works. 'If I had the care of a congregation,' he says, 'I would consider it a duty to receive all as members of whom I could hope they were born of God, though they might not agree with me on a few external matters.' Mr Oulton could not share in such catholic views. He disapproved of Harris referring to baptism as one of the small external matters that were soon to disappear, in that it was an ordination established by Christ himself and intended as a means of grace for the Church to the end of the world. He maintained also that the external matters, to which Harris referred rather indifferently, were clearly taught in the New Testament, and that it was as easy to arrive at a degree of certainty of their meaning as it was of the doctrines of salvation. To do justice to Mr Oulton it must be added that although his counsel of requiring baptism by immersion as a qualification of membership was not received, he did not withdraw his support of the Methodists but continued afterwards to write to Howell Harris as warmly and fraternally as ever, exhibiting as much interest as before in the success of the Connexion. Quite certainly, the establishment of the Association was a matter of deep concern to the Methodist Fathers, they felt their way along every step, and it was, no doubt, with very burdened hearts and fearful spirits that they met together at Watford.

We have already referred to the rules for the societies that had been drawn up. In his *Autobiography* Harris informs us that he wrote them, whereas on the title page it is said that they were composed by 'gentlemen of the Church of England'. The explanation is that it was Harris who drafted the rules and they were then passed to the other leaders for their comments, and were approved by them. They were then published in the names of them all. These rules are important in themselves – they reveal a deep spirituality of thought – but they possess a particular interest also in that this is the first literature distributed by the Methodists to the various churches. Therefore, although somewhat long, we include them in their entirety.[10]

## THE BASIS, PURPOSES, AND RULES OF THE SOCIETIES OR PRIVATE MEETINGS THAT HAVE LATELY BEEN GATHERING TOGETHER IN WALES:

*To which are added some hymns to be sung in the private meetings.*
*By some gentlemen of the Church of England.*

*Prov.* 15:22. 'Without counsel purposes are disappointed', etc.
*Prov.* 24:6. 'In multitude of counsellors there is safety', etc.
[The Welsh for 'counsel', 'counsellors' is 'exhortation', 'exhorter'.]
*Prov.* 27:17. 'Iron sharpeneth iron.'

Bristol: Printed by Felix Farley in Castle Green, 1742.

### INTRODUCTION

To all who have been made willing to deny themselves, and take up their cross and follow the Lamb; and particularly to the Societies within the Church of England.

Of late, we (a few Ministers) have been constrained to meet together as often as we could, in order to watch more carefully over one another, and in order to understand better the condition of Christ's flock, and to confer how best to labour in our Master's vineyard. In the meantime we had it laid upon our hearts to agree to the following Rules. And knowing how scattered you are, and in order to direct you how best to build each other up in your private meetings, we considered it our duty to send you these Rules, hoping that God will bless them to you, and give you hearts willing to submit one to another and to examine yourselves by them, as far as you find them to be just. We thought it best to put them in print so that all could see the truth concerning the basis, purpose and rules of our private meetings; and if any desire to meet with us, for them to see what discipline we consider ourselves obliged to maintain amongst us. Believing, whatever the mocking we might receive from the world, that we have a clear conscience in this, that we dare not do anything in private that we would not acknowledge when all things done in secret are proclaimed from the house-tops. It is in vain that we separate from the world and appear as those who would walk before God, and make rules for our walking, unless our souls are united to God in Christ, and to one another in the Holy Spirit; having been cleansed from all our idols, and expecting nothing in this world but that which our Head received before us, and which he promised to all his followers, namely to be hated of all for his name's sake, Matt. 10:22. And it behoves us to see that it is for his sake that we suffer; and that while we are blasphemed and slandered as proud, idle, deceiving hypocrites, let us be certain that we have an inward testimony that all that they say is a lie: if not, the Spirit of grace and glory will not remain with us as our comfort and support. But if we suffer for his sake, let us not fear: no weapon that is formed against us shall prosper, *Isa.* 54:17; and the gates of hell shall not prevail against us, *Matt.* 16:18. Only let us guard against the proud spirit of the Pharisees; if we see, and others are blind, who is it who made us to differ? Let us show that we have been with Jesus, by our gentle, kind, forgiving and loving behaviour towards our opponents. And though it is by Christ alone that we have been saved, yet let us show our love for him for redeeming and delivering us freely by his life and death, by sincerely obeying all the commandments, loving the law as that rule of our new life in Christ, which we renounce as a covenant by which we come to God to obtain life.

We call upon you to watch in your societies against spiritual pride, revealing itself in a lack of consideration for others, in unwillingness to confess our sins and to receive rebuke; against hypocrisy, or seeking to appear more full of love, faith, humility and light than you are; against self-will and self-love, worldly wisdom, and every attitude which arises from the secret desire of the heart for others to think that you are godly and growing in grace. Do not cease also from searching out every indication of that awful root, which produces all manner of evil, avarice, idleness and laziness. Watch also against idle words, frivolity of spirit, carnal laughter, vain thoughts, and unfaithfulness or flattery when in business, either by using words of double meaning, or by saying more or less than the truth, knowing that we are at all times in the sight of God. Show that you have set him before you at all times. Consider one another's growth in gentleness, kindness and true lowliness of spirit; and may you have sincere love towards all of the family of the faith, and deep compassion towards others causing you to mourn in secret for their sins. Do all things in truth and simplicity as to the Lord.

If you are children, be careful to do your best to win your parents, if they are still in the flesh, by your obedient and humble conversation.

If you are parents, look to your raising of your children and family in the fear of the Lord, praying and searching the Scriptures carefully in the home, and always catechizing them, *Deut.* 6:6,7; *Gen.* 18:19.

If you are poor, be content with what you have, diligent and faithful in your work, living in accordance with your estate.

If rich, see that you communicate, considering yourselves stewards, and that all of your goods are the possession of your Head and being careful that he has his will and way in doing with them as he sees fit.

If you are old experienced Christians, nurture and teach the young in all kindness and gentleness.

If you are young, keep from contentions, from self, and from unbelief, and expect crosses daily, both inward and outward. And when you are closest to the throne, remember us, who are few and full of corruptions, but who have, for your sakes, been compelled to leave all things, seeking nothing except to be faithful, so that we can say at the last, 'Behold us and the children which thou hast given us.'

## THE BASIS OF THE MEETING

1. It is the command of the Holy Spirit that we forsake not the assembling of ourselves together, as the manner of some is.

2. If it is a duty for us to exhort one another daily, while it is called 'Today', as this is the way to keep ourselves from being hardened through the deceitfulness of sin, *Heb.* 3:13, then we should meet together often to exhort one another.

3. It was usual for the godly to meet together in this way under the Old Testament (see Mal. 3:16) and under the New also. The apostles were gathered in this way when Christ appeared to them after the resurrection, and said, 'Peace be unto you.' *Luke* 24:33–36.

4. Our Lord promised to be in the midst whenever two or three (if not more) were gathered together, which promise, all who have gathered together in all sincerity, throughout the ages, have proved. *Matt.* 18:20.

## ITS PURPOSES

1. In obedience to the command, to provoke to love and good works, *Heb.* 10:24.

2. To prevent hardness of heart and backsliding, as we are weak in grace, our corruptions strong and our temptations many, 1 *Cor.* 3:1–3.

3. To understand more of the wiles of the devil, 2 *Cor.* 11, and the deceitfulness of our own hearts, and the work and progress of grace in our souls, 1 *Pet.* 3:8.

4. To enlighten one another in the Word of God, and to support and build one another up in our most holy faith.

5. To exhort one another, and to forestall strife and lovelessness, suspicions and jealousies, 1 *Tim.* 6:4.

6. To watch over one another's lives, behaviours, spirits and tempers, and to bear one another's burdens, *Gal.* 6:2.

7. To glorify the work of God's grace by relating to one another what he has done to our souls, according to David's example, *Psa.* 66:16.

8. To strengthen one another against the enemies of our souls, against the world, the flesh and the devil; to pray for one another, to share together every lesson we have learnt of God, and of his Son, and of ourselves, since last we met.

In order that these Purposes be fulfilled, we agree to the following Rules:

1. After singing praises and praying, 1 *Tim.* 2:1, that we open our hearts to one another, and rehearse in all simplicity the good and the bad that we see within ourselves, according to ability given to us (and according to what is seemly before others). For we experience, because of the pride which is in us, an unwillingness to bring our works of darkness to the light lest we be brought to shame; and therefore a readiness to hide our sins: and while this remains, we will not improve our souls. But we also experience that when we see our sin forgiven, and we bring our hearts to hate it, we are then enabled to bring it to the light; and great is the unity of spirit, the freedom of thought, and the love we experience, resulting from this simplicity.

But if we are not enabled to express with some understanding the wickedness of our corruption and our grief and shame for it, we tend to make light of it, and so bring dryness upon ourselves. And when we speak of God's goodness, if we forget to seek his glory alone and please ourselves with the thought that the brethren will think well of us, or think worse of those who have not our experience: if this occurs, we find that we grieve the Holy Spirit, God distances himself from our souls and coldness and aridness results. In order to remove everything which hinders the increase of love, to confess every suspicion harboured in our hearts against another; whether coming from Satan, the accuser of the brethren or some other way. If the complaint is true, we express it in order to raise the fallen, by rebuking him tenderly, firstly, according to our Saviour's exhortation, privately between ourselves, then before two or three of the brethren, looking to see any indications in him that our love may be renewed. If the suspicion is not true, then it is brought to the light, to our own shame and so that Satan has no place to work his work in our hearts. We have experienced much profit from this. The neglecting of this simplicity has given Satan opportunity for provoking much strife, etc.

3. That we be willing to be questioned and examined by one another; for we are so ready to indulge ourselves, failing to get to the heart of the matter, when we examine ourselves.

## QUESTIONS BY WHICH TO EXAMINE OURSELVES

1. What are our motives in all that we undertake, whether it is the glory of God or some pleasure, comfort, praise, honour or any profit or gain for ourselves?

2. What do we experience within us motivating us in our activities? Love for Christ or love of self?

3. According to what will do we walk and perform all things? Whether the revealed will of God in his Word, or our own wills? Do we deny our own wills in every thing?

4. As we have given ourselves to God in Christ in the covenant of grace, and no longer to live for ourselves but for him who redeemed us and gave himself for us, and as we are to bring forth fruit for every talent which we possess, we are to watch over ourselves, how we may use our souls, bodies, gifts, memory, learning, time, wealth, and every service, to do and receive good, so that we might gain the most glory to God and most benefit to his Church, by laying them out according to the rule of his Word, with all diligence and simplicity.

5. In that Christ has only one body, and in that he prays for all his disciples (or followers) to be one; in that their numbers are but few; in that all the faithful (of whatever judgment over extraneous matters) shall hereafter be eternally one; in that they now prove an inward unity, worked in them by the Holy Spirit; in that they travel along the same road, fight under the same banner, against the same enemies, feed upon the same manna, drink from the same spiritual well, are led by the same Spirit, are clothed upon by the same accounted righteousness, seek the same purpose, and are constrained by the same principle, have all heard the same voice, have been redeemed by and washed in the same blood, etc., so we do not hinder anyone of whatever opinions from becoming a member of the Society, as long as they can find it in their hearts to agree with the aforementioned Rules, and to answer the following questions:

1. Have you been convinced by God's Spirit to see yourself as completely lost and deserving of damnation? and that it would be just for God to command every creature to pain you, and to throw you to the worst miseries and pains, seeing yourself as the chief of sinners?

2. Have you been awakened by grace to see that your light is but darkness? and that you can never know the Father, nor the Son savingly, nor yourself, except your mind is enlightened by a supernatural operation of the Holy Spirit, in that you are by nature as the wild ass's colt?

3. Do you find, not by profession only, but having been taught by the Lord to see and know this, that sin has poisoned your whole nature in such a way that you cannot think one good thought nor do anything that is acceptable before God? and that you are unable to rescue yourself from this condition?

4. Do you believe and prove that it is through the imputation of Christ's righteousness alone that we are justified? and that this is received by faith? and that the Holy Spirit alone can work that faith in us? and that we cannot exercise it, nor any other grace, until that same Spirit blow upon us like the west wind or the south wind?

5. Do you find (seeing that Christ alone is that city of refuge for you to flee to from the revenger of blood) that the Spirit of God has made your affections willing to part, for Christ's sake, with all that was before precious and pleasurable to you? such as your right eye, your dearest friend, your sweetest sin, in public and in private, for Christ's sake and in order to make room for him in your heart?

6. Have you secretly counted the cost? and do you now prove that God's grace has enabled you to deny your own desires, will, righteousness and wisdom, and to submit to the will, righteousness and wisdom of Christ? and you are ready to suffer every cross that you meet with as you follow after him, and by the strength of his grace to seal his Word with your blood if necessary?

7. If as yet you have not received the testimony of the Spirit to witness with your spirit that you are a child of God, is it your desire at all times to seek God with all your heart, seeking nothing but him? Look to see whether you count all things as loss that you might win him; and that you cannot rest even with this, until you have won him.

8. Are you uneasy and have no peace from anything which has been wrought in you hitherto until you prove that Christ is in you – until you know that you have believed – until you have received such a sight of the righteousness of Christ satisfying God's righteousness on your behalf, that will draw out love towards him from you, constraining you to obedience;

and such a sight of his glorious, pierced side that will truly break your heart to mourn over sin as one who mourns for their first-born, and indeed to hate every sin; until you have received the Spirit of adoption crying Abba, Father, within you?

9. Do you believe and assent to the fundamental truths; firstly, concerning the Trinity; secondly, election; thirdly, original sin; fourthly, justification by faith; fifthly, perseverance in the state of grace, etc., as they are declared in the Articles and Homilies of the Church of England? And as for those circumstantial matters in which we might perhaps not completely agree, such as church discipline, ceremonies, the mode and time of baptism, etc., do you promise that you will not weary your fellow-members concerning those things over which God has not brought us to see eye to eye?

10. Is it God's grace that constrains you to join us? And do you, after due consideration, find your hearts submitting without hypocrisy to these rules, acknowledging ourselves, and we you, to be members of the same body, children of the same Father, united, and that you will not tell any outsider what we share together in the simplicity of our hearts (since repeating such experiences to the ungodly is like casting pearls before swine)?

These questions are to be asked of anyone desiring to join with us, after he has first given in his name in the previous meeting and has brought the testimony of some of the brethren concerning his life, character and behaviour, and of the length of time since he came under conviction and received this change in his life. It may be that some who have not been liberated from a spirit of captivity, yet who truly seek but have not yet obtained, having been made willing but not yet tasted of the water of life – these must be sustained with milk. And in order that others be not held back by these, those who are further advanced and have received gifts, should build up others by exhorting, etc. Others again, who have known blessing and profit from meeting more privately in order to examine in more detail, we allow to continue meeting in this more private way; and whoever has been for some time in the general Society, and whose conversation is fitting, is to be received into the private Society when he can answer the following questions:

1. Do you know that you believe? That you are in the faith? And that your sins are forgiven? And that Christ has died for you particularly? And now dwells in you by his Spirit? And that God loves you with an eternal love? Does God's Spirit at all times bear witness with your spirit that you are a child of God?

2. Do you find in your heart a greater sympathy towards those who are tempted? And more compassion, moderation, and love in your spirit towards all, but especially towards the family of faith, whoever they might be?

3. Do you experience more spiritual light within, revealing more and more of God's holiness and the spirituality of his law, and showing you more of the plague and deceit of your heart, the evil of sin, and the appreciation of Christ?

4. Is your conscience more sensitive in reproving the first beginnings of sin in your mind? And every lustful look of your eyes? And the first stirrings of levity or carnal happiness, or hypocrisy, or self, or a bitter nature? And idle words, or forgetfulness of God, or corrupt and vain thoughts?

5. What lessons has the Lord taught you since we last met? How much more do you see of the evil and deceit of your heart? Of the wiles of Satan? Of the depths of God's grace, and the wondrous work of his grace in you? Of spiritual and experimental light in his Word?

6. Are you more amazed at the sight of God's distinguishing love towards you? And does this sight transform you into his likeness, and work in you greater longing for his glory in everything? And for seeing him come to be glorified in his saints?

7. Do the sins of others come home more to you? And do you prove that your souls are more and more rooted and built up in love? So that every view of your weakness and of the strength of your corruption and your darkness, etc., that used to cause you pain (though they still are sources for grief) only cause you to realize more often that your whole salvation is in Christ? And by viewing the righteousness, ability and faithfulness that is in him, cause you to progress comfortably amidst tribulations, saying, 'I know whom I have believed,' when things are darkest for you?

8. Can you say, having been brought to see more clearly through the testimony of the blood and the water, that your names are written in the book of life; and that you know, on the sound basis of the Word of God, after the most rigorous self-examination, 'that neither death, nor life, nor angels, nor principalities, nor powers, nor things present, nor things to come, nor height, nor depth, nor any other creature, shall be able to separate you from the love of God, which is in Christ Jesus our Lord'; and that no-one can pluck you out of his hand for he is greater than all; but when our earthly house of this tabernacle is dissolved, that you have a building of God, an house not made with hands, eternal in the heavens; and that your ground for all this is the eternal and unchangeable covenant of God.

[1] *Christian History*, vol. 5, no. 3 ( Feb.–March 1744), pp. 38–9.

[2] CH, MS (i), p. 276.

[3] Thomas Rees, *History of Protestant Nonconformity in Wales*, p. 384.

[4] CH, MS (ii), p. 323.

[5] *History of Protestant Nonconformity in Wales*, p. 382.

[6] Tyerman, *Life of George Whitefield*, Vol. 1, pp. 541–2.

[7] HJH, p. 170.

[8] CH 48, p. 29.

[9] *Brief Account*.

[10] Occasional sentences within the following section are taken from the translated summary found in Eifion Evans, *Daniel Rowland and the Great Evangelical Awakening in Wales*, (Edinburgh: Banner of Truth, 1985), pp. 181–5.

# 9

# THE ASSOCIATION

The first Association was held at Watford on Wednesday and Thursday, 5 and 6 January 1743.[1] The diaries of both Howell Harris and Whitefield testify to this date and it is confirmed by the dates of a host of letters written directly afterwards. There is therefore no doubt over the matter. On this point it is probable that the author of Methodistiaeth Cymru was again led astray by a misunderstanding of the old ecclesiastical calendar. According to his journal, Harris started out on Sunday morning, 2 January 1743. He was very aware of the immense importance of the meeting before him, important not only to the Methodists but to the religion of Wales as a whole. The first note that day in the journal is: 'Going to meet the Association in Glamorganshire'.[2] He did not take the direct route by which he usually travelled to Glamorganshire or Monmouthshire, through Cantref at the foot of the Beacons, but kept well to the left so as to pass through Cwm-iou in order to confer with the godly clergyman, Thomas Jones, who ministered there and be strengthened in spirit by listening to him preach the Word. His journey took him past scenery as beautiful and romantic as any found in Wales but it does not appear that his spirit was in harmony with the beauty surrounding him. His anxiety of mind was such that he could not obtain any peace except by raising his heart in prayer to God. After praying for Miss Ann Williams, and for his mother, 'I prayed,' he says, 'for our Association, for God to come amongst us and to direct us, and for my going overseas; I was given much liberty to place the matter before God, but was not given an answer. I prayed for our darkened Church and for all who are in sin. I was given strength to mourn and cry for the whole of God's family, seeing the whole Church as belonging to his family, that they might be brought to walk in the light.'

Between nine and ten he met with many of the brethren, somewhere amongst the mountains, who testified to the profit they received from God through him. After deciding on some matters concerning the small society there, and placing them in the care of his brother Joseph, whom he considered to be ordained of God for the pasturing of that flock, he continued onwards. The possibility of emigrating overseas occurred to him again. He saw that the cause in Wales could proceed without him. But his heart was full to overflowing with love towards his spiritual children, making him cry out, 'O! How could I ever leave them?' Surrounded by the wildness of the mountains, his spirit was stirred within him to bless and worship God. 'How can I glorify thee,' he said, 'for Jesus Christ, and the riches stored up in him?' Having reached Cwm-iou, he poured out his heart to Thomas Jones; he confessed the evil of his heart that was much stirred up on hearing that he was about to be excommunicated. As he conversed he broke down, from physical weakness. The old clergyman preached sweetly but Harris did not receive strength. He was however given remarkable unction in prayer by which he obtained much spiritual and physical strength. He departed on Monday morning, having conversed again with Mr Jones, who manifested a truly catholic spirit, and he arrived at Goetre, near Pontypool, about seven o'clock. He preached there on Tuesday morning, warning his listeners against self and the wickedness of the heart. He slept on Tuesday at Llanfihangel. The first entry in his journal for Wednesday is: 'Went to the Association, the care of it all is upon Jesus.' He complains of his weakness and of his misery without the certain presence of Jesus. On the journey he was granted a sight of the Lord and wished he had ten thousand lives to offer up to him. He reached Watford about midday.

Watford lies on the slopes of a valley entering the hills about three-quarters of a mile to the west of Caerphilly, between the Rhymney and Taff valleys. There is no town or village there, but only the elegant farmhouse of Watford-fawr, a well-known stately home in Harris's time. About two fields width away was Watford Nonconformist Chapel, named after the land on which it was built. Methodistiaeth Cymru states:

> Near to Watford house is a very old Presbyterian chapel where the Methodist Reformers used to preach, because of the support of Mr and Mrs Price, who then lived in the mansion. Williams, Pantycelyn, composed an excellent elegy to this Mrs Price, after her death. There was no fixed pastor over the old chapel at the time, I believe, and as Mr Price sympathized with the Methodists he opened his own home to them and obtained permission for them to use the chapel, at least occasionally, to hold their meetings.

It would be hard to include more mistakes in such a small compass. Grace Price, for whom Williams composed his elegy, was not the wife of Price, the justice of the peace, but that of Captain Price, his son; she was not born when the Methodists held this first Association there. Watford Chapel can hardly be called a 'Presbyterian chapel', nor was it old. It had been built some three years before the Association, and it was in the strength of the awakening that resulted from Howell Harris's first visit to the region, that the people were stirred up to build it. Harris called the building 'the new room'. Nor was it without a pastor, in that David Williams, Pwllypant, ministered there as well as in Cardiff.

The Association met for the first time at Watford Chapel at two o'clock. Harris wrote in his journal, 'We stayed in the new room until seven, and then went to the home of Brother Price.' On first sight, it is strange that they were granted use of the chapel, because David Williams, the minister, had stopped cooperating with them. But it must be remembered that the vast majority of the membership there had been converted through Howell Harris, that his visit in 1738 was the occasion for the building to be erected, and that at the time the church considered itself to be Methodist and was to continue to do so until the Arminian and half-Arian views of David Williams forced the Methodists to leave and build the chapel at Groeswen.

Mr Whitefield was chosen as Moderator. He began the meeting with prayer, praise and counsel. Harris wrote that he never saw such a combination of amiability of mind, of love, and of power, as was found in this man. Others present were the Revs. Daniel Rowland, John Powell and William Williams, all ordained clergymen, together with Messrs. Howell Harris, Joseph Humphreys and John Cennick, the laymen. These last six formed the sole composition of the Association at its beginning. The three clergymen were judged to be members on account of their ordination. Howell Harris on account of his unique position as the most active of them all and as the founder of the majority of the societies, and Messrs John Humphreys and John Cennick because of the respect in which they were held by the English Methodists. John Powell was the curate of Aberystruth, near Blaenau Gwent. He had been convicted under Harris's ministry when the latter first visited that region, and had developed into a most evangelical and substantial preacher. For all his great zeal for doing good, he was persecuted fiercely in Aberystruth. It would appear also that his wife was a notably godly woman, and Mr Edmund Jones says of her that the work of some of the chief parishioners, her father being one of them, in refusing permission for Daniel Rowland to preach in the church so affected her mind as to shorten her days. Having suffered much because of his association with the Methodists, Mr Powell received a living in the south of Monmouthshire where he lived until his death.

John Cennick was the son of a Quaker from Reading and was raised in a religious home, being taught to pray morning and evening by his mother. But he became a wild youth. He used to sing bawdy songs, play cards, and visit theatres. His father sent him nine times to London to be apprenticed in different trades, but no one would take him because of his bad habits, except for one carpenter who accepted him on probation but then refused to take him up as an apprentice when the time came. The youth was convicted while walking in Cheapside, one of the most populous streets of London, in 1735, about the same time as Howell Harris. What means were blessed to his conviction is not known, but he remained under intense feelings for some time. He fasted often, and for long periods, and he prayed nine times a day. He feared spirits greatly, and had a terror of meeting the devil. As he judged that bread, even dry plain bread, was too good a food for such a great sinner as himself, he would eat only tubers, acorns and grass, and wished only to exist on vegetables and roots. He found no peace for his soul until October 1737, when God revealed his compassion towards him, and he went on his way rejoicing. Like Howell Harris, he began preaching immediately and he also began composing hymns. Many of these, edited by Charles Wesley, were published in 1739.

In the same year, he met John Wesley, who appointed him master of his school at Kingswood, Bristol, where many colliers had been converted. He reached Kingswood in June but to his great disappointment found that Wesley had departed for London. He was invited to hear a young man read a sermon to the colliers. The meeting was being held under the shade of a sycamore near the spot where it had been intended to site the school. The colliers gathered together, about five hundred of them, but there was no sign of the reader of the sermon. Cennick had to preach to them instead and had a most powerful service. God testified to the word of his grace and many believed to eternal life. He preached the next day, and twice on the following Sunday. Howell Harris arrived on a visit and the two of them, the first unordained preacher of England and the first unordained preacher of Wales, gave themselves to the work of preaching to these congregations that were so eager to hear the Word. When John Wesley returned the following Tuesday, the praise of the two young evangelists were on everyone's lips. Wesley had no thought of restraining John Cennick, so to the latter belongs the honour of being the first lay preacher amongst the English Methodists. It would appear that he was gifted abundantly. He possessed great fluency of speech and unending courage. When Wesley and White-field divided because of the Arminian views of the former, Cennick sided with the Calvinistic party, and he was one of the fifty-two thrown out of the Kingswood society by Wesley in 1741. From then on he was White-field's right-hand man. But in 1745, when Whitefield was in America, he joined the Moravian Church. He died in 1755. Tyerman says of him,

'Cennick had his weaknesses; but, in deadness to the world, communion with God, Christian courage, and cheerful patience, he had few superiors.' And he adds, writing from a Wesleyan standpoint, 'Despite his Calvinism and his differences with Wesley, we admire and love the man.'[3]

Joseph Humphreys was the son of a Nonconformist minister in Burford, not far from Oxford. Although his name is Welsh there is no indication that he was from Welsh extraction. He was born on 28 October 1720, so that he was a little over twenty-two at the time of the Watford Association. He received a good education. His father, who had suffered much scorn and contempt in his day from the hands of Nonconformists and Churchmen because of his zeal and Puritanical life, died when his son was only thirteen years old. Joseph was then sent to a school in London where young men were prepared for the ministry, and his own desire lay in that direction. These young men, intended for the ministry, used to hold prayer meetings and Joseph counted himself privileged to have found himself amongst youths of such godliness and seriousness. He soon found that this was only a cloak, in that they engaged privately in unworthy games and vain, frivolous behaviour. Evil communications corrupt good manners. Joseph was soon as frivolous as the worst of them and in his heart an infidel. He indulged his sinful passions and lived an openly ungodly life. Gradually he recovered his seriousness, he became a member of a Nonconformist church in London, and he began to preach, 'but I had not been convicted'.

In the summer of 1739 he went to hear Whitefield, whose ministry affected him greatly. As he saw the huge crowds pressing together in their eagerness to hear the gospel, he said to himself, 'It was never so seen in Israel.' He sought Whitefield's company, and on one evening had the privilege of supping with Whitefield, Howell Harris and a few other brethren, in an inn in Blackheath. After dining they conversed on spiritual matters. The inn became a sanctuary. Humphreys felt that the place was a heaven on earth. On another day, during the singing of a hymn in the academy (where he was continuing to study) he had such a sense of the forgiving love of Christ that his heart melted within him and his eyes became a fountain of tears. His fellow-students asked him what was the matter but the only answer he could give was that he was happy. Later again, he began preaching in a dance-room. He drew large congregations and a church society was formed numbering some one hundred and forty members. He preached Calvinistic doctrines: sinners being justified before God on the basis of Christ's merit alone. Because of this he was opposed at the academy, his fellow-students mocked him, he was persecuted by his tutor and deserted by his friends. It was believed that he had taken leave of his senses and on 19 December he was expelled from the institution, even though there were no other charges against him. But Joseph Humphreys's one desire was to preach, and he continued doing so, ministering to the societies at Deptford, Greenwich and Ratcliffe. He was persecuted. At times his life was in danger from the stones that were thrown at him, but it did not concern him. In 1741 he united himself with Whitefield, and it was as an itinerant preacher associated with Whitefield that he was present at the Watford Association. Historical accuracy requires us to note that his latter end was not as bright as his beginnings. After a while he left Whitefield and was ordained as a Presbyterian minister. He then entered the Anglican ministry and it is said that he mocked the Methodists, referring to his own time amongst them as a period of madness.

The other participants at the Association are too well-known to need further description. This meeting may be considered as almost unique in the history of the world. Here were six young men, all under thirty, gathered together in a small chapel on the slopes of a mountainside, laying their plans to win Britain to Christ. They were not lunatics, nor were they planning an undertaking without having considered the difficulties. They were intensely serious; their hearts were fervent in their love towards Jesus and in their zeal for saving souls. Some of them were already well-known throughout England and Wales as incomparable preachers, their fluency yoked to the true gospel, able to draw thousands to hear them and then to hold these thousands, for hours at a time, face to face with eternal truths. Hundreds looked to them as their fathers in Christ and many loved them so strongly that they would be willing to pull their eyes from their heads for them. Around them, in the simple chapel, were dozens of men who had been convicted under their ministries and as a consequence had begun exhorting sinners. These now waited anxiously to hear what aspects of the spiritual work would be allotted to them. The meeting was an historical gathering indeed. Its effects are felt to this day, and its history will remain forever sweet to all those for whom a concern for the spiritual good of Wales lies close to their hearts.

The first work of the Association was to examine the public exhorters, that is, those who travelled about preaching in association with the Reformers. Their names were Herbert Jenkins, James Beaumont, Thomas James, Morgan John Lewis, Benjamin Thomas, John Jones, and Thomas Lewis. These will all be referred to later. They were examined with difficult questions, not only on the extent of their knowledge and orthodoxy but also with a view to the work of grace in their hearts, their motives in the work, and the gifts they possessed to fulfil it. After conversing in the chapel with them until seven, they all withdrew to the Watford mansion. It was not until one o'clock in the morning that they were eventually received as members of the Association. Whitefield and John Cennick were the main participants in this examination.

Was Howell Harris hurt by not being voted in as Moderator and by the fact that the two Englishmen had a more prominent role? From a few comments in his journal, we assume this was the case. He complains of the assaults of self upon him, 'Let me strive to be nothing,' he writes, and later, he adds, 'I am the weakest, the proudest, the most blind and the worst of all.' He says that he was afraid to open his mouth, that he was glad that the bulk of the work had been committed to Whitefield, that he longed to be hidden and forgotten about, but that a great sadness had engulfed him. This all suggests that he was fighting against some disappointment received in the meeting. And why not? He also was human, with human faults. But he soon overcame his unhappy feelings and breaks out in prayer for Whitefield, for the clergymen and for the exhorters. The idea of emigrating rises up to disturb him again. He states that he had not received any clear indication of the mind of the Lord on the matter, but it came to this, 'If I am to go, I am content; if I am not to go, I am content; only let me have grace to glorify God.'

On Thursday morning, at eight, Daniel Rowland preached from Romans 8:1, 'There is therefore now no condemnation to them which are in Christ Jesus.' It was a powerful sermon. He described the nature of Christ's righteousness, and the danger of the doctrine of justification without works being misunderstood and misused. He enlarged upon the characteristics of those who have been justified by grace, that they do not live in sin nor delight in it, and he described the behaviour of those who walk in the Spirit. The sermon had a deep effect, especially upon the preachers. Howell Harris felt a particular love for the Holy Spirit and James Beaumont said that he had received new love towards the Three Persons. The Association met again at eleven. The main work was the examining of the private exhorters and the responsibility was committed largely to Howell Harris. In it he received particular power. He says that his words cut to the quick; he referred to the Judgment, to eternity, and the law, until fear spread over all. 'It was an awful place,' he says. He pressed upon them that if they believed that the Holy Spirit had given them the care of the lambs they needed to be filled with the care of a father, the gentleness of a mother, and the sympathy of a brother; that they were in need of Jesus, in all aspects of his names: as king, as priest and as prophet; and in all his graces: faith, love, humility, wisdom, gentleness and compassion. 'I felt,' he wrote, 'as if they were a part of me. I was willing to be their superintendent to watch over them, and I was extremely blunt with them. They were deeply subdued, understanding that they needed every enabling.' They remained in the chapel until seven, discussing various matters, 'and we all agreed on everything,' said Harris.

They afterwards retired to the house and sat up until twelve to complete the work, appointing to each one his place and arranging the Association. 'Again together full of love.' writes Harris, 'Sure our Lord was with us. About two, I went to my bed, very happy in spirit.' We see that the sad thoughts that had disturbed him on the previous day had by now disappeared completely. The influence of the Holy Spirit had united him and all the brethren together just as two bars of iron unite under fierce heat. Some minor matters however had not been fully decided and they rose at half past seven on the Friday to complete all arrangements. 'By ten', wrote Harris, 'we had decided all matters, and were full of love. Oh, what peace, wisdom, love and order are seen when all the work is committed to the hands of the Lord!'

The majority departed about midday but Harris and John Cennick remained in order to preach that night. It proved a remarkable meeting. Harris's comment is, 'God came down.' He felt himself being sweetly drawn out of himself when Cennick preached. His chains fell to pieces, he felt himself in a new world – a world of liberty. The effects were even greater when he came to preach. He wrote later:

> I was now, in exhorting, like the former times, beginning without a text. I showed how that those who possess faith in Christ behold the glory of Jesus, dwell in the Spirit, love one another, have true zeal for the cause of God; but that they frequently depart from the Spirit, that a child having passed out over the threshold of the home may find himself outside amongst the dogs and the pigs, but that these animals do not dare enter inside the home. Many were heated with God's fire indeed. There was a great cry among the people.

It is interesting to learn that this first Association, like so many other Associations after it, did not come to an end without clear indications of the divine Presence. All departed praising and singing. And if the slopes of Caerphilly Mountain and the valleys of Rhymney and Taff were echoing that night with the rejoicing of the crowds returning home having drunk their fill of the sweet wine of salvation, this was only the natural consequences of the influences that had fallen abundantly upon the hordes that had gathered together.

The following are the decisions taken at the Association, as they are found in Howell Harris's handwriting:

Agreed that the following brethren should be public exhorters: Herbert Jenkins, James Beaumont, Thomas James (to be as he is until his affairs are settled), Morgan John Lewis, Benjamin Thomas, John Jones, and Thomas Lewis.

Agreed that Richard Tibbott be the general visitor of the bands.

Agreed the following brethren be private exhorters:

James Williams, to visit the societies at Caeo, Talley, Llanfynydd and Llangathen.

Morgan Hughes, Caeo, Lledrod, and Pontrhydfendigaid.

David Williams, Lledrod and Llanilar.

Price Thomas, Pontargamddwr, and Caron.

John Powell, Defynnog.

William Evans, Llanddewi, Llandegley, and Llandrindod.

Howell Griffith, Llantrissian and Glynogwr.

Richard Thomas, Llanedern and to assist at Watford.

John Belcher, visitor of the single brethren at Watford.

Evan Thomas, Mynyddislwyn.

William Rice, visitor of the married men at Watford.

Thomas Evans, to the care of the outward things at Watford.

William Morgan, visitor of the married men.

Henry Harris, to help brother Price.

Thomas Price, to the care of Watford.

William Powell, to the care of the societies in his house.

Stephen Jones, Glasgoed and Goetre.

Thomas Lewis, Pentyrch and Newhouse.

Richard Jones and John Deer, Aberthin, Llantwit Major and Aberthaw.

Charles Powell, Glasbury and Bronllys.

John Jones, Llanfihangel Cwm Du and Grwynefechan.

Morgan John, Palleg, Creunant, Llanddeusant and Cwmamman.

William Harry and John Richards were approved.

Agreed that the brethren who had scruples about receiving the sacrament in the Church on account of the ungodliness of the ministers, and received with the Dissenters on account of lukewarmness, should continue to receive in the Church, till the Lord should open a plain door for leaving her communion.

Agreed that no exhorter should be reckoned one of us but what was tried and approved, and that no one should go beyond his prescribed limits without previous advice and consultation.

Agreed that each private exhorter bring an account of his respective societies and of those who would be admitted into fellowship next Association, which is to be the first Wednesday after 25 March 1743.

The Lord was pleased to be with the brethren and seemingly to countenance their consultation. Gloria in excelsis Deo.[4]

It may be seen that the spirit of the writer, Harris himself, had warmed within him as he recorded these minutes. His feet are upon the high places and his zealous feelings break out in worship to the Lord who had led them in all their deliberations. There are many things in these notes that call for attention. We see that Watford is being made into a kind of headquarters for the movement. Whether its strategic position – a convenient place both for those from England and from Wales – was the reason for this, or whether it was the suitability of Thomas Price, the owner and inhabitant of Watford mansion, to fulfil the various tasks to be performed, we do not know. The directions encouraging those who were hesitating over the taking of communion, to continue to do so at the Established Church, have been severely criticized. According to Thomas Rees, D.D.:

> The fourth of the foregoing resolutions shows the blind attachment of the early leaders of Welsh Methodism to the Established Church, when they could recommend their followers to communicate in the parish churches with impious clergymen, rather than in the meeting-houses with 'the lukewarm Dissenters' however pious they might be.[5]

That the Methodist leaders, Howell Harris in particular, were very zealous for the Established Church is certain; they considered themselves to be Churchmen, and they did not intend to leave her communion unless forced to do so. But their attachment was not perhaps as blind as Dr Rees would have us believe. The following reasons can be given for the decision that they came to:

1. It was a direction given to those who were accustomed to receive the sacraments in the Church. This is clear from the word 'continue'. There is not the slightest suggestion here that Nonconformists should leave their own denomination.

2. The coldness and spiritual lukewarmness that had possessed many of the Nonconformist churches at this time was just as much an obstacle to true religion, in the eyes of the Methodists, as was the immoral lives of the priests. In their opinion it was impossible for lukewarmness and godliness to dwell together. Any man, filled with the spirit of the revival and with his heart burning with love for the Saviour, could only feel disgust at seeing the communion service being conducted by a minister whose spirit was as cold as ice. And in many places, this coldness was the result of unevangelical views of the person of Christ and of the nature of the atonement he wrought. In the Church, however impious the administering priest might be, the service read by him was excellent, full of nurture for godliness.

3. 'Until such time as the Lord should open the door to us to leave her communion', was the advice. This is what is contained in the rules. This point appeared close at hand to them at that time. The work of some of the clergy in refusing the sacrament to their followers appeared to be bringing matters to a crisis. And if they wished for those who had been convicted under their ministries to remain united, without some joining this party and others a different party, who could blame them?

4. As already mentioned, a low view, and to some degree a persecuting view of the Methodists had by now taken hold of many of the Dissenting ministers and their churches. In some churches they went so far as to refuse communion to those who attended Methodist meetings. In the minutes of the monthly Association of Glanyrafonddu, held on 17 April 1744, there is a reference to one Thomas Dafydd who was excommunicated by the Dissenters for associating with the Methodists. He was admitted into membership and was allowed to serve as a private exhorter, on probation, under the superintendency of Brother James Williams, on the condition that he was not to leave his calling. We have already mentioned an old woman called Betty Thomas from south Cardiganshire who was threatened with excommunication for the same crime. The same feelings were rampant in England where the godly and impartial Dr Doddridge was persecuted fiercely by the Dissenters because of his associations with the Methodists. Such an attitude had naturally produced a corresponding reaction within the Methodists towards the Dissenters, so that, by now, they had in many regions moved a considerable distance from one another.

On taking all points into consideration the decision at the Watford Association with regard to communicating in the Church is hardly surprising.

There is no reference to Howell Harris, or to any of the clergymen, in the deliberations of the Association, but their work is mentioned in the note, already quoted, that precedes these minutes. Harris was to superintend all the societies and exhorters, and the ordained ministers were to itinerate as much as they were able. Howell Harris had received a work after his own heart. If he was anxious before the commencement of the Association, after it his spirit was full of confidence and rejoicing:

> It was decided by the Lord with regard to my staying in Wales, that I was to superintend the societies, to read, and to write, as far as my body allows. On seeing God's plan to be what I had hoped, my soul was filled with love, so that I cried out, 'Oh! let me bear all thy burdens.' My heart went along with those departing from the Association.

He himself left on the Saturday, but not before praying earnestly for an abundant endowment of the necessary gifts for the work:

> Jesus, for thine own glory, name, and cause, give me faith, love, ability, and every grace, in that I ask for them for thy sake, and for thy glory's sake, not for myself, not even for my salvation; and may thy blessing be upon my labours.

Many of the brethren travelled with him, including Beaumont and Cennick. They arrived at Gelli-gaer about twelve. As Beaumont was asking a blessing upon the meal there, Howell Harris experienced a visitation from heaven. He prayed inwardly for help to pastor the sheep, for every wisdom, love and gentleness and for the necessary concern for the task. He noted that he was already aware of a pastor's spirit within him.

Harris continued through Cantref where he spent part of the Sunday, Felin-fach, and Llywel, arriving back at Trefeca on the Thursday. He was there for only two days. The organizing of the societies and the bringing of the exhorters into conformity, according to the decisions of the Association, required him to be on his way. But before beginning his journeying, he saw a glory in Christ that he had never seen before, mainly through reading a book on the nature of the church, written by one of the Baptists. He noted how men divide into parties even though the nature of the church is spiritual, but that the Spirit had blessed something of each of them to himself and that he was free from enslavement to any particular party.

By the time of the Monthly Association at Llanddeusant, held on 3 February, 1743, he had travelled through extensive areas of Breconshire, Monmouthshire and Glamorganshire, forming societies and preaching the gospel. The minutes do not state who was present at this Association, only the decisions agreed are given. These were as follows:

> Agreed that those who exhort privately at one society shall, on condition they will come to our next Association whom we now approve of, namely:
>
> That Bros. W. Williams, Cerrigcadarn; William John, Glancothi; Jenkin Jenkins, Llandefathen; David Rees, Tirabad; Hopkin John, and John Meyrick, should be as they are here under settled, and come to our next Association.
>
> That these hereafter named shall be silenced till the next Association, and are to meet us there, namely:
>
> James Tomkins; David Price, Diserth; Richard Thomas, Ystradfellte; John David, Llandyfaelog; John Watkins, Defynnog, Thomas Price, Llandeilo Fach.
>
> That Bro. John Jones, Caeo, should settle near Neath, and to over-look (every other week) the societies of Creunant, Hafod, Neath, Palleg, Cwmaman, Llandeilo Fach, Llangyfelach, Llansamlet, Llanddeusant, Blaen Llywel, Loughor, Llan-non, Pembrey, and Defynnog, with Bro. John Richard; and to

be assisted by the Bros. Jeffrey David at Llanddeusant, John Powell at Defyn-nog, Jenkin John at Llywel, Edward Meyrick at Pembrey, George Phillips at Neath and Hafod.

That Bro. Richard William David should over-look the societies at Llandy-faelog, Cilgarw, Llanddarog and Carmarthen.

That Bro. John Rees should exhort under the inspection of the Reverend Brother William Williams.

That Bro. William Richard should over-look the following societies, namely, Blaenheinaf, Dyffryn Saith, Blaen-porth, Twr-gwyn, Llechryd and Llanfair-y-llwyn.

That Bro. William Harry should teach school at Caernarvonshire and exhort as much as he can between school hours in the neighbourhood.

That Bro. William John, Llanwrda, and his brother David, should assist Bro. James Williams in the societies at Llanwrda, Llansadwrn, Cilgarw and Tal-ley.

That Bro. Richard Tibbott should teach school in Pembrokeshire.

That Bro. John David should discourse on trial before the brethren at the soci-eties of Llandyfaelog and Cilgarw till we shall have the brethren's opinion.[6]

These are the minutes of Carmarthenshire's first Monthly Meeting. It is very similar in style and content to that of a present-day Monthly Meeting. The notes suggest many interesting questions that we have no leisure to pursue here, but we must quote from Howell Harris's journal with respect to this meeting. He writes as follows:

Monthly Association at Llanddeusant. On the way there I was dry, dead and indifferent, but eventually, by believing that God loves me as I am – hard and indifferent – love began to kindle in my soul, and I found release. I see that God loves me in my sin, for no reason at all, but that it seemed good in his sight. I felt in myself that God would do some great things in me, to me, through me, or for me. For most of the way my heart was like a burning coal within me. I arrived at the place near twelve, and there we sat deciding the business of the societies, and in prayer, until nearly seven. The Lord brought me within the veil, and sweetly kept me there, for most of the time. I am the weakest of them all, but what I feared would be a burden to me was made easy and sweet, we all agreed. Surely the Lord was here. In singing hymns, we were so set aflame that we could not depart. Surely Jesus had compassion upon us; and although previously I was indifferent, I was so overflowed with love to the brethren that I was as one spark of fire. I found one of the brethren was to go to north Wales; my soul truly blessed God for it. On realizing that all the power, as it were, was with brother Rowland, I felt my soul thankful within me. Willing to be robbed of all my power and gifts that he may have all. I truly rejoiced and blessed God on seeing him so full of God. O, how we were all warmed together! After sitting and arranging all our circumstances, I listened to one of the brethren exhorting until after nine. O, what works the Lord will bring forth upon the earth, for me and through me particularly! Never have I heard from Cardiganshire such outpourings of the Spirit here – such flames of love! My heart flamed and burned as an ember of coal, as I saw how the Lord is giving ability, zeal and light to the brethren.

Clearly this first Monthly Meeting terminated with much praise and worship. The brethren were all united and in agreement; Rowland's abilities ensured his pre-eminence amongst them, in Harris's judgment, and Harris himself could bless the God of heaven for the grace revealed in him.

The Trefeca Minutes provide an account of a meeting held at Trefeca on 7 February, 1743; that is, four days after the Llanddeusant meeting. The decisions made were of little import and were required to be presented for the further consideration of the Association. In all probability it was not a regular Monthly Meeting, and we find from his journal that Harris does not seem to have been present.

At a meeting held at Tyfyn, or Tyddyn, Montgomeryshire, on 17 February, it was decided that the brethren Morgan Hughes, Benjamin Cadman and Lewis Evan were to take care of the societies at Tyddyn, Llanidloes, Llanllugan, Llanwyddelan, Bwlch-yr-hwyaid and Mochdre, with Thomas Bowen as superintendent, or missioner. Howell Harris was present on this occasion, but it is doubtful if it was a regular meeting. Most probably, advantage was taken of the presence of the Trefeca evangelist in order to take counsel on various matters. It must also have been a short discussion because Harris informs us in his journal that he was writing until ten and preaching at Trefeglwys, some seven miles away, at twelve. They probably met at the close of the service the previous evening.

The next meeting noted, but without a date, was at Llanwrtyd. All the exhorters of that part of the country were placed under the supervision of the Rev. W. Williams who was at the time curate at Llanwrtyd.

A very important Monthly Meeting was held at Glanyrafonddu, Carmarthenshire, on 1 March, 1743. Many arrangements were made and suggestions to be presented to the Quarterly Association soon to be held at Watford, agreed. Amongst other things, they agreed:

That Bro. David Williams of Llangyndeyrn should exhort only before the brethren, in the nearest private societies till he shall have a testimony from them, and come to our next Association to be examined.

That these should be silenced as being persuaded not sent from God: James

Tomkins, Richard Thomas of Ystradfellte, John Watkins of Defynnog, and Thomas Price of Llandeilo Fach.

That Bro. John Richard of Llansamlet should take care of, and exhort in the societies of Cefnfedw, Blaencrai, Llanddeusant, Cwmaman, Llan-non, Pembrey, Loughor, Llandafen, Llandremor, Llangyfelach, Llansamlet, Neath, Hafod, Creunant, and Palleg; that he should see these once a fortnight, one every day, and to be assisted by John Jones of Caeo, who is to visit them once a month, to go about one week and to work the other . . .

That Bro. William Harry should teach school in Caernarvonshire, etc.

That Bro. Richard Tibbott should teach school in Pembrokeshire, etc.

That Bro. John David of Llandyfaelog should discourse in the society of Llandyfaelog and Cilgarw on trial till the next Association, then to have the brethren's opinion concerning him . . .

That . . . Hopkin John of Llangyfelach; John Meyrick of Llandafen and John Jones of Llandyfalle should (having not come to our Association yet to be examined) remain in their appointed places, as they are settled, on condition they will come next time if they conveniently can.[7]

We include these minutes because they demonstrate the methods adopted by the Methodists in their first Associations and Quarterly Meetings; how detailed they were in their arrangements, how conscientious and without respect of persons. For many of the exhorters to which they refer, everything about them, except for their names, lies forgotten. There is not even a story or tradition concerning them remaining in their localities, not the slightest echo of their history has passed down to us. Yet, certainly, many of them would have been most useful men, though their labours were confined to a limited region. They would have been full of zeal and commitment, and only the last day will reveal the extent of their sacrifice on behalf of Jesus Christ, and of the debt owed to their labour of love by the Methodist Connexion even down to today.

The following decisions were also accepted as suggestions to be placed before the next Association:

That the General Association of ministers and exhorters that are united in England and Wales, by reason of their great distance, should be only every half year.

That the English brethren should meet once between, as also the Welsh brethren (corresponding monthly by letters too) toward the middle of south Wales, where they shall settle.

That once a month (or twice between every Quarterly Association) as many as can of the ministers and public exhorters should meet, or send their letters, etc.

That the general care of all should be immediately committed to the ordained ministers, namely, the Reverend Mr Whitefield, Mr Rowland, Mr Howell Davies, Mr John Powell, Mr Thomas Lewis and Mr William Williams.

That General Visitors or helps, as Stewards under these six ministers, the following six, be appointed, namely, Messrs John Cennick, Thomas Adams, Joseph Humphreys, in England; Messrs Howell Harris, James Beaumont, Herbert Jenkins, in Wales.

That they should have as helps for a more particular inspection, these six private exhorters (or that have a limit and a particular care), namely, John Richard, William Richard, John Harris, Thomas James, John Jones, Morgan John; twelve societies each, in a more limited sphere.
And Morgan Hughes, James Williams, Milbourn Bloom, Thomas Lewis, Thomas Williams, Richard William David, these, six societies each.
Total: Six ministers; six to help them; six exhorters over twelve societies each, and six over six societies each.

That all the rest of the private exhorters should give an account of the one or two societies under their care to the General Visitor over them – that so a regular account may be had in every monthly society by person or letter.

That when one proposes himself for an exhorter, he should first exhort in private societies:
1. To have the approbation of some grave experienced Christian or Christians that have often heard him;
2. The judgment of some two or three private and public exhorters and ministers;
3. To be examined as to his grace, call, qualifications, gifts and doctrine.

That in order to take care:
1. Of the poor and sick,
2. Of money collected,
3. To be a messenger for the society,
4. Peacemaker, etc.,
One Steward should be chosen, or two, in each society.

That as these six exhorters (namely, John Cennick, Howell Harris, etc. before named) should be as helps, etc., to the six ministers before named, yet unlimited as to places, but to the exchange as called for (only Mr Howell Harris mostly for Wales); so the other twelve exhorters (as above) should have their respective changes, and to exchange on consultation with the society.[8]

The second Quarterly Association was held at Watford on 6–7 April 1743. The ordained ministers present were the Revs. Whitefield, William Williams and Thomas Lewis, together with Thomas Lewis, a Dissenter. Of the Superintendents, Messrs. Harris, Herbert Jenkins, Thomas James, James Beaumont, Morgan Hughes, Morgan John Lewis, Thomas Williams and Thomas Adams, were present. Mr Whitefield was chosen as Moderator and he opened the Association with a sermon on the words, 'And Enoch walked with God'. He was granted extraordinary power of delivery. He wrote in a letter:

On Wednesday, at noon, I opened the Association, with a close and solemn discourse upon walking with God. The brethren and people felt much of the divine presence. Afterwards, we betook ourselves to business. Several matters of great importance were dispatched. We broke up about seven, and met again at ten, and continued settling the affairs of the Societies until two in the morn-ing. On Thursday, we sat again till four in the afternoon. Then, after taking refreshment, I preached upon 'The Believer's Rest', after which we went on with our business, and finished our Association about midnight.[9]

This opening sermon by Whitefield is extant and is without doubt one of his best sermons. We are tempted to quote parts of it:

The prevailing power of this enmity must be taken away; for the in-being of it will never be totally removed, till we bow down our heads, and give up the ghost. The apostle Paul, no doubt speaks of himself, and that, too, not when he was a Pharisee, but a real Christian, when he complains, 'that when he would do good, evil was present with him'; not having dominion over him, but opposing and resisting his good intentions and actions, so that he could not do the things which he would, in that perfection which the new man desired. This is what he calls sin dwelling in him . . . But as for its prevailing, it is destroyed in every soul that is truly born of God, and gradually more and more weakened as the believer grows in grace, and the Spirit of God gains a greater and greater ascendancy in the heart.[10]

Later on, he said:

O prayer! prayer! It brings and keeps God and man together. It raises man up to God, and brings God down to man. If you would therefore, O believers, keep up your walk with God; pray, pray without ceasing. Be much in secret, set prayer. And when you are about your common business of life, be much in ejaculatory prayer, and send, from time to time, short letters post to heaven upon the wings of faith. They will reach the very heart of God, and return to you again loaded with spiritual blessings.[11]

He discusses, with discernment, a point with respect to which he himself was so often accused:

And though it is the quintessence of enthusiasm, to pretend to be guided by the Spirit without the written word; yet it is every Christian's bounden duty to be guided by the Spirit in conjunction with the written word of God. Watch, therefore, I pray you, O believers, the motions of God's blessed Spirit in your souls, and always try the suggestions or impressions that you may at any time feel, by the middle course between the two dangerous extremes many of this generation are in danger of running into; I mean enthusiasm, on the one hand, and deism, and downright infidelity on the other.[12]

He ends with an eloquent conclusion:

One word to my brethren in the ministry that are here present, and I have done. You see, my brethren, my heart is full; I could almost say it is too big to speak, and yet too big to be silent, without dropping a word to you . . . I observed at the beginning of this discourse, that Enoch in all probability was a public person, and a flaming preacher. Though he be dead, does he not yet speak to us, to quicken our zeal, and make us more active in the service of our glorious and ever-blessed Master? How did Enoch preach! How did Enoch walk with God! . . . Let us then follow him, as he followed Jesus Christ . . . The Judge is before the door: he that cometh will come, and will not tarry: his reward is with him. And we shall all (if we are zealous for the Lord of hosts) ere long shine as the stars of the firmament, in the kingdom of our heavenly Father, forever and ever.[13]

Such was Whitefield's sermon before the Association at Watford, and it is no wonder that the brethren were melted under the influence of his words. His glorious gifts are revealed clearly in these short extracts. The spirit of life is felt in them. Though we do not have his presence, and cannot hear the accents of his voice, that melting voice that could civilize a mob and completely overcome them, it is said, purely by crying out the name 'Mesopotamia', yet we can perceive the evident characteristics of a true orator. It is clear that the secret of his power did not depend alone on the voice and delivery, but in the fact also that he was a fine theologian; the composition of his sermons were always detailed and philosophical.

The following were the main decisions arrived at during the Association:

Our Saviour being sought unto for direction it was agreed:
That the Rev. Mr Williams should leave his curacies, and be an assistant to the Rev. Mr Rowland.
That Bro. Howell Harris should be the Superintendent over Wales and go to England when called.
That Bro. Herbert Jenkins should be an assistant to Bro. Harris and likewise to the English brethren.
That Bro. James Beaumont should be Superintendent over Radnorshire and Herefordshire and to be assisted by Bros. John Williams, John Jones, William Evans, David Price, and likewise Richard Lewis, a Dissenter, if approved at the Monthly Association – (Approved May 27, 1743).
That Bro. Morgan Hughes should be Superintendent (if he finds freedom)

over Montgomeryshire, and to be assisted by Bros. Lewis Evan, Benjamin Cadman and Thomas Bowen. (N.B. This was, after a long trial, changed and Richard Tibbott set in his place.)

That Bro. Thomas James should be Superintendent over part of Breconshire to the River Usk, and to be assisted by Bros. Thomas Bowen, Edward Bowen, Thomas Bowen of Builth, Joshua Saunders, John Williams of Tregunter, William Williams, Jenkin Jenkins, David Rees and Rees Morgan.

That Bro. Morgan John Lewis should be Superintendent over the societies at Dolygaer, Cwmdu, Cantref, Defynnog, Llywil, which are in Breconshire, and Llanddeusant in Carmarthenshire, and Monmouthshire on this side of the River Usk. And to be assisted by Bros. John Jones, John Powell, Richard Thomas, John Belcher, Evan Thomas, Stephen Jones, Jeffrey David and Jenkin John.

That Bro. Thomas Lewis should be Superintendent over the societies between the Passage and the River Usk, and to assist the English brethren when called for, and to be assisted by Bro. George Cross.

That Bro. Thomas Williams should be Superintendent over Glamorganshire, as far as Llantrisant, and is to be assisted by Bros. Edward Evans, William Powell, Thomas Price, William Edward, Thomas Lewis, Richard Jones, John Yeoman and H. Griffith.

That Bro. John Harris should be Superintendent over Pembrokeshire, and his assistant to be settled at the next Association in Pembrokeshire, the 8th of June next.

That Bro. Milbourne Bloom should be Superintendent over Carmarthenshire, as far as Neath, and to be assisted by Bros. John Jones, George Phillips, John Richards, Richard William David, William John, and James Merrick, who is to be examined at the next Monthly Association to be held at Llandremore, May 10.

That Bro. James Williams should be Superintendent over the other part of Carmarthenshire and to be assisted by Bros. William John, David Williams, John Thomas, John Rees and John Williams.

That Bro. David Williams should be Superintendent in Cardiganshire and to be assisted by ——.

That Bro. William Richards should remain as he is till the next Association to be held at Dygoedydd, the 25th of May next.[14]

As well as these appointments, which show the detail of the care for all the societies, the following decisions were made, amongst others:

That the Superintendents should have the liberty to preach on their journey (if called) supposing they believe in their hearts that the brethren of the Association (if they knew their circumstances) would give them leave.

That the brethren do not think in their hearts that Bro. James Tomkins is called of God to be a preacher, are resolved not to encourage, neither to forbid him, but leave him to the Lord.

That all persons who think they have a call to exhort, should make application to one of the Monthly Associations by whom their gifts, grace and call are to be closely examined into. If approved of, they are to have such a district appointed as the Association shall think fit, and that approbation to be brought to the General Association and approved of there.

That the Superintendents shall send an account of what God has done in their particular districts to London to be there by the latter end of every month, and to direct their letters to Mr John Sims at Mr Abbot's in Charles Square, near Hoxton, London. And that their letters shall be wrote to the minister of the Tabernacle [i.e. to Whitefield].

That each Superintendent shall have a book wherein he shall write the names of each of their private exhorters and the names of each member of their private societies, and divide them into Married Men, Married Women, Single Men, and Single Women, and likewise to bring the state of each society to the general Association.

That a Secretary shall be chosen to every Monthly Meeting who shall take down in a book the Minutes of the proceedings.

That there shall be a Monthly Meeting in the following places:

Radnorshire and Montgomeryshire, with the Rev. Mr William Williams as Moderator.

Cardiganshire and Carmarthenshire, with the Rev. Mr Daniel Rowland as Moderator.

Breconshire, with the Rev. Mr Thomas Lewis as Moderator.

Pembrokeshire, with the Rev. Mr Howell Davies as Moderator.

Glamorganshire and Monmouthshire, with the Rev. Mr John Powell as the Moderator.

That the Monthly Association shall consist of an ordained minister (if possible) as Moderator; the Superintendent of that district and his assistants – supposing the ordained minister should be absent, then the Superintendent shall sit as Moderator.

That each Association shall begin with prayer and end with prayer and exhortation and that there shall be present all the Superintendents, not excluding the private exhorters if they are disposed to come.

That the Rev. Mr Whitefield shall choose Bro. Howell Harris as Moderator in his absence.[15]

It was further noted that the whole Association was carried on with great unity and love, and that the brethren left each other praising and blessing God for what he had done, and expecting still to see greater things than these. Whitefield wrote in a letter quoted below that he had been appointed permanent Moderator whenever he was in Britain. This is not found in so many words in the Minutes, but it is implied in the decision that if he were absent, he would appoint Howell Harris to take his place.

Tyerman views this decision as placing Whitefield as president over the whole of Welsh Methodism, so that the seat of authority was being moved from the Principality and raised up in London. We doubt if this was the intention of the Association. However, when we recall that most of the members advocated Episcopacy, it might well mean that when they were appointing a Moderator they were also acknowledging some element of authority over them quite apart from the duration of the Associations.

Whitefield had arrived in Wales with the intention, not only of attending the Association, but also of conducting a preaching tour through parts of the south that he had not previously visited. Together with the preaching, the journey would involve obtaining the agreement of the religious societies and their exhorters to the arrangements drawn up at the Association, so as to form one strong composite body. Unfortunately Harris's journal for this period is not available, but Whitefield sent a detailed and interesting report of the itinerary to London, to be published in the *Weekly History*. He wrote the first letter from Watford on 7 April, 1743. After giving a report of the Association, he wrote:

> I cannot well tell you what progress has been made since the last Association
> – I remember four years ago, when I rode about Wales, God put Joshua's
> going about taking one city after another much upon my heart – Dear Brother
> Harris reminds me of it now – And the Lord suggested to me, that now I was
> like Joshua, dividing the land. God seems to have given the brethren a holy
> subordination. I am chosen (if in England) to be always Moderator. I trust
> our Saviour gives me a spirit for it. I felt much of the divine teaching. And
> the brethren willingly acknowledged the authority given me from above . . .
> The brethren have put the societies in Wales upon my heart.[16]
>
> Perhaps, in a month, I may come to London. It seems the will of the Lord
> that I should stay in Wales about a fortnight, and take a tour to Pembrokeshire.
> Great doors are open there.[17]

Llantrisant (in Wales), 10 April 1743.

> Yesterday I preached at Cardiff to a large congregation. The greatest scoffers
> sat quiet, and the children of God felt the divine presence. In the evening I
> went to Fonmon. Mrs Jones received us kindly. God was pleased to speak for
> me in the society where I preached. This morning I preached again. It was
> a most remarkable time . . . Dear Brother Harris is preaching in Welsh. The
> people are very simple.[18]

This is Whitefield's account, but according to a letter written by Howell Harris the two men preached at Aberthaw, and went to Fonmon only to lodge. He says also that it was at Pen-marc that they preached on the second morning.

The next letter from Whitefield is from Swansea, and dated 12 April:

Great things are doing in Wales – An effectual door is opened for preaching the everlasting gospel. Yesterday I preached at Neath . . . from a balcony, to about three thousand souls in the street. The Lord was with me of a truth. This morning I preached here to about four thousand with great power. About one I preached at Harbrook, four miles off; and am now returned to preach here again . . . Dear Brother Harris has discoursed in Welsh yesterday and today. Postscript: Past seven in the evening. I have just now done preaching. Your heart would leap with praise had you been present. Swansea is taken! I never preached with more convincing power. Many of the rich and great were present. The congregation larger than in the morning. Jesus conquered for me. To him be all the glory. Praise him; praise him for me.[19]

He is clearly writing while still under the influence of the excitement that had possessed him while preaching, and it is easy to see how his heart is aflame within him. The letter displays the tone of a conquering soldier who has just captured one of the enemy's most important strongholds, and he ascribes all the praise, not to his courage or abilities, but to the presence of Jesus, his captain.

He was next at Laugharne, on 15 April, and writes:

After leaving Llantrisant, the Devil made a great effort to pull me out of Wales, by seeking to persuade me that I should not proceed further; but our Lord was too strong for him. I preached twice [at Llanelli] on Wednesday with great power to a large congregation; and in the evening near Abergwili, five miles from thence. On Thursday, I preached at Carmarthen, one of the greatest and most polite places in Wales; in the morning from the top of the cross; in the evening from a table near it. It was the great sessions. The justices desired I would stay till they rose, and they would come. Accordingly they did, and many thousands more; and several people of quality. Jesus was much with me, and I hope much good work was done . . . Dear Bro. Harris exhorts in every place. Our Saviour seems to have given the towns of Wales to me. I like Wales exceedingly. In about ten days I hope to be near Bristol.[20]

On 17 April, he was at Haverfordwest, and wrote:

I went that evening to Narberth, where I preached to some thousands with great power, they were not unlike the colliers of Kingswood. This morning I preached at Llys-y-fran, and had as it were a Moorfields congregation; and this afternoon I preached to about the same number near this town. I also read the prayers. The authority, power and success, which God is giving to me, amongst rich and poor, is unspeakable. O, help me to praise him.[21]

When he says that the congregation at Llys-y-frân was similar to one at Moorfields, he is, no doubt, referring to its size. Howell Harris estimated it to be twelve thousand. We suspect that the Reformers, in their enthusiasm, tended to overestimate, as is usually done when judging large crowds, but, quite certainly, the congregations in Pembrokeshire at these times must have been enormous, and that the whole population of the county, English and Welsh speakers, had gathered to hear the gospel.

On 20 April, Whitefield writes again from Carmarthen:

> Since I wrote from Haverfordwest, I preached yesterday at eight in the morning to about eight thousand people in that place, and in the afternoon to several thousands at Narberth, both times with great power. This morning I preached with great sweetness at Laugharne, and coming over in the ferry had the unexpected compliment paid me, of one ship firing several guns, and of some others hoisting their flags. I cannot take in the great respect in which I am held here; God has prepared Wales for me. To him be all the praise. This afternoon I preached at a little town called Kidwelly, to a large congregation; and came this evening here. One of the ministers preached much against me last Sunday, and mentioned me by name; but, like my other opposers (and like the viper biting the file) he only hurt himself. I am as it were in a new, but very unthought of pleasant world.[22]

On the 25th, he wrote from Rhayader:

> I preached there [Carmarthen] twice on Thursday to about ten thousand and dear Mr Rowland preached after me with much sweetness and power. Yesterday we had another blessed association; and have now settled all the counties in Wales.[23]

He added that he had preached on the Saturday, the 23rd, at Llangathen, where he had been allowed the church, and a large congregation had gathered. In the evening, he had preached at Llandovery. He spoke again at Llandovery on the Sunday morning, and wrote that God was with him, and by evening he was at Brecon, twenty-three miles away, where a large and most courteous crowd had gathered. On Monday he was at Trefeca, and then in the evening at Gwenfithen, near Hay-on-Wye. He there wrote:

> My body is weak, but I am at the Redeemer's feet, and he reigns king in my heart, and causes me to rejoice and triumph over all.[24]

He proceeded to Builth Wells and then to Gore in Radnorshire, his last preaching stop in Wales on this journey:

> Then I rode to the Gore ... and indeed our Saviour kept the good wine till last; he made our cup to overflow ... having in about three weeks travelled about four hundred English miles, spent three days in attending two associations, preached about forty times, visited about thirteen towns, and passed through seven counties. Here then I will set up my Ebenezer, thank the adorable Jesus

for these and all other his mercies, and from the bottom of my heart give him all the glory.[25]

Whitefield's account clearly does not record all the events of the journey. There is a tradition in Tregaron that at this time, or very shortly afterwards, he visited parts of Cardiganshire and preached at this town from on top of a mounting block, near the old Crown Inn. His hearers were mainly monoglot Welshmen, but the crowd broke out in great rejoicing, though the only word they understood was 'Hallelujah'. This appears strange, but Dr Owen Thomas has a similar story of a lawyer in London who used to hear Ebenezer Morris whenever he came to preach to his fellow-countrymen in the city, and whose face was always awash with tears though he did not understand a word of the sermon.

This visit of Whitefield's proved a great blessing to Wales. The letters of Harris, Thomas Price of Watford, and others, confirm what Whitefield wrote of the power that accompanied him on this tour. It was in Swansea and Carmarthen, perhaps, that he experienced the most remarkable services of all. Price, Watford, wrote to him soon afterwards, saying that he had heard glorious news of many who had been awakened at Carmarthen, one of whom was a notoriously immoral woman, and that a society was to be set up in the town. But the most famous, without doubt, of those converted was Peter Williams who, as a youth of twenty-one, was at the time attending the academy in the town, and had gone secretly to hear the eloquent English preacher, transgressing the prohibition laid down by the academy's principal. The conversion of the man who became afterwards the father of Welsh biblical commentators was reward enough for all Whitefield's troubles on this journey.

The visit was also of great blessing in establishing the obedience of the societies and exhorters to the arrangements of the Association. Whitefield's fame, together with the novelty of his coming, his eloquent gifts, and the general respect afforded him from common people and gentry alike, tended strongly to bring about acceptance to the rules that he presented as the Moderator of the Association. Howell Harris acknowledged this in a letter he wrote to Whitefield on 12 May 1743:

Blessed be God that ever inclined you dear soul to think on his poor, scattered, and leprous, and sick lambs in Wales.[26]

Thomas James, Cerrigcadarn, also wrote to him:

The Lord blessed greatly your coming to us; as regards zeal and good order, all seem willing to submit, seeing it as that which God had wrought and not man. Before long we shall march terribly, as an army with banners.

Let us return to the records of the Associations. One meeting of the brethren occurred at the home of the exhorter Bloom; no date is given, and we do not know if it was a regular Monthly Association or not. Mr Bloom lived at Llanarthne, not far from Carmarthen, and we tend to believe that this was the Monthly Meeting that Whitefield referred to and in which Daniel Rowland preached after himself. The decisions made at the time are unimportant, but it is worth noting the following record:

> In parting, the Lord came in such an amazing manner amongst us that we were enflamed with and united in solid love.[27]

A Monthly Association was held at Gelliglyd on 1 May, 1743, and it seems, according to the minutes, that Whitefield had travelled from Gloucester to be present. Also present were Daniel Rowland, Howell Harris and Howell Davies, together with many superintendents and exhorters. The main decisions were:

> That Bro. George Bowen is to work at his trade till the next Association at Pembrokeshire.
> That the ministers and superintendents collect what they can from their respective societies in order to print Welsh books.
> That Bros. William Jones, Davis Evans and Richard Tibbott should be Welsh schoolmasters.
> That the private exhorters in their journeys should not send before hand to give warnings of their comings to any place, but if desired to speak in any private house they may, to the family and neighbours.[28]

The next Monthly Association was at Watford on 11 May, with John Powell as Moderator, and with Howell Harris and many other superintendents and exhorters present. Amongst other things, it was passed:

> Agreed that Mr Thomas Price should be steward of this society as before and likewise assist Bro. Thomas Williams.
> That men and women should meet in separate bands, as the Spirit of the Lord should lead them.
> That the superintendents should in each private society, discourse with men and women privately [crossed out] separately as they shall find occasion, and as the Holy Ghost directs.[29]

On 19 May, there was a Monthly Association at Llandremor, near Llandeilo Fach. Daniel Rowland was the Moderator but there were few present. The resolutions passed are of relatively little interest but the following note reveals something of the difficulties of their situation:

> That Bros John and Edward Meirig (if they are not turned out by their parents) should exhort privately under the inspection of Bro. John Richards.[30]

A Monthly Association was held at Dygoedydd on 25 May 1743, in which Daniel Rowland and William Williams acted as joint Moderators. Howell Harris, Benjamin Thomas (a Dissenting minister), and James Williams who was superintendent for parts of Carmarthenshire, were also present. It was agreed:

> That Bro. Thomas David (having been examined concerning his call to be an exhorter) should discourse in two private societies, under the inspection of Bro. James Williams, on trial till the next Association, till we shall have a testimonial from him and the brethren that heard him.
>
> That in each society there should be a box under the care of one or two stewards to receive weekly collections towards God's cause, and that each private exhorter should keep a book of names of every one under their care, and should bring it to each Quarterly Association, and what money could be spared by the mutual consent of their societies towards public use.[31]

It is seen that the present arrangements for collecting monies were in place at the very beginning of Methodism.

Within two days there was a Monthly Association at Dolberthog, Llandrindod. William Williams moderated, but the only resolution passed was that Richard Lewis, a Dissenter, should be an assistant to James Beaumont.

On 8 June, a Monthly Association met at Longhouse, Pembrokeshire, with Daniel Rowland and Howell Davies moderating, and Howell Harris also present. Amongst other things, it was agreed that a number of societies should be under the care of Thomas Meyler, John Harris and William Richards. It was passed that Watkin Watkins should qualify himself to act as a scribe or amanuensis to Rowland or to Davies; that John Jones should be silent for a while, until his ordination, so that there might be no obstacle to his being ordained; and that Richard Tibbott should work and attend a private society until he should get a Welsh school.

We have now arrived at the date of the third regular Quarterly Association, which was held at Trefeca on 29, 30 June 1743. This was an important Association, in that the report of the superintendents on the numbers and conditions of the societies were expected. Whitefield arrived from London to take the chair, travelling via Gloucester and Bristol. Also present were Daniel Rowland, William Williams, Howell Davies, John Powell, Thomas Lewis, and Benjamin Davies, the Dissenter. Of the public exhorters, Howell Harris, Herbert Jenkins, James Beaumont, Thomas James, Morgan John Lewis, Thomas Williams, Richard Tibbott, Thomas Lewis amd William Richards were present. Whitefield provided the following account of the conference:

On Wednesday, June 29, I reached Trevecca, where I met a whole troop of Jesus' witnesses. At five in the evening I preached. After I had done, Howell Davies preached and prayed. About eight, we opened the Association with great solemnity. Our Saviour was much with me, teaching and helping me to fill my place in a particular manner. About midnight, we adjourned; but several of the brethren sat up all night, and ushered in the morning with prayer and praise. About eight, we met again, and were greatly delighted at the simple accounts the superintendents brought in from their respective societies. We continued doing business till two in the afternoon, and broke up with much solemnity and holy joy. We had great union with one another. Indeed, Jesus has done great things for Wales. The work is much upon the advance. I was surprised to find so much order. Brother Howell Davies has been blessed to the conversion of a young clergyman, rector of St. Bartholomew's London.[32]

This clergyman, the Rev. Richard Thomas Bateman, came from a noble family and was a man of great abilities. After his conviction, he became an indefatigable worker in Christ's vineyard. He gave Whitefield and Wesley every liberty to preach in his church, and we find that he was present at the Wesleyan Conference of 1748. But to return to the Association. The Minutes state that it began in particular solemnity, with a sermon and an importunate prayer for the guidance of the Holy Spirit, from Mr Whitefield. Its main business was to read and hear the reports brought by the superintendents of the states of the societies under their care. We will refer to these reports later.[33] The only other business to be attended to was a letter received from John Richard, in which he condemned the arrangements drawn up in the Associations and recommended to the societies. John Richard was a native of Llansamlet, near Swansea. He was the superintendent over fifteen societies in Glamorganshire and Carmarthenshire, and was expected to visit each one once a fortnight. In his letter he argues that to divide up the members into single, married and widowed, and to examine them closely as to their spiritual conditions, was Popish; that to subscribe their names in a book was unscriptural; and that to settle superintendents over geographical areas was oppressive. But it was clear from the tone of the letter that the chief cause of his complaint was that the Association had limited his labours to a district, restraining him from going about to preach, as was his desire. He gave the following reasons as those that persuaded him that it was the Lord's will for him to go about:

Firstly, I find my soul most eager to go the more God shines upon me.

Secondly, I go nowhere, without testimony from the brethren, and some marks from God, that the Lord makes use of me as an instrument in his hand to do some good to the churches.

Thirdly, that he does not often leave me without some help, and that not once has he left me, as far as I can remember, completely to myself.

Fourthly, I believe that I feel at times an unquenchable hunger in my spirit for the conversion of sinners to God, and that I would die if I had to remain silent.

Fifthly, I know that if I were to go about I would speak to ten souls for every one to whom I speak presently, and the greater the number of fish, the greater the pleasure in casting the net.

Sixthly, I am now not allowed to speak but once in twenty-four hours, and that once in the evening, and only at some places; but if I could go about I could speak as many times as I was able.

Seventhly, I am having to say that I cannot go to some places, though I am encouraged by God to go, and receive a call from men.

Eighthly, I have too many to take particular charge of, and too few to go about them continually; because the people, after long familiarity with one man, are careless about attending, and you can understand that it is painful for me to go thirty miles and then find that few have gathered, even in daytime.

He ends by urging his brethren in the Association that they look to the Holy Spirit to guide them in their attitude towards himself, and with a suggestion of an inclination for going about on his own, regardless of their arrangements.

John Richards was a simple, open Christian, who clearly was pouring out his disappointed reactions to being constrained in his work, with transparent honesty. He confides that two things caused him to doubt his calling: his brethren's restraints, and his own perception of the greatness of the work. But his religious experience is glorious:

I am glad to be able to do what I can for God, even if he were to throw me in hell at last. But I believe that there is nowhere created by God, let the devil do his worst, where I will not enjoy God, and praise the dear Lord Jesus.

Surely, the reading of this letter would have drawn many tears from the eyes of the gathered brethren. And though they were not able to grant him his wish, as his gifts were relatively limited, they yet felt their hearts warm towards him. A similar letter had been received from Richard William David, an exhorter from Carmarthenshire, of whom we read in the minutes of the second Watford Association that he should be placed under trial.

The Association decided that Whitefield should answer these letters. He read his replies, which he had written during one of the later meetings, to them and these received unanimous approval. These answers are still extant, and are most interesting. The one to John Richard is dated 'Trevecca, June the 30th, 1743':

As far as we can discern you are dissatisfied with the brethren's conduct, and are determined if we do not condescend to your terms, entirely to break from them and go about evangelizing wheresoever you judge the Lord Jesus calls. Did we give you any reason to do so, it would give us some concern, but as we think we have not, and as we know the opposition you can make will be inconsiderable and easily stopped, we can trust the affair with the Lord Jesus and be very easy. Him we profess to be our Head and his Holy Spirit to be our guide.

Notwithstanding, we believe we are liable to err, and therefore would be glad of any information or instruction from the meanest of God's children, and would alter any measure that can be proved to be inconsistent with the word of God . . . you object against our desiring the Superintendents and exhorters to take the names and enquire into the particular state of every member of their societies. What is there, dear Brother, unscriptural in all this? Does not Jesus Christ say a good shepherd calleth all his sheep by their names? Does not every parish keep a register book of their parishioners, and do not the Dissenters put down the names of all that come into fellowship with them? What is the Book of Numbers but a catalogue of the names of the children of Israel? As for enquiring into the particular state of every soul we think it highly necessary – we take it the church is like a hospital, that ministers are physicians, and they are from time to time to come and enquire how is it with their patients. I suppose when the Apostles went about to see how the brethren did they enquired particularly into the states of their souls . . . We do not see how a minister can well preach unless he knows the particular cases of his people, and how could you send us the account you have (for which we thank you) unless you had made some enquiry.

The dividing them into Classes as virgins, single men, married men, married women and widows, is only a prudential rule in order to make the account regular and that the ministers may know of what station in life his people are in, and suit his exhortations accordingly. We find the apostle John writing to young men, etc., and St. Paul mentions the widows indeed that made up a particular class in the Primitive Church.

But you think we lay an insufferable yoke upon the brethren by assigning the brethren a particular district – yours as far as we can judge is about thirty miles extent – a sphere of action we think large enough for one of your gifts, when you have done all that is to be done within these bounds, we shall be very glad of your going further – but till then we think your desire to range proceeds from nature and self, and not from the grace of God.
We think you mistake when you say the flesh don't like going. We think the contrary, nature don't like to be confined. Settling inside work is not agreeable to the old man, though exceedingly useful to the new creature.

Upon the whole, dear brother, we think you are mistaken at present and judge us without a cause. We thank you for your cautions, we have turned them into prayers, and our loving Saviour will answer us. At the same time, give us leave to inform you are entered into a temptation, and seem to have a little of that spirit that reigned in Korah, Dathan and Abiram, who complained that Moses and Aaron took too much upon them. Give me leave therefore, my brother, as I write in the name of the brethren, to exhort you to search your heart and see what manner of Spirit you are of . . .[34]

The message sent to Richard Williams David was that he was to read the letter sent to John Richard.

We tend to believe that Howell Harris considered Whitefield's letter to be lacking in tenderness, and in the grace of the gospel, and so, a few days later, he took upon himself to write himself to the two brethren. To John Richard, he wrote:

I know of tribulations of this kind; for Jesus' sake be patient and prudent. The enemy seeks to tempt you to create a division amongst us, and to cause us to weaken one another's hands. Be humble; fear self; it is a secret enemy, indeed; hard to discern. It is possible that we [i.e. John Richard and Harris] mistake; they [the members of the Association] are many, and a pack of them, at least, are close to the Lord, and search his Word, and attend to the doctrine and guidance of the Spirit as closely as we do. And they are prudent, and having listened to my reasons, in the fear of the Lord, cannot agree with me. I, rather, fear to be infallible, and wait before the Lord, that I might not disrupt his work, and try the spirits of his dear servants, who were in Christ before me, who have offered up their lives for him, and who were privy to his secrets before we were born spiritually. Such thoughts as these gain the victory in me in my tribulations. My soul, dear pilgrim, loves you warmly, and with every tenderness and brotherly love, I end,

Your humble fellow-soldier, Howell Harris.

To Richard William David, he wrote:

My dear, dear brother, since I first knew you, you have been dear to me. Though in my heart I do not feel worthy to wash your feet, give me leave to ask you, before the Lord, who is dear to you, to strive to keep the unity of the Spirit in the bond of peace, and to be vigilant against the general enemy, the accuser of the brethren. We are one body, and one member cannot be without the other, let us forbear one another. The work is great, and we are very unfit for it; let us beware of running ahead of one another. Hoping that you believe me to love you truly and humbly in the Lord, as your brother and poor fellow-soldier, I pray that you greet all the lambs in my name.

No one can compare with Harris as a letter writer; the warmth of his heart is felt in every line of these two letters, and it is no wonder that the two errant brothers soon relented and fell in with the new arrangements.

John Richard is found in the dust as a result, and writes a repentant letter to the next Association:

> I am sorry, dear brethren, that I stood so stubbornly against you for so long. I believe that no one rightly knows, except those who have had experience, how deceitful is the old serpent, as he has been with me on this occasion. And so fully was I in his possession that I considered that you should submit to my judgment. But I believe that the devil has deceived himself. Glory be to God who brings forth good out of evil; for I have been taught by God, as I believe, never again to think that I have more light than all the children of God. And, furthermore, the occasion was a help to me to stand against the same spirit that has lately shown itself in some of the Llansamlet brethren.

> From your unworthy brother,
> John Richard.

So end the Trefeca records for the year 1743. Further records will be introduced into the narrative as we proceed.

---

[1] Strictly speaking, the Watford Association was the first joint English and Welsh Association. There had been several previous Welsh Associations, as mentioned in the previous chapter.

[2] CH 28, p. 34.

[3] Tyerman, *John Wesley* (London, 1890), vol. 1, p. 276.

[4] CH 48, pp. 30–1.

[5] *History of Protestant Nonconformity in Wales*, p. 388.

[6] CH 48, pp 32–3.

[7] Ibid., 48, pp. 33–5.

[8] Ibid., 48, pp. 36–7.

[9] Tyerman, *George Whitefield*, vol. 2, p. 55.

[10] *Select Sermons of George Whitefield* (London: Banner of Truth, 1959), p. 100.

[11] Ibid., p. 103.          [12] Ibid., p. 104.          [13] Ibid., p. 109.

[14] CH 48, pp. 39–40.          [15] Ibid., pp. 40–2.

[16] *Account of the Progress of the Gospel*, vol. 3, no. 1, pp. 49–50.

[17] Tyerman, *George Whitefield*.

[18] *A Select Collection of Letters of the Late Reverend George Whitfield*, vol. 2, 1772, pp. 13–14.

[19] Ibid., p. 14.          [20] Ibid., p. 15.          [21] Ibid., pp. 15–16.

[22] Ibid., p. 16.          [23] Ibid., p. 17.          [24] Ibid.

[25] Ibid., p. 18.

[26] CH, 1980, p. 26.

[27] CH 48, p. 42.     [28] Ibid.          [29] Ibid., p. 43.

[30] Ibid., p. 44.          [31] Ibid., p. 45.

[32] Tyerman, *George Whitefield*, vol. 2, p. 62.

[33] See pp. 348–57.

[34] CH 27, pp. 150–2.

# 10

# SOME OF THE EARLY EXHORTERS

## RICHARD TIBBOTT

*A*ny account of the early beginnings of the Methodist Revival that did not give considerable attention to the efforts of the exhorters and their labour of love for the cause of Christ would be very imperfect and, indeed, misleading. In a machine the small cogs are just as important as the large cogs, although they are not so evident. Humanly speaking, the large cogs in the revival were Harris, Rowland, Williams and Howell Davies. The exhorters in comparison were only small cogs, though some were larger and others smaller, but without their service and support the machine would not have moved forward as it did. We know much of the history of the pre-eminent amongst them; we know of their journeys, their dangers, and their sufferings. We can learn of their characters pretty accurately from the letters that they wrote. They were all full of fire, they were often baptized abundantly in the spirit of the revival, and they possessed a courage which would have had them praised as heroes had they appeared on a battlefield. They were not without their faults; who is so? Some of their impulses and opinions appear to us now to be very foolish, but their honesty, zeal, and loyalty to Christ cannot be doubted.

As for others of them, we only know their names. There is hardly anything of them known even in the neighbourhoods where they laboured; no footnote exists on any book on earth describing anything of their labours. But it is certain that their faithfulness and hard work are recorded fully in the books above, and when Jesus comes to be glorified in his saints, the old Methodist exhorters will reflect his glory as effectively as any. Most of them were uneducated men, homely in their clothing, plain of words, without much sophistication or culture of mind. But they made up for every deficiency by their commitment, labours and zeal for the Saviour. We are sorry that it is the histories of only the most important of them that we have space to provide.

One of the best known of the exhorters, although not perhaps the most gifted, was Richard Tibbott. He was born at Hafod-y-pant in the parish of

Llanbryn-mair, 18 January 1718, the youngest of six children. His parents were godly people, and Richard became a member of the Independent Church at Llanbryn-mair before his fifteenth birthday. It is said that he began to preach in 1738, when a young man of nineteen. This does not mean that he preached regularly – there were no opportunities for that at the time – but he addressed congregations now and again, when asked by Mr Lewis Rees to do so. No doubt Richard Tibbott was one of Howell Harris's most eager listeners when the latter visited the north in 1740, and surely Harris's quickening, enlivening ministry left a deep impression upon him. About the year 1741, he went to the Rev. Griffith Jones's school at Llanddowror. Whether it was Lewis Rees or Howell Harris that encouraged him to take this step we do not know. He soon joined the Methodists. It is thought that he kept a school for some time in the Llanddowror area. Most probably he also exhorted amongst the Methodist societies of the lower parts of Carmarthenshire and the upper parts of Pembrokeshire. Many references to him may be found in the Trefeca records. In the first Association at Watford, he was appointed as a general visitor to the societies. In a subsequent Association, it was decided he would keep a school in Pembrokeshire, and before the end of 1743 he was set as superintendent of the small societies that had been established in Montgomeryshire. In the Monthly Association at Nantmel, Radnorshire, on 18 April 1744, it was decided he was to give himself completely to the weekly visitation of all the societies within Montgomeryshire. But in another Association held in the October of the same year, it was decided he should be sent to John Richard to learn book-binding.

Though Richard Tibbott was a hard-working member of the Methodists, he felt a strong affinity towards the Independents and mixed with them a great deal. This created a degree of prejudice against him in the minds of the Methodists, and some of them believed that he preferred the Dissenters to themselves. Whether he was ever accused publicly of this, we do not know, but he himself knew that such a prejudice existed. A letter of his to the October Association of 1745 is worth reproducing here. It is interesting both for its historical content and for the light it gives on the spirit of the age and on Tibbott's way of thinking:

> We have so many topics in our Quarterly Associations, that very little opportunity is afforded us to express our opinion on many things which it would be of profit to our increase and union, and our fraternal love, were we to do so. There are amongst us also so many different ideas on church government that we are sometimes ready to separate from one another because of them, as have the brethren in Glamorgan, and they cool our love for one another and weaken our unity and fraternity. As I am often amongst the Dissenters, and

in their fellowship, which could be an occasion for you to believe that I am led by them, and that I differ from yourselves in judgment and temperament, I thought it necessary to declare my views concerning the foundations of religion; how far I agree with you, and how far I agree with the Dissenters.

1. To begin with, I will declare my thoughts on the most important principles of religion. Here, my brethren, I must confess my gross ignorance; my heart has been sore for many years over this ignorance; but I trust that I do not rest solely on confession. I do not believe that it is sufficient ground for me that I have many reasons, and have had some measure of light within, and proved some measure of power and authority compelling me to believe some principles; I see that I must have light from the Holy Spirit to illumine the eyes of my soul, that I may see spiritual activity as clear as I see natural objects by the light of the sun, and that I might not change my mind over them in the day of death, in the day of judgment, and to eternity. This is the faith and knowledge that I desire, and I groan because I do not possess it. For this knowledge I will endeavour until I possess it fully and perfectly.

This is my faith and judgment, as I see presently, (a) That there is one God; (b) That there are three Persons in the Trinity, of the same essence, power, and glory, namely the Father, the Son, and the Holy Spirit. (c) That we are all fallen in Adam, and are by nature the children of wrath. (d) That God elected a certain number to eternal life before the beginning of the world. (e) That God's Son became a man in order to save his elect people. (f) That it is by his obedience that his people are justified, and that by faith they gain possession of his righteousness. (g) That the law is the rule of life to those who have been justified through Christ. So much concerning the articles.

2. With respect to Church discipline, I believe it is acceptable for some, under some circumstances, to preach though not having received authority from men, even as we do now; and that our duty and that of others, under such circumstances, is to wait for the leading of the Lord by his Spirit, to follow the rule of his Word, be careful that we do nothing against his written Word, and cry for the guidance of Providence and of God's Spirit to bring us to a more excellent order. Though it is our duty to be of good order, yet our many arrangements should not keep us from fraternizing and fellowshipping with others, who do not follow the same order, but who agree with us on the main doctrines and concerning religious life. But I am happy to remain as we are with respect to church discipline, until God gives us a better order and discipline in his own time.

3. With respect to my union with the generality of the body to which we belong, and to the Dissenters, the unity of my heart is the same as that unity which I profess and manifest in my behaviour. In that I left the Dissenters, as far as being governed by them, and put myself under your government, professing to be a member with yourselves, so I feel in my heart greater unity with the generality of you than with the Dissenters. But the various

tribulations which I have experienced these last years have been so great that I cannot receive any principles of religion nor church orders from any group of people only because they profess them, without myself having grasped the truth of them. Nor am I now so ready to be satisfied of various truths as I once was, since I see that I was deceived into receiving views as true, thinking I was enlightened in them by the Holy Spirit, whereas I have afterwards learnt that my light was only partial and imperfect. It is easy for me to confess that I believed so strongly in some things, that I would not hesitate to stand for them, even if the wisest and best of people judged otherwise; and my zeal had grown so much greater than my judgment, that I would not read any book that was contrary to my beliefs, as if I was perfect in my knowledge and infallibility; and I was ready to condemn any man an ignorant man who said a word against me.

But I had many occasions to change my views of my own infallibility after this. So that now I feel bound to be very jealous of my knowledge, and to discern things clearly before I believe them, nor can I discern anything without being taught by God's Spirit. Though I am in greater unity with yourselves than with the Dissenters, yet I see many things amongst us that need to be reformed: (a) That we are too ready to receive things as true without examining them more closely, and to judge well of them, according to the measure of consolation which they produce within us. (b) We tend to look on every comfort and consolation as the work of the Spirit of God, whereas we should sometimes be much more careful; and we also judge religious life by the degree of zeal and warmth of feeling, condemning others that are not so zealous in their devotions. I would much prefer to judge people by their general behaviour, rather than that which they display during services. (c) There is amongst us too much of a party spirit, which I hate in all. We are too ready to condemn our brethren, the Dissenters, to forbid them our fellowship, and to speak against them; which, if they were to do to us, we would call persecution. An open, unprejudiced spirit is of much value.

4. With respect to the Dissenters, I love that which is good in them; but before I can judge them properly I need to know their circumstances, because they differ as much among themselves as we do from them. I do not agree with the Arminians, Socinians, Arians and Baxterians among them, but the serious and sober amongst them are as dear to me as any, and I maintain the closest relations with them. But I am not led to place myself under their governance, in that I believe that God's will for me is to remain as I am.

5. I have a few things to lay before you that would, I believe, be of profit to us: (a) We should be briefer, if at all possible, in our discussions on externals, and speak more of the chief topics of religion, and examine ourselves on our foundation, and our assurance and experience of them. Having travelled so far to the Associations, it would be well for us to do without some of the time for sleeping and eating, and give ourselves to building one another up spiritually.

(b) I tend to think that it would be profitable for us to set down our principles on paper and print it, so that there might be no misunderstandings, nor room for any to believe that we hold views which we do not. This would also assist us to understand one another's views, and would lead to more unity. It would also be of advantage in leaving behind us a witness to the truth of the gospel, that it might speak to the benefit of ages to come. (c) I believe that should Providence see fit to open the door, we should establish a school in order to provide some measure of instruction to those who exhort. A few months in it, with God's blessing on the education, could be most beneficial.

This, humbly, my brethren, from your unworthy brother and fellow-soldier, Richard Tibbott.

This letter shows Richard Tibbott to be a notably discerning and un-prejudiced man, and in possession of sufficient courage to express his views to an Association that comprised Whitefield, Rowland and Harris. He was more of a Methodist than a Dissenter, and had no intention at all of leaving the Methodists at this time, but he would fellowship with all orthodox parties, loving all who loved the Lord Jesus. As far as we know, it was he in this letter, who was first to suggest the usefulness of a Confession of Faith and of Disciplinary Rules; this is also the first reference to a school. In some things he was no doubt ahead of his time. The reference in the letter to the brethren in Glamorgan is to the message from the Groes-wen exhorters to the Caeo Association in the spring of 1745, to which we shall return later. While the Dissenters at the time were buried in cold orthodoxy and were condemning all warmth in religion, Richard Tibbott anticipated the danger of the Methodists putting too much emphasis on zeal and subjective experience. His soul longed for more tolerance and brotherly love from both directions.

The letter was surely very acceptable to the Association, for soon after this we find Tibbott placed in charge of all the Gwynedd churches. He superintended the societies of Montgomeryshire, Merionethshire, Denbighshire and Caernarvonshire. Once when preaching in the latter county, he was attacked by a nobleman who beat him mercilessly about the head with a cudgel, so that he fell in a faint and was ill for some time. Another time, when on a journey in the same county, he was brought before a magistrate who dealt with him as a vagabond, sending him home from constable to constable, one passing him on to the other, as if he were a dangerous creature. In the disruption between Harris and Rowland, Tibbott joined at first with Harris's party. It was natural for him to do so. Harris was the first of the Methodists to have won his friendship; Harris was the greatest in influence of all the Reformers in Montgomeryshire; and it was with him that all the societies of the county threw in their lot.

The names of Tibbott and Lewis Evans, Llanllugan, were amongst those who were present at the first Association of Harris's party at St Nicholas, on 25 July 1758, and he must have been particularly eager to be present to have travelled from mid-Montgomeryshire down to the Vale of Glamorgan. At this Association it was arranged that Tibbott would bring reports on the Montgomeryshire societies to the next Association, and to take a journey of three weeks to the north. He was also at the Llwynberllan Monthly Meeting of 30 December, the same year, and was one of those who answered when Harris asked who would be willing to give heart and hand to the Lord. He was not at the Dyserth Association on the following Thursday but a note in the minutes recording that he had been sent that morning to the north, shows that it was not through any lack of sympathy for Harris or his party that he was absent.

Gradually, however, a suspicion arose in Tibbott's mind as to the spirit that motivated Harris and his followers. At the Llwynbongam Association of 2 July 1751, matters came to a head. Harris asked for an indication: who was it who had faith to take the land, and to stand alone in the work of the Lord, with none to help? By this, presumably, he meant: who would go through the societies in order to get them to turn their backs on the clergymen? Many refused to give him such indication. On the first evening, Tibbott was uncertain. He saw that the brethren were unsettled and felt a longing to discuss matters with the other party. Harris tried to reason with him and to show the necessity of an unwavering stance. He added that those who had left had offended, and that every possible means had been used in the effort to reconcile them. But all his reasoning was in vain. The next morning, Richard Tibbott was excommunicated for failing to obey the instruction to go about the societies and for his decision to discuss matters with Rowland's party. Out he went, joining with Rowland, and remaining with him until the time that he left the Methodists. His warm regard of Harris continued, however, and when the latter's wife died, Tibbott wrote him a letter expressing his sympathy. It is a Christian letter, full of lofty thoughts and much gentleness.

Richard Tibbott laboured amongst the Methodists until 1762. In that year, the Independent Church at Llanbryn-mair lost their minister when the Rev. Lewis Rees moved to Mynydd-bach, Swansea. Tibbott was pressed to take his place, and he agreed. It may be that, like many of the exhorters, he had a longing to be ordained – a longing that would not have been satisfied amongst the Methodists. At the same time in taking such a step, he was not compromising any principle nor going against his conscience. He had been brought up by the Independents. As a Methodist he had continued to mix freely with his former brethren, respecting them greatly, and party and denomination were never of any great importance in his judgment. He laboured diligently at Llanbryn-mair, his sphere of ministry reaching from Machynlleth to Llandinam. In addition he often travelled through north and south Wales. He was as acceptable amongst the Methodists as ever, and his respect for them was no less. To the end of his life he ensured that he was present at the Bala and Llangeitho Associations, and he was asked to preach in them at the most prestigious times of service. When journeying, he would preach in the chapels of both denominations without distinction, and was welcomed also at Baptist assemblies. He knew nothing of denominational narrowness. His house at Llanbryn-mair was open to ministers and exhorters of every religious party.

Only the last day will disclose the extent of this good man's labours, and the persecution and suffering he endured in his efforts for the gospel. He used to go to Waunfawr, near Caernarvon, though exposing himself to great danger in doing so. He lodged there in the home of Thomas Griffith, the father of the well-known poet, Dafydd Ddu Eryri, who kept a small shop near the bridge. When Tibbott came within sight of the place he broke out into singing, and on hearing his voice, Thomas Griffith would be thrilled, and would cry out in cynghanedd: [1]

Dyna Tibbott, yr wy'n tybied [There is Tibbott, I fancy].

The few Methodists in Caernarvon would gather at Waunfawr to worship. Williams, Pantycelyn, offered to preach in the town itself, but was frustrated by the persecutors. In the face of all the rioters, Tibbott ventured to preach there about the year 1770. It is said that he stood on the steps of the house of a Hugh Owen, a currier, opposite to the tavern, Y Delyn [The Harp], at the bottom of Pen-yr-allt Road. But he was not allowed to continue in peace. First of all a man called Twm y Goes-fawr [Tom of the Great-leg] stood on higher steps and threw wooden platters at the preacher until his head was covered in cuts and bruises and the blood flowed. Later, some scoundrel tried to shoot him, but failed. Another shouted out, his rage as great as his ignorance, 'Why these devils come here to steal the gospel from Christ, I do not know.' How the service ended is not known, but afterwards the preacher and his horse were imprisoned in the castle. They were released the next morning, however, without injury.

He preached on one occasion, accompanied by an exhorter called Edward Parry, at a spot near Henllan, Denbighshire. The vicar of Llan-efydd arrived on the scene, together with Mr Wynn of Plasnewydd, to stop him. Mr Wynn was inclined to stay to hear, so that he might understand the doctrines being taught, but the vicar rushed forward in his zeal and asked roughly, 'How can you dare to preach in this house without a licence?' Edward Parry answered mildly, 'The commandment has been given that we should go out to the highways and hedges, and it is no worse, in my opinion, to go to a house, if there is an opportunity given.' 'I preach to the parish every Sunday,' said the clergyman, 'so that there is no need for anybody else to interfere.' Tibbott understood by this that the man was a clergyman, and said, 'I imagine, Sir, that you preach from the same book as myself, and even perhaps from the same texts.' 'Let me see what book you have,' said the vicar. Tibbott passed him his Greek New Testament. The clergyman and Mr Wynn opened their eyes at the sight of a Greek Testament – they had never imagined that the despised Roundheads knew anything of the classical languages. They both departed without another word.

The last time that Richard Tibbott preached was on 21 January 1798. He preached twice on that Sunday, and administered the ordinance of the Lord's Supper at two places. It seemed as if he was physically stronger and spiritually more heavenly than usual. One of his hearers commented that when speaking of the sufferings of the Lord Jesus he seemed to be almost beyond the veil. He died on 18 March 1798, at nearly eighty years of age. His successor, the Rev. John Roberts, preached at the funeral from the words, 'Know ye not that there is a prince and a great man fallen this day in Israel?' All who knew him agreed that he was an able man of strong mental powers. Though not eloquent or of outstanding preaching skills, he was a fine theologian, and was one of the peaceable and faithful of Israel. In an age when religious prejudices were strong, and partisanship rife, Tibbott clung to the principles of the gospel, scorning the minor issues that divided the denominations. He remains of blest memory to this day.

## LEWIS EVANS, LLANLLUGAN

Another Montgomeryshire exhorter who deserves our attention is Lewis Evans, Llanllugan. We have already referred to his conviction at Trefeglwys in 1740 through the preaching of Howell Harris, and to his activities as an exhorter soon after, without permission from any court, religious or civil. He seems to have been born in 1719 and so was the same age as Richard Tibbott. He was a weaver by profession and worked with his father at a place called Crygnant. It was a talking-point in the locality at the time that a young weaver should go about from door to door, to read the Bible, pray, and exhort. His behaviour raised considerable excitement in the neighbourhood, and persecution soon followed. A very strong man served at Plashelyg, a farmhouse halfway between Lewis Evans's home and another house that he used to visit to read. It seems that the praying and exhorting agitated this servant of Plashelyg considerably, and he used to watch for Lewis Evans as he passed, threatening him with violence should he not stop his activities. This he would not do and the upshot was that the servant beat him cruelly until the path was red with blood. All that he answered his persecutor was, 'Tell me, my boy, what have I done to you, that you should deal with me like this?'

There are many references to Lewis Evans in the Trefeca Collection. In a Monthly Association held at Tyddyn, near Llanidloes, on 17 February, 1743, a number of churches in Montgomeryshire were placed under his care and that of Morgan Hughes and Benjamin Cadman. A fortnight later, at a Glanyrafonddu Monthly Meeting, the fellowships at Llanllugan and Llanwyddelan were placed under his sole stewardship while Benjamin Cadman was appointed to visit all the churches of the county. In a Monthly Association at Trefeca in January, 1744, it was decided, 'That Bro. Lewis Evans should go, as far as he is able, consistent with the call upon him, to Merionethshire.' In Richard Tibbott's report in the same year on the state of the Montgomeryshire churches, it is said:

Lewis Evans, who exhorts in Llanllugan, is blessed of the Lord to many; many doors are opened to him, and many have been convicted by his doctrine.

He was an effective preacher and very acceptable to societies all over the country. In a letter to Howell Harris from a certain T. E. dated, 'Tyddyn, 1 August 1746' is written:

Bro. Lewis from Llanllugan was here a little while ago; the saints' hearts leaped within them at his words. It is a wonder how the Lord increases this man in grace and ability.

In the summer of 1747, Mr T. Bowen, Tyddyn, wrote to Harris:

The coming of Bro. Lewis Evans to us has been notably awakening recently.

We cannot doubt, in the light of such testimonies, that the uneducated exhorter of Llanllugan was a very able preacher and was being blessed by his Master to the saving of sinners and the building up of the saints.

Together with all the societies and exhorters of Montgomeryshire, Lewis Evans took Harris's side in the disruption between him and Rowland. Harris was his father in the faith, and he was present at Harris's first Association at St Nicholas. When it was there decided to send a number of exhorters to the north to persuade the societies that Harris was in the right and that Rowland and his followers had lost their hold upon the Lord, Lewis Evans was one of the envoys. Clearly he was a man who could be trusted. He was present at the Dyserth Association of Harris's party, on 3 January, 1751, and there declared, with a number of the exhorters, his readiness to commit himself and all that he possessed to the Lord. He was appointed to be one of those who were to leave all and to go about continually, serving the cause. He was at the Trefeca Association of the following February; the Neath Association of 10 April, the same year; and the Llwynbongam Association of 2 July 1751, where he again, with many others, reiterated his commitment to serve the cause of religion under the leadership of Howell Harris. He was honoured with the responsibility of preaching during this Association. The last time he is mentioned in this context was in the Trefeca Association of 2 October, 1751. The brethren were there encouraged by Harris to state their feelings freely. Lewis Evans was the second to speak; he said that he felt it an obligation, day and night, to approach the crucified Christ, and to work for him. But gradually, Harris's increasingly autocratic behaviour and his tendency to limit his labours to Trefeca, caused Lewis Evans, along with so many of the exhorters, to leave him and rejoin the Methodists under Rowland.

No one suffered more for the gospel at the time than Lewis Evans. His dangers, sufferings, and escapes read as a novel. When travelling once in the Clwyd Valley, two men, holding large staves, waited for him at a bridge. One of them struck him on the head so that the blood flowed. He was so concussed that he did not realize what a sight he was, covered in blood, until he frightened a passing woman. He was able to reach a friend's house where he could rest and wash his wounds. Another time, when exhorting at Darowen, not far from Machynlleth, about sixty of the town's wastrels came to disrupt the meeting and intending to do him harm. As they were too wild to reason with and too strong to withstand, there was nothing to do but to flee, and as he was light of body and fleet of foot there was every chance that he might escape. As he ran, he fell into a ditch that happened to be dry. This hid him from his pursuers, and he remained there until all had passed and so escaped their clutches.

When preaching at Bala one Sunday, a nobleman who was a local magistrate sent officers to arrest him and bring him for an interview. Lewis Evans was called to the parlour and the following conversation took place:

Magistrate:     Are you the one who preached at Bala?
Lewis Evans:  Yes, sir. I gave a word of counsel to the people.

| | |
|---|---|
| Mag.: | From where do you come, and what is your work when you are at home? |
| L.E.: | I come from the parish of Llanllugan in Montgomeryshire, and am a weaver by occupation. |
| Mag.: | What brought you this way? Do you not have enough work at home? |
| L.E.: | Yes, plenty; but I came here to give some words of counsel to fellow-sinners. |
| Mag.: | There is no need of you here. We have parsons who have had a good education, and who have gone to Oxford at great expense, to preach to us. |
| L.E.: | There is enough work for both them and myself. The people go on their way to destruction for all our efforts. |
| Mag.: | I will send you to prison for your efforts. |
| L.E.: | There have been those better than myself who have been in prison. The Lord Jesus himself was imprisoned, though he came into this world to save sinners. |

The weaver then spoke further of the Lord Jesus and of his great purpose in coming into the world; but the magistrate soon stopped him, saying, 'Do you intend to preach in my parlour?'

'I do not believe, Sir,' was the answer, 'that your parlour is too good a place in which to speak of Jesus Christ.' The magistrate saw that there was no great possibility of his convincing the preacher by any more conversation, he therefore sent him to Dolgelley jail, where the poor weaver lapsed for six months. But the friends of religion began to inquire into the matter and found that the trial and sentence were irregular, and that the nobleman who had carried them out had probably laid himself open to prosecution. The magistrate also realized this, and also that Lewis Evans's friends were looking into his case. He hurried to Dolgelley and to Lewis Evans at the prison. A further conversation took place between them:

| | |
|---|---|
| Magistrate: | Well, Lewis, is this where you are still? |
| Lewis Evans: | Yes, sir. This is where I am. |
| Mag.: | It is likely that this is where you will be forever. |
| L.E.: | No, sir. Neither you nor I will be here forever. |
| Mag.: | If you gave a bit of money I could get you out. |
| L.E.: | Indeed, sir, you should get me out for nothing in that you had a large hand in getting me in. |

Mag.: Tell me, are there many of you?

L.E.: Yes, sir, there are many of us, and there will be many more in a little while.

Mag.: You will all hang from the same bough.

L.E.: Oh, sir, you yourself will have long rotted before that.

Lewis Evans was immediately released at no cost. As a result the magistrate was not prosecuted, but it was made clear to him that an eye would be kept on him from then on, and that any further similar actions would not be tolerated.

Lewis Evans possessed a ready wit and aptness of expression together with a transparent innocence. He and Mr Foulkes, Machynlleth, once climbed to the summit of Snowdon. Having reached the top, Mr Foulkes removed his hat and said, 'What if we were to pray a little?' 'Very good, Mr Foulkes,' was the answer, 'do so by all means; take advantage of the opportunity, for never before have you been so close to heaven.' He was a small man, lively in his actions, quick of speech, and ready with words. He was not considered a great preacher but he proved very useful. He made use of every opportunity to exhort. Some verse of the Bible, or some useful remark, was always upon his lips. He was compared to a circulating school in his eagerness for dispensing knowledge about God and the lost condition of mankind to all with whom he met. He died in 1792, when seventy-two years old.

## HERBERT JENKINS

Another famous exhorter was Herbert Jenkins. He was born in Mynyddislwyn parish, Monmouthshire, in 1721. His parents were religious people in reasonable circumstances who ensured that their son receive a good education. He was for some time at a school at Bristol, a contemporary of Mr Bernard Fosket, afterwards principal of the Baptist College. Most probably he was converted through the ministry of Howell Harris, and he soon began speaking to his fellow-sinners about Christ. As he could preach in both Welsh and English and was a popular preacher, there were many calls for his service. At the first Association at Watford his was the very first name on the list of exhorters received into membership of the Association. At the second Association, he was again the first mentioned on the list of exhorters present. When the country was divided up, no area was assigned to Herbert Jenkins, it was arranged instead that he should be an assistant to Howell Harris and to the English brethren. It is clear therefore that he was considered more able than his fellow-exhorters in some matters. It is said that he received this position after Howell Harris had heard him preaching powerfully on the mystery of the Saviour's Deity. Harris's judgment of him is seen in a letter to Whitefield on 12 February, 1743. He wrote:

> Great power attend the ministers and exhorters in their places. Much does the Lord bless Bro. Jenkins. I saw him this week in his return from Pembrokeshire, Glamorgan and Carmarthenshire. He is universally owned and liked, and called for, and unless his call be exceeding clear to Wiltshire, I don't think he should leave Wales, especially as Bro. Adams is coming on.[2]

It seems however that the cries of the English brethren won the day, for it was in their company that Herbert Jenkins spent most of his ministry. In the Life and Times of the Countess of Huntingdon it is said that he joined with Mr Wesley in 1743 and itinerated with the Wesleyans for some years with much zeal and success, and that he was present at the second Wesleyan Conference, held at Bristol in 1743, where his name appears last of the itinerating preachers. This note however cannot be completely accurate. Herbert Jenkins did not leave his first friends, though he did minister with Wesley's people for some time. Later in the same biography it is said that he reunited with Mr Whitefield, and laboured with Cennick and others at the Tabernacle, and that he preached much in Wales. He was present with Whitefield's people at an Association in Bristol on 20 March 1744.

A letter from him to Howell Harris, dated 11 April 1745, shows him to have cooled somewhat towards the Methodists, and towards Harris himself. He complains in the letter that Harris does not think as well of him as he previously did, and that he had brought serious charges against him. Namely:

1. That his whole heart was not in the work. He denied this completely, but acknowledged that it appeared to him that Harris was inclining too much towards the Moravians, and that this disturbed him.

2. That he did not approve the arrangements made by the Methodists in the Association. He answered that he agreed with the private societies, in which the converts gathered to pray, and sing, and share their experiences; that such meetings had proved extremely profitable; but that he did not agree with placing visitors over the societies, and that the sooner that practice was ended the better.

3. That he remained with the Methodists though disapproving of their arrangements, with the intention of leaving after a while and drawing the people after him. He denied this accusation absolutely.

4. That in some sense he was a different man, and felt differently towards Howell Harris. He confessed that there was some truth in this:

Once, I made you my rule of faith and behaviour; I imagined you were infallible. But now I feel it a duty not to follow anyone, not even a step, except to the degree that he follows Christ.

He ends his letter by saying that he respects Harris greatly, as one who was in Christ before himself, and as one honoured by the Lord in being made an instrument for the salvation of many souls.

It does not appear that Harris took any offence at this letter, but rather that it helped to clear the air between the two men. In 1745, Herbert Jenkins was appointed successor to Harris at the Tabernacle, until the February of the following year. In another letter to Harris (16 August 1745)[3] he informed him that he had fully intended to attend the academy of the Rev. George Thompson, St Gennys, Cornwall, for three months to improve his Greek and Latin, but after many attempts to set out on the journey, so many obstacles had arisen that he had become convinced that it was not God's will for him to go. A Mr Stephens, the minister of the Independents at Plymouth, had encouraged him to go to Gloucester and be licensed as a Dissenting minister; that Brother Adams had done this, and had gone to minister in the west of England, but that he could not consider doing so without first seeking the advice of the Association. As for his being ordained in the Church of England, he had now lost all hope of this. He had been the previous day with the Bishop of Bristol, telling him his story. The Bishop had listened patiently and behaved courteously towards him, suggesting to him that there would be little obstacle as far as his scholarship was concerned. But Herbert Jenkins's Methodism was certainly an obstacle. The Bishop told him it would be difficult for him to obtain a title and a bishop who would ordain him, and even if he found these, the examination would be all the harder for him as he was a Methodist. He ends the letter with the words, 'I hope my dear, dear Brother you'll pray for me. O! When you are closest to the Lamb cry to him that he lead his child all the way.'

As he feared, every attempt on his part to receive holy orders in the Established Church proved a failure. As a result, he threw in his lot with the Dissenters and in 1749 he was ordained minister over Maidstone Independent Church, where he laboured with much success for twenty-four years. He died, at the height of his popularity, on 11 December 1772. Herbert Jenkins was a very able man, an eloquent preacher, and full of energy. Had the Methodists seen their way clear to ordain him, he would probably never have left the Connexion. He wrote many hymns and translated others, particularly those of John Cennick's, into Welsh. He published these, together with hymns by his brother David Jenkins, in a book entitled *Hymnau ar amryw Ystyriaethau* [*Hymns on Various Subjects, by various authors*] in 1744.

## JAMES INGRAM

The name of James Ingram is not found in the Trefeca records but he was certainly an itinerating preacher of some fame. We do not have the history of his birth and youth, but he was converted through Harris's preaching. Soon, Harris made him steward over his property at Trefeca, and the servant followed his master in the work of exhorting. The first letter of his that we have was written to Harris from Brecon prison, sometime in the year 1744. Ingram had been caught in order to press him into the army. This was one of the many forms of persecution against the Methodists used by the clergy and magistrates of the day. They would imprison the exhorters and force them into the army or the militia. At one time in 1745, there were four Methodist exhorters with the army in Gloucester. In his prison letter, Ingram wrote:

> With shame I confess that I was very low last night; but this morning I was enabled to speak on the following words, 'As thy days, so shall thy strength be.' I had liberty last night to expound the twelfth chapter of the Revelation for about an hour; I continued longer today, with extraordinary help. My soul was in heaven, particularly when I prayed for yourself and for the friends. And afterwards, when my father and Sally [his wife] arrived, I prayed with much pleasure. I appeal to you to persuade Sally, who is determined to come with me; but certainly it is not right for her to do so, though to part with her is as if a rib was torn from my side.

The clergy hardly gained an advantage by imprisoning James Ingram. The zeal for exhorting burned within him as a flame, and he spoke regularly to those in prison with him, waiting to be pressed into the army.

Mr Marmaduke Gwynne did his best to obtain his release, but all his efforts were in vain. The last hope of every oppressed Methodist was the Countess of Huntingdon, and Howell Harris appealed to her on behalf of his servant. The reply of the Countess's secretary reads as follows:

> Our only path to help Mr Ingram is to appeal to Lord Stair, the Colonel-in-chief; and he has no authority over the civil servants, only over the military. Therefore if Ingram has not been released to the military authorities, his Lordship cannot do anything for him. There have been two examples of the kindness and equity of his Lordship lately. When I, as steward to the Countess, proved to his satisfaction that two men for whom I was arguing were Methodist preachers, though not ordained, and had been pressed into the army by the malice and trickery of the clergy, churchwardens and rogues,

he released one directly, on condition that he paid the money, and the costs which the regiment had incurred concerning him; which was done immediately. And as for the second, a strong man was found to take his place.

You see therefore that you must send all detail concerning Ingram, and prove that he does not fall under the recent parliamentary bill, as he is your servant and steward of your property, and that you keep a property, which is in your name, and that you have had a good education in the schools and at university, and that you are continuing to pursue your studies. You do not have to say that you are a Methodist preacher. And if you can add that you are a freeholder, better still, for all will be ready on your behalf to release you, should they carry out their vicious threatenings against yourself. You must also note the regiment with which Ingram is connected; who is his captain, and his officer, and you must promise to pay money and costs to the regiment, or have another ready to take his place.

This letter throws much light on the actions taken against the Methodists. We see:

1. That the exhorters were forced to join the army.

2. That to release them, if they made a payment of money or found a replacement, was considered a favour.

3. That this favour was not forthcoming unless the very highest military authority was appealed to.

4. That Howell Harris himself, though a freeholder, was not free from the possibility of being pressed.

5. That the clergy, and their willing servants, were at the root of it all. Ingram was eventually released. He wrote to Harris on 19 June 1744:

I can inform you that I came out of Brecon Prison a fortnight ago, on condition that I appear at the prison when the officer arrives. I was too short for a land-soldier, and was kept to be a sea-soldier, though I am too short for that also, as I am still only five foot and two and a half inches. I do not know at what time, nor in what ship, I shall be taken away. Or even if I am to be taken at all. Many magistrates, and Sir H. H., the Member for Parliament, have promised to do their best to have me released. Others roar like lions. But let them roar; it is God who reigns. I preached usually three times a day, during the three weeks I was in the prison. I am now following my circuit in Herefordshire. Greet all who love Zion in my name.

Your poor and unworthy servant, but by grace your happy brother,

James Ingram.

He remained free, and preached Christ for the rest of his life. On 28 July 1744, Benjamin Cadman wrote to Howell Harris about him:

Bro. Ingram, when he was last at Nantmel, received a call to go over to Montgomeryshire. He answered that he had no authority to go of himself, and that he could not without your permission. We desire for you to pay us a visit, if you are able. And if you are not able, would you give permission for Jemmy Ingram to come.

In October of the same year, John Sparks wrote to Howell Harris from Haverfordwest:

Last night, Bro. Ingram preached in my old pulpit here. He spoke sweetly and comfortingly from the words, 'Unto you therefore which believe he is precious.' Many came to listen, and I hope that some heard in truth.

In January 1745, the old exhorter John Richard, Llansamlet wrote:

I have been with my brother James Ingram at Newton, hearing him speak; many people came to hear him, and I can say from experience that the Lord came also to meet with us. Glory be to his name. Amen. I believe that the service was blessed to open the hearts of some to God's messengers, or even to God himself; for you would marvel at the tenderness of spirit that they showed. Arrange for Bro. Jemmy to go there as often as he is able, because I believe that if he were to go there for a week, the whole locality would be opened up to receive God's servants. I feel in my soul as a lion after its prey, to wrestle those souls from under Satan's rule.

From these and similar letters, it is clear that James Ingram was a very popular exhorter.

Towards the middle of the summer of 1745, Ingram began to believe that Howell Harris was displeased with him because of his carelessness. He wrote to his master:

As I was coming from Erwood, it came to my mind that it would be better for me to remain more at home, in that I, my horse, my laundry, are a heavy charge upon you, but I am of little help at Trefeca. Yet, though it would be pride in me to believe that I could awaken the unfruitful people of this county, I humbly believe that the Lord has a message for them to be delivered through my instrumentality. The Lord's arm was made bare while I preached at Aberedw fair; one of the chief leaders of the fair broke his leg; another fell from his horse last Sunday as he returned from another fair, a neighbour of mine, and he died there and then.

What connection was there between Ingram's preaching and the breaking of the man's leg, he does not say. More than likely he looked upon the accident as a judgment from God. But master and servant were soon reconciled and in agreement. There are many letters from him to Harris after this, in some of which he expresses a wish to be involved with the

English work. However, some time before the Disruption he is lost sight of completely. Whether he died young, or whether he settled as a Nonconformist minister in England, we do not know.

## JAMES BEAUMONT

There are many references in the Trefeca records and the letters of Howell Harris to James Beaumont, an exhorter from Radnorshire. It seems that he lived at Gore, where was an old Nonconformist cause and also a lively Methodist society. He is said to have been a warm-hearted speaker. Harris must have considered him to be one of the ablest of the exhorters because the name of Beaumont is first on every list almost without exception, other than that of Herbert Jenkins. He was received into the Association as a public exhorter, at the first meeting in Watford. At the Monthly Association at Glanyrafonddu he was appointed, together with Howell Harris and Herbert Jenkins, as a General Superintendent over all the societies. At the second Association at Watford he was assigned the societies of Radnorshire and Herefordshire. The following letter to him from Harris shows how highly the Reformer viewed him and the warmth of affection he held for him. The letter is dated 9 July 1743:

My dear brother, Beaumont,
Keep on fighting; the battle is won; behold, Jesus shows the crown purchased by him. Go forth, brave soldier; nothing can withstand you, for Christ is at your side. His bleeding wounds supply all your need; yes, even if death and hell obstructed the way. Listen! Jesus calls; let James obey. Perhaps this letter will find my dearest brother and closest friend sorry for himself, and groaning for release. Well, Jesus will remove your burden; and until then he will support you under it, taking you from the things of time, and showing you things that eyes have never seen the like. At such times, remember your poor, foolish, wicked and sinful brother, who desires to walk in Christ.

The Lord has seen fit to condescend continually to come amongst us, when his providence gathers us together . . . I greatly desire to see my dear fellow-soldier flaming with more and more zeal for the Lamb. Every gift and grace given to you increases my happiness. Soon, we will meet hereafter, amongst the winged hosts, where sin and sorrow will have been destroyed. Assuredly, none there can praise free grace and electing love louder than ourselves, nor with sweeter sound.

I am, my dearest brother and fellow-citizen, ever yours in the Lamb,
Howell Harris.

The letter demonstrates Harris's great affection for Beaumont. The latter was almost as bold, fearless and energetic a man in his travelling and preaching as Harris himself. The following quotation from a letter of his to Harris, dated 2 August 1742, gives an insight into his character:

> Many are under conviction in Llanybister, Meddigre, Llanddewi and Maes-gwyn, where I preached twice with much power. The devil was roaring at his best. Glory be to God, the kingdom of the evil one is falling down about his ears. It is no wonder therefore that he is roaring, in that his time is so short. May the eternal Lord destroy his kingdom more amd more, for Jesus Christ's sake. Amen

He continues by describing how a new door had been opened to the gospel in his own parish, where he had preached the previous evening with extraordinary unction. The churchwarden and his family were at the meeting, many had been quickened, and at the end the churchwarden had invited him to his own home and had prepared him a meal. He preached the next day in the same place. The church officer was again present, and the Word had reached him to such a degree that he had had to sit down and shout out. Some of the family also were weeping aloud. He ends the letter by saying that the Lord had blessed him remarkably amongst the people of Radnorshire, and that his two brothers and young sister were walking humbly before the Lord.

Church officers were not always so kindly disposed towards him. Consider the following quotation from a letter he wrote on 29 November, 1742, to a Mr Grace of London:

> I have been lately in Breconshire, Herefordshire and Glamorganshire. In Glamorganshire, God was remarkably with me; one could think that the devil's kingdom had fallen. I never had such a journey before, glory be to my dear Saviour. I went lately to an evening fair held in the country. The parish priest took hold of me, threatening to put me in the stocks. I answered that I had been in the stocks before for the same reason, and was willing to be placed there again. He did not fulfil his threats but kept me there for some time, until the Lord released me from his hand. I went to a house a little distance away, and preached to many poor souls who had followed me from the place where I had been kept prisoner. The Lord is very gracious to the poor exhorters of Radnorshire. He opens their mouths wonderfully in the fairs and markets.

James Beaumont endured his share of persecution. The following letter, written to Howell Harris sometime in 1744, gives the history of his visit, together with the old exhorter William Evans of Nantmel, to a district in Montgomeryshire:

> When I went to Llanidloes a lady of the town gave me leave to preach under the roof of the town hall. But as the people began to gather, the churchwarden arrived, causing much disturbance. It seems that he had authority from the Chancellor of the diocese forbidding me to speak in the town. When he came

up to me, he asked, 'By what authority do you preach in this place?' I answered that it was by the authority of the Word of God. But he cared nothing for the things of God, but rather how he could pull me down from the place on which I stood. When I saw that he was determined to obstruct me, I told him that I was ready to comply with every law of the land, both of State or Church. He began to lead me away like a prisoner. I took out my timepiece to see what hour of day it was; at this, his heart failed him, his countenance fell, and his speech changed. He said that it was a matter of conscience for him to stop me, as the Chancellor had strictly commanded him that no one should preach in the town; and that if anyone did so, he was to take them prisoner. But instead of imprisoning me, he went away, wishing me well.

I soon returned to where I was to preach and gave out the words of a hymn. Throughout the time we sang, all was quiet; but when I went to pray, the Squire arrived, blowing his hunting horn and calling to him his beagles. [Beaumont, it seems, is referring figuratively to the mob] They appeared as dogs, eager for their prey. But the Lord did not allow them to mistreat me other than to cover me with dung and eggs. They swore that they would lose their lives rather than allow me to preach in the town. I withdrew to a nearby valley, outside the corporation, and many of the people followed. The Lord made me strong and steadfast, and gave me to speak his word boldly, and my labour was not in vain in the Lord.

I failed to preach in Trefeglwys, because of an enormous storm of wind and rain. The lambs of Christ sheltered under a hedge near to where it had been arranged for me to preach, but the rain penetrated through the bushes and the poor creatures were cold and wet. As there was no friend to take me in, I thought of going to an inn about half a mile away. There, in the inn, the number of people increased. The inn-keeper and his wife were persecutors. I asked for their permission to sing a hymn, and it was granted. God enabled us to sing with the spirit and with the understanding. After singing the praises of our Redeemer I took the liberty to exhort and to pray.

About twelve o'clock the next day, we went to Newtown, and the inhabitants surrounded us on all sides. They opened their mouths against us, and gnashed their teeth as lions ready for prey. The town parson told his scholars that whoever of them would beat us most savagely, he would be favoured in his future education. A strange way to buy learning – to pay for it by blood! The first attack upon me was made by the women. They wetted their aprons in the dogs' kennels in order to daub my face with the filth. Brother William Evans stood beside me, seeking to shield me from their blows with his frail body, but in vain. They lashed their horses to get them to ride over us. They raised up a kind of cart, so that it might fall upon us and kill us. The stones thrown at us were hurled with such force that they passed right through a hedge some distance away. In this way the riotous mob continued to beat us most barbarously, until one of them struck me so that I became unconscious. When they saw that I could not take any more, some threw down their weapons saying that I had received enough. Brother Evans held me in his arms until I had come to myself, and then went to look for my horse that had been driven away by the mob. As I stood alone, a malicious woman approached seeking to hit me over the head with a wooden cudgel, but Brother Evans saw her and intervened.

By now, I was covered over in dung and blood, and so weak that I could not stand without help. While my friends tried to help me from the mud where I had been thrown, another woman drew near and threw a handful of dung into my mouth, so that I almost could not breathe. I bled for more than two miles after escaping my persecutors, and when I came to remove my clothes, found that my head and parts of my shirt were soaked in blood. After obtaining a plaster for my head and food for my body, I prayed to my heavenly Father that he would forgive them, and I was contented in my spirit. This was my reception at the hands of the people of Newtown. I pray that God would give them a new heart, for Jesus Christ's sake. Amen, and Amen.

This is how many dealt with the exhorters of old. This is the treatment they received from those whom they sought to help. But notwithstanding the wrath of the parsons and the rage of the mobs, they were not daunted; they continued with a fearless spirit to proclaim God's gospel of grace to sinners. Nor were they provoked to seek revenge for their maltreatment; instead, like Stephen, the first Christian martyr, and like the Lord Jesus himself, they could pray in their blood for their persecutors. They were heroes of which the world is not worthy.

After some years, Beaumont moved his field of labour to England. He wrote to Harris on 11 April 1745, to say that he intended moving towards Bath and London. He complains also in the letter of the coldness that had arisen between himself and Harris. What the cause of this coldness was, we do not know, though we suspect that it was some disagreement over a point of doctrine. And the distance between the two friends widened to such an extent as to become painful. Rice Williams, an exhorter in Radnorshire, wrote to Harris on 29 December, 1748, as follows:

May the Lord hasten your coming to us to hold a private society. If things are allowed to continue long as they are, we can say farewell to any society in Radnorshire. Some are bold enough to threaten that if Beaumont is turned out, many of the exhorters will follow him, as he is certain of the affection of the county. Beaumont preached against us every week. Our little society, which was in perfect unity, is now agitated throughout, and full of party zeal. I fear the consequences. James Probert sent for him last Thursday to the Castle, where they meet weekly, but, as I understand, without the others being informed. He has been invited to come here also, on the first day of the new year; but I intend to withstand him, as Thomas James is to come here, who is a little less dictatorial.

The strife is over sanctification, which is (as they claim) only simple belief. They will not allow any reference to duty or commandment; they do not believe in growth in grace, and hate watching and fasting. Thomas Sheen has drunk deeply of Beaumont's doctrine; he is his right-hand man. Many of our members are caught in two minds, not knowing how to proceed. Our Nicene Creed is abhorred by our new teachers; they claim it should be revised, particularly that part on the generation from the Father before the beginning of the world.

Rice Williams's letter sheds light on the different views held by Beaumont. Were these, perhaps, the source of the mixture of Sandemanianism and Antinomianism that flourished for a while in the Builth area, with Thomas Sheen as leader, after the division between Harris and Rowland, and which is referred to in *Drych Yr Amseroedd?* James Beaumont, probably, died soon after the date of this letter. Certainly, he was dead before the year 1750. It is said that when preaching in the open-air he was struck by a stone and that this subsequently brought about his death. Tradition has it that this took place in Pembrokeshire. He was certainly a committed man, full of zeal and courage, and it is sad to have to record that he departed to some extent from the faith in later life.[4]

## THOMAS JAMES

The next exhorter to be considered is Thomas James of Cerrigcadarn in Breconshire. We have very little of his personal history other than what may be inferred from his letters and the references to him in the Trefeca records. It appears, however, that he was convicted under Howell Harris's preaching and began exhorting immediately. There is evidence that he was preaching at the beginning of 1741. In a letter, dated 9 October, 1742, to Howell Harris in London, he says that he had preached at a fair in Llanfihangel the previous year, and the sermon was blessed to the conviction of some soul. He believed that this constrained him to visit the fair the following year also. The devil sought to hinder him, whispering to him that he would be killed, many of his friends came to him to alert him of his danger, and enemies came to frighten him. But Thomas James would not listen to any of them. He proceeded there, with his life in his hands.

He reached Llanfihangel before the festivities had begun. The inn-keeper came up to him, full of honeyed words, asking him not to disrupt, and that he would be glad to see him there at any other time. He answered that he would not disrupt, but that it was his work to stand up against Satan's kingdom, that he would only speak out against sin, and that if the inn-keeper wished to support sin, he himself could only oppose it. By now a crowd was beginning to gather. A woman, full of the devil, hurled herself against him so that he fell over, claiming that he was standing on her ground. 'Very well,' said the exhorter, 'I will stand on the highway.' They moved to the road and the preacher gave out a hymn to sing, but the inn-keeper began to swear that he could not stay there, and called on the boys to collect stones. These rushed upon the few saints that had gathered on the road, and with murder in their faces and shouts that the highway was free to all, they pushed the small congregation before them so that they could not stand. There were cudgels in their hands, but, said Thomas Jones, 'As far as I remember, we were not afraid. There was a fire burning in my heart the whole time.'

It now became a battle between the two kingdoms; each kingdom fighting with its appropriate weapons. The preacher shouted for quiet so that he could speak with their leader; but when they both withdrew from the crowd, the latter was such a weak man that he trembled before Thomas James and retreated from him. The service was begun a second time. While the saints sang and prayed, the servants of the devil threw dung and pieces of wood at them. The face of William Evans, Nantmel, was covered in mud. But no one was hurt – an open Bible and their clothes were all that were damaged. And Jesus won the day. Thomas James preached for an hour and a half from the words, 'Upon this rock I will build my church; and the gates of hell will not prevail against it,' convicting the ungodly, and confirming the lambs. At the close of the sermon, he felt great love towards his enemies, and he appealed to them with great earnestness to come to the Saviour, showing them that he was able to save to the uttermost. The feast-day was turned into a preaching service. At the end, the inn-keeper approached the man of God, inviting him to his house for supper. Thomas James concluded his letter with the words, 'Not unto us, O Lord, not unto us, but unto Thy name give glory.'

At the first Watford Association he was received as a public exhorter, but no geographical area was given to him to superintend because of some difficulty in his circumstances. By the second Association at Watford, it seems the difficulty had been removed, and he was placed as the superintendent over the Breconshire societies on the Trefeca side of the Usk. The reports sent in show that he fulfilled his duties faithfully. He encountered various experiences while serving the flock. In a letter sent to John Cennick on 26 March 1743, he describes his visit to a society on the border of Radnorshire and Breconshire in the company of James Beaumont and another brother. To reach the place they had to cross the Wye River, and a local gentleman had persuaded the boatmen to charge them an exorbitant fee. When they refused to pay, the boat was tied by rope in the middle of the river. A crowd gathered at the riverbanks, from Hay and other places, to enjoy their predicament of being unable to move in one direction or the other. But these exhorters were full of daring and invention. They turned the boat into a pulpit for proclaiming Christ, and began preaching to the crowd on both sides. The persecutors became enraged and began throwing stones at the preachers. But God wonderfully protected his servants; not one of the three was injured, and it seems that the impromptu service proved the means of saving many. When the three men had been kept in the water for five hours, singing, praying and exhorting, it was discovered that the boatmen had no licence, and they were glad enough to bring them back to land. Thomas James believed that they too had been wounded in their consciences.

The latter part of the life of this servant of Christ is hidden in darkness. The last reference to him occurs in a letter by Rice Williams, dated 29 December 1748. His name is not found in the list of those who remained faithful to Howell Harris at the time of the Disruption. He had either died previously, or, during this crucial period, had thrown in his lot with Daniel Rowland and Williams, Pantycelyn. Thomas James was one of the most useful of exhorters. Temperamentally, he was a combination of the lion and the lamb. He feared no danger, he ventured in amongst his persecutors with no fear whatsoever, but he was notably tender and humble in his dealings with the flock.

## THOMAS WILLIAM AND
## WILLIAM EDWARDS 'THE BUILDER'

The next exhorter we shall note is Thomas William, a superintendent over part of Glamorganshire. Very little of his history is known, but it seems that he was convicted during Howell Harris's first visit to Eglwysilan, in the year 1738, and that he began exhorting immediately. When the Methodists left Watford, because of the errors of David Williams the minister, and settled at Groes-wen, Thomas William was amongst them. In the Monthly Association of 1 March 1743, at Glanyrafonddu, he was appointed superintendent over the societies of east Glamorganshire as far as Llantrisant, and this was confirmed at the next Watford Association. Many of his reports on the condition of the societies are still available and are most interesting. When troubles arose in the minds of the exhorters of Groes-wen over communicating in the Established Church, Thomas William was one of those who sent a letter to the Caeo Association of 30 March 1745. And as the reply received was not acceptable he, together with

William Edwards, 'the Builder', were ordained ministers of Groes-wen in the manner of the Dissenters, and he laboured there, administering the sacraments, until the day of his death. It does not seem that he considered himself to have left the Methodists, at least not completely, and the Reformers often visited Groes-wen on their journeys as before. He did not live long after his ordination but died in the midst of his usefulness, and was buried at Eglwysilan cemetery because Groes-wen did not have its own cemetery at the time.

His fellow-minister, William Edwards, commonly known as 'William Edwards the Builder', is more well-known. He was born in a small farmhouse called Bryn, in Eglwysilan parish, between Pontypridd and Caerphilly, in the year 1719. He was the youngest of four children, and when he was only two years old his father died. He had very little schooling, hardly enough for him to learn to read and write in Welsh. He spent his childhood working about the smallholding. While maintaining the stone walls of the farm, he began to enjoy the work of building. Soon, his fame as a dry-wall builder was known throughout the locality. Having watched stonemasons at work and noted the kinds of implements they used, he felt able to begin constructing houses, and here again he was soon very proficient. Near at hand was the famous old castle of Caerphilly, challenging the storms of centuries with its strong walls and fine arches. William Edwards's aptitude for architecture ensured that his every spare hour was spent studying the design of the structure, so that he soon came to understand the principles involved in bridging a span with an arch.

When he was about twenty-three years old, an iron-forge works was established at Cardiff with a school attached to it. He attended this school, which was kept by a blind teacher called Walter Rosser. He learnt English and the main elements of science. About 1749, he undertook to build a bridge over the River Taff at Pontypridd, and completed the task skilfully. Within a year however extensive flooding occurred. The arches of the bridge were closed by the wood and foliage washed down by the waters from the valleys above. The river was dammed, and under the enormous weight of the collecting waters the bridge gave way. Nothing daunted, he began a second bridge, and in order to avoid a similar catastrophe, he designed it as one large arch. But before it was finished, the weight of its two ends forced out the keystone, and most of the bridge fell into the river. William Edwards would not give up. He worked out where he had been mistaken in his design and set to it for a third time. This third bridge, the longest single-arched bridge in the world when it was completed, is still standing today, a testimony to the genius and courage of its builder.

To return to William Edwards's spiritual history: He was converted under the ministry of Howell Harris when a youth of nineteen. He immediately began to serve the Lord Jesus, beginning to exhort his fellow-sinners. When his friend Thomas William was appointed a superintendent at the Watford Association, William Edwards, as a private exhorter, was made an assistant under him. He himself was not appointed a superintendent, not because of any lack of ability or suitableness, but because of the importance and multiplicity of his secular concerns. As well as being an exhorter, he kept a smallholding, and was busy with his building work. A proof of his popularity is the decision of the Watford Association of 24 April 1744, that the private exhorters were not to speak in public other than in the private societies, with the exception of William Edwards, who was called to Llantrisant and Groes-wen. His name was included amongst the exhorters of Groes-wen in a letter they sent to the Association, and he was ordained a minister there at the same time as Thomas William. When his friend died he became the sole minister at Groes-wen, and there he laboured with much acceptance until the day of his death. He considered himself a Methodist all his life. He accepted a little remuneration from the church for his labours, but never gave up his secular occupations. He continued to build bridges and churches and to maintain his smallholding, as well as preaching the gospel. He died in 1789 when seventy years old and was buried in Eglwysilan cemetery. His family has professed the faith down to our day. His great-grandson is Dr Edwards, Cardiff, who is not only well-known as a physician, but is also a truly religious man.

## JOHN BELCHER AND THOMAS PRICE

Very little is known of the three other Groes-wen exhorters who signed this letter to the Association, namely, Thomas Price, John Belcher and Evan Thomas. Of Evan Thomas, we know only the name. John Belcher was the ablest of the five and the most popular. It was decided at the Watford conference, on 27 April 1744, that a second man be appointed to give himself fully to the work as an assistant to Howell Harris and to help the superintendents in their various localities. After much deliberation on personal gifts and public abilities, they decided upon John Belcher as the most suitable for the work. The Rev. John Hughes concluded that this appointment was made mainly with an eye to the north, but this is incorrect. The resolution states that his area was to be Monmouthshire, Glamorganshire and Carmarthenshire. A note in the minutes of the Monthly Meeting at Llanfihangel on 3 May 1744, suggests that he hesitated much over the question of communicating in the Established Church, but that he promised to keep his doubts to himself. Towards the end of 1745 or the beginning of 1746, he was chosen, along with three other exhorters, to visit Gwynedd in the hope of winning it for the gospel. This is the last reference that we have to him. Whether he died young, or whether he joined the Dissenters, we do not know.

Little also is known of the history of Thomas Price, the owner of Watford mansion, whom Williams, Pantycelyn, calls 'Price the Justice'. In all probability he was convicted under the preaching of Howell Harris and immediately opened his home to the Methodists. He left Watford Chapel because of the heresy of David Williams and joined the Methodists at Groes-wen. He was made superintendent over a number of societies in Glamorganshire, in association with Thomas William, and many of his society reports still exist. Though he signed the letter to the Association, and remained in membership at Groes-wen after they had ordained a minister, he continued a Methodist to the day of his death, and the Reformers were lodged at his home as before. It seems that he stopped preaching quite early on. A letter of his to the Association asking to be released from the work was published in the *Weekly History*. He does not give the reason for the request. It would seem however that his gifts were not as pronounced as some of his brethren and that he was already being troubled by asthma. He was the father-in-law of Grace Price, to whom Williams, Pantycelyn, wrote a famous elegy. His son, Nathaniel, was her husband. And Thomas Price, though weak and confined to the house, was still alive when his godly daughter-in-law died. This is known from the following stanza of the elegy:

| | |
|---|---|
| Price the Justice, you have suffered, | Price y Justis, ti gest golled, |
| Asthma held you in your home, | Rwymodd asthma ar dy stôl. |
| Now your daughter's gone to heaven, | Aeth dy ferch i ganol nefoedd, |
| And has left you all alone; | Fe'th adawyd dithau'n ôl; |
| Wait a little, practise patience, | Aros ronyn, trwy amynedd, |
| In this lowly, desert land, | Yn y dyrys anial dir, |
| Soon you'll join your godly daughter, | Ti gai gyda gwraig y capten |
| Singing with the heavenly band. | Ganu anthem cyn bo hir. |

## MORGAN JOHN LEWIS

Another well-known exhorter who laboured diligently at the beginning of the Methodist Revival was the Rev. Morgan John Lewis. In all probability he was a native of Blaenau Gwent, and was convicted during Howell Harris's first journey to Monmouthshire in 1738. He soon began to exhort and there are many references to him in the Trefeca records. He was one of those appointed to be public exhorters at the First Association at Watford. At the next Association there, he was made Superintendent over the societies of Dôl-y-gaer, Cwmdu, Defynnog and Llywel, in Breconshire; Llanddeusant in Carmarthenshire; and the whole of Monmouthshire on the Welsh side of the Usk. Many of the reports that he sent in are still extant.

At the Association in Llanfihangel on 3 May 1744, there was an important debate on the appropriateness of continuing to receive communion in the Church of England. It seems that it was Morgan John Lewis who opened the debate, and that he was firmly of the view that the Methodists should ordain their own ministers. The decision arrived at was to refrain from doing so until clearer guidance was obtained, and the minutes state that:

Brother Morgan John Lewis agreed by way of forebearance till the Lord should thrust us out or bring in a reformation.[5]

He took a leading part also in the argument at the Llanidloes Association between the followers of Rowland and those of Harris, which terminated in the Disruption. Again, it seems that it was he who raised the matter. He supported Rowland, and it was with the Llangeitho Reformer and with Williams, Pantycelyn, that he threw in his lot. He lived in the New Inn region of Monmouthshire and, after the Disruption, preached mainly to the small flock that gathered there. The fellowship increased greatly when the evangelical Anglicans, who could not abide the unevangelical ministry of the Llanfrechfa clergyman, joined them. As a result a chapel was built with a stable attached to it. This was in 1751. But the members were not able to receive communion. Their consciences would not allow them to attend the services of the irreligious clergy in the parish church, and they did not wish to join the Nonconformists. In their dilemma, they sent two messengers to Daniel Rowland asking for advice. He, having listened to them and considered their case seriously, advised them to call Morgan John Lewis as a minister, with prayer and fasting, and he added:

The prayer of faith will do him much more good than the hands of any bishop under the sun.

Daniel Rowland was a notably liberal man; his commitment to the Church of England was nothing like as strong as that of Howell Harris, and he gave little weight to episcopal ordination. His advice was accepted by the New Inn congregation. All the members met together. After reading passages of the Word, singing and praying, the preacher testified to the articles of his faith, and the church then raised their hands to show their acceptance of him as minister over them. One of the elders then stood up, and in a most serious and deliberate way pronounced Morgan John Lewis as the minister for Christ over the New Inn Church, receiving the care of the Church from the Lord. It is said in *Methodistiaeth Cymru* that this took place at Whitsun 1756, but we judge that it must have been earlier.

This ordination, the first amongst the Methodists, caused much excitement. Churchmen condemned them with much bitterness, as they considered that to administer the sacraments without episcopal ordination was a work of sacrilege and blasphemy. Nonconformists condemned them just as bitterly, in that no other ordained minister had taken part in the ceremony. In their own way, these Nonconformists were just as narrow as the Churchmen, and believed just as strongly in a form of apostolic succession. Morgan John Lewis and the church at New Inn had more open views – views closer to that of the New Testament – as to the nature of ministerial ordination. Mr Lewis would say:

> Much ostracism, bitterness, lack of brotherly love and scorn was directed towards us. We were publicly opposed at the first opportunity. But the way that we profess appears to us to be in more agreement with the way of the gospel, and answers better to the purpose, namely the public choice, or ordination, of ministers. We desire that the Lord help us all to forebear with one another in love.

Because of the ferocity of the storm that arose against the New Inn church, and because the stories and rumours which were spread abroad about them were so untrue, Morgan John Lewis judged it best to publish a kind of Confession of Faith, in which he expressed clearly what he believed.

New Inn was a Methodist church for the whole of the time that Morgan John Lewis was associated with it. Indeed, the Dissenting churches of the land would have nothing to do with it. No Nonconformist minister would on any account supply its pulpit. They were kept outside the camp, just like the lepers of old in Israel. One could imagine that they had committed the unpardonable sin in calling a man to be a minister according to the way that they judged closest to the New Testament teaching. Such is the strength and cruelty of prejudice! However, the Methodist exhorters would visit them on their journeys, cheering the hearts of both minister and congregations by their ministry.

Morgan John Lewis laboured there for another fifteen years, with much success. The whole locality around New Inn was affected by his ministry.

Many came to listen to him from places up to fifteen miles away. The end of his usefulness came about in a very strange way. On a Sunday, the last in which he preached at New Inn, he went in the evening to hold a service at a farmhouse near Pontypool, about a mile out of the town. He slept that night in the house where he had preached. The next day, before he awoke, the owner of the farm arrived with a military officer at his side. He called his tenant and asked him, 'Where is the man who preached here last night?' He received the nervous answer that the man was in bed. 'We must see him,' said the gentleman, 'We wish to speak with him.' The man offered to call him down, but this would not do for the landlord; he rushed up the stairs and burst without ceremony into the preacher's bedroom. There the man of God slept with no thought of any danger. The soldier drew his sword and, standing by the side of the bed and holding his sword above the preacher, he shouted out, 'Heretic, wake up!' Awake he did, and his first sight was of a drawn sword over his head, ready to pierce him. The experience was so sudden and terrifying, without any time for him to appreciate the situation, that it proved sufficient to shatter his constitution and confuse his mind. He recovered to some degree after a time, but he never again preached. He lost all confidence and assurance, and was unable to be of any service to others. Within a year he had slipped into the grave. The Rev. John Hughes used to say:

> As far as appearances were concerned, it would seem that Satan had gained the upper hand. It was New Inn and Monmouthshire; yes, and the whole of Wales that had suffered loss.

Morgan John Lewis was a fine theologian. He possessed a deep knowledge of God's Word and a profound discernment of its teachings. He preached with power and fluency, and men trembled under the influence of his word. He was always deeply serious, and it was said that he was never seen to smile. He was also a true Christian, and a deeply humble man. He died about 1771, having served the Methodist Connexion for about thirty years.

## DAVID WILLIAMS, LLYSWORNEY

Another excellent and useful preacher was the Rev. David Williams of Llysworney. It is stated in *Methodistiaeth Cymru* that he was from Llandyfaelog in Carmarthenshire. Almost certainly this is a mistake, and he was in reality a native of Tregaron. He was born, raised, and came to religion, in that town. He is that David Williams referred to by John Hughes as an exhorter living in Tregaron during the commencement of the cause there. In *Hanes Eglwysi Annibynnol Cymru*[6] it is said that he was at Blaenpennal and a pupil of Philip Pugh, but that when the Methodist Revival broke out he joined Daniel Rowland at Llangeitho. There is no foundation for this at all. The assertion is supported only by an: 'it seems that'. It arises from an inordinate desire to make all the early Methodist exhorters proselytes from Dissent. The probable truth is the very opposite. David Williams was only a seventeen-year old youth when Daniel Rowland began to arouse the country. It is probable that he was typical of his peers in his indifference to God and spiritual matters and that it was the passionate strength of the ministry of the Llangeitho Reformer that conquered him and brought him to religion. Soon, in the warmth of his first love, he began to exhort, and his winning gifts brought him to Rowland's attentions. At the second Association at Watford, David Williams was appointed superintendent in Cardiganshire. Whether all the societies of the county were in his care, or only some of them, is not stated. None of the reports sent to the Association bear his name.

When it was decided to send four of the best-known preachers to the north, because of the low state of religion there, David Williams was among them. His labours were so successful and his ministry so acceptable, that it is said he received a pressing offer to settle in Bala. As he travelled through the north he was often subjected to rough treatment. He was once announced to preach in a small house at Caergwrle, Flintshire. He arrived early but as it began to darken a young girl rushed into the house with the news that a mob of persecutors was at hand. The owner got up and locked the door. At that, the mob arrived and, amidst much swearing and noise, demanded that the preacher be sent out. This the household would not agree to. Their refusal excited the crowd further and they threatened that if their demand was not met they would pull the house to pieces. Some of them ran to fetch crowbars in order to carry out their evil purpose. David Williams therefore decided to go out amongst them. When they tried to stop him, he said, 'Let me go; I must go out to them.' He strode out into the midst of the enraged mob and looking at them fearlessly, said, 'In the name of the Lord, what have you to do with a stranger on his journey? What name or honour would you gain were you to kill me?' One of the mob happened to be a strong man, who had not completely lost all sense of honour. This man stood forward and, together with a mouthful of oaths, said, 'This is a good man. I wish him fair play.' David Williams saw that, almost miraculously, a door had been opened for him to preach. He found something at the side of the road that he could stand upon and, in the light of the moon, he preached to them with great influence, and no doubt the Sun of Righteousness did not hide its face from them. His persecutors were as quiet as the dogs of Egypt and departed peaceably. The Rev. Edward Morgan of Syston narrates a variant of the history. He says that the persecutors dragged the preacher to a nearby lake and were about to drown him when he cried out, ' It will be an eternal shame upon the people of Caergwrle if they drowned a grey-haired old preacher, who had come from the faraway south to preach salvation to them.' And this is when, according to Mr Morgan, the strong man interceded on his behalf.

It seems that David Williams moved to Llysworney in order to supervise the many small societies that had been formed in the Vale of Glamorgan, and that Daniel Rowland had the main hand in his resettlement. He soon married a Miss Pritchard of Tal-y-garn, a member of a very respectable family. When a desire arose in the societies to have some of the exhorters as ministers, David Williams was ordained minister over the church at Aberthin. In Hanes Eglwysi Annibynnol Cymru it is said that this occurred in 1766, but we believe it took place a good deal earlier. Just as it sought to make Mr Williams an Independent when a youth, this same book would make him an Independent from his ordination onwards. It states that he was ordained according to the Independent form. This is not true. The tradition is that his ordination was similar in manner to that of Morgan John Lewis. The little flock at Aberthin had failed to receive a regular administration of the sacraments amongst them from the Methodist clergymen. At this time, Davies had not come to Neath, nor Jones to Llan-gan. The members were not willing to receive communion from the unconverted clergy of their parishes and they sought Daniel Rowland's advice. He suggested that they ordain David Williams. They proceeded to do so, and he administered the sacrament to them until the day of his death. There is no mention that any Dissenting ministers were asked to take part in the ceremony. More than probably they followed the example of the New Inn congregation. The story again illustrates how free Daniel Rowland was, and how he was able to rise above the petty prejudices of Churchmen and Dissenters alike, and also how loosely they were bound to the Established Church. In exactly the same way, Thomas Williams, who was for many years a member with David Williams at Aberthin, was ordained minister over Bethesda-y-Fro, as is shown by a minute in the handwriting of the old hymn writer, John Williams of St Athan.

David Williams remained as much a Methodist after his ordination as he was before, and Aberthin Church is Methodist to this day. He administered the Lord's Supper every month, and on these occasions large numbers of the saints from the surrounding areas would gather. Nor did he give up his journeying. He attended the Monthly Meetings and the Associations and, like his brethren, he travelled throughout Wales to evangelize. He was a man who was mighty in the Scriptures. It is said that it was he who showed the way of God more perfectly to David Jones, Llan-gan, and who guided that excellent man in his theology. His ministry was noted for its tenderness. He was no Boanerges, standing on Mount Ebal thundering curses forth upon an immoral world, but a Son of Consolation, applying the Balm of Gilead to the wounds of those who were already bruised and hurt. His gift was to win people and he did so with the sweetest of voices. John Evans of Bala said of him, 'He was a gentle man and very tender, and a wondrously fresh and reviving preacher.' And of him and John Belcher, the same man said:

> The two of them came to us alternately for many years, in the face of many weaknesses and difficulties. We were all of us poor and could hardly provide them with lodging and a little food, after they had made the great effort to come to us. The brethren in the south were kind enough to support them, otherwise they could not have paid their way in coming to us.

David Williams experienced many difficulties at Aberthin. Sabellianism came into the churches and was the cause of much debate and controversy. But he maintained an orthodox faith and died in peace, leaving Glamorganshire to mourn after him. It should be noted that he was the brother, after the flesh, of John Williams, St Athan.

## WILLIAM RICHARD

We know very little of William Richard, the superintendent of the societies of south Cardiganshire, together with all those along the coast of Pembrokeshire as far as St David's, other than what is found in the Trefeca records. He was one of Daniel Rowland's converts and began exhorting almost as soon as he was converted. The first reference to him is in the minutes of a Monthly Meeting at Llanddeusant when a number of societies were placed under his care. He is mentioned also at the second Watford Association, where it is noted that he was to remain where he was until the Dygoedydd Association. At the Monthly Meeting at Glanyrafonddu, the societies of Blaenhownant, Dyffryn Saith, Blaenporth, Twr-gwyn and Llechryd were again placed in his care, and he is referred to as William Richard of Llanddewibrefi. Whether he was living at Llanddewibrefi at this time, we do not know. He was probably born and raised there, but had now been living for some time in the Cardigan region. In the works of William Williams, Pantycelyn, there is an elegy to a William Richard of Abercarfan in Llanddewibrefi parish, who died of consumption in 1770.

There are many things in the elegy which suggest that this is the same man as William Richard the exhorter.

Williams wrote:

| | |
|---|---|
| Poor Llanfrynach still is weeping | Mae Llanfrynach wan yn wylo |
| To this day, in memory of him. | Hyd yn awr, wrth gofio amdano. |

Llanfrynach lies near the junction of three counties, Pembrokeshire, Cardiganshire and Carmarthenshire, and was therefore close to the region entrusted to William Richard, if not indeed part of that region. If we are correct in our supposition, William Richard experienced strong emotions at the beginning of his religious life. He had jumped and gloried under the influence of Rowland's fiery ministry and he kept his crown to the end of his days. He is described by Williams as follows:

| | |
|---|---|
| Him I saw at his first loving, | Gwelais ef ar oriau hyfryd, |
| At the morn of his awakening, | Ym moreuddydd braf ei fywyd, |
| Jumping, praising, Christ exalting, | Yn moliannu, yn proffwydo, |
| Foremost of Llangeitho's gathering; | Yn flaena' o'r werin yn Llangeitho; |
| With the perspiration streaming, | Chwys fel nentydd clir yn llifo, |
| From his clothes a mist a-rising; | Tarth trwy ei wisgoedd tew yn suo; |
| It is meet, thus to greet, | Cariad pur, gwerthfawr clir, |
| with sweet worship, | yn gwir ennynnu, |
| Till the body gives assistance | Nes oedd corff yn gorfod helpu |
| In expressing heartfelt utterance. | Enaid allan i'w fynegu. |
| | |
| Him I saw upon his deathbed | Mi fum unwaith wrth ei wely, |
| As his soul on glory feasted, | 'Roedd ei wledd fel gwleddoedd gwindy, |
| All his words his trust confessing, | A'i holl eiriau'n tarddu'n gyson, |
| Full of faith and never fearing; | O grediniaeth, heb ddim ofon; |
| Men were blessed while parting | Gwyr yn twymo wrth y siarad, |
| from him, | |
| Women wept, from love towards him; | Merched, hwythau'n wylo cariad; |
| As for me, sinful me, I could see | Minnau f'hun, waelaf ddyn, gwanaidd, |
| before me, | yn gwenu, |
| One who was a child precede me, | Ac yn hyfryd eiddigeddu, |
| I am left, in sweetest envy. | Weled plentyn arna i'n blaenu. |

The description is notable for its liveliness. We can almost see him in his early days, dressed in his thick homespun clothes, as was then the custom. The views of the Saviour's glory that arose before his mind's eye were so glorious that his body had to help his soul to give them utterance. As he jumped and praised, the sweat streamed down his face and his clothes became as soaked as if he had been out in a thick mist. As he clearly combined an extensive religious knowledge with great ability in his dealings with new converts, it is no wonder that societies along the coast of two counties were placed under his supervision. We may suppose that he eventually moved back to Llanddewibrefi, and that he remained there until his death. In his last years his spiritual experiences were not to be calm and placid. He was caught up in heated controversies but he endured faithfully through all tribulations. William Williams gives a further account:

| | |
|---|---|
| You, Llanddewi, almost sheared him, | Ti, Llanddewi, fu'n agosa' |
| With your troubles oft provoked him, | Gneifio'r blew oedd ar ei gopa, |
| Exercised his full endurance | Mwg a thân fu iddo'n galed |
| In the strife twixt Turks and Indians; | Yn y ffrae rhwng Twrcs ac Indiaid; |
| But brave Will stood up before you | Ond fe safodd Wil i fyny |
| When tearful Evan failed to melt you. | Pan oedd Evan laith yn methu. |

We do not know the cause of the controversy, or who the 'Turks and Indians' were who strove together over it, nor the identity of 'tearful Evan' who failed to hold his ground. What is important is to realize that William Richard:

| | |
|---|---|
| Through the barren wastes endured, | O'r anialwch mawr i fyny, |
| Never broken, never conquered. | Heb ei ladd, heb ei orchfygu. |

## BENJAMIN THOMAS

The Rev. Benjamin Thomas was an Independent minister who joined the Methodists. We know very little of his history. In the minutes of the second Watford Association, two Nonconformist ministers are referred to. One was the Rev. Henry Davies of Bryngwrach, who was present, and the other was the Rev. Benjamin Thomas. Their names are included amongst those of the ordained clergy. It may be supposed that Nonconformist ordination was considered as authoritative as episcopal ordination. Howell Harris's name is lower down, amongst the laity. The Methodist Fathers, for all their allegiance to the Established Church, were not men governed by their prejudices. 'The Rev. B. Thomas' was noted as present at the Trefeca Association in the summer of 1743, and at the Abergavenny Association of the following March. In October 1744, at Porth-y-rhyd Association, it was decided that Benjamin Thomas should assist Howell Harris as Superintendent over all Wales, in place of Herbert Jenkins who had chosen England as his main field of labour.

Mr Thomas travelled extensively throughout north and south Wales and did not escape persecution more than others of his brethren. There is an account of him preaching at one time at Minffordd, in a building that had been legally licensed as a place of worship. A mob of persecutors arrived carrying heavy staves, one of which was tipped with iron. They sought to hit the preacher with this, but the blow fell upon a Howell Thomas of Plas Llangefni. It was such a violent blow that the iron head broke off and flew over the hedge into a ditch on the other side. The persecutors followed the congregation for more than a quarter of a mile, hitting and beating them mercilessly, until the road was stained by blood. It seems that Benjamin Thomas escaped comparatively unhurt as he was quick on his feet.

Benjamin Thomas's main characteristic as a preacher was tenderness; the tears would flow down his cheeks as he exhorted sinners. He once preached at Pontuchel, Denbighshire. A man called Thomas Parry, a thoughtful man of strong Anglican allegiance and much prejudiced against the Methodists, came to hear him. His brother had encouraged him to attend the service.

'You will see, Twm,' said the brother, 'that the man preaches from his heart, for the tears stream down his face.'

The message of the sermon was regeneration. Thomas Parry had long desired to hear a sermon on this point, but the clergyman that ministered at his church never referred to the matter. But the preacher from the south more than satisfied his curiosity, and provided him with a full theological explanation of the doctrine. The truth gripped his conscience, and he became a new man from that day onwards. He afterwards became well-known as Thomas Parry, Rhewl – one of the wisest and most useful of all the elders of Gwynedd. We do not know where or when the Rev. Benjamin Thomas ended his career. It seems however that he sided with Rowland at the time of the Disruption, and that he continued to evangelize amongst the Methodists to the day of his death.

## JOHN HARRIS, ST KENNOX, AND JOHN HARRIES, AMBLESTON.

There were two exhorters in Pembrokeshire, of similar names, whose histories have been hopelessly mixed in *Methodistiaeth Cymru*. One was John Harris of St Kennox who, as early as 1743 was appointed superintendent over the societies of Llawhaden, Prendergast, Jefferson, Carew, Llandysilio and Gellidawel. The other was John Harries (or Harris, or Harry), Ambleston, a private exhorter. The first was by far the more famous. It seems that he was a most cheerful man, abounding in genius, a scholar in Welsh and in English, and of great courage. To show his character we can do no better than quote some of his letters to the Associations. This is how he wrote to the Monthly Association at Longhouse, 28 September 1743, addressing Daniel Rowland and Howell Davies:

Dear and kind shepherds,

At last, I am persuaded, from love to the dear Immanuel, to inform you of my condition since the last Monthly Association, when you placed upon me the care of various societies. When I was asked then as to my liberty [i.e., liberty to go about to supervise the societies] I answered as was expected of me. But the thought came to my mind immediately, how could I, who am only a babe in experience, presume to act as a balance for weighing souls? I thought to myself then that if some error in explaining took place, it would be far less damaging to a soul than if I were to judge mistakenly between flesh and spirit, and between true and false love. However, the word, 'At liberty,' by which I then answered you has been as a chain that has bound me to look to that which I undertook. Fear fell upon my soul, lest I be not only unfaithful to the dear Lamb, but also a grief to my beloved teachers, and a disgrace to God's ways and to his children. This burden became so great that body and soul were almost overcome under it. I was in agonies for some time, thinking more of the Association, where I would be called to give an account of my steward-ship, than of the Day of Judgment. I gave myself to writing to the societies to arrange their meetings in order and at appropriate times, appearing to them as someone of authority.

Assuredly, John Harris, who could write like this, was no ordinary man. The same John Harris, St Kennox, related, in a letter dated 12 May 1745, the history of a visit he made to the neighbourhood of Tenby:

By now there is no part of the county which I have not visited to exhort, except for Pembroke town and the borough of Tenby, which is a port about five or six miles from Pembroke. I discoursed last Friday night at a place about two miles from Tenby. Only one believing brother lives in the town; he has often sought for me to visit the place; I wrote to him that I would come to stay at his house, and that if he saw best to invite a number of men and women whom he knew, and who wished to hear me, to come and meet me, then I would expound a few verses in the back room. This he did. But when I was at the middle of the service, the constable entered, saying, 'Sir, you must stop. I am ordered by the mayor to bring you before him immediately.' I said that I would agree to the request, but that as I was now about the work of another Master, that I asked leave to deliver my message from him first. At that, he left the room. But before I finished, the curate entered, together with constables and four or five of the gentry. The curate desired the officer to haul me out. The latter answered, 'It would be a shame to do that before he finished, for he is discoursing sweetly.'

'Down with him,' said the curate, 'otherwise I will bring the law upon you for neglecting your duty.'

Though the men (the constables) were half drunk, I had leave to finish the service. Indeed, it was a blessing to my soul, and to my amiable hearers, who numbered about forty. I got down from the place where I stood and while the officers excused themselves to the man of the house their faces were a wonderful shade of grey.

'We came, Mr Thomas,' they said, 'to see the wonderful pictures that you own.'

'I imagine,' I answered, 'that I was the picture you came to see.'

At that, the officer placed his hand upon my shoulder saying,

'You are a prisoner, Sir, and must come before the mayor.'

'I am ready to come,' I replied.

When we got out to the street it was between nine and ten o'clock at night, and there were about a thousand men and women with lanterns and candles awaiting me, and crying out in horror,

'Away with him! Away with him!'

To the mayor we went. He, without looking at me in the face, asked me for my licence. I answered that I did not have one. He asked,

'How is it you dare come to our town to preach?'

To this I replied, 'I was not announced to preach; but after the people knew of my coming here to stay, they came to the house. I expounded a few verses to them, we sang a hymn or two, and we prayed.'

'You must provide a surety,' said the mayor,' for your appearance here the next Quarter Sessions.'

'I would be glad to learn, Sir, what charge you lay against me?'

'Your work in preaching,' he replied.

'If that is the charge, sir, I will provide sureties willingly. What will be the sum required?'

'Two hundred pounds,' was the answer.

Two of the brethren were willing to be bound over for this sum, but a by-stander asked,

'Would you be willing to give your word that if you were presently freed, you would not come here again to preach?'

'That I cannot do, ' I replied. 'Although I did not come here at this time to preach, there is no certainty that I will not be called to preach here before tomorrow, for I do not have authority over myself.'

'Who is it that has authority over you?' asked the mayor's wife.

'I am under the authority of my Master.'

'Who is your master? Is it the devil?'

'No. My Master is master over the devil, and over you yourselves also.'

'Hush,' said the mayor to his wife. 'Be quiet.'

With that, he called upon me to sign the bond and I was set free.

Such was John Harris's report of his experiences at Tenby. When he went out into the street again a mob of rioters were waiting for him, full of fury and ready to attack him. He was unexpectedly protected by a magistrate, who was sympathetic towards the Methodists. This man took him to his house and looked after him as if he were a king. Harris continued:

I returned home the next day, with the tears flowing down my cheeks from true compassion for the poor souls of Tenby.

What occurred at the Sessions, we do not know. Most probably, the Lord, according to his usual manner towards those who love his name, defended his servant and brought him safely from amongst the lions.

John Harris's history from the Disruption onwards lies in darkness. It is said that he took Howell Harris's side, and that when he realized that his party was weakening and would inevitably die away, he joined the Moravians, following the example of the exhorter, John Sparks of Haverfordwest.

Of John Harries or Harry, Ambleston, it is thought that he was a native of the northern parts of Pembrokeshire who at about the time of the revival moved down to the south. The first reference to him in the Trefeca records surfaces in the minutes of the Llangwm Monthly Association of 16 July, 1744. It was there decided that Brother John Harry be recommended, and that he was to continue to exhort as previously until the next Monthly Meeting, under the supervision of Brother William Richard. At the Haverfordwest Association of 28 January, 1745, it was decided that as Brothers John Harry and John Morris were schoolteachers they should exhort as much as was possible consistent with their school duties. John Harry seems to have been a very hard-working man who made the most of every opportunity to exhort his fellow-sinners concerning their eternal destiny. He lodged once at a farmhouse and did not neglect to warn those who served him. The next morning, the mistress asked her young maid:

'Go and return the stranger's boots to him.'

'No I certainly will not,' was the reply.

'Why ever not?'

'Because he will tell me I'm a sinner,' she answered.

Proof indeed that John Harries wasted no opportunity to do good.

The remarkable Rowland Hill, the minister of Surrey Chapel, London, had a great respect for John Harries's godliness. Mr Hill preached once at Ambleston, after the death of the old exhorter but when his widow and son, the Rev. Evan Harris, were still living in the village. As he departed, he said to them, 'If you get to heaven before me, remember me to John Harry, and tell him that I also am on my way.' On another occasion, the Rev. Thomas Harris, the grandson of John Harries, called at Mr Hill's home in London.

'Who are you,' asked the minister.

'I am the grandson of the late John Harry of Ambleston,' replied the visitor.

At that, Mr Hill stood up, looked at the young man and said with much feeling:

'If there is one man from this polluted world who is in heaven, it is John Harry.'

It may be that it was his kinship with John Harries that lay behind the call to Thomas Harris to minister in the church at Wotton-under-edge, Gloucestershire, where he stayed for many years. The Ambleston evangelist remained faithful to Daniel Rowland during the years of division and was immensely useful in the Methodist circles of Pembrokeshire throughout his life. He preached once a month at the chapel in Woodstock. The Sundays there were named after the preachers ministering. The first Sunday of the month was 'Rowland's Sunday'; 'John Harry's Sunday' was the second. The third was 'Henry Richard's Sunday', the father of Ebenezer and Thomas Richard; and the last, 'William Griffith's Sunday'. John Harries died in the year 1788, in the house of the vicar of Newport, Pembrokeshire. At the funeral, Sampson Thomas preached, from the words, 'Blessed are the dead which die in the Lord.' Daniel Rowland also preached a funeral sermon for him at Ambleston, taking the text, 'And if the righteous scarcely be saved, where shall the ungodly and the sinner appear?' Old John Harry has still some of his kith and kin ministering the things of God to this day. His son was the Rev. Evan Harris, who was amongst the very first men to be ordained by the Methodists at Llandeilo in 1811. Evan's son was the Rev. Thomas Harris, an exceptionally gifted man, whose ministerial career eventually took him into the Church of England. John Harris's great-grandson is the Rev. James Harris, Clarbeston Road, Pembrokeshire; and we understand that the latter has also a son who has recently entered the ministry.

## WILLIAM EDWARD, RHYD-Y-GELE

One of the most remarkable exhorters of Pembrokeshire was William Edward, Rhyd-y-gele. We read of him in the Trefeca records being given permission to visit weekly the societies of St David's, Penrhos and Mounton, on trial until the next Association. He was full of fire and passion, was very gifted, and possessed the ability to address sinners, but was naturally awkward and uncultivated in his manner. He was a Methodist, he had been converted under Howell Harris, but had mixed much amongst the Dissenters and when attending their special services sat with their ministers. They considered him too fiery and irregular. He thought them lifeless and unevangelical. He explained to them once the difference between his way of preaching and theirs, using the illustration of a house on fire:

Your way is to say, 'On travelling one night, firstly, I perceived a fire. Secondly, I saw smoke. Thirdly, I understood that a house was on fire. Fourthly, I knew that the family inside were asleep. Fifthly, I came to wake you and to call you, in case you were destroyed.' My own method, on seeing the house aflame and the family asleep, is to shout out, with no firstly or secondly, 'Hey! Hey! Fire! Fire! Awake! Come out at once or you will be burnt to ashes!'

William Edward was a carpenter by trade. His work took him once amongst the English who lived in the south of Pembrokeshire, and in particular to the mansion of a family of some rank. Soon the story was abroad that the carpenter was a preacher. On inquiring and finding that the rumour was true, the lady of the house arranged that he might address the household on the following Sunday. The Sunday arrived, and William Edward climbed on top of a stool so that he might be higher than his hearers. He took a book out of his pocket and proceeded to read from it in English as a text, 'Whoever sends their servant or maid to dig potatoes or to collect cabbages on a Sabbath morning will be damned forever.' 'That is my text, ma'am,' he said, 'now, with your permission, I will proceed.' But her ladyship's wrath was drawn. She was not innocent before such an accusation, and she shrieked at him, 'No you may not proceed, you fool. Come down immediately. No more of such nonsense!' And down he had to come, without having accomplished anything more than reading his text, and the service was concluded. The story demonstrates the fiery zeal of the exhorter, but also its tendency to break out wildly, not being under the control of a wise and prudent spirit.

His temper was often a snare to William Edward. He once got in an argument with his neighbour, Thomas Hooper. The strife was so fierce that in his excitement William Edward pushed his opponent so that he fell headlong against some tool that cut a deep wound in his forehead. The rumour spread that William Edwards, Rhyd-y-gele, the gospel preacher, had hit his neighbour so hard with a pickaxe as to cut open his skull. It is easier to imagine than to describe the anxiety that this story would have aroused in religious circles. The matter was brought before the society. He denied that he hit Thomas Hooper. But the members did not believe him; the evidence of the wound seemed against him. It was decided that he be thrown out. Before leaving, he asked permission to pray. The prayer was remarkable! The old pilgrim groaned in repentance before the throne, pleading for forgiveness, and appealing to the omniscience of the Almighty that he had not done that of which he was accused. 'My brethren refuse to believe me,' he said, 'but Thou dost know, Mighty Lord, that I did not strike Thomas Hooper in the head with a pickaxe.' His fellow-members were overcome, and having been thoroughly convinced that he had intended no harm, they allowed him to remain with them. The occasion was a lesson to him all his life. He afterwards became as renowned for his gentleness and patience as he had been for his impulsiveness. At the end of his life all who knew him held him in great respect.

## OTHER EXHORTERS

We must now leave the exhorters, though their histories are so entertaining and have so much to teach us. The time would fail us to tell of John Richard, Llansamlet, warm-spirited and honest of heart, who having taken offence at the way in which the leaders of the Association had curtailed his sphere of work, returned to his place eventually, confessing his fault and asking for pardon; or of Howell Griffith, Trefeurig, an educated man of good circumstances, who was of much usefulness to the Lord's cause in the region of Llantrisant, Tonyrefail and the Vale of Glamorgan, and who was not above receiving a loving rebuke from his brethren when they thought that he was tending to wander; of James Williams, the superintendent of the Carmarthenshire societies, whose reports of the state of his societies have been preserved and are full of interest; of Milbourn Bloom, who lived at Llanarthne and at whose house was held that notable Monthly Meeting when the Spirit of God fell as a flame upon his people, warming their hearts and causing them to praise his name; of Morgan Hughes, who was once the superintendent of the societies of Montgomeryshire, and afterwards, together with Williams, Pantycelyn, was superintendent of the societies of the upper part of Cardiganshire, who, for his pains in going about to evangelize, was summoned to the Cardigan Assizes in 1743, but having arrived there was set free because there was no one present to prosecute his case; and of many others.

Taking them as a class, these old exhorters were excellent men. Their only weakness, if indeed it was a weakness, was their longing to be ordained so that they could administer the sacraments, as did the Dissenting ministers. The majority of them had little sympathy with the Church of England; their sympathy towards the Nonconformists was greater. And when their leaders would not allow them ordination, many went over to the Dissenters, taking charge of churches and serving their Lord and their generation faithfully. This is how the Connexion lost such men as Evan Williams, whose flight from the north because of persecution we mentioned; and John Thomas, who settled at Rhayader; and Richard Tibbott, Herbert Jenkins, Milbourn Bloom; and many other talented men. But the majority remained faithful however great the temptation to leave. We lose sight of many of them during the time of the Disruption, and what became of them we do not know. Some became Independents; others wandered from the faith, forming various sects and placing themselves at their head; but for the most part they cleaved to Rowland, Howell Davies and Williams, Pantycelyn, and remained until their deaths, diligent reapers of the harvest, their sickles in their hands.

## SOME OF THE REPORTS SENT TO THE ASSOCIATIONS

We come now to the reports of the exhorters sent to the Associations describing the conditions of the societies under their care. These reports are so numerous that all we can do is to quote some of them almost at random. The very first report contained in the Trefeca records is that of Thomas James, Cerrigcadarn, of which the following are a sample:

BUILTH WELLS SOCIETY. *Exhorter*, Thomas Bowen.

| *Names of members* | *Their condition* |
| --- | --- |
| Thomas James | A full and abiding testimony |
| Thomas Bowen | In abundant liberty |
| Evan Evans | Possesses a profession but weak in faith |
| Sarah Williams | Has been justified and emerged from the furnace |
| Sarah James | A full testimony but in great bondage |
| Eliza Bowen | Similar, but having deserted it to a great extent |
| Ann Baisdel | A delightful experience but weak |
| Mary Bowen | Diligently seeking the Lord Jesus |
| Margaret Lewis | Has lately been justified |
| Eliza Price | A full testimony, but beginning to perceive more and more the hardness of her heart |
| Susan Davies | Justified, but now under many doubts |
| Margaret Bowen | Similar, but possessing many deep defilements |
| Elenor James | Beginning to recover from her backsliding |
| Gwen James, Susan James and Gwen Kinsey | Gone to glory, as I believe |

The number of members here was 13.

LLANAFAN SOCIETY. *Private exhorters,* Edward Bowen and
Thomas Bowen.

| Names of members | Their condition |
|---|---|
| Rice Price | Bearing a testimony in the midst of affliction |
| Thomas Price | Similar, but having lost much of his love and zeal, having been ensnared by the world |
| Thomas Jones | In great bondage. Waiting |
| Stephen Jones | In much darkness |
| James Evans | Weak in grace, but waiting |
| Thomas Bowen | Often a full testimony, but not consistently |
| Edward Bowen | A full and consistent testimony |
| Eliza Evans | Full of doubts because of the strength of defilement |
| Mary Jones | The following word having been sealed to her: 'I have loved thee with an everlasting love.' |
| Catherine Jones | A sweet testimony of the love of God |
| Mary Price | The same |
| Diana Evans | Walking closely with God, but amidst many doubts |
| Margaret Bound | A full testimony |

Here also the membership was 13.

LLANWRTYD SOCIETY. *Private exhorter,* Rice Morgan.

| Names of members | Their condition |
|---|---|
| Rice Morgan | Walking closely but in some doubt |
| David Williams | Has not been left with any degree of doubt |
| Rice Williams | His condition is very dark |
| Thomas Lloyd | He believes he has a testimony but others not fully satisfied with his condition |
| Edward Winston | In great bondage |
| Roderick Rice | In bondage and darkness |
| Ann Lloyd | Seeking diligently, but in great trials |
| Eliza Evans | On the road and seeking |
| Margaret Evans | In her first love |
| Eliza Williams | Burdened by unbelief |

There were 28 members in this society and they are described as proceeding sweetly forward. He gives similar accounts for the societies of Merthyr Cynog, Llandyfathen, Cerrigcadarn, Llanddewi'r-cwm, and Llanigon. His comments on the various conditions of the members are to the point and often very touching. He says of a William Saunders of Llanigon, 'Has been in much doubt as to the deity of Christ, but now believes not only that he is God, but that he is his God.' Of a Mrs P. from the same society, he says, 'She possesses a full testimony, and walks closely, but her name has not been written because the husband threatens and persecutes.' He adds, of the same society, 'There are seven others seeking admission.'

These reports demonstrate the significant difference in spirituality of thought between the Methodists and the Dissenters of their period. The Rev. John Evans, in the pamphlet we spoke of before[7] listed the members of the Nonconformists according to their wordly position. He divided them into magistrates, squires, those who had the right to vote in the county or borough, free-holders, farmers, traders and labourers. The old exhorter of Cerrigcadarn thinks nothing of such divisions; it is immaterial to him whether a member is a magistrate or a labourer; he divides them according to their spiritual condition: those justified; those still seeking; those trodden underfoot by doubts, etc. The early Methodists lived so closely in the divine presence that the minor categories of earth had no weight in their thinking. But Thomas James has not finished his report. This is what he has to say of the following societies:

| | |
|---|---|
| Trefeca | Not in order |
| Llangamarch | Recently established. |
| | Private exhorter – David. |
| | Number – about 14 |
| Llwyncoll | In order, but it is not convenient for me to provide their number. |
| Llanfihangel-Nant-Bran | The society newly established |
| Llanfihangel-Fechan | They will not yet submit to any order |
| Brecon | Not established |
| Llan-gors | Not brought to order |
| Cilhonwy | The society under Mr Beaumont |
| Diserth | Not proved |

He says that the members for whom he could give an account numbered 134, but that the total would certainly be 200. It must be remembered that only a part of Breconshire was in his care. He ends as follows:

Blessed be our Saviour for this much of a beginning, hoping that he will make his Jerusalem a joy to the whole earth, for truly there is yet room. Therefore, pray much for us, and for me, the unworthy – Thos. James.

Consider further the reports of Morgan Jones, the superintendent of parts of Monmouthshire. He writes as follows:

GOETRE:   They are 13 in number with one steward over them, who is a very careful man. There is here only two married men and none single. Two have been received lately, one a woman as amiable in spirit as any of the others. There are some, I believe, who are Christians but who have not yet joined the private society. The members have enjoyed a measure of liberty, or an awareness that they have been justified, all of them except one, some to a greater, and some to a lesser degree . . . They possess much liberty towards one another and towards Bro. Stephen Jones, their private exhorter. I know that the Lord has blessed my labours amongst them. We possess great liberty, one towards another. Blessed be the holy God, who bore them.

GLASGOED:   They are about 9 in number. Bro. Jones, their private exhorter, also serves as steward and, as I believe, serves them faithfully. They have been set in the very best order considering their circumstances. They meet in private as often as they can, and the Lord blesses them, as he blesses all who meet in such a manner. I do not know of one who is not willing to testify that the Lord blesses them exceedingly in their private gatherings; but as to those who resist, they grow dryer every day. All the members have proved the love of God shed abroad in their hearts to such an extent that they are assured their sins have been forgiven and their iniquities covered. I believe that their experience is solid and true, for their lives correspond to it. They are mainly of the poor but are faithful in their callings, and to one another. They are willing to work to support one another, when one is ill or in need. I have much unity with them, and they with me. Blessed be God for bringing it about, Amen.

ST BRIDES:   They are 14 in number, and I believe that they are substantial Christians in knowledge and experience. I examined them privately and had testimony that they all experience the liberty of the gospel to a great extent, except for three; and one of those three has found that Christ is his, though his faith is very weak. As for the other two, they say that they have not yet obtained a hold upon the Lord, but I believe that they have, and that is the judgment of the other brethren. I thought that they showed clearly that it was God's work, though they sought to hide it. They are tempted by the enemy to believe that they were never convicted, though their hearts appear broken and they are as humble as any I saw.

MYNYDDISLWYN: They are 10 in number, with two stewards over them, and the Lord is blessing the means to them. I, and others also, am assisted when I discourse amongst them. They meet privately once a week, and they receive as much benefit from this as from anything. They are irreproachable in their lives. Some of them have a testimony that they are justified, and the others have a continuous desire to be so.

LLANGADOG: A considerable number gather in the public services to hear the Word, and the Lord provides strength to speak in love. 14 have given in their names. They are too young for one of their number to be chosen to watch over them, but someone comes to them from Llanfihangel as often as possible. They are only beginning to meet in private. I experience great liberty in their company, as they are so like children, very willing to be taught.

TREFETHIN: They are 19 in number, with three stewards. The reason that they have three is because two of them are merchants and are unable to come to all the means. They meet three times a week, and experience much of God's presence amongst them, especially in their private meetings. They walk uprightly, and are, I trust, progressing in the knowledge of the Lord. They are, on the whole, assured of the forgiving love of God. There is a small society at Llanheiddel also that is not willing to be brought into order as yet but, at the same time, there are there many of God's dear children.

GRWYNEFECHAN: The number of members here is 20. They are in order, with two stewards watching over them. They meet three times a week, with one of those meetings being in private. They can all testify to an assurance of being justified, though some do not experience as much consolation as they once did. But I trust that the Lord is amongst them. I felt much power when I was with them last.

CWM-DU: The members number 12. The Lord is shining upon them and pouring his Spirit amongst them more than ever. All of them, except two, have experienced the forgiving love of God. They sometimes have so much of the presence of God that they have to cry out, 'Lord, it is enough.' While praying at times they feel so much of God that they wish they could remain where they are until their time to leave to be with Christ.

CANTREF: They are 14 in number, and I believe for the majority of them that they have been sealed by the Holy Spirit until the day of redemption.

BLAEN-Y-LLYN: They are 20 in number. I examined them privately and had more satisfaction than I believed possible. I believe that the Lord has begun a work in their souls. They appear very honest; as far as I can judge they have committed their souls to Christ; but they have not as yet received much indication of the love of God.

LLYWEL (BRECONSHIRE): They are 18 in number and have been settled in as good an order as I am capable of, with a steward to watch over them. They are determined to meet privately, to see what God will do to their souls. They have been very careless of this. Some of them have felt a measure of the love of God. I find them willing to be taught, but there is no great unity amongst them as they do not meet privately. They should be treated tenderly, as suckling babes on the breast, because of their weakness.

LLANDDEUSANT: There are 28 members here; they have been settled in order with two private stewards over them. They meet publicly twice a week, and once privately. I believe that a great work is being carried out amongst them. They can testify that God is pouring out his Spirit abundantly upon them, especially in their private societies. They are all blameless as to their conversation. They testify that the Lord has blessed me to the profit of their souls. Blessed be the Lord for evermore! Amen and Amen. I felt a remarkable power amongst them the last time, when speaking on the wonderful works of God, from Acts 2:11. There were about 200 present.

N.B. There are a few souls also who meet at Llanfihangel-Cerrig-Cornel, about three miles from Abergavenny, who were forgotten the last time at Watford. I would wish you to think of them, and send someone to visit them. Bro. Morgan John Lewis would be best, I imagine, as Bro. Beaumont does not speak Welsh.

The reports of Thomas Williams, the superintendent of parts of Glamorgan, for the societies under his care, are much briefer in comparison. They are as follows, except for the names, which have been omitted:

GROES-WEN:

|  | Husbands | Wives | Single Men | Single Women |
|---|---|---|---|---|
| Justified | 9 | 8 | 13 | 9 |
| Under the Law | 1 | 2 | 3 | 4 |

The number of ordinary members at Groes-wen was 49. If the five private exhorters were to be added, it would make a total of 54. It was noted also that one young girl, called Amy Price, had died, full of the assurance of faith.

LLANTRISANT:

|  | Husbands | Single Men | Single Women |
|---|---|---|---|
| Justified, and possessing liberty | 4 | 2 | 1 |
| Under the Law | 7 | 2 | 2 |

The membership was therefore 18, and if the account is correct, there were no married wives in membership.

The Llanedern society numbered 6, of which there were 4 justified, and 2 under the law; Dinas Powys, 13, of which there were 2 justified and possessing liberty; 6 justified, but in bondage, and the others under the law; St. Nicholas, 32, of which 15 were justified, and possessing liberty; 11 justified, but under bondage, and the others under the law. Pentyrch society numbered 9; Aberthaw, 15; and Aberthin 19. The total number of members in Thomas Williams's care was 168.

A report from James Williams, the superintendent of part of Carmarthenshire, is notable for its shortness. He notes that Caeo society numbered 49; Talley, 45; Llansawel, 46; Llangathen, 37; Cwmann, 32. Cil-y-cwm society was young and not yet brought to order, and so its numbers were not included. He says of some of the members that they possess liberty; of others, that they seem to be in sight of rest; and of others again that they are under the law. Of those who possess liberty, they are not all on the same ground, for some, he states, have only a small measure of liberty.

A particularly interesting report is that of William Richard, superintendent of the lower part of Cardiganshire and the Welsh-speaking region of Pembrokeshire. Take the following example:

### Dyffryn Saith

| *Names of members* | *Their condition* |
| --- | --- |
| 1. Thomas Dafydd | Believes, but under some doubts because of temptations; he desires and longs for more liberty. |
| 2. Dafydd Morgan | Has tasted much of God's love; his faith is enduring; his experiences are very simple. |
| 3. Dafydd Rees | Believes, but is under many clouds. He endured many tribulations but is experiencing more and more victory. |
| 4. Jenkin Jones | Under trials for a season; is dark and dry of spirit. |
| 5. Margaret Thomas | Under much conviction, but very dark. |

We cannot quote the whole sheet, but the Dyffryn Saith society numbered 20. It seems that it did not contain a single married woman. Blaenhownant numbered 10; Twr-gwyn, 9; Llwyndafydd, 10; and Aberporth, 20. In Pembrokeshire, the Longhouse society numbered 20; St. David's, 11; Fishguard, 35; Dinas, 7; Newport, 13; Pen-caer, 7; Llwyn-y-grawys and Eglwyswrw, 35. The total comes to 190, with 19 members on probation.

To end, we give the report of John Harris of St Kennox. He wrote as follows:

On the 13th of the month, I met with the lambs of Prendergast and Ismason in Ponton (25 in number). The windows of heaven were opened and the dews of God's love rained down upon us until we were all but drowned in the great ocean. I was given to experience wisdom, knowledge, understanding, humility, and sympathy, together with my dear lambs, so that I could say, 'The kingdom of God is within me,' and also, 'God is love.' The lambs were as bone of my bone, and flesh of my flesh. We sang the new song, and we sang with one breath.

On the 14th of the month, at Llawhaden. There were only 11 in number, but my love was continuing and increasing. While in prayer, it was not sufficient to kneel; two fell upon their faces on the floor and could only just manage to get up. And as I presented to them the love of the Lamb, they could not remain in the room but departed, one by one, rolling in the dust and shouting, 'Michael, you sing, we cannot!'

On the 15th of the month, at Jefferson. Shaking the tower of Babel, which was set to fall, both in private and in public. I was enabled to believe it had fallen; the lovely strains of free grace were upon all lips, and every heart was full of love.

On the 18th of the month, at Carew. Number, 25. After exhorting publicly it was revealed to me that nothing troubles the devil more than the private societies. This was evident in his instruments, namely, fleshly people of all denominations; they hate them above all things. Though the door was closed at the beginning, the dear Lamb visited, standing in the middle, and saying, 'Peace be to you!' Then the dear lambs were dissolved in tears, and were filled with love, so that one shouted out, 'Pity! Pity! It is overflowing. Do not be partial but fill others also.' And the others broke out into cryings, ' Blessed be God for Jesus Christ.'

On the 19th of the month, at Mounton, near Narberth. We had sweet communion with the dear Emmanuel. As the weather was wet and other circumstances hindering, they did not expect me, so that 11 members were absent.

On the 20th of the month, at Gellidawel. Number, 16. From the beginning, yes, even until now, the dear Lamb did not take his sweet smiles from me, but he entertained me, as it were, upon his knee, until I, and the lambs also, were full of love, causing us to cry out to the host of heaven, ' O, you blessed saints, sing, for you have been released from the clay. Treble your song, until we come to you!'

Therefore, as I call you dear brethren, I have been given to receive of your labours and efforts in the great work. I consider that I have undertaken the burden with yourselves. And as I believe that our dear High Priest assists you, I believe that as he is the author, so also he will be the finisher of the work, though Satan and his instruments say like Tobiah to Sanballat of Nehemiah's work in building the walls of Jerusalem, 'If a fox go up, he shall even break down their stone wall.' Go on, the Lamb of God has indeed a hand in the work in which you are engaged, and you will reap of the fruits of your labours. This, from the unworthiest of all who seek the face of the Lamb

– John Harris.

These reports reveal much ardour of spirit and much skill in discerning the various spiritual conditions of souls – souls entrusted to the care of the exhorters. They are all reports on the state of affairs about the beginning of the year 1743. We should keep in mind that the numbers of members mentioned are no indication whatsoever of the numbers of those who heard the gospel from the lips of the Methodists, and who considered themselves followers of Rowland and Harris. It was no small thing to join a society in those days. The door was so narrow, and the discipline so strict, that we find many of the superintendents acknowledging that there were those who, in their judgment, had been saved to eternal life but without having joined themselves to any society. At Llanddeusant, the number of members was only twenty-eight, but the superintendent estimated that the number of hearers listening to him was about two hundred.

---

[1] *Cynghanedd* is a traditional Welsh poetic form observing strict metrical and alliterative rules.

[2] STL, vol. 1, pp. 79–80.

[3] Ibid., pp. 172–5.

[4] CH 4, p. 46, provides a reference from a Moravian manuscript (Lorenz Nyberg, *Account of the Awakening in Pembrokeshire*, 1767), which gives a different explanation of Beaumont's theology, and a completely different account of his death:

'In 1750 James Beaumont of the Gore in Radnorshire came to a place near St David's for his health. He visited Haverfordwest and preached. He preached Christ's humanity and the sufferings of Christ. He knew the Moravian tenets and wished Cennick would visit Pembrokeshire. On June 17 he preached his last sermon. He got ill, and died in old Mr Sparks's house in Bridge Street on the 22nd; he was buried on the 24th in Prendergast churchyard. His preaching was blessed to the Moravians here.'

[5] CH 48, p. 78.

[6] '*The History of the Independent Churches of Wales.*'

[7] See footnote 20 on p. 28.

Top: Llangeitho Chapel and the statue of Daniel Rowland
Middle: An early portrait of Howell Harris
Bottom: Talgarth Church as it was in Harris's time

Top: Trefeca College and the Howell Harris Memorial Chapel
Middle: The Countess of Huntingdon's College at Trefeca. The
photograph is taken from *The Evangelical Register*, 1824
Bottom: Trefeca College from the north-east

Top: Defynnog Church, where, in 1737, Harris and Rowland met for
the first time
Middle: Trefeca College Library with Harris's pulpit and oak chair
Bottom: The interior of the Howell Harris Memorial Chapel

TOP: AN EXAMPLE OF A LETTER BY HOWELL HARRIS
BOTTOM: HOWELL DAVIES

Top: Llys-y-fran Church, Pembrokeshire
Middle: St. Daniel's Church, near Pembroke
Bottom: Woodstock Chapel, Pembrokeshire

Top: Mounton Church, near Narberth, Pembrokeshire
Middle: Newchapel, Pembrokeshire
Bottom: Howell Davies's home at Prendergast, Haverfordwest

Top: Prendergast Church, the burial place of Howell Davies
Middle: Llwyn-llwyd, near Hay-on-Wye, Brycheiniog
Bottom: Llwyn-llwyd Academy in 1900

Top: Maesyronnen Independent Chapel
Bottom: Examples of William William's handwriting

# ALELUIA,

### NEU,

## CASCLIAD

#### o

# HYMNAU,

Ar amryw Yſtyriaethau.

O Waith y Parchedig
Mr. WILLIAM WILLIAMS

Eph. v. 19. *Gan lefaru wrth ei Gilydd mewn* SALMAU, *a* HYMNAU, *&c.*
Col. iii. 16. *Gan ddyſgu a rhybuddio pawb ei gilydd mewn* SALMAU, HYMNAU, *&c.*

Y DRYDYDD RHAN.

Argraphwyd *Ymrhiſto* gan *FFLIX FARLEY*
Yn y Flwyddyn M.DCC.XIV.

TOP: PORTRAITS OF WILLIAM WILLIAMS. THE LEFT-HAND PORTRAIT WAS
DRAWN ABOUT 1779 AND THE RIGHT-HAND ONE PUBLISHED IN 1867
BOTTOM: THE TITLE-PAGE OF WILLIAMS'S FIRST BOOK OF HYMNS. THE
CORRECT DATE IS 1745, NOT 1714

PLACES RELATING TO WILLIAM WILLIAMS: 1. LLANFAIR-AR-Y-BRYN CHURCH
2. LLANWRTYD CHURCH  3. PANTYCELYN  4. CEFN-Y-COED  5. PANTYCELYN
6. THE MEMORIAL CHURCH, LLANDOVERY  7. GRAVE AT LLANFAIR-AR-Y-BRYN

Top: Watford Independent Chapel
Middle: Plas Watford near Caerphilly, Glamorganshire
Bottom: William Edwards 'the Builder'

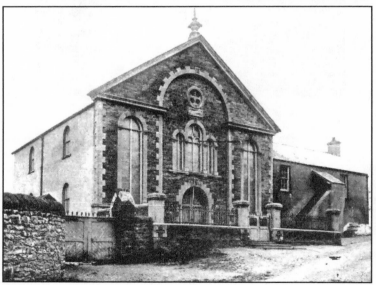

Top Left: The gravestone of David Williams, Llysfronydd
Top Right: The grave of John Harris, Ambleston, Pembrokeshire, his
son Evan Harris, and his grandson Thomas Harris
Bottom: Groes-wen Independent Chapel

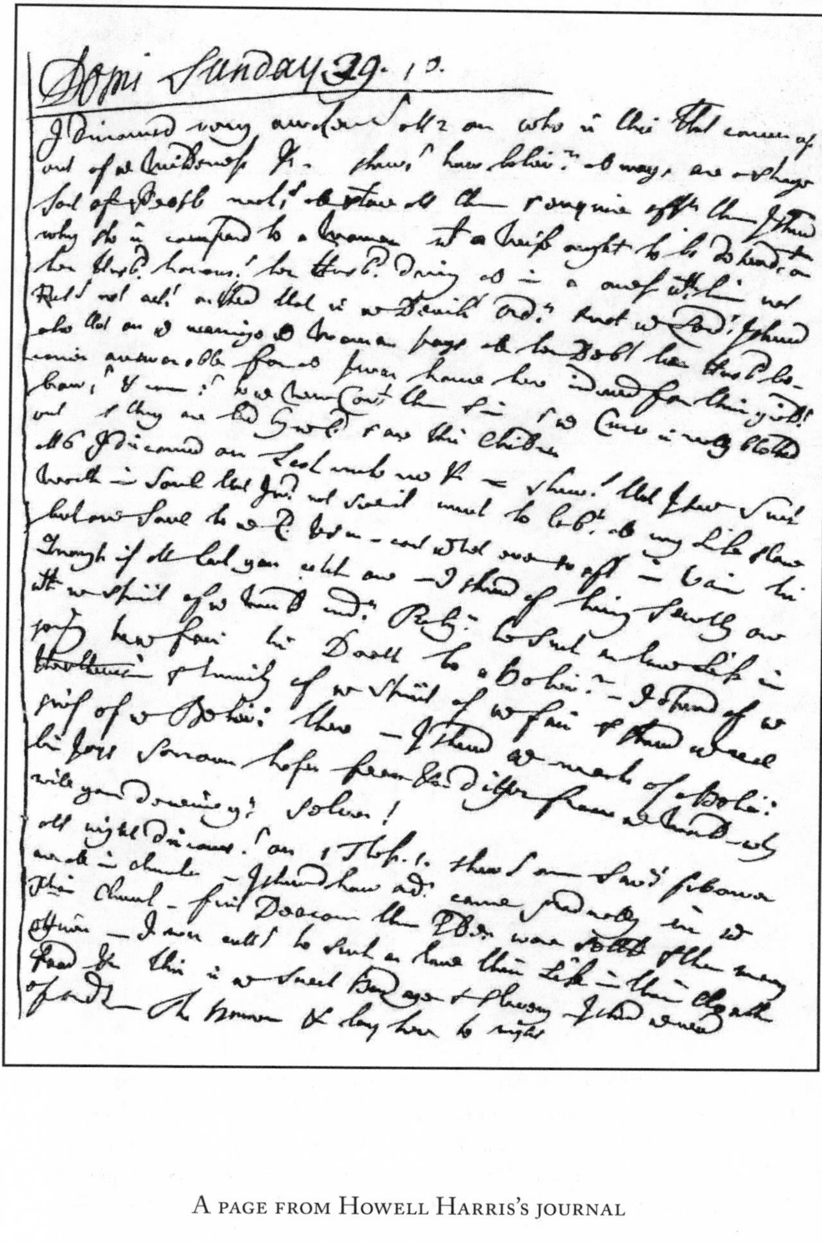

A PAGE FROM HOWELL HARRIS'S JOURNAL

Places of interest in Carmarthenshire:
1. Cil-y-cwm Chapel (built 1740)  2. Ystrad-ffin Chapel  3. Llansawel
Chapel (built 1744)  4. Penlan, near Llansawel  5. Llanfynydd
Chapel  6. Abergorlech Village  7. The home of Mrs Griffiths,
Glanyrafonddu-ganol  8. The home of Mrs Lloyd, Pant-yr-esgair

Sr.

Talgarth Feb. 27 1735-6-

When first I was inform'd yt you took upon you to instruct
your Neighbours at Trefecca on a particular Occasion, I mean
of ye Nature of ye Sacramt, and inforce yr Duty by reading a
Chapter out of yt excellent Book The whole Duty of Man; I
thôt it proceeded from a pious and charitable Disposition. But
since you've advanc'd so far as to have your publick Lectures
from House to House, and even within ye Limits of yr Church,
it's full Time to let you know ye Sin and Penalty you incur
by so doing. The Office you've fondly undertaken, belongs not
to ye Layty any farther yn privately in yr own Families: And
if you'll be pleas'd to take your Bible in Hand, you'll there
find ye heavy Judgmts wch God inflicted upon ye Sacrilege and
Impiety of those who audaciously presum'd in invade the
Office ministerial. If you'll consult ye Histories of this as
well as other Nations, you'll see ye dismal & lamentable Effects
of a factious Zeal, & a Puritanical Sanctity; for 'tis an
easy Matter to seduce ignorant and illiterate People, and
by cunning Insinuatns from House to House, induce them to
embrace wt Tenets you please. I've yet one heavy Crime
to lay to your Charge, wch is this That after you've expatiated
upon a Sunday in ye whole Duty of Man to your Auditrs,
wch in my Opinion is wrote in so plain & intelligible a
Maner yt it's incapable of a Paraphrase, unless it be to
obscure, & confound yt Authrs Meaning, you conclude wth a long Extempo
:rary Prayer, wth Repetitions, Tautologies &c. Pray consider
how odiously this savours of Phanaticism & Hypocrisy.
Wt I've already sd will I hope disswade you, for ye future
from such Practices; But if ye Admonition of yr Minister
ônt prevail, I will acquaint yr Bror of it: and if you
will persist in your Way, I must acquaint my Diocesan
of it, wch will prove an immoveable Obstruction to yours
ever getting into holy Orders: for your Continuance in
it will give me as well as others just Reeson to conclude
yt your Intellectuals are not sound. I am yours well
wisher & afsrd. humble Serv P Davies

If Sir Letters sent you Mr Nelson & by seriously weighing wt is there sd & if yr Sacred function, a you
see markt in ye e, if you will be convinc'd of your Error.

A LETTER OF REBUKE FROM THE REV. PRICE DAVIES, TALGARTH, TO HOWELL
HARRIS (SEE PAGE 144)

TOP: ALPHA CHAPEL, BUILTH WELLS. THIS IS THE SECOND CHAPEL. THE FIRST
ON THIS SITE WAS BUILT IN 1747
BOTTOM: AN ACCOUNT IN PETER WILLIAMS'S HANDWRITING OF THE
PERSECUTION HE SUFFERED AT ADWY'R CLAWDD

Top: Aberthin Chapel near Cowbridge, Glamorganshire
Middle: Llantrisant, Glamorganshire, where the first Association
of Rowland's Party Met
Bottom: Wern-llestr, the house where Harris first preached in
Llansamlet

TOP: LLANSAMLET CHAPEL IN 1900
MIDDLE: ST NICHOLAS CHURCH, GLAMORGANSHIRE
BOTTOM: TRE-HILL CHAPEL, ST NICHOLAS

# 11

# HOWELL HARRIS (1743–4)

## HARRIS'S HEALTH DETERIORATES

We have followed Howell Harris's history up to the middle of the year 1743. We have seen how he travelled without stop, labouring by day and night, exhorting sinners, confirming the saints, arranging the societies, and superintending everything involved in the powerful movement which the Lord had begun through himself and Rowland. From the first Association at Watford, held at the beginning of January, to the middle of August when he went for some days to London, he could hardly be said to have had a single day's rest. On top of this, his correspondence was extensive. He received letters from many individuals whom he had never met and on all kinds of matters, and he was so conscientious and careful that he would not pass one letter without replying to it. Under all this weight, it is no surprise that his health gave way. It is no exaggeration to say that he impaired his constitution to such an extent that he was never again as strong as he had been. As he entered the details of each day in his journal, his first comment is nearly always that his body is ill and bruised. When travelling in Pembrokeshire in June, he complained of unbearable pain shooting through his head and throat, and that his eyes, ears and tongue were not functioning properly. This made him wonder whether he should stop the exhorting and devote his time wholly to the work of superintending the societies. In a letter to a London friend, dated 4 June 1743, he says:

It is now much upon me that I am called from the public to a more private work. My reasons I shall lay before you; I know you will lay them before the Lord and your praying believing acquaintances. First, God seems to lay this more on my heart than the other. Secondly, my nature is so worn out and spent and my body so impaired that I have not sufficient strength; nor have I had for a long time but what I had by faith miraculously. Thirdly, my voice is so habitually taken away that indeed I cannot make a great auditory hear, at least not without uncommon pain. Fourthly, by a series of uncommon trials from all quarters, from men, from Satan, and from my own cursed nature, the Lord seems more immediately to be fitting me for inside work. Fifthly, he has poured public gifts of calling, convincing, and holding forth Christ to the unawakened on many of our brethren more than on me, and I believe they are more blessed in this work than I am. Sixthly, there seems to be a necessity for somebody for this work; and 'tis work enough separate from the public. Seventhly, I could thereby have more time for reading, writing letters, and perhaps doing and receiving good in private. These reasons, especially my hoarseness and illness, make it impracticable for me to come to London unless some brother comes with me for the public work.[1]

He states, however, that his low condition had taught him valuable lessons – his duty to sympathize with those in pain; to understand the sympathetic association between one part of the body and another; and the readiness of one bodily member to support another, which is a mirror of the mysterious and spiritual unity between the saints. He felt certain that his suffering had been intended for his good, to make him more humble, and so more prepared to receive any gift that God had soon to grant him.

## EDMUND JONES ATTACKS THE METHODISTS

It seems that the division which had already begun between the Dissenters and the reformers, widened greatly in this period. On 30 May, Harris writes in his journal:

> I heard from Bro. H of a public declaration against us by dear Bro. Edmund Jones and his adherents, the Independent ministers, (1) because we communicate with carnal ministers, (2) because of our not being ordained, etc.[2]

This *Bro. H* was Herbert Jenkins, in all probability, who was at the time on a visit to Trefeca. The declaration must have been a kind of call to arms, as a result of the work of the Watford Association in advising members who regularly received the sacrament in the Established Church to continue doing so, until the Lord should open a door that would enable them to leave its communion. The declaration appears to have been a denominational Assembly decision and to have been sent to the churches in an Assembly newsletter. The reference in the second part of the accusation, namely preaching without ordination, is to Howell Harris directly. This was considerable ungratefulness on the part of Edmund Jones and his brethren, to say the least. After Harris had visited their localities on their request, and had been the means under God of convicting a great many souls, of which many had joined their churches, it was most unworthy of them to turn against him and accuse him, in a public proclamation emanating from their Assembly, of being unordained. But Harris did not take offence. He says:

The Holy Spirit, my dear Guide, kept me from my own spirit, humbling me, and sending me to God, giving me love towards all those who separate from me. I was enabled to cry out in secret, 'O Father, show me thy will concerning this; see how I am attacked from all directions. O lead us, and arrange us as you wish, and sanctify all to us. Bless those who are against us. For how long will your children strive in the way, and be divided? (Here I was given a spirit of mourning over this.) O keep us from harming them, or weakening their efforts in any way. Bless them and grant them success in gathering souls to thee, and be amongst them.'

If there was ever an unselfish prayer, full of the spirit of Jesus Christ, it was this prayer of Howell Harris on behalf of Edmund Jones and the Independent ministers. He clearly felt that he had been raised above his corrupt nature, because he comments in parentheses, 'This is far from the old man.'

Edmund Jones's proclamation bore fruit, causing many of the Dissenting ministers who had up to now been supporting the revival to turn their backs. Within a few days, Howell Harris wrote as follows in his journal:

I again heard that many dear brothers, ministers, intend to leave us because of prejudice against us. It was very painful. But God's Spirit, through whom I can do and suffer all things, kept me from myself. I was brought very low and made to love God for it; in that I saw him as a protection from self and from gathering according to the flesh. I felt neither anger nor offence towards them; I could wash their feet; and I sent them a message, that if they departed from us, we could not depart from them.

It would be difficult to meet with a more liberal spirit. Perhaps the phrase 'gathering according to the flesh' refers to the danger that Harris once feared, namely that he and his followers would be driven by circumstances to join with the Dissenters, but without any unity of spirit and heart. From now on Harris would have little support from the Nonconformist ministers. The fact that he was going about to exhort without having been ordained by bishop or minister, was a stumbling block that they could not surmount.

## BEGINNING TO BUILD CHAPELS

By this time a desire for building chapels had arisen amongst the Methodists, not in opposition to the parish churches but for the convenience of the lay preachers, in that homes were becoming much too small for the congregations, and also as places for the societies to meet. In all probability the first Methodist chapel raised was Maes-gwyn Chapel, Radnorshire. This is not the same place as that Maes-gwyn near Hay where the famous

Dissenting minister, Vavasor Griffiths, used to minister. It is more to the north, lying between Rhayader and Llanybister. James Beaumont, in writing to Harris, who was at London, on 2 August 1742, says, 'Justice Vaughan threatens to pull down the Maes-gwyn meeting-house.' If it was a Nonconformist chapel it would have been licensed according to the law and as far beyond the reach of any justice of peace to demolish it as the cathedral at St David's.

Beaumont must have known this. But as the Methodists of old did not obtain licences for their chapels, in that they did not consider themselves Nonconformists, their buildings were to a considerable degree at the mercy of their persecutors. The probability is that Maes-gwyn was a Methodist chapel. By 1742, Howell Harris was excited by the prospect of building places of worship. In that year, he wrote to a noblewoman who was in danger of being persuaded of spending her wealth on trivial things, listing many worthy causes that cried out for support, and amongst other things, he notes, 'There are books to be published and distributed, and society houses to be built.' The society was an uniquely Methodist institution, so that in referring to society houses Harris must have been thinking of building chapels for their use.

The chapel at Groes-wen appears to have been built in 1742. The deed for the land on which it stands is dated 2 June 1742. The Methodists of the Watford area, having tired of arguing with David Williams, the Independent minister of Watford Chapel, were looking for a more peaceful home. Thomas Price of Watford Mansion, one of their exhorters, was the main mover in the business and it is his name that heads the list of trustees on the conveyance deed of the chapel land. The society at Groes-wen was ruled by the Association in exactly the same way as all the other societies, and its reports, sent to the Association, may be found amongst the Trefeca records.

We tend to believe that many chapels were raised in different parts of the country in the years 1742–3. In March 1743, the Rev. Benjamin Thomas, a Nonconformist minister who joined the Methodists, wrote to Harris:

> The Churchmen have locked the doors of one of the meeting-houses against me, and I preached there with my back to the door. Some believe that they have written to London in relation to this. Would you be so kind as to inform me what it is they can do. I am willing to give my body and soul to suffer for him, if he gives me strength.

We find it hard to believe that he is speaking of any of the Nonconformist chapels. He knew, as did the whole country by now, that the In-

dulgence Act protected these and that nobody, not even the Archbishop
of Canterbury, had any right to interfere with them. The probability is
that he is referring to Methodist meeting-houses, which were unpro-
tected as they had not been licensed. In the Porth-y-rhyd Association
of 3 October 1744, one of the decisions made was to build a house for
religious purposes at Llansawel. There is no reason not to believe that
this decision was fulfilled, and its wording carries no suggestion that this
was a new approach.

Howell Harris always maintained a deep interest in the days of the
year associated with important stages in his spiritual life. He wrote on 6
April, 1743:

> On this day, eight years ago according to the days of the month, Easter
> Sunday in that year, I received the sacrament for the first time. I had been
> convicted of the necessity of this the previous Sunday, namely 30 March. At
> this time was produced such an influence upon my soul that did not leave
> me for the next fortnight. I then found Holl Ddyletswydd Dyn [The Whole
> Duty of Man] by which I came gradually to appreciate my wretchedness, and
> which terminated in conviction.

On 20 April, he writes, 'Today is the eighth anniversary of my first
conviction, through reading Holl Ddyletswydd Dyn.' On Whit Sunday
of the same year, he says:

> This is the eighth anniversary since I had my first sight – through faith – of
> Christ dying for me, and I felt peace and joy. About this time, eight years
> ago, Satan was cast out of me. Now my soul was made to cry out, not with
> feeling alone, but with a degree of light, 'Satan, thou dost know that thou art
> cast out from me, by the power of God; that God is now in me. Thou dost
> know, Satan, that I am now a child of God, and an elect vessel for him. Thou
> dost know that I am thy lord, that thou hast not ruled over me ever since that
> time, and that thou wilt never rule over me. Thou dost know that I belong
> to the Lord, and that thou canst not harm me.' My soul was now enabled by
> faith to obtain the victory over all my enemies, by seeing that God had loved
> me, and had saved me from them all. I was, in truth, made thankful for being
> saved from the kingdom of the devil, with his power and misery. I now saw,
> by faith, my privileges, that I was the Lord's, and he was mine. Eight years
> ago I was taken from the devil's claws to God, but now I long to be freed
> from the influence of the flesh and of nature, in which Satan works. O God!
> save me from myself! O save me from nature!

Clearly, only a man that lived much in the spiritual world could write
like this.

## THE IMPRISONMENT AND TRIAL OF MORGAN HUGHES

One of the great events of the year 1743 was the apprehension of the ex-horter Morgan Hughes and his imprisonment at Cardigan, until his case was heard in the court there. He was refused his liberty on the payment of bail in the meantime. These events greatly disturbed the Methodists; the future of the revival would appear to hang upon the results of this episode. As Howell Harris passed through Cardigan on the way to the Monthly Association at Longhouse, poor Morgan Hughes was a captive inside the walls of the prison. He was not allowed to enter the prison to see him. It seems he did not have a licence from the justices for this. But his feelings are evident from the following entry in his journal:

> Cardigan, Wednesday. In secret, I found the case of Bro. Morgan Hughes, the prisoner, weighing heavily upon me. I felt such love in me that it was as if I had taken the place of the captive and was feeling as he felt. Everything that I had, life, money and all, were for his service; I could have suffered in his stead. I felt the same fatherly love towards all the exhorters, that I could suffer with all of them. I wrote a letter to Bro. Rowland instructing him to seek the brother's release by obtaining bail for him.

It was a trial for one as sympathetic as Howell Harris to have to turn his back on Cardigan prison without having seen his friend, or having helped him in any way. The attempt at releasing him by bail also failed. He remained imprisoned until the day of his trial. Thomas Price of Watford, and the society of which he was a member, were much disturbed by the issue.

Mr Price wrote to Howell Harris, 'I am sorry and yet rejoice to hear of Bro. Rowland and Bro Hughes's persecution.' This suggests that Daniel Rowland also had been summoned to stand trial at Cardigan but that the justices did not dare to imprison an ordained priest. Mr Price adds:

> I thought to come up to Cardigan against Sessions, and Bro. William Morgan and Bro. Thomas Evans, but as we both were obstructed as being summoned to appear on the day and the last being out of order. Therefore this comes with all our hearty love to Bro. Rowland and Bro. Hughes and as we hear that they must appear at Sessions we have sent you by the bearer this small sum as a token of our love to give them and I think it best if they proceed against them that you would get it removed to Westminster and we are all here willing to assist you to carry it on rather than choose to be defendants, but if they drop it I would have you draw a bill of indictment for abusing Bro. Morgan Hughes upon the king's highway. There he will have no need of any witness because it was done in such a place.[3]

It is easy to see from these words that Thomas Price was deeply concerned, and also that he was very knowledgeable in matters of the law.

On a Monday morning, 28 March, Howell Harris and Daniel Rowland set out from Llangeitho towards Cardigan court-house. Their journey led them through the beautiful Aeron Valley, one of the most scenic in Wales. By three o'clock they had arrived at Clwyd Jack, half farmhouse, half mansion, about three miles below Talsarn, where their animals were fed. They arrived at the home of a certain Walter Watkins by six, and eventually reached Cardigan by nine. Their fellowship along the way was of the sweetest; they felt the greatest delight at being called to suffer together. Howell Harris saw the great tenderness and wisdom of God in the details of their suffering. At the first, when they were weak, they were not persecuted other than by mocking and laughing, but it was enough to exercise their weak grace. But when, about four years since, a great storm had arisen against them, they had sufficient brethren, friends and money to support them. It came to his mind to write and publish Welsh books, so that all might come to know Christ, but he felt that his first duty was to visit the societies where clearly the Lord was blessing him. After reaching Cardigan, he first visited Morgan Hughes in prison. Harris wrote:

When I saw him my heart became aflame; I was drawn out in the power of faith, love and warmth, so that all fear, lowness of spirit, and anxiety at appearing before the bench, disappeared; I could face them all bravely, and suffer with my brother. In the power of this strength, I could even go through fire; the fear of the mob was removed from me; I had the courage to confess my Lord. I met Morgan Hughes at a time when he was low, seeing all against him and none to take his case in hand. But I had sufficient strength of faith to declare and show that God was above them all, that we have no need of the support of the arm of flesh, in that God laughs at the devil and his every effort, and that he would bring forth good from all this. I comforted my brother, and felt myself full of love and compassion towards our opponents.

Harris relates the details of this visit to Cardigan, from the Monday night to the afternoon of Thursday. He says that his body was weak but as for his soul it was living far above the creature, blessing God for ever considering one like him. Many believers had gathered to them so that there was no lack of sympathy or money, and in the midst of their fears they continued to hold meetings for prayer, singing, and praising, the like of which had not been heard before in a court of law. The senior juror was a man called W. Lloyd, who proved himself to be a friend of the revival. Harris wrote, 'I felt my soul expanding with love towards him, like to that of the angels.' They conferred with a lawyer and an advocate, explaining the case. Mr Lloyd took Harris to the coffee room of the main inn, amongst all the jurors and men of importance, and it seems that a favourable impression was made. On Thursday the trial began. It followed the cases of five lawbreakers – three who had stolen horses, a cow, and some money; and two housebreakers. After dealing with these, Morgan Hughes was brought forth. But by now it was understood that the jurors had dismissed the case, chiefly through the influence of Mr Lloyd who himself had been entreated by his wife, a young noblewoman. Harris promised Mr Lloyd that the Methodists would not proceed with counter-charges against their persecutors provided they paid all the costs of the case. All that was left for the judge to do therefore was to release Morgan Hughes, and in so doing he showed the utmost respect towards those who were persecuted for no cause other than their religion. 'O Lord,' wrote Harris, 'this all comes from Thee.' This concluded the case at the Cardigan court, and the whole affair was of great significance, both in striking fear in the hearts of opposers and in encouraging those who sought to worship God according to their conscientious convictions.

## HARRIS'S CONTROVERSY WITH
## THE BISHOP OF ST DAVID'S

During the year 1743, Howell Harris was also in correspondence with the Bishop of St David's over the refusal of the clergymen to administer the sacrament to himself and those converted through him. No letter from the Bishop's side of the correspondence has survived, but in the Trefeca records is a copy of Harris's letter sent to the Bishop's secretary and dated 1 August 1743. It is clear from this copy that serious complaints had been laid against Harris with regard to his doctrine and behaviour, and he, in his reply, does not hesitate to speak his mind, not even fearing to suggest that the Bishop himself is not completely orthodox in the faith. The following is a portion of the letter:

> I still doubt whether his Lordship agrees with respect to justification, that the only cause of justification before God is the passive and active obedience of Christ, without any work of our own; and that this merit is imputed freely to us by God, and discerned in the conscience as being ours through the grace of faith, which also is given us. This faith is proved to ourselves to be a true faith by the Holy Ghost testifying to our hearts; and proved to the world by an upright life and conversation. In this sense, I believe that both an inner and an outer sanctification are necessary; it is necessary to display these in our walk to our eternal home; and they are ever necessary as the fruit which follow justification – but still I fear his Lordship meant good works as a

necessary condition to obtaining justification, and not what follows justification . . . As regards to the charges listed in your letter, I confess to some, but
deny others. But you admit that they are full of bitterness and bad feeling. As
far as the places at which I have been speaking are concerned, I acknowledge
that I have taken up collections towards religious projects overseas, but I paid
every penny to Mr Whitefield some three years ago, and he transferred them
to the cause involved.

As to the charge that I hold to sinless perfection, I have not ever believed or
taught this. After having been in the company of Mr Wesley, some three years
ago, I acknowledge that I did make use of expressions that were not perfectly
clear, but having learnt that he held to this view I wrote a long letter to him,
and divorced myself from him on a point of doctrine. Yet, I still believe that
he is an honest man who labours to do good, and as such, I love and honour
him. I believe that his Lordship would be more favourable towards us if he
were not to believe all that he hears.

I am accused of saying that no place is more sacred than another. I hope that
you also believe this, that there is no difference, under the gospel, between
any one place and another, other than a difference of convenience, and that
there are no promises in the Scripture for God's presence to be found in one
place more than another, except for the case of Solomon's temple. And that
was only so, insomuch as it was a type of the Christian Church, and was to
remain only until spiritual worship was established, when all shadows would
be abrogated. Now, whenever two or three gather together in Jesus' name,
and in faith, there is the presence of God. At the same time, for the sake of
external order, we desire that there should be no reason against, and that it
might be possible for us all to meet in the same place.

As for the accusation that I speak at the same time as divine service at
Felin-newydd, I believe that you have been misinformed. If I did do so it
was done in ignorance; it was near to sunset when I arrived there, as far as
I can remember. If I am thrown out of communion under the pretence of
a sensitive conscience, when no complaint can be brought against my conduct, while others are received though they live in open sin, it will one day
become evident even if it is not so now, whether or not this is conscientious
behaviour. You know that if we are not given relief from this, and from other
similar unreasonable and unloving actions in the church courts, that the civil
courts may be appealed to. If church members are thrown out purely because
they go to hear where they can understand what they hear better than in
the parish churches, and where they gain more profit, and feel more of the
Divine Presence, I do not know how such a Church can be free from a spirit
of persecution, nor claim that it possesses that catholic love and tenderness
which we consider to be the main characteristics of a Church.

A letter worthy of an apostle. It is easy to see that it was written in
all honesty and with complete fearlessness, while still wishing to

acknowledge every due respect to the Bishop and his Chaplain. In the light of this letter we can learn the nature of the accusations brought against Howell Harris, namely:

1. That he held that good works are not a condition of justification, and that he preached John Wesley's doctrine of the sinless perfection of the believer.

2. That he took up collections during his services and then used the money for his own needs.

3. That he preached that episcopal consecration did not make a building more sacred than any other, but that any place might be used for religious purposes, whether consecrated or not.

4. That he held his meetings at the same times as the services in the parishes.

He proves that he was innocent of some of the points brought against him, and as for the others, that his own views were more scriptural than those of his accusers. Regarding the refusal of Holy Communion to him and his followers, while men of open immorality were received, he writes with an irresistible authority, and it would be hard to believe that the Bishop of St David's could avoid a blush of shame when reading such a vigorous defence. We are glad to see that Harris's churchmanship was not as strong as is sometimes made out, and that he considered the consecration of a bishop to be of very little weight. We respect his courage and honesty, as well as his conscientiousness towards the truth and towards Christ.

## HARRIS'S FIFTH VISIT TO LONDON

On Wednesday, 3 August 1743, Harris departed on horseback to London; his fifth journey to that city. The purpose of the visit was to meet with the English brethren at their General Assembly. He did not take the direct route but travelled through south Wales, partly in order to use every opportunity for preaching, and partly in order to confer with his brethren so that he would be able in the Assembly to pass on the views of the Welsh leaders, as well as his own. On the first day, he visited Beiliau where he preached on, 'I am the way.' It proved a good service and he felt much liberty. The next day he reached Myddfai and preached on, 'Feed my sheep.' He did not stay here long but continued to Parke in Pembrokeshire, estimating the day's journey to have been about fifty miles. He stayed here until the Saturday afternoon when he proceeded through Llansteffan to Capel Ifan. A Monthly Association was in progress here.

Howell Davies preached first, to a congregation comprised mainly of saints. After him, Daniel Rowland spoke from Galatians 2:20, 'I am crucified with Christ,' – an extraordinary sermon of much light and warmth. He showed:

> Firstly, how the soul sees itself void of all good in itself, and sees all for time and eternity. Secondly, what sort of death this is: a painful death, a lingering death, a shameful death, but it brings joy at last. Thirdly, what is this life he had, and what a mystery is a Christian, dead but yet living, weak but yet strong, sinful but yet pure, blind but yet seeing, falling but yet up. Negatively, it is not a natural or moral or legal life; positively, it is a holy, just, sweet, growing, and eternal life. Inference: is everyone who is void of this spiritual life under the curse? Then what will become of you? O come out of the law and sin and self and the world, to Christ.[4]

He was given extraordinary power; Harris's heart leaped within him throughout the sermon, and he felt an assurance that God would descend and bless the work.

From Capel Ifan, Harris continued through Carmarthenshire, Glamorganshire and Monmouthshire, preaching the gospel of the grace of God in Swansea, Neath, Llantrisant, Watford and Llanfihangel-on-Usk, and arriving at Bristol on the Wednesday, a fortnight after leaving home. With his companion, James Beaumont, he hurried to the New Room to hear Mr Mansfield preaching. The subject of the sermon was justification without the works of the law. The preacher explained his subject so clearly, showing the emptiness of the principle of doing this, that or the other, in order to obtain life, that Harris's soul was filled with thanksgiving to God for raising such a light in the land. He also felt his pride being somewhat hurt in that he had thought that such light would not be seen 'without one of us amongst them'. Whether it was the Welsh that he intended by the 'us', we do not know. He had intended being present at a Monthly Association at Bristol but this was over before he arrived. Having heard the decisions carried, however, he felt that he could approve them all. On Thursday morning, he set out again for London, arriving about five o'clock on Friday afternoon. He entered the city through Hyde Park, passing some of its most superb buildings, but he was hardly aware of the magnificence around him; God had opened his eyes to behold the glory of another world and the splendour of his Father's house, whose glory is eternal, whereas the greatest pomp of this world soon passes away. Putting aside his tiredness, he went that night to the Tabernacle to hear Mr Whitefield preaching and felt his soul being humbled within him by the influence of the truth.

On Saturday morning, Howell Harris and Whitefield visited John and Charles Wesley. He felt unworthy of being amongst such companions and that it would be a privilege to be at their feet in service. The topics of their conference was the great work of the revival; the possibility of a union between them; and of appointing persons to meet together to arrange possible co-operation. Considerable discussion was given to their receiving of the sacrament together. The two Wesleys did not feel able to agree to this, they felt that the meeting of Whitefield's followers with theirs would lead to arguments. They agreed the appropriateness of unordained preachers – they were present in all denominations; that it was better not to form themselves into a separate party until they were actually forced out by the Established Church; and also to resort to the law against any who might attack them, in order to maintain their liberty. But they had no desire for revenge. They intended to forgive those who ill-treated them once they had realized that they were breaking the law. They agreed also to appeal to the law of the land against the tyranny of the Church courts. They departed in the sweetest of tempers, having humbled themselves before the throne of grace.

On the Wednesday, within a week, the Association for all the English brethren began. The first topic of discussion was the appropriateness of separating from the Established Church. Howell Harris wrote:

Bro. Whitefield and I stood against it, and at length the brethren were reconciled to stay as we are, etc. I find the Lord is not for destroying the poor National Church. Firstly, he has many good souls (Mr Griffith Jones, etc.) in it, that don't join with us. Secondly, he keeps and blesses Bro. Wesley much. Thirdly, he over-rules the malice, etc., of the clergy. Fourthly, he has impressed it upon Bro. Whitefield's heart that he shall be a bishop, and by that means keep him too as he is. Fifthly, he has providentially kept us from a separation. The discussion continued for long. I argued: firstly, the beauty of the form of ordination amongst us; secondly, that he who desires to be ordained must have the approval of those who know him, as he must put his name forward in his parish church, three weeks beforehand; thirdly, he must obtain a good character from three clergymen of his acquaintance; and fourthly, he must be examined by his bishop. I said I declared I did not go at first to set up any party but to reform all, and so do now act consistently.

We agreed Bro. Humphreys should be as he is unordained. He talked of joining the Dissenters wholly and taking a congregation, which I said I had freedom he should do to answer his own conscience, but I was united to him in that act, I made it my own, and so if I would not be ordained in the same way would act inconsistent with myself, but that I should hold fellowship with him as a Dissenting brother and not as Methodists, who are properly

Church of England, and there stay unless they are turned out. We agreed that among such Dissenters as join with us, some Dissenting minister, that would, should give the ordinance, and among the rest some of our ministers that should be free (though against the Canons, as we deny the authority of them) to such as can't have it in the Church, etc.[5]

This discussion greatly illuminates the attitude of mind of the Methodists at this time. The issue of whether to remain in the Established Church had become a burning issue amongst them. Whitefield and Howell Harris were the most anxious to remain. It is clear that Whitefield thought he would be made a bishop. His friendship with the Countess of Huntingdon, and others of the nobility, strengthened this belief. Many references may be found in Harris's journal expressing the hope that they would gain a bishop in sympathy with the revival, and, no doubt, this had something to do with his determined allegiance to the Establishment. We do not intend to imply any vain attitude in Whitefield, that he was ambitious for the appointment for his own personal promotion. More probably he thought that the best means for evangelical religion to root itself in the kingdom was the evangelization of the Established Church, and if the Methodists were to turn their backs on it, and to form a separate party, this aim would be postponed, or even made impossible. And yet, perhaps the thought of promotion was not completely absent. Who of us is completely free from thoughts of advancement?

As for Howell Harris, it is not easy to understand the strength of his loyalty. On one hand, we find him a man of liberal attitude, belittling the traditions and ceremonies of the State Church, breaking various forms which he considered authoritarian, and daring to state to the Bishop's face that there was no difference between a consecrated house and one not consecrated. On the other hand, he would not hear of leaving its communion, other than through being forced out. However, we are certain that he was completely selfless in the matter. His eyes were not blinded by hopes of a position and he was not eager for promotion. If he desired ordination it was only in order to gain advantage for doing good.

But to return to the decisions of the Association. It was agreed that it was acceptable to take legal action against those who disturbed their meetings and who attacked worshippers. 'At this,' says Harris, 'my soul was filled with compassion towards the rioters; I had such a view of their wretchedness, and such love towards them, that my heart was near breaking.' On placing any action in the hands of a lawyer, care was to be taken that the person prosecuted should not be harmed in any way; to strike fear into them was the only aim. They then went to dine at the house of a Mr

Richardson. Around the table they discussed the Moravians and their errors, and Harris endeavoured to moderate the bitterness of some of the brethren towards them. In the evening a society meeting was held.

'And although,' says Harris, 'I had been far from the light throughout the day, and without spiritual communion with the Lord, in the singing the divine influence came upon me, so that I was drawn closely to the Lord, and caused to cry out that I might not return to the creature.'

## HARRIS LOSES HIS TEMPER

The Association reconvened shortly after seven the next day, Thursday. Howell Harris felt himself to be in darkness and comfortless; the previous day's argument had wounded his spirit.

There was considerable doubt in my mind whether I should continue my connection with this Association. Though I could stay to wait for it, I cannot feel the same brotherly union towards them as towards the Welsh brethren. A little after seven I went to the brethren, and we sat until two settling the affairs of the Tabernacle, appointing a visitor for the sick, a school teacher, a bookseller, and a leader for each class. A long talk about preaching the law as a rule to believers: Bro. Cennick and others against it much, that we should preach Christ until we became like him, and sin be destroyed. I said I could not agree with that, it was Antinomianism, I thought. That I thought that just as the new creature is nurtured by the knowledge of God in Christ, so also by the holiness of God in the law is seen the evil of sin, and the old man is destroyed, that is, the corrupt nature. That it is not until we believe that we are under the law, but until there is none of the old nature remaining; and that the law is to remain a schoolmaster for us until we are brought to a full subjection to Christ. I saw that he [Cennick] was far beyond me in liberty, but I could not unite with him in this. I had strength to declare how it was with me about my failing to find union with them in soul wrought by the Lord, that I was scrupulous about coming to London any more, and declared my thought of coming no more. I was dead, dull, dark and dry; far from God, and not able to feel communion with God or with them. I was brought low; I saw that I was not worthy to be in their company, yet I was full of love towards them. We then discussed many things . . . Then, having arranged visitors with respect to the Tabernacle and the new room, we dined together; I was sick in body and weary in soul. I retired and sought to pray and draw close to my Lord, but I could not. I saw little of God in my understanding, my will, and my affections; but plenty of the devil, and of that nature which is ready to be inflamed at any difficulty. I am the weakest, the most blind, the most corrupt and the fullest of self of everyone; and while wishing for an inward union to be formed, I desire to be in external union with them. It was painful for me today; yet I am thoroughly happy, because I am resting by faith in the faithfulness of Christ.

So wrote Howell Harris, and the Association closed with a sermon from him on Hebrews 10:19, 20.

This was the first heated argument, resulting in wounded feelings, which arose in the Methodist Associations. It is clear that Harris lost his temper. He admits this sorrowfully, complaining bitterly of his corrupt nature that was ready to ignite at any provocation. We have a glimpse, for the first time, of the heated temper, and the spirit that would not brook any opposition, which damaged his usefulness subsequently and caused him to turn his back on his brethren. Certainly, the state of his health, the natural result of overwork, was a factor in the rise of this spirit that was beginning to possess him.

## FURTHER ARGUMENTS BACK IN WALES

Harris returned from London at the beginning of October. The first thing he notes after his return is a conversation he had with a Richard Jenkins, who had left the Methodists and had joined the Dissenters. He writes:

I saw that he thought mistakenly of me, that I had changed my view with respect to the written and living word; and that I received and indulged in lying tales about them, seeing them as a party that had united against us and that I had forced people to keep away from them. I replied that the light which they followed happened to weaken our hands; for myself, that I was called to remain in the Established Church; and that they preached against us. But with respect to Mr Edmund Jones, that I believed of him that he was a child of God, a true minister of Christ, and did everything from conscience; but that I remained in the Church because of conscience and not from prejudice. I then expressed myself with respect to the written word, that God is not in it essentially, nor continually, nor works in it constantly, but when he wills to; that the word is an instrument through which the Lord works to call sinners to himself, and to reveal to them the Lord Jesus Christ. But in and of itself, apart from God, it is only a dead letter, empty of light and life; that the life is alone in God. The word is a written testament, containing bequests for God's children, and a mirror of God, representing him before the world; but that we cannot see God himself unless the Spirit reveal him to our souls; that the Spirit is apart from the word, and has not bound himself to it, though he has bound us to it; and that to say he is always in it, were our graces active to behold him, is the same, to my mind, as saying that the Spirit is always in the waters of baptism, or in the elements of the Lord's Supper; and that it is a denial of the sovereignty of the Spirit, who shines according to his own pleasure, both in the word and in our own souls. That we appreciate he is often present to others in the word, when we do not perceive him, and to us, when others see him not. That I find for the book which we call the Bible, that it is only for time, whilst we are in the flesh, and that it will not be needed in the spiritual world, in that God can there speak directly to our souls. When the Lord speaks through the word, that the voice and power is something apart from the Bible, which even then is dead, though life comes to us through it; it is only an instrument.

This quotation proves that Harris was an able theologian, with a keen discernment for theological distinctions. It is also seen that the barrier between himself and the Dissenters was gradually widening and that each had become suspicious of the other. He had only two days of rest, if it could be called rest, after returning from London before setting out again on his journeying. He had arrived back on the Sunday night, and on the following Wednesday morning was heading towards Glanyrafonddu, where a Quarterly Association was to be held. Along the way he overtook some of the flock, whose fellowship was enough to fire his soul.

On the way heard of Dissenting Ministers turning against us and turning some out for joining with us. Work going on gloriously through Bros. Rowland, Williams and Davies, many coming under conviction, and many hundreds coming to the ordinance. My soul flamed within me, and I was drawn out to bless the Lord.[6]

At Llwynyberllan he met the three clergymen, Daniel Rowland, Williams, Pantycelyn, and Howell Davies, of whose successes he had been informed and his spirit was again warmed by their company. He felt bereft of power for journeying to north Wales, but wrote: 'I felt that my soul could appeal to God and cry out, "O Lord, thou knowest that I am ready to go there to die, and then to come to thee."' At Llwynyberllan, Howell Davies preached a powerful sermon on Isaiah 1:6. The next day, these ambassadors of Christ reached Glanyrafonddu, and Herbert Jenkins was given a remarkable hold on God in prayer, as he opened the Association. Harris preached first to the gathered brethren, until about half past two, speaking of the greatness of the work; of order and subjection; of reading the Scriptures, and other good books, in order to educate their minds; and that he saw his place as an assistant of the ordained ministers.

But a storm arose in the Association:

Had a dispute about the Moravians. Bro. Rowland being prejudiced for them and I declaring against their errors. The Enemy ruffled my spirit. Again, Bro. John Lewis opened his convictions about leaving the Established Church; that its foundations are Jewish; its canons unscriptural; its ministers God's enemies; and its worship intermixed with Popish superstition; and that he

thought we should now leave it. That now we are a Church and should separate. All the Brethren agreed against this motion ... We are guilty of none of
the evils in our Church, as having all borne our testimony against them; and
I also declared my faith and reasons for it, that this work shall fill the land,
and that I am persuaded I am called to labour in this Church.[7]

Quite clearly, the discussion became heated and Howell Harris was
greatly agitated. The remark that 'the Enemy ruffled my spirit' is significant, but shows also a degree of honesty that is not often met with. Was it
out of respect for Harris's feelings that the brethren agreed unanimously
not to separate, or from a real conviction that to remain in the Church
was their duty? We do not know. But it is good to note that the storm
subsided, and peace returned to the conference. According to the journal,
'Then, having agreed to remain as we are, and having answered some
things to those who hesitated, we prayed and sang, and power and fire
came down amongst us.'

From this time, until its close, the Association proceeded sweetly. The
superintendents presented their reports, which were greatly encouraging,
and many matters were decided. During discussion, remarkable light was
received from the contributions of Morgan John Lewis and William
Richard. John Richard, Llansamlet, was restored to his place after having
been under some discipline; then, in Harris's words:

After deciding all matters, and having found that the superintendents of
Monmouthshire and Montgomeryshire were lukewarm, the Lord opened my
mouth and with, I trust, divine wisdom, ability, authority, love, and sweetness,
I addressed the exhorters on their work; on the importance of their correct
behaviour amongst the lambs; of our unfitness, all of us, for such responsibility; of the importance of giving ourselves to reading; of the building up of the
saints as living stones; of receiving the work as directly from God's hands; and
of loving one another. Life and power accompanied the words, signifying the
greatness of those things that God will shortly perform amongst us.

The next morning, Thursday, he continues:

The sound of singing and praying was to be heard throughout the night. A
complete cloud of the Lamb's witnesses had gathered, namely, three priests,
two Dissenting brothers, twelve superintendents, and a large number of exhorters. I felt a great closeness towards God. I spent the morning paying my
farewells to the brethren, and arranging my journeys, which I do every time
with much care and prayer.

He stayed at Glanyrafonddu until the Saturday, and then departed
for Llangeitho. On the Sunday, he greatly appreciated the service in the
church, and Rowland's sermon on Hosea 1:10. He was in closest fel-

lowship with God during the communion also. He states that amongst the congregation that had gathered were representatives of eight different counties. At five in the afternoon, Harris preached from the words, 'Continue ye in my love,' and was given remarkable fluency of speech. On Monday morning, he rose at five; he felt such intense love towards Rowland and Williams, Pantycelyn, that he found it hard to part with them; at six, he set out for Llanbryn-mair. He travelled extensively through parts of Montgomeryshire, Radnorshire and Breconshire before returning.

In November, he was present at a Monthly Association at Llanddeusant. There was no anger or argument on this occasion; everything proceeded sweetly. Harris delivered a most solemn charge to the exhorters with respect to their behaviour, their dress, and their reading. He portrayed the greatness of their work, the worth of the lambs, and how they should be loved and tenderly cared for, for Christ's sake.

> I was particular in showing how self and pride come in, in various lights, such as dress, etc. Then my lips were opened, by God I believe, to rebuke a brother for being unfaithful to that entrusted to him. While I rebuked him I was in the dust, I was being pierced by love towards him, and I showed the injurious effects of unfaithfulness to our charge for all of us, that it was a dishonouring of God's authority amongst us.

Harris was never more contemptible and mean in his own eyes than when he was administering a rebuke to another, and here he breaks off to cry out, 'O Lord, who am I to be placed in a position of such authority! I feel it to the quick, that he places me more and more in the position of a father, and this drives me to the dust.'

He travelled without stop throughout the November and December of 1743. We continually find him either at Llangeitho or, in the company of Daniel Rowland and Williams, Pantycelyn, in other parts of the country, which suggests that important issues to do with the revival were causing much concern and calling for serious and frequent discussion. But Harris's spirit was on the high places of the field. On Christmas Day, he writes:

> I am now returning from a four-week journey through Cardiganshire, Pembrokeshire and Carmarthenshire, where the work proceeds remarkably. I never before saw, in so many places, such fire, life, power, and liberty of faith. May Christ keep us ever mindful of the extraordinary work of the Holy Spirit. Surely, the Lord has returned to his temple. Last night, in private, my soul burned with desire to glorify God; my soul was on fire of worship to God. I cried out, 'O God, I love thee and bless thee for Christ. I bless thee for his life, my perfect title to heaven; I bless thee for his death, my deliverance from the curse; for conquering death and sin and the devil; I bless thee that he is now in glory, and all authority is his.' O, such liberty! My faith was

greatly strengthened through reading Matthew 1:21, that I could be saved from my sins. I was given much strength to pray for this county, particularly that God might stay here, and make me a blessing to it.

The year 1743 was a remarkable one in the history of Welsh Methodism. During it the constitution of the Connexion arrived at a permanent form, and the societies and exhorters were brought to order. It was a period of much anxiety, of heroic activity, and of powerful visitations. And we find Howell Harris, at its close, in a glorious spirit, praising and worshipping God.

## A QUARTERLY ASSOCIATION AT WATFORD, 1744

On the first Wednesday of 1744, a Quarterly Association met at Watford. Harris's experience on the way there is worth recording:

I cried out in deepest humiliation, 'O Lord, except for the grace which is in thee, O Jesus, I could not go on; I was terrified by the trials and crosses; upon thee and upon thy grace I lean.' I was given a blessed view of the glory, love and sweetness of God; I inclined most comfortably upon him, crying out, 'Regarding going to London, show me, O Lord, whether thou art sending me. It is the same to me whether I go or do not go. Only let me possess thee, and then send me to hell, if it is thy will, to preach to the demons there. Thou art king over them, and they are part of thy kingdom.' I saw this so clearly that I was ready to go or to remain. Then, quite unawares, the following cry rose within me, 'O Lord, send me to London; send a message with me to the blessing of the lambs.' I felt a deep love and a desire to be sent amongst them. With respect to the mighty before whom I must appear, bishops, etc., my soul was made to cry, 'O Lord, thou art in heaven; upon the grace which is in thee I lean . . .' Yesterday was the day on which the lambs from Montgomeryshire were to appear before the enemies at Bangor; I felt a deep communion with them in their sufferings, and an assurance that God would be with them. As for myself, I felt myself willing to go amongst the mob, and amongst deaths of all kinds, for I saw Christ far above all things.

As far as this summons of the Methodists of Montgomeryshire to Bangor is concerned, the following quotation from Howell Harris's letter to the Rev. Griffith Jones provides some light:

Since I saw you I have been in Montgomeryshire, and yesterday they went to Bangor, and according to your advice I consulted some judicious persons, and find that the way of removing causes from that court to the arches is by a writ from the Lord Chief Justice, called nolle prosequi – or non pros – and next Saturday at Trefeca I am to have information what were the proceedings against them, and whether that with the other business may call me to

London immediately. Last night I met with Mr Whitefield here and he is for my going up and is for carrying the matter on, but as 'tis our Lord's cause I doubt not but he will incline all his, that are under the government of the law of his love to join heart and hand in carrying his cause on. Blessed be God, the work is moving on, 'tis on the increase everywhere, fresh doors are opening daily.[8]

This letter was written from Watford in January, 1744. It is seen that Griffith Jones, although not formally united to the Methodists, was heartily sympathetic to the revival and was an adviser to them on any difficult issue. How matters developed at Bangor Assizes is not known, but we can be sure that the Lord, as is his wont to those who love his name, took care of his own. The 'other business' that Harris notes might call him to London was the legal case being brought against those who attacked the Methodists at Hampton, breaking up their meeting. The result of the case was very significant to the Methodists as it ensured their right to conduct their meetings in peace according to their principles.

The Watford Association was a small one. Daniel Rowland, Williams, Pantycelyn, and Howell Davies were absent. The Trefeca records show that it was the rough weather that kept them away, and that their horses failed. But Whitefield had arrived faithfully and had taken the chair. The Rev. Henry Davies, Blaen-gwrach, was present and most of the superintendents. They began at twelve with prayer and praise. Harris wrote:

> I looked for enabling to lay my life down; I felt myself willing to do so, and yet the terror of death was not removed; I saw the dissolution of nature and the change of state as something to be greatly feared. I saw death as a terrible monster, but I saw Jesus Christ above it, and above the devil; and in the consciousness of Christ's power the terror was taken away.

The Association's first work was to receive the reports of the superintendents. Then Whitefield delivered an address to the exhorters. Whitefield then preached, with considerable power, from Hebrews 8:10–12. The fraternity then reconvened to decide upon various matters of which Harris supplies the following précis:

> 1. Whitefield spoke of the legal case, and God's Spirit came down; I had strength to see that it was for the Lord, and so also did all the brethren. It proved to be a means of pressing us closer together, and so we all contributed what we could towards the case.

> 2. Whitefield asked me to write the story of my life; I received great liberty towards Christ, perceiving that he wished this from me; I had strength to decide to do so, for the lambs' sakes, and out of love to him, as all the work is his.

3. When I was asked to go to London to see many of the mighty, and when I feared the trial, I had strength to direct my sight to the wounds of Jesus, and the cry arose within me, 'O Lord, let me go; let me go, and send me.' Then after praying with some liberty with the brethren, my mouth was opened to exhort, and fire, life and power came down amongst us. About eleven, we went to Watford, and sat there until five, speaking freely with the brethren of many things, such as the pre-existence of souls, the journey of the Israelites towards Canaan, etc. All my assurance is in the grace which is in Christ. O, how we are favoured, and how the Lamb leads us and pities us.

It is easy to see that the best of spirits existed between them and that the brethren were very free in each other's fellowship. With a few lines, Harris draws a beautiful picture of the company about the fire in the Watford mansion, having finished their work, and staying up until five o'clock in the morning, discussing such intricate and speculative matters as the pre-existence of souls. We see also that the meetings were held in the chapel. But whether this was the Watford chapel or the Groes-owen chapel is uncertain. The form of words suggests the latter.

The following is the report of the Association's resolutions, as found in the Trefeca records:

A letter was read from the society of Cnapllwyd wherein they requested that Bro. George Phillips should come over to help them. The request was weighed by the brethren, and it was agreed he should be sent to them.

Bro. Beaumont's account of his society is that it is, in the general, very sweet and in a growing state. But wants an inside labourer to nurse the souls. He is to take care of them himself (so far as is consisting with his plan) till the Lord shall raise up one with that particular gift.

Bro. Thomas Lewis is to be given wholly to the English brethren.

The brethren think that Bro. Jacob Jones is called of our Saviour to labour in his vineyard, they agree he should be an assistant to Bro. Morgan John Lewis. The same of Bro. Richard Edwards.

That Bro. William John should be superintendent over Carmarthenshire in the room of Bro. Bloom who has resigned.

The accounts of Bros. Morgan John Lewis, Thomas Williams, William Richard, William John, Thomas James, and Richard Tibbott, for the societies of Montgomeryshire, Breconshire, Monmouthshire, part of Radnorshire, and Carmarthenshire, were read and were very sweet indeed. The rest could now come.

The Monthly Associations have been kept since our last meeting as usual in every Superintendency, namely in Gellidochlaethe, Caeo, Trefeca, and Watford. At Dygoed, disappointed. And the Lord was with us everywhere, settling all things, we trust, according to our Saviour's will, in love, peace and union. Our next Association to be at Abergavenny, the first Wednesday after Lady Day, 1744.[9]

It seems that all the business of the Association was concluded on the first day, but Whitefield preached the next morning at eight on 1 Cor. 15:53 with remarkable unction. About ten, he and Harris departed for Abergavenny. On the way, they passed through the Pontypool area, the field where the Rev. Edmund Jones laboured. Howell Harris was greatly encouraged when he heard of the efforts and success of that good man. He says, 'I had much union with him, and love for him, though Satan, at the first, attempted so to pull us apart that I did not like to see him.' On recalling that it was Edmund Jones who was foremost in drawing up and distributing that declaration against the Methodists, the spirit manifested by Harris in the above quotation is truly magnanimous.

The following letter, sent by the members of the Mynyddislwyn society, is self-explanatory, and casts a gloomy light upon the corrupt lives of the Church of England clergy at the time:

> Dear brethren, we are at a quandary because of not being able to receive the ordinances. Because our curate is one of whom it is said that he is sworn against as an adulterer, we cannot partake with him, without breaking God's commandment. We desire to have your opinion on this matter. We believe that the ordinances are means that should not be neglected, but nor should we depend upon them inordinately. We wish to receive your advice, and for you to remember us before the throne of grace.

This letter is dated 11 January 1744. No doubt it was intended that it be read and considered at the Watford Association, but there is no record of it in the minutes. Whether it was discussed, and if so, what answer it received, is not known.

## A SIXTH VISIT TO LONDON

On Wednesday, 11 January 1744, Harris set out for London. He reached Ross-on-Wye about three in the afternoon, having had unusually profitable fellowship along the way with the brother, Morgan John Lewis. They learnt many valuable lessons together: that it is through experience that one knows God, oneself, Christ, and the devices of the devil. He reached Gloucester by five, and having eaten, went to the society where he had occasion to rejoice. He rose the next morning at six in order to address the members of the society, from the words, 'For thine is the kingdom.' On Saturday night, he arrived in London, proceeding immediately to Mr Whitefield's house where he heard glorious news of the success of the work. On Sunday morning, he went to St. Paul's. He could not hear the clergyman preaching, but was given strength to pray for the Church of England:

> O Lord, return; Thy glory is on the threshold of the door, nearly having left us. O return, rebuild our ramparts; so that, if there is here any remembrance of Thy name, if any of Thy seed remain, if your glory has not completely departed, I may stay in this poor Church.

He felt such love for the benighted souls within the Church that he could not leave them, but was constrained to cry out:

> O Jesus, Thou hast opened meeting houses (many have been opened lately) and, Lord, I bless Thee for that; but wilt Thou not bless us also, and open the doors of the churches?

He felt a spirit of mourning. He confessed his own sins, the sins of the Church, the sins of the nation, and cried:

> O Lord, I see that we are dead, in a deep sleep, and not only that but that we rebel against Thee, and tempt Thee in every way. O have mercy upon us, and return to us again.

When the sermon was over he approached the communion table and saw in Christ all of which he stood in need. That night, he went to hear the preaching of Whitefield, who was excellent, speaking from the history of Samson, and in the society that followed Harris addressed the fraternity. He heard there of the Bishop of London writing against them.

On Monday morning, he went with Whitefield to a lawyer to discuss the legal case. He heard that it was likely that the mob would not defend the case, which caused him to cry out, 'Glory!' On Tuesday, a Monthly Association was being held at the Tabernacle; it does not appear that there was much business to discuss, the only matter referred to in his journal was the marriages of some of the brethren, to which the fathers of the brides-to-be objected. What was decided on the matter is not stated. He was in London until 15 March, preaching, exhorting in the societies and in many conferences of ministers.

He visited the royal palace at Kensington; some prisoners sentenced to death at Newgate, and the Countess of Huntingdon a number of times. London was in a ferment at this time with fears of a French invasion. Harris also shared in the fears and wrote that an enemy fleet had once sailed up the Thames. It appears too that his health was bad throughout this time; he was sometimes not able to rise from his bed until noon. He reached Gloucester on Friday, 16 March, and intended to be present in court for the trial of the Hampton rioters. These did not provide much of a defence and were judged guilty, but the decision on the amount of fine they should pay was left to the court of the King's Bench in London. According to Whitefield, who was also present, 'I have heard that the rioters have been terribly affrightened; but they do not realize that our purpose is to show what we might do, and then to forgive them.' There are few examples found of men as willing as the Methodists to forgive their enemies, and so fulfil the law of Christ.

## VARIOUS QUARTERLY AMD MONTHLY MEETINGS

On Sunday night, 19 March, Harris arrived at Trefeca, weak and weary. On the Wednesday of the following week, he was at a Quarterly Association at Abergavenny. Whitefield had arrived, to take the chair. Daniel Rowland, Williams, Pantycelyn, and Howell Davies were present, together with a considerable number of superintendents. As he arrived, he heard of the fall of some of the brethren.

> The Lord gave to me a burden of grief that we were sinning in this way against our dear Father; that we, who have been so favoured, should sin against him. I met another brother, Mr William Evans, who was under some burdens, and I felt more than ever before that his burden was pressing upon my spirit.

He then states that he departed afar from the Lord, that the pollution of his nature broke out in anger, that he lost his temper, and was enflamed, and he heard that his passion had caused someone to faint. He saw how unfit he was for his position, and how unworthy to be a married man, the thought of which was now pressing heavily on his mind, and he went to his room to humble himself before the Lord. It proved a painful time for him, but he was enabled, before emerging, to thank God for hiding his face from him and for allowing his pollution to manifest itself, in that this was a help to keep him humble. He became willing to give up his prospective wife, his place in the church, and every gift and ability he possessed.

Whitefield began the Association by preaching from the words, 'Lovest thou me more than these?' He explained the characteristics of love to Christ: rejoicing on hearing of the success of the gospel; willingness to die; willingness to love one's enemies; thinking and speaking of him; loving God's children of whatever religious party; that he enables us to open our hearts to one another; that we cannot love Christ without our knowing it; and that he causes us to give up all things for him. The prayer at the close of the sermon was of extraordinary power. In the private meeting, Harris was charged with administering discipline to a brother who had transgressed. In doing so, he saw himself as worse than the one being disciplined, but that God had concealed his evil, whereas this man's evil had been revealed. This pierced him, as a dagger in the heart. The next day, he preached with much power.

Apart from the arranging of the Monthly Meetings for the following months, the only resolutions of the Association noted in the Trefeca records are the following:

> It was solemnly agreed upon that no one should be absent from an Association except he can give a reason for it at the day of judgment.
>
> That the next Quarterly Association is to be kept at Trefeca, the first Wednesday after next Quarter Day.
>
> That Bro. John Richard should continue going his rounds till next Association, and in the meantime Mr Harris is to visit the societies on account of their bearing fruit to him. He was absent but sent an account of the societies and they were pretty sweet.
>
> That Bro. David Williams should be summoned to come to our next Quarterly Association to answer to things laid to his charge.
>
> That there is to be preaching at every Quarterly Association by the ministers alternately . . . the Association to begin at twelve and the brethren to refresh themselves before. Mr Rowland to preach the next.[10]

There is little in these resolutions that requires comment. We learn that the old brother, John Richard of Llansamlet, was in poor circumstances and that the purpose of Harris's visit to his societies was to encourage them to provide him with some financial support. We see also the large place given to preaching in their Associations from the beginning.

On 2 April, 1744, Harris was at an English Association in Wiltshire. Whitefield was Moderator. It appears that he was the permanent chair of the English Associations as well as of the Welsh. At first, Harris felt hard and carnal; but when the Moderator began praying for the king and the country, and against the papists, his heart melted within him, and his spirit was liberated. They sat until about five, deciding upon general regulations, and setting each in his place: clergymen, preachers, exhorters, and superintendents. While they did this, Harris felt a desire to go to the war, to die on the field of battle. He states also that he was made an instrument for taking a step forward towards separating with the brother, J.W. – John Wesley, no doubt.

On 13 April, there was a Monthly Association at Nantmel, Radnorshire; Howell Harris was present, but Williams, Pantycelyn, chaired. Harris wrote in his journal:

Truly, my lips were opened to address the brethren generally, asking of them whether they felt the work placed deeply within their hearts; whether love for souls was present in them; and whether a view of the majesty and nature of the work, and the value of souls, had caused them to cry for strength and wisdom? Also, whether the Spirit had shown them: 1. The glory of Christ? 2. The evil of the heart? – that the one is not sufficient without the other. Has God given them two faiths, one for their souls, and another for the work? Whether a sense of the majesty of the work drives them to the ground, and a sense of the privilege belonging to it makes them humble, and excites them? Then the brethren replied, most sweetly. Bro. Beaumont showed how the Lord had freed him from self-love by showing him that he and the work were in God for time and for eternity. Then, after examining the brethren (I saw that the Lord was equipping me for the position, and blessing me in it), I was enabled to excite them to industry, and to show them how to behave in families. I spoke for a long time to Bro. – regarding his marriage and his prospects in life, showing how a minister should not be hindered by the things of the world but as little as possible. I had much faith, warmth, zeal, and liberty to exhort, and particularly to pray, and I then left sweetly in love.

It may be seen that Harris had realized, as early as this time, that the duty of ministers of the Word is to give themselves wholly to the ministry, as far as that is possible for them.

The following are the resolutions decided upon in the Nantmel Association, as they are found in the Trefeca records:

Agreed that Bro. Richard should be wholly and altogether on the work of visiting the societies, all every week.

That Bro. Edward Bowen should retard his marriage now as not clear it is of God.

That the exhorters should take care in the families they are in, to exhort, instruct, etc., the children, servants, etc. We had much of the Lord, teaching and enflaming our hearts; and giving us much spiritual light in our work and places; showing us the greatness of the work and visiting us in it.[11]

Howell Harris departed about five o'clock, in the company of Williams, Pantycelyn. The fellowship of the two friends, as they crossed the mountains of Maesyfed and Breconshire, was of the sweetest. Williams directed his path towards home, past Llanwrtyd, where he had once been a curate, and Harris headed for Dolyfelin, where he was appointed to preach. His journal reads:

I had much pleasure in the company of Bro. Williams; I was favoured with a sight of God as all in all, similar to that I received in the morning.

He spent the Sunday at Llanwrtyd and went to the church in the morning, but it was not a Williams who now ministered there but someone very different as far as the discernment of the truths of the gospel, and the ability to expound them, were concerned. Harris wrote, 'I had pity for the poor blind clergy, crying for them earnestly as for blind people at the side of the road.' After the service, he himself preached from Psalm 23 and had much liberty both in preaching and praying. In the evening he preached to a large gathering, numbering many hundreds, in a place called Pen-y-lan, about three miles outside the village. On the Monday, he was at Llwynyberllan, going from there to Cil-y-cwm, where he preached, again to many hundreds, and again on Psalm 23, from under the large oak tree in the middle of the village. It was a most powerful service. He met there with a clergyman called Lewis Lewis, an able man, who seemed to Harris to be full of power and life, and yet who frequently fell in an abominable fashion. He journeyed on to Caeo, after preaching at the roadside on the way, and went in the evening to the private society. On Tuesday, he was at Cwm-y-glaw, proceeding from there to Abergorlech Chapel where Daniel Rowland preached from Jeremiah 8:7. On Tuesday, 17 April, they gathered for a Monthly Association at Glanyrafonddu. Harris, Rowland and Williams were present, together with the Rev. Benjamin Thomas, and a great number of superintendents and exhorters. The meetings began at six in the evening; they conferred together, arranging matters and praying, until about eleven. Harris was in excellent spirits. It is clear from his comments that the previous Association at that place, when he had been overcome by the evil one, was much on his mind.

> I was in a prayerful spirit, and pleasant to the brethren; all things occasioned my subjection; I was low, and tender, and so content. When praying, I saw that death, hell, war, and all things of a terrible nature, were within Christ's authority; I saw him above them all. While exhorting, I was given freedom and boldness; I showed their duty towards the lambs; that Christ came to redeem them, so that they might use soul, body, time, breath, talent and money in his service, etc., and not to serve themselves. I had liberty to cry, 'Lord, all things are thine; thine is my soul and my body, so they cannot be lost.' By this light my spirit was broken down, so that I could endure being opposed and could accept all things.

These words show surely that he was in the gentlest of states of mind. The following are the resolutions that were passed:

Agreed that David William Rees should go and acknowledge what he has spoken amiss in discourse to Mr Griffith Jones before Mr Davies, and on their being reconciled to him to be admitted again as an exhorter, and that he should desist exhorting till then.

Agreed that as Thomas David has been turned out by the dissenters for communicating with us, that he should be wholly united to us, and received by us, and should exhort on trial under the inspection of Bro. James Williams as superintendent, not leaving his calling in the meantime.

Agreed that the exhorters should discourse by way of exhortation and not in the form of a sermon.

Agreed that Thomas Griffith should be a private exhorter under the inspection of Mr Rowland and Mr Williams.

Agreed that Benjamin Rees should exhort as a Dissenting brother as before, till next Association.

Agreed that John David should exhort in his neighbourhood on trial under the inspection of Brother James Williams till a report of his gifts, qualifications, etc., be had in order to examination.

Agreed that the Bro. Evan John should have an answer to his letter by Mr Williams that we are not so persuaded of his call to exhort as that we can give him the right hand of fellowship and therefore we give him up to the Lord.[12]

We see that the method of proving preachers in those days was very similar to that of today, with the difference that those who had no clarity of vision with respect to their own talents were not quietened but committed to the Lord. What that involved is not clear. Perhaps it meant some period of probation until light was obtained on their case from the Head of the Church.

Within another two days, namely, on 19 April, there was a Monthly Association at Llandremor. It must be appreciated that these Monthly Meetings, following on each other's heels, belonged to different regions, but that Howell Harris, as much as possible, was expected to be present at them all. Here it was Howell Davies who chaired. The two Howells were at this time on the point of marrying, and they conferred together with the sweetest of fellowship on the matter.

It was a small Association; few had gathered together, and there was very little business to discuss. But it appears that they had ample evidence of God's favour. Harris preached to begin, from Matthew 28:18 and was given particular strength to address both saints and sinners. On beginning the private meeting with prayer, the Lord came down, humbling them all, enlightening them, and kindling them. After establishing the brother William Christopher as a catechizer, Harris spoke very plainly to some brother, that he should either join the Dissenters or the Methodists. 'Then,' he says, 'having arranged all in their places, we departed as in a flame.' Only two resolutions from this Association are to be found in the records, namely:

Agreed that William Christopher should be a Catechizer to catechize only and that we should all endeavour to set catechizing everywhere. There being a great call for Bro. Richard William David to Gorseinon and great need there and at Pembrey we consented till next Association at Abergorlech that he and his brother should go there and visit them.[13]

## A MONTHLY MEETING AT WATFORD – THE FIRST EXCOMMUNICATION

After journeying through extensive areas of Carmarthenshire and Glamorganshire, Howell Harris arrived at the Monthly Meeting at Watford, and as not one of the ordained priests was present, he took the chair. He had preached the previous evening in the new room, that is, either Watford Chapel or Groes-wen, with much unction. With power greater than he had ever before experienced, he described how great a king was Jesus; how excellent was his kingdom; that heaven, earth and hell belonged to it; the way in which he ruled over all things – grace and sin, light and darkness, life and death, the spiritual world and the natural world. He then explained the security of the citizens of this kingdom, that the word of God, the oath of God, the faithfulness, strength, wisdom, mercy, and nature of God, were as strong chains keeping them from falling; and that bad men, sin, Satan, were only God's servants for bringing the saints forward, by barking like dogs at their heels. He continued:

> Then I strengthened those who were afraid of being pressed to go to war by showing that a cannon ball would do as well as anything to send them home. I shouted out, 'If you could only see how rich you are, how secure, how happy; the kind of King you have; you would be ashamed of yourselves for your fears and barrenness; cry to him that you and all your talents may be used by him, being aware of what a privilege that would be; wherever you go, and amongst whatever peoples, you will always be within Christ's realm. O, glorious King! Let your faith be extended to see the glory of his kingdom!

It appears to have been an extraordinary powerful meeting. He himself states that he had never had its like before, and that he had never had such remarkable thoughts before. Perhaps that was indeed the case, but the latest memory is always the best memory. Their rejoicing increased as they sang and prayed at the close.

> I saw the glory of Jesus' kingdom in such a beautiful light that my soul flamed and was strengthened, and I was brought to join with the heavenly choir in singing, 'Worthy is the Lamb that was slain! Worthy, indeed!'

About twelve o'clock on the Wednesday, the Association began. As they prayed at the beginning, Harris was constrained to ask whether the Lord intended to give the Methodists up? He was persuaded otherwise, and felt that this conviction was from God himself. They conferred, with some breaks, until twelve at night. They had great trouble with one exhorter, William Rees, as they sought to convince him of his errors. He held that he was perfect, and he would not promise to keep quiet in the societies about his supposed perfection. Harris continues:

> So, for the glory of God, for the good of the lambs, for the benefit of his own soul, we turned him out of the society, in that he appeared to be so full of himself. As we sought God's guidance in this matter I had assurance that as it was the Lord who had sent me, he would ensure that I be supplied with every necessary knowledge and light.

They sat together until about four in the morning, speaking freely of various matters: of communion in the Church of England, and the persecuting spirit of the priests; of Harris's imminent marriage; and other things. The brethren also judged that John Belcher was the most qualified in knowledge of Scripture, gifts, and grace, to be an assistant to Harris in his important work.

The Trefeca records provide the following list of the resolutions passed at this Association:

> Agreed that Bro. Price should as before take care of Monmouthshire societies in the moors, and assist Bro. Thomas Williams as far as he can.

> After some consultation, we agreed about regulating the private exhorters, that they should not exhort publicly, but only in the private societies, except William Edward who is called openly to Llantrisant and Groes-wen. Joseph Simons [to be] as before, and Evan Thomas to go to Machen and Mynyddislwyn as before on trial, and that we should look out for proper persons to catechize all within and without in order to establish the lambs, etc., in sound knowledge of the principles of religion, by Mr [Griffith] Jones's Catechism.

> [Agreed] that for the better regulating of Catechizing after proper persons are called to the work, that the Superintendent should be present to assist in the work.

> [Agreed] that it should be proposed to Edward Lloyd to be a Catechizer at Groes-wen; to Samuel Jeremiah at Llanedern; to William Thomas at Aberthin, Llantwit and Llanharry; to Edward Edwards at Dinas Powys and St. Nicholas; to Kitt Basset at Aberthaw; to Howell Griffiths or Morgan Howell at Llantrisant; to William Hughes at Nottage; and Jenkin Lewis at Hafod.

> Agreed that as the rounds of the Superintendents are so large that they can visit the societies but once a fortnight, and as Bro. Herbert Jenkins (though

called to assist Bro. Harris as a General Superintendent) is called to spend half his time in England, that there should be one chosen that should give himself entirely to go about as an assistant to Bro. Harris in such a district to help the Superintendents. After debating about his inward and outward qualifications, that we propose to John Belcher as the most proper person to fill the place above mentioned, in part of Monmouthshire, Glamorganshire and Carmarthenshire, by the sea side, in the rounds of Bros. John Richard, Thomas William, Thomas Price, and part of Morgan Johns. That the Superintendent should meet his assistants to settle the lambs once a fortnight, Friday evening.

Agreed that we are not persuaded of Bro. Williams Rees's call to exhort, we should send to him to desire him to desist till we are more satisfied. That Bro. William Powell should go on still waiting to see where the Lord calls and settles him. That as Bro. Richard Jones is to blame on several accounts for cleaving to the world, being unfaithful to his charge, regardless of his duty to us his brethren, etc., and has continued in these and other blameable faults after frequent admonitions and reproofs, we have agreed to speak to him that if he does not penitently own his faults and promise amendment we should desire him not to discourse any more as one of us, and acquaint the societies of this, but if he seems penitent to let him go on trial till our next General Association.

Agreed that through the help of God we should begin to discourse strictly within an hour or less to the time appointed.

That Bro. Richard Thomas should come to our Association at Llanfihangel on Holy Thursday to be settled.

We discoursed on several heads of divinity and agreed, and that we are not, nor should not call ourselves a Church or sect, but societies called in the Established Church till turned out, and that such as discourse are not, nor should they, be called ministers, but exhorters.

We see also [that] what is to God's glory and edificial for a rule in one place can't answer the end in another.

That as the gifts, etc., of the private exhorters are but short, it is left to the discretion of the Superintendent to exchange them as he and they shall agree in their meeting at the fortnight's end, only that they should not settle themselves without consent.

After talking a long time with William Rees about some antinomian errors that he is fallen into, and offered to let him stay among us notwithstanding if he would promise not to disturb us and the lambs by propagating his errors, and when he would not promise this, but said (though he owns he has wanderings in prayer, etc.) that he has not sinned several days, and that he has no sin in his understanding, will or conscience, etc., we agreed that it is our duty to turn him out of the societies and Association, and to warn all the society against his errors, and to have no close fellowship with him. So we solemnly (after a long debate and prayer together) turned him out, and had our hearts broken with love to him and concerns for the glory of God, with holy fear and concern for the lambs.[14]

So end the minutes of this Monthly Association at Watford; one of the most important held. In it, for the first time in the history of Methodists, a member was excommunicated for doctrinal error, and the hearts of the brethren were almost broken on having to discipline him. The first heresy to trouble the Methodists was Antinomianism. Perhaps one reason for this was their tendency to move to the opposite extreme of that of the Dissenters, who were ravaged by Arminianism. The William Rees who was thrown out was not the brother of the same name who was kept from exhorting because of the inadequacy of his gift. The first was present, and a long argument with him took place; the second was absent so that a message had to be sent to him. We see a strong allegiance to the Church of England in the decisions not to label themselves a Church or a sect, and to refuse to allow the exhorters to call themselves ministers. Howell Harris was almost certainly responsible for these decisions; he was more loyal to the Church than any. Rowland, Williams, Pantycelyn, and Howell Davies were absent, and they had much less respect for the Establishment and were readier to leave it.

The following Friday, Harris was at Pen-tyrch, about six miles from Cardiff, and his comment in his journal is worth recording:

My nature was completely worked out, and I did not arise until after ten. As Bro. T. P. and I opened our hearts to one another and finding that my failings were being spoken of in secret, I had a sight of the nature of self and pride, seeing it is a mountain within me, raising itself up against God, and that to such a height that only God could forgive and destroy it. I was given a heart to mourn because of it, and faith to commit my selfishness and pride to God's hand to be destroyed. I find that the brethren draw closer to me, seeing that their cause is similar to mine.

It is clearly amongst the Methodists that Harris's failings were being spoken of in secret; his enemies proclaimed the faults that they found in him from the housetops. It appears therefore that the hot temper of the Reformer, which broke out whenever he was opposed, or when any mention was made of leaving the Church of England, had become a topic of conversation amongst the exhorters and the ordinary members. He was aware of his weakness and grieved because of it, taking it to the Lord for forgiveness and deliverance from it. On Saturday, he was at Aberthin,

and on Sunday, he attended Wenvoe Church, where an evangelical clergyman called William Thomas officiated. He partook of communion,
and thanked God that he had allowed the ordinance to continue in the
Church. He prayed:

> O God, do not let us be deprived of this ordinance in this poor, orphaned
> Church; rather let us become salt in it. Do not allow our corruptions, selfish-
> ness, pride and tendency to despise others; nor the corruptions and persecut-
> ing tendencies of others, to turn us out. O return to us, and may we become
> a light to the whole land.

The following note in his journal, written at Watford and dated the
following Tuesday, is self-explanatory:

> They try to take from me that which I have already given away, and which
> is not in my possession but Christ's, namely my life. I see in this a trial of
> my faith. There is a warrant out to press me into the army. When I began to
> think of this I was given relief by crying to the Lord, 'O Lord, that which
> thou dost perform shall stand. Thou art King. They cannot work without
> thee. Now, teach me only to glorify thee, and to rejoice that I have a soul and
> a body to give to thee.' Never before had I such sweet experience. The news
> (about a warrant) is so far from being painful to me that I would not have
> taken a thousand worlds for not hearing it. Those words came to my mind
> which had been blessed to me seven years ago, namely, 'No man can shut it.'
> I saw them all in Christ's hand,

A blessed experience indeed! We never see Harris so uplifted by grace,
or showing such excellent spirit, than when the storm is rising against
him.

A Monthly Association was held at Llanfihangel-on-Usk on 3 May.
Again, there were no ordained clergymen present and so Harris was
Moderator. The following resolutions were agreed:

> Association at Llanfihangel-juxta-Usk. Agreed here, as at Watford, about
> catechizing to propose it to the brethren and to use Mr Griffith Jones's
> Catechism, especially on the creed.

> Agreed that Bro. John Belcher should assist Bro. Harris in assisting the
> Superintendents, as at Watford.

> Agreed that the private exhorters should take the immediate care of visiting
> the private societies in secret, except on causes extraordinary, when any to be
> received or turned out, or some scruples to be removed, or something to be
> consulted as marriage, etc.

> Agreed as at Watford to regulate the private exhorters.

> Having discoursed together and communicated our light to each other
> freely about our duties toward all mankind and the relation we stand in to

all in general as fellow creatures, to the whole Church in particular all over the world as being Christ's body and to that branch of [it] in this nation especially, and more immediately to such as associate themselves with us; we agreed, in order, as far as we can remove stumbling blocks, to communicate in the parish churches and to advise the people to do so, in order to prevent our appearing like a sect (having before agreed not to call our societies churches, but societies in the established Church, and not to call the exhorters ministers, etc.) and especially as the scruples of most seem to rise from their corruptions and darkness and not their grace; firstly, looking to, and stumbling at, the faults of others with them receiving, which savours much of the Pharisee pointing at the publican, and betrays too great an ignorance of themselves and want of pity to others; secondly, looking at the meanness or sinfulness of the minister, and saying, 'How can we expect a blessing or receive benefit from such a one, etc.?' which argued a weakness of faith to look through the means to God, looking and depending on the grace of the person administering instead of that in Christ. Bro. Morgan John Lewis agreed by way of forbearance till the Lord should thrust us out or bring in a reformation; only he said their parish church was now all in confusion, having no settled order as to times, etc., and when he proposed having the ordinance at St Bride's, the minister did treat him very kindly saying he had no objection to him, etc., but said there was a canon against it. Bro. Belcher said he had not quite freedom, but would be kind to himself. The rest were satisfied.[15]

It is seen that the same matters were being discussed, and the same resolutions being passed, in different Monthly Meetings. This was in order to form a common understanding amongst the various societies and exhorters in all parts of the country. It can also be seen that the relationship between the Methodists and the Established Church was again the topic of long discussion during the meeting. But this time Harris did not lose his temper, as at Glanyrafonddu. Instead, the reasons for and against departing were deliberated with care; and eventually they agreed to remain until the time came that they were thrown out. Whether Harris added something of his own opinion to the minutes when he mentions that the suggestion not to partake together with ungodly men and from the hands of immoral clergymen, was fuelled more by corruption than by grace, and savoured of a Pharisaical spirit, we cannot tell. No doubt, this is what he thought, and it is natural to assume that his thoughts influenced him as he wrote.

## HOWELL HARRIS'S WEDDING

On 3 May 1744, Ascension Thursday, during this Association, he wrote as follows:

Seven years today the door was just going to be shut against my going about and Miss Williams's father sent his son to ask me to discourse at his house, which proved the means of opening the door for me and now I am going to have his daughter.[16]

We conclude from this reference that Mr Williams of Skreen was the gentleman from Radnorshire who invited Harris to preach in his house in 1737, and was the providential instrument for spreading the revival across the country. It appears that Harris's imminent marriage was greatly disturbing the gentry of Breconshire and Radnorshire. Mr Williams, Skreen, was a gentleman, and belonged to their particular circle, and a marriage with Miss Williams would draw Harris, the Methodist, whom they despised in their hearts, into some connection with themselves, which they could not tolerate. The frustrating of this marriage was the main purpose in raising a warrant to have him pressed into the army. Harris wrote:

I find that the ire of the magistrates increases greatly against me. A J.P. told Miss Williams's father that he would send me to the war, were it only in order to prevent me from having his daughter as a wife.

They succeeded in so disturbing Miss Williams's brother that he opposed the marriage and joined in their conspiracy.

At last the storm began to close in upon him. On 8 May 1744, he wrote:

Near one o'clock, William G— and the constable came there to take Jemmy to be a soldier.

This 'Jemmy' was James Morgan, the overseer of his house, and an exhorter with the Methodists.

I had been warned that they were coming; so I ran up the stairs and fell before the Lord. But for some time I was left so that I could not pray, nor draw close to God. I was committed, but because I had sunk into myself I did not feel the strength and life that I generally knew. I was in bondage to a slavish fear, so that I could not be bold. I was brought down like a partridge; the enemy was nearby; I felt the flesh fearing lest the house of clay be undone by a blow on the head. Gradually, however, I recovered myself so as to go down to the workers.

These workers were preparing the house at Trefeca, which he had received as a gift from his brother, Joseph, for his prospective bride and himself. Clearly, Harris's faith failed him for an instant. The mighty man, who feared not all the hosts of evil, weakened for a while and became like other men. We are not writing the history of a perfect man, but of a godly man, whose grace, at times, comes under a cloud. And the episode was not yet ended. Fearing that the magistrate and constable would return to take him, he fled in the direction of Tyn-y-cwm, Radnorshire. Can this really be Howell Harris? No wonder that he notes on the way that he is still in bondage and crying out, 'O my weakness!' But he also declares, 'The Lord knows me.' This fit of despair did not last long, however. 'My soul was filled with strength,' he wrote, 'I saw that my life, though I lost it ten thousand times, was nothing beside his glory. I saw all my enemies as nothing.' He continued towards Skreen so as to comfort and prepare Miss Williams for what might lie ahead, and the next day he returned to Trefeca to await the outcome, whatever that might be.

On Thursday, 11 May, his state of mind was glorious:

> I saw that my body is not my own, but the Lord's. I would prefer to descend into hell a million times than to give place for a second to any complaining thought; that he should rule my soul and do with me as he sees fit, even if he were to destroy me, or sentence me to eternal punishment. As I have been purchased by him, may he not do with me as he pleases? I heard again and again today the certainty how I am to be taken tomorrow, how all the Magistrates are enraged against me especially on account of my marriage.[17]

The next day, a Monthly Association was to be held at Trefeca, and it appears that his persecutors had decided to enforce the warrant as Harris was addressing the public meeting, so as to strike fear into all hearts, especially those of the exhorters who would have gathered from all parts of the country. But God's man was quite fearless.

> I saw such a view of God as above them all, and such an assurance that he would give me an open door that no man would be able to shut, that I looked on my opponents as insects and vanity.

God did not leave him without comforts during this storm. One brother travelled all the way from Neath in order to encourage him. Another came to give him the news that the mayor of Bristol had proclaimed that he would not send one of the Methodists to the war.

> This melted my heart, I saw that God always revealed himself on our side. Many advise me not to speak tomorrow, as I am sure to be taken; but I see that my duty is to go forward with the work, and that I am called to suffer in it. I am often filled with joy at the knowledge that my suffering is at hand; other times I fear and tremble at the sight of God, and at their ferocity and hate, which is God's rod, being applied by him to our flesh; it goes like a thrust of a sword through me. But, together with every cross, I receive some addition of strength to the new man, and something of self and nature is removed.

The day for enforcing the warrant was Friday, when the Association would be under way. Harris awoke in cheerful spirit. He saw God sitting upon the flood.

> I wrote my journal, and arranged all my affairs in preparation for my imprisonment; and I was happy and contented. I was kept from looking for carnal protection; I could escape should I wish to do so, but I saw that my duty was to stay.

He proceeded to the meeting, to stand up for his God. Before departing, he prayed for his mother, that her faith should not fail. He was in the private meeting with the brethren until one o'clock and then went to the public meeting. A large number had gathered and he was given extraordinary power as he spoke. His text was the house on the rock and the house on the sand. Before closing, he opened his heart to the congregation. He said that he was ready to suffer, and that it was love towards God and towards their souls that brought him there that day. For some reason, the warrant was not enforced. Was it the power of the words of the man of God that weakened the arms of his persecutors? Or did they fear to lay hold on such a famous name as Howell Harris, a free-holder, and a man supported by some of the chief noblemen of the kingdom? But God watched over his servant. He disarmed his enemies as effectively as he closed the mouths of the lions long ago.

This Monthly Association at Trefeca was a small gathering. None of the three clergymen was present, and only two of the superintendents, Morgan John Lewis and Thomas James; perhaps the persecution had kept the others away. A large number of exhorters had gathered however. The main decisions taken were as follows:

> Gave our opinion to Bro. Walter Hill about his scruples of receiving the sacrament with carnal ministers, etc., that for the present till we should be turned out or a reformation should come on we should as far as possible bear and forbear for the sake of the work.

> Agreed that Bro. John Williams (as other private exhorters) should not be settled continually to overlook the one or two same societies, but should be sent here or there at the discretion of the superintendent as he should see his gifts and the condition of the people called.

> Agreed that Bro. Thomas Jones should hire himself with John Richard and be as before till next general Association and visit Radnorshire once a month. After consultation about Morgan John Lewis's marriage we had all freedom to it.

> Agreed that the determination of Bro. Edward Bowen's affair of marriage should be made by Bro. Thomas James and Bro. Thomas Bowen after they should consult the both societies that he and she belong to.

Agreed that Bro. Walter Hill should go to service to Bro. William Evans and that Mr Roberts should be written to on his account to release him and that the brethren should be spoken to to ease Bro. Evans of some of the burden of his wages. [Agreed] that Bro. William Evans should give himself wholly to the work so far as is consisting with his family cares and overlook all the societies under Bro. Beaumont in his absence while he is in London, being assisted by Bro. Thomas James.

[Agreed] that all should, in this time of trial, use double diligence and strive to bring up catechizing in families.

We thought Bro. Thomas Jones's affair of marrying not of the Lord.[18]

Within three days, that is on 15 May, there was a Monthly Meeting at Brynbychan. A great many attended, among them, Daniel Rowland, who was Moderator, Williams, Pantycelyn, the Rev. Benjamin Thomas, Richard Tibbott, and others. Howell Harris travelled there through the district of Buallt, speaking at many places along the way. At ten o'clock on the morning of the Association, Daniel Rowland preached at the Anglican chapel of Abergorlech, about four miles from Brynbychan. His text was Psalm 2:6, and he had a notable service. He showed how safe was God's Church, how impossible it was to overcome it, however much hatred there was against Christ. He closed by calling upon all of God's children to triumph in hope, and not to be concerned on hearing of wars, etc., as our Caesar (Christ) is alive. 'Not only is he alive,' cried the preacher, 'but he reigns. Rejoice; Christ reigns!' Harris's soul cried out within him as he listened, 'Glory to Christ!' It was a remarkable service. And when the preacher prayed at the end for all classes of men, including the king, an unusual light shone upon the congregation. Said Harris,

> My soul blessed God for dear Rowland; for the ability, power, wisdom, courage, and authority that he has given him; and I felt satisfied to be of no ability for these to blossom to God's glory.

They reached Brynbychan in the afternoon. At five the Association began, and they sat until ten at night. Harris felt quite ill, but God opened his mouth to address the brethren on the nature of humility, of a broken spirit, and of true personal knowledge of God. He had such a sight, during the meeting, of the strength of the enemies, the greatness of the work, his own unfitness for it, and his need for every grace, that he cried out,

> Lord, nothing can enable me to go out [to preach], except that Thou send me; this, and this only, is the foundation I build upon, that I have been sent by Thee.

The next day, he went as far as Dygoedydd, in the company of Rowland and Williams. There, Daniel Rowland preached on Song of Solomon 2:14, with great unction. Then the friends departed. Rowland and Williams continued to Cardiganshire, and Harris to Trefeca.

The resolutions of the Brynbychan Association were few and comparatively unimportant:

> Agreed after a long debate, that Evan John should be left to the Lord, till we should have more light, as we had no light to see his call and he had no liberty to give over.

> Agreed that when any place to be published for exhorting, that the name of him that is to exhort be mentioned in publishing.

> Agreed that catechizing be set up and ordered in such a manner as is most to edification, to stir all to the more searching of the Scripture.

> Agreed that William Samuel should exhort on trial at and about home.[19]

As the day of Harris's wedding approached, the opposition to the union increased. The Williams family itself was bitter and persecutory. The father, who at one point had given his consent, now offered his daughter £1500 if she would withdraw; her mother threatened to beat her; and her brother was full of rage. Furthermore, stories were being spread around against the Reformer's character: that he was only marrying her for her dowry, and that they were not entering marriage in an honourable condition. The expectation of the humbling of the man who went about preaching, threatening the wrath of God against all workers of iniquity, caused much rejoicing amongst the magistrates of Breconshire and Radnorshire, as ones that had found great spoil. But the young girl had courage and integrity, and, notwithstanding all the opposition, she was united in marriage to Howell Harris at Ystrad-ffin Chapel on 18 June 1744. In order to put a stop to the enemies of religion, Harris refused to take a penny of dowry with his bride and, as a married couple, a little time proved the falsity of the other rumour.

## FURTHER ASSOCIATIONS

On 27 June, the Quarterly Association was held at Trefeca. Nearly all the fraternity was present, Rowland, Williams, and Howell Davies, amongst the others. At eleven in the morning, Rowland preached from Hebrews 6:18, showing the necessity of faith before works, and the duty of approaching the promises before the commandments. Harris felt heavy and sleepy during the service. Not even Rowland was able to fire a congregation every time. After him Herbert Jenkins preached on

Philippians 4:4, and he secured a better grasp of his hearers' interest. Harris wrote:

> After he had finished, we dined, and I felt much pleasure in serving the brethren at table, being thankful that I have a house where I can welcome God's messengers. About three, we joined the other brethren at the Association, where we sat until ten. We had several affairs of moment to consult about, especially about the ministers giving the Sacrament in houses; and I was drawn out in great warmth, zeal and earnestness. As I had been against it, so now, seeing such uneasiness in the lambs for it, and so many leaving us on that account, it seems to me like a voice of Providence calling the ministers one step further. But as they had no liberty, we agreed to set aside some time next week to consult the Lord about it. We agreed in all our determinations and consultations. How gradually does the Lord lead us, according to what we can bear. As we read the reports of the superintendents on the lambs in their care, we had great satisfaction. But I was dry. We then supped, and had sweet fellowship together, arranging our Quarterly Meetings for the future.[20]

The next day, Morgan John Lewis preached, with much power, from Habakkuk 3:19, and the brethren then departed.

For once, we see Harris being more radical than Daniel Rowland, Howell Davies, and Williams, Pantycelyn. He had become willing for the clergymen to administer the sacraments in homes, in those parishes where the incumbents were immoral or where communion was refused the Methodists. The three clergymen were not yet ready for such an important step. No doubt they feared that this would lead to the Bishop revoking their licences, something he could easily do as not one of them was more than a curate.

Here are the resolutions passed at this Association:

> Agreed after debating about the necessity of an assistant to Bros. Morgan John, Thomas Price, Thomas William and John Richard, that Bro. John Belcher should give himself wholly to assist them till the next Quarterly Association.

> Bro. Evan William determined to leave us, and go among the Dissenters.

> Agreed that Bro. Morgan John should exchange a round with Bro. Thomas William and Bro. Thomas James.

> Answered a letter from Bro. Richard Charles about working on the Sabbath, that he should cease from all servile employment to keep holy the Sabbath day.

> Agreed that Bro. [Herbert] Jenkins should come from England a month before our next association and then to be more determinately settled.

> Agreed that Bro. Thomas Jones should go about under the inspection of Bros.

Howell Harris, James Beaumont, Morgan John, Thomas James, on trial till our next Quarterly Association.

Agreed that our next Quarterly Association should be at Porth-y-rhyd – three miles from Llandovery, the first Wednesday after Michaelmas. Mr Howell Davies to begin preaching at ten in the morning. Monthly Association at Abergorlech, Tuesday evening, July 10; in Pembrokeshire at Llangwg, Monday morning, July 16.

Agreed that all the brethren should keep a day of private fasting and prayer next week about various things. The whole accounts were read and we had sweet accounts.

Agreed that Bro. Williams should visit the societies in the upper part of Cardiganshire once every six weeks on trial till our next General Association.[21]

Almost certainly, Williams, Pantycelyn, was this visitor. But it must be understood that it was not he, an ordained minister, who was on probation, but rather the plan in which he was to visit the societies every six weeks. The Association was not sure how this arrangement would work.

Howell Harris waited at Trefeca, renovating his house and preaching in the surrounding areas, for some nine days after this Association. On 7 July, he and his wife began a journey of some three weeks, through parts of Radnorshire, Breconshire, Carmarthenshire, Glamorganshire and Pembrokeshire, arriving at Llangwm on 16 July. A Monthly Association was being held there. But on their way, they paid a visit to Howell Davies at Parke. Harris was in a sweet frame during the journey:

I had such love for God's glory that all other causes were swallowed up in this. I desired no grace or gifts, but for his glory. My own salvation was nothing compared to this. I cried, 'O Lord, give me Thy grace, faith, love, wisdom, humility, and courage to rise above sin, death, and Satan, only for this, that I might glorify Thy name, and behave as Thy child and minister. For myself, let me serve Thee, and then do as Thou wilt with me, for time and for eternity.' We sat as a meeting until six, arranging the exhorters, and deciding many matters. I believe the Lord blessed us greatly, the one to the other, giving us considerable light on various matters. I heard from Bro. William Richard how terrifying it is to go before the Lord even one step, and how severe will be our suffering for so doing; and also how much of a judgment it is not to have our time filled by the Lord with one duty or the other.

This William Richard was the exhorter of Llansamlet, and, no doubt, it was he himself who, on some occasion or other, had run before the Lord had sent him and had been punished for his presumption. As to the nature of his step, together with the judgment that befell him, we can only conjecture. Harris continues:

I learnt lessons from many other brethren, particularly when Thomas Miles said that if we do not have an inner voice, we do well to follow an outer voice, that of Providence. Much was said of William Edward (Rhydygele) and George Gambold.

Then Howell Harris departed for Haverfordwest, where he preached that night with considerable power from a text in the Book of Job. The resolutions passed at this Llangwm Monthly Meeting were:

Agreed that Bro. John Harry (being approved) should exhort as before till our next monthly association, under the inspection of Bro. William Richard.

Agreed that Bro. George Bowen should continue diligently in his present occupation and exhort in his neighbourhood under Bro. John Harris.

Agreed that Bro. William Gambold (being approved an exhorter) should exhort under the inspection of Bro. Thomas Miler.

Agreed that Bro. William Edward should come to speak to Mr Davies to be admitted to communion, before he should be admitted for examination for an exhorter.

Agreed that Bro. George Gambold (being received and approved as an exhorter) should go about as much as he can with taking due care of his grandmother.

Agreed that Bro. John Morris (being approved an exhorter) should continue to teach a school, as he now does, till providence opens another door and assist Bro. Thomas Miler as much as he can.

Agreed that Bro. John Sparks and Bro. John Evans (being received and approved Exhorters) should exercise their gifts under the inspection of Bro. Davies.

Agreed that Bro. John Lloyd and Bro. John Gibbon, should exhort in private as they did before, and in public under the inspection of Bro. William Richard.

Agreed that Bro. John Hugh (being approved) should exhort as he did before as much as he can, with following his occupation under the inspection of Bro. William Richard.

Agreed that Bro. John should exhort as before on trial, and Bro. William Jones, under the inspection of Bro. Thomas Miler.

Agreed that Bro. William Lewis and Bro. John Thomas should assist Bro. John Harris in private work.[22]

So read the minutes. We know hardly anything of many whose names are mentioned here, but it is worth recording these decisions as examples of the methods of the Fathers in pursuing the work. Howell Harris and his wife continued through parts of Cardiganshire, calling at Newcastle

Emlyn, Blaen-porth, Llanwenog, and Cil-ffriw. By 26 July they were at
Glanyrafonddu. There, Harris met with a trial, which we give in his own
words:

> I was tempted in this place on hearing of an attempt on Satan's part to sepa-
> rate between us and the ministers with respect to the fire which is amongst us.
> Last night I gave testimony against the extreme behaviour of some, laughing
> out loud, leaping and jumping, which the ministers condemn. After I had
> spoken my mind, from the Lord, as I thought, I was strongly opposed by the
> flesh, and by earthly reason; I committed it to the Lord, after I had strength
> to behave like a Christian . . . I had an answer regarding what I said of the
> fire, namely that what I had spoken pleased the Lord. O, how God stands by
> me, clearing and justifying me, when I destroy myself and my character, and
> lose my authority, through not behaving as a messenger of heaven.

The meaning is not completely clear, but we may conclude that Harris
had spoken with some warmth against the extreme expressions of emotion
displayed by some; that someone had dared to argue against him, claiming
that such expressions were legitimate, and that he in return had lost his
temper, and had reacted in a way which, in his judgment, was unworthy
of a minister of Christ. When the incident had passed, he committed the
whole affair to God in heaven. In time, he received an assurance that he
had been correct in his view, but was ashamed of his lack of self-control,
realizing that he had not behaved as an ambassador of God. This is why his
conscience condemned him, though he felt his judgment was correct.

Harris had hardly returned to Trefeca when it was time to set out again
for the Monthly Meeting to be held at Cwmbrith, near Llandrindod, on
1 August, 1744. Williams, Pantycelyn, was in the chair, and the following
are the minutes of the meeting:

> Having examined the state of Bro. Richard Tibbott's societies in Mont-
> gomeryshire, we agreed that as his time is not taken all up he should now
> for the harvest assist the brethren, etc., till he should find out some employ-
> ment.

> After a close examination of Bro. Edward Bufton about the knowledge of
> the divinity of Jesus Christ and of his bearing his people's sins away on the
> tree, and of the perseverance of the saints, etc., by the revelation of the Holy
> Ghost, and of the misery of all mankind by nature, and having been satisfied
> of his grace and call to speak for the great God, we agreed that he should
> assist Bro. Beaumont as a private exhorter.

> That as there is very great opposition and mobbing at Leominster and as the
> Lord gives them power of faith in their souls, the brethren should continue
> to meet together as usual, and commit themselves to God, and if any abuse

should be made so as the word be stopped and their lives in danger to use the law in faith – and that Bro. Beaumont should go and visit them as soon as his wife is brought to bed.[23]

In addition, we learn from Harris's journal that the Association decided that Daniel Rowland and Williams, Pantycelyn, should take a journey to north Wales, or, that Williams announced that this was their intention. Harris wrote:

I felt that all the powers of hell were in league against us. I then had great love towards, and deep sympathy towards, Bros. Rowland and Williams in their work, in that they go soon to north Wales, to the midst of dangers. I then had much sympathy with all the Methodists and priests in Wales, then those in England, and then those all over the world, as I saw that they were all engaged in one spirit against hell. O the difference between understanding with the spirit, and a mere discernment of truth in the letter!

Within ten days, namely on 12 August, there was a Monthly Association at Llangeitho. Harris journeyed there through Llanidloes and Llandrindod, preaching at various places in Montgomeryshire. Richard Tibbott accompanied him for some of the time, and as he conversed with that godly exhorter he was made to feel how small his own appreciation was of the glory and mystery of divine things. He arrived at Llangeitho late on Sunday night. On his journey he felt such brotherly love for Daniel Rowland that he could not refrain from crying out,

O Lord, send a message of love and power through me, a weak creature, to him, my eldest brother; and, O Lord, save me from my old nature, for Thy name's sake.

On Sunday morning, he went to the church by nine. Williams, Pantycelyn, was preaching on Zechariah 13:9, 'And I will bring the third part through the fire, and will refine them as silver is refined, and will try them as gold is tried.' Harris quoted many of his comments, and we include them here as an example of Williams's preaching:

He showed what is the nature of the fire by which he refines his people. Firstly, that he sends a spirit of bondage upon them; not a legal bondage arising from a slavish fear, but the hiding of his face. That he leaves them with faith, but yet removes his face, which is worse than hell to those who love him. Secondly, that he refines them through the fire of providential crosses, giving David and Job as examples. Thirdly, by allowing some liberty to the sin and pollution within us, which is the most secret fire, and the heaviest burden of all, to every Christian. His comments here were searching. He showed further the effects of the fire, that it gives light and consumes every sin.

Such was the preaching of William Williams at Llangeitho Parish Church. Harris commented, 'It was a sweet sermon. O what a blessing is the ministry of the word!' But he also felt that Williams was not sufficiently clear on some points, 'Though this was an excellent discourse, yet some things were so delivered that had I been in the flesh or not freed by another portion I could have been brought to bondage for want of more distinctions.'[24] He came out of the church a little before twelve. In the afternoon, he went to Llancwnlle Church; it is not said who was ministering there. In the evening, Harris himself preached to a large congregation from the words, 'That your joy might be full,' and it seems the service was a notable one.

According to the journal, the Monthly Association was held on Sunday night, once the public services of the day were over. Harris wrote,

> We arrived home happily, and there was delightful unity amongst us. We sat up until twelve in an Association, speaking of many things, and we were very happy together.

Few superintendents and exhorters were present, and the following discussion was the only one recorded in the minutes:

> After examination of the affair of Bro. Morgan Hughes and not agreeing in our light we did put it to the vote whether he should discourse in private or not, and we were equally divided, and waited again and each continued the same in his light – one half thought he should, the other that he should not; and so it was left undetermined, and his societies to be inspected by David Williams and Thomas Griffiths.[25]

Harris's comments in his journal show that though the brethren were not of one mind, there was no ill-feeling between them, but that they agreed peaceably to differ. He suggests also that others matters were discussed, 'I am assured that the Lord is to present me with the privilege of reading and writing. This I cannot do until I have liberty.' Whether he is referring to the writing of books to help the new converts, we do not know. Again,

> Now, as Bros. Rowland and Williams are going to the north, I was made to bear a little of their burdens, and to argue on their behalf, for the Lord to keep their hearts in victory and liberty; seeing myself as too weak for such great trials, and yet willing to go were I to be sent. I cried, 'O Lord, do not let Thine enemies have the victory.'

On the Monday morning a sermon was preached at Llangeitho Church, probably by Rowland. In the afternoon, Harris went to Lampeter where he preached from a stone on the road to a large crowd, from the words in Job,

'I have heard of thee by the hearing of the ear.' He returned home through Cil-y-cwm and Dol-y-felin, reaching Trefeca on Friday afternoon.

In less than a week a Monthly Association was held at Trefeca, on 18 August.

It was a small gathering, with no minister present, Harris chaired, and the following decisions were passed:

> Having read what we agreed on before and consulting together, we agreed that Bro. Thomas Jones should give himself wholly to the work and be an assistant to Bro. Thomas James, Richard Tibbott, James Beaumont and Morgan John, visiting Breconshire, Montgomeryshire and the Welsh part of Radnorshire, with Longtown society, under the inspection of Bro. Howell Harris.

> Agreed that as Bro. Evans is in some straits for some money, they should be immediately borrowed, and that it should be laid before the society to ease him.

> Agreed that Bro. Joseph Saunders should as soon as his circumstances are settled give every Saturday evening and Sunday, to visit the neighbouring societies alternately.

> Agreed that the brethren should do all they could to have two places to discourse every Sunday and to settle them so as not to hinder any from other places of worship.

> Agreed that Bro. Thomas Bowen should abide in Builth for half a year without removing, to wait to know more of God's voice.[26]

There is little need of comment here. The decision for arranging services so that none would be hindered from attending other places of worship shows how determined the Methodists were not to form a separate party. The arrangements for supporting Brother Evans, that is Williams Evans, the fiery spirited exhorter of Nantmel, show how full of sympathy they were, and how ready each was to bear another's burden.

We have already mentioned that persecution from the populace had almost completely ended by now in most regions of the south, and particularly in Breconshire. General opinion had turned in favour of the Methodists. But a persecuting spirit agitated the gentry more than ever. In the Sessions held at Brecon, 28 August, 1744, the following decision was presented to the presiding judge by the Breconshire Senior Jurors:

> Inasmuch as we, the Senior Jurors of Breconshire, have received as a charge from the Honourable Judge of this circuit, amongst various other learned and worthy matters, that we should draw attention to every obstacle in the way of our sacred religion, the most precious part of our national constitution; and inasmuch as it is only too familiar that many illegal meetings (as we are informed) are being held in the open, and in other places, by persons calling

themselves Methodists, whose preachers claim that they are expounding the Holy Scriptures while under the influence of inspiration, by which they gather together large crowds of unruly people, to the endangering of the peace of the realm of our lord King, and which, unless it is soon put down, may imperil the peace of the whole empire generally; and insofar as these preachers, or false teachers, in their irregular meetings, confuse the minds of many of his Majesty's citizens by their hotheaded doctrines, which, in time, may prove very dangerous, even to the destruction of our established religion, and so overturn our good government, both ecclesiastical and national; we, in order to be as precise as possible in denouncing this malicious conspiracy, would present to your attention the following houses, namely, Pontwal, Bronllys parish, the house of John Watkins; and the house of Howell Harris in Trefeca, the parish of Talgarth, both in this county, as places which hold and maintain these irregular meetings; and we request our Honourable Judge, should the power of the court not be sufficient to subdue these irregularities, that he appeal to some higher authority to do this, that our religion, the peace of the nation generally, and the possessions of this county particularly be preserved on the basis of our ancient and excellent Establishment.

It would be hard to imagine a document containing more lies, and more likely to stir up the national authorities against the Methodists. The memories of the Civil War had not all yet passed away, and the war with France meant that the government watched jealously over every gathering where they suspected that revolutionary thoughts were fermenting. So the Senior Jurors of Breconshire had tied a fly appropriate to the condition of the water. They surely knew that the Methodists were loyal to a man; that they desired as much as possible to keep the peace; that they never held a meeting without praying for the king and for all in authority; but the animosity of the gentry towards them, no doubt excited by the malice of jealous and persecuting clergy, was such that it was not too much for them to present to a state judge, during the main county sessions, a portrayal which they knew to be untrue, of a people who sought to worship God according to their consciences. How the judge responded to this situation is not known, but nothing came of the matter.

There was an Association at Abergorlech on 4 September. It was probably, from the small number present, a Monthly Meeting, though this is not stated in the minutes. The Moderator was Daniel Rowland, and Williams, Howell Davies, and many superintendents were present. Rowland preached in Abergorlech Chapel on Hebrews 2:11, 'For both he that sanctifieth and they who are sanctified are all of one.' He expounded the means by which Christ sanctifies his people; the greatness of the work of sanctification; the putting aside by Christ of his glory in order that he might fulfil this work; and the way in which we are being made like God, though not to the infinite degree of his divinity. 'He had uncommon light . . . and now we are turned out of the chapels and my soul is made to rejoice in it, looking to the Lord and seeing him above all.'[27] The phrase 'turned out of the chapels' refers to the issue over the Church of England chapel at Abergorlech, which we shall meet with in the minutes. All that Harris says about the Association in his journal is that they experienced a sweet meeting together. The minutes are as follows:

> Agreed that a petition should be drawn up to the Bishop about the Chapel at Abergorlech to declare with all humility their intention to continue Mr Williams their pastor and, if needs be, to suffer for it.

> Agreed that for some time till our next association, Bro. John Morgan should be silent and not discourse.

> Agreed that some time should be laid aside for humiliation and intercession the week after next by every one of us.

> Agreed that a house should be built in Llansawel for religious uses, such as preaching, teaching school, etc.

Abergorlech was a Church of England chapel-of-ease. It was probably not in use at this time by the Church, and so the Methodists took possession of it for preaching, and perhaps for administering the ordinance, as it was a consecrated building. No doubt Williams, Pantycelyn, was the 'pastor' who had charge of it. It appears that the Bishop wished to frustrate them and to close the chapel. This was the reason for the petition and the decision to continue preaching there, even if that was to mean punishment for them. 'Then,' says Harris, 'we came to Glanyrafonddu. When I heard of the unusual success of Bro. Rowland in north Wales my soul was filled with thanksgiving.' He proceeded with his wife to Llangathen, and heard a young clergyman in the parish church preaching the strangest doctrines instead of the gospel, and what with bodily weakness and listening to such folly, he felt a pressure that could not be put into words. Once the service was over, he preached outside. His subject was the prodigal son, and the clergyman was amongst the listeners. He received extraordinary strength, but when he came to show how God's child longed for home and did not fear the day of judgment, the young clergyman rode away. On Saturday, Harris was back at Trefeca. On arriving he found that black clouds were gathering overhead, for a rumour was abroad that his enemies were again about to press him into the army. But he encouraged himself with the thought that all things were under God's control, and he could overrule everything to his glory.

## VARIOUS MANIFESTATIONS OF INDWELLING SIN

Harris's journal at this time is most interesting, but we must be satisfied with a few references only. On 10 September, he wrote:

Today, I was favoured with two letters from Glamorganshire, each of which contained a feast from God. One had news of the success of the gospel amongst the soldiers in Glamorgan. As I read, I was a flame of love towards God, and towards dearest Price. [Probably it was Price of Watford who wrote the letter.] The second implored me to come over and feed my spiritual children. I cried that I might be sent there, to feed my lambs, and not to be sent empty handed.

On 11 September, he wrote:

About eleven, I went to Tredustan meeting house (the Congregational chapel); I feared going, in case I caused offence to anyone, and yet I longed to go that I might meet with my God. So I went, in all simplicity, trusting all to him. Though I could not judge anything as to the grace of the man who preached, and though his topic was more of reason than of Christ – 'O that they were wise' – yet, I had clarity to listen and to receive all in love and thankfulness. At the start, I cried on behalf of this congregation, and all the Dissenting congregations of the nation, that the Lord would return to them and fill them. Then, when he said that one part of wisdom is to have a true sense of the glory of God, and to have fellowship with him, I felt a strong desire for this, and for this alone.

This quotation shows: (1) that amongst the Methodists there were those so full of prejudice towards Dissenters as to cause Harris to fear he might offend them by going to a Dissenting chapel; (2) that Harris himself did not share in any way in this prejudice, though himself so loyal to the Church, but rather that he expected to meet with God under the ministry of a Congregationalist brother; (3) that the Dissenting ministry at that time, if the Tredustan sermon was a typical example, had too little of Christ, in the Reformer's opinion, and leaned too heavily on duties; (4) that Harris felt that God's presence had departed from the Dissenters in Wales to a large extent, at that time, and that he was full of prayer that God might return to their midst.

On Saturday, 17 September, Howell Harris and his wife set out on a long journey, partly in obedience to the request of the Glamorgan brethren, and partly in order to be present at various Associations. He preached that night at the chapel-of-ease at Grwynefechan with much power. He saw that God had children there. He proceeded to Lampeter, near Crickhowell, and on Sunday morning he was at Cwm-iou,

listening to the godly clergyman, Thomas Jones. The latter preached sweetly on Revelation 3:3, expounding the promises. In the afternoon, Harris
preached. His bodily weakness was such that he was unable to continue.
He prayed to the Lord in faith for strength, saying, 'Whatever I receive
from Thee, will I not spend it all for Thee?' In answer to his prayer came
strength. The text for his words were the words in John, 'That your joy may
be full,' but instead of being a son of consolation he was made to thunder
until the whole assembly was disturbed. From there they continued to
Aber-big; he was so ill that he could hardly speak, but while preaching
from 1 John 3:1 he received spiritual and physical strength. The Lord
came down amongst them in a remarkable way. His lips were wonderfully
opened to demonstrate the privileges of the godly and the nature of God's
love towards them. On Sunday they were in Goetre; on Wednesday at
Llanheiddel; Wednesday at Tonsawndwr; Thursday at St. Bride's; and on
Thursday night, they arrived at Watford where the Association was to be
held. Harris was Moderator. He wrote,

> I saw the privilege bestowed on me, that I am here as moderator; I was
> humbled in my spirit because of this, and I was made to tremble for fear of
> pride. The Lord came amongst us, and he pulled down much of Satan's work,
> such as prejudice, etc., and gave me wonderful wisdom, teaching me many
> lessons through everything.

At the close of the Association he preached to an unusually large gathering. The records of the Association read as follows:

> As the enemy had begun to work some prejudice between some of the la-
> bourers, which arose for want of more love and humility in public discourses
> and private behaviour; after waiting humbly on God and each laying open
> his heart and acknowledging some fault each of himself having learnt many
> great lessons, and especially seeing that it is not enough to have the eye single,
> but the rule and motive must be right, and the whole in a right spirit ere our
> conduct is safe: we agreed, and were united. Glory be to God. We saw many
> of the enemy's stratagems. Bro. Howell Griffith having been overtaken in a
> fault and having shown sufficient proofs of true repentance to the brethren,
> it was agreed he should be again received on trial on condition he take care
> of the occasion of his fall for the future.

> Agreed that Bro. Richard Jones should be talked to by Bro. Harris, etc., and
> received only on signs of amendment from his indifferency, etc., which he
> accordingly showed two days after being spoken to before all the societies at
> St. Nicholas, where it was settled that he and Bro. Thomas Lewis and ___ of
> Pwll-y-march should exchange alternately every Sabbath and keep up their
> fellowship with the brethren.

There also were stewards settled in St. Nicholas society, and so likewise in St. Andrews and Burthyn and Aberthaw societies.

Whereas Bro. Thomas Williams had spoken something against the gown and cassock, he owned he did not mean as being against it, but the idolizing of it, etc.

Bro. Powell too acknowledged his fault in speaking of Bros. Price and Belcher as being unsound in some principles, etc., and was thought unguarded in speaking to the people against showing any difference to the preachers than others. That being weakening their hands and hindering the people to honour the office, though his aim was right to prevent idolizing them or respecting persons in the flesh.

These minutes show that the Methodists were beginning to face internal difficulties; that some of the most respected exhorters were falling into sin and were in great need of being restored; nor were they completely free from envy and prejudice, one towards another. Clearly, a powerful revival and deep, arousing feelings are not enough to destroy the old man in the best of people. It is hard not to laugh at seeing the great care taken that none should speak a word of condemnation of anything pertaining to the Church, and especially not of the clothing of the clergy. But it is worth noting that not one of the clergymen was present at the meeting so that it was not one of them who was responsible for this zeal. Howell Harris proceeded slowly through parts of Glamorganshire and Carmarthenshire, heading for Porth-y-rhyd where a Quarterly Association was to be held on 3 and 4 October. The following quotation shows his state of mind:

I had strength to desire that I might be made a blessing to all, along the journey; to the exhorters, and to the lambs; that I might bless every house that I come to, and be of use to everyone who hears me. I saw the honour that God bestows upon me by placing me in such a position. I prayed for the workers, particularly that they might be one.

The day before the Association they arrived at Abergorlech Chapel, where Rowland preached from the words, 'Get thee behind me, Satan.' It seems it was a very timely and pointed sermon. The 'Satan' to which he encouraged the brethren to say, 'Get thee behind me,' was pride. Harris provides a précis of the sermon:

He showed how there is somewhat in the saints to be nourished and discouraged. He was home in showing of pride in gifts and pride in graces. He spoke to such as have no gifts; how happy they are, like a shrub safe from many trials and temptations which blow on those that have great gifts, and how the Lord regards faith not gifts. He showed home the danger of pride of gifts: 1. They are not given for our own use but for the use of others, and so not our own;

2. Where is much gifts there is but little grace; the growth of these generally hinders the growth of the others. 3. Thou art not anything better in God's sight for all thy gifts nor more than if thou hadst none of them. God only looks on faith. 4. Gifts are only given on condition, and may be taken away, and often are, but grace is never taken away. 5. Gifts expose us to much temptation, as in Joseph's coat. He showed the nature and danger of pride of gifts, how God is against all pride, and nothing done in pride will prosper. First sign [of pride in graces] – when we admire our graces; and second – when we look at and trust in our own grace, instead of Christ. It shows itself, too, in self-admiring and a show of humility in not coming to Christ because of our sin and sinfulness, which is self and unbelief to the utmost.[28]

This was a sermon mainly for the exhorters; every word told on Howell Harris:

My soul was made to submit under the word, I prayed for humility for myself and for the exhorters. When I heard that the sacrament was to be administered, after the chapel had been shut, my soul was filled with thanksgiving, seeing that the Lord was returning to us. But who is so oppressed by such a body of pride as myself! Such falls do I have because of it!

We see that the Methodists' efforts with regards to Abergorlech Chapel had been successful. Rowland preached again at Glanyrafonddu, the night before the Association. His text was Revelation 12:1. On proceeding towards Porth-y-rhyd they met up with many brethren heading in the same direction. Harris heard news that greatly encouraged him: 1. That the Archbishop had offered to ordain one of Whitefield's people. 2. When the complaint against his house at Trefeca was presented (by the Senior Jurors at Brecon Sessions) that Mr Joseph Hughes had stood up and prevented it. 3. That the Lord had blessed Mr G. to open his doors to preaching. 4. That the gospel was gaining ground in many ways and in many places.

The Association was begun by a sermon from Rowland whose subject was the Lord, a wall of fire about his people. Harris then addressed the exhorters on the privilege, majesty and nature of the work; their unfitness for it, showing what kind of men they were, and who and what kind were their enemies; the nature of true humility, that it means we are nothing in our own eyes, and are as concerned for the affairs of our brethren as we are for our own; and the necessity of wisdom for all of them.

All separated that night in a happy frame of mind, but a storm arose amongst them the following morning. Harris relates the story:

This morning we had a cross. I rebuked Bro. Rowland and others for self-indulgence, and for not going about as much as they should. He became angry. But soon, the Lord destroyed the snare, and we were reunited. I reasoned against the two, and the Lord shattered my heart, and brought me low in such a way, that I was willing not only for the brethren to see my weaknesses, but to rejoice that this was the case. And from a sense of my pollutions and weakness I cried to be put aside, seeing every one of them as filling their places far better then myself. I was truly brought low; I could not but weep before them, confessing what was wrong. I could lie before the feet of them all.

It is clear that Harris's hot temper had got the better of him again, and caused him to offend his brethren. We find him in the dust as a result, groaning and weeping, and earnestly seeking their forgiveness. Surely, the sight of this man, so bold when before all dangers, now in tears before his brethren, must have deeply affected the fraternity, and it was an easy and happy task to extend forgiveness to him. They departed in the best feelings. The following records provide the resolutions passed:

After some consultation about the importance of our work and about seeing and feeling the burden of it, we agreed to observe two days henceforth to be together. That one of the ordained ministers preach at the Quarterly Association alternately, and if the one that is to discourse should be hindered by Providence to come, the next in course should preach.

Agreed to write to Bros. Davies and John Harris that did not send the reasons for their absence, and likewise wrote to Bro. Thomas Miler for wholly neglecting our associations.

Agreed that Bro. Jenkins, on account of the present necessity and call in England, should be wholly there, excepting a fortnight in every three months he should give us at the time of the Quarterly Associations.

Agreed that Bro. Benjamin Thomas should assist Bro. Harris instead of Bro. Jenkins, to superintend all Wales.

Agreed that Bro. James Ingram (who was a hired servant with Bro. Harris) should assist him as exhorter and clerk, to be sent by him to assist in England and Wales as the occasion shall call – both he and Bro. Thomas on trial till our next Quarterly Association.

Agreed that Bro. Roger Williams should go to Merthyr and follow his trade and assist Bro. Thomas James and Bro. Morgan John on trial till next Association.

Agreed that such of the superintendents as have light and qualifications should take their liberty in opening the Scriptures, but that the private exhorters should continue in their exhortation and not discourse by way of preaching from a text but privately exhorting or expounding – this to be confirmed on further light.

Agreed that Bro. Harris should carry a reproof in the name of the brethren to Bro. John Williams, for his negligence in watching over the society in his care; and to let him go on for one month on trial, and to be turned out then unless he shows obedience and faithfulness.[29]

There are many things worth commenting upon in these minutes, but we cannot go into detail. It is delightful to note that Howell Harris visited John Williams and succeeded in bringing him to submit humbly.

> I was not as I should have been, yet he was brought low and was melted; and there came upon me what I never felt before, namely the burden of the Lord. The Lord was truly near to the both of us; he broke our hearts, and we wept.

Howell Harris was not given much time at Trefeca after returning; he soon set out for the Monthly Association held at Nantmel, Radnorshire, on 18 October. On the way to Nantmel, he had two remarkable services, indeed the two most remarkable of his life. He wrote:

> The Lord made this day a great day to me. In a place called Gwernfyddai, about ten miles from Talgarth, I preached and prayed from 1 John 1:7; I had great liberty; I was taught how to pierce, and wound, and convict those who were without God, and who lived in sin. The light was extraordinary. Then I came to Trefilod, about three or four miles further on. On the way, I had a clearer view than ever before of the glory and majesty of God, and that as an assurance that he would bring me through all trials to himself. I had a view also of the glory of Jesus, and great liberty when speaking from Revelation 12:1. I showed how the divinity of Christ was manifested to the Church; the great authority seen in God's manifestation of him; how this affects our souls. I was reaching home at this point. I explained the way we should listen and pray; that we are approaching God, and how that when we come carelessly, we do not see him. I was now piercing to the quick, and speaking with immense authority. I showed that some sins and evil habits that a child could fall into, and some that he could not; and the way they were slaves to themselves and to the world. It was, in truth, an awful place. Many, I trust, were converted.

It is seen that it was the clear and simple truths of the gospel that Howell Harris proclaimed; nor do his remarks appear to be particularly well organized; but there was the divine unction upon his words. The gathering before him felt that he was delivering a message from the Lord of the whole earth, and they trembled as aspen leaves before the irresistible power displayed.

Harris hurried to Nantmel, where Daniel Rowland was preaching. The painful feelings engendered at Porth-y-rhyd were by now fully healed. Harris wrote in his journal:

> About five, I went to the Association, and felt in my soul, by the Holy Spirit,

a union with Bro. Rowland. O how great is the mystery within the Church that the world knows nothing of! Such communion with himself does the Lord grant to the poor creatures who gain his favour! I had such unity with all the brethren that I could not think of leaving them behind; I was one with them. I had extraordinary light while examining a young exhorter, and showing him the greatness of the work. We discussed many things, arranging a day of subjection and prayer, once a month; aid for the persecuted saints at Leominster; and pressing on the lambs to walk more closely and to bear fruit. I felt my heart burning within me. Then my lips were opened by the Lord to speak of Christian liberty; of victory over sin and Satan; the privilege of being believers; the danger of being lukewarm; and the necessity of zeal, fire and life; that we should not be in captivity, otherwise we should not be able to lead the lambs into liberty. But even if we ourselves be under Satan's feet, that we should not pull others there, but rather rejoice at seeing others conquer. I was in the Spirit; and we were all happy and delighting. I felt myself more a conqueror over sin and the devil than ever. One brother had written a letter against myself and Bro. Rowland for our frivolity. I had strength to answer him in love.

So wrote Harris of the Nantmel Association. It is easy to see that much brotherly love was evident. The Reformer of Trefeca, particularly, was on his high places, sin and the devil under his feet, and his heart bound to those of his brethren. The following are the minutes:

After examination and opening the nature and weight of the work of exhorting, it was agreed that Bro. Thomas Meredith of Mochdre should exhort on trial in his own society.

After a long discourse about the state of the societies and of the danger of lukewarmness and necessity of divine fire and life, agreed that all the brethren should stir up the people to hear where there is life and to receive affectionately every lively messenger, etc.

Agreed that as there is a general negligence about bearing fruit to the Lord, and much carelessness in the walk of some, that all should stir the people up zealously to a strict walk and to bear fruit.

Agreed to keep a day of fasting and prayer every month to humble our selves for our sins of the whole visible Church and the whole world and especially on account of the war.

Agreed that the first day of next November be kept a day of humiliation in all the societies on account of the persecution and mobbing at Leominster.

Agreed that Bro. Richard Tibbott should go to Bro. John Richard to learn the trade of book-binding.[30]

Within five days was the Monthly Meeting at Trefeca. Howell Harris was Moderator. The only record of it is as follows:

After opening our hearts to each other and acknowledging our lukewarmness, carelessness, want of growth in holiness, etc., with some measure of broken-ness of heart, and a sense of the evil of our own and other sins ... [we agreed to keep the resolutions passed at Nantmel].[31]

The following note is very significant as regards Howell Harris's posi-tion in the revival:

No more Monthly Meetings were held this quarter. Bro. Harris went to London.

Howell Harris and his wife set out for the capital about mid-November, and returned home on Saturday, 29 December.

[1] HJH, pp. 265–6.
[2] CMHO, pp. 96–7
[3] STL, vol. 1, p. 87.
[4] Eifion Evans, *Daniel Rowland*, p. 232–3.
[5] HHRS, pp. 51; CMHO, p. 98.
[6] CH 28, p. 158; CMHO, p. 99.     [7] Ibid.
[8] Transcribed by Eifion Evans.
[9] CH 48, pp. 70–1.
[10] CH 48, pp. 72–3.
[11] CH 48, p. 73.
[12] CH 48, p. 74.     [13] Ibid.
[14] CH 48, pp. 75–7.
[15] CH 48, pp. 77–8; CMHO pp. 100–1.
[16] CH 36, p. 12.
[17] CH 36, p. 13.
[18] CH 48, p. 79.
[19] CH 48, p. 80.
[20] CHMO, p. 102.
[21] CH 49, p. 22.
[22] CH 49, pp. 23–4.
[23] CH 49, pp. 24–5.
[24] CH 31, p. 21.
[25] CH 49, p. 25.
[26] CH 49, pp. 25–6.
[27] CH 25, pp. 14–15.
[28] Transcribed by Eifion Evans
[29] CH 49, pp. 28 and 84.
[30] CH 49, p. 85.
[31] CH 49, p. 86.

# 12

# HOWELL HARRIS (1745)

## THE WATFORD QUARTERLY ASSOCIATION, JANUARY 1745

*T*he Methodists began the year 1745 by holding a Quarterly Association at Watford on 2 January. Surprisingly, there is no reference whatsoever to this conference in the Trefeca records. Harris had arrived the previous evening. His experience was mixed. To begin with his mind was joyful and at liberty on seeing in Christ all his right and title to eternal life, but at Watford, it seems, he heard of errors and arguments that were abroad and this disturbed his spirit greatly:

> I saw that the enemy had been let free amongst us, and just as he dwelt in our corruptions previously, he was now amongst us as a spirit of heresy and deceit. Then, on considering our arguments, I had liberty to cry, 'O Lord, if thou dost intend to unite us as one, and to bring us all here, and to forbid that we should be scattered or divided here, then let me have such a view of them (the gathered brethren) and of the work, that will make me to triumph in joy, and also to mourn.' After waiting for a while, I had such a view of the greatness and majesty of God, of the glorious home on high, of his work, of how glorious is the Church, and of the work we have in hand, that I had a spirit to mourn both for myself and for others.

It is clear that he was troubled in mind in case the Association became a scene of warring, and would end in division. He then went to hear Williams, Pantycelyn, preaching with much power from Song of Solomon 3:8. Harris commented:

> He opened up the whole book to this point, and then described the night that is referred to here as (1) the night of a legal spirit; (2) the night of persecution; and (3) the night of tribulation and affliction. He illustrated these in the history of the Church in Egypt, in Canaan, in Jerusalem, and up until now, referring particularly to Job, Joseph, etc. He showed that though the enemies of the Church were so numerous, that God defended them. He was particularly powerful when describing that persecution was, perhaps, at the

413

door. He reached to the quick in exciting all to be diligent, now, while we still have liberty.

Clearly, Williams had had a remarkable service. The Association then conferred until about eight in the evening and, contrary to the fears of some, unity and sweet harmony pervaded the meeting, except that one exhorter was removed from his office because of his carelessness. Harris continued:

> Then, we discussed some arguments that had taken place amongst the brethren. I saw the worth of the Scriptures, and the great mercy that we had them, and that we were to believe the truths they contain without arguing over them. I said that there were six mysteries to be believed, though they could not be comprehended. (1) The Trinity; (2) the Incarnation; (3) the reckoning of Adam's sin to us, and our partaking of it; (4) the reckoning of Christ to us by grace and our partaking of him; (5) that God has loved his people with an eternal love, and yet, until they are convicted, they are the children of wrath, and under the curse; (6) that God has an election, but not a reprobation.

It is clear that not only was Harris thoroughly orthodox and an excellent theologian, but that he also had correct views of the limits of human reason, recognizing that there are mysteries that belong to religion that do not allow of speculative examination but require rather a worshipping subjection before the excellent glory which they contain. Harris proceeded:

> We then discussed Supralapsarianism, and Sublapsarianism, that God loved us freely, and that Christ is the way by which this love runs freely towards us; we discussed the sense in which he wills sin, namely, that he allows it; and as we dealt with these great matters I saw our ignorance.

This is not surprising – the brethren were launching their boats on to deep waters. But it is interesting to note that these great mysteries of the gospel, which human minds will never fully encompass, possessed a great attraction for these Methodist Fathers. In order that the reader should not be frightened by the long and strange terms used, Supralapsarianism and Sublapsarianism, we should explain that these have to do with the order of the purposes of the divine counsel. The first holds that the purpose to save men in Christ came before the purpose of allowing them to fall, while the second maintains the opposite.

But to continue with Harris's description of the Association;

> I had liberty when singing to ask the Lord whether what I had done was pleasing to him. When praying, I was drawn out in deep humility, love and a broken spirit. On hearing good news of the way in which the Lord was prospering the brethren, I rejoiced greatly, seeing myself as the weakest of them all. Then, after eating, we sat down until about twelve.

The next day, the Association conferred again until eleven, and terminated with a sermon from Daniel Rowland, from the words in Nehemiah, 'Remember them, O my God.' The service was a remarkable one, even by Rowland's standard. Harris wrote:

> As he prayed, I felt my spirit being drawn out with him in his petitions; particularly when he prayed for the king and the nation; and I was given proof that the work would continue, and that the persecution would cease. Truly, he was full of God. I had power to strive together with him in his sermon. Such an influence, I never before witnessed, and I was compelled to honour the dear brother Rowland. Certainly, the power was remarkable this time. He was given remarkable wisdom, inwardly and outwardly, to show that just as every member has its place and purpose in the body, so also in the Church. 'If you are a backslider,' he said, 'read Hebrews; if devotional, read the Psalms; if you are prone to be rebellious, read Joshua and Judges; but if you would accomplish great things, read Nehemiah. He went beyond all in the greatness of his undertakings, and that without appropriate means.'[1]

We must resist the temptation to continue quoting Rowland's sermon. Harris commented:

> A wonderful power is given to him to draw souls to God, and to draw God towards them. It was as if he could not give over striving. Blessed be God that he is still in our midst in such a way. I see that greater degrees of ability have been given to him than any other I know. As for myself, I possess but little ability and little influence.

It is no wonder that the brethren, after such a manifestation of the presence of the Almighty amongst them, departed happily.

On 16 January, a Monthly Association was held at Trefeca. The following are its minutes:

> After we spent many hours in singing and praying together in a love-feast wherein our hearts were enflamed in an uncommon manner as each witnessing the presence of the Lord in a very uncommon manner after each of the brethren gave an account of the societies under their care, we agreed to see to the easing of Bro. James as to his outward affairs that he may be the more free to go about.

> [Agreed] to pray as to Bro. Thomas Jones's motion about marriage, and to agree that he should entirely leave his school.

> [Agreed] that Bro. Thomas James should inspect into Bro. Edward Bowen's affairs and see whether he shall think the Lord call him to move where he is.

> [Agreed] that Bro. Lewis Evans should go as far as he can to the north to Merionethshire in obedience to outward calls.

[Agreed] that Bro. Joseph Saunders should give every Sunday to some societies or other and be stirred up as means of reviving, and was reproved for his
lukewarmness.

After Bro. Harris had spoken on humility, faith and zeal and about searching the Scriptures and to see that our zeal and warmth go not beyond our
knowledge and sight of God by faith, agreed that Bro. Harris should settle
some differences in Llanafan's society arising from the Dissenters coming
to the house where they met, at the time of their meeting, and complaining
that they have no benefit in hearing them.

After having been more than usually happy, sweet and full of divine love, and
settled every thing – each having a witness of the uncommon presence of
our Lord among us, we parted about twelve o'clock; having been together in
Preaching, Love-feast and Association, near twelve hours.

Gloria in Excelsis Deo![2]

It had been an extremely successful Association. Harris commented:

As we sang and prayed our hearts and souls were as if filled with new wine.
Wisdom was given to me to arrange our circumstances, after having enquired
into the state of all the societies and exhorters. I encouraged them to humility,
wisdom, searching the Scriptures, and warned with respect to fire and zeal.
But after receiving more fire than faith could bear, the flesh received it and
I fell. But, O, the gentleness of the Lord towards us. I received a little light
to see that God was for us.

It is hard to understand what he means by 'receiving more fire than faith
could bear'. Is he perhaps suggesting a tendency, verging on the unhealthy,
to over-analyse the state of his heart and the nature of his feelings? Or,
more probably, is he referring to a zeal in the meeting that was not completely according to knowledge, and not completely corresponding to
inner convictions? The comment certainly reveals a tenderness of conscience that is not often encountered.

## THE FIRST EMPHASIS ON 'THE BLOOD OF GOD'

The next day, he prepared to set out on a long journey of over a month,
which would take him through many parts of north and south Wales. The
following note reveals his feelings at the time:

Today, I wrote a Welsh letter to Merionethshire having been filled with love
for them particularly, and having realized that it is the will of the Lord for
me to visit them, and perhaps to die amongst them.

Was he referring to the possibility of overwork proving too much for his
constitution, or to the possibility of persecutors bringing about his death?

On Friday, he arrived at Erwood, where he preached with much power:

> Had vast liberty to preach the blood of Christ, seeing it as the blood of God. Never had such a sight of it in my soul, and never had such power to set it forth as now.[3]

This sermon at Erwood was a turning point in his career. It was the first occasion of his use of the phrase 'the blood of God', which was the expression that caused so much offence to his brethren, and was one of the main reasons for the eventual disruption. His journal provides the outline of the journey:

> Proceeded sweetly to Builth, and on the way Christ's blood was held powerfully before me as the blood of God. It was this light that kept me happy. I never saw before this mystery of the blood as the blood of God. Came to Builth. As I saw the children playing, my heart was pierced by godly grief; I could hardly bear it.

He preached there with considerable unction. He went to Dol-y-felin where he met Mr [Marmaduke] Gwynne whose presence always fired his spirit. He preached from Galatians 4:2. He lodged with Mr Gwynne that night and read a book by Griffith Jones on the eternal love of God:

> As I read, God tore away the veil; I had such light whose like I never had before to see that he loved me with an eternal love, and that in eternity he purposed to bring me to glory. Before this light I saw all things disappearing away, and myself the object of the eternal love of the Trinity, so that I despised myself because of sin, and I understood the nature of sin, root and branch, more than ever before.

He went to Llangamarch and preached a powerful sermon from a text in Hosea. Passing through Merthyr Cynog, he preached from Philippians 4:4. From there he proceeded to Llanddewi where he received the sacrament, and then to Glyn where he preached from Isaiah:

> I had here more strength than ever to preach the blood. I showed that this was not being preached, but only reason, and that this is why we have lost the power from amongst us; and that some despise it. I referred to the power of God; that it is the blood of God; and of knowing Christ only.

It is seen that this one idea was uppermost in his mind throughout the journey. He continued through Blaenllywel, arriving at Llanddeusant on the day before the Monthly Association at Abergorlech. His experience here deserves recording:

> Today and yesterday, I was melted completely, and brought low before the feet of the Lord, as I received light from the Holy Ghost to perceive the outward

mercies that surround me. So, under divine influences, I fell on the floor, and worshipped, confessing as follows, 'O Lord, Thou art all love; it flows freely towards me. I am all sin, and self, and ignorance, and enmity; and, particularly, unbelieving and ungrateful. Yet, Thou dost forgive all. O incomparable love!' Then I was drawn out with the desire that he reveal his glory in Christ. There I had liberty to pray that he would be amongst us, and influence Bro. Rowland to be more amongst the lambs, to feed and enflame them.

We see that Harris was again convinced that Daniel Rowland was not itinerating as much he should have been. We cannot decide whether there was any degree of truth in this, or whether Harris was not giving sufficient consideration to Rowland's differing circumstances – that he was curate over three important churches. The date of the Monthly Association at Abergorlech was 22 January. Rowland and Williams, Pantycelyn, were present, with the former in the chair. Proceedings began with a sermon from Rowlands on Micah 6:5. Harris commented:

> On uniting in the most powerful prayer that I believe I have ever heard, I felt myself brought low; I saw myself the worst creature that God ever created; that more sin streamed from me than anyone in the world. I saw myself as the last in God's vineyard. I saw Bro. Rowland as my older brother, but yet that God had sent me.

After the sermon the sacrament was administered. At about five o'clock they met to discuss various matters, continuing until about ten. Harris does not mention the decisions taken; he only notes that he and Rowland were lodging together. The following are the minutes of the Association:

> After hearing of the state of the societies and finding that in Glamorganshire and several places there has prevailed great lukewarmness – we agreed to keep a day of humiliation between this and Feb. 21.

> Agreed that Bro. John Morgan should go immediately about and gather in the money for the books to pay Mr Farley [the publisher of the Weekly History].

> Agreed that Bro. David Williams should go and discourse with Mr Griffith Jones next Saturday and should assist Bro. John Richards what he can, with teaching the school.[4]

There is not much of importance here. We see that the Rev. D. Williams, Llysworney, had moved to Glamorganshire by 1745.

## IN DEEP WATERS IN PEMBROKESHIRE

Harris travelled with Rowland to Cil-y-cwm, where he preached twice. He then passed through Glanyrafonddu, where he preached and addressed the society, Llanarthe, Llan-non, and St. Clears, reaching Parke,

Howell Davies's home, by the Sunday. He found himself in deep waters that Sunday, as he explains:

> I saw myself as without concern for God's glory, without love for the brethren, without compassion, nor any consideration for the consequences. I saw that I sinned against love and grace; against mercy, means, relations, and blessings. I see that I sink deeper, deeper. O the depths of the evil of sin! I was in such misery and confusion that I could not come out of it. But though I was weakened and broken, I felt pure love toward the brethren and I saw myself as unworthy to be amongst them, in that they are all favoured more than me in grace and sanctification. Went down about three, and could not be free to go to the brethren. Saw also the evil consequences of my not going, seeing myself unworthy to be among them; but I could not help it. I had help only to cry to the Lord that he would fulfil his will, whatever it may be. But as I was returning towards Llanddowror and arriving at the place where I had to decide, the Lord had compassion upon me and gave me suddenly such a love to the brethren, that I could not but cry out in my spirit that I might be with them, and live and die with them. I was peculiarly one with them. I had such union with Bro. Howell Davies that I never had before, feeling a flood of love towards him, body and soul, as the temple of God, as one in God's favour, and as the messenger of God.

It is clear that he had been through a great storm; one that probably arose because of some offence received from one of the brethren. Possibly he had heard of some story, either on the way to Pembrokeshire, or at Howell Davies's house the previous night, which had caused him to be angry. Perhaps he heard some criticism of his sermons, or that some of his choicest plans had been opposed. He raged terribly because of it. His temper rose until he lost all control of it for a while; and having recovered himself to a degree, though he felt ashamed of himself, he could not bring himself to seek the company of his brethren, who had gathered together a day before the Association and were spending the afternoon in prayer and praise. He was undecided what to do, whether to break all connection with them and return home, or to go amongst them. Mercifully, his heart was filled with love, so that the latter course was followed, but the episode was a foretaste of the tempest that was to carry Harris out of Methodist circles before five years had past.

After a storm comes the calm, and it appears that the sun was shining upon the fraternity that had gathered at Haverfordwest for the Association on the Monday afternoon. Harris wrote:

> I was close to God, and we were enabled to arrange our plans beyond all expectation. No wonder the enemy hindered my coming here. Sure there was much work done, and we settled many things that seemed intricate – about a

new superintendent, settled the private exhorters, removing prejudices, and settling this new house here, opening our hearts to one another as regards justification, and how far souls can proceed without saving grace. Saul, an example, as well as Judas, Balaam, Demas, the foolish virgins, and those mentioned in Hebrews 6. We had much love for one another, and union and co-operation. Then I went to preach.

Of his sermon, he said:

My heart was enlarged, my lips were opened, the people felt, and the Lord descended in an uncommon way; particularly when I showed how gloriously he would be with them in death, when their eyes would be dulling, and their hearts failing; 'Then,' I said, 'Then, you – yes! – you poor and despised sinners who believe, will see the glory of our Father's house, will unite with the heavenly host, and stand around the throne, to praise and worship.'

It was a very powerful service and as he departed his heart was full of love towards his Saviour and his brethren. The following are the main resolutions passed at the Association:

Agreed that Bro. William Edward should (on trial till next Association) weekly visit the societies at St. David's, Penrhos and Mounton, and that he and all other private exhorters should visit other places only so that neither their charge nor their calling be neglected; and as directed by their superintendents.

Agreed that Bro. Christopher Mends should weekly visit the societies at Walton West and Studder, with the liberty and restraint above – following his calling – under the inspection of Bro. Davies.

Agreed that Bro. John Sparks should exhort as before on trial at and about Haverfordwest under the inspection of Bro. Davies.

Agreed that Bro. George Gambold should go out wholly and leave the school to discourse publicly as a superintendent on trial until our next Quarterly Association at Caeo, and then to be settled and fixed.[5]

After the Association Harris visited many areas of Pembrokeshire, passing through St David's, Tre-fin, where he had a remarkable meeting, Bwlch-y-groes, Llwyn-y-grawys, and Eglwyswrw. The topic of ministry in every place was the blood and the wounds. He then traversed Cardiganshire, visiting Llechryd, Cwmcynon, Cilrhedyn, Lampeter, Capel Betws, and Llanddewibrefi, where he lodged at an old mansion called Foelallt, on the slopes of a mountain. Again, at every stop, he laid great emphasis on the merit of the blood, in that it was God's blood. 'I see that I am preaching the truth,' he wrote. On Sunday, he sat under Rowland's ministry, and went from there to the church at Llancwnlle. He preached himself in the evening at Gwynfil village, near Llangeitho, to a congregation of between two and three thousand. He was hindered from continuing to north Wales as he had planned, and he returned home, via Caeo and Llwyn-y-berllan. He provides the following account of the journey:

> This day month I went from home through Breconshire, Carmarthen, Pembroke and Cardiganshire, near 300 miles. Enabled to discourse about 50 times. Had unconceivable and immeasurable blessing . . . together with uncommon mental and physical strength to proclaim Christ.[6]

Within a few days of returning there was a Monthly Meeting at Trefeca. The matters discussed were unimportant, but during the Association a love-feast was held in which he received particular indications of the presence of the Most High:

> It was a love-feast indeed; we were there singing, praying, and exhorting until gone ten. But what am I alongside many of them? The brethren were enraptured to such degree that they were singing and praying to near two. Glory to God, who is yet amongst us. In the love-feast I had strength to seek, and to knock; I felt a measure of closeness to God; but he came not in that enflaming way of old, removing the covering and revealing his glory, so that my soul melted and I had the nearest access. But we continued to wrestle with God, and soon I had strength to ask the Lord whether he intended to visit the nation in his grace, and to return to us? Did he intend to support the poor Methodists, leading and defending us? Afterwards, I had assurance in my spirit that he had approached us in love. I then had liberty to ask the same thing in public prayer, and the Lord revealed himself in the brethren's consciences and they were as assured as I was. I then had great liberty to encourage them to effort, to life, to zeal, and activity.

These quotations reveal a soul living very close to the Lord. Whether his actions in questioning the great God, and requiring a definite answer from him with a view to the future, and then in interpreting his own assured feelings, and those of his brethren, as a positive reply to his question, reveals a completely healthy state of mind, we would not take it upon ourselves to decide. It appears as a first shoot of that mystical tendency which developed to an extreme degree in him afterwards.

## DANIEL ROWLAND CAUTIONS HARRIS AS TO HIS THEOLOGY

Another Monthly Meeting gathered at Trefeca on 2 March, and Daniel Rowland came to preach to the outlying areas for several days before the meeting. Harris went to hear him at Erwood. He preached remarkably from Philippians 3:8, 'Yea doubtless, and I count all things but loss for the excellency of the knowledge of Christ Jesus my Lord.' Of the full notes that Harris wrote of the sermon, we can only provide a few:

He showed how our condition in Christ excelled that of Adam.

1. Had Adam continued without sinning, we are not told that he would have been removed from earth; but we are to be removed to heaven to be with God.

2. He was only in a paradise to which Satan could obtain access; but we are to be moved to a place where he can never come.

3. Though he was, in one sense, full of grace, yet he did not have an abundance of supply; so, although he could have stood, it was possible for him to fall; but we have inexhaustible treasures in store, no matter how much we expend.

Then he emphasized perseverance in grace, showing that if Satan had destroyed us through sin so that we could not save ourselves, yet that Christ was a better worker than he; therefore shall he not save us so effectively that we shall not be able to damn ourselves? He showed how those who abuse this doctrine are carnal. Next, he explained the excellency of the knowledge of Christ, showing the majesty of this knowledge, its usefulness, that it brings pardon, grace and happiness. He was full of learning and godly wisdom . . . To Trefeca with him. Strengthened in hearing him say how the Lord gives me with them to strengthen his hands and to preach the same things with him, withal cautioning me to guard more in my doctrine.[7]

This last phrase is most significant, showing that the Reformer from Trefeca tended, in his brethren's judgment, to be unguarded in his expressions when explaining the great doctrines of the gospel. He, however, received the warning in the same spirit as it was given:

We had love and union, and I had a degree of humility in seeing myself as being noticed by anyone. On hearing him preach (at Trefeca) on 'If any man will follow, etc.', I think I never heard such wisdom. There came power with the wisdom.[8]

Harris felt a soldier's spirit rising within him as he listened.

The following are the resolution passed at this Monthly Association:

We met before on February 10 and spent some time very edifying in taking to consideration the state of the nation and Church; observing the signs of the time and asking each what light he thought the Lord gave about the present work, when so many things concurred to threaten sore judgments; and each had faith clearer or weaker that the work should go on and that it was as yet but begun, and some of the opinion that trials might go before. The Lord was then in an uncommon manner with us, and the brethren were kept up to sing and pray, etc., till past 12 at night.

After opening our hearts to each other and asking questions about our work, we agreed to meet again on Friday at ten in the morning, March 29. To be kept on monthly, every 4th Friday from March 1st, and that every day of our private association henceforth be a day of fasting and prayer together.

Agreed that each should lay the circumstances of Bro. Thomas Jones before the private societies.

Agreed that next Tuesday fortnight, 19th inst., be kept a day of private humiliation among the faithful, on account of the division in England, and the lukewarmness and other sins in England and Wales.[9]

The last entry shows that the situation amongst the Methodists in England was critical: divisions and formation of parties had occurred, and their president, Whitefield, was in America since the previous year. As a result, the burden of the care had fallen mainly upon Howell Harris. At the beginning of March, an Association was held at Bristol, and he went there, together with Beaumont. His spirit was grieved because of the disputes amongst the exhorters. In the boat, as he crossed the Severn, he was given much nearness to God, and strength to ask him to deliver him from his own spirit in the day of temptation that was at hand, in case he should offend God, or offend the brethren, which he feared above all things. God assured him that he would keep him. Once he arrived at Bristol he called the brethren together. A meeting was held in which they humbled themselves before Almighty God and asked his guidance. Then Harris addressed them, stating that God had a quarrel against them. On the morning of the Association he wrestled intensely with God before leaving the house; he viewed the day as a day of trial, a day of mourning and of humiliation. A desire to return home came upon him but he was willing to remain as long as that would result in God's glory. He wrote:

Such a number, even of those who profess to know the Lord, exult in our divisions; some condemn our teachings, others condemn our spirit and zeal. O Lord, how long wilt thou allow us to be a laughing-stock? Are we not thy children, thy poor ambassadors, sent by thee? O, have compassion upon us.

In this spirit he met up with his brethren. A feeling of brokenness passed over the gathering as they read the minutes of the previous Association. Harris's comments continue:

Then, I debated with Bro. Bishop, who intends to separate and join the Baptists. After speaking freely we came to an understanding with him with respect to those who have not been baptized but who are convicted. He believed that we should obtain a licence to preach; that the baptism of infants is a human device; that he has a right to administer the sacraments without ordination or laying on of hands. With this we all disagreed. Some of us, myself amongst them, had no liberty to apply for a licence. We were all unwilling to administer the sacraments without being ordained, and unwilling also to ordain amongst ourselves. We were unanimous also with regard to the baptism of infants, but we agreed that he could come amongst us, if he wished. On being pressed, I went to the hall to preach, to a large gathering.

The Association continued over the Thursday and Friday, and peace reigned in all the sessions:

Certainly, the Lord heard our prayers, and he sweetly united our hearts and souls. I felt that the Lord was giving me simplicity, love and liberty, and victory over prejudice, to speak simply, and not to dispute over words. I saw that we all thought the same:

(1) With a view to Christ our righteousness; they meant the same in calling him our sanctification, as we do in calling him an imputed righteousness, or personal sanctification.

(2) They mean the same thing by the fruits of faith, or the fruits of the Spirit, as we do by the new creature, namely a principle of grace within the soul.

(3) They mean the same thing by the word faith in exercise, as we do by faith, or communion with God.

(4) They mean the same by faith out of exercise, as we do by the word unbelief, or backsliding in the heart.

(5) When they speak against experience, they only mean that it should not be put in the wrong place, that is as a substitute for Christ.

We then agreed that if we used a phrase that is not in the Scriptures, we should explain it with Scriptural expressions, and as far as possible to confine ourselves to Biblical terms.

Again:

We agreed upon justification and sanctification; that Christ, and not faith, is the foundation on which we should lean; and we had uncommon light and liberty when discussing the necessity and place of fruits, that is holiness of heart and life, and the place of the law or the commandment in religion. We had meant the same things previously, when we had seemed to be contradicting one another. We agreed also on how to deal with those who were breaking the law in their lives; that they are not believers, in that Christ writes his law in the heart of the believer. We opened all our hearts to one another on every point; we also wrote down the things we agreed upon. We agreed also on the various degrees of faith – weak faith and strong faith, notional faith, believing faith, and saving faith. We agreed also with regard to Bro. Cudworth; I had felt uneasy about him as a fellow-labourer; but when he expressed himself as agreeing, simply, without deceit or guile, with what had been written down, I had liberty to receive him. Circuits were arranged for each one; and having arranged the young preachers in their various places, we departed sweetly and happy, having offered up praise and prayer to God, who gave us the victory.

So ended the Bristol Association, and its effects were very important for Methodism in Wales, as well as in England. For the first time some kind of Confession of Faith and Rules of Discipline were drawn up and set down on paper, so that appeal might be made to them in the future.[10] Clearly, this was a time of great agitation, and in the excitement all their religious beliefs were being reviewed and argued over, one by one. They viewed lack of orthodoxy in the same light as lack of morality, and it was easy for brethren to quarrel over words when there was no significant disagreement in reality. It was wise of the fraternity to agree to make use only of Scriptural terms as much as possible in their discussion of doctrines; and no wonder that Harris called the Association a 'blessed Association'. There had been a very real possibility of division. That at least was Howell Harris's judgment; and we believe that it was his wisdom and prudence as Moderator that was instrumental in re-establishing peace and in keeping the brethren from disruption. He discussed the occasion in a letter, dated 12 April 1745, to James Erskine:

> Your concern for us when we met at Bristol I trust I shall never forget – it was indeed a critical time, but the prayer-hearing God opened his ears to the cries of his many wrestling children. Things indeed had gone to that extremity, that it was gone beyond the reach of all means to do any good, but God pities us, and would not let his glory and his work and his poor wretched children and messengers be trodden under foot, nor his enemies rejoice. He performed wonders for us. Never was his arm made so bare for us. Satan's wiles were detected, and his hellish aims brought to nothing. As you have heard particulars, I am persuaded, by Bro. Edwards, I need only observe to you that the means he made use of to reunite us again were: He first laid before us (at least, some of us), the dreadful consequences that were like to follow a division; the dishonour brought upon our dear Lord; the stumbling block laid in the path of the unconverted; and the disorder that would come amongst us and those who love us. Next, having created in us, or at least, in some of us, a desire to be one, and under the influence of this desire to pour out our hearts before the Lord, he removed our prejudices, giving us a faith that he would yet have compassion upon us, and unite us in his truth, though that seemed so unlikely. Then opening our hearts to each other the veil that kept us from understanding one other before was removed, and we found our misunderstanding and differences arose from mistaking each others' expressions; for as to justification and sanctification and saving faith we meant alike but had different ways of expressing the same truth. As you, I suppose, have

seen in the minute of our Agreement, Brother Cennick had been unguarded in some expressions in the warmth of his zeal, and from the earnestness of his desire to exalt the God-man, the glorious Emmanuel, and in removing the false rests that kept so many securely without coming to live by real faith on his blood and wounds, the enemy sometimes hurried him a little to slip in speaking and confounded some of the people in hearing, so as to mistake him in both extremes, and some of the young men I believe have been more faulty, but I believe of all sides we have been humbled and brought hereby nearer our kind and compassionate Master.[11]

We cannot go into detail on the contents of this letter, though it has much in it of interest. Howell Harris spent the Sunday at Bristol, and returned home by Thursday, 29 March, so as to be present at the Monthly Meeting at Trefeca. He met his brethren with a happy heart because things had turned out so well at Bristol, though, at the same time, every success in the work made him humble and filled him with submission. He wrote:

> Our meeting was full of good news. In prayer, I was remarkably drawn out, and the Lord made his face to shine upon us wonderfully. As I placed before them the offer from Scotland of keeping a day every three months, and every Sunday morning, to thank the Lord for the recent awakening in England, Wales and America (a suggestion to which the brethren agreed), I had strength to see that this related to no one more than myself. Firstly, no one has been favoured more than myself – the worst and most unworthy of all. Secondly, no one has offended and tempted the Lord as myself, and so no one has greater obligation to praise him and to submit before him. Thirdly, no one is so bound over to desire the success of the work. I have cried out to be conscientious in this. After we had examined the conditions of the societies, and of the way in which the days of humiliation were kept, we departed in the sweetest of spirits.

In the Trefeca records the minutes are as follows:

At an Association held at Trefeca, March 29, 1745; Mr Howell Harris: Moderator.

After relating how the Lord had heard our prayers in uniting the brethren in England, we settled our next monthly Association at Bro. Thomas James's house at the month's end, Friday, 26 April.

As a proposal was sent from Scotland to keep one day in every three months, beginning November 1st, a day of prayers, for two years, and to meet every Sunday morning on account of the late work in England, Scotland, Wales and America, both to praise God for it and interceded and pray for its furtherance and to be humbled for the sin that attended it, we agreed to it – to keep the first of May next (the quarter's end) and every Sunday morning with as many as we can have, and also in private to give it a place in our hearts and time as much as we can every Saturday night, and to recommend it to others.

## THE GROES-WEN LETTER AND
## SUBSEQUENT DEVELOPMENTS

The following Thursday and Friday, the first week of April, a Quarterly Meeting was held at Caeo. This was an important Association on many counts, but its history is not to be found in the Trefeca records. The conference was opened by a sermon from John Powell, the clergyman from Monmouthshire. Harris commented:

> I was solemn and heavy, but not in the Spirit, when listening. But I had strength to wrestle for him, that God might shine upon him, and the Lord came down. Then we dined, and Bro. Gambold preached on John 1:1,2 etc. He had great fluency of words, but the Lord did seem to set a contempt on laymen preaching. He was quite left, so that all were dry, seemingly. The Lord did not seem to be near us, and I was afterwards cut in hearing Bro. Rowland saying that the Lord seems to be leaving the exhorters, and I saw it too as to myself and others. This was blessed; there was given to us a degree of watchfulness, and zeal, and mourning, for our continual backsliding from the Lord; our idolatry and spiritual whoredom. But, certainly, our meeting was not yet full of God. In reading a letter from the Bro. Howell Davies declaring what an honour he sees it to preach the blood of Christ, I had light and convictions. I see the glory of his blood is but beginning to come in sight. We did read two letters from Monmouthshire and Glamorganshire about their going to leave us.[12]

What society in Monmouthshire sent a letter is not known, but the letter from Glamorganshire was from the exhorters of Groes-wen, and is so important, and so typical of the feelings of many of the exhorters at the time, that it is worth quoting in full. It reads as follows:

> To the dear brethren in general, and the ministers in particular, assembled at Caeo, greeting. Grace be with you all, Amen.

> We believe of you that you are such as are beloved of God, that God is loved by you, that you have been specially called by God to the work of the ministry, that God's cause is dear to you, a burden on your souls; that his will has been made known to you in great measure, and for that reason we have felt it necessary for us to send word to you as men who have received a spirit to sympathize with us, and with many others who at the present time are to a considerable degree lacking liberty, because of the disorder prevailing among us. Our consciences are so constrained by the word of God, that we cannot go on thus contrary to the order of God. Because we see that God, from the outset, has given his Church an order, which is to continue until the end of

time. We think it is your duty to sympathize with us in this weighty matter, because it was at your advice we became messengers of God in an irregular way; and for all we know God has given us a measure of success; and will you, as good stewards of God's house, strive to carry on this great work until order is attained? It is most unlikely that any body of people ever remained in this fashion for all time. We have been expecting to get your views on this matter for nearly two years, and we do not see any indications that you have deliberated on this question as it deserves; but we fear that too many of the prejudices of your upbringing cling to you. We are of the opinion that you are too much attached to the Established Church. We think that if you received ordination in the Church of England, as also you expect, that would not suffice to set at rest numerous brethren and sisters in the country; because what they require is a number of men to minister the word and ordinances to them regularly; to undertake their oversight as shepherds over flocks; or remain as we are, and to this we cannot think of consenting.

We have placed our case in God's hand, hoping that, if you fail in compassion for us, God will open for us a way to a better order. Brethren, it pains us to hear that you cannot grant us liberty to exhort because we are not ordained, and that, as far as we can see, you do not care whether we shall be ordained or not. If your sympathy fails us, we feel that we must turn our eyes to some other direction; and may God direct us. We confess that we are the [fruit of] your labours, and it pains us to be obliged to leave, to make room for others to come into your labours; we are, however, compelled to break through every obstacle, for the sake of the name of the Lord Jesus and a good conscience. We do not take this course rashly, but with much and earnest thought; and the more we consider it, the more it weighs on our minds, so that it becomes hard to bear.

One reason why our consciences are so oppressed is, because the rule of laying on of hands was practised in former times (viz., the time of the apostles), in the case of all men who ministered in the word; not only in the case of the bishops, and the elders, but also deacons, as you may see from Acts 6:6, 'Whom they set before the apostles: and when they had prayed, they laid their hands on them.' Then we have the account of the splendid results which followed, as you may see in the next verse. It is probable that these men, like ourselves, had preached many times, and that God had prospered them; yet it may be that the bishops and elders had [up to then] not permitted them full liberties, more than you clergy permit us today. Therefore we pray you to do what they did; by doing so you cannot offend any man who takes God's word as the guiding rule of his life; then we may expect the same effects, increasing our number, and strengthening such as are already called. We beg that the brethren may not regard us as having relapsed into lukewarmness, because we thus convey our thoughts to you, or think that we can expect to make a name for ourselves here. No, because, if you will permit the exercise of your reason, you will see that we do not so act. Besides, we could leave you quietly, and so be ordained, and have congregations under our supervision. No, brethren, we are willing to labour together with you, as we have up to the present, and to be governed by you as hitherto, but 'in the Lord', and according to his word. We have been trying to place our matter before you for some time, but have not been permitted to do so. May God have compassion upon us at a trying time, when our fathers in Christ, and our brethren in the Lord, are leaving us comfortless. This at present from your most affectionate brethren,

Thomas Price,
William Edwards,
Thomas William,
John Belcher,
Evan Thomas,
Eglwys Ilan, March 30, 1745.[13]

This is certainly a strong letter, though it contains some personal references that are not completely respectful. It was hardly appropriate for these exhorters to suggest that if some of the leading men of the Association were ordained according to Church of England rites, the Association would not care what happened to others. Reading between the lines, it is easy to see a strong desire for ordination; they were ready to remain with the Methodists as long as they were ordained; they were determined to leave if they were not. No doubt, the same inspiration was working its way as a leaven amongst exhorters of many of the societies. It would be interesting to know what answer was given to this letter, if, indeed, it was answered at all. But this is not known. Harris's journal however sheds much light on the state of mind of the gathered fraternity at Caeo over this matter:

There was a strict and long examination of the nature, evil, and symptoms of pride and self appearing in the exhorters, and I had some cutting lashes given, but not lasting. We opened our hearts to each other, and saw that we must declare against the Dissenters. That they sleep and leave the Lord . . . the Lord did indeed give me a message to deliver to the brethren, most awfulsome and cutting, about humility and poverty of spirit, and sure the Lord was there indeed, and all seemed affected, and several declaring how they felt the words coming like swords to their souls. It went mostly about the absolute danger of pride, and how abominable it was to see us [the exhorters] proud, seeing we have but little gifts, very little knowledge in anything, no learning or parts, mean and contemptible in the eyes of all; and so, really, the vilest, etc. Showing how we should be inwardly ashamed and confounded before God when we see any inclined to come and hear such mean ignorant and contemptible creatures as we. Very searching about being truly poor in our own eyes, showing how pride appears in our not bearing and loving reproof.[14]

This entry shows that Harris and the brethren considered that spiritual pride amongst the exhorters was the motive behind this passionate desire for ordination that had raised its head, and was causing heated argument and division. The following points seem clear:

1. That the Methodist leaders at this time, and Howell Harris in particular, clung firmly to the Established Church, and were unwilling to acknowledge the right of the ablest exhorters for ordination to the complete work of the ministry. They desired that many might receive episcopal ordination, but without this they were not willing to undertake the responsibility of ordaining amongst themselves. They preferred rather to suffer the neglecting of the societies, and the departure of their ablest exhorters.

2. Whilst some exhorters possessed abundant gifts and deep understanding of the Scriptures, there were many others who were weak in ability, shallow in discernment, and defective in taste and judgment. It is however very possible that the desire for ordination, and thus the obtaining of a higher standing in the church, was stronger in this second group than any. If therefore ordination of the exhorters was to commence, it was very possible that this would open the floodgates, and jealousy and envy would flow in upon the brethren as rivers.

3. It is fairly certain that many of those, perhaps the most respectable class, who followed the Reformers and called themselves Methodists, were more faithful to the Church than were the leaders. If they were to see the least tendency in the Association to become a Dissenting denomination they would have turned their backs on them immediately.

For all these reasons, Rowland and Harris saw no room for manoeuvre; they waited eagerly for clearer and more decisive light. At the same time, however, we believe they were deficient in enterprise at this period, and were waiting for clearer signs than they had any right to expect. Because of this they lost hundreds of followers who left them for other groups. This, however, was no loss to religion, for it became the means of spreading a much more evangelical and more aggressive spirit in these other parties, and perhaps also of attenuating effectively the erroneous tendency that was so prevalent amongst them.

The first thing Harris did on returning home was to call on Price Davies, the vicar of Talgarth, to obtain from him permission for the Methodists to receive communion at the church, which privilege had been denied them for nearly two and a half years. Harris wrote,

He objected to me:

1. That I discoursed at home in time of divine service. I said I never did it designedly.

2. That I had acted against the Canons. I said the Canons were no law, as never ratified by Act of Parliament.

3. That I had wronged the Bishop of London. I said I thought I did not; that I believe his Lordship is not clear in justification, and that if I was to be called before him I should think it my duty to tell him so; but if I misquoted him in the letter I sent to Mr Glyde, I owned my fault in another letter, and it was owing to my not having his Lordship's letter by me when I wrote it.

4. That I did not come to my parish church. I said that I was but seldom at home, and sometimes I went to meetings. That I had heard some good discourses there; and sometimes to Talachddu; that I had heard there what suited my taste better; but that I did not go, as he said, out of curiosity, and that I would come easier here were it not for Mr Edwards the curate.

5. That I did backbite the clergy, which, if they are faulty, we should pity, etc. I said I did not allow myself in that spirit to any; but that I thought it my duty to declare against their sins, etc., as they are means of leading others in sin by their even seeing many a one drunk, and even at cock-matches, and others are encouraged thereto thereby . . . I showed him how I have laboured to keep several in the Church who scrupled coming because of the ungodliness and ignorance of the clergy – preaching works instead of Christ. Then he objected, and I corrected [myself] that they ought to be preached in their place as fruits of faith. He objected that when the people come from hearing me they looked scornful and despising on him; and I said I hoped I never did so; and he said no. I said I hated that spirit in myself and all others, and always reproved it. I said I asked to come only to show my spirit, and as I was at peace in myself with him, I was free if he would let me come. But if not, that he knew I would lose nothing by it; that I may, and do, have it elsewhere . . . He was very bitter against Bro. Rowland, threatening him with a citation if he came again. When he said I could not trouble him for refusing me the Sacrament, as I had said in a letter to him. This I showed from the trial that passed between the Bishop of the Isle of Man and the Governor [to] whom he refused the Sacrament, and was sued.[15]

So ended the discussion between Howell Harris and old Price Davies, and it is fascinating as an example of the feelings of both parties. The clergyman does not appear to have given him a definite answer at the time, but he did yield, because, for Easter Sunday, the following entry is found in the journal:

Talgarth Church – being admitted to the Sacrament again . . . In the sermon on Colossians 3:1, I was surprised in hearing the soundness and spirituality of it. My soul was fed and enlightened . . . To the Sacrament. Having under the sermon been near the Lord, and made more then commonly thankful to hear such a sermon here.[16]

As had previously been agreed, a Monthly Association had been arranged at the home of Thomas James, Cerrigcadarn, on 26 April. Its decisions are not recorded, probably they were unimportant, but Harris gives something of an account in his journal:

We sat together till after four, and the Lord made me cutting and severe towards the brethren. I showed that we must be taught by God in all that we seek to teach the people, otherwise we cannot speak with authority, and life, and boldness; that they should realize our relationship to all of God's creatures, and to all men, and to all believers, and see that we have been born into the world as wicked as devils. When we go before the people, that we are facing creatures that are dead in sin, upon whom neither words nor arguments will have any more effect than if we were trying to drill stones with our fingers, unless God speaks to them and convicts them; that we should decide not to go to the people when we are without God, and to take care, having gone, to keep our eyes firmly on God, because when we go in the flesh, when we see in the congregation some wise and experienced man, we will forget the people and direct all our remarks to him, and try to establish ourselves in his opinion, and so forget the Lord. I then showed how the people had fallen into deep sleep, how, though they are touched by the word of God, they do not in their lives acknowledge the Lord, and will not receive rebuke. I observed that it would be better for us to cease from preaching if we were not effective in piercing and convicting. I referred to pride – pride in clothing – our ways of seeking to hide it, and how we are slaves to it. There was great power amongst us. I believe this will be a blessing to them, and to the lambs. I saw that the Lord had sent me with this message. Then, having arranged a day of humiliation, and having ordered our circuits, I went about eight to Llangamarch.

He preached there with great power, and slept at Mr Gwynne's house. Next week, he went on a journey to parts of Monmouthshire and Glamorganshire so that he might be present at the Watford Association, and also in order to confirm the exhorters. The agitation and discomfort amongst them pressed heavily upon him. He said:

I feel my soul trembles because of the exhorters; self-seeking is prevalent amongst them, poverty of spirit departing, and head knowledge increasing. O my God, lead us into thy doctrine, that we might see and glorify thee, and might become like thee. It would be horrible if the Methodists were to depart from the Lord after all that he has done for them. But the Lord is gentle towards me in this day of trial. I find that they seek only ordination, discipline and congregations. O, are they not like the Israelites in this, who wished for a king that they might be like other nations?

After preaching at Cantref, Dol-y-gaer, Llanheiddel and New Inn, he reached Watford on the night before the Association. Here, within two miles of Groes-wen, was the centre of all the agitation for ordination, and it was from here that the letter had been sent to the Caeo Association. Of necessity therefore, the exhorters' desire for ordination and the disturbance resulting, must have been uppermost in the minds of all as they gathered, and the matter had to be discussed. Harris took advantage of the presence of so many brethren to raise the topic before the formal Association sessions, sharing his own views at length and answering questions and objections. His journal relates the events:

In discoursing with the brethren I declared I differed with them in three things:

1. That I never looked on the societies as churches, but little branches of a Church.

2. The exhorters never as ministers to dispense ordinances, nor, many of them, even the word, by way of preaching, but by way of exhorting.

3. On us never as a sect, but a people in the Church, called to reform till either we should be heard, or turned out; and that whoever is called to labour as a reformer must have a strong love to bear much; and that I look on all these uneasinesses as arising:

i. From Satan's secretly working on the conscience to attempt to divide us; and my reasons for this are, (1) I can't think God lays the scruples [of receiving the sacraments in the parish churches], because the time is not for removing and easing them; (2) those that have yielded to them as from God, have never prospered; (3) we could not agree with Dissenters, if we would go among them, because of the Baxterian doctrine, lukewarm profession, etc., and they, looking on us as inferiors, would not let us have any authority to reform; (4) the thought of going out as a sect is shocking to me.

ii. I think these scruples have place (1) from the prevalency of self-judging too well of our own judgment to understand the Scriptures; (2) from want of feeling the work coming with weight on our souls enough; (3) from want of seeing the consequences, etc.

iii. I believe that the Lord would show the lesser things to such as he has shown the greater things, and that he would begin the separation [from the Church] by such as he has given, and does give, most of himself to, and with them, etc.

I answered objections:

1. That none dissented from the Established Church till they were turned out: so the Apostles from the Jews, the Protestants from the Popish, etc., the

latter having ordination and ordinances from the Popish nearly a hundred years before they made a Church.

2. Objection: that there was no likelihood of many of them being ordained in the Established Church for want of the languages, etc. Answer: that when the door should be opened for us, it must be by the Lord opening their hearts to ordain out of conscience, and not stick to the forms, etc., or else thrust us out, etc.

3. I showed ordination, though used, yet, as many preached without it, it is evident it was no great thing in the Apostles' days. When Apollos did preach, he was not charged for going [about] unordained, but for want of better light to know Christ; and so the brethren that went about on Stephen's death. Objection: But then was a time of persecution. Answer: And so 'tis now when we shan't be ordained.

I spoke my mind and [that] of Bro. Rowland of some of the exhorters, that seeing, (1) such self and pride, and (2) instability, etc., growing among many of them, I trembled for them, and could not coquet to any of them; and also, as to the people, that they are growing asleep for want of preaching to them the life of faith; i.e., living now, the present time, on Christ; and putting home to them not what they did feel, but what they now do, etc. And I believe the Lord blessed our being together very much, beyond my expectation, etc., the brethren having more love, humility, and subordination than I expected, taking it kind when I declared my mind to them – that I thought they would not prosper if they would go on, and they would put a greater hindrance in the way of the work (according to my light) than anything that has yet happened. I declared my mind too with respect to the form of worship that I would be glad if that of the Church were to be revised, and its use be left to the minister's discretion. I answered an objection too: That ordination, we see, can't keep carnal men from taking the work in hand.

This was undoubtedly an important meeting, and it appears that Howell Harris on his own, without the help of any of the other brethren, overcame the demand for ordination that was increasing amongst the exhorters. His main reasons for not separating were: firstly, the fear that the Spirit of the Lord was not behind the movement, and as a result it would prove a great obstacle to the revival; secondly, the hope that bishops sympathetic to the revival would be appointed who would then ordain the more able and qualified of the exhorters, without querying too much as to their academic education. It is no surprise that later, privately, he humbles himself before God for the privilege granted to him, and that he saw Satan's kingdom falling to the ground. The next day, at the Association, all was serene. Harris addressed the exhorters powerfully, they decided to forget the issue and to continue as before. But it was agreed to draw up a paper explaining their situation and to present it to the bishops. That night, Harris went to

Groes-wen, to those who had separated from them, to preach. His text was the phrase in the Book of Revelation, 'Fear not; I am the first and the last.' To use his own words, 'The Lord came down.'

> My soul's one desire was that the Lord should presence himself amongst the people, in that words, or matter, or raising the voice, or weeping, are nothing without God. I had great liberty to show how Jesus Christ is the first, and the power this truth has to conquer fear; that he is first before men, if we fear men; the first before devils; and the first before sin. That Jesus could say, 'I know the beginning of men, and the beginning of Satan, and the beginning of sin; I know the full extent of their strength, and wiles; I am able to plumb their depths.' Then, I showed the way in which he was the last, and that he proclaims, 'I will be last after sin, men and devils; I will remain on the field until they are all conquered; I will remain in your soul to purify it until all is perfect. I am dwelling in your soul, to wash you until you are clean and pure, not having spot or wrinkle. I am in you to fight your battles, until all the enemies that surround you have been conquered. Do not fear, in the last day, when everything will be burned with fire, I will be last. I, who have loved you, and whom you love; I, whom you desire above all things, and for whom you have left all things; I will be there, the last. I have been dead, it is true; I completed your salvation upon the cross; I descended into the depths to defeat death and Satan; but though I was dead, I am alive.'

By now, the meeting was full of awe; all had involuntarily risen to their feet. The preacher proceeded to apply his doctrine.

> This is enough! The Lord is alive! Come now, lift up your eyes to the blood! Look, and you will see death's citadel pulled down, the lion in chains and conquered, hell defeated; you will see light the other side of the grave.

The preacher now had complete mastery over his congregation. He was full of faith and of the Holy Spirit, and every word spoken reached home. He then proceeded to thunder against the enemies of Christ: Socinians, Arians, Deists, the Pope, and Hell, and he concluded the sermon by exhorting them all to submit to the Saviour. He wrote:

> I had remarkable strength; my soul was free and full of faith, light, and Christ's Spirit. O, how glorious is this light!

Very probably the powers felt in this meeting contributed as much to the producing of a better spirit amongst the exhorters as did Howell Harris's arguments in the Association.

From Watford, Harris went towards Aberthin in a happy state of mind, leaving the exhorters whom he had rebuked in a low spirit. His text there was Isaiah 30:2,3 and he was given considerable power to show what the Lord had done for them, and how they were departing in their whoredoms. In the society afterwards, the issue of leaving the Church was raised and they were all unanimous not to separate. On Saturday, he went to St Nicholas. He heard there that the press-gang was out, and his spirit rejoiced within him at the thought of the dangers which he faced. The clergyman at Wenvoe Church was very evangelical and according to his custom when he was in the neighbourhood, Harris went there on the Sunday to hear the Word, and to receive the sacrament. He then turned for home, passing Watford, and preaching with much unction at Mynyd-dislwyn, Gelli-gaer and Pontsticill, arriving home by 1 May, which had been appointed by the Association a day of prayer and humiliation.

## BACK TO LONDON

Within a few days, he received a letter from London calling him there, as there were many important matters to be arranged, and Whitefield was in America. He spread the letter before the Lord. He felt completely at his service, as clay in the hands of the potter; and considered it a privilege to go, if God was calling him. Before setting out for the capital however he took a long journey through West Glamorgan, visiting Llansamlet and Gower, then through Carmarthenshire, and as far as Parke in Pembro-keshire. What brought him here was his sympathy for his dear friend, Howell Davies, who was in deep waters, having lost his wife. After spend-ing a Sabbath at Llanddowror with the venerable Griffith Jones, Harris returned to Abergorlech, where a Monthly Association was under way. Daniel Rowland was to preach there. He was given remarkable power at the prayer at the beginning. The journal states:

> The dear Brother Rowland prayed wondrously. When he began interced-ing for the nation, and to call God to return to dwell again amongst us, the place was filled with the presence of God. I feel sure that this prayer travelled straight to heaven.

Rowland's text was 2 Corinthians 7:1, and his message was that the doctrine of free grace is destructive of sin. The Lord was present to a re-markable degree. There is no record extant of the Association, other than what Harries noted in his journal:

> I sat late with the brethren, as there were press-warrants out. We examined each other about our willingness to go to the war, and each was willing if called, but agreed to be prudent. About more regulations among us as to our rounds that the lambs may be more regularly fed. We had much love and communion of spirit.[17]

He returned home through Glanyrafonddu and Llanddeusant. It

appears that Harris's own mind was not completely easy with respect to the decision to remain in the Established Church. He refers to it on many occasions during the journey, and on his return to Trefeca there is a remarkable note in his journal:

> I prayed earnestly for the Lord to return amongst us, but when I received a favourable answer regarding the work, I had none as regards the Establishment, the bishops, and the clergymen, though I had argued much in their favour.

These words certainly convey a considerable unease of spirit.

In mid-May, he and Mrs Harris set out for London. He was not without concerns for the cause in Wales in his absence:

> But I had faith to commit all the labourers to his care, as I was to leave them for a while, and I prayed that the Lord might be wisdom and power to them, and enable them to tread Satan under their feet.

On arriving in the capital, he found that the societies there were in considerable disarray. Divisions and disagreements had arisen among them, and doubts over the moral behaviour of some of the members were rife.

> I hear such things here, and see such divisions, that I do not know what to do or say. It is good for me that Christ is all my wisdom and strength; I see my life and health in his hand. O, how shall I conduct myself in this hour of trial?

A Mr Cudworth was at the root of the trouble, the same man that had been agitating previously at Bristol. Not only had he been introducing debate on the nature of the soul's reception of Christ's righteousness, but some troubling issues about his personal character had also arisen and he had been accused of some immorality. Harris believed that the man was not born again, and eventually all connection with him was broken. Mr and Mrs Harris were about a fortnight in London and it appears that he was eminently successful in smoothing out the difficulties of the English brethren and in drawing them back together again. We cannot quote the journal for this period, though it contains an interesting and detailed account, but it has also this significant remark:

> Last night, I disclosed that I have usually had only one concern when ascending the pulpit, namely that all in the meeting should profit from my words, and that Christ should be revealed to all; but now I am troubled over another matter, and that is a fear lest I offend anyone. And if I see many of God's children coming to hear with suspicious ears, attending only to see if I fail, it is a sad proof why I cannot believe that they seek to assist me and to uphold my arms with their prayers. O, how painful is strife! How glad

would I be on all accounts to be able to withdraw, except that it is the Lord who has called me here.

The note suggests that some of the London brethren were beginning to suspect whether Harris was orthodox and were coming to hear him with the intention of catching him at fault. He and his wife spent some time around Bath and Bristol on the way home and it was 22 June before they arrived back at Trefeca.

Howell Harris was much encouraged when he heard that the work had proceeded successfully whilst he away. He heard particularly of the power accompanying the ministry of Howell Davies, and his soul was immediately quickened by the news.

My soul was filled with thanksgiving, and also with love towards him, and for every witness that God has in the world. O, the goodness of my Lord in blessing me as if I never at any time sinned against him! My soul was drawn out of me in rejoicing because of the gifts, graces, success, wisdom and power which he gives to others.

He here demonstrates exemplary benevolence of spirit. He then heard that a man was coming that day from Brecon in order to take him and press him as a soldier. He felt the strength of his corrupt nature as he became pale on hearing the news. But he withdrew in secret, and there had a view of the glory of the Lord Jesus Christ as one with all authority in his hand. He saw that the devils and every kind of evildoer, including the man from Brecon with the warrant, were in chains before Christ. This filled his spirit with peace. He saw the value of the promises, particularly that promise, 'When thou passest through the waters I will be with thee,' so that he was enabled, not only to have peace of mind, but also to comfort his family. But the story proved to be untrue, or, if there had been such an intention, it was not carried out.

## FURTHER ASSOCIATIONS AND JOURNEYS IN WALES

On 3 July, a Quarterly Association was held at Blaen-y-glyn. Daniel Rowland was not present but Howell Davies and Williams, Pantycelyn, had journeyed there, together with the Rev. John Powell, the clergyman from Monmouth. As might be expected, Howell Harris was also present. The following are the minutes:

Having received a letter from Brother George Gambold about his call whether public or private, finding that his gifts are rather for edifying the saints than of conviction, and so seemingly blessed in several places in public – having weighed the matter before the Lord we referred to Bro. Howell

Davies to direct where he should discourse in public and where in private only, and that on trial until the next association.

Having received two letters, one from Bro. John Richards and another from Richard Tibbott, being under some scruple at the present time how to act, being sure to be pressed if they go to some places where they used before to go, asking our advice how to act, whether it be not a call to put themselves out of the enemies' power by taking a licence – we all agreed, that taking a licence at this time would dishonour the Lord, as would also leaving the work; most therefore of the mind that such as are out of the power of the enemies should go publicly to places of most danger and others to go more private, and so to use all innocent wisdom, as this is only a trial for a time and not to be looked upon as a persecution. But Bro. William Richard had Daniel's case laid so on his heart that he finds himself under a necessity to go on just as before – and we agreed that if the persecution should become general, and the gospel wholly stopped then appeal to the legislation, and if rejected to the bishops, and then if our liberty be wholly taken our way will be clear to separation.

The accounts of the brethren were read and full of comfortable news of the progress of the gospel in most places. Bros. Thomas James and Thomas Williams unwritten.

We agreed that the brethren should do all they can to take in subscriptions to print Elizeus [Elisha] Cole's book on God's Sovereignty in Welsh against our next Association.[18]

The brethren's opposition to separation and forming a new denomination must have been considerable, when they chose to be torn from the bosoms of their families and removed from those societies which were so dear to them, rather than placing themselves out of reach of danger by obtaining licences to preach and become Nonconformists. It must be remembered also that those who took this decision were themselves also open to this danger. Howell Harris expected every day that the authorities would issue a warrant and apprehend him. Furthermore, many of the exhorters who had already been pressed were present at the meeting, having had permission to visit their brethren; and for some time they, with the others, wept together and together raised their groans to God. Those mentioned as being out of danger were those who had been ordained, either in the Church or as Dissenters. Howell Harris judged that the best way to bring the meeting to an attitude of quiet confidence was by referring to the eternal truths of salvation:

I spoke powerfully on the danger of our own understandings, and on the mystery of the Godhead, that it is not possible to comprehend it other than by faith in the light of the Spirit. I showed how my eyes are beginning to be opened to perceive the great mysteries of the Godhead. (1) In the Word being made flesh. (2) In the Trinity in unity. (3) In the reality of our union with Christ. I believe that this proved to be the means for stirring the brethren from trust in their own understandings, to gaze upon the divine mysteries; and in particular they were stirred up by gazing upon the blood. There we see the Father, the Son, and the Spirit. There we perceive the eternal love of God. And the Lord came down and we were joyful together.

It would be difficult to find a better example of saints trusting in the Lord, and in the power of his might, so that the fear of danger was swallowed up out of sight by the majesty of the glory that excelleth which is in God. On 16 July, there was a Monthly Association at Erwood, recorded as follows:

> In this Association, nothing particular was decided, but the time was spent in singing, and praying, and opening our hearts to one another regarding the nature of the work and the state of the Church and of the nation. We were there for some hours, and God came amongst us, supporting us.

Towards the end of the month, Harris travelled through Glamorganshire. His journal gives the following account:

Trefeca, Sunday, 29 July, 1745.

> As I am today beginning a journey through Glamorganshire, I fell before the Lord, and obtained notable closeness to him as I prayed for my dear wife and family. I was assured that I would see them again, and receive them from the hand of death, as I did that morning on awakening. I had liberty to plead as regards my journey that I might be blessed, and be made a blessing to all, wherever I go. After praying with the family, I departed. When I reached Cantref, the brethren were leaving the church. I was greatly encouraged on meeting them; and my soul flamed on hearing how good he is to the brethren who have been pressed. On the road towards Watford, I had much closeness to God while singing, and praising his name for his mercies to others. I arrived there about seven, having travelled about forty miles in eight hours. There, I fainted before the people at the end of the prayer. Having recovered myself, I spoke to them from the words, 'And the Word was made flesh.' I had great liberty when referring to the union of natures, and to the blood of the Godhead. Power came down mainly as I applied the doctrine, showing that as mankind in Christ has been united with God, so we in him have been united with God. I had help to explain this union, how that the soul and body are one with Christ, our souls one with his soul, and our bodies one with his body. Then I referred to myself, that though fire burn my body, and worms consume it, yet I would receive it gloriously again. I had great liberty to stir them up to live as in the sight of Christ, and to keep close to him.

It was intended to hold an Association at Watford, as the following note in the Trefeca records explains:

> We intended to hold an Association, but Bro. Price had gone to Carmarthenshire, and we are unable to meet with Bro. Richard Jones, towards whom all means were used to restore him from his indifference and carelessness in the work. He was again asked not to speak in public until he was restored through repentance, and the brethren decided not to call for him until God's cause weighed more on his heart.

But to return to the journal:

Watford, Monday.

Today, I saw the mystery of the blood more than ever before; it was before my eyes throughout the day. I saw the whole of my salvation, my strength, my fountain in which to wash, as a sea flowing out from God, by virtue of the secret union; so that its root is in God. I cried that the glory of the blood and this righteousness be manifested throughout the world, in that every truth meets together and focuses upon this truth – the Word made flesh. Had freedom to discourse with Bro. Thomas William, showing how God is the Master-builder, and knows where each stone will fit in the building, and till 'tis where he intended it, it will weaken and not strengthen the rest of the building.

These comments were probably directed at the desire of the Groes-wen exhorters to be ordained, so that they might have the right to administer the sacraments and have the status of the Dissenting ministers.

I declared my mind that I saw somewhat of God in each way of worship – Episcopal, Presbyterian, Independent, and perhaps somewhat of man. Each may be right at some time, place, and circumstances; but not universally, without tolerating each other. There is a great difference also when the king and Government are Christians compared to when they are the enemies of Christ.

I continued to Dinas Powys. I had much liberty in praying, and in speaking on Matthew 1:21. I had authority to pierce, to awaken, and to convict. I showed how God hated sin, that he came to destroy it, root and branch; and that wherever the Spirit of the Lord is, there is war, until sin is conquered. I showed how he destroys it, by revealing the blood. Here I was reaching to the quick. I spoke convictingly both in Welsh and in English, declaring that my reward for my labour was seeing them walking in the Lord. Though I was weak, ill, in pain, and nearly fainting, I spoke home in private on walking in holiness, keeping discipline, excommunicating whoever behaves improperly, and forbidding all to exhort unless there are signs that the work lies upon their hearts. I had great freedom with this part also. I realized the enemy was seeking to blacken me, and weaken my hand, by spreading abroad that I had fallen into errors. In this also I was kept in peace and thankfulness, though in the midst of pain.

## Dinas Powys (Tuesday)

Last night I was kept close to the Lord, and far above the flesh, in the midst of all my pains. I find that Bro. Wesley, together with the brethren, depicts me as having fallen into error. In this I rejoice, that they make me to be nothing, despoiling me of my fame, and of the souls (that were convicted through me) that the wonderful Person on high be glorified. I cried, 'O Lord, let me be forgotten, except to the degree that you will use the remembrance of me to extend thy praise. Teach all to know thee; enable us all to think and speak rightly of thee.'

I went towards St Nicholas, some five miles away, in great pain because of toothache. I called on Mr Hodge, and found him full of love. When the time came to speak, the Lord gave me strength to face the work, and I was given much authority and light. I was severe against those who excuse sin, or who seek to place the blame upon God; I showed that the root of all evil lies within us, and in the devil. I was reaching to the quick as I described truth increasing in the head, but not in the heart. Privately, afterwards, I was very close regarding weeding the society and forbidding any wickedness in ourselves or in others, otherwise the Lord would leave us. I declared that I would spare no one, but that I would turn out any who walks improperly, whoever they might be. Objection: Then, we will become few. Answer: Were we only two, let us be together with the Lord. Objection: The societies will decline. Answer: Let them decline; unless we have societies in the Lord, let them all be broken into little pieces. I then placed before them the case of Richard Jones, that he has been silenced because of his indifference, yet some were still asking him to speak. I declared that he has grieved the Lord, and that he was showing that God's cause was not close to his heart; and until repentance is given to him, I cannot work with him, nor will I come to those societies that invite him. I do this out of a conscience towards God. When I thus declared, the Lord shone in my soul; my heart melted sweetly within me, bearing testimony that I was doing his will. We departed full of love.

I directed my steps towards Aberthaw, reaching there by six. The pain of toothache was nearly unbearable, but my soul was brought to bless and praise God because of it; I saw that it was a rod, as I had been wandering from God, and I loved God for it. I called at Fonmon, but so great was the pain that I could only stay there for a few minutes. When I arrived at Aberthaw I was released from the pain sufficiently to speak to a large gathering on, 'Rejoice evermore,' but my words were turned to become cutting and stern. I arrived at Pentrythyn, some six miles further on; the pain was coming on again. I felt that I had been delivered from death, but, O, how weak would I be in pains were I not to have God! I was given forebearance on having the tooth removed, but when the pain returned again I asked the Lord regarding pulling another tooth. After removing a second tooth the pains ceased.

Pentrythyn (Wednesday)

Last night, at Aberthaw, many of Mr Wesley's people were in attendance and I said that we and they agreed with respect to this, that we had to be freed from sin at last, and that the Christian rejoiced in the knowledge of this; that he rejoices even in the midst of his grief because of the corruption of nature, because God loves him, forgives him, and views him as perfect in Christ. This morning, in secret, I had a further glimpse in my spirit that I must be on Mount Zion, in the company of multitudes of the saints, and I therefore saw myself as a stranger here. I went towards one to speak at Aberthin, and had an uncommonly powerful service, preaching on, 'Continue ye in my love.' I was severe with those whose whole delight is not in God. O how sweet it is to preach in the Lord! The congregations were more numerous than usual in most places. I then went to the private society, and we sat up the whole night, until nearly six. It was strange how the Lord strengthened me, both in soul and body. He was present with us; he made us as a flame of fire and love; he endowed us with life and power and warmth. I was severe with them, that they should not endure sin amongst them, or anything like it. I then strengthened their faith in the work, showing that there was every sign that it was from God, and that it had spread over the whole land, both on our side and the other side of the sea. As far as the objection that the instruments are poor is concerned, I answered that it was the same in the time of the apostles, and that, in God's hand, the poorest instrument was as good as the best. I referred to the stopping of Richard Jones from preaching, because of his indifference, and his refusing to accept rebuke, and showed that we must be united in refusing his kind, otherwise there would be no authority amongst us. I then showed powerfully the necessity of all being taught of God, and filled by him, for the fulfilling of their ministries. Then, by singing and praying, our souls were enflamed; the Lord was with us indeed. My eyes were kept fixed upon the new Jerusalem; I was full of feeling, and longing to be there. I stirred up the brethren against the devil, showing how he destroyed us at the first, and how he continues to divide us, and to make us unhappy. By now, the brethren were full of life. O, glory to God for returning to us again! I referred to the great mystery; the Word made flesh, and the way he illumined me at first. After this, they dealt with many complaints they had against one another, and were now completely free from any temptation to separate.

For all the fascination of the journal, we must hasten to proceed. He went from Aberthin to Penprysc, a farmhouse nor far from Llantrisant, where he preached powerfully from Matthew 28:18. The congregation melted under the influence of the word. He preached another day at a place called Hafod from the words, 'For to me to live is Christ, and to die is gain.' He thought that he had never before had such power while preaching. The Lord was truly present. Many wept freely, others shouted out under conviction, Satan was wounded, and death was gloriously made bare before believers, as Harris himself wept sweet tears of joy. He shouted out, 'I do not care if there is order in my preaching or not; it is not order I need but power.' He proceeded towards Neath and heard that the townspeople had determined to mob him. The flesh protested at this for a while, but God soon quietened his spirit. Before arriving there, he preached at a place called Cwrt Herbert on, 'Rejoice evermore.' He was given much tenderness here as he invited the whole congregation to come to Christ. He was left in peace by the Neath inhabitants. At Llansamlet, the steward of the land on which he stood to preach took possession of his horse, and the horses of the other exhorters, in lieu of the rent owed by the tenant-farmer. Harris went to speak to him, and showed him that God's work would proceed whatever the opposition. The steward offered him his horse back provided he promised never to return there again to preach. He replied that he could never give such a promise, not for a thousand horses, nor even for his life. He had sufficient love to desire to see that unjust man in heaven; he not only suffered his horse to be taken but he blessed God for it, in that previously he had inclined to be proud of the animal.

He journeyed next to a farmhouse near Swansea, called Perllan-Robert, where Howell Davies was preaching. What brought the evangelist of Pembrokeshire to Swansea we do not know. He preached, with influence, from Zechariah 12:8. Harris's comment was that Davies was riding on the wings of the Almighty and that the service was a notable one. The meeting of the two friends, who spent themselves in the Lord's service, proved a refreshment of spirit to both. Mr Davies described the amazing success of the work in Pembrokeshire, in the English parts as well as the Welsh areas. Howell Harris continued through Abergorlech, Glanyrafonddu, Llanddeusant and Llywel, reaching Trefeca after being away a fortnight. Throughout the journey he had been weak in body; he had fainted at times from the severity of the pain he endured, but the Lord had strengthened him wonderfully when he stood up to speak and he had had services that were as powerful as any previously experienced. The state of the churches in England was also weighing heavily upon him. He says that he had received letters from London stating that the confusion amongst the societies was continuing. His comfort in the face of all was that the Lord was God.

On 8 August a Monthly Association was held at Trefeca, and Harris was Moderator. The following were the decisions agreed upon:

Bro. Harris laid open the several branches of the work of the Lord in England, Scotland, Wales, America, France, etc., and each opened his heart, what his heart is about the present work, and the state of the nation. Bro. Morgan John having it much on his mind to draw up a petition to the Bishop and each society send one or two proper persons to the parish minister to treat with them tenderly to see what they may do in God's hands to further the reformation. Others thought it was not time yet but that the work would go on.

We took to consideration the iniquity of the Land, the state of professors and our own sins and infirmities. We were much refreshed in hearing of the means the Lord has now used in north Wales, where the door had been shut against the word, to bring the gospel to the towns. A young man who had been pressed into the army, had been encouraged, indeed compelled, to preach by his captain, who stood with a naked sword in his hand to defend him, while he spoke. Some of our reasons that God would not give up this nation, notwithstanding all, were (1) the infinity of his grace; (2) his having a Church and that countenanced here from the Reformation even till now; and (3) this late revival that he has begun, and that in so eminent a manner, even without the ordinary; (4) his continuing to carry it on against all opposition even still; (5) his keeping the minds of all the labourers still catholic and public, and from separation etc; (6) his keeping liberty hitherto, keeping the laws free from persecuting. Bro. Harris gave a warm exhortation, and having prayed and sang and opened our hearts, we were happy and blessed and sure the Lord was among us, and gave us many blessings.

These notes suggest many questions, but we must proceed. It seems that Morgan John Lewis's proposal of petitioning the bishops and drawing nearer to the clergymen in the various parishes pleased Harris much and he wrote in his journal that he considered M. J. Lewis and James Ingram pillars of strength to the cause. He goes on to describe how he related to the meeting the controversy that had arisen between himself and John Cennick. He notes that the next day would be a day of trial for him. He had come across a pamphlet written by the Archbishop of Canterbury and directed to the Methodists. Having read it, there did not appear to be any hope of the work progressing (in the Church), humanly speaking; and he was made to look to God alone, leaving the matter with him.

On 22 August, there was an Association at Tyddyn. Daniel Rowland was Moderator and Williams, Pantycelyn, was also present. Before setting out, Harris heard that two of the English brethren had turned their backs, and the news pierced his heart as a dagger. Williams preached on the first verses of John 15. The service was lifeless, but when Rowland turned to prayer a sweet breeze played upon the meeting. This Association is the last that has its minutes noted in the Trefeca records, from now on we have to depend on the journal and on letters. The minutes are as follows:

> Agreed that Evan David go on as before – and likewise Andrew Whitaker.
>
> After much debating with Bro. Benjamin Cadman, as he is not determined in his own mind whether to join with us or the Dissenters, that he should cease from exhorting till our next Quarterly Association, and that his mind, and the minds of the societies, be sent there by Bro. Richard Tibbott.

In the journal Howell Harris states that an applicant from the Dissenters had come to them. The fraternity reasoned with him for some time, showing that there was a considerable difference between themselves and the Dissenters and that he could not be in agreement with both. They believed that those who joined with the Dissenters were following carnal reasons and became lukewarm. They wished him every success and power, but if he were faithful, as they were, in cleaving to the Established Church and at the same time declaring against her corruptions, he would be sure of being empowered. All agreed on this. In the evening, after the Association, they travelled to the house of Thomas James, about thirty miles away, and on the way the topic of conversation was ghosts and hobgoblins. Such tales were related of them, and of the things they did, that Harris felt shivers passing through him.

## LEADING THE ENGLISH CALVINISTIC METHODISTS

About the middle of September, the Quarterly Association of the English brethren was held at Gloucester, and because of the turmoil amongst them Harris felt obliged to be present. As soon as he arrived, John Cennick came up to him and opened his heart. He explained how God's cause was pressing on his mind and how the behaviour of some of the brethren was a weariness of soul, causing him to weep streams of tears before the Saviour's feet. He said further that he had sought the advice of many whose counsel he respected, and they had agreed that the two of them, Cennick and Harris, must take over the leadership of the work, and place the younger brethren under discipline. 'When he said,' wrote Harris, 'that he needed someone who would go with him to the stake, I felt great closeness to him; but my sinfulness and weakness were staring me in the face.' His decision was to lay the whole matter before the Lord, by means of the following prayers:

> (1) I cannot refuse this privilege, and remain obdurate against such a call, for a thousand worlds. (2) I have no answer to give, except to spread before thee all my sins, my unworthiness, my impurity, my pride, my temper, my lack of qualification. (3) If thou art calling me, then I know I will receive of thy

treasure grace to fulfil the office, and a fuller conviction of thy will. (4) Give me a new sight of thy Church, and of thy cause; let me feel it placed within my heart. (And this I was given. I was granted a wider revelation of the glory and mystery of the Church, as the Bride of God, and raised up out of sin and hell to glory. In this light, though it was but weak, I saw every obstacle as nothing before the glorious Church). (5) Therefore, give me the eyes of an eagle, for wisdom and understanding; the strength of an ox, for patience, diligence and consistency; and the heart of a lion, for courage, boldness and determination, that I might honour thee, and fulfil this office. (6) Raise me above this life, in that everything that belongs to it is but vapour and vanity.

No imposition of work was too great that the Reformer of Trefeca would not undertake it. It was mainly on his shoulders, though he had able assistants, that the weight of administering the revival in Wales rested. The resulting labours and responsibilities were almost too much for him, and now, together with John Cennick, here he is shouldering all the responsibility of the cause amongst the English brethren. It was the awareness of the presence of God alone that could have endowed him with such valour. After a meal, they attended the Association, and continued through the night until six the next morning, arranging their affairs. 'Surely, the Lord was amongst us, and was over-ruling,' wrote Harris. Cennick gave a fluent address, showing how they should engage body and soul in the Lord's work, until he come. After completing all arrangements, they discussed various doctrines, amongst them the doctrine of universal salvation. Cennick said that he believed the doctrine, but that it was not one to preach, except by an angel, about a thousand years after the resurrection. They considered the Godhead, and all saw eye to eye. As they sang the hymn, Harris had a view of the mystery of the Godhead in man, and his soul was humbled within him. As the decision of the London Association with respect to the excommunication of Mr Cudworth, who was going further and further away, was confirmed, Howell Harris felt great closeness to the brethren, and he expressed himself very openly to them.

Before the end of September a Welsh Quarterly Association met at Erwood. Five exhorters and one clergyman lodged with Harris for the night before the meeting. He was grateful for the privilege of accommodating them. Williams Richards, the exhorter from Cardigan, preached on grace, its nature and excellence, and had a good service. The next day, at Erwood, Daniel Rowland preached first, from the words, 'Oh that I had wings like the dove!' and, as usual, it was a powerful sermon. After him preached John Sparks, in English, from the message to the Church at Laodicea. Harris felt greatly for him, because he was young, and he prayed that the Lord would prosper him. His prayer was abundantly answered. In the private meeting, Rowland gave a severe word, reaching to the quick, with respect to the behaviour, and even the vanity, of some of the exhorters. But gradually, Harris felt that too light a spirit had entered the meeting and had affected himself also. 'I reproved Bro. Price home,' he states, 'declaring that he corrupted me. He offended and went out. Then the Lord shone upon me, and I saw that all would come well, in that he is God, And so it turned out.'[19]

To read of this occurrence, and others similar, is to be reminded that the first Methodists were but men, and were open at times to be childish and to be offended at the least thing. It shows also great tenderness of conscience, that the very least sense of lightness was unacceptable to them. The next day, an early start was made in order to finish all remaining tasks. Having opened their hearts one to another, they found that all were loyal to the king, and Harris declared that King George was the only legitimate sovereign.

Then William Richards, Rice of Llanwrtyd, James Ingram, and Morgan John Lewis, prayed, humbling themselves because of their sins and of the sins of the nation. The Lord came down among them. On their knees, they confessed in prayer and to one another that their bodies were not their own. They encouraged one another to follow Christ more closely, and to preach more on the fruit of the Spirit. Harris also appealed to the ordained clergymen to visit Glamorganshire and Monmouthshire, because the need was so great, and their gifts so excelled his own. They departed sweetly, having had a happy Association.

## A VISIT TO THE REV. GRIFFITH JONES

On a Wednesday, early in October, Howell Harris began a long journey through Pembrokeshire. He went first to Glyn and from there to Cray, where the people had not gathered, probably because they had not heard of his visit. He preached that night near Trecastle and had a powerful service. The next day he was at Llanddeusant and Glanyrafonddu, and the Saturday at Glancothi.

After preaching the Word in many places in Carmarthenshire, he arrived at Llanddowror on the Sunday afternoon, in time to hear the Rev. Griffith Jones. Mr Jones's subject was the brazen serpent. Harris thanked God that there was such a light amongst the Welsh. He stayed at Mr Jones's house and soon realized that the good man had heard many tales of the disorders of the Methodists:

> To Llanddowror, 6 or 9 miles. Mr Jones preached on John 3:14. Seeing that the Lord has set me as a peacemaker between Bro. Whitefield and Wesley,

Bro. Adams and Cennick, and here, between Bro. Rowland and Mr Gr. Jones. To Mr Jones's house, where by all accounts I heard of our irregularities, misbehaviour in private societies, exposing secrets and falling to gross sins. Mr Jones said that too many of us were open to being accused of pride, foolish judgment, together with bitterness of spirit; and that we were deficient in humility and love, and called others persecutors. He had heard of our unwise actions in England and Wales; of our division in England; and he was offended with the screamings and crying out under the Word. [He spoke] again and again for catechizing, else that all would come to confusion and nothing. I replied that could not be; that whatever would become of us as a Body, that I was persuaded several hundreds have been converted and are safe. I said that I believed everything he had said from his own personal experience, but that it was a grief to me that he had listened to our accusers, and had believed them, without having brought us face to face with them, and that if he had done that he would have found that the work is of God. I thought that we should have more room in his affections.

I spoke to him and Madam Bevan, having strength from God to say all I knew, how they all (the Church people) had weakened our hands, disowned us, and had prejudiced some in Bath against us. I told him also of his book on the Articles, when he had charged me with hindering the sale of it. I said that I did not agree with the book, and that whatever I had said or wrote, it arose out of conscience. He asked did I not feel a desire for all to be saved? I said that I was strongly tempted at times to pray for the devil, but that I could not see any middle way between the salvation of the elect only and the salvation of all. When he pressed me for my belief, I said that I thought it was the elect only who would be saved; for the rest, there was an impossibility in their way, an impossibility arising, not from God, but from themselves, and that I thought it was an error to put forward the possibility that all would be saved. He referred to the work of Tillotson, *The Whole Duty of Man*,[20] and praised Tillotson as the best man that ever sat in the archiepiscopal seat. He argued that his book was one of the ablest on that subject, and that it was so full of Christian kindness that it hardly left anyone unsaved at the end. I replied that he might find such ideas in the works of philosophers but that such was not the doctrine of Paul and Christ.

I told him of his English pamphlets [*Welch Piety*] where he gave such scourges to us as a Connexion, that I thought of the first attack, though it smelt overmuch of the wisdom of this world, that his intention was honest in writing it, as he was seeking greater freedom from the bishops. But when I saw him repeating the same, and referring to our weaknesses, and not mentioning anything else, that such behaviour could not be loving, and would strengthen the prejudice against us, particularly as it was in print, and also coming from him, whose work would be read, it may be, for a thousand years. He admitted that he and she [Madam Bevan] were prejudiced against our Connexion, calling it unscriptural and an ordination. I explained to him our purpose, namely to understand the spiritual state of the converted and not to establish ordination. As to catechizing, I thought he had raised it too high, that the use of it is not universal but subservient to preaching, that I had done what I could to set it up, but did not find the Lord succeeded that.

He objected much to our private exhorters as being ignorant and unfit for the work, and that they had a copy of our societies and the places where they met. I said that we only sent them out to watch over each other's souls, and that when we found any behaving improperly we stopped them. When I was asked if we had found ourselves a sect, I said no, we waited either to be engrafted fully to the Established Church, or to be turned out, and then, either join some other party or form ourselves into a separate party. He had been prejudiced against the Moravians by Mr Tennent and Bro. Wesley's Journal. I said I believed they walked nearer our Saviour than most I knew but were unsound in their judgment in several things. I said that I heard Mr Rowland reproving those that cried themselves, but that many I believe could not help it, and that I had rather see them cry than gape.[21] He acknowledged that he liked to see people weeping in the services and even groaning. I told him in private about making somewhat up between him and Mr Rowland that the enemy may have no room to work between such as loved the Lord, and desired him as I believed he wept daily for us before the Lord, not to be prejudiced, because of our mistakes and apparent disorder. I made emphasis, though in all humility, that God was most certainly amongst us. He and I (after some heat in the midst of both sides, he charged me with heat, and I could receive it kindly indeed, and refused his praises) parted broken and affectionately, I could hardly forbear weeping several times and at parting. I owned I honoured him, and so far as I knew each of the brethren did so. I desired him to come among us, that I believed if it were not for others, he would be nearer to us, and that I was also to blame because I did not visit him more often. They [Griffith Jones and Madam Bevan] more friendly to us than before, but had listened to insufferable reports.

He said we were charged as going to Quakerism and all errors, and to leave the Bible and to follow our experiences. I said that was not true, but what is the Bible but a dead letter to us till we do experience the work of the Spirit in us, not one of the other separately, but both together. All he said against warmth of affection without judgment, I said also turned the other side against light without warmth – catechizing.[22]

Such was the conversation between Howell Harris on the one hand and Griffith Jones and Madam Bevan on the other. It is easy to see that the arguments were at times heated; that both sides expressed themselves very forthrightly. But it is delightful to appreciate that they were ruled by a spirit of love through it all, and that when they criticized they were nearer to tears than to losing their tempers. Not only are the arguments interesting but they also shed a stream of light on many things connected with the Methodists. We see:

1. That while Griffith Jones was very sympathetic to the Methodist Revival at the beginning, he had by now become a judge, and had given too much credence to the untrue stories spread around about the Reformers. Perhaps the desire of some of the exhorters to be ordained according to the Nonconformist practice had something to do with this.

2. That Howell Harris was more of a Calvinist and, we might almost say, an abler theologian, than Griffith Jones. The latter, clearly, was too much under the influence of Archbishop Tillotson, who had wandered far in the direction of Arminianism.

3. That Howell Harris, although he thought highly of Griffith Jones and honoured him greatly, was too independent to follow him slavishly, and dared to disagree with him over some of the truths of the plan of salvation.

But we must follow Harris on his journey. 'Was thankful for dear Mr Jones and all his reproofs', he says. 'I cried that I might never be left without someone to warn me.' On Monday, he preached at the Pale to an enormous gathering, from the words, 'For unto you it is given in the behalf of Christ, not only to believe on him, but also to suffer for his sake.' The Lord was evidently present; many broke out in praising, and he used his influence to moderate what he thought was inappropriate.

In the afternoon he was at Carew, where he preached from the first Psalm. This was an awe-stricken service. 'At the beginning,' he writes, 'I was very terrible against the ungodly. Truly, the Lord was in the place in a wonderful way.' He spent time also counselling the lambs, who in their zeal were too ready to wander from the straight way. On Tuesday morning, at Carew, one brother got such a hold in prayer that Harris rejoiced that the Lord was so evident in Pembrokeshire. In a place called Lamphey, near Pembroke, a Leet Court was being held with many gentry present. He took advantage of the occasion and preached from Exodus 20:1, 'I am the Lord thy God.' With much graciousness, he rebuked the gentry, the clergy, and all the people, for their careless lives. He took advantage on these occasions to pray for the Church, the king, and the nation, which was full of ferment, and to thunder against those who supported the cause of the Pretender. On Tuesday, he was at Neath, near Milford Haven; on Wednesday, at Pembroke and Walton, where he spoke on Romans 8:15, with much comfort. On Thursday, he had a remarkable service at Haverfordwest. He then went to Hayscastle; God was evidently present; then to Llandeloy and Longhouse. On Sunday morning he went to Morvil Church, not far from Woodstock, to hear Howell Davies. On Monday, there was a Monthly Association at a place called Ffynnon Gainc. He wrote in his journal:

At the Association, the Lord opened my mouth to speak home about the fire and the power of God, he being in the Word, all in all. All the brethren agreed the fire among us to be of God. Bro. Gambold declared that we must be dead to ourselves, nor expecting anything as we go about but coldness, nakedness, hunger, poverty, and being reproached, and that by Christians; but that we should go for Christ's sake even if we were in rags and bare-footed, contributing our clothes and food to one another, and being without our-selves if need be. All agreed. I spoke home too of not giving offence to the clergy, etc., as much as possible, as we are in the Established Church. Showed their bigotry in Scotland and America [towards lay preachers]. I spoke of the place of each: how, though Bro. Howell Davies and Williams are my spiritual children, yet as being ordained I feel a subordination to them, and we are called all to be their assistants. I spoke also of Mr Griffith Jones, to come as near him as possible, and to honour him, and to set up catechizing in the most edifying way; as much as possible to keep to the written Word, drawing all men to it, for it is our only rule. All agreed. Agreed also to keep a day of fasting November 1.[23]

There is one new piece of information in this passage, namely, that Howell Harris was the spiritual father of Howell Davies, as well as of Williams, Pantycelyn. It is stated definitely. Harris proceeded in the evening to Llwyn-y-grawys; he thundered there against the Pretender, and praised King George, and had remarkable power. He then turned towards Eglwyswrw and Cerrig Ioan, crossing to Cardigan, and visiting Blaenporth, Cwmcynon, and other places. On Friday night, he arrived at Llangeitho. The next morning he crossed the mountain and, passing through Abergwesyn, he arrived at Trefeca by evening. He had only the Sabbath to enjoy the company of his family. By the break of dawn on the Monday, he was away again, arriving at Caeo by midday, where he preached powerfully from the first Psalm. Early in the afternoon, he was at Llwyn-y-berllan where a Monthly Association was being held. Daniel Rowland was the Moderator. It does not appear that any important decisions were taken, but Harris addressed the exhorters with great solemnity. He said:

I declared that perfection was the goal before me; if I fall I must arise, and that it is self-denial that places a value on the work. I exhorted that the societies be stirred up to read the Scriptures, and to bring all their experiences to the touchstone of Scripture; and if they are not consistent with the

Bible that they are not to be received. I said that the people must be given preaching as often as is possible, and to be advised not to make a noise in the public meetings.

It can be seen that Griffith Jones's rebuke of the more fiery-tempered for shouting out under the Word was being passed on through Harris to the societies. The next day, Rowland preached at Abergorlech Chapel from Hosea 9:12. After the sermon there was communion, and Harris came from the chapel very cheerful of heart and a liberated man. The two friends travelled together to Glanyrafonddu. Their fellowship was of the sweetest, the one opening his heart to the other. Harris was then pressed to preach, which he did most effectively, on the mystery of godliness. Rowland preached the next day, and they then went to Dygoedydd, where Rowland had an ever to be remembered meeting. They then separated – Harris returning through Ceincoed, Llangamarch and Gwernddyfwg, arriving home late on Saturday night.

In the following week there was a Monthly Association at Watford. Harris and Rowland were both there. Their labours must have been never-ending. Harris returned on Thursday night, and by Sunday morning was setting out for a journey through Montgomeryshire, preaching at Tyd-dyn, Trefeglwys, Llanbryn-mair, Blaencarno, Llanllugan and Mochdre. At the last place, he expressed his opinion of the Dissenters very forcibly to Richard Tibbott, that they did not appear to him to be seeking God as their main aim, but rather orthodoxy, order, sound notions and mo-rality. For himself, he would not care if he but spoke one word over and over again, if the Lord was to use that word to wound some and to heal others. His whole aim was to deal with hearts.[24] He was a supporter of orthodoxy, and even to the study of books and of the original languages, as matters subservient to the Spirit, but that he wished for God to qualify the preachers for the work, by revealing himself to them. His heart was catholic and he was against prejudice of every kind, and for an increasing of every kind of knowledge, but not through and in the letter only, but in the Spirit, through the operation of faith, and that the essence of faith was the knowledge of God, as he reveals himself in Jesus Christ. What instigated this discussion we do not know; probably Tibbott had pressed on Harris to take a leaf out of the Dissenters' book and set up some kind of academy to train the exhorters, as he had suggested in a letter to the Association. But to proceed, Harris bade farewell here, with much af-fection, to many dear lambs of the Lord Jesus who had come here from Caernarvonshire and Merionethshire, and he returned through Llwyn-ethel and Llandrindod.

## LONDON AGAIN

In the last week of November, he and Mrs Harris were in London. Matters were still confused amongst the English brethren and, in addition to everything else, Cennick was threatening to leave them and to join the Moravians. In the Quarterly Association held at the Tabernacle on 4 December, the issue was raised:

> Bro. Cennick opened his whole heart and conviction about his first knowledge of the Moravians, and of his light to join them immediately. I also declared my knowledge of them and love to them, and how I could not agree with them about many things.
>
> (1) Because they refuse to declare the Law to sinners, to show them their need of Christ.
>
> (2) Because they have only one point in their ministry, namely, the Person of the Lord Jesus, and so they refuse to hold to any degrees of faith.
>
> (3) Because they hold that all shall be saved in the end.
>
> When he committed his care to me of the Tabernacle, I could answer that I had a passive resignation and submission to his going away and to my coming here till Mr Whitefield comes, or some other way opens. I had already spread the matter before the Lord, and he had already placed them [the English brethren] upon my heart, so that they were bone of my bone and flesh of my flesh.[25]

It is difficult not to be amazed at his boldness. The care of the cause of the Methodists in Wales was mainly upon his shoulders; his labours amongst them was very nearly too much for him; and here he is now on his own, having lost John Cennick, undertaking all the care of the work in London and in England. That night Harris went to the Tower of London to his brother.[26] The next day Cennick said farewell to the Association and, amidst tears, committed all the work to Howell Harris.

> He spoke gloriously of the mystery of the Person of Christ; he pointed the eyes of the people towards the blood, calling upon them to worship the wounds. The people wept copiously; I also had liberty to weep. At the end, he prayed earnestly for me, and light shone into my soul.

This is certainly not how men generally behave when turning their backs on their religious friends and joining a different party. If Cennick was deviating in his judgment, we cannot but still admire his conscientiousness. But this was not the end. The next day, the last day of the Association, many of the leading brethren, Hammond, Heatly, Salmon and Thorn, expressed their intention of following Cennick and joining the

Moravians. One other, Godwin, said that he intended leaving but would wait for further light before deciding whether or not to join the Moravians. Of those considered leaders, the only ones remaining to support Harris were Herbert Jenkins and Thomas Adams. His spirit did not fail him in this crisis; he strengthened himself in the grace that is in the Lord; he wrote to Whitefield to inform him of all developments, and comfort flowed into his soul from the words, 'And the government shall be upon his shoulder.' After arranging matters as well as possible at the Tabernacle, and throughout England after such a serious crisis, Harris and his wife returned to Wales shortly before Christmas. But he did not return to rest. Two days after Christmas he set out on another long journey through Monmouthshire and Glamorganshire, and was at Dinas Powys, some three miles from Cardiff, when the dawn of 1746 broke upon him.

[1] Eifion Evans, *Daniel Rowland*, p. 262.
[2] CH 49, pp. 87–8.
[3] CH 37, p. 22.
[4] CH 49, pp. 88–9
[5] CH 49, pp. 89–90.
[6] CH 31, p. 25.
[7] CH 31, p. 25.
[8] CH 37, p. 22.
[9] CH 49, p. 90.
[10] Eifion Evans suggests that to state that a 'Confession of Faith and Rules of Discipline were drawn up' is to claim too much; they were engaged only in a discussion of faith and its relationship with good works.
[11] Trefeca Letter 1312. Transcribed by Eifion Evans.
[12] CMHO, pp. 106–7.
[13] CMHO, pp. 103–5.
[14] CHMO, pp. 107–8.
[15] CMHO, pp. 108–10.
[16] CMHO, pp. 110–11.
[17] HHVP, p. 114.
[18] CH 50, pp. 28–9.
[19] CH 37, p.26.
[20] John Tillotson (1630–94), Archbishop of Canterbury (1691–4) was not the author of *The Whole Duty of Man*. The book was published c. 1658 and its probable author was Richard Allestree (1619–81), Regius Professor of Divinity at Oxford.
[21] i.e., yawn.
[22] HHVP, pp. 115-6.
[23] Ibid, p. 117; CMHO, p. 127.
[24] CMHO, p. 128.
[25] HHVL, p. 78.
[26] Thomas Harris (1704–64), Howell's older brother, was then Deputy Assay-Master at the Mint in the Tower.

# 13

# HOWELL HARRIS (1746)

## OPPOSITION TO HARRIS'S DOCTRINE ON
## THE PERSON OF CHRIST BEGINS TO ARISE

*A*s we have said, the first dawn of 1746 broke on Harris when he
was at Dinas Powys, and his comments on the day in his journal are
worth quoting:

Dinas Powys, New Year's Day. This morning, I truly received *calennig*[1] from
my dear Lord. He showed me he was stronger than my heart, and stronger
than my corruptions, though they are so powerful, stronger than all devils,
stronger than men, and stronger than my fears and trials. On perceiving this
by faith my soul worshipped and praised him gloriously. I went to Aberthaw
by one. There I preached from Romans 7 on the body of sin. I had great
liberty to explain the original sin, that the children were sinners, and that
they were truly damned and fallen in Adam. I showed how the Spirit convicts
the soul of this, and causes it to grieve because of this rebellion against God.
I had strength to declare the glory and mystery of Christ, and the privilege
of being able to worship the man Christ; and of those who neglect one
opportunity, how they might never receive another, were it not for God's
eternal love, and they would be unbelievers for eternity. I showed them the
wise men, the disciples, Thomas and Stephen, seeing him and worshipping,
and how he and the Father are one, as he said to Philip. Truly we had *calennig*
here, and it was blessed to us also.

We went by six to Aberthin. Here, the Lord honoured me more than ever
when praying and preaching. Though Satan had armed the minds of the
members against the mystery of Christ, through reasoning, yet the Lord, as
they acknowledged themselves pulled down all their reasoning by his Word
and Spirit. At the same time, they at first held firmly against worshipping
his humanity. We truly received wonderful *calennig* of love. I preached from
the words in Isaiah, 'For unto us a child is born, unto us a son is given.' I was
close to the Lord; I felt myself dead to self. Truly, the Holy Spirit was present.
I showed that the great God was the Babe of Bethlehem; so the wise men
worshipped him; so also Stephen worshipped the man Jesus, as he saw him as
God; so also confessed Peter to the man (Jesus) that he was God; that is why

he said to the Jews that they crucified the Lord of glory, namely, God; that is why Peter called his blood, the blood of God himself; so Thomas called the man (Jesus) his God. Certainly, he is God, and whoever sees him, sees also the Father, as he told Philip. Though there are three Persons in the Trinity, there is but one God. I showed how the veil was torn away, many years ago, on the way to Montgomeryshire, and God shone down upon me by this word, 'Great is the mystery of godliness,' and that this now is my food and life. I was humbled by a sense of the honour afforded me in allowing me to carry this message to the lambs.

We have quoted his words extensively in order to show how completely his meditations were taken up by the mystery of the union of the two natures in Christ's Person. This was the great emphasis of his ministry at this time. We do not believe that his views, on the whole, were erroneous at this time, but his choice of words was not happy, and we feel he was prone to go into too much detail and to carry his conclusions too far. It is clear also that opposition to his views was beginning to grow in the societies but that his presence, with his fluency and enthusiasm, was sufficient to quell all opposition that arose. But to continue with the journal:

Aberthin, Thursday. We had a private Society to past 10, and I had much freedom there to mention my fear about the Societies, lest they rest in something without coming to the blood of Christ, to see all there. This is the reason for their quarrels and arguments, and we will never be united without coming to this blood. I showed, both publicly and privately, how I saw in Jesus, human compassions, tenderness, and sympathy, and divine infinity, joined in one. In what way, we cannot say, nor can the angels. I showed the way that carnal reason tried to divide the God and the man because it cannot discern the mystery. In secret again I heard how the Lord brings Bro. Thomas William [back] again, and has prevented their being divided and scattered at Llantrisant. I was nourished through seeing that the Lord is God. One brother who had been in deep trial with respect to Christ's divinity was liberated tonight. I showed them how the Lord had called them to reveal his glory in them. Do not rest therefore in forms and knowledge and order and externalities.

I went hence to St. Nicholas, 3 or 6 miles. There I had liberty and power when speaking on words from the Book of Revelation. Went hence, at 3, toward Llantrisant, 5 or 8 miles; hearing on the way that some there opposed me. It proved a blessing to me, and a means to humble me to the dust and to make me poor in spirit. I knelt to pray in the dust, in the sight of a large congregation, feeling my unfitness, but the Lord raised me giving me the spirit of a lion, so that I carried everything before me. I had previously proved the divinity of Christ out of the Scriptures, showing that this man was God. Never before did I have such authority. I proclaimed to all who could hear that the God-Man is my life, and my all, to eternity. If he is not

God, that his blood holds no merit, and that we are all lost forever and ever. I preached on the wise men coming to worship the sacred babe, Jesus. It is strange how carnal reason and nature kick against this truth; I feel it in myself. But I was enabled to terrify, to plead, and to open the Scriptures, so that reason was silenced, manifesting its darkness, its ignorance, and its enmity towards God.

I was also led to show of the Church, how death and lukewarmness is come to the Church of England and Dissenters too, since they lost the preaching of the blood. Formerly all churches rang with this doctrine, and then there was life and power; but now form, human wisdom, and order, etc., is come; but the blood and the Spirit is the life. Opened about these too. I excepted some few Dissenters and people; showed how I offend parsons and ministers by declaring of their faults, etc. Answered [an] objection against us: That our preachers are unlearned, etc. I showed that is an argument for us; whence have we these gifts? can we get them ourselves? There are others as gracious and more learned, and of several parts, can't preach for the world; and I declared tis not by my memory (for I have very little indeed) nor by my learning, that I have discourse; but as I have it from the Lord. When I go before the people, I do not know what I shall say, but that I give myself to God. I had much authority to apply the truth, and to show that if this babe, this man, was not God, how was it that the wise men were not sinning as they worshipped him? and Thomas, as he called him, 'My Lord and my God'? and Peter, as he called him Lord, and Son of God?

In the private Society, Bro. Thomas William opened the whole how his temptation about dissenting began to come upon him this four years; firstly, scruples about ordinations; then, seeing little things great; and then, we not yielding to his scruples, he thought us bigoted, and his heart began so to warp from us, and then began to despise us, and to see our infirmities, and think us young and raw and selfish, etc. And still, though he was following his conscience in all till just now, when it came close about dissenting, the Lord opened his eyes, and he sees now as clear as can be, it was all of the devil's work and snare; and he thinks so of all that left us, and is now free to communicate in Church, which before he could by no means. The same light too had another brother that did dissent last Sunday, and so he comes back. O Lord, this is thy work! Humble me! Thou dost favour us, because it pleaseth thee, and because thou art God.

I showed them of the whole of the Reformation, how God has honoured this Church of England, in that in it shone that first light through Wycliffe; I referred to Hus, Jerome of Prague, and from them went to Luther, Calvin, the establishment of the Protestant Church; then to Henry, Edward, Mary, and Elizabeth, in this country; how the Church has been a bulwark against Popery above all others, and how we should not now have the toleration we have in any other Church in the world; and opened how all [of us] were called [while] in the Church. Showed how they suppress lay-teachers in

Scotland and America now, and even imprisoned a Moravian missionary there lately, that preach nothing but the blood of Christ as I do. I opened out the whole about the Dissenters, Mr David Williams and Edmund Jones, how they were when I first knew them, and are now; and how I see such as go to them sink gradually to their formality, and how they drew all they can from us. And there was such wide difference between them and their doctrine, spirit, scheme, and us, that one can't be in close connection with them and with us.[2]

There are many things that strike us as we read these quotations:

1. That the main topic, and nearly the only topic, of Howell Harris's ministry at this time was the mystery of the unity of the two natures in the Person of the Lord Jesus Christ. He felt that he had received a revelation from heaven on this truth. All the merit of the passion and the blood seemed to him to depend on the union being so close that, in a sense, the human nature had been deified and become the object of worship. We, presently, can see that there is considerable confusion in his thought, yet, at the same time, that he stresses an important element of the truth, but that he separates in his doctrine that which was never separate in fact, namely, the human nature of the Saviour and his divine person. While reasoning on this point, he uses unscriptural phrases that could not but give offence, on serious consideration, though his warmth of utterance might conceal their impropriety at the time. And he would push his ideas to extremes, ignoring contrasting truths.

2. Almost certainly, Thomas Williams of Groes-wen, who was appointed minister at Groes-wen by a Nonconformist ordination, was the brother who confessed his repentance for leaving the Methodists. Perhaps we should not press his repentance so far as to believe that he did not now intend to administer the sacraments again. But it is clear that he had been disappointed in the Dissenters and wished to draw closer to the Methodists, acknowledging that more of the divine influence was to be found amongst them, and that henceforth he wished to be considered a Methodist.

3. We see Howell Harris's reasons for cleaving to the Established Church, indicating that he was not governed by a blind partisanship. He thought, as did John Elias after him, that the Church was the only effective bulwark against Popery; that no other religious institution would accept lay preaching, which had been blessed so evidently in Wales; furthermore, the formality, lukewarmness and doctrinal errors of so many of the Dissenters were a stumbling block to him.

From Llantrisant, he went to the home of William Powell and then, weak in body but strong in faith, to Craig Wen, in the parish of Eglwys-ilan. He had there a powerful service, though many of the opposers of the doctrine of the unity of the two natures were present. He did not take a text but showed from the Scriptures the glory of the mystery. Many were melted as they listened but some remained unconvinced. His journal continues:

> Then I called a private Society, and opened the whole about Bro. Thomas William; and he did too, as last night. And about Edmund Jones, showing he was bigoted, etc., till my acquaintance with him. Asked all if they were now fixed about their being in God's way, and had no scruple to dissent, etc.; and all said they were.[3]

Harris then enlarged upon the differences between Methodists and Dissenters; that the Dissenters rested in form and plan, whereas the Methodists pushed forward full of spirit and light; that the Dissenters did not perceive the wickedness of various sins, that was apparent to Methodists.

> Afterward one said he could not agree with what I delivered; and the exhorter of this place too said, if he would speak, he must speak against what I delivered.

It is clearly Harris's views on the Person of Christ that are being referred to.

> . . . and I had authority given me, and said as to convince him, I had no more to say than what I had in the pulpit, and if he opposed it, he was a heretic, and I could not labour with him. And so put to the Society if they believed the doctrine I delivered or not. And they said all they did; and I said I could have no fellowship with him till he should be humbled for darkening the glory of Christ, and stumbling His lambs, and reasoning and opposing what he did not know. That this was my message I had from God, and can't yield one jot of this – tis my life. Through grace I must die for it. If Christ is not truly God and as truly Man, and as such has lived and suffered, then I am lost forever and ever. I showed that it was not enough to say that God was in this man; that God was in believers; that it was an error to call the Sav-iour God and man; that there was an eternal union between us who believe and God; but that the Word was made flesh. In what way, I do not know. If he, the exhorter denied that God had suffered, and that Christ prayed to the Father, then I should not reason with him, in that it is a mystery, and it cannot be received but by the Holy Spirit. I referred to Christ sometimes calling himself God, and other times man; sometimes claiming authority to lay down his life and to receive it again, and other times praying to the Father

and confessing that he could do nothing of his own, without the Father, and that it is the same person who does these two things. This is the truth, but I cannot comprehend it.

Then, when he would cavil, I insisted now on his being silent, as he had cut himself from having anything to do here. He then was very stiff and obstinate, and denied my authority to turn him out; that that was [vested] in the Society, and not in me. Not in me myself, I replied, but in conjunction with my fellow labourers, nor with them unless this Society freely chooses me and them to watch over them. If so, I judged it, we had power to turn out and to receive in, if they chose us. (Here some light came in that this came now to put me to read and think more about this). Then I sang a Psalm. I was before when speaking, melted down, and the Spirit of God in the singing, washed my heart, so that I felt I was willing that God should take away all my gifts and graces, and clothe him [the exhorter] with them all. I cried, inwardly, that I might have the privilege of seeing him shining more brightly than myself in glory. As we prayed together the Lord came down in an uncommon manner, breaking our hearts. I was so broken that I was obliged to desist, and then to weep and mourn over all our sins, and to cry to love him again; and to cry, How long shall we thus always tear, and devour, and rend, and divide!

When I had done, I thought he would come to me, and own it was a temptation; but he did not. I went to him exceeding broken and loving, and fell upon his neck; and he only said he had union with them and me, but was in the same mind. Then, with all calmness and weeping brokenness, I said that what I did, I did for the Lord and his truth, and out of conscience; and though 'tis like tearing flesh from my bones to do it, I must do it, and said, This may have a voice from God to you. Perhaps you have been going long ago (for so it was in me) – I could not be knitted to you, but only on what the brethren said of you. I would yield to their light. And, as to this, as a younger brother, you should be silent as to what you knew not; but I thought you were wise in your own eyes, and very stiff, though so seemingly very humble – (for so he appears), to bring head knowledge, and a scheme, and a lukewarmness among this flock; and now, at length, the Lord found you out. But I only mention this as a caution. Perhaps the fault is in me; but let the Lord judge. I refused to dispute any more, it being 11 o'clock. I like him, and parted with him and the brethren, and went away with my heart more broken, and weighed, and oppressed than ever, that I am the vilest and unworthiest by far of all, and am obliged to do thus. But, on the way, I had freedom to lay all before the Lord, and to ask if he would prevent all evil to his soul . . . I see, I think, that this rises from the pride of the young teachers.[4]

It is clear that Howell Harris had received glorious views of the Person of the Lord Jesus, and of the closeness of the union between the two natures in him – views whose extent went beyond that of any of his brethren. Glorious truths had dawned upon his soul; truths to which the other Reformers, perhaps, had not paid sufficient attention. However, we find scattered amongst his journal entries many unscriptural phrases which show that his views were to some extent confused and, as already mentioned, some of his expressions were inappropriate. And here he now is, turning out from the society, for the very first time, an exhorter who could not fall in with his own particular views. It is easy to see that the ingredients for a storm were beginning to gather. Harris continued towards Watford, ill in body and ready to faint. As he considered the particular message delivered to him, and the opposition he saw beginning to gather, he cried:

'O Lord, thou dost know, my only aim is to bring everyone to thyself, to see thee, as thou hast revealed thyself in thy Word.' . . . I then received a spirit of grieving over every word I had said out of place, and of desiring that he would reveal his glory. I feared going to the Association in case they opposed the message. Yet, I trusted in the Lord, crying out, 'O Lord, I cannot deny thy truth; and I cannot disagree with my brethren.' I then came to Gelli-gaer where I received witness that God had sent me and had forgiven all my sins up to now. I had freedom to speak from, 'My words, they are spirit and they are life.'

He judged that the congregation received a blessing. He then proceeded to Mynyddislwyn, still ill and weak and near fainting, but he who sent him there strengthened him, body and mind. His text was, 'Unto us a son is given.' He felt that he had been called here to testify to the mystery, an impression that he had not received at Gelli-gaer:

I was enabled to speak of the excellency of the knowledge of this Son; how all must come to know him; the misery of those who do not know him; the way in which the Scriptures witness of him; that they are the fields and he is the pearl hidden in them. I showed the revelation of Christ which is given only by the Spirit. I had liberty to expound the mystery of Christ; that this man is God. The Spirit accompanied the word; many felt, and many wept.

He arrived at a place called Pen-heol-y-badd on Saturday night. On Sunday morning, he continued another mile and preached at Tonsawndwr from the words, 'And this is eternal life.' The Lord was present, and many wept. He showed that a glorious day was dawning in that the cockerels, that is, God's ministers, were crowing all over the country. He referred here also to the mystery. From here, he went to New Inn. 'Unto us a son is given,' was his text here also, and the mystery of Christ was his theme. Great grace was upon the people, and he hoped that the glory of the Saviour was about to shine on the Church. Howell Davies had been announced to preach at Tonsawndwr on the Monday, but he had failed to arrive because of illness. Harris therefore returned there to take his place.

He had a remarkable service while preaching on the body of sin. He still found a path to arrive at the theme that was now engaging all his attention, namely, the mystery of the two natures in Christ.

> Surely, God blessed his people, and myself, and he appeared in me, as well as for me, while I was preaching him and his mystery. He showed how I will soon, through his truth and blood, meet the people again in glory, out of the reach of sin.

He next visited Llanheiddel, and in another powerful service felt that the promises were meat and drink and power to him:

> Never before have I had such feast-days; he has kept the best wine till last. I said that, even if I were a Dissenter (I showed how I was not against them, but for them, in that I loved them), I would join with the Methodists because the Lord is with them.

But while on earth, the sweet is always accompanied by the bitter, and Harris proved this at Llanheiddel. He wrote:

> Tuesday morning. I received a blow on hearing that the brethren at Watford had sunk deeper into their error of refusing to worship the humanity of Christ, and that they had drawn to themselves Mr Davies and the young man who was with him; and that someone from amongst them had referred to the dead body of our Lord as being stone-dead. With this burden I had faith to cry to the Lord that he might sanctify it to me, and humble me. I had great liberty also to pray for the brethren, who speak of that which they do not yet know; then, Christ's glory was held up before me, his glory from the cradle to the grave, and God was close to me.

Who this Mr Davies was, who was bewitched by the Watford brethren, we do not know. It is clear that Harris's preaching on the mystery of Christ's Person was beginning to agitate the societies; that the extreme and incautious words possibly used by him were provoking opposite extremes in others. He comments in his journal:

> What an intolerable load should I have to go to the Association, what fear of the brethren, lest this error should run, and Christ be stabbed among his friends, were it not for faith. I feel light, love, tenderness, courage and authority to reprove them as younger brethren given to me, and that even this shall work for good, and this opposition shall [work], as it hitherto has worked, for good.[5]

## THE GLYN ASSOCIATION OF JANUARY 1746, AND SUBSEQUENT JOURNEYS

The Association was to be held at Glyn on 9 January 1746. The day before, as he travelled towards Taf-fawr, Harris tried to evaluate what opposition would arise from the brethren against him and his doctrine. He had a fresh view of the glory and deity of Christ on appreciating that the government was upon his shoulders. At Taf-fawr, he received considerable strength when preaching the blood. He also referred severely to the carnal Dissenters who spoke endlessly on order and on church government, and called themselves a Church, but were wholly deficient of life. From there, he went to Glyn – a journey of ten hours on horseback – and arrived late on the night before the Association.

Howell Harris was clearly aware of what might occur at the Association. He expected a fierce attack upon himself and upon the particular doctrine that he preached, and he sought to strengthen himself against it:

> I felt within me a desire to meet with the brethren, even though I might be trodden underfoot, condemned, and opposed; I saw no other prospect before me; but I rejoiced in it, seeing it as the means of pulling down my pride. But I had a view also of the dishonour to our Lord when we opposed one another, and of the sheep being scattered and divided; this was very painful to me. I had strength to pray that God would keep us together.

The Association was opened by a very successful sermon from Williams, Pantycelyn, on Ephesians 6:11. 'A powerful breeze came down upon us,' wrote Harris, 'My soul was kindled within me, and I was brought down to the dust. I was grateful for the ability, grace and power being given.' After the sermon the brethren dined together, and after a sweet prayer from Morgan Jones, they began discussing various matters. During that prayer, the 'Amens' were so loud and excited, that some were offended, but Harris argued that the fire was from God. A number of letters were read, and the faith of the fraternity increased in proportion to the increase of their trials:

> Satan tries us from all quarters, but the Lord did wonderfully appear for us today, and made up the great breach that I did so dread from Glamorganshire. Oh! The tenderness of the Lord. That which I feared was removed, and our spirits were united; but this shows what kind of children we are; how little sympathy we feel for one another; how ready we are to divide, and to place the worst explanation on one another's words. The brethren acknowledging their mistaking me, and their sin in starting up carnal questions about worshipping Christ's manhood, and their work in raising carnal views on the humanity of the Saviour, as if his humanity was apart from his deity in his sufferings, so that it is not to be worshipped; and their work in claiming that it is his humanity that is the way, the door and the offering, so that it is not to be worshipped at all.

On their confession of their fault, I had liberty to speak of the mystery of Christ and how it was first revealed to me. Bro. Rowland noted how

Ainsworth comments that God died, according to the degree that he was God-Man; and if one were a doctor and a lawyer, it would be appropriate to say that the doctor died, or that the lawyer died. And that he himself had preached, on Christmas Day, on the mystery of Christ, from the words, 'And the Word was made flesh.' O tender Father! I showed how there was deity associated with the soul and body (in Christ) when they were separated from each other; the way that this shines upon me; that I believed that they only saw it according to the light of reason, and that they should therefore be silent. I said that I thought the Moravians were correct on this point, and that I had not changed my mind on any truth, but only grown and strengthened in the light. I find the enemy is endeavouring to divide them in Pembrokeshire. The Moravian spirit coming down, but I endeavoured to mollify and pacify. It is good that the Lord is God. I said to John Belcher that I believed I saw in him an unfitness to deal with weak souls. I had great liberty in prayer at the close.

Thus this most important Association concluded. We apologize for such a long account of its history from the journal, together with the history of Harris's journey. This is the point at which the leaven of the disruption was placed in the bread. That which he called the mystery of Christ had so swallowed up Harris's attention that he hardly referred to any other topic when preaching. He was so convinced of its truth, and its importance as a truth, that he was willing to die rather than to submit an inch upon the matter. It is clear that the first objection to the doctrine arose from amongst the exhorters. Harris, no doubt, feared that Rowland and Williams would take their side at the Association, and would agree with them in their attack upon himself. On this point, he was very glad to be proved wrong. They rather persuaded those who opposed to confess that they had misunderstood his words and had raised carnal questions concerning our Lord's person, and as a consequence they submitted to him. If Rowland discerned the foolishness of some of Harris's phrases at this time, he did not suggest it at any point. He set it down to a difference of expression, believing that they were united at heart. No wonder that Harris was in such a triumphant temper, and his feet on high places.

The extent of his joy is seen in the following letter to Mr Thomas Adams, one of Whitefield's exhorters at the Tabernacle, which he wrote from Trefeca the day after the Association:

My dear fellow-labourer and most dear brother, I have been a fortnight's round and came home last night from our association and such accounts I never had to send you. Our Saviour, I think, has not at all so thwarted and confounded His enemy and so blessed His dear bought lambs, and so opened His loving heart, as now I have been made a witness, ever since I came home, of his glory and majesty. But tongue can't express what mighty acts He is doing by the hands of His ministers here. The clergymen are like flaming seraphs, and many of the lay brethren are blessed with unconceivable success. Three counties especially, Pembroke, Carmarthen and Cardiganshire seem to be the Lord's peculiar dwelling place, and to be, as it were, the centre of the work. In several parts of Glamorgan, Monmouth, Brecon, Radnor and Montgomery shires they grow most gloriously, and though the enemy is continually sowing his tares, yet brotherly love and simplicity prevails, and such is the manifestation given of the glory of God in the face of Jesus Christ, that it quite overpowers nature in several places. Several are so baptized with the promised fire of the Holy Ghost that they cannot contain themselves. The loud 'Amens', 'Allelujahs', and praises to Him that has redeemed them, frequently drowns the voice of the preachers. Several hours, nay, whole nights are spent in singing, praying, etc. O! Glorious days! The cocks have crowed and the dawn of a bright morning appears. Surely the Captain is in the field. The Lord has indeed visited His Temple. The blind receive their sight daily, the deaf ears are unstopped, the lame walk, and the dead are raised. The kingdom of God and of our Christ is come among us; woe be to those that oppose openly or secretly, or [those who] (Meroz-like) are neuters . . . At our association we were more happy than ever and had glorious accounts from all parts, for every Superintendent brings an account of all the souls under his care, etc. Satan is confounded. Dear brother, go on boldly, he will be trampled upon completely before long. Our God will bless us and give success; let us always wash our feet.

Tomorrow, I preach at home; on Monday, I begin a new journey. Immediately on returning, I intend, if God wills, to go to London. Your horse is strong. On this next journey I intend to hire a horse to take me from place to place. My wife joins me in loving remembrances to you and your wife. Yours, in our dear Redeemer, Howell Harris.[6]

As mentioned in the letter, he set out on his next journey on Monday, 13 January. He describes his experiences in the journal:

Today, before beginning my journey to Glamorganshire and Carmarthenshire, my soul was raised above sin, fear and Satan, and I was made a conqueror through faith. I went towards Cwm-camlais, a distance of 10 to 15 miles; along the way, my soul was quickened within me on seeing that I had no God other than the man Christ Jesus, and that he is a forgiving and loving God, who justifies me, blesses me, and leads me. I saw that there is an inexhaustible treasure in the mystery – God manifest in the flesh. I had great liberty in praying and preaching from 1 John 5:7; I was directed more particularly towards the lukewarm and carnal, those who had left us and joined with the Dissenters; I showed how they had departed from God's way; what is the number of those continually drunk on God's new wine, and that the work is divine, as the signs prove.

It is difficult to understand the reference to those drunk on new wine. It could, in the context, mean either that few of the Dissenters, or many of the Methodists, were so. Here again, he preached on the mystery. He continued to Llanddeusant, where he preached from John 17:3. He had much power; speaking at times against carnal professors, at other times, against the openly ungodly. He saw that he was being led in different ways: at some times to thunder, at other times to comfort and heal. Here again, before concluding, he proclaimed the mystery that is in Christ. 'I opened the whole with authority,' he wrote, 'showing that this man is God, and that he is the only God.'

On Wednesday, he arrived at Ty-gwyn. Here his text was, 'And they overcame him by the blood of the Lamb.' He was close to the Lord while speaking, and happy; the people, also, appeared loving. But no great power came until he began speaking of the victory of the godly man over sin through Christ. On Thursday, he was at Gellidochlaethe, and wrote, 'Last night, the lambs skipped and jumped after being fed by the mystery of Christ. Now the light is beginning to shine upon them.' At Llangadog, he spoke with some considerable power and light from 1 John 5:7, and as he was describing the difference between the followers of Christ and sinners, a light from eternity shone into his soul, brighter than anything he had seen previously. He saw this world as a pale shadow of the world to come. His message here was evangelistic, sweetly inviting all to come to Christ but the power did not fall until he began to deal with the mystery of Christ:

> I showed that fear vanishes when Christ's glory appears. I opened the whole, as usual, about Christ, particularly of him as standing mutely before Pilate, and his work in taking our sin and guilt upon himself, through which God can deal with those who believe as though they had never sinned. I showed that if Christ died for all, then all must be redeemed, that they cannot be punished a second time. I was powerful when dealing with the birth, life, passion and death of Jesus, and when explaining the confessions of Peter, Paul and Thomas. Here also the lambs were fed.

We find him next at Llansamlet. The previously mentioned Llangadog was probably some parish in Glamorganshire. He was feeling weak and faint on the journey, but when he began preaching, physical strength was suddenly given to him. His topic was God's sovereign knowledge in Christ and he was led to emphasize the mystery of the blood, showing that this was the foundation of all that they enjoyed, and crying out that he was willing to venture eternity on the basis of this blood. It was a most powerful service. At the end, he held a private meeting, and wrote:

We stayed until ten; the power and life made us like flames; it came home to me how open we are to the wiles of Satan; but I had peace in committing all into God's hand.

There clearly were some unpleasant symptoms amongst the congregation, mixed in with the spiritual warmth, and discerned by the Reformer. He preached next, both in Welsh and English, at Perllan Robert. It was a most melting service, but without as much of the fire, power and crying out as was experienced under the ministries of the clergymen.

I had much tenderness in conveying my usual message of the mystery of Christ; many seemed as if they were feeling; and power accompanied the word as I spoke on the mystery of the Saviour, and the mystery of the Trinity, and exposing carnal reason.

On Friday, he continued to Loughor where he preached on the words, 'One thing have I desired of the Lord.' He heard here that the gentleman who had taken a horse from him near Neath, on his last journey in this region, had himself lost two of his horses, had been very ill and was not yet fully recovered. Harris commented:

I am learning many varied lessons from the different kinds of people that I meet, but I find no one as wicked as myself, nor any who has received such favour.

He here met a young gentleman called Mr Dawkins, who appeared under considerable feeling, and who had much pleasure in discussing spiritual matters with him.

A great work is proceeding; a young clergyman was ordained here recently, who is a Christian. O Lord, visit thy Church!

The condition of the Church of England clergy at the time must indeed have been dreadful if the ordination of a clergyman who was a Christian was a matter to be drawn attention to, and to be grateful for.

On Saturday, he travelled to Pembrey by two o'clock. The people had been waiting for him for four hours. He was amazed how he lost his time continually, but says that he could not help it. He had liberty in speaking here but the influence was not great. He had intended to reach Llanddowror by the Saturday night, but failed to cross the estuary to Llansteffan until it was so late that he could not proceed any further. He did not however waste his time. The people at Kidwelly heard that he was in the place, a crowd gathered, and he had opportunity to preach to them. His sermon was similar in nature to those he used to preach at first, namely a denunciation of the carnality and blindness of the clergymen of the Church, the wickedness of the gentry, and the low morals of the common people. It was a very notable service. The effect on Harris's own feelings was almost overpowering. On seeing how the Lord was succeeding the work, he cried out:

Alleluia! Amen! O sweet eternity! I see now why the Lord kept me so long in captivity by the fear of death, in order for me to become familiar with the dark cells of death, and so be able to comfort others when they cross over.

He arrived at Llanddowror at about one o'clock on Sunday; he was afar from the Lord on the way. The Rev. Griffith Jones's text was, 'And this is the condemnation.' Harris received a blessing during the sermon and particularly during the communion afterwards. But while the old clergyman was discussing 'the conditions of salvation', Harris felt that Christ was his condition and his title to all the blessings of the covenant.

An Association was held on the Monday at Glancothi, and Harris arrived there by two o'clock. Daniel Rowland and William Williams were present, together with the Dissenter, Benjamin Thomas, but Harris does not record any discussion that took place nor anything that was said, except by himself. He wrote:

I had great nearness to the Lord in prayer; my heart was humbled and the Lord came down as I showed how the eyes of all were upon us, and I exhorted to watchfulness, and to not giving offence to any in anything. I explained that to behave differently proved a lack of love to souls. I was powerful in showing the necessity for humility, and that while we were being kept in the dust the Lord would honour us. God came down amongst us; many were melted and many wept freely. We sat together for five hours. The Lord was with us remarkably, giving us love and wisdom to suffer one another, while we dealt with matters of utmost importance, and with the breach that Satan had attempted to make among us. We were all humble and united here.[7]

He then records an address he gave in which he referred to the mystery of Christ; how Christ's death had destroyed death; how the body and soul of the Saviour were united to his divinity while separate from one another; how this mystery was first revealed to him, and how he had not been disobedient to the heavenly vision. He showed also how Satan was seeking to cause some to err by opposing the phrase 'an application of the blood', choosing instead the term 'a reception of Christ', and thereby encroaching on to the Antinomian doctrine of an eternal justification in substance, and an operative justification when Christ died. The brethren agreed with all he said. He was powerful and sharp when showing that God had loved the elect from eternity, and that Christ, as their head, had died for all their sins and in their place, and yet that they were dead and the objects of God's wrath until they had been born again, and believed, and had had Christ applied to them. All saw eye to eye, and departed happily about nine o'clock.

Though it was so late, Rowland, Harris and Williams journeyed to Glanyrafonddu for lodging and arrived there at twelve. Harris rode by Williams's side and received sweet blessing from the fellowship. On Tuesday, Rowland preached at Abergorlech Chapel, Harris noted, 'A most excellent sermon indeed I heard from the great man of God, on Psalm 105:14,15.' The Lord was near, it seems, during the communion also. Howell Harris was struck by three great mysteries – God, Christ, and the Church. Of the last, he saw that it was truly glorious. As he spoke on these mysteries, some were offended. He rebuked them for what he saw as being out of place in them, but there was sweet unity between himself and Brother Rowland. After returning to Glanyrafonddu, Rowland preached again, from Joel 3:13. Once more, it was a remarkable service. Harris's soul was aflame within him. He saw in Rowland the same spirit as was in himself. It seems there was much public rejoicing during this meeting. Harris, in a brotherly way, counselled those who were on fire for love and a sense of victory, and they were humble enough to receive his advice. The friends travelled together on the Wednesday to Llwyn-y-berllan, where Rowland preached on Jeremiah 33:6. There were here evident indications of the Lord's presence. Harris spoke also and he wrote that his tongue was as the pen of a ready writer. Then, after much happiness in Rowland's company, he turned his face towards home. He was at Bronnydd on Thursday, at Dôl-y-felin on Friday, and he arrived at Trefeca later that night after a journey of nearly a fortnight. His journal entries show that the mystery of Christ's person continued to be the main subject of his meditations. This is what he preached nearly everywhere and, on the whole, there was no great objection being raised to his doctrines. In particular, Daniel Rowland and himself were in perfect union.

The first thing he did on returning was to establish a six-weekly meeting, open to all who spoke publicly. The agenda for the conference involved a sermon at ten, then a private society and love-feast for all the members that could come from all parts, and afterwards an Association for the exhorters, not so much for arranging matters but in order to meet with one another before the Lord. On this occasion Harris preached. His text was, 'Great is the mystery of godliness,' and God filled the place with his presence. In the society afterwards, the heavenly influences continued to descend without interruption. Harris defended the rejoicing in the services by referring as proofs to David dancing before the ark and Christ riding victoriously through Jerusalem. After dining, the Association met. The Lord was with them as a flame of fire. For some time they could not utter a word other than to cry out, 'Glory! Glory! Hallelujah!' After a break, Harris spoke on pride, laziness, and carelessness, that through these things they grieved those who were close to the Lord. He wrote:

> We opened our hearts to one another; some of Satan's snares were broken, and the Lord revealed himself again so as to obstruct the breach that Satan had intended. I spoke to Bro. Beaumont about some of the unclear phrases that he makes use of. The Lord came upon us as flaming fire; we were full of love and joy and of victorious song. After supper and some private talk, we departed drunk with God's new wine.

It was certainly a conference of life and joy, and of very powerful influences.

At the beginning of February, Howell Harris visited London to fulfil his duties as the General Superintendent of the English churches. Though the responsibility was great, he was not unaware of the honour placed upon him. While being amazed at the goodness of God towards him, he refers again and again to the fact that he had been made head of the work in England. He was not free of ambition, and this high status and important role was satisfying to him. He was in London for more than a month, and the governing of the brethren proved almost too much of a task for him. We cannot go into the detail of the history (though it is written fully in the journal) as it does not bear essentially on the story of Welsh Methodism.

On his way home he attended a Bristol Association that was held on 7–8 March. As well as internal troubles, the relationship between the societies and the Moravians was causing difficulties, and the Association decided to send a letter to the Moravian Connexion calling on them to establish causes in Wiltshire. The journal notes that considerable disorder and agitation were present at the Association because of the unwillingness of Herbert Jenkins to co-operate with his brethren. Harris returned home, preaching in many places in Monmouthshire: Llanvaches, Goetre and New Inn, for example.

At the last place, a small Association was held and he was much comforted by the submissive attitude and religious experience of Brother Morgan Jones. On comparing views, the two found that they agreed in all things. They both judged that they should not confine the Spirit's activities by the making of any plans, nor by any ordering of their sermons; that both Spirit and word were essential; that the two together was the light and rule of the Church.

## A STORMY ASSOCIATION AT WATFORD

Harris had little rest after returning home. At the end of March and the beginning of April, he journeyed through Breconshire, Montgomeryshire and Radnorshire, visiting Tyddyn, Bwlch-yr-haidd, Mochdre, Llanllugan and Llansanffraid. In all places, his meetings were most powerful; the people broke out in singing and praising; their 'Amens' and 'Hallelujahs' would often drown his voice, and they remained behind to rejoice for hours after the service was over. At the beginning, Harris opposed such actions; this was due mainly to Griffith Jones's influence upon him; but by now he supported them, and defended them from commandments and examples in the Bible. On 9 April, a Quarterly Association was held at Watford. On the Tuesday night before the Association, Daniel Rowland preached at Groes-wen Chapel and Harris attended. The theme of the sermon was the spiritual effort required from all with respect to the Lord's cause. Harris also preached, and he says that the Lord filled the place with his presence. It appears that the society at Groes-wen was, by now, after some degree of estrangement, as Methodistic as any of the societies. Harris preached with such vigour that he was in some pain afterwards. He answered the objections of those who asked, 'Are you Arminians or Antinomians?' 'I have not come to deal with such things,' said the preacher, 'but to ask who is on the Lord's side. God has declared himself against Satan and against sin; if your heart is on the Lord's side, give me your hand in fellowship.'

It was, to some extent, a stormy Association. The Moravians wished to establish causes in Wales, and tried to attract to themselves those who had been converted under the ministry of the Methodists. They first sought to establish a foothold at Haverfordwest in Pembrokeshire. Perhaps the influence of John Gambold, afterwards a Moravian bishop, was the reason for their choice of Haverfordwest, in that many of the Methodists of that town were close relatives of his. It was natural that the issue became a talking point at the Association. Some tended to condemn the Moravians severely. But as for Harris:

> However, I expressed my view that there was too much narrowness and prejudice both in ourselves and in them, and that we would give advantage to the devil unless we were more humble; that I was as firm as any against the errors of the Moravians, and against their work of coming to Wales to cause division; but I could not agree with the expressions of some of the brethren at the Association and I saw in them a lack of faith for not leaving the work in the Lord's hand.

Howell Harris was on friendlier terms with the Moravians. He often used to visit their fellowships when in London. He knew that it was mainly through their instrumentality that John Wesley had been brought to evangelical religion, and he believed that the root of the matter was in them, though he did not agree with many of their ideas. It was therefore natural that he should feel affection towards them. However, the debate at Watford became heated, and because Harris argued for maintaining as tolerant a view as possible of the Moravian beliefs, someone accused him of being an Antinomian. He felt the the insult keenly. He was very hurt in his feelings on departing. He felt that the brethren looked upon him as a poor thing. The following morning he was no better. But Howell Davies and Williams, Pantycelyn, called upon him and were gentle and attentive to him. He recited his complaints to them, and they had sweet fellowship together. The reason that Rowland was not with the other two clergymen was that he had been appointed to preach that morning. After their conversation, they hurried to hear Rowland, but on arriving found that the service had ended. Privately, Harris grieved on seeing the brethren with their differing views so bitter against one another, and on seeing Daniel Rowland so stubborn against the Moravians. His mind was considerably confused.

He raised the matter again as they reconvened. He was against all the wrong things of the Moravians, and opposed their entrance into Wales that would cause division, but he could not condemn them in that he believed they were part of the body of Christ and that though their heads were to some extent in error, yet, many of them knew in their hearts a closer relationship with Jesus than many of the Methodists. He argued further that the Kingdom of the Lord did not depend on prejudice and on hot zeal for what was considered to be the truth, but on gentleness and love; that he himself was only a servant and had no authority to obstruct others. He suggested that it was not by open opposition that they would best obstruct the Moravians but by a moderate and loving spirit, and gentle remonstrance. He feared lest the agitation would hinder the work and take away the simplicity of the ministry amongst them. He does not state definitely how the discussion ended, but we can conclude that the brethren's decision was to ask Harris to visit Haverfordwest. He set out on that very day, reaching Hafod, some twenty-five miles away, by nightfall. By Saturday, he was at Llanddowror. He spent the Sunday conversing with Griffith Jones and listening to him preaching. In the evening, he arrived at Parke, Howell Davies's home. On Monday night he attended the private society at Haverfordwest and had much liberty to describe the wiles of Satan and his use of prejudice, pride and self-dependence. The next morning, he and John Sparks did their best to avoid any division. Harris preached from Romans 7:24, and in the sermon he succeeded in delivering a final blow, for the time being at any rate, against the devil's devices. He explained the error of the Moravians; the necessity of preaching the law; the importance of searching the Scriptures and of rooting the converts in them. He felt that he had succeeded with his message and he departed happily towards Wolf's Castle.

From there, he proceeded to Llaneilw, St David's, Longhouse, Fishguard, Ty'r Yet, Cerrig Ioan, Cwm Cynon, and Llangeitho, where he spent the Sunday. On the Sabbath morning, Daniel Rowland had a remarkable service at Llancwnlle. His theme was resisting the devil. The effect of the sermon upon Harris was almost more than he could bear. He says that only once previously had he heard Rowland in such a spirit. It is easy to read between the lines that Harris felt he had been too heated at Watford, and that his temper at the Association was not what it should have been. He says that he came to Llangeitho with a spirit of self-denial. He wrote:

> I had such union of soul with Bro. Rowland as I never had before, seeing it is my privilege and happiness to strengthen his hands, to live and die with him, and live with him forever. I loved him as my own soul. After the Sacrament we went to Llangeitho. At six, I discoursed, [being] refreshed in seeing Bro. Rowland come in.[8]

It appears he had a hard service of it:

> [Having] not the liberty I [am] used to have somewhat straitened me; the Word did not seem to run . . . none cried or showed any signs of being affected.

Perhaps there is a degree of childishness in the feeling he expresses, but it is very natural.

> But I was made humble, and I was ready to be mean in his sight.

On Monday morning he records that his heart is overflowing with love towards Daniel Rowland:

> I told him that I felt it an honour to be able to wash his feet and to perform for him the meanest tasks; that I was happy and thankful for the gifts he had received and the success that crowned his efforts, and for being numbered as one of his friends. I felt faith that Bro. Rowlands and I should triumph over all.

It is good to see how the souls of the two friends cleaved to one another, though clouds arose between them at times. Harris preached at Llangeitho on the next day, Monday, before departing and was thankful to receive the usual power when preaching:

> I had burdens on my soul . . . the word would not run by me at Llangeitho but I was kept low and humble . . . but there, in prayer and discoursing, the Lord took it all away by giving me freedom of gifts and spirit before Bro. Rowland.[9]

He then retraced his steps, visiting Glanyrafonddu, Llandeilo, Gellido-chlaethe, Trefeurig near Llantrisant – where a horse was given him by the fraternity, Aberthin, St. Nicholas, and Dinas Powys. On Sunday, he was at Groes-wen, and when preaching on the words, 'And they overcame him by the blood of the Lamb,' he brought fear to the hearts of unbelievers and carried all before him. He was at Watford on Monday, and it appears that a degree of sharp dissension still prevailed here amongst the brethren. He warned them that Satan had been loosed among them and wished to divide them by his wiles, as he had the brethren in England. He charged them to examine themselves whether they had every grace in operation, particularly evangelical repentance, self-examination, and tenderness of conscience. 'It is a wonder,' he writes, 'how the Lord keeps us from error, though we be so often on the brink. I trust that Arminianism and Antinomianism received an effective blow.' On Monday night, he visited Mynyddislwyn. His text was, 'Rejoice evermore', but instead of comforting the saints, as he usually did when speaking on these words, he was led almost unconsciously to thunder forth terrifyingly:

> I pierced to the quick those who rejoiced but were not born again, and had not God's grace in their hearts. In particular I was fearful towards those who live in ostentation, and towards our persecutors. I could not help it. The Lord led me; I had no thoughts of my own. I condemned those who rejoiced because they had the world, and because they were healthy, and likely to live long. I was led to thunder most awfully against carnal clergymen, who swear and get drunk and are ignorant of God. I showed that it was not strange that these abounded seeing that there was none in the parish who prayed that a good man should come as clergyman. I ended by showing that it was out of love to their souls that I spoke in this way.

A strange sermon, certainly, from such a text, but Harris felt that this was the direction which the Lord desired him to take. He was at Llanfihangel, Monmouthshire, on Thursday. From there he proceeded to New Inn, but no great power accompanied his preaching. He continued through Coedcae-mawr and Llanheiddel, returning home the next day after a long and important journey.

In early May, he set out again for London. There is a significant note in his journal:

> I arrived at Fair Oak before dark. On the way, I had a view of the glory of Christ's person. But I was told that Bro. Rowland was determined to oppose any preaching of the blood. The news fell heavy upon my soul; but God made me humble, and I had strength to cry that he would bless those whom he sent. I was happy to be deprived of all gifts, as long as the truth, the whole truth, be proclaimed.

He stayed at London until after the Association held on 18 June, and then returned to Trefeca.

## THE FIRST SIGNS OF A DISAGREEMENT BETWEEN HARRIS AND ROWLAND

On 27 June, a Quarterly Association gathered at Trefeca. It proved to be an important but tragic event for it was the occasion of the beginning of that disagreement between Howell Harris and the other leaders of the revival in Wales, which eventually concluded in a complete separation. We will let Harris relate events in his own words:

> About eight, Bro. Rowland came here and several other brethren and sisters. Seeing the lambs of God with love and tenderness for each other, but bitter and condemning over all that is wrong among all the ministers and exhorters . . . Bro William Richard prayed and exhorted, and I prayed in English too. I see I am ready to lose my place and authority.
>
> Felt especial unity with Bro Rowland in spirit and at the same time my soul was exceedingly sorrowful under the sense of my own and the brethren's sin and stubbornness, self and want of love and tenderness. When Bro. Rowland asked me for a book, I felt ready to give him the blood from my heart. I found some who laid upon me to speak to Bro Rowland, discoursed in private with him and instead of having my burdens removed they fell heavier, so that I may say that I begin to suffer with Christ. I saw something of the burden that Christ had to carry because of the perversity and rebellion of his children; and when I feel so much from an attack upon me from one direction, how much did he feel when all the weight of his people's sins were upon him? Rowland so despised the exhorters, disowning their labours. After, I told him of his not honouring them in the Lord, as sent of him. I cried that he would clothe them with humility and give them power and life and success, and if some were not sent by him that he would weed them out. I prayed also that he would show their sending to dear Bro. Rowland who thinks they only bring a reproach on the gospel and do no good at all and drive the people away. Soul mourned over Bro. Beaumont and myself over all our pride and self and unguarded expressions. In conversation with Bro. Rowland, opened my

whole mind of all I saw amiss in him – his lightness and want of a fatherly spirit, showing that we should go before the brethren in faith and humility, love and longsuffering. He owned it, but said the Lord did not set him in the place of a father, else he would fit him for it. I said I felt it wrought in me to honour him as such, and withal was sorely grieved in seeing him not valuing to lay burdens on his brethren.

I said I preached in London against the Moravians in public and private, against their pride, errors and selfishness. I declared I am of the same mind in every point of doctrine and have not changed these nine or ten years. As to the brethren's charging me with changing, 'tis only an answer to my prayer that God would use some means to keep me from being exalted in their eyes. When he charged me with Moravianism because I mentioned of the blood of Christ and worshipped that Man, and used the term 'Lamb', etc., I declared I had the light of the glory of Christ's Person before I knew there was a Moravian, and to the extent that they preach the mystery, I agree with them; but that I have had nothing from them but from the Lord. When I used the word 'Lamb', that it was sweet to me, but that I was free to use all his names alike. That one name would be made sweet to me now, and another at a different time, and am never offended at my brethren's using any of his names. We should not cramp each other's freedom in that.

I said further that I did not know one God outside of Christ; that I saw all of God in this Man, in that the Father and the Son are one; and when I consider God with my reason that I see him as a great God, but in Christ I see his infinity. He cavilled at using the word 'mystery'; I said how Paul uses 'the mystery of Christ' frequently. He was quite stiff whilst I declared I was only for peace and love and moderation, being persuaded that they [the Moravians] are children of God as well as we, and we are fallible as well as them, and that we seem to have the same pride to censure them as they have to censure us, which I think is our sin on all sides. He said that he had heard me preach Antinomianism; I said that I did not know what careless remarks I might have used but that, unless I was mistaken as to the meaning of Antinomianism, I did not hold to the smallest part of that doctrine. At the same time I saw a glorious liberty in the gospel, and I had been led to distinguish between the dispensation of the letter and the dispensation of the gospel, in that the first leans on the letter but the second is the fruit of the Spirit of the Lord. I told him that I had heard him preach it also, much more than he now does, namely of justification, and of the righteousness of Christ, which is complete, and in hearing so little of it now I was tempted to think he had it only in his head, but not in his heart, but that I could receive his message on the conditional promises very well and believe the Lord sends him with it. I desired him to mention what Antinomian expressions I had (but he said he could not remember them); that I spake in the name of the Lord to him in order that we may go on as brethren with[out] the jealousies of each other, but if he would persist in entertaining surmises from the enemy that I was free to commit it all to the Lord and would leave every workman to his own Master. When he wondered I was so weak when I said of the loads I had on me, I said that it was not my nature that made me thus concerned for was I left to myself I would go on and fear no brother, and as I have received my message and ministry from the Lord I would go on with it in his strength by myself, as I began by myself, but it was sore to go on thus and I thought it best to withdraw to England till this storm should blow over.

I declared I was not for any party as such, that I was a member of Christ's Body and loved the Moravians as belonging to Christ as I loved the brethren here and laboured only for love and peace as I thought it was his duty too. He carped at the saying, 'We are not more holy, etc.' [I asked him] 'Do you think you see so deep to the mystery of Christ now, as you will ten years hence?' But as to our way of expressing these spiritual truths we must be tender and bear with each other else we may make one another speak what we will. But he was so stiff (though I hope the Lord will bless somewhat too) that none but God can prevent a breach. I mentioned the pride of the people with them [i.e. the clergy] and also his criticizing and captiousness that tis not the fruit of the Spirit. Then having discoursed with him, I took up my burden and laid it before the Lord; I then wrote my journal till twelve o'clock.[10]

To describe this quarrel between these two men, the very pillars of the revival, is a sad task. We must remember that it is only one side of the story that we have here, and if it were possible to have Daniel Rowland's account, it would be very different. We must notice also that Harris wrote his report while still in the heat of the moment, a bitter spirit still boiling within him. If he had written at a later time, when the storm had passed, he would no doubt have moderated much of what he wrote. His journal continues:

To hear Bro. [William] Williams preach . . . most excellently well on union among believers. It shot into my mind that it was the Lord that had given him his matter. I saw such opposition to this union that only the Lord could move. Afterwards Bro. [Howell] Davies preached in English from Joshua 1:9. The words fitted my case; I believed them by faith; but what I lacked was a direct application of them to me . . . [Afterwards] to the Association, which I feared so much because of the prejudices that had arisen in the minds of the brethren against one another. I opened my mind and laid open Bro. Rowland's prejudice against the brethren. He owned he had no freedom toward many and he despised the exhorters tonight that had been so blessed to many, and also despised my discourse on the mystery of godliness, and also despised the brethren's ignorance. When the brethren were asked about me, some owned they were jealous of me leaning to Antinomians and Moravians. I declared I had not changed in any article of my faith this nine or ten years since I was established about Perfection six years ago, but even then I did not mean Sinless Perfection, for when I understood what Bro. Wesley meant, I declared against him. Bro. Rowland laboured to declare me a changeling, self-contradicting and a liar and Antinomian. I said how amazed I was when he first told me that many considered me fickle, until I remembered that I had prayed earnestly that the Lord would humble me in the eyes of my brethren, lest they think too highly of me, and it shot into my mind that this was the way the Lord chose to answer my prayer. I spake very home as to my own ministry, I had received it from God so it stood or fell to my own Master, and as to the brethren, I loved and honoured them in the Lord and could not bear him to despise them. As to their faults, I hope the Lord that sent them would remove them and qualify them more and more, but that I loved his ministry and honoured him in the pulpit, but out of it I was grieved to see [his condition], and if all men had told me of it I would not believe there was so much self and pride in him; that if I had not a love to him from the Lord I could not stay with him, but as 'tis from God let him do and say what he will. Seeing he did own the Word to be the rule, I wish it was brought nearer his conscience, [that] his dark, witty, cutting and carnal way of speaking I could not see came from the Spirit of God, and I was grieved to see him live in them. We spoke about sanctification and when they mentioned conviction necessary absolutely before we come to Christ and all are drawn that way, I stood up and declared I was a witness against that, that I and many others were drawn by love. I stood for that he might draw them that way he will.

He, and many more, declared:

1. Against my preaching the blood of Christ as what they could not receive.

2. That God did not suffer.

3. Against preaching a mystery; that it must be explained.

I declared that I had this from God and not from man and would preach it and God would cut my way through men and devils and if they would all stand against it, it was no more to me than to see butterflies. I was only grieved to see their ignorance of this mystery, which is my food. How God did not and could not suffer, but God-man did – neither the man nor God separately, but the two natures in one Person. And that I never saw him as man, but that I saw him as God also. If I had seen him in the manger, I would have worshipped him; and I would have worshipped his sacred dead body at the side of the grave, in that the body, as well as his soul that was in heaven, was also united to the Godhead. This, through grace, I would seal with my blood, and until I believed it I had not yet been freed from the fear of death.

I said that I loved the Moravians in that I believed they belonged to the Lord, but I never agreed with all they held. This time, six years ago, I left them and joined Mr Wesley when he preached the necessity of using the means of grace which they refused and denied, and [I] preached against their errors in Haverfordwest and in London, publicly and privately, and also here warned the brethren against their errors. When they said [in the Association] that I worshipped the blood of Christ, I said that I did, as being part of Christ, in that not one part of him is separate from his divinity. When they said that I changed; that I first preached thunderings, then all the freeness of grace, then the fruits of faith, all this I owned and 'tis by the same Spirit. I am led still to thunder at times; that I must preach as 'tis given me; all must as the Spirit gives them freedom and one is not to bar the other. When objections were made against our not preaching scripturally, I owned I was faulty here and that tis owing to my carnality and sin that I don't meditate more in the Scriptures and other books, with care and fear.

Afterwards there was a discourse with Bro. Beaumont and he had great tenderness and we both declared for our growing by faith. When Bro. Rowland spoke authoritatively, I denied his authority, that I looked on his [office] as nothing, that I received him as a brother but no other. Then the accounts were read, and one prayed, and I prayed, and the Lord came down. I spake to the brethren (Rowland and the ministers being gone), stirred them up to more diligence in reading the Scriptures and reading good books, in being sober in the work, and in being certain that they do all for God. After supper (the ministers having gone to bed), the Lord came in a wonderful measure down indeed. I felt my heart a flame, and my soul full of light and faith. A good company was kept all night till about four in the morning to sing and rejoice; we were like David before the ark. I exhorted to more watchfulness, humility and godly fear. But I was overtaken by the enemy and fell for a little while; I was raised again as I asked simply of the Lord. I then arranged my journey. I slept none at all all night or the morning.[11]

So ends the account of this sad Association. On the following morning, Rowland, Williams and Howell Davies were leaving for their homes, but before they went, Harris requested an opportunity to speak with Daniel Rowland:

> Had a dialogue with Bro. Rowland again. I told him to be careful of preaching less out of books and more out of his heart, which he received as from God; that I was grieved at seeing so little of the fruit of the Spirit in his behaviour; and that I was glad to see the ministers so united, though I was a black sheep amongst them.[12]

He also noted that Rowland was softened on parting. After their departure, a Baptist minister preached with much acceptance. He said that none but Christ had authority over his ministers and he encouraged the people not to attend carnal clergymen. No doubt, the reference was to the three who had recently left them. The emotions expressed by Harris at the end of the day are inexplicable:

> I came to the last Association full of joy and cheerfulness and went away under heavy loads; I came to this Association burdened and weary, and departed full of rejoicing.

Rejoicing! At a time when Methodism had received a blow that was to paralyse all its activities for a period, and from which it suffers to this day! But we must remember that we are writing the histories of imperfect men.

We will leave to a further chapter any discussion of the orthodoxy or otherwise of Howell Harris's theological views, but this account in his journal suggests certain points immediately.

1. Almost certainly he mistook the meaning of the words of Daniel Rowland and the other clergymen. We can hardly believe that they belittled his ministry. His words had been blessed to the salvation of two out of the three, and they must naturally have considered and spoken of his preaching with great respect. It is hard to accept also that they would have condemned him for speaking of Christ as the Lamb. Quite apart from its Scriptural use, the term is found throughout Rowland's sermons and Williams's hymns, and Harris himself acknowledges that the three of them submitted to the Bible's authority. He narrates what they said according to his understanding of it at the time, when he himself was considerably agitated and probably incapable of discerning the drift of their remarks.

2. It is clear also that Harris ruled the Association with a high hand. He would not allow any comment from the brethren on the content of his preaching, as he considered that he had received it as a revelation from God. If they opposed him his only response would be to threaten to drive on through men and devils, and that his opponents were but as butterflies to him. It is evident also that he used sharp and bitter words. He accused Rowland of possessing only a religion of the head and not of the heart, and that he was motivated by pride. As far as we can gather, the spirit of the clergymen was not to any extent as bitter. Stubbornness is the main fault that Harris attributes to them.

3. It must be acknowledged that an element of jealousy had entered in amongst the leaders. The three clergymen, Daniel Rowland in particular perhaps, were not free of it. They saw Howell Harris, though not ordained and wanting in some of the ministerial gifts possessed by themselves, yet because of his energy and fiery zeal, exerting greater influence than they

within the societies, and exalted to be head over the Calvinistic Methodism of England. As imperfect men, and possessing, no doubt, various
degrees of ambition, it was natural for them to be envious and to pay too
much attention to the failings of one who had been raised so high. On the
other hand, it is not improbable that Harris's promotion had gone to his
head to some extent, and caused him to think less of these clergymen, who
because of their ordination were so much more respected than himself by
the more Established element of the Methodists. We fear that the age-old
question, 'Who shall be greatest?', had gained a hold in their hearts.

4. It would appear that Harris in this Association, if not previously,
had succeeded in forming the exhorters into a party in opposition to the
clergymen. We find that they remained together in session after the three
clergymen had left. They remained together also until dawn, singing, praying and in discussion, when the other three had departed for their beds.
Previously, Harris had often stressed the lack of knowledge amongst the
exhorters; he now exalts them as those sent by God. His clear aim was
to bind them to himself. It was easy for him to influence the exhorters.
He was the spiritual father of so many of them. Furthermore, he and
they were on the same ground, so to speak, that is, without ordination,
and it was not difficult for them therefore to agree in their envy of their
ordained brethren.

5. We fear that it was Harris's belief that he had established a strong
party, by whose aid he could remove the influence of the clergy, which
was at the root of his confident feelings at the close of the Association.
He did not believe that the clergymen could defeat him. He saw himself as head over Welsh Methodism just as he already was over English
Calvinistic Methodism, and therefore without any to oppose him. We
are not suggesting that pride of heart was at the root of such a desire; we
believe better things of him. He no doubt persuaded himself that in such
an exalted position he could serve the Lord Jesus and the gospel more
effectively. Were he to have foreseen the tragedy that was to result from
his dispute with his brethren, his heart would certainly have been bitter
within him, and his pillow awash with tears.

In the morning, Harris was assailed by different feelings: a sense of
grief that the brethren had refused the message concerning the mystery
of Christ and the glory of his blood, and that they were despising himself
because of his simplicity and ignorance. At the beginning of the week
following, he set out on a journey to Monmouthshire. One of his aims, no
doubt, was to confirm his authority over the societies. He preached first
at Fairmeadow, between Talgarth and Crickhowell. His text was, 'This

is a faithful saying', and he fiercely attacked pride. That night, he was at Cilonwy preaching on, 'All power is given unto me in heaven and earth', and he rejoiced that he received again the power that used to accompany his very first sermons of old. On Wednesday he was at Grismond parish, where he encountered much opposition from the Nonconformists. He says that he received a message from the Lord on the way that he was not to go to Cardiganshire, but that he would receive power and authority while preaching the blood and mystery of Christ – that message which his opponents would not receive. He continued through Abergavenny, where he had a good meeting, and heard that the news was spreading like wildfire across the land, that Rowland was against the exhorters. He visited Goetre, Llanfihangel, Tonsawndwr, and New Inn, where he powerfully addressed the exhorters. He returned to Trefeca by the following Sunday. For all his boldness, there are indications that he felt very lonely after losing the friendly support of his brethren. We find him turning to Christ and writing, 'Thou art my brother! Thou wert my brother when before Pilate; thou wert my brother on the cross; and thou art now my brother in heaven; and in thee I am glorious and a conqueror.' He says that the Lord blessed him remarkably on this journey, honouring him to the same degree as Brother Rowland was dishonouring. 'The worst of characters,' he says, 'bear witness that I am an honest man.'

## A RECONCILIATION

At the beginning of the following week he set out on a long journey through Carmarthenshire, Montgomeryshire and Radnorshire. On the first night he was at Trecastle, where he was given great power to show forth the infinite merit of Christ's blood, and in the private society that followed, he described the lukewarmness, prejudice and head knowledge of the Dissenters, adding that he loved them but desired that they should press closer to God. He was next at Llanddeusant, preaching again with much power. He asked himself whether he would continue to pay two pounds a year to support the monthly sermon from Daniel Rowland in this county. This probably refers to Rowland's monthly preaching visit to Abergorlech, and Harris's assistance in paying for someone to take his place at Llangeitho. The following is Harris's account of his experience at Llanddeusant:

> Last night I had a willingness to suffer everything from every quarter, from the carnal and the spiritual, and even from Bro. Rowlands who has been suf- fered to despise, disparage, and trample on me, twitting me with want of gifts and want of stability and of Antinomianism. This morning I dreamt that my

heart was broken with love and that his was too, and we fell on each other's necks, and he kissed me, and I humbled myself to him.[13]

It seems that the dream affected him greatly, for he believed that dreams could provide a message from the Lord. Daniel Rowland was preaching at Abergorlech, most probably there was a Quarterly Meeting there, and after much hesitation and a considerable battle against his own stubbornness, Harris decided to go to hear him. Rowland's text was Revelation 2:17, 'To him that overcometh will I give to eat of the hidden manna, etc.' Harris commented:

He began excellently by showing that all grace is active grace; he expounded the error of the Antinomians who appropriate merit to grace, and who say they love Christ while they live in sin.

As he listened, Harris's heart was melted. A cry arose in his heart that they might love one another and understand one another better, and he asked of God:

How long will I be suffered to bear the fruits of pride, stubbornness and the flesh? I hear the same language from all thy faithful ambassadors, with each thinking of the other that they are the enemies of the truth.

He wished for the storm to blow over:

There was light and gospel in Bro. Rowland's sermon. He showed that the Christian war is a holy war; that the Holy One is the Captain; that the ground on which the fight takes place, that is, the Church, is holy; and that it is to be waged by holy means. Who can write the light and power that was here?

The two men travelled together to Talyllychau:

On the way, my dream was fulfilled. I opened to him my whole soul; much of the enemy's work was washed away, and we drew closer to one another. I told him how I agreed with his sermon today. He said that he had much respect for my ministry, and that all must acknowledge that I was sent of the Lord, and blessed. I told him my burden; that I felt that he did not honour the Moravians sufficiently, and that therefore he was sinning before the Lord. He replied that he did not feel anything against them, and that they could preach in his church, as long as they did not proclaim their particular opinions. I said that if they came to Wales, I would oppose their errors, but that I would do so in God's love, in that I judged they knew more of God than I did. He complained that I was drawing too close to Bro. Beaumont; I acknowledged it, but that I did so in order to moderate him, that he might not be turned out from us.

Here are the two leaders, to a great extent, reconciled.

Howell Harris preached at Talyllychau, but Rowland, speaking on Revelation 12:9 after him, was given extraordinary power and feeling. Harris felt that the Lord was much more evident in Rowland's ministry than in his own:

> He discoursed most wonderfully; all the time I felt union of soul with him, as if I was preaching myself. With him to Cwmyglaw. I hope this storm is blowing over; we rejoiced and jumped and sang and were merry like drunken folks.[14]

So much rejoicing filled their hearts on being reconciled that they hardly knew what to do with themselves. They almost appear like children, in their quarrelling and subsequent reconciliation. Harris told Rowland that in London he had preached against the Moravians, and in Wales against the Antinomians, and that in almost the identical words that Rowland had used the previous day. Harris noted:

> He confessed that nothing he had heard from me had caused him to be offended, but my work in cleaving to Bro. Beaumont, thereby justifying that which was not right. I hope that we went to our rest in the truth again. I told Rowland that he had sinned against my ministry. He denied this, and declared that he looked upon me as God's messenger, but he confessed that he despised the exhorters. Lord, destroy this feeling in him. He believes even now that I am too tender to the Moravians; but I am for peace, and love, and rest in the house of the Lord.

The two travelled to Llwynyberllan. Harris preached on the glory of the church, and then Rowland spoke from Matthew 9:49, and had a most powerful meeting. They then separated; Harris went to Bronydd, where power and influence accompanied his message; and from there to Merthyr, Erwood, Builth Wells and Llangamarch. Extraordinary light and power accompanied his words at Llangamarch. On the morning of the following Sunday, he was at Dôl-y-felin, from where he passed on to Rhayader, where he felt as if he was in chains when endeavouring to speak, and he arrived at Tyddyn that night. An immense congregation had gathered here, and he had a good meeting. After the sermon, a private society met until twelve o'clock. In the society, Harris spoke of Christ's blood, his Deity, his glory and mystery. This, he said, was the foundation, and that God and ourselves are one at this place. He said further that five things are attributed by the Scriptures to Christ's blood: (1) Infinite merit; (2) The ability to propitiate divine wrath; (3) The destruction of death to the believer; (4) The extinguishing of the eternal flames for the believer; (5) The introduction of everlasting blessings. 'There is no God but Christ,' he said, ' and if you are united to Christ, you are united to all that is in God.'

Though the hour was so late, Harris did not go to his bed on ending the society but remained up throughout the night addressing and warning the exhorters. The next day, a Monthly Meeting was held there. It does not appear that any of the clergymen was present, but many of the exhorters had gathered. They had begun to look to Harris as their Captain. He expounded the mystery, showing how his soul was in union with Christ's soul, and his body with Christ's body, to all eternity. He next explained the way in which divisions entered among them, namely through some placing emphasis on one truth, for example, justification, and calling those who emphasize sanctification, legalistic; others who lay stress on sanctification, called the advocates of justification, Antinomians. In the Meeting they discussed the doctrine of the Trinity, and the unity of the Godhead. Harris notes that he was so tired from the length of the journey and from the number of times that he preached, that he could not eat. He left about four o'clock on the Monday, and received a rebuke on some matter from a dear friend that he found most painful to the flesh, and even to grace.

He next travelled to St Harmon, on the Radnorshire border and from there visited the home of a man called Hugh Edwards. He was here taken up remarkably by the glory of the body of Christ, and the phrase 'eating his flesh and drinking his blood' ran through his mind continually. He then journeyed to the home of William Evans, Nantmel. Along the way it seems that, as the personal influence of Daniel Rowland weakened within him, the old quarrel began to take up more and more of his thoughts:

> I saw clearly how God had kept me in the middle amongst so many errors, and how that Bro. Rowland, by opposing me, had reduced my boldness and weakened my arms. I saw that God's glory had departed from his heart, and self had intruded. I saw that God would raise me up and stand at my side.

It is amazing to read that such unworthy thoughts concerning his friend could find any place in his mind, when they both a few days previously had danced for joy because of their reconciliation. This episode only dishonours both Harris's head and heart. But we are not narrating the histories of perfect beings. He was troubled in heart on entering William Evans's home. It seems that the old exhorter of Nantmel had been one of Rowland's supporters at the Trefeca Association. But he was given much unity of spirit with the brother and, as they departed, they understood each other much better. He next journeyed to the home of Brother Buffon, where he preached on the blood of Christ and at the same time encouraged the brethren to bear with one another. James Beaumont had preached before him, on the mystery of God. They sat together privately until late, opening their hearts to one another, and removing prejudices.

Beaumont was much more extreme in his language than Harris, and his defending of Beaumont had been one of the charges brought against Harris. He was to be found here at his best, seeking to moderate some of Beaumont's ideas, particularly the latter's explanation of the phrase 'eating the flesh and drinking the blood' of our Lord. He told him that, even if he were in possession of the truth, the time to proclaim it had not yet come. He then continued through Dôl-y-berthog, Llansanffraid, Ty'ncwm and Dôl-y-wilod, returning to Trefeca after a journey of three weeks. A note in his journal, written at Llansanffraid, is worth recording:

> Spoke to the Minister [of the parish] Mr Williams . . . I endeavoured too to soften him toward Bro. Beaumont who had offended him as well as vast many others.[15]

The reference proves that Beaumont's doctrine had become generally unacceptable, and it would have been well for Harris had he not made such a friend of him.

The day after his return, a Monthly Association was held at Trefeca. None of the clergymen was present, and Harris presided. He spoke for a long time on the blood of Christ, and directed the exhorters how to conduct themselves while he was away in London. The marriage of the exhorter Thomas Jones was also discussed and consented to. Howell Harris took in a Quaker as a lodger in his home. This action may be seen as a firstfruit of the 'Family' at Trefeca. He says also that he was guided by the Lord to send his horse to the exhorter Thomas James. He set out for London in the middle of August, passing through much of Glamorganshire and Monmouthshire and being present at a Quarterly Meeting at Groes-wen. Again, no clergyman was present and he presided. It does not appear to have been a particularly happy Association. There was considerable unease at Watford and Groes-wen at his strain of ministry. Indeed, in these churches was to be found the core of the opposition against him.

> I went amongst the brethren, that is, the preachers, and told them that I was not hearing sufficient complaining amongst them for their ignorance of God and of Christ, and for their tendency to Antinomianism; and that I feared for them that they were not convinced of their ignorance, or rather, that they were too selfish to confess it. They acknowledged this to some extent, but they were offended that I did not differentiate clearly enough in my ministry. I then opened to them the words, 'Eating the flesh of the Son of God,' as I did at Aberthin. I sought to remove their stumbling block. I rebuked their pride, but they would not receive it. I opened my heart to them as a father would to his children, that I believed in the Trinity, but that my faith was too weak

to feast on the doctrine and to preach it; but that I was called to preach the
unity of the Person of Christ, and that this was my nourishment. I persuaded
them that I was not about to join with the Moravians. I then departed for
Watford with a heavy heart.

On his way there, he felt the importance of the office that he occupied,
that he had been placed amongst the fathers of God's house, side by side
with the ordained clergymen.

The Association, we may surmise, was being held jointly at Watford
and Groes-wen. The next day, Harris again met with the exhorters and
addressed them on their relationship with himself:

I explained to the young brethren their place, and my own place, and the
way in which I believed the Holy Spirit had placed me as a father over the
exhorters; that they were my assistants, but that they were not allowing me
the authority of a father to chastise them; but that I was being catechized by
them, my hands being weakened and my ministry frustrated, and that they
appeared to me to be lost in pride. I said that I was convinced that I had gone
too far in attempting to satisfy them, and in explaining myself and submitting
myself to them. I rebuked them for their pride and their lack of care for God's
glory. One of them melted as I was praying; another said that I was bringing
errors into the church. I asked God to forgive him, and I departed.

No indeed, it was not a happy Association. There are suggestions that
Harris was dealing with the exhorters in a very high-handed manner,
expecting personal submission and fealty from them, and assuming a
headship over them that totally excluded Daniel Rowland and the other
two clergymen.

## FURTHER FRICTION AT NEATH

He was in London for two months. We will pass by the events of this
period as they bear no direct relation to Welsh Methodism. He returned
about the end of September. The day after his return he preached at Trefeca, and complained that his brother – he does not say whether it was
Joseph or Thomas – refused to come to hear him, though staying there at
the time. Within a few days, a Quarterly Association was held at Neath,
and he journeyed there. On the way he heard, at Glyn, that his brethren
had, in some sense, cast him aside, and that he was being portrayed in very
dark colours. This produced a very bitter spirit in him. At Gellidochlaethe
he heard a very wonderful sermon from Morgan John Lewis on the son
of promise, the most wonderful and strangest sermon he had ever heard.
Harris was grateful that such light was among them, and he could do no

less than honour him. But the knowledge that the brethren were closing ranks against him was weighing heavily on his mind, and he asked the Lord whether it was a rebuke to him for some sin committed, or an honour set upon him that would yet turn out to be a jewel in his crown.

The Association met at seven on Wednesday night, and proved a tumultuous meeting. In Harris's words:

I told the brethren that they were dear to me, that I could wash their feet, and that I was willing to be without gifts, success or ability, so that they might receive all. I was then broken and burst out weeping. Before this I was in my own spirit because I had been tempted. I had heard that they agreed at an Association they had together [about a fortnight ago] for Mr Rowland to take my place and to settle who to go out and where to send all, and as for me, to send me to Carmarthenshire and not to Glamorganshire where, it was told them, I was not received and preached errors. I opened my belief about the Person of Christ and I saw there is no difference [between us] but the enemy's coming down [among us]. [I discussed] my first settling here, by their choice and Mr Whitefield's, and how it was made clear in my own soul and how I went on in this persuasion until now, till I find I am turned out, but as to the consequences of it I am clear. How I am in England called a Legalist, because I preach against the Antinomians and the Moravians and because I turned out Mr Cudworth; while in Wales I am called Antinomian and Moravian.

When they said how formerly when any jars would arise between me and Bro. Rowland I would cry and fall on his neck and take his words and so it would be over, but now it was not so, I was more stiff. I said I did not know of anything [for which] I opposed him in unless it was in reproving his licentiousness in eating, drinking, laughing, beating, etc., withal I know I am by far the worse, but that I was recovered through repentance. I don't know of anything I have to be stiff in, unless you go to rob me of this truth, that that Man is God. If so, I shall be stiff, and perhaps I went too far then in humbling myself [before Rowland]. I think the sin is in his and your side in blackening my character and weakening my hands and sinning against my ministry and calling me Antinomian. Though I so often declared I agreed with all I heard them preach, yet they without any just cause from the beginning have entertained jealousies of me. But as to give up my place, I can't, though it is not out of slavish fear I thus every time open my heart and declare I agree, for the Lord has told me He has set before me an open door which no one can shut. I can't and dare not give up my place, and if the Lord has set me in it, let them see to it for turning me out. I also mentioned how I am willing to withdraw, and reproved their ignorance and wisdom that rises against this profound light. I see now that Satan has been permitted to blind the eyes and make fat the hearts of the brethren, setting one against another. It is a sore storm but some great good is to follow.

I showed what pride and want of love they show toward the Moravians and they to them. If you had power of all sides you would persecute each other openly. I opened again about the mystery of Christ and his sufferings. I saw others – Luther, the Puritans, Dr Watts, Mr Whitefield, etc. – using stronger expressions than I ever did. When they charged me with worshipping the blood of Christ, I said I did not as separate from him but as part of him, how the propriety of one nature is often reckoned to the other, that God bled and died because the man that suffered was God. The incomprehensibleness of the union between the two natures I can't explain because tis a mystery inexplicable, and will be a matter of our adoration forever. When Christ preached his Godhead and Manhood, he did not explain but simply spake of himself as equal and inferior to the Father, insisting on all to receive it because he said it without explaining it. I declared against John Belcher that he seems to me to be puffed up and I can't labour with him. I named places where they charged me with Antinomianism and how they gathered Associations without me. I think that possibly they have sinned against me [though] I am the father of most of them, and am very free to go on as before. I knew them by myself, hoping I shan't be left to fling any by-words against any of them, but to preach the truth as I have it from God. I am also charged with introducing Mr Wesley here, who has professed enough against Antinomianism. I hope much chaff will be blown away by this means, and no union shall abide among us but that wrought by the Lord, and backbiting, carrying tales, etc., and a trifling spirit will be destroyed.

About ten the brethren went to supper and I wrote my journal, being all of us in ourselves and but little of the Lord among us. As they had a proposal to lay before the brethren here about settling Bro. Rowland in my place, to take and to turn out the exhorters and to settle each his round. I declared I was free to deliver up my place as general Superintendent but could not put myself under his authority to be sent here or there as he saw fit. That freedom I had from the Lord to go where I was enlightened in my own mind, and could not give it up for fear of sinning against the Lord. That they had sinned against my ministry, and I thought things would not be right till they should be humbled for their sin before the Lord.

October 3, 1746 Neath. Association continued. Last night, in joining in prayer, I was set free and had love and liberty, loving and honouring them all in the Lord. [Crying], 'Lord, thou knowest thou hast humbled me to Bro. Rowland and hast made me to labour for peace and union and thou knowest they have sinned against my ministry and weakened my hands,' my whole soul crying they may be forgiven. I felt I could go on my knees before them all and take any shame to myself. [At the Association], when they charged me with correspondence with the Moravians and I said I did not, but that I wished for it in that I honoured them greatly because they knew Jesus Christ, several of the brethren spoke home. Mr Powell [a clergyman] reproved the exhorter that opposed me very home. Another brother spoke home that he felt their words in rising against me cut him; another said I was the spiritual father of most if not all. I could appeal to the Lord about my uprightness in my behaviour towards the brethren in this affair, though they without cause have judged me and received false [reports]. I declared how Bro. Morgan John Lewis preached stronger gospel than ever I had but it was truth, and if I had spoken so I should indeed be charged with Antinomianism. Though they begin on me they won't end here, they'll at length disagree among themselves. I thought many of them were legal in their hearts and know but little of the glory and mystery of that Man. Slept a little from four to seven.

I was indeed willing to go to England and leave here for a time and willing to stay here and go hither and thither, and willing to stay at home, or anything. What is stumbled at is the preaching of the Godhead, the blood, the mystery and glory of Christ. O Lord, help me to behave now in the hour of trial, right toward all. Wrote this to eight.

Discoursed, declaring that:

1. From a sense of my own infirmities for the place;
2. Thinking Mr Rowland would be more blessed to them;
3. As a motion had already been made and agreed among so many at Caeo, and Bro. Williams (Pantycelyn) declaring, 'I saw him [that is, Rowland] the fittest as being a minister';
4. As I am called so much to England;

I am free to resign my place to Bro. Rowland but could not without sinning against the Lord give him any authority over my ministry so as to order me where to go or how to preach.

After I declared [that] I looked on myself as removed out of my place till I should be resettled by a new choice, Bro. Morgan Jones stood up and declared he did, before God and men, choose me to be over him in the Lord, seeing that the Lord had fitted me more than any for my place. Bro. John Powell had declared [the same] before. Several spoke now, so that I saw God re-establishing me in my place, as he showed me on the way coming here. He would, though, [that] I did not know such a motion had been made toward turning me out, but I was afraid the brethren should speak too earnest for me against Bro. Rowland having my place, lest that would heighten his prejudice against them, but as Bro. John Belcher had so caused a breach by carrying a railing accusation to Bro. Rowland, and as the Lord had showed me that he was puffed up, I could not labour with him till he should be humbled, and as to Bro. B. Thomas, as he had condemned my doctrine and preached against me, and I having had burdens about his conduct long ago which I did bear with, hoping the Lord would convince him, I could not labour with him till I should see him humbled too. This occasioned a fresh commotion and I insisted on it because it was on my conscience.

Then we went to breakfast, after the accounts were read. I prayed and exhorted the brethren and was enabled to satisfy them about everything. How when their love was lost and their hearts were open to receive accusations against me, how many [stories] they had heard to increase their jealousies: that I loved the Moravians more than them and that I preached so as to blacken their preaching, but they had power to believe me now, and if they were humbled before the Lord for their sin, I had freedom to come again to them ... the brethren that had accused me, Bros. John Belcher and Price and Davies, came to me after we had parted and they fell on my neck and the offending brethren desired me to forgive which I most readily did and owned I could not stand before humiliation, and then we were all set at liberty and rejoiced with unspeakable joy.

I settled to meet with Bro. Rowland a fortnight hence. I reproved them for not showing care about my brethren at Bristol, the £25, but such a storm and so much of the hatred of the devil against me I never saw before ... The Lord indeed gave me a fresh commission and reinstated me in my place.[16]

Howell Harris wrote these notes whilst in the middle of the ferment of these events, and with his spirit still warm within him. It is difficult to gauge to what extent his own feelings coloured his account. Unfortunately, it is only his own words, almost exclusively, that he relates; he provides very little indications of how he was answered. We may imagine his profound disturbance on the way to the Association when he first heard the rumours that were circulating; his head-on attack, having arrived at the meeting, on the gathered brethren, accusing them of attempting to supplant him in his absence, of sinning against his ministry, and blackening his character; his declaration that he would not submit to being ruled by Daniel Rowland, and to be sent from place to place according to arrangement; and his refusing to allow the content of his preaching to be determined by others.

He was a man of strong feelings, and his roaring from the floor of the Association must have been terrifying to the fraternity. Most probably, he hardly allowed them to make any kind of defence and certainly they would not have been allowed to refer to any fault they saw in him, even when he, in full flow, was denouncing their own failures. At last, after many of the exhorters had declared afresh their trust in him and, probably, after Daniel Rowland and the other two clergymen had assured him that the rumours he had heard were not true, they succeeded in quietening him. At the same time, there was probably some foundation to these stories. In that many of the Glamorganshire exhorters were very opposed to Harris's doctrinal views, with many of his meetings in that county terminating in fierce argument and bitter spirits, it is quite probable that the

Association judged that it would be better under the circumstances for him not to visit Glamorganshire so often but to concentrate his labours on Carmarthenshire.

There are unmistakable signs by now that Harris and Rowland were envious of one another. Both were men of strong character; both, it would appear, loved to rule, and their followers, almost certainly, were stoking the fires. Unfortunately Rowland's papers are not available, so that we cannot give the history as he saw it. But it is natural to suppose that Harris's increasing influence over the exhorters, together with the promotion he had received on being appointed over the English societies, had produced a degree of envy in the bosom of the man from Llangeitho, particularly as he must have been conscious that he possessed greater ministerial gifts than his friend. On the other hand, we believe that there are clear indications, even from his own account of the Neath Association, that Harris was demanding a lordship and supremacy over the Methodists. He accuses the brethren of holding an Association when he was absent, as if his presence was an essential necessity for such a meeting. He refers to his 'place' as a general Superintendent, as if he stood above Rowland and Williams, Pantycelyn, and Howell Davies, whereas in the first years he held himself in submission to them, because they were ordained men and he a layman.

It appears that when he proclaimed that he would not collaborate with certain brethren, he presumed that he could shake off from the fraternity whomsoever he wished, not excluding Rowland himself. He was confirmed in this spirit by his belief that he was in direct communion with heaven and therefore bound to be correct in all particulars, and those therefore who opposed him to be in error.

He would not enter into debate upon his doctrinal views; he saw them as a revelation he had received from the Lord. All who dared to see things differently were carnal. He believed further that it was according to God's voice that he planned his journeys, arranged the circumstances of his home, organized the societies, and decided upon the best means to advance the revival. As a consequence he saw no need to confer with anybody over anything; all should submit to his arrangements, because they were divine arrangements. Yet it must be added that his conscientiousness in all things is undeniable. He was, to a considerable degree, without egotism. If he wished for the highest seat, it was not that he might feed his vanity but as an advantage for carrying forward the work of the Lord more effectively. In energy, effort, and willingness to spend and be spent for Jesus' sake he surpassed all his brethren.

Howell Harris returned from the Association, passing through Llansamlet and Blaenllywel, preaching in many places on the way. He noted in his journal:

> O Lord, may the brethren be humbled before thee. O dear Father, I cannot be willing to give up the crown which thou didst give me in this work. But I bring the brethren before thee; grant that they may recognize their place, and bow to thy Spirit.

## A HAPPIER ASSOCIATION AT WATFORD

After being at home at Trefeca for about a fortnight, he set out for Watford, to the Association, and the appointed conference with Daniel Rowland. At Gelligaer, on the way, he wrote:

> I loved Bro. Rowland; I felt that I could never leave him, though he was willing to leave me; but as for the other brother – Benjamin Thomas – he remains a burden upon me, and I prayed that the Lord might humble him.

He arrived at the Association in the afternoon. At first, all were very quiet, as if they were frightened of each other. Then Harris opened his heart, declaring that the brethren had sinned against him by harbouring suspicions of him and envy of the doctrines he taught and of his warmth when preaching. Rowland confessed that he had been at fault in reading too many letters of complaint against him, and that he felt quite free towards Harris and his ministry, as long as he denied the particular views of the Moravians. Harris replied that he had never endorsed them; that he had preached against them in London, and against the Antinomians by name. Then, they opened their hearts to one another and found that they agreed in all things. Daniel Rowland preached and had a powerful service. Harris was delighted at the doctrine. 'I had peace in my soul; I saw that Bro. Rowland had one gift, and myself another.' This meeting was probably at Groes-wen, for we read that after the sermon they proceeded to Watford. Harris walked with Morgan John Lewis. The fellowship between them was sweet, and he shared all his thoughts with him. They all remained in conversation until five o'clock in the morning. 'We understand one another,' wrote Harris, 'our latest union is the clearest and best that we have ever had.' The next morning, Harris spoke to them again, explaining how they had all fallen into sin; describing how he hated Antinomianism, and that he was one with his brethren in all matters. He referred to the accusation against him that he spoke too respectfully of the Moravians, and stated that this must arise from the grace within him, in that he was very opposed to them on many points. He then left for Rhiwderyn, where he preached on the glory of Christ. At St Bride's, his text was, 'For he shall save his people from their sins.'

He reached the home of a Robert Evans, near to Caerleon, on the Saturday, and preached with warmth and power from the words, 'For this purpose the Son of God was manifested that he might destroy the works of the devil.' His meditations on the Sunday morning show that he was not completely healed of the hurt that he had received:

> I see that our latest distress has led each one to recognize better his own place, and to study more of church government. I see that my place is to be free, to look after the societies that I have gathered, except they refuse me. I see that many of the brethren despise me, and are pained by my weaknesses, but I receive strength to commit all to the Lord, and to ask him to keep me in my place.

We find him next passing through Llanvaches and New Inn. In the latter place, in a private society, he took the opportunity to explain the difference between the Methodists and the Dissenters. He said:

> 1. We preach mainly to the heart and the spirit and we reach them, wounding the flesh and causing it pain. We emphasize faith in the heart rather than light in the head. Their light comes from the head, it eases the soul and does not strengthen faith.

> 2. We disturb the soul to its depths, carrying conviction to its core, giving further knowledge through Christ's Spirit. They leave the soul quiet and undisturbed.

> 3. They do not search the heart and show their faith, which they have in doctrine, as it works in action.

> 4. They are not free from the tendency to draw souls towards them (from the Methodists). Someone once claimed that the societies had the right to ask whom they wished to come to preach to them. I answered that I was against forcing any to receive someone against their will, but if they considered that I was the instrument that drew them together at the first, and if they had taken up the order established by Mr Whitefield, in consultation with the brethren, that I must as a father watch over them, and that I must also know, and give my consent concerning those with whom I will be co-labouring. With a view to the exhorters also, that I must watch over them, call them together to counsel, strengthen, and rebuke them, and also to have them preach on probation.

It is clear that he would not allow any autonomy to the societies.

At Goetre, the next day, the theme of his meditations is again the appropriate form of church government for the Methodists in Wales, and his place amongst them. He wrote:

I wish to know the nature and extent of the place in which the Lord has settled me, so that I might not sin hereafter, either through fear or the opposite, but fill it as the Saviour desires me, for the edification of the lambs. I see that we are led to be to some degree similar to Episcopacy and Presbyterianism, with Bro. Whitefield as archbishop; myself, although I am not ordained, even as Paul was not for a period, having been taught to be a general Superintendent over the labourers and flock; and the ordained clergy as evangelists, to preach everywhere. But one thing is unclear to me. Perhaps it remains dark in that we do not know how the movement will end, and possibly we will be grafted into the Church, and light will be given as the circumstances change. That which is unclear to me is, Are the clergymen and myself to be equal in our care for the societies and in the preaching? Or, Does the work in private belong more appropriately to me, with them assisting? Or again, Should an area of the country be given to each one? Or once more, Are we to proceed as we are at present until we shall be forced out, or received into the Church? However, I feel the care of the societies which I have been instrumental in gathering together, and those that have chosen me to watch over them, to weigh upon me in such a way that I cannot give them up. Lord, I do not know anything; show me what is necessary for the present time that I might not wander to the left or the right.

Hitherto, the work in Wales has been divided up for all, but it is evident that we need to come to some order. It is good that the government is upon thy shoulder, O Lord. I need to know the will of my Lord that I might not sin against him. I think that we are being led to some kind of discipline. Lord, go before us. I think that the work of the clergymen would be to go about preaching, and to administer the sacraments, be present at the Associations, and serve communion at them. My work would be to go to the Associations, speak there, preach when I can, visit all the private societies and the Monthly Meetings as far as I can, in Wales and in England, even though the care of London is also placed upon me. What else pertains to me, I do not yet know. With a view to our relationship, the one to the other, Lord lead and enlighten me.

It is seen that a plan of church government is beginning to form in Harris's mind. It is clear also that this plan would shut the clergymen out from any direct control over the societies and the exhorters. Harris considered this a right that belonged to himself, and he limited the clergymen, mainly, to the ministry of the Word and the administering of the sacraments. Goetre was the last place he visited on this journey before returning home. The first thing he heard on arriving at Trefeca was that Rowland was continuing to accuse him of departing from true doctrine. It was one of the exhorters who brought him this tale. It is not unlikely that Harris was too ready to receive such groundless stories. He decided to ignore it, however, so that no division might result. On 1 November, a Monthly Meeting was held at Trefeca but not one of the clergymen was present.

Beaumont delivered a sermon in which he declared that the law was not to be preached as a means of convicting and awakening sinners – that what should be preached was faith. He said that the law was not the rule of life for the believer and he also denied the eternal generation of Christ. It appears that Beaumont was by now a complete Antinomian. They stayed down for most of the night trying to reason with him, but in vain. After Beaumont had left, Harris and about fifty of the exhorters remained until the morning praying, singing and praising, and they felt that the Lord was truly amongst them.

About the middle of November there was a Monthly Meeting at Tyddyn and Harris attended, preaching in various places in Breconshire and Radnorshire along the way. Williams, Pantycelyn, was present and preached with much power. A man from Bala had arrived to ask advice because Bro. Lewis Evan had been thrown into Dolgelley prison. He was directed what action to take, and a collection of four guineas was immediately taken up to assist him, though only thirty men were present altogether.

They felt thankful for the imprisonment, in that it gave them an opportunity to show some sign of their love and affection. Harris said that they all must make an effort against the devil in north Wales. He referred to his own position: that he was not in any man's debt in the world but only a debtor to the Lord; that he often refused money as an acknowledgement for his work, in that he was not at liberty to receive it, other than when it was given in faith, being considered an honour to be able to give to the Lord. They also conversed with a man who denied the doctrine of the blood. Harris said that he himself received and felt the doctrine and that it was to be found in the Bible, not figuratively, but substantially and spiritually.

During December, Harris went on two journeys through parts of Glamorganshire and Carmarthenshire. On the last day of the year he was at Llanddowror, in conference with the Rev. Griffith Jones. He was greatly encouraged on hearing of the intention to establish catechizing schools in every part of the land, should the Archbishop, together with the bishops and clergymen, be willing. He said that the Methodists were ready to assist in this, and to submit to the Bishop; that they were determined not to leave the Church; and he explained the degree to which catechizing had been introduced into the private societies. He earnestly pleaded for

Griffith Jones to unite with them, so that crafty men might not divide them by carrying lying tales of one party to the other. Fellowship with the godly vicar of Llanddowror was balm to his soul.

[1] A traditional New Year's Day gift.
[2] CMHO, pp. 129-30.
[3] Ibid., p. 130.
[4] Ibid., pp. 130-2.
[5] Ibid., p. 134.
[6] Transcribed by Eifion Evans.
[7] CH 25, p. 20 ff.; HHVP, p. 119-20.
[8] CH 31, p. 58.
[9] Ibid.
[10] CH 31, pp. 86-88
[11] CH 31, pp. 88-90.
[12] Ibid.
[13] CH 25, p. 22.
[14] Ibid.
[15] CH 37, p. 57.
[16] CH 31, pp. 91-5.

# 14

# HOWELL HARRIS (1747–8)

## VARIOUS ASSOCIATIONS

On the first day of 1747, Howell Harris was preaching in Haverfordwest, Pembrokeshire. After the sermon he conferred with the Moravian ministers, who had by this time established a cause in the town. He thought it might be wise to set up a meeting between the Moravians and the Methodists so as to remove any stumbling blocks. It was not that he intended that there should be any union between them but that both sides should consider one another more lovingly. The next day he was at Longhouse, and in the evening at St David's, where an enormous congregation had gathered. He continued through Felindre, Llechryd, and Ty'r Yet, reaching Newcastle Emlyn, where a Quarterly Association was being held, on a Wednesday. The meeting was opened by a sermon from Williams, Pantycelyn, and then Harris preached, mainly on the state of the nation, both politically and spiritually. It was a happy Association throughout. Harris felt that his spirit was united with those of his brethren forever. Various matters were discussed, such as catechizing; the duty of the societies to confer with the leaders before receiving anyone to preach amongst them; the need to refuse entrance to all but members to the private society. After reading the reports – amongst which was a reference to the society house that had been built at Llansawel – and after arranging the following Association, they departed in sweet fellowship. No mention is made of Daniel Rowland or Howell Davies; they were probably both absent. Harris commented, 'I believe that I see great things drawing near, after the late storm and distress which, I hope, is well nigh over.'

He returned through Maesnonni, Llangamarch and Llansanffraid. In the last place he had a remarkable escape:

> In the private society, we were upstairs, about two hundred of us, when the main beam broke so that we all fell down. Not a bone was broken amongst us. There was a small child in a cot beneath everything, but a floorboard fell over the cot so that nothing touched the baby; indeed, it did not wake from sleep. Had it happened five minutes earlier, many would have been injured.

He went with Mr Williams, the vicar of Llansanffraid, to the church, where he heard an excellent sermon. After preaching himself – a remarkably solemn sermon – he returned home.

The next week there was a Monthly Association at Trefeca. It was opened by a sermon by Harris from the words, 'Hitherto have ye asked nothing in my name, etc.'

> I truly had the Spirit with me. I explained to them the nature of justification; the way in which we are just through the righteous of Christ; gentle in his gentleness; and obedient in his obedience. I showed how we have no righteousness of ourselves; and how far we can go in grace, and yet be greatly ignorant of the death and righteousness of Christ. Indeed, the veil was rent today, and many saw themselves as complete in this dress.

Clearly, Harris did not cleave closely to his text, but felt at liberty to depart from it and take up any truth that he considered profitable at the time. After the sermon there was a general society for all members. It seems to have been an unforgettable meeting; the divine influences filled the place. In the warmth of his emotions, Harris cried out:

> You who are able to leave, go. We do not wish for any here except those who feel constrained to come. If you have not been born from above, if you are not of those who must pray and must be zealous for your salvation, keep away. But you cannot keep away; you must come; for the Lord is God, and everything must give way. O, how many things are drawing you forward! The covenant cries, 'They must come!' The blood cries, 'They must come!' So also grace and the promises.

It is evident that God's fire descended, and that Harris's heart burned within him. In the Association, no decisions of major importance were made, but the Reformer encouraged the exhorters, with all solemnity, to set up catechizing in every place and to exhort the members to familiarize themselves with the Scriptures.

At the end of the week, Harris set out for a journey of some weeks through Somerset, Devon and Cornwall, and on the way over to England he preached in many places in Glamorganshire and Monmouthshire. On the first evening he was at Blaentawe, and as he crossed over the mountains he meditated upon the Scriptures and felt that God was his companion. This quiet meditation had softened and prepared his spirit for the service. His topic was the gospel as the power of God unto salvation, and he had much liberty. The next morning he preached at Gellidochlaethe, and in the evening at Neath. Here, the society was in considerable disorder and contained some of Arminian views, a system that Harris could not endure. He spoke strongly to the members, stating that they must choose between one party or the other, that they could not belong to both. He then explained the doctrine of election and answered objections. 'Why does God require of us to turn, if we do not have the ability to turn?' asked one opposer. He replied, 'If we have lost the ability to obey, the Lord has not lost his right to command.' He explained further that God gave the law to man to convict him, to show him that he was lost and under condemnation. Afterwards, he described his own position, the way in which the Lord and the brethren had placed him in his office as general Superintendent over the societies and exhorters; but fearing ambition, he had not used his authority, and he commanded them that they refuse to allow any to exhort amongst them unless they had been authorized to do so. He believed that, under God's blessing, he had been instrumental in avoiding a division at Neath.

He next visited Hafod and Nottage. In the latter place, he declared his view that the Methodists, Wesleyans, and Moravians, would be united to the Established Church. Certainly, the wish was father to the thought. Next day, he was at a place called New Furnace-on-Taff. He wrote that in the private society Satan raised up opposition to the doctrine of the mystery of the blood, through the person of a private exhorter. Harris rebuked him but as the man remained obstinate, he had to turn him out. On the following day was a Monthly Association at New Inn, Monmouthshire. He spoke fully on his position as general Superintendent; on his decision not to leave the Church of England, though he loved the Dissenters; he exhorted them to maintain discipline in families, and for all to recognize their place.

> After I had done, I had a trial from Bro. Morgan John Lewis, as [I had] last night from another brother, that I imposed on them and kept them in bondage, that all that opposed or contradicted me were reckoned dark or the devil, that I had no rule from the Word for what I did, and that the discipline about giving up ourselves to Christ and his Church was from the Moravians. He said that he sided with Rowland. Mr Powell backed him up again and said I had some prejudice against Mr Edmund Jones. Then much confusion arose.[1]

What his answer was to Morgan John Lewis, we do not know, but there must have been much unhappiness, 'There was much heat present, and Satan came down.' Matters seem to have calmed down later and various affairs settled peacefully.

He continued through Bristol, where an Association was held; Bath; Wellington; Exeter; Kingsbridge; Plymouth; and St Gennis in Cornwall. The journey lasted five weeks and for much of it John Wesley accompanied him.[2] He was only three days at home on his return, before departing for the Monthly Association at Builth Wells. Many exhorters had gathered there, together with two clergymen and the godly gentleman, Mr Marmaduke Gwynne. Harris grieved because Antinomianisn was on the increase in the area. 'I examined a preacher,' he wrote, 'and we settled outward affairs about the house.' This 'house' was Alpha Chapel, which is often, but wrongly, referred to as the first chapel of the Methodists in Wales. It was, rather, their first chapel in Breconshire. He then visited Tyddyn, where he spent the Sunday. Whether there was some kind of Association here, we do not know, but he and the brethren decided to set the following Wednesday as a day of prayer for Lewis Evan, who was still in prison. He prayed earnestly for north Wales, that the word of the Lord might run; he saw that all the opposition was in reality against God. Next day, he was at Bridgend, Radnorshire, and was very severe in the private society against lukewarm believers:

I showed the duty of giving all that we possess to the Lord, and having all things in common; and the way in which the Lord had behaved towards them, and themselves towards him. I gave them my history, that for years I have been travelling fifty miles a day but that they will not come a few miles to the meeting for fear of catching cold. I declared I would turn out of the societies all as would absent themselves [from] two societies, let them be who they will (God's house shall not be slighted thus) . . . We have received a message from God, and although we do not call ourselves bishops, priests or deacons, yet we are the ministers of the Lord. God knows us. [I was then] cutting to them about their not having a house here to meet, showing them that the least they could do, many of them, would be to give £5 or £10. Many were humbled and broken and affected and recovered, and said, 'I am the man', and a few proposed to meet and to build a house.[3]

Two points are worth noting from this account:

1. That chapels had been built in quite a number of places by the Methodists, so that Harris felt able to rebuke the society at Bridgend- a rural area in Radnorshire – for not doing so themselves.

2. We have here, for the first time, a suggestion of that practice, which Harris acted upon afterwards at Trefeca, that Christians should hold no personal possessions but have everything in common.

The following day, Howell Harris hurried to Trefeca, where a Monthly Meeting was held. He opened the conference with a sermon on the words, 'When I am weak, then am I strong.' He says that this was a dreadful place to him, standing between the living and the dead.

I was severe towards the Dissenters and all carnal believers, showing that they were all angry against me because I rebuked them, but that it was in love I did so, and that if it were in my power, I would raise them from the dust. I showed that we are complete in Christ, secure in Christ, and more than conquerors in him.

In the private society that followed, the Lord came down, and Harris was given things old and new to declare. He showed that they could no longer return, they had to go forward. In the Association, no new resolutions were passed; the time was spent listening to Harris's report of the success of the work in England.

At the beginning of March he went to London, and stayed there until Easter. He had hardly returned before he set out for the Quarterly Association at Watford. On the Friday before the Association he preached at Goetre, Monmouthshire, and in the private society there he treated the members very severely:

> I showed them how opposed in spirit they had been to my ministry from the beginning; how lazy they were, that they would not come three miles distance from New Inn to our general meeting, so that therefore they did all they could to hinder the work. That they absented themselves from the Church and departed from its communion, whereas it is clear that the Lord has called us to this; and that they weakened my hands more than any. I said that, unless they moved forward, that I would not come amongst them; that I could not come where the doctrine of the blood, and the blood itself, through the Spirit, was not allowed to run freely. If the doctrine is a burden to you, I said, in one sense it is to me also, because, as God is my judge, I cannot refrain from preaching it. I did not receive it from man or woman, but from God; I have had it for seven years. I said that this would be my last visit unless I saw a change. I then spoke sweetly on the blood, and the Spirit came down, and we were very tender.

The Goetre society was very near to that of New Inn, where Morgan John Lewis ministered, and who greatly objected to Harris's particular doctrines. This explains the strong opposition the Reformer from Trefeca encountered there. It is a significant fact that Harris on this occasion did not visit New Inn.

He went to Llanheiddel on the Saturday, and spent the Sunday in the home of Robert Evans, near Caerleon. He preached at Llanvaches on Monday and was again severe towards those present. He arrived at Watford on the night before the Association, and heard various news and rumours that grieved him deeply. He did not know how to act in that a certain exhorter had been brought there whom he had turned out because his spirit was not sympathetic to the Methodists. There was also present a Dissenting minister who, against Harris's wishes, was visiting the societies. In his grief, he retired to pray. The Lord shone upon him while he was on his knees. He returned to the brethren, and after discussion much of his load was lifted. He then went to Groes-wen to hear Daniel Rowland preach. The text was Hebrews 6:7 and the service was greatly blessed. Harris felt a deep affection for his dear brother as he listened – deeper indeed than ever.

The first resolution of the Association was the appointment of three of the brethren to assist Howell Harris in his work as Superintendent, namely, Benjamin Thomas, the Dissenting minister, Thomas Jones and Thomas Williams. The last was Thomas Williams, Groes-wen, and this appointment proves that he had committed himself again to the Methodists completely. A degree of agitation and disagreement arose amongst the brethren with reference to the exhorter whom Harris had excommunicated. Although it is not definitely stated, the journal suggests that the sentence was not confirmed. In an interval between sessions, Harris had a long private conversation with Rowland, and it seems that they were warm in their affection for one another. According to Harris:

> The Lord took away the unbearable burdens that were weighing upon me. I had liberty to tell all the brethren that which I thought was error amongst them, and the way in which we should strengthen one another's hands. The clergymen and myself should tell one another the things we hear, otherwise we will lose all authority. I had strength to rebuke the pride of the brethren, showing that courage, wisdom, faithfulness and tenderness be always amongst us, and that everyone should recognize their place. I found a cry in me that the Lord should come amongst us. After deciding many things, and arranging the brethren's journeys, we departed sweetly after having once been brought to the edge of separation.

At the end, Daniel Rowland preached from the words, 'Is there no balm in Gilead?' At first, Harris was dry, but when the preacher began to speak of Christ's blood, though he only said a little on the point, his spirit was stirred. He saw in himself a mountain of self, and a world of pride, but he saw also that he would be freed from all, as it is the Lord who is King. 'I find that preaching experience does not feed me, but when the Man Christ is spoken of, then I am fed.' His next words are hard to understand:

> I mentioned to Bro. Williams that he is legalistic and deficient in doctrine, with a veil over his eyes. But on seeing the Lord with him, and himself so simple, I was made thankful for all the gifts given to each of us.

Williams, Pantycelyn, deficient in doctrine! We are used to consider him as almost the pre-eminent of theologians. One who, as by some spiritual instinct within him, discerned divine truths that the philosophical theologians, with all their reasoning, had failed to reach. We imagine also that he of all the Methodist Reformers was the one who was nearest in his views in those doctrines with respect to the two natures in the Person of our Lord for which Harris was long criticized. We find in his hymns many of those expressions that the Reformer from Trefeca was blamed for using. Yet, here we have Harris accusing him of doctrinal deficiency and of being blind. We have no explanation for this; we must take the journal as it is.[4]

On Saturday, he went to St Nicholas, where he had a sweet service. At the close, he had a conversation with one of the private exhorters, William Harry, with regard to strengthening the unity between himself and Daniel Rowland. The exhorter perceived that a division between the two leaders would be devastating to the societies. He next visited Aberthin, where he spoke strictly, explaining how it would be worse for those who did not obey the gospel than for pagans. On Saturday night, he arrived at Llantrisant, and preached on the same theme as at Aberthin. In the private society that followed he did his best to unite the members. He encouraged them to set up catechizing. On Sunday morning, he went to the church where he was encouraged by a good sermon, and afterwards, in the sacrament, he experienced great sweetness. On Monday, he was at Hafod where he spoke on the nature of the work that God had now been carrying out in Wales for over ten years. He advised those who communicated in the Dissenting chapels to continue doing so and, similarly, for those who took communion in the churches to remain there. He reminded them of the way the Apostles remained in the Jewish Church, though they had the same reasons for turning their backs on it as had the Methodists for leaving the Church of England.

He proceeded on to Neath. On the way, he saw that God was infinite; infinite in his perfections; infinite in his truth; infinite in his love, so that there is nothing anywhere that can be compared to him. At Neath, he met a religious sister who intended to remarry and who claimed that she had received an answer from the Lord that was different from that which Harris had received. This weighed him down, causing him to call upon the Lord, 'Why hast thou placed me in this position?' But he was quietened in his mind, recognizing that it was the Lord who had ordained his place and had given him the necessary qualifications, and all for his own glory. He preached with great liberty on Galatians 6:1. He explained the privilege of following Christ. He thundered against lying, showing that the eternal covenant was opposed to sin of every kind. In the private society he laid certain conclusions before them and exhorted them to discipline. He went on Tuesday to hear Daniel Rowland, somewhere near Neath:

Bro. Rowland preached gloriously today on the unity of believers; he showed the necessity for them to agree in love, and for each one to know his place, and remain in it, so that the reed might not consider itself a cedar, nor the snail imagine itself an elephant. I enjoyed him greatly; I was made to rejoice because of him; and I felt the greatest unity with him, desiring to live and die with him. Uncommon power accompanied the word; souls were filled with the Lord, and balmy breezes blew upon us.

After the meeting Harris went to visit a sick brother who was full of faith. Then Rowland and he travelled together to Glanyrafonddu, a distance of twenty-five miles. It seems that Williams, Pantycelyn, was of the company.

Had freedom to tell Bro. Rowland of the union I feel toward him; that we should be one so as to strengthen one another's hands and to maintain authority. I hoped that he would assist in this. I referred also to the need for discipline. He was strongly against the doctrine of the witness of the Spirit, and pained at Mr Griffith Jones. I succeeded in moderating him on both matters. Other things were discussed, such as, my call to preach; the Urim and the Thummim, etc.

The next day, after reaching Glanyrafonddu, he wrote again:

Yesterday, when journeying with Bro. Rowland, I had much liberty, but I see that much work has yet to be done by the Lord. I spoke of the holiness of the work; of our disorder, of our lack of discipline, our party spirit; and of our need to agree in private on all things so that we go amongst souls with one voice. I showed how the work is to be carried out among us, and I believe it will be somewhat between the Presbyterian and Episcopalian way. [I spoke] of Bro. Wesley coming into our field of labour, and of deciding a place for each one. We discussed of the war, and of the cry in my soul that I might leave a blessing behind me wherever I went. I spoke home to him and Bro. Williams with a view to their levity, that they might be careful, so that I might rebuke the other brethren, who would otherwise run to hide in their example; and that they would allow me my place in the private work, which belongs to my place and office.[5]

We have space to comment only on one point in this account, namely the levity of which Rowland and Williams, Pantycelyn, were accused. We have no evidence at all to believe that they were frivolous or light men, in the usual meaning of the words. They lived too much in the company of the profound truths of the gospel to practise any frivolity. It rather seems that they were naturally of sunny tempers, able to enjoy healthy laughter and see the humorous side of various circumstances. Howell Harris, on the other hand, was so extremely solemn and serious that every appearance of humour, however innocent, seemed to him to border on the sinful. The friends separated at Glanyrafonddu and Harris turned towards home, preaching on the way at Llanddeusant and Cefn-y-fedw. He was only two days at Trefeca before setting out again on a journey to Montgomeryshire. The exhorter, William Evans, was with him, it seems, as a companion. They passed through Tyn-y-cwm and Llansanffraid in Radnorshire and arrived at Mochdre. He preached there in Welsh and English to many simple people, who had begun to gather to hear the gospel. His text was Matthew 11:28. He wrote:

> I had great liberty and much power to invite them to Christ. I showed that they could not be saved through their works, and that if they trusted in their works they were idolaters, and the love of God was not in them.

After the sermon a private society was held. The Reformer spoke on the blood of Christ. God came to the place, and they were there until three in the morning, singing, praising, and exhorting. Harris kept crying out, 'The blood! The blood! THE BLOOD!' until his voice was drowned by the shouts of the other exhorters present. From here he went to Llanfair where he spoke on pride and had a powerful meeting. He was next at Llanbryn-mair, and as he preached there on the blood of Christ, the Holy Spirit came down powerfully. He showed that it was God's blood, and that there was an absolute necessity for it. He then expanded on the divinity of Christ, and there was no one present to oppose the doctrine. In the private society following, in that many were present from Anglesey and Caernarvonshire, he explained the nature of the societies; the discipline of the Methodists; together with the history of how he began to go about preaching. He described further the difference between themselves and the Dissenters, how that:

1. They were different in doctrine, as many of the Dissenters were Baxterians.

2. They were different in discipline, in that the Methodists were part of the Established Church.

3. They were different in spirit.

He was next at Blaen Trefeglwys, where he preached from 1 John 5:4, 'For whatsoever is born of God overcometh the world.' He had an uncommonly powerful service. God came down so evidently that the preacher had to stop because his voice was drowned by the cries of the congregation. He journeyed from there to Tyddyn and heard of some dear brother of an exhorter who had fallen in some way and was to be turned out. Harris's heart was smitten by the news. He drew near to the throne of grace in order to know the Lord's mind on the matter, and the answer he received was that the glory of God and purity of the discipline required that the rebuke be administered, and that it would be the means of restraining sin and Satan. Many from Anglesey, Caernarvonshire and Merionethshire were again at Tyddyn; indeed, it seems that they were following him throughout the journey. In the private society after the sermon, he took advantage of their presence to inform them of various matters:

> I went to the private society of I believe four or five hundred members[6] . . . I placed before them the matter of the house in Carmarthenshire; the lawsuit; and bearing fruit for the Spirit, namely, pre-eminently, humility. I said that we must be victorious, whether we win the action or not, for God is with us. I exhorted them also to discipline, showing that if there was only six in the society, that this was enough to go forward in the Lord, and that he would add to them. After preaching, I was with the preachers; I saw my place and that the Lord had given me light and gifts to fill it. Then, after praying, we departed sweetly from the lambs of the three far-flung counties.

'The house in Carmarthenshire' is probably a reference to Llansawel Chapel. Which lawsuit he is referring to is not known – the poor Methodists were being persecuted continually in some court or other at that period. He travelled from here to Dôl-y-felin and Builth Wells, arriving home after an absence of nine days. He noted that remarkable influences had accompanied his ministry during this journey. At Builth Wells there had been a Monthly Meeting with four to five hundred members present.

In the week following there was a Monthly Meeting at Merthyr Cynog. The exhorter, Beaumont, came to Trefeca a day early and Harris told him of the matters that needed correcting in the society under his care, referring particularly to the arguments and jealousies among them. They agreed on two points, namely that each one was free to preach the message in his own way, as long as he did so in all simplicity; and secondly, that what was all-important in a sermon was that the Lord should be in it. They travelled together to the Association. On the way, Beaumont argued that the only purpose of the law is to explain the wretchedness of the sinner; that no one should be exhorted to live virtuously according to the commandments of the law, but that all should be directed to Christ. Harris answered that this doctrine savoured of Antinomianism. At Merthyr, Harris sought to reconcile some religious members who had quarrelled, but in vain. The Association was begun with a sermon from Williams, Pantycelyn, on the foolish virgins. Harris grieved because there was so little of Christ in the sermon. He thought it legalistic. He was comforted, however, in believing that the preacher was in God's hands, and that he would lead him into all truth. After the service, Harris rebuked the preacher for some legalistic phrases that he had used, but Williams did not receive the rebuke humbly. Instead, with rising temper, he said that he loved all, and was concerned as to the means he used in order to drive them from their sins.

Harris feasted his soul in listening to Morgan John Lewis preaching on the mystery of salvation in Christ. He showed that Christ did nothing as God, and nothing as man, but everything as Emmanuel; he explained how Christ had declared in past eternity, 'Lo, I come to do thy will, O God'; and the way in which the Lamb had been slain from before the foundation of the world; he said that not only our guilt was laid upon him, but also our iniquities. 'I had more unity with him than ever,' wrote Harris, 'I could not but love him.' The two travelled together lovingly to Trefeca, and Harris opened his heart to his friend, emphasizing the need for more unity between them, and the necessity of understanding one another before going before the people.

There are many references in the journal to the work of the two Wesleys in entering into the field of labour of the Methodists in Wales. It seems that John Wesley had preached in Cardiff and Neath, and possibly some other places in the Principality, during the year 1746, and the Welsh brethren feared that there would be two parties of Methodists in Wales, with one undermining the other. In order to come to an agreement on this, John Wesley was invited to an Association held at Bristol towards the end of January 1747, and the decision arrived at is important and interesting. In the Association records we read:

It was feared, because Mr Wesley had preached in Neath that the result would be a division in the society. Mr Wesley replied, 'I do not intend to set up a society at Neath, nor in any other place in Wales where there is a society already, but to do all I can to oppose any division.' And we have all agreed that whenever we preach amongst one another's people, that we will do our best, not to weaken, but to strengthen one another's hands, and that particularly by endeavouring to frustrate any divisions. And as one division had occurred in the west of England, it was agreed that the brother who came with Mr Wesley should go there with Mr Harris, to seek to heal the wound, and to encourage the people to love. It was agreed also to protect carefully one another's character.

We have to do with that section of these decisions that relate to Wales. Certainly, John Wesley kept faithfully to this agreement, and this is the reason why Wesleyanism did not make an appearance in the Principality until the beginning of the next century. The two wings of the Methodist army, though having differed and divided over some important doctrines, yet felt that they sprang from the same fountainhead, were ruled by the same spirit, and were too closely bound with one another to set up opposing societies.

In the middle of May, Howell Harris set out for London and was there for nearly two months. A mere two days after returning he was called to attend the Quarterly Association at Cil-y-cwm. His journal states that the meeting was held at the 'New House', which proves that a Methodist chapel had been built here. The conference was opened by a sermon by Peter Williams on the text, 'O how I love thy law,' and according to Harris he preached wonderfully. Harris felt that here was a message from the Lord to himself, his soul was melted within him, and though the sermon contained some legalistic phrases, he felt grateful that God had such a man to stand up for him. 'I had the witness within myself,' he wrote, 'that God had come to the camp against Satan and sin, so that we were sure of the victory.' After much persuasion, Harris agreed to preach and had a very happy meeting. It appears to have been a very happy conference throughout. He comments in the journal:

> We were happy and loving and decided upon many things tending to better discipline, completely united, which we had failed to agree on before. We strengthened one another's hands, and arranged rules concerning marriages. We had great pleasure in singing and praying; and it was sweet that the Lord gave us a rest amidst a great storm.

From the Association, Harris went to Cefncoed, where Williams, Pantycelyn, lived at the time. The next morning, Thomas Williams of Groes-wen preached, and Harris after him. His content was the blood of Christ, its virtue, glory, and infinity, and he adds that Bro. Williams, Pantycelyn, was amongst the hearers. After the service, Howell Harris and Thomas Williams travelled together to Trefeca and had sweet fellowship along the way.

## VISITS TO LONDON, SOUTH WALES AND NORTH WALES

In July, Harris set out on a long journey through Carmarthenshire, Cardiganshire and Pembrokeshire. He first preached in the main street at Builth Wells to a vast crowd of people. 'A fountain opened to the house of David and to the inhabitants of Jerusalem', was his text, and he evangelized sweetly, inviting all to the fountain. In the private society he discussed the intention of building a meeting-house in the town. From Builth, he and Mr Gwynne went to Glanirfon, near Llanwrtyd. He judged the

congregation there to be near two thousand. The mystery of our justification and sanctification in Christ, through his being made sin for us, was
his message, and he seems to have had a powerful meeting. He then had
a twenty-mile journey to Caeo and arrived late so that the congregation
that had gathered for him was forced to disperse. He preached the next
morning however. He notes here that he had no need of preparation, nor
of a text, when preaching:

> It is the Lord who speaks. I convict, thunder, exhort, or declare that God has
> loved the world, exactly as I am directed.

This comment suggests that he took no text when speaking at Caeo.
He preached next at the new meeting-house at Llansawel, 'the fountain
opened' was again his text, and he says that he was extremely severe towards those who professed religion but who approached the Scriptures in
the light of nature. 'The Lord was evidently amongst the people,' he wrote,
'many were broken, and were blessed.' He was travelling quickly, and by
the next night had crossed the chain of hills across the north-west corner
of Carmarthenshire and had arrived at Maesnonni. He had travelled there
in the company of a young man, newly begun as a clergyman. Harris
charged him to be faithful to God and to the souls under his care, and to
confess Jesus before men, not consulting with flesh and blood. His text
at Maesnonni was Romans 7:21. Two other clergymen and an exhorter
were at the sermon and he charged them, as they should answer to God,
to preach the blood of Christ to the people. He then returned to his main
theme, the mystery of the Godhead and the mystery of Christ:

> This Man is God, there is no other God. I showed that some Christians make
> three Gods, and see the Father as above the Son.

The next day, he notes again:

> Last night, I showed that there is no God except Christ; that the Father and
> the Spirit are not other Gods, otherwise not one of them would be God; yet,
> that it is the Word, and not the Father nor the Spirit, that was made flesh. I
> showed how God became man, and died, and that his blood was the blood
> of God.

He next preached at Cwmcynon, the mystery of the blood being again
the theme. From there, he went to Pengwenallt, Llwyngrawys (where he
felt ill), and Fishguard. The meeting at this last place was very barren.
On the Sunday, a week after he left home, he was at Wolf's Castle, and
in the morning attended the church at Hayscastle, 'where now the Lord
gathers his flock to feed them by Bro. Howell Davies'. It was Davies who

ministered that morning. He preached on 'The just shall live by faith', but Harris felt hard and carnal as he listened. But at the Communion table that followed the Lord came down and made Calvary wonderfully sweet to him by the ministry of the Spirit:

> I saw more wonderfully than ever the blessings and treasure of Calvary. I am going up to him there, where sin and death are conquered. O Calvary! Calvary! This is where pardon and every blessing is to be had.

He himself preached afterwards from Ephesians 3:18 and had an unusually powerful meeting. That night he went to Longhouse where he led a private society, discussing many things, such as the pleasure of meeting Paul, Peter and David in heaven; the rewards of the faithful; and the necessity for tolerance. He then addresses his favourite theme, the mystery of Christ.

On Wednesday, a Monthly Association was held at Haverfordwest and he was present. On the way he prayed earnestly for the brethren that self might be destroyed in them and that God might be all in all, and for all to recognize his own place, and the place of others. He does not mention who was at the Association, nor does he note anything that was said, other than by himself. He began the meeting with an address in which he discussed many different points: he described the time when enlightenment on the conditional promises first shone upon him; the way in which faith, grace and work should be preached in their appropriate places; and the necessity of spiritual poverty. He was very severe when referring to pride and carelessness, and on the necessity of all remembering their place, their relationship to the body, and to the Head. It seems that some were guilty of breaking their engagements, and Harris said that they should be stopped from preaching for a year. He continued:

> I was cutting about some of the ministers [clergymen] saying I changed in my doctrine, calling me Antinomian. [We] consulted about the way of receiving in and turning out [of the society]. I see the same methods are not practicable everywhere, and we must not follow our own reasonings. I was cutting in referring to having respect of persons, and about strengthening each other's hands; how I always study this, and especially when I came here, to strengthen the ministers' hands . . . then at the room I discoursed on Matthew 8:26.[7]

After the sermon, a society was held. The exhorters sat up with Harris until two in the morning, and he comments that they were greatly blessed. He describes it as a happy Association with all present agreeing, but it must be remembered that probably none of the clergymen was present, and that Howell Harris was therefore having everything his own way. He continued through Walton-West, Llangwm, and Mounton, returning to Trefeca after a journey of sixteen days.

It is worth noting that he did not on this occasion call on Howell Davies at Parkes, though he was passing close by, nor either at Llangeitho. Although he was still co-operating with his brethren at this point, it is easy to see that his feelings towards them were cooling and that he was not longing for their company, as in previous years. With respect to the accusation of Antinomianism brought against him by one of the clergymen, perhaps there was some element of truth in it. He was too much in Beaumont's company, who had erred far in the direction of Antinomianism. When having been in his company for some time, Harris would use expressions that could not be justified, and describe the preaching of duty as being legalistic, but when freed from Beaumont's influence he would return to himself again.

In October he took a journey to north Wales. He wrote to his wife from Llanbryn-mair on 21 October. The letter has a postscript from Bala written on the following Friday, 23 October:

> We arrived here safely, and it is remarkable how the Lord has been with us. God has taken this place; we had no opposition, but everything was quiet. It is not likely that we shall be hindered further. Within twelve days I hope to see you again. We are going to Caernarvonshire and Anglesey, and then through Denbighshire and Merionethshire.

It is probable that James Beaumont was his companion on this journey. On 31 October, on the return trip, he was at Shrewsbury and writing:

> We came here last night after a journey through north Wales, where I expected to be murdered, and where the door was closed against me for several years by the wrath of the populace, and bitterness of the clergy, who were agitated all the more as the people were leaving the Church completely after hearing me. Now, the door is open, and though I have been in Bala and Caernarvonshire, where I once was in danger of my life, the enemy was chained, and I hope that much good was done. Societies were formed; many of those who had left the Church [of England] were persuaded to return and to remain within it. I was strengthened supernaturally to travel about thirty miles every day; to stay down until twelve, three and six o'clock in the morning; to arrange societies, to question souls, and to preach. O Lord, thou hast heard our prayers, and have allowed me to return. Thou hast granted me to see thy salvation coming to poor, dark north Wales. Thou hast visited the people that sat in thick Egyptian darkness. It is likely that a great work shall be done in Merionethshire, Caernarvonshire, Anglesey and Denbighshire; one could think there was a tendency to hear in the people. O, that I might be considered worthy to bear the message of the Lord.

## A STRONG LETTER TO EDMUND JONES

Before departing for the north, Harris wrote an important letter to the Rev. Edmund Jones. Though the letter is long, we feel it should be inserted fully because of its clarity, its Christian spirit, and the light it provides on various questions:

Dear brother,

I find by a letter of yours to Mr Price that I am charged with asserting things contrary to God's word, and to my own saying at other times, and not only so but asserting that it is God that gives it me immediately, and so belies the Lord. This you think is shocking and I think so too, and since I have heard it I have examined myself and summoned my conscience to do its office and can't find myself guilty, and what was this foundation, on which such a charge was founded, I can't tell, or what I could [have said] from which perhaps some good people by misapprehending me and by Satan's temptations or by my not explaining myself in my zeal at some time or other, I can't recollect, as neither having heard who my accusers are, and when and where I dropped such expressions, but if I dropped anything bordering to such a charge, I here declare I am sorry for it.

But I was surprised to find myself charged, found guilty, and as such used, and I myself never hearing one word of it. I thought dear Mr Jones would not have acted so to any, but your writing of it to another without acquainting me was perhaps with a design that I might take the reproof the kinder from another than from you. However, that was not following the rules we are to walk by. Though I am thankful (I trust I can say without dissimulation) to come at the true knowledge of my faults by any means – for I am conscious I am full of them – but if you can allow me in any sense to be employed of the Lord, allowing me according to your light to be misled, yet if you can look on me as your brother, and in some senses or other a fellow labourer, it would be well not to entertain such reports as hinder brotherly love, which I trust I can say I find in my soul for you. Though I have thought that your zeal for Independency carried you too far in some sense, to hinder the work I humbly hope the Lord has committed to me – and so have thought it my duty at some times to testify against some steps, and if I have not done it with love, humility, prudence and holy fear enough, I put this among the many, yea, innumerable things I am obliged to be humbled daily for.

Some things in our light and judgment to be sure put us at some distance from each other, but notwithstanding, I have and do (for myself) wish that all that the Lord in any measure uses may have some general times for meeting, conversing, and settling some rules to prevent coldness, prejudice, lies and weakening each another's hands.[8] With regard to the proofs you bring forward that it would be better for me to leave the Established Church, and the accusation that we intend to set ourselves up as a church, I am not happy with the one or the other. As to the last, I have never heard anything of it before. As to the first, I would be glad if you could inform me of the usefulness of any of the brethren who have left us. You acknowledge that the bulk of the people that are dying from lack of knowledge are in the Established Church, and new doors are opening to them continually within the circle of their own Church. As for the brethren who have left us, they themselves confess that they receive more of the Lord when they meet with their old friends. I do not find that they are blessed to the reawakening of the sleepy professors amongst whom they find themselves. And as we have need of help to go out against a dark and suspicious world, I cannot but believe that their circle of usefulness has been greatly confined, in that they have left the public work for one much less public.

With regard to the accusation that we refuse people to join with some Nonconformist brethren, I cannot but judge the accusation as completely unfair, for it is well-known that most Dissenting congregations, in whose neighbourhoods we have settled, have been increased and quickened through our instrumentality. According to the light we possess, it appeared to us that souls were not improving (amongst the Dissenters), and they would confess themselves that it was with us they were fed. As for others, who were lively, and throwing their souls into the work, while with us, after they had dissented, they became lukewarm and careless. Instead of increasing in spiritual life, they declined. Others were offended and kept from coming to hear us by imagining we were deceitfully claiming a relationship with the Church of England. Their prejudice was insufferable; they did their best to draw people from those places where the Holy Spirit had saved them, and fed them for many years. If, on these considerations, I happened to speak against the behaviour of some of you, if you would keep in mind the rule to do with others as you would wish others to do with you, your wrath will be greatly placated. If anybody came amongst the people, who through your instrumentality were called and gathered out of the world, and led them into error, particularly if they were completely happy if left to themselves; and if you found that they went in consequence to hear preachers that you were not satisfied with their doctrine, would you not feel it hard that these (those that led your people into error) were complaining that you were seeking to hold your congregations together, while in truth it was they who were the aggressors, intruding into the labour of others?

Our reasons for remaining in the Established Church appear to us to be of much more weight than the reasons for leaving. So, we believe we would sin against the Lord and his work if we turned our backs upon her; and we would be giving an opportunity for the enemy to frustrate the glorious revival, which is widening its borders day by day. In my humble view, if a reformer were to arise from amongst the Dissenting churches, and not setting up separate congregations, he would do more service to God's Church, and cause less offence to others. I say this only as my view of the matter; I do not judge; I know that God has various intentions, so I keep silent . . . My judgment is, and this was your judgment once, that the Lord is leaving the Dissenters, and intends to quicken his work in the Established Church. If you came amongst us, as before, and in a way that gave us no room to think that you came seeking to divide us, I believe that you would see the way that the Lord intends us to be; and that he was amongst us, for all our corruptions, our weaknesses and our confusion. If you came thus, you would strengthen our hands instead of weakening them, seeing that we are bearing the heat of the day, and that the whole world and Hell is against us. On seeing the difficulties against which we battle, your brave heart would be stirred up once more, and your spirit would burn in sympathy towards the young men who go out, with their lives in their hands, against the Philistines. Come. Let there be no further strife between us. Let us agree in this, that we will not weaken each other's hands; and if you cannot believe that we are correct in remaining within the Established Church, do not condemn us, when we assure you that it is completely a matter of conscience.

We are seeing such a work begun; some notable clergymen having been awakened; many persons of the most honourable ranks attending, and some of us having been called to preach privately before nobility, of which there is one marquis, one earl, two ladyships, and two ladies of title. We are seeing prejudices fall, and doors opening throughout England nearly, and, at last, in north Wales, and even in Ireland. Therefore, do not condemn us, if there is in us any fear of running before the Lord . . . He that believeth shall not make haste. Let us be taught by God, and be patient, longsuffering and faithful to him; then we shall see the truth succeed in God's good time, driving error and latitudinarianism out of the Church; or else, Satan shall be granted to raise such persecution within the Church so as to drive out all the faithful . . . If the old Church is to be left to refuse the light, and separate congregations to be formed, which I hope will never be, then Providence must decide the time and instruments.

O, by God's help, may you not suffer a little longer with the old Dissenters, labour amongst them with patience, and seek to find young men, full of love, to follow the old ministers, not forming new congregations by drawing people from amongst us, but leaving us within the Church of England. We could then meet you privately or in the Associations, to settle matters, and to honour you as one whose feet I am not worthy to wash. I could then open all my heart to you, as before. I hope that I write in the simplicity of the gospel. And without hypocrisy I am able to write to you, as loving as ever, as your most unworthy Brother and fellow-sinner, but saved by grace; and truly desiring to meet you above, to worship together to all eternity; and to live presently as your fellow-citizen and fellow-labourer,

H. HARRIS.

This is a strong, yet gentlemanlike letter, written in a Christian spirit, and full of good nature. Some points in it are difficult to understand, such as the encouragement of Edmund Jones to work in co-operation with the old Dissenters. Is there here a suggestion that the prophet of Pontypool, for all his godliness, was not only persecuting the Methodists and seeking to steal their people, but was also a thorn in his own brethren's sides, and unable to labour together with them? Be that as it may, other things are very clear in the letter:

1. It shows that there is no foundation whatsoever to that which has been alleged by Dr Rees of Swansea, and other historians who have followed him, namely that the first members of the Methodists were proselytes from amongst the Dissenters. Harris says specifically that it was a well-known fact that the Methodists did not build upon the Dissenters nor draw people from them, but rather that the establishment of societies in the neighbourhood of old Nonconformist churches proved of advantage to those churches by increasing their numbers and their activity.

2. Though Harris clung to the Established Church, he was not in any way a persecutor of those who left it. At the same time, he feared that they had limited the sphere of their activities by turning their backs upon it, and had diminished their possibilities of doing good.

3. He dreamed that the Established Church would be leavened throughout by the revival; that its leaders would support evangelical preaching, and would even become active members of Methodist societies. No wonder therefore that he opposed separation. While any hope of the realization of his dream remained, he judged that to leave the Church would be to run before the Lord.

During the week after he returned from north Wales there was a Monthly Association at Trefeca. None of the clergymen was there, so Harris presided. He opened proceedings with a powerful sermon, and in the society that followed he addressed the members on various matters, and called their attention particularly to the blood of Christ. He cried:

> The blood! It is an almighty blood, an infinite blood; who can plumb its depths? It was this blood that united my soul with God. If you have any desire to be holy, wash in this. If you wish to conquer sin and Satan, come to the blood. If you wish to go to heaven, take the blood with you.

And as he expounded the virtue of the blood a great shout rose from all, so that his own voice was completely drowned by the cries of the congregation. He felt that he had received an authority that he only rarely experienced.

In the second week of November, he set out for London. He passed through Hereford, and attended an Association held by the English brethren at Ross. He arrived back at Trefeca, after his visit to the capital city, on the last Monday of the year.

He was only three days at home before beginning a long journey to the west of England, which was to last a month. On New Year's Day he was at Cwmdu, a place between Talgarth and Crickhowell. The next day, he was at New Inn, Monmouthshire. As well as preaching, he was collecting for the new chapel that had been built at Builth Wells, but contrary to the usual practice of collectors, he would not receive any money or promises at the time, in case the gifts were given out of love to him rather than in faith.

On the same day was a Monthly Meeting at the place, the main business of which was the restoration of William Edward of Groes-wen, who had been placed under discipline because of an error in doctrine. Howell Harris asked him two questions, and the specific form of the questions are characteristic of the particular views of the questioner: (1) Was he willing to worship the baby Jesus? (2) Did he believe that a spiritual revelation of Christ was to be had over and above the knowledge of him that is found in the letter?

William Edward answered these questions acceptably and was reinstated as an exhorter. At the Association they also discussed marriage and the care of the chapel at New Inn, and two men were given permission to begin preaching. He also received a letter from two brethren accusing him of some wrongdoing. The Association was throughout happy, he and the brethren agreed on all matters. In the west of England he visited Exton, Plymouth, Kingsbridge, and other places and did not return until the beginning of February.

The day after his return there was a Monthly Association at Trefeca, and he began it with a sermon from the words, 'I am black but comely.' He took the opportunity to refer to an untrue story about him that was spread abroad by the Dissenters, namely that he was their enemy. He wrote later:

> The only reason they have for saying this is that I speak out against their sins; and on exactly the same ground it could be said that I am an enemy of the Church of England, in that I do the same of it. But I said that I always differentiated between the guilty and the innocent, and that I knew many gracious and godly people and preachers, whom I love, among the Dissenters; and that if it was within my power I would not close down neither church or chapel, but rather fill it with God.

In the private meeting of the Association, he and the preachers discussed many matters and arranged their journeys, and all was accomplished very amicably.

On the last day of January, he set out for Carmarthenshire, Cardiganshire and Pembrokeshire. A note in his journal written when he was at Llangamarch is worth recording:

I sought the Lord's counsel on many things, and had great strength to strive with the Lord concerning Sir Watkin Williams Wynn; I called upon him boldly that he might reveal his power. 'Do not let this effort of Satan succeed,' I cried, 'save the soul of the nobleman, but defeat his plans.'

## PERSECUTION FROM SIR WATKIN WILLIAMS WYNN

At this time, Sir Watkin was persecuting God's saints with a high hand. The following quotation from a letter written by Harris to a believing sister in London throws light on the behaviour of the baron of Wynnestay:

You heard a little of our brethren and sisters' treatment in north Wales by Sir Watkin Williams Wynn, and much more I have heard of it since. He has raised the penalty of £80 on the poor people for hearing and receiving two of our brethren; so that many have been quite ruined thereby, and the Gospel stopped for a time until it be tried. This makes me spare a moment to send you a line of it, to desire Brother Jenkins if he is there or wherever he is to call the souls together to pray on some appointed time after the general fast on March 11, and to write to all the societies everywhere to make conference of it. Be of good courage, my sister, this is good news; the Lord is coming and Satan roars. Let each one look to his armour, there are excellent and glorious times nearby.[9]

There is a letter written by Peter Williams that describes how that good man had to suffer the wrath of Sir Watkin.[10] In addition, he was threatening to evict from his estate all that dared to associate with the Methodists, and in that he owned more or less all the land in the district, his threats, if they were carried out, would have resulted in the uprooting of all religion from the area. There were scores of people therefore, as well as Harris, seeking the Lord's intervention in the matter. Their prayers were answered in a dreadful way. One afternoon, about a year after this, Sir Watkin was riding upon his horse at Wynnestay Park. On what was level ground the horse somehow tripped so that the rider was thrown onto his head on the ground, and died on the spot. Truly, there is a God who judges the earth. Another tradition concerning these troubles in the north, is that a number of poor people had gathered in a prayer meeting, and one of those praying obtained such a hold on God as he pleaded with him to halt the persecution that he was assured on rising from his knees that his requests had been heard in heaven. He gave out a hymn of his own composition to sing, noting his feelings:

| | |
|---|---|
| Queen Esther now is near | Mae Esther wedi cychwyn |
| To entering the King's chamber, | I mewn i lys y Brenin, |
| A pardon to her he'll extend, | Caiff pardwn iddi ei estyn, |
| Sir Watkin's evil works will end. | Ac ofer waith Syr Watcyn. |

It is at that moment, so it is said, when this verse was being sung in the prayer meeting, that the baron met his end at Wynnestay Park.

## ASSOCIATIONS AT LAMPETER AND CARMARTHEN, AND A COLLECTION FOR WHITEFIELD'S ORPHANAGE

From Llangammarch, Harris went to Llanwrda and from there, in intense cold, to Lampeter, where a Quarterly Association was meeting. He heard unhappy stories on the way concerning his brethren's feelings towards him, so that his spirit was weighed down on nearing the town. After much pressure, he was persuaded to preach on the morning of the Association. A sentence or two will show the nature of the address:

> I showed that there is but one God, there is none other God above or below, but Jesus Christ. I explained how some make an idol, and call him the Father, and place him above Jesus Christ, and worship this idol instead of the only true and living God. I showed how they were just so much Arians, in having Christ give satisfaction to the Father. If he did this, then who gave satisfaction to the Son, and to the Spirit? Objection: But do you then worship Jesus? Answer: We worship the Father, the Son and the Spirit in him (that is, in Jesus): three in one, and one in three.

This quotation shows how confused Harris was in his views on the Trinity, and that he was getting very close to Sabellianism.

In the private meeting of the Association there was keen argument and some degree of bad feeling:

> When I wished in faith to give up the law in north Wales, and I rebuked the selfish and carnal spirit of one who came from there, wishing direction, Satan came down. Someone accused me of pride. I refused to act until the brethren acknowledged their fault and expressed sorrow, placing me in my proper place; and I told them that I had no purpose in coming there save to serve Christ, and that everyone must stand in his own place. The Lord came amongst us again. I had opportunity to explain our reasons for remaining

in the Church. I find that the Lord, through various means, is bringing the brethren to settle within the Church. We agreed to collect in order to proceed in law against Sir Watkin Williams Wynn. The brethren arranged their journeys. Privately, I had an answer from the Lord with respect to the law, and with a view to employing Mr Williams, Caerleon, to carry it forward. I find God's Spirit within me crying out strongly against Sir Watkin.

It would be interesting to know what became of the lawsuit, and whether it was the sudden death of the nobleman that brought it to an end. The next day, matters proceeded amicably, though Harris gave a severe lesson to some brethren for their lightness and carnality, and an argument arose between him, Rowland, and Williams, Pantycelyn, over the rules for excommunicating carnal professors. The other two argued that this was difficult and dangerous. But, for Harris, 'I argued strongly that there was a spiritual light or eye within the Christian, which judges and measures all things.' He insisted that all who were careless should be placed under discipline.

How the argument ended, we do not know, but many arrangements were made and the brethren separated with happy feelings on the whole. It is impossible to read Howell Harris's own account of the meetings without being aware that he was very autocratic and claiming the rule, and that he referred too often to 'his place' in the Association, as if he had been placed higher than his brethren. It is sad to see one so full of good nature and so affectionate in spirit, being so taken up by such a feeling.

From Lampeter, Harris embarked upon a very full itinerary of the lower parts of Cardiganshire, parts of Pembrokeshire, Carmarthenshire and Glamorganshire. As well as preaching and arranging matters in the societies he was also collecting for the Orphanage that Whitefield had established in Georgia. On the cover of his journal is listed the sum collected at each place, and as this is the first report of any collection taken up amongst the Welsh Methodists, we record it below. As well as being interesting in its own right, it informs us of the relative strengths of the different societies. 'I received,' wrote Harris, 'for the Orphanage:

|  | £. | s. | d. |
|---|---|---|---|
| Maesnonni | 0 | 13 | 0 |
| Twr-gwyn | 0 | 11 | 1 |
| Cwm Cynon | 0 | 11 | 0 |
| Newcastle Emlyn | 0 | 7 | 8 |
| Llechryd | 1 | 4 | 3 |
| Trefdraeth | 0 | 10 | 3 |

| | £. | s. | d. |
|---|---|---|---|
| Fishguard | 0 | 3 | 6 |
| Tre-fin | 0 | 9 | 3 |
| Llanferan | 0 | 0 | 8 |
| Hayscastle | 1 | 6 | 10 |
| Haverfordwest | 1 | 6 | 6 |
| Llangwm | 0 | 6 | 3 |
| Carew | 1 | 1 | 1 |
| Jefferson | 0 | 12 | 1 |
| Meidrim | 0 | 12 | 2 |
| Carmarthen | 1 | 3 | 5 |
| Llanddeusant | 0 | 2 | 2 |
| Ffoi (near Llanelli) | 0 | 4 | 1 |
| Llan-non | 0 | 3 | 2 |
| Swansea | 0 | 8 | 4 |
| Llansamlet | 0 | 6 | 1 |
| Neath | 0 | 8 | 9 |
| Hafod | 0 | 5 | 9 |
| Penprysg | 0 | 12 | 0 |
| Llantrisant | 0 | 15 | 0 |
| How. Griffiths | 0 | 2 | 6 |
| Aberthaw | 0 | 3 | 7 |
| St Nicholas | 1 | 1 | 6 |
| Groes-wen | 1 | 8 | 0 |

Harris travelled unceasingly throughout this spring; there was no stop to his efforts. He was at times in Glamorgan and Monmouthshire, at other times in Montgomeryshire or Carmarthenshire, and when he was not far from home he would visit nearby places in Breconshire and Radnorshire. It would be difficult to follow him on all these visits, and hardly profitable to the reader. In the first week of May, a Quarterly Association was held in Carmarthen. Harris says that he went to 'the Room' and preached there to a large congregation. This suggests that the Methodists had built a chapel in the town. His text was 'By grace ye are saved', and he had unusual power and light to glorify God's grace. In the private meeting of the Association a sweet breeze blew upon them as they sang at the beginning. They then read the Minutes of the last Association; monies were received from various places for the lawsuit and they then discussed how best to proceed with the case. It was decided that Harris and Price of Watford should visit the lawyer. The brethren that should visit north Wales were also agreed. On the second morning, the reports were read and were very acceptable. Harris continues the account:

But Bro. Rowland was still jealous of me about the Trinity, and had been offended at somewhat I said of our carnal distinction of the Godhead, setting the Father above Jesus Christ, and afterwards [feelings] rose high. I told him I feared he did not know the Lord, and I shouted with authority, 'There is but one God, and this light will extend all over the world, no matter what the opposition. When I read the Puritans, I do not find that they differ from me in anything. He despised me, said I did not read or preach the Scriptures, and I fell under it, cried, ''Tis true, I don't study or meditate in the Scripture enough. I would desire to meditate in them continually, and my sorrow is that I fail!' He opposed the witness of the Spirit. I answered, that though many fool themselves, yet, an answer is given to prayer. The storm blew over, we were calm, and he heartily invited me to Cardiganshire.[11]

It is clear that both men had hot tempers, and in their excitement would say unkind things of one another. Peace had scarcely been restored when a letter to the Association arrived, indirectly from the students of the Academy in the town, containing a challenge to a debate over something Harris had said in his sermon. On responding to the letter, the students rushed into the meeting and chose one of themselves to act as spokesman. This was very inappropriate behaviour, and in that the majority of them were the young preachers of a Dissenting Academy, it was even more inappropriate. Harris noted that much bad temper was displayed on both sides, particularly by himself, when he rebuked them for their pride. They began by charging Harris with denying reason:

He began about reason, that I denied it. I said that it was enmity against God. Opened to some (the students that were absent and did not hear me preach) how I only insisted on it that at some times the Spirit of God through the law and the gospel did so work on souls, that they could not contain them-selves without expressing it in an external vocal manner. I spoke respectfully and lovingly to such of them as were loving and humble, but fell upon the others home, and when they complained, we bantered them. It came to me, 'Answer a fool according to his folly.' I reasoned logically with them, and on their not keeping to the point, I accused them of not having learnt how to dispute by rule. They should have brought their master with them. I declared we were wholly against disputing and had wrote to them to signify it as far as we could, without giving their pride room to triumph and to say we were afraid. But I was amazed at their pride in coming to attack a body of labour-ers in this manner, which was the first open attack we ever tasted . . . [They said] that I had said the Dissenters wished, or would set, if they could all the bishops and clergy in hell. I disowned such an expression, and that I could not bear to hear anyone say so, for I loved and highly esteemed many Dis-senters, and was for being with peace with all. If they would leave us alone, I assured them I would leave them alone, unless they would go and pervert the Scriptures and draw souls from us to them. I reproved the young man, Evan William, that had sent the letter from north Wales that has set all the Dissenters on a bad spirit toward the work of God.[12]

It is surprising to see the name of Evan William, who had been an exhorter with the Methodists, now numbered with the disrupters that had broken in on the Association. Harris also rebuked another young man who had spread through the town the story that twelve clergymen were to come to oppose the Methodists openly at their Association.

I hope it will be blessed to them to check their pride, for I felt love to their souls, wished well to all of them that were humble, the rest I said I would let all know of them that the Church of God may not be filled with such a spirit.[13]

## ON THE ROAD THROUGHOUT THE
## SECOND HALF OF 1748

On 9 May, a school was opened at Trefeca, and he went around the local families encouraging them to send their children there. For some years he had been building a house at Trefeca. Whether the idea of gathering together a large family from various neighbourhoods, in order to provide them with religious advantages, was already in his mind at this time, is difficult to decide. The next week he was at a Monthly Association at Dyserth. He gave the brethren an account of the Association at Carmarthen and the opposition received from the students; he explained his attitude to Dissenters; they made arrangements for setting up a school in the area; and agreed that the following Thursday be set aside for prayer. Some exhorters from Montgomeryshire, who had been placed under discipline by Howell Harris because of pride, were present. He hoped that they might now be restored. But their sin had not been brought low; the discipline had to continue. He spoke to them many times, hoping to persuade them. The dawn was breaking before he gave up on them, and having failed himself he sent the exhorter, Thomas James, to them. But both attempts were in vain. Their true faults were errors of doctrine. In the middle of May, he went to London and stayed there until the beginning of July. During this time, he had to see to the unhappy work of turning Herbert Jenkins out of the Connexion.

On 19 August, Daniel Rowland and Harris travelled very amicably together to Monmouth. Harris opened his heart to his friend, explaining the reasons for Herbert Jenkins's excommunication, and also explaining the meaning of some remarks he had made in north Wales. We imagine that they were returning from escorting the Countess of Huntingdon back to England after spending some time in Wales. They both, along with Griffith Jones and Howell Davies, had met the Countess at Bristol. They had all travelled slowly through most of south Wales. Some of the clergymen or the leading exhorters would preach in the villages through which they passed, and some of these services were remembered by the godly noblewoman as long as she lived. They stayed for some days at Trefeca, when Griffith Jones had a remarkable service while preaching in the open air. In *The Life and Times of Selina, Countess of Huntingdon* it is said that this journey took place at the end of May and the beginning of June, but this cannot be, because Howell Harris's journal has him ministering in London for most of May and the whole of June. Probably it was at the end of July and the beginning of August, 'between the two harvests', as it is said, that the Countess undertook this journey.[14]

He next travelled through Cardiganshire and Pembrokeshire. We cannot follow him from place to place, but it is good to see that in Pembrokeshire Howell Davies proved a friend and companion. Immense congregations came to hear him in every place. At Parke, he was in some distress what to preach, in that a large number of clergymen and many prejudiced Dissenters were present. It seems that he and the Dissenters were rapidly distancing themselves from each other. After taking counsel in prayer, he decided on 1 Corinthians 2:2 as a text, 'For I determined not to know anything among you, save Jesus Christ, and him crucified.'

I showed the way they had wearied Paul with their arguments, but now he had decided that they would weary him no longer; he would have nothing to do with any other knowledge, save Christ crucified. I was then led to speak on the mystery of godliness. I emphasized that it is a mystery, and it is beyond all arguing. According to my custom, I spoke strongly on Christ's divinity, that he was God in the manger, and God on the cross. And though it was the human nature that suffered, yet his sufferings were divine. I explained his words concerning how he was below the Father, and also equal with the Father. I referred to the thief on the cross praying to this Man, that he ventured his soul upon him, seeing him as Almighty Ruler and God over that eternity into which he was to leap. He, also, did not refuse the prayer, but answered it with the majesty worthy of God. I mentioned Stephen praying to him. I showed not only that he – this Man – this Person – was God, but that he was eternal God; that he is the only God; that he made the worlds, and that there is no other God apart from, or above him; that we believe in the Godhead, according to the creeds of Athanasius, Nicene, and the Apostles, that there are three co-eternal Persons, but there is only one God; and that it was this one God, in the person of the Son, who became man, and offered up his life. Then, I turned to them, and asked them, 'Did they not make three Gods? And did they not go past him to the Father, whom they considered greater than he?' I showed that there was no such Father, from his own words to Philip; and that there is no greater or smaller, no before or after, in the Godhead; and that he that sees the Son, sees the whole of the Godhead, that fills every place and every thing at one and the same time. Now, if he is the only God, and if there is only he, have not some of you been worshipping a strange God? Yes, worshipping an image and idol of your own mind? You pass by the living God, to worship this, this imaginary God whom you call the Father. I was strong on this, though I must exercise tenderness towards all, yet I must stand by this blood.

We have noted his comments fully, in order to show the nature of his views. He continued by explaining his relationship towards the Dissenters, that he respected them, and preached in their chapels; that his whole aim was to raise them up to God; that the Methodists had no intention of forming a party, that they had been called while in the Established Church. He referred also to some letter that had been distributed throughout Wales and England, and contained accusations that were completely untrue.

The English press was pouring out all kinds of abuse of the Methodists at this time. In one pamphlet it was said that they made their followers mad, that many of them in Wales had committed murder and were hanging in chains at the time. Whitefield was described as a man with a windmill in his head who was going about the world seeking any whose brains he might dash out. But Griffith Jones, Llanddowror, was slandered more than any. Another writer, who was an educated man, more's the pity, claimed that the Welsh Methodists were adulterous, and that prostitution was not considered a sin amongst them. He said, further, that the Methodist preachers would make the members confess their sins to them, and that one of them, Will Richards, a cobbler, when he would be forgiving the sins of any would hand them a piece of paper, ensuring them that this paper would open the doors of heaven to them. Harris was probably referring to some pamphlet of this kind.

The next day, he received a letter from two Dissenting ministers, discussing the sermon of the previous evening. He saw that he would have to suffer because of the Word preached. He went down to talk to them:

> Went to them to discourse, and immediately Thomas Morgan [Henllan Amgoed] said that Man that died was not eternal God. I said then he was a heretic and I would preach against him to blood, but if he called it back, or owned he was blind in the matter, I would withhold until he had further light from God. I said it was a matter of conscience with me, and that I must strive for it to blood, that he is the eternal God. I showed them their ignorance, and that no one can know Christ but in the light of the Holy Spirit; that the union between the two natures in Christ is eternal, and so, in my sight, it

is the most shame-faced blasphemy to say that he suffered or accomplished anything as a man, and not as the eternal God.

Then I went away. We parted sweet, and begged of them for the future not to bring such blind and wicked distinction, but blaze abroad the fame of that Man ... I find they would have me say 'tis the Person of Christ that suffered, and was God, and not to say that Man.[15]

From here, he returned through Laugharne, Carmarthen, Pontargothi, Llanlluan Chapel, Llandremore, Swansea, Gellidochlaethe, and Hafod, reaching Trefeca on 24 September. He preached to immense gatherings at each place and with considerable unction upon his ministry. The mystery of Christ, and the closeness of the union of the two natures in him, so that the humanity was made divine as part of the one Person; these were the content of his sermons at every place, though he would vary his texts.

On Boxing Day of that year, a general Assembly (so Harris called it) was held at Trefeca. Whether this was one of the regularly arranged Associations, we do not know, but there is no mention of any of the clergymen present. The meeting was opened by a sermon from Harris on the visitation of the angels to the shepherds at the birth of Christ. It does not seem there was much order to the sermon; he covered a number of matters; he says that he spoke for three hours, and that considerable power accompanied the message. As usual, he expanded on the mystery of Christ, proving that he was the true and living God; that there is no God higher than him, and that the Trinity, through the unity that is in the Godhead, dwells in him. He showed the divine condescension when dwelling in the womb of the virgin, and in taking our nature, and in this way, becoming such a Person whose like was never before seen. He then spoke of the Pretender, declaring that they had no desire for any king to rule over their bodies but King George, but that over him was King Jesus:

Wherever we shall go, we shall be in the kingdom of Jesus. When this work was beginning, Satan created an opposition to it; but it came to nothing. Where is Satan now?

In the society that followed, he was severe on the members because they were not bearing fruit. He said that he had for some time been paying the rent himself for the room at Trefeca; that no one had come to him to ask him whether he could afford it; that it was enough for him to do to preach the word to them without providing the room as well; and that he had kept a school at the place for some time at his own cost. He condemned them for not sympathising with their brethren, in that some of the exhorters were poor men, and in danger of being sent to prison. 'Why could not a number of societies support them?' he said. We can imagine that his words cut them to the quick. They were there until two o'clock in the morning, with Harris showing them their deficiencies. Various matters were then arranged. James Beaumont's case was one matter under consideration and it was judged that a spirit of error had taken hold of him. Harris argued against excommunication, asking that they behave towards him in an evangelical manner in the hope that God would retrieve him. Before closing, the heavenly influences fell upon them abundantly. The brethren leaped, so great was their joy. And after singing and shouting victory, it was five o'clock before Harris got to his bed.

It is likely that Harris had more time for the work in Wales in the second half of 1748 than had been the case for a considerable period, in that Whitefield returned to London in July after having been in America for four and a half years. In the Association held in London on 20 July 1748, Whitefield presided. As far as the English work was concerned, Harris viewed himself as a kind of Captain under Whitefield. The latter, however, was not completely ready to take his place amongst them as before. He said that so much disorder had entered amongst them, because of the young preachers going beyond their appropriate limits, that he did not know what to do. He wished to hear from different parts of the country before he made up his mind, but was determined not to labour together with any who would not be willing to be taught and to be under discipline. He did not, he said, desire to be head, but the young preachers must know their place, and view themselves as candidates under probation, and himself as a father over them, otherwise he would hold no connection with them. As a result of this address, the brethren said they wished to submit themselves fully under him, and to use every means to increase in usefulness. Whitefield's return removed a heavy burden from Harris's shoulders, and no doubt the advice and sympathy of such a sincere friend was a balm to his soul in the midst of the trials through which he was passing.

---

[1] HHVL, p. 118.

[2] This is unlikely. HHVL relates meetings with Wesley only at Bristol, pp. 119, 120.

[3] CH 38, p. 40.

[4] Gomer M. Roberts argues that it is Peter Williams, the future Bible commentator, who is being referred to here and not William Williams. He cites a further comment from Harris's journal which shows that PW preached at this Association. PW in his autobiography confessed that at this time he hardly knew the difference between Arminianism, Baxterianism and Moravianism. *Bywyd a Gwaith Peter Williams* (Cardiff, 1943), pp. 25–6.

[5] HHVL, p. 140.     [6] CH 38, p. 42.     [7] HHVP, pp. 134–5.

[8] Transcribed up to this point by Eifion Evans.     [9] Transcribed by Eifion Evans.

[10] See p. 668.     [11] HHVP, p. 147. CH 25, pp. 101–2.     [12] HHVP, pp. 147–8.

[13] Ibid. p. 149.

[14] Faith Cook acknowledges the difficulty in dating this journey. She believes it was in early April 1748. See *Selina, Countess of Huntingdon* (Edinburgh: Banner of Truth, 2001), pp. 107–8.

[15] HHVP, pp. 154.

# 15

# HOWELL HARRIS (1749–50)

## HARRIS DEFENDS JAMES BEAUMONT

The morning of the first day of the year 1749 saw Harris waking at Aberedw, where he had arrived at about eleven the previous night, on the way to a Monthly Association at Builth Wells. His experience on the road from Aberedw to Builth is worth recording:

> I feared in my heart to lose the sight of God's face; I cried more than ever before, 'O Lord!, I fear thy frown more then hell! I have greater fear of losing sight of thee, of frustrating thy work, and grieving thy Spirit, than of any persecution. If thou dost frown, who can comfort me?' I felt in my soul a fear of having any gifts, success and power, in case I did not give all the glory to the Lord.

At Builth, he preached on Luke 2:5. After the sermon there was a society for all the members. Here he was very severe towards those who lived in sin, emphasizing to them that God saw them, and would reveal them, if they did not repent. He rebuked those who were careless about communion with the Lord, and viewed sin as a small thing, their consciences being corrupted. But he comforted those who were broken because of their faults and prepared to forsake them. He told them that they were children of the free woman, namely, Sarah, and that they belonged to the new Jerusalem. In the private society, James Beaumont's case was again raised. Many of the exhorters wished to turn him out because of heresy, but Harris could not agree. He did not believe that God desired it at present, and thought that the demand arose from prejudice amongst the exhorters:

> How I see the brethren too fierce against Bro. Beaumont, and ready to turn him out without meekly talking to him in private about his odd words. I could not agree to a sentence that I saw God did not approve as just in all respects, but if, after all evangelical means, he would prove obstinate then I was free, though I know him to be a child of God, having more gifts and light than all of you here, but pride comes on it all, and he sees himself the greatest, and would have others think so too, and that proud spirit catches the people

when he is blessed to them, and rises heats and disputes. [I showed] how he would own his odd words and was against divisions. Making right both for and against Bro. Beaumont.[1]

He succeeded eventually in keeping Beaumont within the society. Howell Harris was always a loyal friend. He then expanded on the nature of the work and the way in which he considered the trials and burdens relating to it as privileges. He travelled next to Glanirfon, a farmhouse in the neighbourhood of Llanwrtyd. He preached here on heaven and the judgment. He could not say how well he had spoken, but the Lord came down and his voice was drowned by the 'Hosannas!' of his listeners.

On 3 January, he was at Llwyn-y-berllan and at the private society he encouraged the members to establish a Christian school – one of Griffith Jones's schools, no doubt – immediately. This seems to have been a particular concern for him at this time. He pressed them also to contribute something weekly to the Lord. At Llansawel he met a young schoolmaster to whom he explained the best method of educating, namely first of all to direct the eyes of the children towards God, to submit their spirits to the yoke of Christ, and to instruct them in the various branches of morality, as well as in the principles of the Christian religion. After preaching on the birth of Christ, he held a private society. He there discussed the education of children; the necessity of establishing a Christian school; the need for the members to submit to their leaders; and he rebuked them firmly for not respecting James Williams, their superintendent, as they respected himself and Daniel Rowland. Before closing, however, he turned to more comforting matters and they broke out in singing and praising.

He passed on to Glanyrafonddu, and during the day gave seven addresses, either preaching in public or speaking to societies. He visited Llangathen, Llanegwad, and Glancothi, before arriving at Carmarthen for the Quarterly Association of 5 January. He feared that great trials awaited him here and he sought the Lord's help. His theme for the opening sermon of the Association was the visit of the angels to the shepherds in the fields of Bethlehem, but he does not appear to have kept closely to his text:

> I had much authority to rebuke sin, to show the necessity of repentance, and to warn those who remain in darkness. I was terrible when speaking of the omniscience of God, of his threatenings and his rods.

## THE DEATH OF HARRIS'S DAUGHTER

As he finished preaching, and before the private meeting of the Association had begun, he was met at the door by his servant, with awful news:

Met my servant coming to tell me that my little girl [Anne] is dead, and I immediately retired. Though dear she was witty, beautiful and sharp, yet I found it easy, through my Lord being present, to give her and my dear wife and my life to the Lord. Saw the Lord's tenderness to me in that I was not there to see her dying, my affections being so strong.[2]

He went immediately to the Lord to ask for guidance. He expressed his readiness to continue his journey and leave his wife to bury the dead, if that was the divine will. He was answered, that he was to arrange Association matters and then return home the next day. This he did. He explained the place of the brethren and his own place; that there was a Moses or some other, full of authority, always present in the church; that his mantle fell from his shoulders on entering heaven; that there was continually another that received the mantle; and that the gifts and authority of the apostles were presently in someone's possession, in that there was always the necessity for them. There is here more than a suggestion that Harris himself was the present bearer of the mantle. He encouraged the exhorters to deny themselves and to possess a united spirit and heart. There was much singing and praising. He left Carmarthen at three o'clock in the morning and arrived at Trefeca, a distance of sixty miles, the next morning:

This morning at two I came home, and found what I had not believed before, that my little girl, which was the prettiest and most sensible, loving, winning, sharp and amiable I ever saw, was dead. When I heard the news and went to her corpse, I was so full that I was obliged to withdraw. If it had not been for her faith and the presence of the Spirit, the trial had taken away my life, I felt so strong were the strings of nature. Speaking to [my] mother, who was overwhelmed with sorrow. Went to her dear mother, who, if she had not been supported by the Lord, must now have sunk. To lose one who had so engaged the hearts of all. We continued weeping on each other's necks for a long time – to seven in the morning. Wrote a letter to Mr Whitefield on their relating the vast pain the child went through, and the circumstances of her death. It touched me sore, I feel on remembering some particulars about the child, that it at once takes away almost life. I had now a letter from London to invite me to take care of the London society. Afterwards all my cry was, 'Lord, home, home, home, home, home, home, home, home.' O let it not be thus. Remember my unfaithfulness to thee, my carelessness, my presumptuous falls, my inability to stand against anything, my corruptions, spiritual ignorance, blindness, and so utter unfitness to deal with souls. When the people were come together to the burial, I sang the 49th Psalm and prayed. The Lord came down so that all were affected to weep. I trust my little girl's death was a general blessing to them, then I exhorted them. Then I took her out under my arm, and rode before my dear wife to church. My mouth was suitably opened to all home. Showed that this trial was not as a scourge for sin, but to try patience and to bring glory to God. Afterward we had freedom to eat hearty, which before had been taken from us all for a good while.[3]

On Wednesday, 12 January, he set out on another journey. It was night and almost completely dark when he eventually arrived at Cantref, at the foot of the Brecon Beacons. The wind howled dreadfully, the rain descended as a waterfall, and the weary traveller was cold and wet. But he did not feel the least degree of discomfort, 'The Lord made the darkness and storm sweet to me,' he wrote, 'I saw myself the happiest man in the world. I would not change my place with the wealthiest.' The next day he passed through Glyn and Blaenglyntawe, arriving at Gellidochlaethe, a large farmhouse near Neath, by evening. On the way, he meditated on the greatness of his privileges, the glory of God and the incarnate Three in One. On Friday, he preached at Cadoxton-juxta-Neath from 1 John 3:8. He showed the majesty of redemption, that God created the world in six days, but that he was preparing the work of salvation for four thousand years. He then took up his favourite theme, the mystery of the two natures in Christ.

A Quarterly Association was to be held here, but before it began Harris received two items of unfortunate news. The first was of a man whom he knew who had fallen into debt, and the second was of an influential man who was decrying the Methodists, saying that they would come to nothing and that Harris himself had changed. This troubled him but, as usual, he took his burden immediately to the Lord. In the private meeting, he addressed the exhorters and members solemnly on the need to read the Scriptures and to make them the rule for all things; on making collections more often; on self-denial, when he said that he lately had refused the opportunity of a hundred pounds a year. He charged them to be faithful to the light they had received. 'You will be as nothing before the devil, if you sin God away.' He felt a deep unity with the fraternity as a whole.

## THE DUTIES OF STEWARDS

He passed through Nottage, where he preached on Christ having come to seek and to save the lost; and Hafod, where he was very severe on carnal professors; and Cefn Cribwr, where he had greater power than ever to urge the placing of Christ's yoke firmly upon the necks of young Christians. On Monday, he was at Llantrisant. He says that his clothes were worse than those of all his brethren and that he was riding the worst horse, but that he was completely satisfied. He held a private society there, and encouraged the members not to mix too much with the Dissenters, who were to a large extent dead to God and given to formality, and without the authority to keep out the world and self. He then explained the Methodist way and his own place in it. He saw that the Lord was fitting him more and more for his role, going with him and doing all things for him. On Tuesday, he visited St Nicholas. Here he encouraged them to divide their possessions into three parts – one part for paying just debts, a second for maintaining parents and family, and a third for doing good, about which they should consult the Lord. When praying at the close, the Lord came down so evidently that the preacher's voice was drowned by the cries of the crowd. Before leaving, he spoke with the exhorters and preachers. He explained the necessary qualifications for the superintendents, namely that they should know God, and have communion with him, so as to know his will, and that they should be familiar with temptation, so that they possessed patience. Their work was:

1. To receive all the collections, keep an account of them, and bring the sum to the Monthly Association.

2. To watch over the door of the meetings, lead strangers to their seats, keep the children and dogs quiet.

3. To visit the sick and the poor.

4. To notice those who attend the means and to turn to them and speak with them.

5. To look out for those absent, and find out if they have fallen or tending to levity.

He then explained that the Methodists were but a part of Christ's body; that the Wesleyans, the Moravians, and the Dissenters also belonged to it. It must be borne in mind that these superintendents or stewards of the societies were what we presently would call deacons.

He next went to Aberthaw, and his text there was, 'Learn of me.' From here, to Dinas Powys where he preached from, 'Take my yoke upon you.' At Groes-wen, he preached for three hours. He started at eight, and continued until eleven. At the close of the service, he held a private society for another six hours, that is, until five. He himself gives these times. It seems that many of the societies had gathered at Groes-wen, though no Association was usually held there, and he took the opportunity to put in place everything that he considered out of order in each of the societies. He started with Llantrisant, calling forward the members and dealing severely with them for the disorder amongst them, the lack of love, and the carelessness for the glory of God. He said that the Lord blessed them when they were together but once they began quarrelling they broke his heart. He then prayed on their behalf and obtained a strong hold, and God came down, humbling them deeply, until at last they had the victory. After this, he settled two other societies in order, though he does not say what their faults were. Afterwards, he gave general directions, encouraging them to come to the Monthly Associations that they almost all were failing to attend. He said that they had to leave all things, as he had done, and that he was determined to serve those who possessed the same faith as himself, being dead to themselves, not concerned with what they ate or wore, nor who would be greatest and who least. He thought it an honour to be soaked to the skin, to be worn out, to be in desperate circumstances, to be hated of all because of the gospel; he would go to prison for years; yes, he would be willing to die, for their sakes. He said further, that he did all for nearly no pay, that he could travel a hundred miles without anyone asking him what his circumstances were, but that many came to him for help when in trouble, thinking that he was rich because he occupied such an important role amongst the Methodists, and so many societies were in his care.

He pressed them to take Christ's cause to their hearts; he described to them the case of the new chapel at Builth and encouraged them to take up a weekly collection towards God's work. Someone answered that they were unable to contribute, but Harris gave him a lesson that he would not have forgotten for a long time. He said that all were to contribute, even the poor, referring to the two mites of the widow; they were all part of the Body; they sinned in possessing anything, unless they possessed it in the Lord; that no fruit was acceptable, even if it had been washed in the Lamb's blood, if it was not the fruit of the Holy Spirit. After closing the society, he addressed the exhorters and stewards in the same vein as at St Nicholas, showing them their various responsibilities:

> I met the preachers and stewards, and showed the latter their places and work, as at St Nicholas; and called them all to account here for giving the Sacrament here in this house (Groes-wen), as it affected the whole Body, without consulting us all. And if they want to do what seems to me to hurt the work several ways, I would withdraw from them. I showed that I had come to remove what was too heavy for them, and to support them. I gave them advice concerning discipline, and we sat together till eight. I had been in the work for twelve hours, without food or drink.

This was surely a strange meeting. The account provides a clear confirmation of the tradition that it was following encouragement from Daniel Rowland that some were first ordained to administer the sacraments at Groes-wen. Harris's complaint, that they should not have taken such a liberty without conferring with them all, suggests fairly strongly that they did consult some person or persons. And who would this be, other than Rowland? It is clear also that this was completely against Howell Harris's judgment and feelings. Of all of the fathers, it was he who clung closest to the Church. The fact that he was at liberty to visit them, to point out to them their duties, and even to rebuke them for what he considered to be wrong amongst them, is an indubitable proof that the congregation at Groes-wen was as fully Methodist after this ordination, as before.

## HARRIS'S IDEAS ON EDUCATING THE EXHORTERS

The next day, at Watford, Harris had a very interesting conversation with Thomas Price:

> I showed him the nature of our place, that such a large body of people depended on us and were to us as children, that we should be for their sakes in the way of being lawyers, physicians, as well as theologians, and fathers. That we should read legal and medical books as well as theology, church history and doctrinal controversies. I spoke freely to him of the nature of the work, the way in which he proceeds in all strength, and the way in which we should use some means to educate the preachers, and establish a college in order to raise prominent young men to the ministry. I also thought that Mr Whitefield was too definite when he claimed that knowledge of Latin was essential.

This is the seed, planted by Richard Tibbott in his letter to the Association concerning the education of the exhorters, now bearing fruit in Harris's mind. The nature of the college he envisaged is evident. It would teach the elements of law and medicine, as well as the various branches of theology. He laid great emphasis on the basic things because many of the converts were very ignorant of them and depended completely for light and guidance on those whom they considered their spiritual fathers.

Harris travelled through Fair Oak and Redwick, he then had to return suddenly to Trefeca. But he was back at Goetre by Tuesday, 24 January, having journeyed all night.

> I arrived here at three in the morning and rested in my clothes for two hours. I had to proceed to a meeting with Mr Whitefield at Gloucester in that the King's work calls for speed and determination.

We do not have room to give the history of the Association of the English brethren at Gloucester, but it is clear that Harris was a loyal admirer of Whitefield, and loved him deeply.

> I had such a view of Mr Whitefield that greatly warmed my heart towards him, in that the Lord and his love dwells within him. I loved him deeply and rejoiced that such a man was ever born.

On 6 February, there was a Monthly Association at Trefeca opened by Harris with a powerful sermon on the words, 'They that trust in the Lord shall be as mount Zion, which cannot be removed.' He did not remember having such a meeting before; the Lord was truly amongst them. In the private meeting of the Association the brothers' journeys were arranged; the venues of the Monthly Meetings decided; and the superintendents over the various societies appointed. He encouraged the younger brethren also to come once a week, now and again, to Trefeca to be taught. It is not said who was to instruct them nor do we know to what extent the suggestion was taken up. He notes also that Bro. William Griffiths from Caernarvonshire was present.

On Monday, 14 February, he began a journey to Radnorshire and Montgomeryshire. He preached on the first night at Erwood, on the nature of faith. The next day, at Builth, his text was, 'O wretched man that I am!' In the private society that followed there were many exhorters present and he took the opportunity to emphasize the privilege it was to be allowed to serve the Lord:

> [I] showed of my leaving a £100 a year, and a place where I might wear my ruffles and gold lace, and nothing but conscience stood in the way. With the work of the gospel I am often wet to the skin and cold. Do I complain? Do I feel it hard? No, no, I am amazed that I am allowed such an honour. [I talked also] about gathering weekly, not each a penny, but each according to his ability, and seeing it an honour too.[4]

He also exhorted the labourers that, when they contracted with their masters, they should keep some time for the work of the Lord. At Llansanffraid, his text was, 'Rejoice evermore.' At the private society he showed that the rule of God's Word and the example of the Lord Jesus were one and the same; that to argue about the differences between them was like arguing on the difference between one and two making three, or two and one making three. He encouraged them to be free from party spirit, and to give all the preachers that came to them the same respect, whatever might be their various gifts. At Dolswydd, James Beaumont was amongst the congregation, and the two travelled together to Llwynhelyth. His text at Mochdre was, 'O Israel, thou hast destroyed thyself,' and he had a sweet meeting. He said that he had left £200 a year for the sake of the work, and that he would do so again. He showed the great work that God was carrying forward, and that presently it was only beginning; that his own main work presently was the moving of thorns and briers aside; that hell had been greatly agitated against this work from its beginning, but could not destroy it; that all that they possessed was the Lord's, when they gave themselves to God, they gave their possessions also, they could not now call them back, nor would they wish to do so.

On Friday, he was at Berriew, where he preached on the prodigal son. At Llanllugan, he preached at the home of a believer called Robert Thomas. His text was, 'It is a faithful saying', and at the close he had a very interesting conversation on the nature of pride, with Lewis Evan, who had recently been released from Dolgelley prison. On Saturday, he was at Llanfair Caereinion, and his text was Ephesians 2:8. He proclaimed to his hearers that there was no difference between themselves and the damned, other than for God's grace, and yet they were so ungrateful and so unfruitful. Authority and power accompanied the ministry. In Blaen Carno, he preached on, 'Ye are come unto mount Sion', a hard service, though he had a measure of light as he applied the truth.

He was at Llanbryn-mair on Saturday night, preaching from the words, 'Adam, where art thou?' A private society was held on the Sunday morning at the same place, with twelve present. Harris began by explaining that the societies were like hospitals, where all were ill and were in daily need of an application of the blood of Christ to their innermost being; that it was possible for the mind to be enlightened and the emotions affected, and yet for sin, prejudice and the fear of death to remain still in the depths of the soul. Again, the societies were like schools, where all were taught of God. He continued by praising the Established Church and seeing the Methodists as reformers in its ranks; he described his own position – that the care of all the preachers and societies throughout Wales was upon him; he referred to Richard Tibbott, and to the difference between themselves and the Dissenters. After the society, a public service was held. Lewis Evans preached first and thundered forth the law, so that Harris, after him, felt constrained to present the gospel. In the afternoon, he travelled on to Llwytgoed, a distance of eleven miles. On the way, he asked three questions of the Lord:

1. Was there anything in his spirit that was refusing to bend and submit to the Lord? He received the answer that there was not.

2. In answer to a second question, he was reassured that the doctrine, discipline and order of the Methodists was acceptable to the Lord, and that he would dwell amongst them.

3. He asked would it be profitable for him to repeat this journey in a few days, in order to educate the exhorters and, after a while, he received a positive answer. He saw the benefit that might accrue, but it was a new work, and he feared to take it on without it being given to him of the Lord, and knew the absolute necessity of God's support, if he was to undertake

it. He rejoiced to think that the Lord was to make use of all his (that is, Harris's) abilities, even the teaching he had received in the various schools he had attended.

This episode shows that Harris was planning to add to his other responsibilities the role of an itinerant teacher, providing for the exhorters the kind of education they might have received in a theological college.

He also had a long conversation about the Dissenters with Richard Tibbott. He said that his heart was upright towards them, that he loved them and grieved over their errors, that his only purpose in speaking against them was to move them from their deadness and formality. He mentioned also how they had begun to cold-shoulder him when he first saw the light of the gospel clearly and began to invite sinners as they were to Jesus Christ. He considered that many of the Dissenters were the children of good men and had received a good education, as a result of which they had made a profession, but that they had not been moved from out of themselves nor received the gospel in truth, though he believed that many of their preachers and people did belong to the Lord. Tibbott agreed, and said that he was quite willing to commune in the Church, although this was rather uncomfortable for him because of his education and upbringing. It was only occasionally he had received the sacrament with the Dissenters, but that as he now was labouring amongst them, he thought that he might offend them if he took communion in his parish church, and that it would be better for him to travel to some other parish to receive. With this, Howell Harris agreed.

An immense crowd had gathered at Llwytgoed. Harris's text was Romans 7:24, and it was a powerful service. Afterwards, a general private society was held, that is a society of members and exhorters from various places who happened to be present, and he was there, and with the exhorters afterwards, until one o'clock in the morning. He exhorted them to redeem the time, and to teach their children; he adjudicated on some difficult issues amongst them; they arranged superintendents to read the Bible and expound it for the various societies; he also referred to his intention of returning there within a few days in order to teach the exhorters. As he pressed them to give themselves to the service of the Lord, he said:

> I do not offer to you any dish that I have not tasted for myself; we must be taught ourselves, and that through hot temptations, before we can teach you . . . The Lord is soon to take possession of the land. I am not asking for anything less presently than Great Britain. At the start, I asked for no more than my relatives, my neighbours and my parish, but now, nothing less than the whole country will do.

A remarkable society was had. 'It was a glorious time of liberty,' wrote Harris.

On Monday, he was at Ty-mawr, Trefeglwys. From there, he proceeded to Llanidloes, where he preached in Welsh and in English, but mainly in Welsh. He dealt with the case of the exhorter, Thomas Bowen, who to a large extent had lost all spirit of religion. Harris talked with him for some hours, answering his arguments and reasoning. He was given much wisdom in this respect, but Thomas Bowen continued stubborn. The next morning, Harris made another attempt. He called at his home, and answered all his objections so that Bowen could find nothing more to say, but the attempt was in vain, the exhorter's heart had sunk back into the world. From here, he continued through Rhayader, Dôl-y-felin, and Erwood, returning home on Friday after nearly a fortnight of laborious journeying.

During the brief period in which he was at home, he notes that he received four backsliders to the Trefeca society and he refused one woman from the Dissenters to give her time to consider the matter seriously. He met twice with the exhorters, in order to teach and qualify them for the work. He says that they spent some time with the basic elements of spelling, reading, arithmetic and grammar. He felt great pleasure in this work. He received news that his brother-in-law had been appointed to a public position worth five hundred pounds a year. He responded:

> I was glad of the position that I have. I also am a servant of the King, a servant of the King of kings, and I have an honourable place in his Privy Council.

## A JOURNEY THROUGH CARDIGANSHIRE AND PEMBROKESHIRE

About the end of February, he set out on a long journey through Cardiganshire and Pembrokeshire. At Bolgoed, a farmhouse about two miles from Brecon, he spoke from the words, 'I am black, but comely.' At the private society at Bronwydd, after the sermon, he was led to give an account of the beginnings and growth of the revival and the way in which he was appointed at Watford as the general Superintendent. He then showed that the societies were not churches, but reformed branches of the Church of England, in which they were to remain until the darkness that remained in the Church was swallowed up by clear light, or until they were thrown out of it. He said also that he loved the Dissenters and could not abide any who despised or were disrespectful of them. He went on to Cil-y-cwm, where he preached on the duty of abiding in Christ. He had a remarkable society after the sermon. As he was explaining how much the Lord had done for them, such glorying and praising of God broke out that he had to stop speaking for some time. He proceeded through Llwynyberllan, Llansadwrn, Caeo and Llancrwys, and on the way was assured that the Lord would give him the languages – Latin, Greek and Hebrew – so that he might be more useful for the flock. He had faith to pray for this; he would not cease from such prayers, because he saw that it would tend to God's glory. Early on a Sunday morning, he was crossing over the mountains that led to the fruitful Teifi valley and to Capel Betws, about two miles south of Llangeitho. He stayed here until Rowland came from Llangeitho to administer the sacrament.

He was probably quite troubled in mind as he waited, in that he had not visited Llangeitho for two years, because of the coldness that had arisen between Rowland and himself. During the ordinance, he had particular indication of God's favour. That afternoon, at Capel Gwynfil, the name by which the village of Llangeitho was known locally, he preached to an immense gathering in the open air. His text was, 'I am black, but comely.' It had been raining heavily during the day, but as soon as Harris's prayer ended, the clouds scattered and the sun appeared and the weather was ideal for holding the sevice.

After the sermon, he held a society for three hours. He spoke of many things; of following the example of Christ, and that he never saw himself as a devil in human flesh except when meditating on the humiliation of the Saviour; of the tenderness of Christ towards Peter in not reproving him for his fall; and on the reading of the Scriptures, showing that the benefit of this remained even after emotional warmth had cooled. He gave rules for the men and the women in the society on how to read a chapter, and pray, and how, unless God opened their mouths to speak to edification, they should not speak at all. The divine presence was so evident in the meeting that Harris failed to continue:

> I cried out; I could not desist; it was a day of reconciliation. I had increased strength for the task. Many prayed, and tongue cannot express the rejoicing that was there.

That night, he was very weary in body. Before leaving, he begged Daniel Rowland to visit Breconshire. There was certainly a better understanding between them than had been the case.

On Monday night, he preached at Abermeurig – a severe sermon, full of threatenings, law, and thundering. He found out afterwards that the place was very ungodly and corrupt, and that such a sermon was what was needed there. On Tuesday, he was at Cwm Cynon, and in the society, after the sermon, he said that self and the devil should not be allowed to dwell in God's house, that he had a commission against all devils and was opposed to all things within believers emanating from hell. He thundered also against the carnal methods of courting which were current in the land, and he examined them whether they attended the church each Sunday to hear either Rowland or Howell Davies. At Dyffryn Saith he preached on, 'And this is life eternal,' and in Newcastle Emlyn on, 'Wretched man that I am.' He continued through Pen-y-wenallt, Dygoed and Ty'r Yet. In the last place, many exhorters had gathered and he encouraged them to establish everywhere a weekly collection. He described to them his own circumstances, that he had nothing but the promises to fall back upon, and that he would have given up the work long ago had he not the witness in himself that God had called him to it. He next visited Longhouse and Hayscastle, where he listened to Howell Davies in the parish church, and received the sacrament.

The next Monday, he hurried to Haverfordwest where a Monthly Association was being held. He found that the Lord was there before him. When they made a rule to make weekly collections, some were opposed, and Harris advised them to proceed slowly in case God was not in it, and if they pushed it through all opposing arguments, they might lose their influence in the gospel, that influence which Christ had purchased with his own blood. He showed that the best way to overcome obstinacy was by love and patience.

He referred to his own circumstances, that he had not received five pounds in the last six months, that he had refused a hundred pounds a year, which shortly would be two hundred pounds, but that he rejoiced for being in poverty and discomfort, counting it an honour. After arranging other matters, he went to the room to preach. His text was Ephesians 5:20 and he discoursed on Christian morality. The Association met at the close of the service. Harris explained the nature of the education that he would like the exhorters to receive, namely, spelling, English grammar, rhetoric, logic, geography, history, philosophy and languages. He described the lessons he had been giving at Trefeca. All the exhorters agreed, and it was decided that John Sparks would prepare a spelling book with copies, for the next Association. The stewards also were expected to take lessons.

> I then showed the necessity of education in all things, otherwise they cannot be useful, and as fathers. They should learn to behave at table in company according to their character, not like a fop, nor like a fool; and how to address others. I taught what I could; and for them to be dead to themselves, and to

the world, and to fashions, so that it should be of no matter to them what they wore. I showed the honour of our office, that we are allowed to draw near to the person of the King.[5]

It may be seen that Harris's idea of an academic education was extensive. He realized that the initial provision would have to be very basic. Some of the exhorters had hardly received any early education and so had to be taught spelling and reading, but he intended the course to develop and extend so that those who followed it through would not be behind the clergymen of the Established Church in culture. The reference to instructing the young men in table manners and in addressing others shows how practical Harris was in all his plans. Many of the young preachers came from poor families. They knew much of the doctrines of the gospel but very little of the rules of etiquette and social practice as taught by Lord Chesterfield, and as they might be invited, quite frequently in those days, to the houses of the gentry, many of whom were associated with the Methodists, there was a danger that they might become objects of scorn to the wordly in those places. But the Reformer was very anxious that they should not become proud, whatever honours were placed upon them, and so he pointed out that to draw near to the person of the King was of greater privilege than to enter the house of any gentleman.

From Haverfordwest, Harris passed on to Pembroke, where he preached to a vast throng, from Matthew 1:21. He spoke on the name of Jesus, showing that he was King, Priest and Prophet, and much power and light accompanied his words. He was next at a place called Caino, where he was weary in body, and had no liberty at all while speaking but he hoped that someone might have received blessing. 'They that trust in the Lord shall be as mount Zion', was his text. In the private society he had great liberty when counselling the members to live by faith. He said of the exhorters that they were determined to continue preaching even if they had to go about without clothes and barefoot. He explained the duties of masters and servants; that they should practise more self-denial, that Jesus Christ was the great example in this, and that it would be profitable for them to live below their station so that they would have something to contribute to the Lord. He told them that as for himself, he considered it an honour to be wet and to travel a hundred miles a week, preaching two or three times a day, without any pay for his labours but what he received from the Lord. His next stop was Jefferson. As he travelled there, he was very displeased on hearing some rumour:

Hearing how Bro. Rowland said of me that Whitefield had influenced him to change my mind about [the doctrine of] the Trinity, etc., and how Bro.

Howell Davies said I was not now the same as I was. I felt self rising strongly, and would defend myself and have satisfaction of them. After consulting the Lord, as I always do, called a private society.[6]

His temper cooled and he decided to bear all things. It is clear that his spirit was often disturbed by talebearers. At Jefferson, his text was, 'Great is the mystery of godliness.'

I showed in what way it is a mystery:

1. In that it is completely hidden from the carnal man; he knows nothing of it.

2. In that it is through faith and through the teaching of the Holy Spirit only that it may be known and not through natural means such as reading, studying, and meditating, though the Holy Spirit often approaches through these means and so they should be used.

3. It is a mystery in that its depths cannot be plumbed, not even by those who have seen deepest into it.

He also notes that he applied the doctrine powerfully to careless sinners:

I was dreadfully cutting. I hurled the terrors of God upon them, showing that they sinned against law and gospel. I showed how the old and young, the rich and poor, were fellow-sinners along the wide road, and yet claim that there is no need whatsoever to go about exhorting the people. I showed the state of the county. I thundered terribly and warned them.

It must have been an awful place, and the influences too much for flesh and blood to bear. In the society following, with John Harris present, he encouraged them strongly to continue in brotherly love, and not to be absent from the means. 'You do not realize your loss in missing even one opportunity', he said. He preached powerfully at St Kennox, and while passing from there to Maenclochog he had to part with John Sparks, who was very dear to him. But John Harris continued with him, and Harris pressed him to encourage the members to be at their best for the Lord. 'As for myself,' he says, 'I said that I could not rest, and that I was determined, through grace, to die in this most honourable work.'

From Maenclochog, he travelled to Parke in the company of his old friend, Howell Davies. He compared themselves to travellers brought together after passing through terrible storms. Harris opened all his heart to his friend, describing the greatness of the work and of his success, and his belief that the storms of the past through which they had passed had been the means of keeping them from pride. His text at Parke was, 'This is a faithful saying.' He then journeyed through Gilfach, Mounton, Laugharne, Merthyr and Llanpumsaint. In most of these places he preached without a text, and great power accompanied the ministry. At Carmarthen, he heard John Richard preach on the humiliation of the Saviour and preached after him on the mystery of Christ. At the Monthly Association meeting there, he solemnly emphasized to the preachers their need for further education. He finished the journey at Llanddeusant. It was the depths of night before he arrived there, and as he crossed the Black Mountain he was cold and wet to the skin. Though it was so late, he had to preach, and began his sermon at twelve o'clock. His theme was 'A finished salvation', and the Lord came down. He continued on immediately to Trefeca, arriving at four o'clock in the morning, the day before Easter Sunday. He wrote in his journal:

This morning I came home after a journey of three weeks in Pembrokeshire, Cardiganshire and Carmarthenshire, and after travelling over eleven hundred miles. The Lord favoured me remarkably in every place as I preached, counselled in the private societies, and arranged matters concerning the eternal kingdom of our Saviour. For all our sinfulness, yet the Lord carries forward his work in every place. I believe that I have the honour of leaving a blessing behind me wherever I go, to the church, to the world, and to the exhorters. Many revelations of his glory were given me of the Lord.

Harris had returned home on 25 March. The following Tuesday, there was a Monthly Association at Trefeca:

In the general society I had such a sense of the love and presence of God that I could not speak. Everyone was full of God. My mouth was then opened for two hours, in great tenderness and love. I showed them of the love of God, of the honour of being in his service, and of the life of faith.

In the private meeting, he examined the exhorters closely and arranged the journeys of each one. On the first day of April, he set out for London, and did not return until 11 May. One night, soon after his return, the Rev. Price Davies, the vicar of Talgarth, came to visit him and he was more humble and gracious than Harris had ever seen him. He described his whole history to Davies, the way he had been awakened by Davies's call to the people to come to the sacrament, and the manner in which he began going about to preach; that he had no kind of plan at the beginning; that he had not heard of Whitefield or Wesley, and that he had no idea that the work would increase as it had. He declared further his determination to remain in the Church of England.

I said that those who were brought up in the Church should remain in it; if any hesitation arose in their minds they should take it to the minister; if he were to have no patience and give them no satisfaction, they should go to another clergyman; if they could get no help from any clergyman, they should come to me or any one of us, the Methodists; and if they had no satisfaction from any of us, they were then at liberty to follow their own light and conscience.

He described further the persecution that he received from the hands of the clergy, that he often preached against them, and that he had been in danger of his life from them, but that he was for reformation and for doing as much good as possible, and that if the Methodists left the Church, he would leave them. Mr Davies acknowledged that reformation was greatly needed.

> Then, I showed Mr Davies that the prejudices [of the clergy against the Methodists] had lessened greatly in that many faults of which we were guilty had been corrected, and in that they saw that we clung to the Church. I confessed also that I and others had been too warm in our zeal. He stated that this is what had been carried to the ears of the clergy and bishops, yet, he confessed that many of them were bad men, and that he himself was quite bad.

On hearing this confession, Harris broke out in praise, 'Wondrous, Lord! What canst thou not do?' He then proceeded to commend the Church, that its service was most sweet. We record this account being mindful of historical accuracy, as well as because of its inherent interest. It shows that Harris's spirit, which was always warm and loyal towards the Established Church, for all the faults that he saw within it, was by now entwining ever more tightly about it, and that he was determined never to forsake it, even if this would result in his having to leave the Methodists. Quite possibly it was his renewal of fellowship with Whitefield that had brought about this change in his feelings.

In May, Daniel Rowland passed through Trefeca, and Harris went to hear him preach. His text was Romans 8:13, and he spoke on grace in conflict with sin. He said that grace would not yield to corruption until it was fully conquered; that the Christian has put to death the works of the flesh, and hated them with all his heart; that there were many Pharisees to be found, who were only moral outwardly, and that nothing was acceptable to God and grace but the complete destruction of sin. The doctrine thrilled Howell Harris's heart:

> I saw that the Lord was proceeding against sin; this was clear in that he had given a commission to his servant, and my soul was made to rejoice because of it . . . Blessing God because of this message.

## LONDON, CARMARTHENSHIRE, AND GLAMORGANSHIRE

At the beginning of August, Harris went to London and stayed there until the middle of September. The main event during his stay was Whitefield's resignation from the Superintendency of the English Connexion and the transferral of this responsibility to Howell Harris. This took place in an Association held at the Tabernacle, London, on 1–7 September. Many things had brought Whitefield to this:

1. Though he was an able organizer, and a good manager and leader, this was not his main gift, nor the work that pleased him most. Above everything else, Whitefield was a preacher, and his favourite work was calling sinners to Jesus Christ. And in order to be at liberty to go wherever there would be a call, and to preach Christ wherever a door was opened to him, he felt he had to free himself from every responsibility and care for external matters.

2. The continual controversies and arguments that pervaded the Connexion in England had wearied his spirit. He felt that he could not put up with his intractable brethren much longer. And although he did not wish to disassociate from them, he would not be further wearied by their strife.

3. It is very probable that his views of the Established Church had changed. At first, he believed that revival within it was impossible; he judged that the Methodists, as a body, would very shortly have to leave it. But now, through associating with many of the nobility, and particularly with the Countess of Huntingdon, he came to believe that it was by reforming the Church that the nation might be reformed. He thought that he would be made a bishop, and that evangelical clergymen would be promoted to positions of authority, and that in this way the Church as a whole would become evangelical. He was not eager therefore to multiply Methodist societies nor to be himself the leader of them. It is very probable that he influenced Howell Harris, and made him also more loyal to the Church of England.

Towards the end of September, Harris visited parts of Carmarthenshire. In a society at Llwynyberllan he declared he was willing to be out of sight in the work; that Whitefield should be head of the work in England, and Rowland in Wales, and if they were willing, that John Wesley should be over them all. The least portion would do for himself. To carry about the truth, to be hidden from view, would be sufficient honour for him, and he did not mind if others received all the respect and popularity. He was undoubtedly honest in such remarks. This was his feeling at that moment. But the sentence that follows this comment suggests some degree of underlying bitterness: 'Soul cried indeed that Bro Rowland may not have a fall, as it seems to threaten.'[7] Soon, he was on his way to Glamorganshire. He describes himself as being weak in body, and with his spirit troubled because of the disorder amongst the Methodists. On the first night, he preached at Cantref; the next morning, at Taf-fawr, and he complains much of the roughness of the road; in the night, he was at Llanfabon. On the way to Groes-wen, he heard of some trouble that had arisen at Goetre. He felt an unbearable burden weighing upon him as a result; he thought that party spirit was likely to cause immense damage to them, and he groaned on seeing Satan given permission to tear them. But while preaching on Matthew 11:28,29, the Lord came and it proved a powerful service. In the private society, he opened his heart. He said that he saw himself the worst of all, but in Christ it was as if he had never sinned, and as if sin had never entered into the world:

Powerful breezes of the Spirit came down when I showed our union with Christ. I asked them, 'Do you travel on this way?' This is my life. I am not debtor to the flesh, but to the Lord, to live to him.

After the society, he was with the preachers and stewards until twelve o'clock at night. A strong breeze descended here also:

I showed them the eternal God in the manger. I questioned them home on the Godhead of the Saviour; I showed the way this truth was revealed to me; I explained my unity with the Moravians on the mystery of the Trinity, and the way in which the Holy Trinity dwells in Christ; that they should not do anything without inquiring of the Lord, acknowledging him as Master. A strong gust of wind came down, and we decided many things.

The next day, he and Thomas Price, Watford, went to Cardiff. On hearing the rude shouts of the mob he feared, and could not compose himself for a while, but soon he was strengthened and enabled to evangelize sweetly, from the words, 'O death, where is thy sting?' He had a long conversation with Price which is worth recording.:

I offered to give up my place as far as any title is involved; that Rowland could be head in Wales, Whitefield in England, and Wesley over those two. I said that I would serve in exactly the same way then as now, and that I have no great trust in any; that I see a lack of the practice of the rule of love towards one another, and that envy has come amongst us. I showed how Bro. Rowland weakens my hands; that in England I am blamed for keeping the Moravians and Wesleyans out of Wales, and that in Wales I am accused of betraying them (that is, to the Moravians). I spoke of pride, of love of the world, and that he, Price, was not as simple as at first. He opened all his heart and fears to me. He said that Bro. Rowland would not take my place, that he united with them to honour my talents and service, but that he (Rowland) believes that I do not always exercise my judgment but act from the feelings of the moment. He also said that he and the brethren would not accept Rowland in my place. We departed sweetly.

We next find Harris at Dinas Powys, where he preached from Christ's answer to the disciples of John the Baptist. His theme was the deity of Christ. At St Andrew's, he met Morgan Jones who told him of the state of the legal case in north Wales. He makes no comment on this. It seems that Morgan John Lewis was also there, and Harris went to him to discuss the situation amongst them at the time:

> I said that the work was too much for me, unless I had help from souls who would be dead to themselves, and who saw it an honour to be given up to the work of the Lord, having the cause in their hearts. I showed that my work was so great that it would be good for someone to follow in my steps, nurturing the young exhorters and stewards, and going about families to awaken them, so that the Lord would be head over all . . . I offered to place the ministers as heads over the work in England and Wales, and for me to be out of sight.

It may be seen that he is still to some extent bitter against the clergy-men and that the question, 'Who shall be head?', was still too prominent in his mind. He went next to St Nicholas, where he had opportunity to hear Howell Davies. After the service, Davies told him that the devil was roaring terribly against him in Carmarthen and at Dygoed; that he was being accused of some immorality and that bawdy songs had been composed about him.[8] The news was as the stab of a sword in his heart. He could not speak when travelling to Aberthin because of the extent of his grief. Having arrived, however, he was given much strength to speak from the words, 'I am the Lord thy God.' In the society afterwards, he said much of the Person of Christ, his blood, and merit; that he was eternal in the womb, eternal at his birth, and eternal in his life, in his obedience, and in his death. He rebuked the members severely for their pride, their miserliness, and the way they spent their money, and he warned them against judging the exhorters, otherwise they might fall into the same sin as Korah. After the society for the members, there was another society for the exhorters and stewards, and it seems that Harris was arranging matters just as if these meetings had the authority of Monthly Associations.

He passed through Penprysg, preaching the gospel of the kingdom, and came to Nottage. He here heard that it was intended to name him as a trustee of the chapel that was nearing completion at Aberthin. This threw him into some confusion. He feared that the Methodist ministers might be offended that his name was on the deed and theirs not, and that they would not come to preach in the building because of it. 'I am willing,' he wrote, 'to take my part in all the difficulties arising with God's house, but not in the honour of it.' He passed through Hafod from Llangatwg, and arrived at Llansamlet where a large gathering awaited him. He had a powerful meeting as he spoke on the glory of Christ, and the eternal nature of redemption. His text in Swansea was, 'For he shall save his people from their sins,' and he was at his best in proclaiming the mystery of the Trinity. In the private society, he rebuked the members strictly for their civic pride in refusing to receive brethren of lesser abilities to exhort amongst them, and of frustrating the work by such behaviour:

> This is but pride and a lack of mature judgment; what we need is the power of God attending whoever is speaking.

From here, he traversed Gower and parts of Carmarthenshire thoroughly, returning to Trefeca about the middle of October.

## MADAM SYDNEY GRIFFITH AND JAMES BEAUMONT

As well as his deep spirituality and strong common sense, Howell Harris had a streak of credulity that bordered on superstition. He believed that he received direct messages from God by allowing his Bible to fall open of itself, and reading the first verse that would take his eye. He brought questions to the Almighty on every matter, large and small, and believed that his state of mind subsequently, provided the answer from the Lord for his query. And at this point in his career, this tendency brought him into a severe and bitter tribulation. A woman, who had been brought to religion under the influence of his ministry, arrived at Trefeca. Her name was Mrs Griffith or, as she is always referred to in the journal, 'Madam Griffith'. Her husband, after abusing her terribly, had left her. She claimed that she was filled with the gift of prophecy and was able to test the spirits. Amazingly, Harris believed her claims, and in his innocence he imagined that the Head of the Church had honoured the Methodists with one of the extraordinary gifts of the apostolic age. He believed that she could be of great help to the revival by being as a pair of eyes for him, directing him how to respond in difficult situations, and to enable him to distinguish hypocrites from true believers. He decided immediately to take her with him on all his journeys, although he realized that some would draw wrong conclusions from such a practice. But his wife did not believe in the prophetess. And when he came to lay the matter before the brethren whose judgment he trusted, they also expressed their concerns. As usual however, opposition had no effect upon his plans; indeed, it only served to make him more determined in his conclusions:

> This opposition must stop, just as all who have opposed me from the beginning have been brought to nothing. I am certain that Mrs Griffith is a pillar in the house of God.

There is not the slightest evidence to doubt the purity of Howell Harris's life. All his views were as undefiled as the light of the sun. His danger, indeed, arose out of his naivety and his inability to see occasions of suspicion in matters that seemed very suspect to others. At the same time, it does appear that a degree of spiritual fanaticism had overtaken him. Strangely enough, John Wesley, one of the most discerning of men in his judgments, was also overtaken by similar circumstances. It is clear, however, that Harris's credulity in this matter gave occasion to the enemies of the Lord to blaspheme for a season.

At the beginning of November, Harris set out on a journey through parts of Montgomeryshire and Radnorshire. We will not go into the details of the journey but only notice two points of some importance. The first was that he drew closer still to James Beaumont, who held very peculiar views of the Trinity and was well down the road to Antinomianism. Harris manifested a particular tenderness towards Beaumont. In some senses the man was his Absalom. He now took him as his travelling companion, praised him for his preaching, and commended him for his humble spirit and his willingness to be taught. How he could do this is strange, in that he and the exhorters had recently spent a whole night at Trefeca endeavouring to persuade Beaumont to stop using certain unscriptural expressions, and had failed. Harris knew that by taking Beaumont as a companion, he was deeply offending his brethren.

The second point is that during the journey he took the opportunity to inform the exhorters that the difference between them and John Wesley was not very great:

> I opened of our meetings with Mr Wesley, and how we did not differ much about perfection, only about the nature of it, in that Christ is our perfection, and that we slowly grow up to his stature by faith. And also about falling from grace and perseverance, only differing about the point where to fix it. And with a view to universal redemption, we believe that Christ died for all, but [his death] only applied to the church. We agreed also on justification, that the life, as well as the death, of Christ is applied to us.

We are inclined to believe that Harris was open to be influenced to some degree by his friends, and that their ideas, for a season, would colour his own views, as long as they did not begin to argue with him and oppose him. Beaumont also pressed upon him the idea that he would shortly be the real head over all the societies in Wales.

At the end of November he set out for London, and did not return until 27 January 1750. Before leaving London, he broke off all connection with the English brethren. The reason for this was a disagreement between himself and Whitefield. The latter asked him not to mix any further with the Wesleyans and the Moravians, nor to attend their societies, as he was in the habit of doing. With this Harris could not agree. He said to Whitefield:

All my view is union; that the outward church may be, like the invisible church, one, that Christ be indeed preached in spirit according to the Scriptures. And that he, Mr Whitefield, be no authority over me any more than I over him, save to tell one another what we see out of place in each other.[9]

Whitefield's conduct in this matter is strange, particularly as he had begun again to exchange pulpits with John Wesley, and had also conducted services together, one reading and praying and the other preaching. However, the quarrel cooled Harris's feelings towards Whitefield and he decided not to work again in the same Connexion.

On the last day of January, a Quarterly Association was held at New Inn, Monmouthshire, and Harris attended. The conference was opened with a sermon from Daniel Rowland. To begin with, Harris appreciated the doctrine. When the preacher said that redemption was complete, a sweet breeze floated over the congregation. But according to Harris:

Matters were darkened by carnal comments on the Trinity; it could be believed from him that the Father was on his own when he created; that the Son was on his own when he redeemed; and the Spirit on his own when sanctifying. He said also that the best men doubted sometimes because of their corruptions and their work in not looking to the Lord.

His condemnation of this comment of Rowland's suggests that he had been influenced to some extent by Wesley's ideas on perfectionism. He says further that Christ's glory was not made evident, and that he found his mind wandering on to the subject of whether he should buy saplings to plant at Trefeca. This shows a considerable change of spirit in him; this was not the way that he usually listened to a sermon from Daniel Rowland. In the private meeting of the Association Rowland accused him of continually changing his views and of domineering over all who would not submit to him, as if his command was law. Harris answered that he was not guilty of either charge. As to the first – fickleness in doctrine – that he had not changed at all since he first began to speak in public. And as to the second – being autocratic and domineering – that this was the sin which he had least exhibited, that his main purpose always was to glorify Christ.

I said further that I would convict them of the sincerity of my intentions by withdrawing, and giving up my place amongst the preachers, and amongst the people. That I had only laboured amongst them as long as they were ready to receive me in faith, but if things were as he (Rowland) said, and that they were afraid to express their thoughts to me, I would leave, and would go about only to those places where I had an open door from the Lord. I would go to the preachers and people who were willing to receive me, that nobody could stop me doing that.

Harris added, in his journal, that this storm had arisen because of Whitefield, and because of their prejudice against Joseph Beaumont. He may have decided that Whitefield had written to Rowland to inform him that Wesley's particular views were colouring Harris's sermons to some extent. At this point, Howell Harris rose to his feet to leave. Rowland answered that it would be better for Harris to stay and for himself to leave. Matters quietened for a while:

> Then the storm returned on considering Bro. Beaumont. I said I was happy for them to rebuke him for anything that was not in order in him, in doctrine or behaviour, but that I could not agree with turning him away only because of prejudice and without just cause. I said that I knew his faith was true, and was used of God, and that I was unwilling to bind him, as with a chain, with regards to the places where he might preach, in case the Lord had some message to send by him. I saw that they (the clergymen) were misusing their authority. I saw, and I said, that we were blessed that there were none amongst us who were in authority, and that it would be a judgment upon us if someone was to be made so.

He proceeded to speak of Christ and the ignorance of many about him, the infinite nature of his suffering, his wounds, his blood, and the infinite nature of sin.

> When Bro. Rowland spoke carnally, I told him to pray that all his knowledge might not be only out of books. It was a terrible storm, and Bro. Rowland threatened to leave if we did not turn Beaumont out.

Harris took the matter to the Lord. He saw clearly that retaining Beaumont was the cause of so much agitation in Wales and England. In the event, matters were left as they were, at least for the time being. A brother called Phillips quietened the fraternity by explaining that Beaumont believed in the Trinity. Other matters were then decided, and a certain brother was rebuked for writing against Griffith Jones and interfering in a matter that did not concern him. The next sentences in the journal are worth recording:

> At this point Bros. Rowland and Price departed, and directly, the Lord came down. I showed them the glorious and infinite nature of the work; I explained how it is spreading, and that if the exhorters will be faithful over a little, they would be raised to be fathers. I proclaimed, in the hearing of all, the infinity

and glory of Christ; that every attempt to oppose him would be in vain. I was severe upon one who opposed him and who viewed him carnally. I saw, and I showed the brethren, that God did not come down upon us until Rowland and Price, etc., had departed, and that it was their unbelief and selfishness on this point that was keeping God away.

This was surely a most unkind comment, manifesting a spirit that was considerably disturbed.

Before leaving New Inn, Howell Harris had a further long conversation with Rowland, Price and Howell Davies. They told him that Whitefield had indeed written to them about Harris and his views, and that Whitefield wished the preachers to come under their care. Harris argued on behalf of Beaumont, but they did not wish to hear him on that point. But, while conversing, they drew closer to one another and were more tender in their thoughts of one another. Harris warned them to keep close to God; he tried to get them to meet privately and to open their hearts to one another and declare what they saw amiss in one another. He complained that Daniel Rowland opposed the Moravians and the Wesleyans, whereas he, Harris, saw the followers of Whitefield and Wesley as two branches of the reformed Church. After showing that they should feel each other's sins as if they were their own, and that their work in blackening one another was as if they blackened themselves, the storm blew over and, as they sang a hymn, they felt that the Lord was amongst them.

There were two very injurious influences upon Harris in this period, which, despite all warning and counsel, he would not shake off. The first was the influence of James Beaumont. At this time, it seems, Beaumont was not only far from orthodox in the faith, but was also full of pride, and was seeking, as much as he could, to turn Harris away from those with whom he had worked together from the beginning. Had he agreed to throw over Beaumont at the New Inn Association, as he surely should have done, the storm would have quietened immediately. But he would not. He was determined to keep Jonah in the boat. The other damaging influence was that of the woman who claimed a spirit of prophecy. He believed that she had been raised higher into the divine light than anybody else on earth, apart from himself, and that the Lord had a great work to accomplish in Wales through himself and her, and that every opposition to her was an opposition against God's will. She herself was deceitful and filled his mind with prejudices against his brethren. She had prophesied, said Harris, that he would separate from Whitefield, and also that all unity between him and Rowland would cease. She now pretended that she had received a revelation that he would soon be head over all the preachers and societies of Wales. She wrote to him from London to warn him to be faithful in preaching the Man Christ Jesus, and he perceived the letter as a direct message from the Lord.

The influence of this cunning and hypocritical woman did untold damage to him. It caused him much trouble in his home, and it gave opportunity for his opponents to spread abroad untrue stories of his immoral and impure behaviour. There was no suggestion of evidence for these stories; no man on earth has been freer from the power of carnal lust. The spiritual tone of his references to the woman in his journal testifies to the light in which he viewed her. We would not now mention her influence over him, were it not certain that she had a great part in the development of the disruption that occurred between Howell Harris and his friends and fellow-labourers.

## PREPARING THE WAY FOR A SEPARATION

Harris was only a few days at home before beginning a journey to Pembrokeshire. We will refer only to a few matters of interest that occurred. At Llandeilo, he met Daniel Rowland, but very little of the old friendship was in evidence:

> I find no brotherly fellowship and Christian communion with him now; but rather, my spirit is closed. I told him that we saw little of the nature of sin, otherwise there would be more fear in us; and that I did not see the burden of the work being felt by any, so in consequence I would go out on my own. We discussed also about a house here to preach.[10]

At Longhouse in Pembrokeshire, he met Benjamin Thomas whom, next to Daniel Rowland, he considered his main opponent. He noted in his journal:

> I spoke freely to Benjamin Thomas, showing what children we all are, and the way in which we all are out of order, with no one knowing his place, and all of us ignorant of Christ. He accepted all from me. I saw and felt how great is the task of bringing Christ before the people, that we were not doing it correctly, and I cried that I might be before the Lord, in that I do not allow any sin (in the societies) and I do not allow any place for self. As a result the opposers are not against me, but against God.

This last quotation throws a strong light on the state of his mind, namely, that he considered that the Lord had appointed him to rule over the societies, and in that he to the best of his ability had been faithful to his stewardship, any opposition to his rule was an opposition to the divine will.

Harris was next at a Monthly Association in Haverfordwest, where Howell Davies was present. It does not appear that anything of importance was decided here, but his conversation on parting with Howell Davies is worth noting:

I told him that the glory of Christ was beginning to be manifested and that all who opposed it would be destroyed. I showed him the carnality and formality of Bro. Rowland; that he is not increasing in the knowledge of Christ and appears to be increasing in selfishness. I referred to the pride of Bro. Beaumont, and also to the way in which, ever since the glory of Christ had been first manifested amongst us, I had endeavoured to search the Bible, and the works of good men. And now, God would destroy all opposition. I said that I thought Bro. Rowland would be the last to come in.

The last to be brought to a recognition of the glory of the Lord Jesus, is what he meant, presumably. What answer Howell Davies gave to all this, we do not know. Perhaps he realized that there would be no point in attempting any defence of Daniel Rowland at the time.

A Monthly Meeting was also held at Carmarthen, and Harris addressed the exhorters and superintendents with great solemnity. He declared to them:

This is one responsibility that belongs to my important office, to which indeed belong many branches, many of which I never saw in the right light before. I see that more branches have been given to me than to any of the preachers, the clergymen, or the exhorters, other than Mr Jones, Llanddowror. I was led here to rebuke for lightness and drinking, and for being one with Christ; and I showed how many had fallen through pride. I was severe for increasing in poverty of spirit. I showed how the work, for all the difficulties, is progressing wonderfully, and the way in which my bow abides in strength. I refused one who had fallen and was applying to come to us, and who appeared very humble, because his spirit was not sufficiently broken, and as I did not feel any spirit in his words.

After much journeying through Carmarthenshire and part of Glamorganshire, he arrived at Llangatwg, near Neath, and the account he gives of his experience here is important:

Last night, after I had preached in public with considerable blessing, Mr Peter Williams contradicted me openly about publishing myself but more so after the private society and went away. I was severe and rebuking here, as at Haverfordwest, but here particularly because of their carelessness towards God, and their party-feeling and carnality toward Mr Rowland. I said that I saw no one who knew his place, and I was therefore determined to go about myself and see who the Lord would unite with me, laying his work upon them, as they passed through all things. I showed how I saw a slavish and schismatic spirit possessing the people; that it was the ministry of the Word alone that had been given to us, and the sacraments were meant for the parish churches.

I counselled them on many matters. I then exhorted them strictly to be one with Christ in all things. The Lord came down at this. Many of the exhorters and stewards confessed the greatness of their sins, their duties, and their privileges. I expressed my love to them, and that I rebuked them in love. I heard of so many corruptions and schisms breaking out amongst them that I could hardly forbear, and of brethren breaking their engagements after their being announced. So many things I have to do. It is good that the Lord is God.

Here is the first example we have of Peter Williams siding with the clergymen, Rowland, Williams and Davies, in opposition to Howell Harris. Whether he disagreed with his doctrine, we do not know; the main accusation mentioned is that Harris preached himself. This suggests that his position amongst the Methodists, and his disagreements with his brethren, were often mentioned in his sermons during this journey. We find also that Harris, by now, has made up his mind to separate, and to form a party of his own, hoping that the majority of the exhorters and of the people would follow him. This had been in his mind for some time and he had mentioned the possibility to Daniel Rowland when he had met him at Llandeilo, earlier in the month.

At Rhos-fawr, a village in west Glamorganshire, he had a long discussion with two of the exhorters, John Richard, Llansamlet, and William James. His purpose clearly was to win them over to his side at the separation on which he had determined. He wrote:

I showed them our fall from God into the spirit of the world, and they saw that the Lord Jesus is not now being loved, but that corruption is entering like a flood. I showed that the clergymen are preaching head knowledge, that they are addressing the head and the emotions, but that the spirit of the people are becoming more wordly, selfish, jesting, sensual and carnal; that the people ignore all but the clergy, respecting the gown and the name. I explained the necessity of looking at everything in God, and perceiving all things in the light of the last day. I requested them to gather together, not for the sake of a party, but to encourage one another in the light given to them by God; to go amongst the people, to save them from this plague of frivolity, and of looking to the flesh for all things, which is devastating us; to endeavour to raise the people up to the light; and for them to let me know how matters are progressing. I showed how I had none now to help me; that many direct the congregations, but they do not increase in the love of Christ nor are watchful over his commandments; that the word of God does not increase in its influence, in that they do not see Christ in its threatenings, in his promises, and in his commandments; that they do not see him and his word as one, and that they perceive the word carnally, as the world does. We see that it is time now to stand, and to oppose any respect to the head and to the flesh. I spoke my mind about the clergy, and particularly Rowland, that I thought he would be the last to come to the light; and that he was hostile to every threat and careless over knowing the mind of the Lord.

He proceeded to accuse the clergy of avarice, and that their ministries were not effective in producing spiritual life.

I saw that it was time for me to come from England to Wales to withstand this self which has entered. I must expect to be severely judged and be mistreated by the people, who are as mischievous children, throwing off the yoke.

He then declared his faith in his position and that the work had to proceed despite all opposition.

It is not in any way pleasant to relate this account. There is no pleasure in seeing old friends separate and misunderstanding one another so completely. It must also be that Harris's own spirit was greatly damaged as he accused his erstwhile companions and fellow-labourers of possessing head knowledge only, and of having only a carnal understanding of the glorious truths of the gospel. But in all this, he believed that he was fulfilling the divine commission.

At Cefngleision, he encouraged the stewards of the societies to meet at least once a month on their own, to pray, to open their hearts to one another, and to organize their affairs. He did not wish for the arrangements to be discussed before the whole society in that there might then be danger of them being publicized before the world. He wrote:

I showed that secrets should not be trusted to babes and children; the first need only bread, and the second, nurture, clothing, discipline and work; and unless you keep them down, they will destroy themselves and all connected with them.

It may be seen that he believed in ruling the societies with a rod of iron, more or less, and that he would not allow any voice to the ordinary members in the making of decisions. He adds:

I spoke to the quick of making idols of the gown, and the name, and other things relating to the clergy. I showed the necessity of looking at everything as God sees it. That these names and other things belonging to the clergy are but carnal, and for those who are carnal, but that there are many of the Methodists that will not look at any minister but the clergy, and so also the clergy themselves; but that the gifts of the Spirit and the work of Christ is gloriously equal in all. I referred to the work of lay people who taught, such as Paul, Apollos, and the scattered brethren from Jerusalem; that Calvin, and even the bishops, acknowledged that a layman might preach in situations of necessity or persecution. I explained who was great in my view, namely, those who fear, love, and honour God in truth, who have his cause upon their hearts, who walk humbly before God, and are watchful. I saw that things were more in the Spirit than ever, and that the Lord was abroad, beginning to gather stones together.

The last sentence would seem to refer to his belief that the time was ripe for him to form a party separate from the Methodists. He continues:

I showed the way in which they even honour a clergyman purely because the name 'priest' belonged to him, but that we should honour them only as far as the Lord is blessing them and no further.

He was no doubt correct in this, but it may be seen that his spirit is completely changed from what it was at Watford, when he rebuked some unfortunate exhorters for saying something disrespectful about the clerical gown. He adds:

I had faith to present all that I had said about the clergymen, namely, Rowland and Williams, to God, in that I am for exalting the Lord, and for each man to remain, and be seen, in the position where God has put him. I had a letter from Cil-y-cwm asking me to take charge of the society there; I spread the matter before the Lord, and had permission to take it over in God, and for God.

This last sentence is very important. It shows that the quarrel between Rowland and Harris had affected the societies and that they were beginning to line themselves up with the one or the other. It is rather surprising to see the Cil-y-cwm society sending such a message to Howell Harris. It was at Cil-y-cwm that William Williams, whom Harris considered one of his opponents, was a member, and the hymnodist's influence in his own neighbourhood must surely have been considerable. We shall see later that the letter had not been sent by the society as a whole but only by some persons in it.

On 5 March, he arrived in Trefeca after a fuller journey through south Wales than he had ever undertaken before. There was a letter from John Cennick waiting for him. He felt such affection for this brother that he felt he could run in his company around the world, and he cried that he might have his fellowship in the work again. Howell Harris must have been feeling very lonely at this time. He had quarrelled with Whitefield, whom he had once considered a prince from God, and he had estranged himself from his old companions in Wales. He names Cennick, Beaumont, John Sparks, John Harry, John Richard, and Thomas Williams, Groes-wen, as those who sympathized with him. He was now preaching publicly against the Methodist clergymen, as the following quotation from his journal shows:

10 March. I was led to speak severely against the pride and self in our young professors, that the religion of Jesus is not seen in them. I showed the way in which the Methodist clergymen and people are falling more and more into Self and pride. How many of them will go forward, God alone knows. For the majority, I showed that they were at root, Jews, Pharisees, and enemies of the Saviour; that their religion is but a little head knowledge with light touches upon the emotions, while self is below it all, and that they grow in the flesh, bearing fruit to the flesh and to the world.

It would be difficult to find harsher words, and he must have caused the people to view Daniel Rowland and his party in a very unfavourable light.

He was only at home a few days. He soon set out for a journey through Montgomeryshire. He referred to the clergymen in nearly every one of his sermons – that they did not know their place, and that they lived in the flesh. At Tyddyn on 14 March, he wrote:

Bro. Richard Tibbott asked me what to do, in that the fathers, that is Rowland and myself, disagreed. I opened to him the whole of our differences; the way in which the Lord had enabled me to begin this work by myself, to go out before Whitefield, Wesley and Rowland; how he placed me as father over the Association, and how they used to submit to my rebukes until, a few years ago, Rowland refused them, and opposed the preaching of the blood, in prejudice against the Moravians. I showed the way I had received the glory and death of our Saviour four years before I came to know them, and that I united with them when I learnt that they acknowledged his Godhead and death. I explained the way I gave up Cardiganshire and Carmarthenshire, where he [Rowland] had influence, because our lights did not agree when it came to arranging external matters, and because he does not increase in his preaching except in formality and in studies that affect the understanding and emotions. Now I have been called to go to Carmarthenshire but I will not respond to the invitation unless they choose me to arrange all private matters, and he [Rowland] only to preach, or instead, for him to arrange and myself to preach. This is what I have offered to the exhorters in every place, and here also.

He was probably referring to the Cil-y-cwm letter when mentioning a call from Carmarthenshire. He was mistaken in his times; there were not four years between his conversion and his meeting with Daniel Rowland, but more like two years. After visiting Mochdre, Llanbryn-mair, Llwytgoed, Dôl-y-felin and Llangamarch, he returned through Brecon to Trefeca on 24 March. He saw that the whole of Wales had been given to him by the Lord; that he had been placed on the pinnacle of the temple, but he felt his insufficiency in his position and responsibility.

On the last day of March, he was preaching to a large gathering at the house of a man called William Powell. His text was, 'With his stripes we are healed.' This house was probably in Glamorganshire. But Harris's mind was entirely on the plan of establishing a party apart from the Methodists. He wrote in his journal:

> I talked to Bro. Thomas Williams on having another private meeting with him and W. Powell, Thomas Jones, John Richard, Beaumont, etc., and others similar who are up to us in light, to exchange ideas with one another, and to enquire with respect to gathering souls together, and to see who amongst the people are increasing in knowledge of Christ crucified, and in the life of faith, living on Christ, and dead to self and the world.

He is next at Llantrisant with Thomas Williams as a companion, and he says that he preached with power, courage and boldness, to an immense audience. In the private society, he commanded them authoritatively to obey Christ, and he was severe on all who united with anyone to sin against Christ. A large congregation awaited him also at Aberthin. He saw that many were coming to the light, and that he was to be victorious, and he prayed out loud, 'Glory for the blood of the Lamb!' After the sermon, he gathered all the societies in a private meeting. He told them that they would respect him more if he was worth a thousand pounds a year and wore a clergyman's gown.

> I showed that Paul was contemptible in the eyes of many; that Calvin was only a layman; the way that God had made me the father and founder of this revival, and that I had gone out to preach four years before Whitefield, Wesley or Rowland . . . Perhaps God intended this in order to bring low the pride of the clergy, and to show that he works in his own way, and that he himself performs the work. I told them that unless they returned to the Bible at the feet of Jesus, that I would dash the societies in pieces, that Christ might not be mocked by a show of obedience.

By coming to the feet of Jesus, he meant of course an acceptance of the doctrine which he taught concerning the Person of Christ. After the general society, he held a meeting of the exhorters and stewards and it seems that matters became very unpleasant. Some complained of William Powell. Harris answered that this was because of Powell's faithfulness to God. 'Satan came amongst us; I turned two out, and three others walked out.' He says that his soul was fearful within him as he rebuked and disciplined, but that it was the Lord who had placed it upon him.

After journeying through Nottage and Aberthaw, he arrived at Fonmon Castle, where he had a good service, preaching on the man who was lowered through the roof to Jesus. William Powell and Thomas Williams were with him at every place, and he would direct them with a view to gathering together those of the same opinions. The society at Dinas Powys was rather stormy, 'I turned out one exhorter, and received another in.' At Cardiff, he preached on the sufferings of Christ. Thomas Price of Watford was there, and the two travelled together to Groes-wen. On the way, Harris said that Daniel Rowland did not love Christ, and that he rarely preached him; that the influences that came by Rowland were only light, external breezes, alighting on the people, which soon disappeared; and that those who produced the most noise in the meetings were often those who were most careless. We grieve at reading these comments. They cannot be explained on any other ground than that a bitter spirit was prejudicing all his judgments.

I then told Bro. Price that he had sunk into the world, that he loved the world and had left the Lord. A great storm arose, and he showed an enmity towards the mystery of Christ. I departed, burdened of soul; he came after me; we conversed over all things quietly, and he said that he received my doctrine as I preached it at Cardiff, and that he was determined to begin anew. I then suggested to him that we went together to north Wales, but he was not free to do so.

The purpose of the trip to the north, we believe, was to take possession of the societies there.

His sermon at Groes-wen is so thrilling that it deserves to be described. His text was 1 John 3:1, 'Behold, what manner of love the Father hath bestowed upon us, that we should be called the sons of God.' He said:

I showed, with much liberty, how close God is to believers, and the way in which he frees them from their sin. This truth is explained in the Bible as not accounting, not remembering, not seeing, forgiving, hiding, and placing upon the scapegoat. I showed how there are those now on earth that God beholds, in Christ, as if they had never sinned. I said, 'By declaring his glory, God has opened heaven for you; by uniting you to himself he had set you in heavenly places, by making you as if you had never sinned. I ask you, which of you, having risked your life to save a friend, and having overcome all obstacles, would then leave the friend at last to the enemy? You who are fathers, could you remain in a warm house, full of every kind of provision, and leave your child to die outside from lack of food and warmth, especially if he were to cry out to you, even if you were angry with him? O come, and return to the Lord. He will forgive all your sins, as long as you will not live in them. He will throw rubbish, such as ten thousand pounds a year, at those who are his enemies, yes, at dogs; what has he therefore in store for you, his children?' I showed that we must have a picture of the believer and the unbeliever in the two worlds before we have a complete picture. I explained further that believers, in truth, live on angels' food, namely, the bread of life, and that they drink the blood of Christ, so that they will live eternally. 'We will live forever!' I said. 'We will not die eternally; we will only sleep; close our eyes on the world, and open them again in God, with all our sins and tribulations, and snares, behind us. And when we shall appear in Christ's glory there will be no old man or baby there, no one lame or weak. Our bodies and souls are now united to Christ, and can he dwell in purity and glory, above sin, above death, and above Satan, and leave you, his children, under them? No! He can never do so. Awake, therefore! Rise from the dust!' I then showed the Christian's majesty from the robe which he wears, the same robe as worn by God the Father himself, the same robe as worn by the whole family in heaven and on earth, and that Jesus Christ is their brother, and that he is not ashamed to own them.

He records that he had a glorious service, that the power of the old days accompanied the message. In the private society that followed the same sweet blessing was felt.

## HARRIS QUARRELS WITH THOMAS PRICE AND DAVID WILLIAMS

When Howell Harris could forget his slights and his place in the socie-ties and be filled by the spirit of the gospel, as at Groes-wen, he carried everything before him in the power of his preaching. He was a hurricane, uprooting the strongest trees and sweeping aside every obstacle that stood in the way. The illumination of heaven was upon this service, but it was a shining through a gap in the clouds, and we find that the darkness soon returned. After the society, he conferred with the exhorters and stewards. The same spirit that had manifested itself at Aberthin got hold of one of the stewards. Harris turned him out. The man replied that he was lording it over God's heritage. Harris continued, showing that the preachers and he had the same ministry as Moses, the prophets, and the apostles; that they fought against the same devils, and were filled with the same spirit; and though they were, according to their feelings, willing to be under the feet of all, yet, that they must magnify their office, otherwise Jesus Christ would be dishonoured. This affair with the stewards at Groes-wen was but a small gust in comparison to the immense storm which arose at Watford the next day. In Harris's words:

This morning I had a great battle with Satan in Bro. Price and Bro. David Williams, concerning the stewards I turned out at Aberthin. When Satan gets in it is hard to remove him. At last, I said to them that I would leave them, and go about on my own as before. I told them they were Jews, not knowing Jesus, nor loving him, and yet that they considered themselves fathers. That they had increased in the flesh, and that the Lord had put up with them until now, but that he would not tolerate further, and that he had gone out against all carnality. 'If you,' I said, 'are enslaved to man and to the flesh, I am not.' They were interceding for the stewards, saying that to turn them out would create great disorder. I said that I saw the work depending on the Lord, and not on the shoulders of such men, and that I was ready to leave the consequences to him. I showed that they were, by their behaviour, trampling my place underfoot, and constituting themselves into some kind of higher court, but that I was determined of claiming the liberty that Christ had purchased for me. 'Not one of you has authority over me', I said. 'You have not had such authority from God or men. If the whole carnal Association, as you call it, were to excommunicate me, I would do the same thing again. I pay no attention to anyone, but to the Lord.'

He then withdrew to pray. He had previously received a letter from Madam Griffith predicting the approach of much disorder.

David Williams, the minister of Aberthin, was, no doubt, the brother standing with Thomas Price during the altercation. This quotation shows that Harris's temper was sometimes uncontrollable; that he claimed a dictator's authority over all the societies, and would not allow anyone to interfere with his work, not even in the form of advice or intercession. We almost think that an element of madness had begun to possess him. In private, he says that he saw deeper into spiritual things than ever before. Then:

As I saw that the opposition was against the Lord, and not against me, I returned to the brethren and showed them how they had sunk into the flesh, and had allowed the devil to enter God's house, and were not now willing to turn him out; but that I was determined to press forward, and I would stand on my own. I said that I could agree with their request, namely, to reinstate the stewards, except that I feared to anger the Lord. I said, 'We cannot continue to go on together, in that we do not see eye to eye, and you do not have faith to submit to my light, and to leave me to the Lord. I am God's free man. I pay attention to no one but him.' I showed the way the stewards had behaved, judging the preacher behind his back, without saying one word to him, nor to me. I demanded of Thomas Williams that he insist on finding out if the people were of this spirit; if they called for me, for him to send for me, otherwise I would not come.

It is clear that he was in no mood to be argued with. He considered himself as being in constant communion with heaven, and being guided directly by the Spirit of God in all that he did, and that therefore any opposition to him was an opposition to God. However, the storm abated a little. Thomas Price and David Williams went with him, to hear him at Machen, and this lightened his spirit considerably. He journeyed through

Monmouthshire, particularly through those parts bordering on England, and did not return until 15 April.

## THE LLANIDLOES ASSOCIATION, MAY 1750

On 5 May, he set out for an Association at Llanidloes, with James Beaumont as a companion. He was in a glorious frame of mind. He shouted out continually, 'Glory for the blood of the Lamb!' At Builth, he took Beaumont aside and rebuked him severely for using Greek words during a sermon:

All know that you have no knowledge of Greek. It is spiritual pride that animates you. And if you did know Greek, how foolish it would be to show it when preaching. I am afraid that you are riding for a fall. You have corrupted all the preachers, and although you have the light of the gospel, you are a Jew in spirit, and unworthy of the sheep and of Christ.

Harris could rebuke Beaumont himself, but would not tolerate anyone else doing so. But on hearing his friend preach at Llansanffraid on the humanity of Christ, he saw that Beaumont was further on than himself in the knowledge of faith, and a strong breeze passed over his spirit, and over the meeting. From there, he proceeded to Llanidloes.

His record of the Association begins:

As soon as I came to the town I felt the devil an awful weight upon me, so that I had to cry out for my life, 'Glory for the blood of the Lamb!' in order to keep my temper in place.

His cries were inward cries, presumably. The Association was begun by a sermon from Peter Williams on the misery of man. He said that man was legally dead, under the sentence of eternal damnation, and an enemy of God; that the door of communion between him and God was closed; but that Christ had come to redeem us. It seems it was a powerful service, but Harris feared that he and the other hearers had felt little of the edge of the truth.

I then went for food, but Mr Rowland and Williams were so full of enmity and, as I think, of self and pride, that I felt obliged to tell him that, though I could accept him as a brother, he had not been set as an archbishop over me, nor had any authority over me from God or from men, and that I would not submit to him in any way. I said the same of Williams.[11]

What they answered him, we do not know. Then Harris preached. His text was 1 Corinthians 2:2. 'For I determined not to know anything among you, save Jesus Christ, and him crucified.' While in prayer he was given great boldness. He then showed that many things were good in their place, but that the apostle turned his eyes from them all and towards

Christ crucified, as to the centre; that the knowledge that was in Christ explained the nature of the Fall, the infinite nature of the resulting need; the infinite demerit of sin, and the truth of hell; and that the danger of refusing Christ was great. He continued:

> Then, I proclaimed the doctrine of the blood, and God came down, while I showed that it was through the blood that we were bought, and brought near to God. After this we went together (to the private meeting of the Association), and the Lord kept the devil bound in a chain; we had peace; I felt in my spirit that we were obtaining the victory through faith; we decided upon the journeys to north Wales, and various other things, and we set aside two preachers for north Wales. As soon as Mr Rowland left, God came down gloriously; my spirit was set free, and I showed them the glory of the Saviour, exhorting them to look to him, to be one with him, and to build their souls upon him.

The Association continued the next day, but the two preachers for north Wales had to leave immediately. Harris charged them to be vigilant against self and pride, and to lead the people to Christ. In the private meeting, Howell Harris attacked Morgan John Lewis vehemently, accusing him of possessing head knowledge only:

> My voice and spirit were raised against the devil that was in his spirit, and after three had testified against him, I told him that he could not preach with me, unless he was to submit, and confess his fault.

He then says that he arranged a number of matters, and addressed the exhorters, showing that he had been placed by God as father to the Association.

## SEPARATION NOW INEVITABLE

So ended the Association at Llanidloes, the last in which both Harris and Daniel Rowland were present together. The report shows that Howell Harris carried everything before him. In Montgomeryshire, Radnorshire, and Breconshire, his was the greatest influence by far. In an Association where most of the exhorters came from these counties, he could do as he wished, it was useless for the clergy to attempt to oppose him, and it seems that Daniel Rowland departed, leaving the field to him. Once the clergy had gone, he was as a king amongst his court. The preachers obeyed him, and he was allowed to arrange all matters according to his wisdom and judgment. It is no wonder therefore that he was on his high places. In formal terms, no separation took place at Llanidloes. Nor does it seem that any heated argument took place at the Association, but the emotions present were very unpleasant and it appears that the two sides departed having privately decided that they would not meet again in any further Association. With the energy and alacrity which characterized him, Harris immediately acted upon this decision. On the way home, at Erwood, he sat down with the exhorters John Richard, Thomas Williams, Thomas James and Thomas Bowen, until late at night, arranging the work and the means for them to draw together in a closer union. Harris told them that this was absolutely necessary and they agreed:

> After showing the way in which we should consider one another in God, and what to do concerning the preachers, and the way in which we should lead them towards the light, as the Lord used to do, I told them to watch over the societies, and inform me of their conditions. We would then meet again in a month's time and confer.

A decision to gather the societies together and to place them under Harris, is evident in this quotation.

During the remainder of May, Harris travelled in Breconshire, and managed affairs at home. On the first day of June he began a long journey through Glamorganshire and Monmouthshire. On the Sunday, he was at Aberthin, where he says that he had an enormous congregation, the biggest that he had ever had in the county, and there was authority in his ministry. But in the private society, matters were much more tumultuous. Harris wrote that the devil was in the place, and he turned out the stewards that had attended without first conferring with him. These left. He continued to rebuke. He told them they were full of self and pride, and in the end, many broke down and wept. After preaching at St Nicholas and Cardiff, he arrived at Watford. He was powerful in the ministry; he shouted out continuously, 'The Blood! The Blood! The Blood! Unless you drink it you will be damned forever!' In the society he said that they were all in the flesh, that they were not convicted of their sin against Christ, they were blind, and he compared them to Judas:

> I said to Price that I would go out on my own, and that I would see who it was that the Lord would send with me. I opened to him all that had passed, and about Rowland; the way in which he (Rowland) has fallen since many years, that his views are legalistic, and that the devil is in him so strongly that he cannot withstand him.

He proceeded to Llanheiddel and New Inn, and there was an awful quarrel between him and Morgan John Lewis and David Williams. He finished the journey at Goetre, where he wrote:

> I found out that an agreement had been made here against me, and against the doctrine of the blood; I knew nothing of it, but now it has come to light.

It seems that the attitude of the people here, together with the spirit he had sensed throughout the journey, brought him to the decision to return to Trefeca immediately.

He had hardly returned when he received a letter from Monmouthshire informing him that all the preachers had turned against him, and that they blamed him deeply for taking Madam Griffith, the woman who pretended to a spirit of prophecy, around with him. We have referred to this woman many times before. He believed that she possessed a gift of prophecy, and had been given by God as an eye for him, to judge and prove the spirits, so that he could discern different characters and doctrines. It is amazing that such a spiritual and discerning man could be so credulous. Without doubt, this hypocritical woman greatly harmed his spirit and his cause. At Trefeca, he called the fraternity together. Exhorters from the neighbouring societies were also present, probably. He explained to them the situation and the necessity of a separation: 'But,' he said, 'the brethren have already themselves separated from us.' They took the matter to the Lord:

> I had an answer from the Lord that we are the body and centre of the work of the Methodists. Here in this body [we have] the mind, spirit, truth, blood, and glory of the Lord; that God is in the midst of us to supply us with all graces and gifts, etc., which attend his presence.[12]

Having conferred further, it was agreed that they must separate before they could ever be one, in that Rowland and his party were preaching grace instead of Christ, and were exalting themselves more and more against the doctrine of the blood.

---

[1] CH 41, p. 33.                    [2] HHVP, p. 159; CH 25, p. 103.
[3] HHVP, pp. 159–60.             [4] CH 41, p. 35.
[5] HHVP, p. 163.       [6] Ibid.            [7] CH 41, p. 61.
[8] He had already begun at this time the practice of taking Madam Griffith about the country with him on occasions. See p. 549, 553–4.
[9] HHVL, p. 263–4.       [10] HHVP, p. 169.
[11] Geraint Tudur, *Howell Harris: From Conversion to Separation, 1735–1750* (University of Wales Press, 2000), p. 191.       [12] Ibid, p. 192.

# 16

# THE DISRUPTION

## HOWELL HARRIS'S DOCTRINAL VIEWS

This is perhaps an appropriate place to discuss the doctrinal views of Howell Harris. No one who has familiarized himself to any extent with his sermons, his letters, his controversies with various individuals on various subjects, can doubt that he was a considerable theologian.

He possessed an eagle's eye for discerning the difference between one statement and another, and with respect to one important doctrine it appears that he had plumbed the depths beyond any of his contemporaries in Wales, with the exception perhaps of William Williams. The topic involved was the closeness of the unity of the two natures in the Person of our Lord. He felt the repugnance of separating the natures and of saying that the Saviour accomplished one thing as God, and another as man; and he dared to proclaim that the whole of Christ's Person was in all that he did, and in all that he suffered. While it is not correct nor scriptural to say that God died, yet Howell Harris was perfectly orthodox in arguing that there was a closer relationship between the divinity of the Saviour and death, than seen alone in the strengthening and upholding of the human nature throughout his suffering; perfectly orthodox in arguing that the Son of God died; in arguing that the Infinite Person was made an atonement. We believe also that he did not hold that God died, because we often find him demonstrating that the divine nature of the Lord Jesus held an unbreakable grip upon his body when it lay in the depths of the grave, and upon his soul when for a little time it dwelt apart from its body in paradise. We do not like the phrase 'the blood of God', it tends too much to materialize the Godhead; but the phrase upon Harris's lips was only a strong expression of that important truth, which filled his soul with its glory, that the whole Person of the God-man was involved in his death, and constituted his sacrifice. He believed that he had discovered this truth by a direct revelation from heaven, and the brilliance of the discovery blinded his mind for a while so that he could barely see any other truth. He had inquired deeper into this doctrine than any of his co-labourers.

But Harris's vision was not clear, and it must also be acknowledged that he was either considerably confused in his thoughts or else unfortunate in his expression of them. He appears to believe that the human nature of our Lord, when united with his divine nature, was somehow transformed and glorified so as to share in the specific attributes of divinity. When he says that the blood was infinite and that it filled eternity, he compels us to believe that he meant more than the infinity of merit. Everything mystical had a great effect upon him.

It is not easy, either, to understand his view of the Trinity. At times he seems perfectly orthodox; he states explicitly that he believed in three Persons; that it was the Son, the Word, who became incarnate, and not the Father nor the Spirit, and that he opposed Sabellianism. At other times there is confusion. He says that the Holy Trinity became incarnate in Jesus; that there is no God outside of Jesus; that the Trinity was in him; and that those who believed that the Father was in any way above Jesus were setting up an imaginary idol, before whom they were bowing down and worshipping. He denied therefore that the Saviour expiated the Father's wrath, and would ask rather scornfully who it was who expiated the wrath of the Son and of the Holy Spirit. Every thinking man must sympathize with him when he says that the Trinity is a mystery to him, and the doctrine too much of a mystery for him to feed upon and, ultimately, it may be that the confusion existed more in his expression of his views than in the views themselves.

The following is the comment of Mr Charles of Bala upon the disruption:

It is probable that Mr Harris was a man of warm temper, and whatsoever took hold of his mind he would receive and pursue it with much warmth of vigour. It is probable also that the people were not educated too closely in these great topics, in that they were not generally found in the path of doctrinal teaching. An aged believer told me once that he and many other brethren were members together of a society for more than five years without knowing anything of Christ, not even of a historical nature, and when they heard a preacher mentioning him specifically they did not understand him and did not know of whom he was preaching. I asked the godly old man what was it that was preached to them. He replied that they would hear of nothing but the evil of sin, the fires of hell, and damnation, until they trembled with great fears and horrors of heart.

It is almost certain that this old man was misrepresenting matters, or that he had heard no one during these five years except for the most ignorant of exhorters, because the sermons of Rowland and Harris were full of Christ, and whenever they did dwell on the evil of sin they would go to Calvary in order to show it in its blackest colours. But to continue with Mr Charles's words:

> Harris was opposed by some of his brethren who were wearied by his way of speaking about the person and death of Christ, namely that God had died, etc., etc. They judged that the phrase was unscriptural and tending to Sabellianism. Opposition from his religious brethren was a completely new experience to Harris; up until then they had listened to him as a father and chief teacher, as he was in truth to most of them. Instead of reining himself in, and judging prudently and impartially as to whether such expressions were appropriate for these topics, his spirit was embittered towards them, and gradually they distanced themselves from one another, until, eventually, matters came to a head in the sad disruption.

## A CONVERSATION BETWEEN AN ORTHODOX AND AN ERRONEOUS METHODIST

In order to understand Daniel Rowland's position we include a short essay published by him in 1749, when the argument between him and Howell Harris was at its most heated. Its title is *A Conversation between an Orthodox and an Erroneous Methodist*. It hardly needs saying that Rowland himself is the Orthodox, and Harris the Erroneous.[1]

*Orthodox:* All hail, my brother; I am pleased to meet you and to have this meeting for conversation. I hear that you and others do bring false accusations against us by alleging that we are Arians.

*Erroneous:* Quite true. I have said so, and I again —

*Orthodox:* You do. Then how dare you maintain such a falsehood? We believe that Jesus Christ is the true God, and that he is co-eternal, co-equal, and consubstantial with the Father.

*Err.:* I affirm that you are Arians, and I publish it to the world.

*Orth.:* What reprehensible conduct. Consider, I pray, who is the father of lies; for you are not only given over to believe what is false but you shamelessly proclaim it; and this is not the only particular in which you misrepresent us. May the Lord forgive you your evil report; and may you learn in future to confine yourself to the truth. I am informed that you deny that there are three persons in the Godhead.

*Err.:* Three persons! I object to the term 'person'; it sounds carnal and I cannot adopt it.

*Orth.:* It has the sanction of Scripture (*Heb.* 1:3) and has been in use from the beginning. I judge it a sufficiently correct expression; but you are wiser than your ancestors. That there are three persons in the Godhead is evident

from several passages in the inspired Book. Our Lord commands his disciples to baptize all nations in the name of the Father, and of the Son, and
of the Holy Ghost. Saint John says that there are three that bear record in
heaven, and these three are one. Athanasius also, and the Church of England,
most worthily exhibit this great truth when they teach that the person of the
Father is one, of the Son another, and of the Holy Ghost another. But I hear
that you contend for the Patripassian heresy. You declare that the Father as
well as the Son, became incarnate.

*Err.:* I do; it has been so revealed to me.

*Orth.:* Revealed! What revelation can be contrary to the revelation of the
Scriptures? These teach that it was the Word who became flesh. It seems that
you are tainted with Patripassianism as well as with Sabellianism.

*Err.:* You can easily apply hard names; but this is what I believe – that the
Father as well as the Son was made flesh, suffered, and died. But pray, do
you believe that God died?

*Orth.:* God is a spirit without body, parts, or passions; and as such he neither
suffers nor expires. He is called the immortal God, and he cannot therefore
cease to live.

*Err.:* I aver that God suffered and died.

*Orth.:* I believe that the second person in the Trinity, God the Son, assumed
a human nature which became one with the divine person in the God-man;
but the two natures are so distinct and distant that his humanity only tasted
suffering and death. That humanity, however, being united to the divinity,
what Christ did and suffered was of such infinite merit that the justice of
God was satisfied for the sin of man. The following Scriptures prove con-
clusively that it was as to the human nature alone Christ died: 'Being put
to death in the flesh' (2 *Pet.* 3:4); 'he was crucified through weakness (2 *Cor.*
13:4), that is, as he was a man; 'who his own self bare our sins in his own
body on the tree' (1 *Pet.* 2:24).

*Err.:* I hold that there is such a union between the two natures of Christ
that God as well as man died.

*Orth.:* And so you have added Eutychianism to your other two heresies. I
believe with Athanasius that our Lord Jesus is perfect God and perfect man,
but one Christ; and that not from confusion of substance but from unity
of person: one not from conversion of his divinity into flesh, bur from the
assumption of his humanity into God.

*Err.:* Does not the Bible set forth that the Word was made flesh?

*Orth.:* The pious bishop Beveridge, I think, elucidates this truth very clearly.
'When our Lord,' he says, 'took our nature upon him he became man as well
as God; but the two natures were not made one but remained unconfounded.
The two natures, therefore, being in themselves distinct, were yet united so

as to constitute one person.' In my judgment to assert that God died or suffered, is fearful blasphemy. To renounce Christ as your mediator and advocate with the Father is Sabellianism; to regard Christ's body as omnipresent is Eutychianism.

*Err.:* I contend that the union between the two natures is such that where one is there the other is also.

*Orth.:* My Bible informs me that the body of Christ ascended to heaven, and must remain there until the time of restitution of all things. The Apostles' Creed and yours do not agree. You have piled together an astonishing jumble of heresies. You are Antinomian, Sabellian, Patripassian, Eutychian, and Ubiquitarian all in one.[2]

*Err.:* My opinion is that whatever Christ performed in one nature he did it in both; he did nothing in one nature contrary to what he did in the other.

*Orth.:* Such being the case the Deity must have hungered, slept, and been subject to weakness – a conclusion that amounts to a shocking blasphemy. If what you assert is correct, namely, that what Christ did in one nature He performed in both, then Christ even as God could not foretell the time of the Day of Judgment; he was therefore not omniscient, and consequently not perfect God. You now perceive which of us is the Arian.

*Err.:* I again declare to you that the things you are now gainsaying have been revealed to us; and if you, instead of being guided by carnal reason had been truly enlightened, you would behold these glorious mysteries as they appear to us. In your benighted condition you cannot apprehend them.

*Orth.:* Granted that we are ignorant and in darkness, would you pass judgment on all our forefathers, the compilers of the Church Service, the good old Athanasius, and upon the whole body of orthodox divines?

*Err.:* I see. You gather your knowledge from books. For my part all books could be in flames. But pray, is it not your contention that the Deity forsook our Lord at his crucifixion?

*Orth.:* I hear that you so misrepresent me; but it is only another of your mis-statements. What I say is, that God hid his face in such a way that the human nature was unsupported by the divine, and hence the cry, 'My God, my God, why hast thou forsaken me?' Such was the desertion in my opinion; but I believe that the personal union of the two natures continues, and that our Lord was God-man in the womb, God-man on the Cross, and God-man in the grave. I will again implore you to confine yourself within the bounds of truth; and I would advise that instead of committing good books to the fire you should study them, and especially the best of books – the Bible. You would give over traducing and condemning others, and so far from being dominated by your present ungovernable spirit you would be restored to the old ways and be free from the degrading bias of your present heresies; and may God give you a good understanding in all things. Amen.

A third edition of the *Conversation* was published by the Association in 1792, and printed by the press of John Daniel, Carmarthen. This edition contained the following preface:

Impartial Reader, the unanimous view of the Association, when encouraging the re-publishing of *A Conversation between an Orthodox and an Erroneous Methodist*, did not in any way intend to dishonour, ignore or slander any specific person, nor any branch of the church which professes faith in the eternal name of the Son of God, and fellowship. But inasmuch as there are now so many new labourers in the vineyard: some fathers, some teachers and assistants; the purpose is to provide an honest account of the orthodox opinions of the fathers, evangelists and assistants at the beginnings of the Association, particularly those of the Rev. D. Rowland. 1 *John* 2:24: 'Let that therefore abide in you, which ye have heard from the beginning. If that which ye have heard from the beginning shall remain in you, ye also shall continue in the Son, and in the Father.'

Next to this preface were the initials J.E. and J.T. Mr Morris Davies, Bangor, states, on the basis of evidence which he considers sufficient, that J.E. is the venerable John Evans of Bala, and that J.T. is the faithful old preacher, John Thomas of Llancwnlle, who concluded his ministry at Denbigh.

This *Conversation* shows that Daniel Rowland's opinions of the topics at issue were the same as those held by men who are generally considered orthodox divines, and that he was well read in church history. It also shows, unfortunately, that he was thoroughly indignant and that his bitterness of feeling had led him to use sharp words like the edge of a sword. Nor are we convinced that he has portrayed Harris's viewpoint completely fairly, although this perhaps could hardly be expected during such heated controversy. It is not correct to say that Harris had completely rejected the word 'person' when referring to the Trinity; we have come across the term many times in the quotations he gives of his sermons. Nor is there any evidence that he believed that the Father became incarnate, except perhaps that Rowland considered this to be an unavoidable consequence of believing that the Trinity dwelt in Jesus Christ. It is not impossible also that in his sermons Harris expressed things in the heat of oratory in a more extreme way than when he came, in a cooler state, to write them later in his journal. But as for the other allegations, that he condemned book-knowledge; that he accused his opponents of being Arians and Deists; that he claimed that the body of Jesus was omnipresent; and that, when pressed, he would fall back on the revelation which he believed he had received; there is plenty of foundation for these in Harris's journal. Even if his views on the Trinity and on the mystery of the person of Christ had not been incorrect, he was overemphasizing them, and giving them more attention than was appropriate to the harmony of the faith. In the last years of his connection with the Methodists he hardly gave attention to any other matter in his ministry. Whatever his text he returned to this topic, just as a compass needle is drawn to the pole. One of the main accusations against him was that a complete change had occurred in the tone of his preaching. One reason for this, no doubt, was the opposition that arose against his doctrine. His invariable reaction to criticism was to become more stubborn and determined. He would also express his ideas in a wilder style and more excitable phrases. He said once, 'I recognize no God except Jesus Christ. You may take all the others; I challenge them all.' Such statements, together with his claim that his opponents were worshipping idols of their own imagination and denying the true deity of the Lord Jesus, became insufferable to the feelings of Daniel Rowland and his friends, and made any continuation of fellowship with him impossible.

## FACTORS OTHER THAN DIFFERENCES IN DOCTRINE AT THE ROOT OF THE DISRUPTION

It must also be remembered that there were other reasons for the disruption, apart from differences of opinion over doctrine. Harris claimed a dictatorial authority over the societies and exhorters. Time and again he called himself the father of the Association. He compared his position to that of Moses, who was placed as judge over Israel, and he considered himself to have been invested just as directly by God. He would not ask counsel of his brethren and considered opposition to himself as equivalent to opposition to God. He excommunicated from the society and threw out exhorters on his own authority, without submitting to any Monthly Meeting or Association on the matter.

The responsibility of the clergy, he believed, was to go about preaching and administering the sacraments, while the exhorters and stewards should fulfil the arrangements that he would make for them. And in that he was easy to excite, and possessed strong, if not ungovernable feelings, he often acted on the spur of the moment. Rowland accuses him to his face of throwing out exhorters in his temper. It was not possible to reason with him; he considered that the rule of the societies lay in his hands, and that all others should remain silent; and he believed that he acted under the direct guidance of God. It is no wonder therefore that a revolt occurred; and it is easy to see that his dictatorial ways became painful to Daniel Rowland, Howell Davies and Williams, Pantycelyn; all ordained men whereas he was but a layman. They might very naturally have noted his position and refused to consider him their equal, let alone accept him as one placed in authority over them. They did not react in this way, but they were unhappy for him to take the reins completely into his own hands.

Dissatisfaction with Howell Harris increased enormously through his determination to take Madam Griffith, a woman who maintained that she had a spirit of prophecy, about with him. He brought her to the societies and to the Monthly Meetings; he called her his 'Eye' and believed that she was given to him by God to enable him to discern hypocrites and to be guided in his judgment. As has been mentioned already, there was never the slightest evidence to suspect his moral purity in this association. We do not believe that there was any real suspicion of this at the time. Yet his behaviour provoked strong feelings. Most, even of his own followers, believed that she was a complete hypocrite, and they were perfectly correct. When once returning from London, through Erwood, one of his closest friends told him that things had come to a strange state that a woman was at the head of the Association. Thomas James, the exhorter from Cerigcadarn, wrote to him, complaining. His answer to them all was that he had no will in the matter; that he had himself fought against it at the beginning but that God had defeated him; and that by now many of the preachers believing as firmly as himself that she was an 'Eye', would not remain in the Connexion unless she was given her place. His behaviour was particularly childish, and displayed a degree of gullibility not often found; yet all was completely compatible with the character of Howell Harris who, for all his strength and acumen, was in some things exceptionally superstitious. We believe that this, as much as anything, hastened the approach of the disruption.

## ROWLAND'S PARTY BREAK WITH HARRIS

After the Llanidloes Association, the two sides felt that they could not remain together; but having come so near the precipice, Harris hesitated from taking the step into darkness. The decision was taken out of his hands by the other party. On Saturday, 4 July 1750, Daniel Rowland, Howell Davies and Williams, Pantycelyn, met, together with another clergyman whose name is not known, at an Association at Llantrisant. Present also were eleven public and four private exhorters. In this meeting it was agreed to break every connection with Howell Harris. At the time, he was journeying in the Capel Ifan neighbourhood of Carmarthenshire. He was greatly moved in spirit when he heard of it but mentioned to the society that he was determined to continue; that he had on previous occasions seen the devil rising to oppose him through the peasantry, the clergy and the gentry and that all had come to nothing; that he would see this opposition also evaporating away; and that he felt inside him a spirit which was unconquerable. He further stated that the true disruption had in reality occurred four years previously. We now find him beginning to organize his own party. The following Monday, 6 July, he collected eight preachers together at Llansamlet, probably at Wern-Llestr where the society usually met, in order, as he put it, to 'lay down the foundation of God's house'. He said that they had an exceptional meeting; that they partook of the same bread and were enlivened by the same spirit. Harris was appointed by them to be head over all the societies; the brethren rejoiced over the split; and Harris told them that Rowland and his party were arisen against the Lord, against his Spirit, and against his truth.

'Secretly,' he said, 'I perceived that the Lord willed that we should depart from the brethren and their Association, because: (1) They have in spirit departed from the Lord. (2) They are in truth his enemies. (3) Because they hate the government of the Spirit. (4) Because they despise the Urim and the Thummim. (5) Because they do not have life to feed upon the Christ. (6) Because they despise this doctrine of the flesh and blood, and I love in truth this dear and infinite flesh and blood.'

What he meant by 'Urim and Thummim' we do not know, unless it is a reference to the 'prophetess'.

On 13 July he was leading a society at Llwynyberllan and complained bitterly that the societies had become formal, carnal and nurseries of pride, but he added that he was willing to visit them for as long as his visits were welcomed and of blessing. The next day, at Cefnygweision, he noted that he had emerged victorious from the hottest warfare he had ever encountered. It would seem that he and Daniel Rowland had met, perhaps at Llwynyberllan, and that a bitter argument had arisen between them. Rowland had accused him of falling from grace; of constant change; of paying attention to parts only and not the whole of the Scriptures and of the truth concerning the person of Christ; of excommunicating members from the societies in his temper; of schism; and of stating that there were not six in Wales who knew the Lord. Harris answered that he feared that Rowland and his party did not know the Lord; that they were enemies of the blood and opposed to all that was of God; that in their sermons they did not reach the depths of their hearers' spirits, but that they mainly appealed to the mind and the feelings so that the hearers were becoming flippant and carnal. He said further that by meeting with one another and excluding himself, they had shut him out of the house (that is, the chapel) at Cil-y-cwm. This note demonstrates that the previous invitation from the society at Cil-y-cwm to superintend them had not come from the society as a whole but only from certain individuals amongst them. It is most painful to see these two fellow labourers so bitterly opposed to one another, mainly through misunderstanding, but the conversation reveals the accusations that they had brought against each other.

Within a week, on 17 July, Harris heard of the death of James Beaumont. It appears that he died very suddenly at Haverfordwest, in the house of John Sparks, an exhorter. His last words before his spirit fled to his Saviour occurred when his wife was offering him a little wine, and were, according to the minute-book, 'I will not drink henceforth of this fruit of the vine until I drink it new with you in my Father's kingdom.' Harris felt the loss of his friend greatly. Beaumont had a very particular place in his heart, and he writes that his own spirit longed to go home. We believe that the root of the disruption was to be found in the old exhorter from Radnorshire. He laboured much and suffered long for the gospel, but he was a man of many failings and had wandered far from the faith as it is in Jesus. And we feel sure that he had influenced Harris to the detriment of his spirit.

At this time Harris made every effort to maintain the sympathy of the societies and to keep the exhorters on his side. He travelled tirelessly and wrote letters to those whom he thought he could influence. A week before the meeting of the clergy at Llantrisant, he wrote to John Sparks:

The Clergy and several of the labourers have declared against me for my principles, practice and spirit. I write not to you to secure you with me in this, for the Lord Jesus, the only wise God who is my all, knows that I have no party but am alone as I first went out, only that a few that know and love his flesh and wounds and blood hang on me and can't leave the chief of sinners [Harris] and I thought it my duty to let you know this briefly; for particulars I refer you to the bearer. If our Saviour inclines you to desire, before you determine which side you'll join, to labour to be further informed, I shall give you the meeting at Laugharne in the morning next Tuesday fortnight, 17 July. I shall be that Sunday before, 15 July, at Carmarthen and if you and Brother Gambold and Brother John Harris can come to Laugharne, if you'll send a line against that Sunday to Carmarthen. Or I would strive to come that Monday night to St. Kennox to meet you all, or either of you, if you desire it, that you may know the whole truth. As Mr [Howell] Davies and Benjamin Thomas have all joined in rejecting me and as he [Howell Davies], and perhaps the people, look on Pembrokeshire as his labours, I shall think it my duty to keep away except I am called afresh by the people or preachers or both. I am now, in greatest haste in the mangled body of our God and Saviour to all eternity, Yours, How. Harris.

It is impossible to read this letter, with the deep sense of loneliness that runs through it, without a tear coming to the eye, whoever we may consider most responsible for the disruption.

## THE FIRST ASSOCIATION OF HARRIS'S PARTY AT ST NICHOLAS, JULY 1750

On 26 July 1750, Harris and his party held their first Association at St Nicholas, a small rural village in the Vale of Glamorgan, about six miles from Cardiff. Why this place was chosen, we do not know. It is not central for the whole of Wales in any way. Perhaps there were numerous societies in the area and that these were sympathetic to Harris. Those present were, Howell Harris, Thomas Williams (Groes-wen), John Richard (Llansamlet), Henry Thomas, William Jones, Roger Williams, Thomas Bowen (the elder), Thomas Bowen (the younger), Richard Tibbott, Thomas Sheen, Thomas Meredith, Lewis Evan, Edward Davies, John Lewis, David William Thomas, Stephen Jones, Richard David, John Davies and George Phillips; nineteen in number. Why the Pembrokeshire exhorters were absent, we do not know. There were many of them in deep sympathy with Harris; perhaps they had not yet decided which party to support. Harris journeyed to the meeting in company with a clergyman, Henry Lloyd, but he does not appear as one of the participants. It seems that some of Rowland's supporters had journeyed to the place out of curiosity. Harris's journal reads:

> When I saw the enemies of Christ there, my dear Lord met with me and exalted me above all in singing victoriously, in praying, and in preaching from 'we beheld his glory'. Truly, the Lord my God was here as a warrior, declaring war upon the Arians, Deists and their God. I proclaimed [to the Rowlandites] that I was determined to proceed, maintaining the same spirit as was in me at the beginning; and if that spirit was from the devil, it made me truly blessed and led me to Christ. I said, 'We are determined to continue; there are many scores of us here congregated, and while you only believe what you can understand, we believe God and his word, and reject our own understandings.'

He added that he was ready to venture to eternity with that spirit which worked in him, and he compared the opposition to Korah, Dathan and Abiram.

The Minutes state:

> This is the first Association that was held after the four clergymen and the fourteen preachers met to oppose the doctrine and spirit of Brother Harris. We met to wait upon the Lord, to see what could be done in that the whole work had come to a stop. All felt something which they had never had in an

Association before, and saw that the Saviour had established many important works. As many again had united with us but were unable to be present because of circumstances. There seems to be a new face on things. We are now in hope to see our Saviour's glory and the discipline of his Spirit and the life of faith brought into the reformation and a more catholic spirit towards all; and of seeing the wisdom and pride of man exiled once again, and the name of Christ exalted amongst us. After a sermon on, 'We beheld his glory', as we were singing most triumphantly, the Lord came down to declare war against those other preachers who had taken counsel together against God, his death, and his Spirit. The Lord gave us one heart; but when we found that the Spirit was not running as freely amongst the younger brethren, lest they take offence from Madam Griffith, we called on all to open their hearts with respect to her.

'Madam Griffith', the false prophetess, had come to St Nicholas for the Association. Harris gave an account of all her history: how she was established as a mother in Israel; how he had not found such faith in any other; how she had prophesied of the separation before it happened; how she had been of great assistance to himself in serving the Lord in faith. He said that there were three types of light: the light of nature; the light of prophecy; and the light of faith, transforming and taking possession of what is seen.

As a result of Harris's explanation, the nine men whose names are given first on the list above, admitted that they had been tempted, but had now been convinced in the Lord that Madam Griffith had been raised to be an Eye for them, to bless them in that in which they were deficient, to judge the spirits and to discern the mind of Christ amongst them. It was agreed to invite her to the Association to assist them in their discussions on various matters.

There arose next some difficulty with an old brother called 'Old Adams'. The Minutes state that he had been deceived by the devil and had attended the Association in order to harm and frustrate it. 'I told him,' said Harris, 'that if John Wesley and George Whitefield offered their societies I would take the matter to the Lord. But when he was commanded to leave, he began to roar. My own spirit was aroused and I called him a deceiver, an enemy of God, and a false prophet, and in the name of the fellowship as a whole I excommunicated him.'

The next note in the Minutes is particularly interesting: 'Mr Peter Williams came in and would stay in but not join.' It is difficult to judge his motives, whether he wished to mediate between the two parties before matters went further, or whether he sought further information on points of controversy.

We declared we are determined not to join till the separated brethren repent and are brought to the Lord. I showed the three things in which we differed. (1) They preach Christ mainly to the head, and they oppose the glory of our Saviour, which we seek to lay before the people. (2) They build on old ideas and experience; we exhort souls to continual belief in the Lord. (3) We are for the true discipline of the Spirit, whereas they have departed from the Lord, and souls could listen to them continually without being awakened to perceive the sinfulness of unbelief, self-righteousness, legality, and failing to feed upon the Lord. We explained further that our point was not, who would be greatest, but who would be least. Brother Harris said he saw himself as the poorest of the brothers, but that there was a difference between workers in the church and private members; that some were babes, others young, and others fathers; and that there were differing gifts and degrees of faith, and a difference in the spirit of the preachers; and that we all needed to submit before the Lord in order to recognize everybody's place. He said also that we took the example, spirit, and command of our Lord as our rule. In all this we agreed as one. Afterwards, he [Peter Williams] went out.

Perhaps Williams judged that all hope of reconciliation was over. The following were the resolutions:

We agreed that the preachers were to meet in Associations as before; the next to be at Builth, 26 September, and in the meantime we would take into consideration the appropriateness of holding an Association for the whole of Wales once a year, and every six months in south and north Wales, separately.

We discussed the appropriateness of maintaining private societies, and agreed so to do after Brother Harris had explained the nature of societies from the Old and New Testaments. We decided also to nurture in small folds the souls that have been awakened to see their need of a Saviour, but not to accept any into this Body nor to call any by our name except those that either see the glory of the Saviour, or their ignorance of him, and who live by faith upon him. It was agreed also that those who perceive the glory should meet apart to view Christ, feed upon him, speak of him, and pray to him. And that the others should be met by an appropriate person to be nurtured for as long as they are willing to be taught, and remain submissive, diligent, and in the exercise of the means of grace.

We agreed that all our members should unite in the worship and ordinances of the Established Church; that it is the word of reconciliation only that has been entrusted to us; and that we are to proceed as reformers in the Church, as we did at the beginning, and in the same light and spirit.

We agreed also that Brother W. Powell and Brother Thomas Williams should bring a report on the state of the cause in Monmouthshire and Glamorganshire to the next Association; Brother John Richard and Brother Rue Thomas to do the same for West Glamorgan, Carmarthenshire and Pembrokeshire; Thomas Jones to do so for part of Breconshire and Herefordshire; Charles Bowen for the remainder of Breconshire; and Richard Tibbott for Montgomeryshire. They were also to discover where doors might be open, and where Brother Harris might establish new societies or re-establish those that had been scattered.

It was said that a certain Stephen Jones had been thrown out by Rowland's party for stating that the blood of Christ was so great that he could not comprehend nor explain it. Furthermore, Rowland and his supporters were accused of claiming that they only believed what they could understand. Naturally, this Stephen Jones was warmly received at the St Nicholas Association. Our Lord was described as a Lion as well as a Lamb; that the spirit of rebuke proceeded from him as well as the spirit of tenderness. It was decided also to send representatives to north Wales, in that the departed brethren were restraining souls from coming to Christ. These representatives were also to seek to persuade people not to attend the preaching of any of Rowland's supporters until that party had returned to the Lord. It was arranged that the first man to visit the north would be Roger Williams; he was to leave immediately. Rue Thomas was to follow within a fortnight and Richard William Dafydd after him. Lewis Evan was to meet each man and be his companion until he returned. Lastly, a month before the next Association, Thomas Williams and David Thomas were to go. They would decide on the meetings to be held and to invite the preachers who wished to unite with Harris to the Association at Builth. It was further noted that the Lord opened the mouth of Madam Griffith, the Eye, 'most home indeed to show that if we were spiritual we should see the spirits of people as plain as we should see their faces'.

So terminated the first Association of Harris's party. We would judge that it was of a very mixed nature. There is no doubt that Harris and his followers were completely sincere, that they believed that the truth was with themselves and that the clergy had departed from Christ. They believed that true religion would endure in the land only if they obtained the victory. On the other hand, it is difficult to accept that all the enthusiasm was from heaven. While they condemned carnality, they themselves were not free of the flesh. The sending out of these missionaries provoked a dreadful strife in the Methodist camp. After preaching, these representatives would gather all professors together, they would forewarn them against the clergy who, they said, had lost God, and according to the spirit of the command that had sent them forth, they urged them not to listen to Rowland or his supporters. As a result, the societies were torn apart and members of the same family found themselves on opposite sides. Rowland was refused admission to a great number of places where previously he had been welcomed as an angel from God. It is quite possible that there was a considerable degree of bitterness and of a persecuting spirit among the clergymen and their followers also, but we have no record of their activities.

The first Association held by Rowland's party sent a demand to Harris that he should provide an account, within three weeks at the latest, of the monies he had collected for legal fees against Sir Watkin Williams Wynn. He replied that all that he had received from the Rowland party was five pounds from Rowland himself, five pounds from Benjamin Thomas, and a guinea from Williams, Pantycelyn. As for the rest of the money, he was not responsible to them for it. He then describes how the money was paid out.

As proof that Harris's affection towards Daniel Rowland had not grown completely cold, and that he still held some appreciation in the depths of his soul that they remained one in their views of essential truth, we would wish to note the following letter written by him:

> My dear brother Rowland, Where are you gone? What spirits are come about you? What battles are you fighting and against whom? O, come up, come up and return. If you think me viler than you 'tis right you should and I have therefore the right to cry louder, 'Grace! Grace!' However, you want washing as well as me; let us both then come to the fountain. Don't stumble at the stumbling. Can you think it possible for me to have sin and leave the dear Lamb of God? I have been more unfaithful and more weak than all but I leave him to show the other side of the leaf to you, whether I would allow myself to grieve him or whether I would not die to show all his glory to you. Come, fight no longer; rather stop to see or to find . . . Daniel! My dear brother Daniel! Away with them that again will crucify him. Come lay aside the prejudice lest others measure to you the same measure you measure your brother. Don't oppose the coming of our Saviour's kingdom and glory.

On the back of this letter is found the note, 'This was written at Old Abbey,[3] Cardiganshire, but not sent to Rowland.' What a pity that the letter was not sent. Were it to have failed in bringing about reconciliation it might still have been the means of removing much of the bitterness of spirit. The letter reveals however the deep vein of affection retained in Harris's heart, though hidden for a while under a heavy cloak of bitterness.

## HARRIS'S SECOND ASSOCIATION

On 26 and 27 September, Harris's party held their second Association, as previously arranged, at Builth Wells. More were in attendance than at St Nicholas. Before the formal meeting Harris inquired of the Lord, and of John Richard, 'of the rightness of allowing those who had come to the light, and had shown an obedient spirit by not going to listen to the others when we asked them, and who came to the meetings on the Sabbath to be counselled and to be spoken to personally,' to attend the preaching of Rowland's supporters. It was decided that permission was to be given as Rowland's people had now made a statement of their orthodoxy with respect to the death of Christ. When, and in what form, this statement was made, is not said. Harris justified the prohibition made previously on the grounds that there was reason for believing at the time that, because of their tendency to deny the mysteries and to hold that the two natures were apart, the opposing party were near to Arianism. This shows that Howell Harris was beginning to realize that there was no great difference of doctrine, after all, between himself and Daniel Rowland. But he writes in his journal:

> We are convinced that there is no change in their spirit. This declaration about the divinity of our Lord might be only a conviction of the head, or it might arise from some trick, and be not the product of a new vision given to them of the person of the Saviour.

He adds that it was still necessary to warn those souls who were presently growing in the faith from going to hear Rowland's people because of the latter's legality of spirit.

The Association was begun with preaching. John Relly preached 'a great and glorious sermon' from Philippians 2:8, 'And being found in fashion as a man, etc.' 'To have the gospel is such a blessing,' was Harris's comment as he listened. He describes how the meeting was filled with glory and that the preacher had to stop for some time before proceeding. After Relly, John Richard preached from the words, 'There are three that bear witness on earth.' Glory was displayed during his sermon also. Harris, before the meeting began, had charged those present not to hide nor restrain their feelings:

> I showed that we are the body of Christ; that we had been called within the veil out of the flesh, and if we did not rejoice in the Lord and demonstrate our sign from the rooftops, we would be carnal, and not dead to the world.

Thus all the emotions aroused in the meeting were given free rein.

The first task of the private meeting was the questioning of all exhorters present.

1. They were examined on their knowledge of the Lord. Many were found to be ignorant of him, but gave the appearance of simplicity and

of a united spirit; others had received a glimpse of him; whereas others again were ascending to the light.

2. They were examined as to the disruption. All agreed that it was of God, and that the spirit of those who had left them was one of departure from the Lord. They were building on the sand of self-wisdom, whereas Harris's people were building on rock, by constant faith.

3. They were examined about Madam Griffith, whether they viewed her position as correct and scriptural and whether they were easy in their hearts that she should be present at the Associations and be one of the fraternity. Many confessed to having been bound in the shackles of reason, but that now they had been strengthened in the Lord and in his Word and Spirit; that Madam Griffith had been of great blessing to them, proving the hearts and spirits of those that remained and driving away the carnal.

The result of the examination was the dividing of the exhorters into three groups. There were twelve in the first group. These were in the light and perceived the glory of the Saviour. The group was divided into two parts. The first part consisted of those qualified to be fathers, namely John Sparks, John Relly, Thomas Williams, John Richards, William Powell and one other who is not named. The second part was formed of six young men who had come to the blood, namely Roger Williams, Stephen Jones, Thomas Jones, Edward Jones, Edward Bowen and Thomas Davies. The second group also numbered twelve and comprised those who also were strong, who saw their all in Christ and who were drawing towards the light with all their might. These were Rue Thomas, Henry Thomas, Richard Edwards, Richard Tibbott, Richard Watkins, Rue Morgan, John Williams, Thomas Meredith and Evan Thomas, together with another three whose names are not given. The third group was made up of twenty-four men who were weak, but possessed of the same doctrinal views and spirit. It was noted that some of this class were doubtful of Madam Griffith.

The following resolutions are found in the Minutes:

Seeing such powerful errors working in the other brethren [Rowland's people] and such an evil spirit manifesting itself in them in various ways, and the means they use to beguile the weak, we had considerable discussion on the rightness of attending their ministry and speaking to them. All the brethren agreed to give liberty to those who wished to go, so that they could judge for themselves, until such time that they had made up their minds to leave for them or to remain with us. But afterwards they were not to hear them until the whole Association was satisfied with them.

We discussed those who invite both the other party and ourselves. We agreed: (1) With respect to those who are undecided on whether to invite both parties to their houses to preach, that we preach amongst them until the next Association, or until they make up their minds to unite with ourselves or with the others. (2) That we should preach amongst those carnal ones who invite both them and us on condition that they keep a place open for ourselves, without a breach, at whatever time we come.

A working party was also agreed, of about twenty people, with Howell Harris as its leader, in order to decide any matters that arose. Brethren were appointed to lead the societies and to visit various parts of the country. But the Association was not to end without some degree of unpleasantness. A certain Joseph Saunders presented complaints against Madam Griffith. Harris turned him out immediately. He threw out also Thomas Sheen, because the latter could not see the work of the Lord in Madam Griffith or in William Powell. This raised again the issue of the appropriateness of Madam Griffith's presence at the Associations and in the societies. Richard Tibbott questioned the right of women to speak publicly. This brought Howell Harris to his feet. He said that they should not only tolerate her presence but feel honoured by it; that she was a pillar of truth, and that the testimony was sealed in her heart. Tibbott was reconciled. Harris believed that they had been given a glorious Association; that the work was now truly beginning, that the other brethren were in the wilderness, that like Saul they had lost the kingdom and were using carnal instruments to draw the people to them. He added that James Relly, George Gambold, John Harry and John Harries, the last three from Pembrokeshire, had joined their party three weeks after the Association, and that many in Flintshire, Denbighshire, Merionethshire, Anglesey and Caernarvonshire had also joined, though were not yet put in order.

## PREACHING IN PEMBROKESHIRE AND NORTH WALES

On 1 October, he began a journey to Pembrokeshire, calling on the way at Llwynyberllan, Carmarthen, and other places. John Sparks and Madam Griffith were his companions. On the road, he explained to them the constitution he had drawn up for the societies that supported them. Firstly, a General Assembly was to be held, comprising the evangelists, exhorters and elders, about fifty in all, from all parts of the land. Its purpose was to provide a general affirmation of what had already been decided by the inner circle, but every member would have opportunity to reveal the light that was in him. Furthermore, public rebukes and discipline would be administered there, and all matters relevant to the Body as a whole would be there discussed. Next in line would be a more select Association made up of about twenty-five of the evangelists and elders. Every member attending would be expected to arrive with full comments on all he had observed of their temporal and spiritual condition, ready to spread it before the Lord. Matters were to be decided here before bringing them to the General Assembly. Here too the preachers were to be examined and accepted, different cases to be heard and adjudicated upon, and directions given as to marriages and discipline. Thirdly, a more select body again, comprised of those evangelists who were fathers, those who had the mind of Christ and who lived close to him, and possessed spiritual senses sharpened so as to be able to discern between truth and falsehood. To this inner cabinet was to be brought any cases of difficulty, there the spirits would be tested, the most secret matters would be there revealed, and each would there have allotted to him the position where the Lord would have him be. According to Harris:

> It is this body that is the life and heart of the Inner Association, and also of the General Assembly, together with the total number of those souls which have been placed under our care.

It is clear that this form of church government was in his mind during the Builth Association, although he was only now revealing it, and that it was with such a constitution in mind that he had examined the exhorters and had divided them into three different categories.

He was in Pembrokeshire for three weeks, attempting to bring the societies there under his wing, in which he was zealously assisted by John Sparks. He lived at Haverfordwest and would make forays into the surrounding countryside. He expressed his great disappointment that the exhorter John Harry had not come to him at St Kennox; his absence had pierced him like a sword thrust. The note in the Builth Association Minutes about this man could not therefore have been true. One night, in the private society at Haverfordwest, the devil entered. He revealed his presence by permitting someone to question the appropriateness of attending the preaching of Howell Davies. Harris was not ready to answer and so rebuked the man for asking such a question. He said that it was too late to consider the matter that night; that no one was to speak but himself, and that he, for the time, was the voice of God. He said further that the majority of the exhorters and members connected with the Haverfordwest meeting house agreed with him, but rather than fighting, if the opposite party claimed it, he and his followers would go out to the street. In the same Association a disagreement arose between himself, John Sparks and Madam Griffith, because the other two kept whispering together when he was addressing the Association. He was so upset that he abruptly left the meeting and the town, and headed towards St Kennox. There, he asked himself whether Madam Griffith's work might be at an end, or whether it might be the Lord's will that the Methodist Connexion be wholly broken up. Gradually, his feelings became calmer and he returned to Haverford-west and to his brethren and sisters, and confessed his repentance.

From Pembrokeshire he journeyed through the lower parts of Cardi-ganshire and the nearer parts of Carmarthenshire, but found that the greater number of the societies sympathized with Rowland. He was extremely stern with them because of this, stating that he would not visit them further unless they acknowledged him the place allotted him by God. On returning to Llwynyberllan, he crossed the mountains to Hen Fynachlog, situated about a mile from Pontrhydfendigaid, and not ten miles from Llangeitho. It would seem that this particular flock was opposed to Rowland and had sent an invitation to Harris to visit them. As he passed through Tregaron, his spirit was filled with a great love for Rowland:

> I feel vast love to Bro. Rowland, and that he is my brother. I am glad that he
> is at the head [over the brethren that had separated from Harris] and mourn
> to see so many vipers about him poisoning him.[4]

It is seen that in the depths of his soul, Harris could not but embrace Rowland, and that he blamed those about him rather than Rowland himself. He found a large congregation at Hen Fynachlog and having preached, he conducted a private society. He mentioned there his love for Rowland, but that presently he had to fight against him. It appears, how-ever, that it was not for spiritual purposes that they had sent for him, and he told them that he would not return unless they constituted themselves formally, and applied to him not from prejudice against Rowland but from the fear of God and in a spirit of love. The next day he crossed Mynydd Mawr and after visiting various places in Radnorshire and Breconshire, returned to to Trefeca.

On the last day of October he met with the inner group of the As-sociation at Trefeca. Harris spoke extensively on coming into possession of the same enlightenment, otherwise the unity between members would not be spiritual at all but carnal, as with the party that had separated. Two exhorters, William James and Rue Thomas, were sent out of the meeting to pray, because they were not growing and the burden of the work was not weighing upon their spirits, and also because they were not able to press onwards within the veil. Harris could find little difference between their spirits and those of the opposing party. It is clear that his standard for what he judged to be spirituality was rapidly rising and was soon to reach a level higher than was attainable for the generality of the godly.

On 4 November 1750, he started on a journey to the north. After visiting various places in Radnorshire on the way, he reached Llwydcoed, Montgomeryshire on Friday, 9 November. There was no faltering of his courage as he considered the difficulties that he foresaw before him. 'I felt my spirit,' he said, 'above all the devils of the north, seeing them all like flies.' He rested only an hour at Llanrhaeadr-ym-Mochnant in order to feed himself and his horse, and then travelled through the night, reaching Mwnglawdd, not far from Wrexham, on the Saturday morning. He preached there, with great influence, on the Trinity, on eating the flesh and drinking the blood of the Son of Man, and he showed that the death of God is above the comprehension of the flesh. He stayed over the Sunday at Mwynglawdd and preached again there, from the words, 'Do ye now believe?' It would seem that it was a most powerful meeting. He described the three marks of the elect, namely, that they are taught of God; that they recognize the voice of Jesus and hear it; and that they look upon him whom they pierced. He thundered mightily against the proud and selfish spirit that had entered into those who were once simple and ready to be taught.

> I warned the people not to listen to reason, and encouraged them to listen only to the Lord. I said that I had come to turn their hearts to the Lord; that I had no other work, and, 'If you hear anything other than Christ's voice in us, reaching your hearts,' I said, 'then leave us. It is of no weight what you were; what matters is what you are now. Saul was once amongst the prophets, and the foolish virgins amongst the wise virgins, but they are not with them now. Objection: So you therefore hold to falling from grace? No we do not. Those who are on the rock cannot fall; but who are they? We call many brethren that God will yet not accept. I must speak plainly with you. It is of no weight what is said about myself, because I have not come for myself, but for the Lord.' I said further that we are Reformers within the Church, and that we were not a separate church or sect.

No doubt this sermon is a typical example of his ministry at this time amongst the societies of north Wales. On the Sunday afternoon he went to Wrexham, where he preached from the words, 'And with his stripes we are healed.' He describes it as a service of 'much freedom in the simple way.' He returned to Mwynglawdd in the evening and preached there again. After the sermon he held a private society and spoke for long on the birth, sufferings and blood of God. He wrote:

> I spoke. There are only a few here, in all probability, whom God will find willing to be taught of him, while the others, after proving him for many years

and finding him faithful, will leave him, trusting in their own wisdom, and in their memory and in books. The glory was here, and the Lord came down in truth to strengthen souls. Afterwards I was with the preachers until two o'clock in the morning. My lips were truly opened to commit the care of the souls of this place to them, in the same words as used by Paul to the elders of Ephesus. Yet it was not I that spoke, but the Lord in me.

On Monday he was at Llansannan, preaching with much liberty to a few simple souls who were willing to hear the gospel. At evening he was at Hen Blas with a sermon from the words, 'This is a faithful saying, and worthy of all acceptation.' His text at Plasbach on Tuesday morning was, 'Behold I stand at the door and knock.' He says that a wonderful authority accompanied his words:

I showed purposefully how the Scriptures testify to the glory of this Man; that it is not enough to believe that God is in him or with him, but that he is the Perfect One, and that his blood is the blood of God . . . Such chaff is now to be found at every hand. Many are thrown about and are being tested by this disruption. Few in these parts of the country have been awakened though there is here much preaching.

On Thursday he was at Waunfawr near Caernarvon and saw for the first time Daniel Rowland's pamphlet. He states:

Last night I saw dear Brother Rowland's charges against me as holding four heresies: denying the term 'Person'; holding that the Father suffered and that God suffered and died, and that Christ's body is everywhere, and that I am puffed up. I weighed each charge before the Lord and was acquitted and saw myself nothing before the Lord and was only grieved for Bro. Rowland for exposing himself and for his ignorant bitterness.[5]

It is unclear what he meant by 'acquitted'. He could hardly deny that he held to some of the doctrines fathered on him by Rowland; he used the phrase 'the death of God' often in his sermons during this journey. Perhaps his meaning is that the opinions he is said to hold were not heresies. But it is clear that his feelings towards Rowland are becoming less painful:

I cried that [the Lord] would take the paper and wash it in his blood. I gave it to the Lord.[6]

He travelled to Lleyn, to Brynengan most probably, on the Thursday, preaching from Zechariah 12:10. In the private society he described how the Lord had come amongst them with his winnowing-fan, and he narrated in full the details of his own history from the beginning, together with the reason for the disruption between him and Rowland's party. By Saturday he was at a place called Ysgubor Fawr on Anglesey. His text was, 'In the world ye shall have tribulation.' He was taken ill here, so that he failed to proceed to Llanfihangel as he had intended; he says also that he was low in spirit. By the Sunday however he managed to arrive there and preached on the infinite nature of Christ's sufferings. On Tuesday, he was again at Waunfawr having begun his return journey:

> Now, I [am] turning again my face from the north toward home, having I trust done my Lord's work and settled a few stones together and separated between the believers and unbelievers, and helped those who are in the way to grow.[7]

The next sentence refers to some event of which we know nothing:

> My life was only scarcely saved from the mouth of the lion; it served its purpose of piercing my flesh and destroying the dross within me, as good as if I had been brought to trial. They persecute, not with stones and staves, but with poisonous words.

By Thursday night he had reached Bala. His text was, 'Hereby perceive we the love of God, because he laid down his life for us.' He wrote:

> I was kept from sinking and had great authority, light, freedom and power indeed (so as I never had before here) . . . I showed the necessity of having the Spirit and the weakness of every means without him. I was severe against unbelief and against ignorance of Christ I said that I had to be faithful, and speak the truth on this point; that I left everything in order to go about. I then spoke severely to the believers for them to stay in him by continuing to believe; that this is our duty, and that every other grace we have received is as nothing compared to this.

We do not know in what way he influenced those at Bala, he does not say whether he gained the support of the society or not. The following Sunday he was at Llanfair Caereinion, where he preached from the same text as in Bala. He preached there on Sunday night also, from the words 'This is a faithful saying', but he says that he did not receive much liberty until he began speaking on the mystery of Christ. 'This is the message which I am given everywhere,' he said. The following Tuesday he was at Bedw preaching from, 'This man receiveth sinners.' He wrote:

> In praying and singing and discoursing, my spirit was raised above the devil in all, and I had vast freedom indeed in setting out the glory of that Man. I showed that he is the infinite God; that every flesh will ultimately acknowledge his Divinity; that he is the omnipresent God, but that God did not die. I explained that the Immortal died, that he lived, and was great and glorious, while in death. They (Rowland's party) do not acknowledge he is God, but only that God is with him and in him and that he is perfect.[8]

Quite certainly, this is not a correct depiction of Rowland's thought; he believed in the full deity of Christ as assuredly as Harris himself. Harris adds: 'I called a private society afterwards but there was so much of the devil amongst them that I went out and left them.'

He then went towards Cardiganshire and visited Hen Fynachlog again. It is easy to see that he was eager to gain some of the Cardiganshire societies, in that the county was considered to belong exclusively to Daniel Rowland. He says that he heard of some woman in Northampton who had prophesied that there would be one spirit, one doctrine, and one church throughout the kingdom. He believed in prophecy, and this story impressed him greatly.

> If the nation would not reject the gospel, there would be great, great glory, peace and plenty here, but if it will reject, the earthquake were but preceding great judgments in a year's time.[9]

From here, he returned home via Llwynyberllan.

His activity at this time was unremitting, and there must have been considerable tensions in the societies throughout the land. Indeed, the agitation spread into the Established Church and into the Nonconformist denominations. Both Churchmen and Nonconformists took Rowland's part in the controversy. On December 18, 1750, we find him writing at St Andrew's near Cardiff:

> These are glorious days in truth. All are being proved, shaken and winnowed. All the Nonconformist ministers, all the clergy, and our own brethren, are up in arms against me. Here I find Mr Lewis Jones has remained and opposes me. He exposed me yesterday while preaching. One of the false brethren went to the local clergyman to expose me, and he wished to send immediately for the constables in order to take me. When I heard of these things my spirit rejoiced within me. I felt the exceeding sweetness of the cross, and the idea of being taken was very pleasing to me.

There is no doubt that a persecuting spirit was running high in both camps and much bitterness being poured forth by both sides. On December 22, Harris preached at Pontypridd and once he had succeeded in gaining the attention of the crowd, some Nonconformist, full of the devil, interrupted him, opposing him publicly. Harris turned on him. The man left the meeting together with another, as full of the devil as he. After this the Lord came down.

## OTHER ASSOCIATIONS OF HARRIS'S PARTY

On the last day of 1750 and the first of the new year, a preparatory meeting for the Association was held by Harris and his party at Llwynyberllan. It would appear that it was a meeting of the 'inner Body', and about twenty-five were present which, together with Harris and Madam

Griffith, included Richard Tibbott, John Sparks, John Richard, and others of some importance. The self-denial that Harris required of the exhorters and the discipline that he maintained over them was beginning to become intolerably severe, and one of the main duties of the various Associations was the examining of the preachers to see who came up to the standard. They were set a difficult examination at Llwynyberllan. Three questions were asked of them:

i. Was their knowledge of Christ of the spirit, or of the head only?

ii. Did they possess a full assurance that they had been called by him to preach? And if so, were they dead to every kind of personal motives, and willing to suffer every kind of hardness, cold, hunger, nakedness, and similar crosses?

iii. Were they committed to this work of reform presently proceeding within the Church of England?

Harris is almost demanding of them to forsake all personal judgment and will and to neglect their personal circumstances completely, so as to be so many machines under his control to be sent and to act according to his commands. Though the demands were so high, the exhorters managed to answer satisfactorily, some with more and some with less faith. But there was one burning question that disturbed their minds, namely the presence and function of Madam Griffith, 'the Eye' of the Association. In reality it was she who had the rule, to a large extent, for Harris believed that she had the mind of God, and when he took any action without first consulting her, she would not hesitate to rebuke him severely. Her influence hung as a nightmare over the preachers, and the issue could not be avoided.

'After this,' says Harris, 'when Madam Griffith was not given liberty to speak, I went out, and the meeting broke up in disorder.' Was it the exhorters who would not allow her to speak, by their refusal to listen, or did she feel that she could not address them as usual because of a lack of sympathy in the meeting? We do not know. The latter is the more likely. The confusion and disorder continued for five hours: Madam Griffith threatening to leave, and Harris and some of the exhorters begging her not to. 'And the Lord kept her from leaving,' notes Harris's journal. About midnight they reconvened, and the argument raged until three in the morning, with Harris having prevailed. 'After a long and fierce encounter with Satan,' he writes, 'about three in the morning, the Lord came down and united them with her and myself.' There is no doubt that it was their respect, verging on worship, towards Harris which caused the brethren to give way. Harris stood up amongst them, asking them who it was who had it in his heart to give himself, body and soul, to the Lord and to each other. The first to answer the call was Thomas Jones; the next was Thomas Williams, with great seriousness; afterwards many others, including Richard Tibbott. According to the journal:

Then these had each a visible glory resting upon him as soon as they had yielded, and felt a relation they never had before, and felt all things in common.

Harris, at this point, saw the foundation of God's temple in Wales being laid. It is easy to see that he had lost all sense and judgment, so buried was he in the mystical and the imagined. But, after all this, some of the brethren still hesitated and refused at that time to commit themselves.

On January 2, the Association was at Dyserth. On the journey there Thomas Williams and John Relly preached at Builth Wells. The Association began with a powerful sermon by John Sparks. Harris then arose and spoke on the absolute necessity for all to give themselves up to the Lord, to his work and to one another; that the time had now come to lay down the foundation and to unite together. He then asked, as he had done at Llwynyberllan, 'Who now is ready to leave everything for God and for this work? Who is able to give his soul, his body, his spirit, together with all that he is, and all that is in him, to the Lord, and to us, his brethren and God's servants?' He mentioned that ten of them had covenanted together at Llwynyberllan to do so. A great many stood up to show their willingness, and upon seeing them on their feet, the exhorter William Powell whispered to Harris, 'The Lord is doing a great work.' But many left without answering, amongst them some who had submitted themselves at Llwynyberllan, namely, John Richard, Llansamlet, Thomas Bowen, Builth Wells, Stephen Jones, William Jones, Rue Thomas, etc. The number of those who committed themselves was twenty-seven; they bound themselves, together with all that they possessed, to be ruled and directed by the general body; that they would preach, or not preach, and give all their time to itinerating; according to the direction given to them; that they gave the whole of their service to him and to each other, each taking the other for better or for worse. 'I showed them,' said Harris, 'the majesty of the work. That it was far above that with which we were previously engaged; that that required of us to be dead to our own will and wisdom, but that this required a particular wisdom, to discern who has been sent by the Holy Spirit.' It is clear that those exhorters who followed Harris were forming themselves into a kind of league, and pledging themselves by a promise whose severity of discipline and absolute nature of obedience was not unlike those of some of the strict Papist societies. It is noted that Richard Tibbott was not at Dyserth because he had been sent on a journey to the north, and Lewis Evan with him.

The following morning, at Gore, Harris heard that his mother had died. He hurried home, and when viewing the body was very much perturbed, but on hearing that her last words were, 'Lord Jesus, receive my spirit,' he became quieter, and longed to go home himself. He preached at her funeral from the words, 'O death, where is thy sting?' By now he had reason to fear that the tide was turning against him in various parts of the country. At Erwood he received a letter from Dyserth, where he had held his Association the week before, informing him that the society there had left him and placed themselves under the care of Thomas Bowen. At Cwmcynon, on the way to Pembrokeshire, he noted that all who used to listen to him there had either been convicted or quietened; that no one opposed him but that they had all departed. In many places in Carmarthenshire, he writes that he left the society without having examined them because he felt the presence of the devil there. He itinerated extensively throughout Pembrokeshire noting that he had good services, 'but I find myself blackened considerably because of my doctrine, my followers, and Madam Griffith, so that it requires a great deal of faith to receive me to the house.'

We next find him journeying through Glamorganshire and finding matters considerably confused. On February 10, he wrote as follows from Dyffryn, near Tai-bach:

> Last night came here after discoursing at Hafod and declaring the Lord left them, and so refusing to stay there because the Lord did not stay there. While I preached to them, all my words condemned them because they have left the Lord.[10]

On the afternoon of the same day he preached at Neath and went that night to the home of John Richard, Llansamlet, for lodging. But there he found that John Richard had not advanced, had not come through to the light, being persuaded by his wife, by carnal reason and by his lack of faith. Furthermore, he had turned against Madam Griffith. Harris left immediately, travelling all night, and arriving at Llandeilo Fach. While on the road, he wondered whether the Lord would raise up another body of people to continue his work, and whether he and Madam Griffith would be left to themselves at last, with all the people having departed to follow the other side. At Gellidochlaethe, the next day, he refers to the house of the exhorter George Phillips as another house at which he had refused to stay because the Lord was not head there.

On February 14, 1751, a meeting was held at Trefeca to arrange the routes of the preachers on their various itineraries. It was agreed that five would journey regularly in the north, and four in the south. By this arrangement it was hoped that every society would receive a visit once a week. It was further agreed that the exhorters would visit those members of the societies whom they thought ready to unite with them, informing Harris and Madam Griffith of them so that they might confirm their place. No one was to be considered a member unless they possessed the faith and had given themselves to the Lord, but those who were seriously seeking and were striving to arrive, were also to be visited. At this meeting it was again found that many of the brethren were weak with some tending to turn back.

A similar meeting was held at Neath on April 10 and 11, where, as well as Harris and Madam Griffith, John Sparks, Richard Tibbott, Lewis Evans and many others, were present. Next to Harris himself, John Sparks was the main leader of the Association at this time, and it was usually he who began the various conferences with a sermon. Harris then spoke at length on the attributes necessary for a 'father', for the 'young men' and for the 'children'. 'Fathers' required a paternal spirit and heart and sufficient growth in faith and experience for them to possess a spiritual stability. They needed to be more forward than others in being ready to face every kind of danger and opposition. They were expected further to be animated in all their spiritual senses so that they could discern spirits and understand all the secret wiles of the devil. They must possess within them also the mystery of the Lord, pure love and a mortification of self. They were to be the eyes, lips, and ears of the flock, and to watch over the other preachers. It is no wonder that, after a thorough examination, no one was found up to the mark of such a standard, though it was hoped that the Lord was preparing some. We note that John Richards, Llansamlet, asked permission to attend the Association. This permission was granted, but he did not throw in his lot with them, being captive to his carnal reason.

Passing by many minor meetings, we arrive at the important Association held at Llwynbongam on July 2 and 3, 1751. Harris's required standard, as is evident, was being raised higher and higher continually and his discipline becoming ever more severe. His exhorters accordingly were falling away from him, one after another. During this summer also, Whitefield visited Wales, preaching in support of Rowland and his party and opposing Harris's work in taking Madam Griffith about with him. It is certain that this visit influenced many. John Sparks failed to attend the Association because of illness, others sent word that they could not come, and others again had taken offence. Richard Tibbott, Lewis Evan, and many others, however, were present. At the commencement Harris suggested that all bare their hearts, so that they might see who it was who had faith to go and possess the land, and to stand upon the Lord's side on his own, with none to help. As a result, many were turned away, not possessing the necessary faith. By now, Richard Tibbott was beginning to hesitate, he felt less inclination to itinerate, and wished to speak to the other brethren (Rowland's people).

To counter this, Harris got to his feet and expanded on the necessity for all to be established in the Lord and in the work, that none should stumble because of those who had left for these had all departed from the truth, and every means had been applied for their recovery. He showed also the differences between the preachers: that some had been called to be fathers, others young men, others children, evangelists and prophets; and that some possessed the spirit of Moses and Paul to arrange and command. He then referred to Rowland's party: that they could not in all conscience, be received back until they had repented the sinfulness of their spirit and the unbelief of their hearts. As for Madam Griffith, he said that she continued to be a blessing to him, by being an Eye and a discerner of spirits. At the end of the meeting that first night, many gave in their names as being willing to submit to that detailed discipline which had been outlined, amongst them were Thomas Williams and Lewis Evan. The first decision made the next morning was the following:

> Richard Tibbott was turned away for refusing to undertake a journey and for visiting the other brethren, in that every means has been applied to them, and because we have no faith that it is the Lord who has sent him to them.

The Association came to an end, after various other arrangements has been decided upon, with a sermon from Lewis Evan on the sufferings of Christ and one from Thomas Williams on the building of the temple.

On 2 October 1751, an Association was held at Trefeca. Not many attended, although Lewis Evan and Thomas Williams and others were there, together with Howell Harris and Madam Griffith. But both John Sparks and Richard Tibbott were absent. It was said of the latter that he had sunk from the Lord, but that he had written a letter to the Association. A Thomas Roberts from Anglesey was examined, received as a preacher, and called upon to preach to the Association. It seems that many homes in which Harris used to preach were now closed to him, and particularly to his exhorters. He therefore instructed his preachers to speak in the open air. He gave the following reasons for this recourse:

1. This is the general commission, 'Go and preach the gospel to every creature.'

2. Until they went out into the highways and hedges they would not be taking full advantage of the glorious liberty available to them through the gracious permission of the Government.

3. In that many carnal people would come to hear them in the open air that would never attend at a house.

4. In that it was in the open air that the work began and that it seemed reasonable to continue the work in the spirit with which it began.

5. Until they went out to the highways and hedges they could not feel confident that they had done the utmost in their power for the salvation of the land.

This Association is the last for which there are any records in Harris's journals.

On the first day of January 1752, a General Association was held at Llanllugan, Montgomeryshire. About twenty-five were present. It is not thought that Lewis Evan was amongst them because soon afterwards Harris had to administer a severe rebuke to him as one who had failed to come up to the light and had shown an opposition to the Lord. The first undertaking of the Association was to disassociate themselves from the name 'Methodists', in that the term had become badly defiled by their doctrines, selfishness, and enmity to the blood. From now on, Howell Harris's people were to be called Exhorters, a name not used by any others. Their main meetings were to be known as Councils and not Associations. Most probably, those who went about warning sinners were beginning to be called speakers or preachers, and the word exhorter, as a formal office, was falling out of use.

At this Council, Harris was excessively severe. He told the brethren that they were not growing, that they did not possess the spirit of the revival; that God's love did not burn in their souls; and that this was the reason why so few came to hear them. He said further that the devil had no fear of them but that they, rather, feared the devil. He complained also that all seemed to be against him and those who clung to him, and that some of the brethren were in danger of being killed in Anglesey and Denbighshire. One of the Council's decisions was to discontinue building any more chapels, but to preach in the open air, at fairs, markets and in the villages.

On the way home from the Llanllugan Council, Harris called at Bedw, and it is here that we find the concept of a 'family' at Trefeca forming. He wrote:

I conversed with Sarah and Hannah Bowen, who feel themselves obligated to commit themselves to the Lord, and to me. I encouraged them to come to Trefeca, as it seems likely that the Lord is to lay down a foundation for a house there, and it maybe that they shall be the first stones. I am now to be more domesticated, in order to write, etc.

These two were the daughters of Mr Bowen, Tyddyn, and they went to Trefeca as was suggested to them. Miss Sarah Bowen afterwards became the wife of Simon Lloyd, Bala.

The next Council was held at Trefeca on 11 February 1752. By this time, many of the leading exhorters, who had stood bravely together with Howell Harris at the beginning, had left him. Of these were John Sparks, John Harris (St Kennox) and Thomas Williams (Groes-wen). He still maintained a great strictness over those preachers remaining. He told them that they were not to lead societies; that not one of them had become enough of a father to do so, but only to itinerate for preaching. It is quite certain that those preachers who were still with him were more ignorant, more uncultured in their manner, and fuller of a fanatical spirit, than those who had departed. Directly after the Council, Harris went on a long journey through Carmarthenshire, Pembrokeshire, part of Cardiganshire, and Glamorganshire. He had huge congregations in every place, particularly in south Cardiganshire and Pembrokeshire. He preached each time in the open air. He stated that the crowds were too numerous for any house, but there is reason to believe that many of the houses, where once he was received as the angel of God, were now closed to him. At Cilgerran he wrote that his congregation was made up almost entirely of unbelievers who were not used to attending preaching at any place, and that professors were absent, and that such was the case in the majority of his venues. At Haverfordwest, he preached on the street, and noted that Howell Davies, John Sparks and John Harris, St Kennox, were amongst the hearers. He preached with great severity, and it does not appear that he had any fellowship with his old fellow labourers. There must have been a measure of sadness in the hearts of both parties.

From Carmarthenshire he crossed the hills to Llanddewibrefi and recorded that a multitude of many thousands had gathered there. What induced him to go so far out of his way to preach is hard to say, unless it was to throw out some kind of challenge to Daniel Rowland, who was the curate of the church there. But he found the people of Llanddewibrefi to be full of prejudice; none of them seemed to be striving for the light. After visiting more places in Carmarthenshire and Radnorshire, he returned to Trefeca. This was the last important journey with respect to the cause of the gospel in Wales that Howell Harris was to undertake for many, many years. He felt that his work was in decline throughout the country. The standard that he had set was too high, his discipline too strict, and his demeanour too high-handed, for the exhorters and societies to abide by them. And it is clear that Rowland's people were gaining ground. The sympathy of the other denominations, Churchmen and Nonconformists, were with them. Whitefield returned again to Wales, that summer, and preached over forty times for Rowland's people, being present at one of their Associations. Although Harris felt that the tide was flowing against him, he did not become disheartened in any way, but began a new aspect of the work, namely, the collecting together of a family at Trefeca and the disciplining of preachers and others there, so that the place could become a focal point of spiritual activity that would extend throughout Wales and parts of England.

[1] The translation is that of Hugh J. Hughes, as found in HJH, pp. 334–8.

[2] The *Sabellians* were heretics; the followers of Sabellius (a bishop or elder in Africa in the third century) who taught that there was no difference between the three persons of the Trinity, but that they were all one; and therefore that the Father and Holy Spirit suffered death along with the Son.

The *Patripassians* were heretics (about the end of the second century) who said that the Father had suffered as well as the Son. (From the Latin, pater and passio – father-suffering).

The *Eutychians* were heretics who alleged that the two natures were so co-mixed in Christ that the Godhead suffered and died. (From Eutyches, an abbot of Constantinople, c. AD 448.)

The *Ubiquitarians* claimed that Christ's body, as well as his deity, was omnipresent. (From the Latin, *ubique* – in all places. They were a branch of the Lutherans and flourished about 1560.) [The above notes are by Hugh J. Hughes.]

[3] Strata Forida.

[4] HHVP, p. 185.

[5] CH, 28, p. 50.

[6] Ibid.

[7] Ibid., p. 55.

[8] Ibid., p. 60.

[9] CH, 32, p. 9.

[10] CH, 27, p. 175.

# 17
# HOWELL HARRIS AFTER
# THE DISRUPTION

## HOWELL HARRIS AT TREFECA; HIS SERIOUS ILLNESS

*I*t appears that the idea of forming a religious settlement of some significance at Trefeca had been in Harris's mind for some years, though he had no clear vision of its nature and form. He had been building there for some time without really knowing for what purpose. Now, after the disruption, the concept took on a definite form. He states in his journal that Trefeca was the most central position possible; that it lay half way between Carmarthen and Gloucester, and between Bristol and Llanfair Caereinion; and that it was about equidistant from Tregaron, Llanidloes, Newport, Cardiff, Llantrisant, Neath and Swansea. On 13 April 1752, he laid down the foundation of a new building, larger and more attractive than the existing one. He had no money at all for this work, nor anything to fall back on in attempting such a venture, other than the promises of the unchanging God. For all Howell Harris's labours and immense efforts, he had received as reward for this labour scarcely enough to maintain himself and his family; certainly not enough as far as money was concerned. He often commented, though not as a complaint, that his clothing was poorer than any, and his horse the poorest. We find him often in debt and in great distress in his attempts to raise a sum of money to meet some need. Yet, notwithstanding this, he began on a work that would entail thousands of pounds, when he had not a penny behind him. The day after the laying down of the foundation he set out for London, and he says that he left behind at Trefeca sixteen workers, three women, and a further four to arrive soon. He committed them to the Lord upon leaving, declaring that he left him as head over them.

In the summer of 1752, two very important events in the life of Howell Harris took place. The first was the death of Madam Griffith, which took place at London on the last day of May. He greatly mourned her loss, believing that her departure was an irredeemable loss to the work. But it is certain that her death proved a blessing to him, in that while he was linked to her, she remained one of the most influential factors in poisoning his soul. The second event was that he was struck down with a serious illness, which he thought would prove his death. This was the result of overwork. For all the strength of Harris's constitution and his toughness of character, no mortal flesh could have maintained the labour, weariness and travelling which he had endured, without breaking down. In addition, for the last two years since the disruption, he had nobody of comparable stature to assist him and the whole weight of the work had been borne by him. Whitefield had his sea voyages, when he would obtain relief from his endless labours, and these had long kept him strong and healthy. By 28 June 1752, one wing of the building was complete and a Council had been arranged to meet on that date at Trefeca to celebrate the opening of the place, as well as for the usual administration. Howell Harris was very ill; he considered that he was on the brink of Jordan. Yet, he insisted on dragging himself to the Council, on both days, in order to speak to the gathered preachers. His addresses brought with them the solemnity of another world:

> I am bidding you an eternal farewell; I do not expect to see your faces again. My confidence is alone in the blood of the Godhead, yet I have called you, wishing to express my love to all who have come to him. You, who have backslidden, let me in my death do that which I failed to accomplish during my life, namely, to excite you to follow on, with palm leaves in your hands, so that you may shine forever before the throne. The blood of Christ cleanseth from all sin. Although Satan has blinded you and hardened you, come to this fountain, and you will overcome and will meet with God. O, that I could make the whole creation hear me! I would send them all to the fountain. Let me greet you from the edge of eternity. Come to the cross; you will see there every mystery, the Father, the Son, the Holy Spirit, the Three in One, shining upon you. Let me depart with the strong hope that I may see you before the throne.

As he delivered this address he nearly fainted, and he had to be carried back to his room. It must have been an unforgettable experience for those who heard him. It is noted that there were some present from every county in Wales, except for Cardiganshire and Flintshire.

But, contrary to his expectations, he slowly recovered. As soon as he was able, he began preaching three times a day to the workers and to those who had come to live at Trefeca. The result was that people gathered to him from every part of the country. Some came as whole families, but generally they were single people, both men and women, who believed it was their duty to give themselves to the service of the Lord. He had not expected anything of the kind. When he first laid down the foundation of the building he had only been thinking of a place for some half a dozen families and a number of single preachers, together with a few women as servants. He was always one who would fight to overcome all difficulties however, and so he now hastened to extend the house and to raise other dwellings around it, so that a small village was formed. Devout farmers would also come to the neighbourhood, either renting or buying land in the area, so that they might be close enough to take advantage of the spiritual privileges that were to be found there.

Within eighteen months the Trefeca 'family' numbered over a hundred, and contained representatives from nearly every county in Wales. Each prospective member, before joining the 'family', had to donate all their wealth to the general treasury. Some of them were particularly wealthy, but no doubt the majority were poor, and the burden of maintaining this large family fell completely upon Howell Harris's shoulders. He purchased land to farm; he bought wool for the women to spin and knit; and Trefeca became a centre for various businesses. And God watched over them so that they did not want for anything.

> Being often in straits concerning temporal things, wanting twenty or fifty, or even a hundred pounds, I had nowhere to turn to for assistance but the promise, the Lord not relieving till the last pinch, and even then appearing from a quarter that none could ever imagine, some bringing and some sending me £10 or £20, and even £100, though living at a distance of seventy or eighty miles, being compelled to do so only by the Word sounding in their conscience night and day, and no man in the world knowing or imagining anything of it. Thus the Lord appeared for me many times. This seems strange to many, and well it may; yet it is the real truth.

There was nothing to attract the lazy or soft to Trefeca. The whole family was under severe discipline, having to live and behave at all times according to detailed rules. The food was spartan, the clothing was rough, and the discipline called for great self-denial. Howell Harris was not a man to load a table with delicacies, and to provide support for idleness and indifference; he had never indulged in these himself, and had no intention of maintaining them in others. But there was one thing available, and that more valuable than any material advantage in the judgment of those honest souls gathered there, and fully meriting the sacrifice of natural comforts. The gospel of Christ was preached there in its purity; the bread of life was distributed in abundance and with great regularity. According to Williams, in his elegy to Harris:

| | |
|---|---|
| You were faithful in your family, | Ti fuost ffyddlon yn dy deulu, |
| Strict in your communal hall, | Llym yn dy adeilad mawr, |

| | |
|---|---|
| Pulling down man's empty glory | Ac a dynaist flys ac enw, |
| And the pride that moves us all. | A gogoniant dyn i lawr. |

| | |
|---|---|
| And you made your children faithful | A ti wnest dy blant yn ufudd |
| To their calling every one; | At eu galwad bob yr un, |
| Laid down, by your rule and order, | Byw i'th reol, byw i'th gyfraith, |
| Every duty to be done; | Byw i'th olau di dy hun; |
| There's no other in the country, | Fel na fedr neb yng Ngymru, |
| By whatever means at hand, | Trwy na chleddyf fyth na ffon, |
| Could have formed so many people | Ddod â thy, o'r un rhifedi, |
| Into such a heavenly band. | Tan y dymher hyfryd hon. |

| | |
|---|---|
| Before sunrise at Trefeca | Y mae gweddi cyn y wawrddydd |
| Could be heard the voice of prayer, | Yn Nhrefeca ganddo fe, |
| While their neighbours all around them | 'Ramser bo trwm gwsg breuddwydlyd |
| Still slept on without a care; | Yn teyrnasu yn llawer lle; |
| And before the meal was taken, | A chyn llanw'r bol o fwydydd, |
| Harris then would preach and pray, | Fe geir yno gyngor prudd, |
| Before nightfall, prayer and reading – | A chyn swper, gweddi a darllen – |
| Worship offered thrice a day. | Tri addoliad yn y dydd. |

The erection of the building and the settlement of the family at Trefeca prompted many untrue stories to be spread abroad in Wales. It was suggested that the Reformer's purpose was to get rich on the backs of the wealthy people that were drawn there, and to make money out of their labours and energies. There was no truth in these tales. Whatever were Howell Harris's weaknesses, a lust for money was not one of them, nor yet a lust for wordly honour. Nevertheless, he was not completely free from giving occasion to suspicion. Whenever wealthy people, especially if they were young women, would pass over all they possessed into the Trefeca treasury, it was only natural for their relatives who expected to benefit from their wealth in one way or another, to become bitter and spread rumours abroad. And after monies had been received, it was not without great difficulties that it could be retrieved again, even when the circumstances indicated that it should be. We could refer, for example, to the case of Sarah Bowen, one of the two sisters from Tyddyn, who was of comfortable circumstances and had given all to the establishment according to the general practice. One day, Mr Simon Lloyd of Plasyndref, Bala, arrived, partly perhaps out of curiosity and partly in order to obtain spiritual benefit. Having knocked, who should open the door to him but Miss Bowen. The gentleman's heart was drawn to the young lady immediately, and as he succeeded in producing a corresponding response from her, the two made arrangements to marry. But how to regain the lady's wealth was the problem. There was a considerable to-do over the matter. Eventually John Evans, the well-known preacher from Bala, mediated during a visit to Trefeca and after some argument, a satisfactory marriage contract, which survives to this day, was drawn up.

## CAPTAIN HARRIS OF THE MILITIA

About the year 1756, the whole nation was in considerable excitement in the anticipation of a French invasion to conquer Britain. Howell Harris was a patriot to the core of his being; he believed that religion, as well as politics, called upon him to support King George. Nor was he in any way lacking in war-like spirit. Under the influence of the excitement the Breconshire Agricultural Society presented an address to the king with the offer of forming themselves into a troop of light horse, ready to proceed at their own expense to any part of the kingdom if called upon to do so. When Harris heard of this he informed the Society that if their offer was accepted he would provide ten fully armed soldiers at his own expense, for the troop. In the event the Society's offer was not taken up, but as an indication of their gratitude to Harris they elected him an honorary member of the Society. Soon afterwards he discussed the war situation with the family at Trefeca and as a result five of their devout young men enlisted. They took part in many fierce battles including the attack upon Quebec when it was won from the French, and when General Wolfe was killed. While fellow soldiers fell around them a wall of defence seemed to surround these five and not one of them was killed. Four died natural deaths in foreign lands, and the fifth, after being taken prisoner of war by the French returned to Trefeca, living there until the day of his death.

In the spring of 1760, through the suggestion of his brother Joseph and of the members of the Agricultural Society, Howell Harris joined the County Militia together with twenty-four men from the Trefeca family. He was soon commissioned as captain. It is strange, from one point of view, to find an evangelist such as Harris becoming a soldier, but he considered that Protestantism was endangered. He thought that if France were to win the day, Popery would reign, and Bibles would be banned from the country as a result. He believed that he was as faithfully serving God by the sword as he had previously served him with his itinerating preaching of the gospel. Before his departure he placed the establishment at Trefeca in the hands of trustees until his return, and he appointed Evan Moses to manage the place in his absence. Evan Moses was from Aberdare. He was an uneducated but serious man, who had an unending respect for Harris.

The first garrison to which the Militia was sent was Yarmouth, and on the way there Harris preached at every place. When he arrived at the town he inquired whether there were Methodists there. He was informed that many had attempted to preach there but had been stopped by the rage of the mob and had barely escaped with their lives. Not lacking in faith, he sent out the town crier to announce that a Methodist preacher would be speaking at the market-place at a certain hour. A huge crowd gathered at the spot, armed with stones, bricks and mud to throw at the preacher, and vowing that they would put him to death. Harris at the time was drilling his men on a clearing nearby. When the hour announced arrived he went up to the crowd and asked them what was the matter. They answered that they had been expecting a Methodist preacher, and that it was a good thing for him that he had not arrived. He replied that he was sorry they had been disappointed, and that he was willing to sing a hymn with them, to pray, and also provide an address. He climbed on to a table that stood nearby; his men gathered around him; their singing reverberated around the market-place; he followed them, praying with great power. The novelty of the scene, the armed men surrounding and defending their captain, their loud 'Amens', together with a divine influence that pervaded the place, overcame the mob so that Harris had every opportunity to preach. He was granted a most effectual service. Such influences fell upon the gathering that many were convicted where they stood. From then on, Harris preached in his uniform at the market-place every afternoon, almost without exception, and to large congregations. Gradually, other preachers joined him; a strong society of many members was formed, and Yarmouth became as famous for its religion as it had been previously for its irreligion.

The next winter the Militia was sent to Brecon, and Captain Harris preached throughout the region, as he had used to do. It appears also that much more kindly feelings now prevailed between himself and Rowland and his party. The two sides had begun to realize that they had misunderstood each other, that to a large extent their quarrel had been a mere striving over words, and that both parties had departed from the brotherly love required by the gospel. The Methodists felt the loss of the courage and organizational gifts of the Reformer from Trefeca amongst them. In 1759 they had gone so far as to send a message to him asking him to return; the request was carried to Trefeca by Daniel Rowland in person. Harris did not see his way clear to consent at the time, but no doubt the request greatly affected his spirit. It is thought that it was about this time, when the Militia was at Brecon, that the disturbance in the Llandovery Association occurred. The tradition is that Harris, while approaching Llandovery town, met with Daniel Rowland, William Williams, and many exhorters, fleeing for their lives, having failed to proceed with an Association because of the violence and persecution of the mob. He encouraged them to return with himself. Having reached the town he climbed up on to the milestone which served as a pulpit, and facing the mob like a lion, he cried out, 'Peace, in the name of the King of heaven!' This had no effect upon the crowd, they continued with their foul language and threatening. At that, he pulled off his outer garment, appearing before them in his military uniform, and cried out, 'Peace, in the name of King George!' They were frightened by the official uniform and became quiet and pale; a deathly silence took hold of them, and he took the opportunity to convict them of their sin at being more terrified before the King of England than they were before God. After this, the Methodists had perfect peace to continue with their Association.

In December 1762, the Brecon Militia disbanded and Harris gave up his captain's commission. He had gained considerable praise for his patriotism and bravery. The Breconshire gentry held him in sincere respect, and we see the once contemptible evangelist, so often threatened in the past with fines and prison, and who had been arraigned by the magistrates of the county before one of His Majesty's judges, now high in the favour of his erstwhile persecutors. His men had behaved in an exemplary fashion. Sir Edward Williams, the regiment's colonel, wrote to him as follows:

> Captain Harris, I have no time to do justice to the behaviour of your men; but in a few words I assure you, that in every respect their conduct does credit to the religious principles you have taken so much pains to instil into them.

## THE FIRST MOVES TOWARDS RECONCILIATION

On 23 January 1763, Howell Harris commenced his fiftieth year, which he called his year of Jubilee. By now his heart longed for reconciliation with his old friends, and four days previously he had sent Evan Moses, his chief servant, with a letter to Daniel Rowland, Llangeitho, asking for a reunion. Rowland and he, no doubt, had discussed the matter before when the former called on him with the letter from his brethren, and he knew that the Reformer from Llangeitho shared the same desire as himself, otherwise he would not have sent his servant with such a request. This was a blessed period for Wales at the time. After many years of failure and great barrenness, a revival had broken out at Llangeitho in 1762 upon the publication of a hymn-book by Williams, Pantycelyn, and this had spread throughout the whole country, so that the villages and valleys were full of praises. No doubt, the prevailing spiritual warmth melted the hearts of the Reformers and brought them into a more loving regard for one another. On 30 January, Harris received a letter from Evan Moses asking him to meet with Rowland at Trecastle on the following Wednesday. It appears that Rowland was on his way to a Monthly Meeting to be held at Llansawel. Harris wrote in his journal:

> When I read it, I felt so happy that the Lord was opening a door of usefulness to me. I had heard of the life that was amongst them, and of their success; and my only fear was in case I, through my selfishness and sin, should bring a curse upon them. I was brought low; I was so free from envy that I blessed God for raising them up, and longed not that they should share death with me, but that I should share in their life. I was made to rejoice in the hope that I might go amongst them again.

It is evident that his thoughts towards Rowland and his followers had changed completely and that a new spirit had possessed him. He set out for Trecastle to meet Rowland, and a great fear possessed him that he might prove unfaithful to God in one way or another. Of his meeting with Rowland he writes nothing but surely there was a warm clasp of hands, if not an embracing and many tears. Rowland pressed him to accompany him to the Monthly Meeting at Llansawel. He told him that such was the desire of the believers generally, as well as his own. Harris, in anticipation of such a request, had decided to refuse, but his friend's urgings proved too strong for him, and after praying on the matter, he judged that the Lord was willing. The next day, the two set off together and they reached Llansawel about six o'clock. There they met Williams, Pantycelyn, Peter Williams, and many exhorters. He wrote:

> I had heard of the spirit of song that had fallen upon many parts of Cardiganshire and Carmarthenshire, and of the hundreds that gathered to hear. The Lord opened my mouth to speak, that we should not receive nor deny these external signs, but should judge them according to their influence on the heart and life, and especially according to whether they produced poverty of spirit.

He also referred in his address to William Williams's book, *Pantheologia, neu hanes holl grefyddau'r byd* [*Pantheologia, or the history of all the religions of the world*], and praised it as a most useful book. That night he lodged in the same house as Williams, and they were up until twelve o'clock. Harris wrote:

> Williams confessed his sorrow for the way in which he opposed me before, and he explained how he came thereafter to preach and publish the teaching which he had opposed. He said also that I was his spiritual father.

No doubt the fellowship between them was sweet. That night, having retired to bed, Harris was taken ill with acute abdominal pains. It may well be that his emotional excitement and his overjoyed state at finding himself amongst his brethren once more, was the cause. He was very weak the next day, but he met with the exhorters and spoke to them seriously and at length. Amongst other things, he told them to be careful of the spirit of singing that was manifesting itself, in case it either disappeared, or gave occasion to the flesh. He advised them further not to mix too much with their hearers but, having preached, to withdraw. He was then compelled to preach in the chapel, the construction of which had been due mainly to himself and for which he had collected all over Wales. His subject was Zechariah 12:10, 'And I will pour upon the house of David, and upon the inhabitants of Jerusalem, the spirit of grace and of supplications.' We cannot give the sermon, but the service pleased him greatly. That night he returned to Llandovery, and his experience the following morning is worth recording:

I returned here last night, having received the most urgent invitations to visit Neath, Cil-y-cwm, Cardiganshire and Carmarthenshire, from Rowland, William Williams, Thomas Davies, John Williams, and others. I find that the exhorters have been placed on my heart as if they were my children. Surely, this is the year of the Jubilee! The time has come; the shadows of prejudice are receding; the old love and simplicity are returning, and it seems that all the barriers that were previously in the way have been removed. This spirit of prayer that has descended appears completely free from any lightness, and the self, that was evident before. Upon seeing so many new places begun by them, and not one by me, I felt it was an honour to be in their midst, and it is a comfort to me to see that my place, and my work, and my people of old, are offered to me again after a rupture of thirteen years.

## ITINERATING AGAIN

No formal decision was passed at Llansawel with respect to the reunion of Harris with the Methodists but he was invited with great kindness to come amongst them as before, and every door was thrown open to him. On 18 March 1763, he set out on a short journey through parts of Carmarthenshire and Cardiganshire. His first preaching stop was Cil-y-cwm, the spiritual home of William Williams. The service was held in the open-air because of the numbers attending. The text was 'Search the Scriptures'. He preached for two and a half hours, with extraordinary power and influence, and he was particularly severe on those who scorned or were careless of God's Word. After the service he returned to the chapel to lead a society; there were some hundreds there and he exhorted them all to pray. He dined with the curate of the church, with Williams, and many others of his old friends that he had not seen since the disruption; he then retired to his old lodging, Llwynyberllan, to sleep. On the journey there he gained much information from his guide of the revival that was spreading throughout the land. He says:

> I cried that some of this fire might catch hold in my own spirit; for I learnt that many had been awakened in these parts, through the spirit of song and of blessing the Lord which has broken out, which lasts sometimes throughout the night.

His comments show that we presently have no real conception of the influence wrought by Williams's hymns in the rekindling of God's fire in Wales, when it had almost been extinguished by quarrels and disruptions. We find him next preaching at Llansawel Chapel after a Mr Grey. Almost certainly this would have been the Rev. Thomas Grey, the successor to old Mr Philip Pugh at Llwynpïod, Abermeurig and Ffos-y-ffin. Sometime after this, Mr Grey joined himself to the Methodists. It must have been quite soon after.

A friend has informed me that he searched diligently through the old records of the associations of the Congregationalists, as they are found in the Evangelical Magazine and other publications, and they do not even re-fer to Mr Grey; whereas he is found preaching regularly in the North and South Associations of the Methodists. A huge congregation had gathered. Llansawel chapel at that time had become a centre for the Methodists throughout Carmarthenshire. He was given a powerful service, speaking sternly to those who were enjoying liberty without first having been in captivity. After he had finished, the people would not leave. They flocked into the chapel and he had to speak there again. His topic was the neces-sity for self-examination.

From there he journeyed to Carmarthenshire, preaching on Castle Green at two o'clock to the largest audience that he had ever had in his life up to that time. He calculated that they were about ten thousand. He spoke in Welsh and English from, 'We beheld his glory', and he showed that the way to produce high morality was to preach Jesus Christ. He was not satisfied with doctrine alone, but thundered forth terribly against swearing, drunkenness, prostitution, and other sins; and he cried out with all his strength, 'With those who know him and who love him, let my home be eternally!' He went that night to Pant Howell where his text was the same, but his sermon was substantially different. He was at this time very contented in spirit. He says:

I see the great honour placed upon me, that I am called by my dear Lord to his work, and that he has again given me a place in his house.

On Good Friday he was at Cardigan and while journeying there he recorded how all had overtaken him in light, faith and communion with God. He went to the church in the morning and in the afternoon preached himself; and although the people had been informed of his visit only the previous night, a vast crowd had gathered. His topic was the sufferings of the Saviour. At night, he was at Twr-gwyn, where a chapel had by now been built. Matthew 11:28 was his text. He noted that a large congregation had gathered and added, 'Such singing and such rejoicing I had never before heard.' We saw previously that he was at first rather suspicious of the singing and warned the believers to be careful about it; by now, however, he is quite overcome by it.

> I was moved to justify the singing that is now in the county, where many sing God's praises and worship him throughout the night. I showed to the carnal who take offence because those who are religious praise God to excess, that they should consider that they (the carnal) do not praise God at all, and so believers must praise him not only for themselves but for the carnal also

After the service he went to the home of Mr Bowen, J.P., Gwaunifor, and arrived there at midnight. The next morning he preached beside the chapel which Mr Bowen had built at his own expense, to a huge gathering. Here he parted with Mr Grey and Mr Popkin, who had accompanied him from Cil-y-cwm, and he returned immediately to Trefeca. It may be seen that he had taken great strides forward, and why he preached only in these places noted we do not know.

On the Tuesday after Easter he went to Builth Wells, which he had visited only once in twelve years. He preached with much strength. He met there with John Richard, Llansamlet, and another exhorter called Evan Roberts. The two returned with him to Trefeca, and the next morning, John Richard commenced on a journey to the north. A few days later he noted that he had been reading the works of Daniel Rowland, and those of Williams, Pantycelyn, and that he had been much subdued upon seeing how little he had been used when compared to his brethren. 'I had nothing to say for myself,' he writes, 'other than that I am lazy, unused and polluted.' He was too hard on himself, because he might have said as truly as the Apostle Paul, 'I laboured more abundantly than they all.' But he was probably thinking of his retirement to Trefeca.

On 2 May 1763, he began a long journey through Cardiganshire, Pembrokeshire and Carmarthenshire. The first place he visited was Llangamarch, where he preached with no specific text to a very large gathering.

'I instructed the young converts,' he says, 'and built up the faithful.' This shows that very many from that neighbourhood had recently been converted. That year saw one of the most powerful revivals that ever visited Wales. It spread as an unstoppable flame throughout the country, until the mountainous valleys as well as the plains were full, as it were, of the worship of God. Whether it had broken out as early as this in the year, we do not know, but already, certainly, there were 'young converts' at Llangamarch. The next day, Tuesday, Harris crossed Mynydd Mawr and came to Tregaron. Here, Daniel Rowland awaited him, and he wrote:

> I was humbled on seeing that the Lord had opened doors to me, to go about with my old fellow-labourers, which position I had forfeited through my sin.

He was given remarkable freedom in prayer, and when preaching was terribly severe upon those who judged and opposed God and his work, and he showed the spirituality of the law and the personal and detailed nature of its commands. He records that three clergymen, as well as Daniel Rowland, were listening. From Tregaron he went to Llwyn Iorwerth, not far from Aberystwyth. The people followed him, singing and praising the whole way. Upon seeing and hearing them, he felt that the Lord had been furthering his work without him, and that he had honoured Rowland and his exhorters so much more than himself. But he was far from being envious and ready to commit himself to help them, hoping that he would receive blessing also amongst them. He began to converse with the people and found them to be honest, willing to be taught, gentle and self-denying. 'Christ Jesus came into the world to save sinners', was his message here, and he evangelized sweetly.

That night he was at Lledrod; the whole countryside had gathered to the service, and he was given remarkable power to preach on, 'For he shall save his people from their sins.' The next day was a day of national thanksgiving for the peace that had been obtained, and he went to the church at Lledrod for communion.

We find him next at Llangeitho, where he had not been for fourteen years. There were here at least ten thousand people to hear him, and after being granted to wrestle powerfully in prayer, he preached with great liberty from the words, 'For we which have believed do enter into rest.' He showed that it is faith that purifies the heart and that overcomes the world, and he was very severe with those who seek to identify faith with fanaticism. He noted that over two hundred men and over forty fairly young children had joined the society there. After the service he was asked to lead a private society in which he spoke on various matters, and ended with earnest prayer for Mr Rowland. He wrote:

> I see that the Lord has raised him higher than myself; that he has given him all this work and honour, together with all the societies and the exhorters.

If Harris, as he observed all this, was as completely free from envy as he says he was, God's grace must have been poured out plentifully upon his spirit.

On Friday he was at Abermeurig and then, leaving the beautiful Aeron Valley, he crossed the hills to Lampeter, in the Teifi Valley. His text here was, 'It is a faithful saying and worthy of all acceptation.' Many of the gentry were in attendance and so he preached in English as well as in Welsh. He referred to two ladies in particular, Miss H. Lloyd and Miss Evans. After calling at Dolgwm, a large farm below Lampeter, he came on Friday night to Gwaunifor. Rowland was still accompanying him, and on the road Harris opened his heart to his friend, sharing his hope of getting John Wesley and one of the Moravians to go about Wales with him, and of forming a general union between the parties involved, under the wing of the Established Church. What Rowland thought of this plan is not known. At Gwaunifor he preached with authority on the blood of Jesus Christ cleansing us of all sin. In the private society that followed he impressed upon the believers the necessity of mourning as well as of rejoicing. After preaching at Twr-gwyn and at Cwmcynon, he arrived on Sunday night at Llechryd where he had the greatest attendance of his life. He calculated that some twelve thousand were present. 'Great is the mystery of godliness', was his text:

> I preached his sufferings and wounds, that these are the only refuge; I called and invited all to him, showing that God is in him as in his temple. I was severe with those who opposed the present work and desired it to come to naught, showing that they are of the same spirit as Cain.

He had opportunity here to talk to Mr Enoch, the superintendent of Madam Bevan's schools in the three counties, and found him an honest and humble man.

It seems that Daniel Rowland departed at this point and that Mr Popkin was appointed to accompany him during his time in Pembrokeshire. Popkin was a man of proud spirit, tending to Antinomianism, and it is remembered that Daniel Rowland had great trouble with him later, and eventually was forced to excommunicate him. Popkin began to rebuke Harris for leaving the Methodists and for wasting so much of his time, and he kept on praising Rowland excessively. The Reformer suffered it all patiently for a while, but eventually turned on him and informed him that

he (Popkin) would not be allowed to be a bishop over him. After passing through Llwyn-y-grawys, they came to Newport. 'My flesh is meat
indeed', was his text and he was moved at first to thunder terrifyingly,
referring with great solemnity to death and eternity. But before concluding, he offered the gospel sweetly, proclaiming that Christ Jesus was
immutable. A gathering of many thousands had collected at Fishguard.
'This man receiveth sinners', was his message, and he rebuked those who
did not feel their sinfulness. For the first time on his journey he found
that there was considerable prejudice against him in the people's minds.
The revival had not yet reached here; there was not the singing found in
Cardiganshire. That night he was at St David's, and says that the congregation was of many thousands. After passing through the English region
of Pembrokeshire, he came to Haverfordwest and preached in the chapel,
but not so many were present because of some misunderstanding in the
announcement of his visit.

During the sermon he mentioned the desirability of achieving unity between the various religious parties, that they were brethren, and that they
would spend eternity in one another's company. When discussing with Mr
Howell Davies, who had come to hear him, the appropriateness of having
John Wesley, together with one of the Moravians, to travel the country
with him, he discerned that Mr Davies was very prejudiced against the
idea. The next day he went to Woodstock, where a chapel had been built,
and preached powerfully from the words, 'Look unto me, and be ye saved,
all the ends of the earth.' In the company of the exhorter, John Harry, he
went to Mounton, and from there to Laugharne, complaining of much
bodily weakness. He was here in the vicinity of Llanddowror, but his old
friend Griffith Jones had died over two years before. But he called to see
Madam Bevan. He tried to talk with her on various matters to do with
religion, but she was not ready to embrace his suggestions as regards pro-
moting unity between God's people, and was moreover strongly opposed
to lay preaching. He refused an invitation to dine with Madam Bevan and
hurried to Carmarthen where he preached for two whole hours on the
words, 'Thou shalt call his name Jesus,' with life and authority and much
effect, to a crowd of many thousands.

Later that same day he preached at Brechfa, Carmarthenshire, on justification and sanctification. The following day he was at Llansawel, where
Williams, Pantycelyn, met with him. Williams preached on unbelief. He
portrayed it as the worst of sins, and said that when we have faith to see
this world and its toys as nothing, we will think nothing of all its great
men and be able to rejoice always. 'I loved the spirit and the voice', wrote
Harris. He himself preached after Williams on, 'With his stripes we are

healed.' This sermon was always appreciated and so it proved at Llansawel also. After preaching in the street in Llandovery to a congregation of over three thousand, he returned to Trefeca, happy in spirit. He had been greatly encouraged by the company of friends, many of whom he had not seen for thirteen years.

## AN ASSOCIATION AT TREFECA, THE FIRST FOR THIRTEEN YEARS

During his previous tour he had invited the next Association to Trefeca, where no such gathering had taken place since before the disruption, and the brethren had willingly agreed. His heart leaped within him in anticipation of the honour of welcoming God's servants. He states that he had twenty beds available for them at Trefeca, together with sufficient lodging places in the farmhouses nearby. He wrote:

> Trefeca, May 18. The first General United Association. O! Jubilee! Last night, at seven, Mr Rowland and son, Mr Edwards, David William Rees, William Richard the first, and William Richard the second, four exhorters, John Thomas, Thomas Grey, the Dissenting minister, a curate called Lewis, and two exhorters, Popkin and William John, came here, and eight women and seven men came also. Being pressed I discoursed on our Saviour's poverty. I received extraordinary strength and authority. I received them all with a humble spirit and in the Lord, and cried that the Lord would come amongst us and bless us, which he did abundantly. This morning up at six, breakfast at seven, went together at eight. Several were coming, Mr Peter Williams, John Williams, Jeffrey, Stephen Jones, David Williams, etc. A letter from John Richard was read. Absent – Howell Davies, William Williams, John Harry, etc. I opened how it was that they had sent for me four years previously, and how I came to the meeting at Llansawel; that I can't join them till I was satisfied whether they are in the Church of England. If they don't join in their Parochial Council and worship, they are a new sect, and when Mr Rowland and a few others die they must have Dissenting ministers over them all. I showed my reasons against the name Methodist and why I ever renounced it. Declared I was not against their coming to chapels to have the sacrament of Mr Rowland, under discipline and examination. How I have been kept in the Church, and how I have showed such as leave it not to prosper. Mr Rowland said the same. All agreed to stay in it, only they could not persuade souls to this. When I urged [discipline] home, beginning at the Association with the exhorters, who should be examined carefully; then, in the societies with an appropriate arrangement for families; without this all would become disorder. All agreed and joined to call for my help in this, and they saw my place vacant since I went off . . . After appointing a further meeting in a fortnight the meeting was ended.[1]

The above quotation reveals Harris's particular genius: his love for order, his care for discipline, and also his continuing strong attachment to the Established Church. After the private meeting there was a public service in the open air in the village. A large gathering had collected, not only from neighbouring districts but from the further regions of the county and from Glamorganshire. No doubt stories about Trefeca and the remarkable establishment which it contained had spread over the region, and these, together with the romance of the reconciliation between Harris and his old friends, had drawn the people to the place. Popkin preached first. His text was, 'For thy Maker is thine husband.' Harris notes that it was notably Calvinistic; it is possible, reading between the lines, that this means it was tending to Antinomianism. 'But,' he says:

> ...when Rowland rose after him, and opened his lips, I felt the Lord fill my spirit and all my graces were stirred up. I felt that he was my brother, that I loved him, and that I rejoiced to be hearing him that day. His text was, 'Comfort ye, comfort ye my people.' He was most convicting, showing that those who are happy in the flesh have no need of comfort. Sweet breezes were blowing over the meeting; great and excellent glory descended; all were shaken; truly, God has visited us in his love.

When Harris's spirit was right, Rowland's ministry would always overcome him, and clearly he was now melted completely under his influence. He wrote, on the following day:

> Yesterday I had liberty to ask the Lord to come down and bless us, as I saw that it is an unusual thing to make up a rending in the house of God, and bring Israel and Judah back together again. I cried that he knew it was for his sake that I had invited them here, and in order that I might benefit from their life and blessing. I was happy as I listened to them. At three we went to dinner; and we were glad. I expressed my love to them; I saw that Rowland was their prince, and that they submitted to him, and I was glad of that.

It is easy to see Harris's strong love towards Rowland in every sentence of the above. At four, Peter Williams preached on the pure river of water of life and the tree of life on either side. He had great influence. 'There were many here,' says Harris, 'from Cardiganshire and other places singing and praising; surely, God has answered our prayers and has taken away our reproach.' All departed happy and full of love. The only unpleasant occurrence during the Association was the work of Popkin, who possessed an acrimonious and bitter spirit, in seeking to snub the Reformer from Trefeca.

With the exception of that day when he experienced release from the burden of his sin, at the time of his conviction, this day, when he felt he was being received back into the bosom of his brethren, was the happiest known by Howell Harris on earth. 'This is from the Lord', he said. From now on, calls rained upon him from all directions. The week after the Association he noted that he had received invitations from Blaen Crai, Trecastle, Merthyr, Tirabad, Hay, and other places. After spending some time in Bristol, he went to Bath, and returned on June 1 to Cardiff. At Llandaff he met with a Mrs Jones, Fonmon, 'a simple, sincere woman', who informed him of the onset of persecutions, and that the judges on the bench were declaiming against the revival, and that she was warned to obtain a licence for her house. Harris objected to this. To him it tended too much to Nonconformity, and he advised her to speak to the Bishop.

He journeyed to Aberthin where he had promised to meet with Rowland in a Monthly Meeting, but the meeting had ended before he arrived, and all had dispersed. But another congregation was gathered and he preached to them on, 'They shall look upon me whom they have pierced.' From here he journeyed to Pyle, to Swansea where about four thousand heard him, to Llansamlet, and to Pontneathvaughan, and then returned to Trefeca, weary in body. In July he visited London in order to attend the Wesleyan Conference. Charles Wesley there asked him to address the preachers, which he did. He told them that he was glad to see such love and simplicity amongst them; that the work was being carried forward with the same spirit as at its beginning, that he had received the privilege of being the first layman to go about preaching; and that he had sought ordination from the bishop on four occasions, and been rejected each time. He closed his address by calling for a general uniting of Moravians, Wesleyans and Methodists. He was asked to preach also at Spitalfields Chapel to a large congregation. Harris was very much taken up at this time with the hope of union. This was his main reason for coming to London. To secure it he was willing to make any sacrifice, other than a sacrifice of the truth.

## FURTHER PREACHING TOURS AND ASSOCIATIONS

On 3 August he set out for an Association at Llangeitho, passing through Abergwesyn and Llanddewibrefi. He felt that Rowland was far in advance of him; apart from being an ordained man, the present revival had begun under him, and all the exhorters deferred to him. 'But,' he wrote, 'I am not jealous of him; so full of glory he was when I first saw him in the pulpit at Defynnog.' When he arrived at Llangeitho the Association had already begun, and Thomas Davies (Haverfordwest?) was praying. The same man then preached on the Christian as a soldier, with Popkin after him, on the

Deity of Christ. After dinner, Howell Harris preached. It is clear from the journal that Daniel Rowland made much of him and honoured him in every way. The exhorters were weighing on Harris's mind and Rowland gathered them together in order for him to address them. His burden was the necessity for discipline; without it they would not be able to stand. His main complaint was that the exhorters were itinerating as they wished through the country, without anyone arranging their engagements, or controlling them, and that they received collections from the congregations. Williams, Pantycelyn, agreed with his complaint; he stated that Rowland excelled in the pulpit, but that he was not able to control the exhorters, and that before the latest revival had broken out matters in the societies had sunk very low.

'All agreed to have discipline,' noted Harris, 'Brother Rowland said that they all knew that he, from the beginning, had refused to be the leader when it was offered to him; and that he had told them continually that my place was empty ever since I had departed; and that he was of the same mind, and called me to my place, which I had occupied before.' This would involve placing Harris, as before, as general superintendent, with a wide-ranging authority over the exhorters. Rowland must have been most magnanimous when extending such an offer, and he must also have had a high view of his friend's wisdom as an organizer. Howell Davies however was inclined to disagree, because of Harris's efforts at the time to unite them with the Moravians and Wesleyans; he said that this was not possible, and he complained about John Wesley's actions in visiting Pembrokeshire. He was however brought to agree.

Harris then suggested that the three clergymen together acted as superintendents. They each refused. Unanimously, they called upon him to take the position. Harris required time to consider such a step, but he promised he would do what he could to meet with the societies. Rowland and Williams, Pantycelyn, were firmly in favour of Harris, and Howell Davies too, to some extent, but many of the exhorters, Popkin in particular, tended to oppose him secretly, and whispered to one another that he had been received back like the prodigal son.

There is one sentence of historical importance to be found in the journal at this point:

I find that Mr Rowland is turned out and not received into his churches.[2]

Some historians of the Established Church deny that Rowland was ever excommunicated in that there is no record of it in the diocesan papers, but they forget that there was no need of any record or decision in the case of a curate. But if there were any need for further proof of a matter for which there is so much eye-witness account, it would be found in this record by Harris – written at Llangeitho, and most probably when under Daniel Rowland's own roof.

From Llangeitho, Harris, in the company of Howell Davies, went to Abermeurig, where he preached on perseverance in grace. He then crossed, through Llandovery, to Trefeca. He spent much of August in Bath and Bristol. On 20 September he set out for Llandovery, there to confer with Rowland, Williams, Pantycelyn, and William Richards on various matters of importance to the Connexion. While there he refers more specifically to Rowland's removal. He states:

> Mr Rowland has been turned out and is not received by the churches. I feel it is hard on him, that he is the first to be turned away, apart from Mr Harris, Exon; and perhaps this is the beginning of a general persecution. I pleaded with them to persuade the people, (1) not to turn to the Toleration Act, that it is an arm of the flesh, and could be changed; (2) not to think of leaving the Established Church on this account, lest this should be out of revenge, or be seen to be so, or seen as anger against the bishop because of his severity; (3) for them not to speak bitterly of the bishop's work, in case that becomes an evil seed causing us to rise against the government.

Nothing could be clearer than this in affirming Rowland's excommunication by the Bishop of St David's, and it is all the more forceful in that it comes from Howell Harris, who adhered to the Church of England through thick and thin. As far as his counsels were concerned, they required a good deal of grace to be carried out, and there is considerable doubt as to the wisdom of the first two, at least. Should he not rather have asked whether this was not a providential suggestion of the need for forming into a party apart from the Church? This was precisely the kind of indication for which he had looked twenty years previously. The only thing agreed by the friends at Llandovery was the postponement of the disciplining of the exhorters until the approaching Association, also at Llandovery.

Howell Harris spent the whole of September and October on a preaching tour through England. He visited Leicestershire, Yorkshire, Bedfordshire, Lincolnshire and Rutland, and spent some time in London. He preached for the Wesleyans, the Moravians, as well as any of the Church of England who would receive him. His main burden, together with the gospel, was for uniting all the societies that could be considered as the fruits of the revival into one strong movement within the Established Church. On the last day of November, having been back at Trefeca for only a week, he departed for the Llandovery Association. Daniel Rowland was not present, but Williams, Pantycelyn, had arrived, together with William Richard, John Thomas, William Harry and Peter Williams. Harris here came to the decision to take up again the position of general superintendent over all the societies, as he had been requested at the Llangeitho Association. He saw that he was not only loved, but respected. It seems that he and William Harry were becoming close friends, and Harry returned with him to Trefeca. But Popkin tried his utmost to bring about a rupture. In his journal Harris mentions two other points of importance in the period to the end of the year: that he bought Lower Trefeca Farm from his brother, Thomas; and that on the advice of Evan Roberts, one of his chief men at Trefeca, he bought a chaise. Evan Roberts brought the chaise down with him from London. But, having received it, Harris was almost too shy to use it. 'Strange indeed!' he said, 'A carriage coming to this place! This is thy work, O Lord.'

Having reached the beginning of the year 1764, we must suffice with a few references, taken almost at random from the journal, which throw some light on Harris's history during this year.

3 January 1764. Price Davies, vicar of Talgarth, granted permission for communion to be administered every month at his church. The news was brought to Harris by John Morgan, the curate, and his soul rejoiced within him.

22 January 1764. Harris left for Cardiganshire to establish societies, using the chaise for the first time. He preached to a crowd of many thousands at Cil-y-cwm; he was willing to hold a private society but was not asked. He visited Caeo, Lampeter and Abermeurig, reaching Llangeitho on the 25th. He there preached to many thousands in the open air and then addressed hundreds in the chapel in a private society.

He was told by Rowland of the answer received from the Bishop of St David's in response to an appeal to him concerning his opposition to the revival. The Bishop had replied that people were leaving the Church, and reproaching the clergy; that this was the reason for removing the curates; and that no further ordinations would take place of any that associated with the Methodists. He visited Lledrod; preached to a vast crowd and, in the society, placed each one in his appropriate place. He visited Morfa, Gwndwn, Gwaunifor, Dolgwm, Talley and Llandovery. On this journey Harris was leading private societies for the first time since the Disruption, that is after an interval of fourteen years, and was convinced more and more that Rowland was the father of the exhorters and the mainstay of the revival in Wales.

19 February 1764. The Trefeca Family sat for the first time in the gallery of Trefeca Church and sang gloriously, so that the whole church was full of glory.

27 February 1764. Harris travelled to Blaen Crai, Blaenglyntawe, Neath, Swansea and the Gower peninsula. He returned through Gellidochlaethe, arriving back at Trefeca on 4 March.

1 April 1764. Harris was again on his journeys. He preached on the road about five miles out of Llandovery to a large crowd, he then arrived at Cross Inn towards evening. The next day he preached to a great multitude at Carmarthen, on the Castle Green, and was given much authority. On being pressed, he preached also at the chapel, where Williams, Pantycelyn, Thomas Davies, William John, Evan Richards, and others of the preachers were among his listeners. The next day he went to Capel Newydd in Pembrokeshire; then to Newport; to Fishguard – where he sternly rebuked the sin of unbelief; and then Woodstock, where he expected to hear Howell Davies and receive the sacrament from him, as it was the Sabbath, but the service was over before he arrived. He had travelled there in torrential rain. He visited Wolf's Castle, Solva and Haverfordwest. In the last place, he met Mr Nyborg, the minister of the Moravian church, and travelled with him to Pembroke. There, Harris preached in the chapel to a large congregation, on 'It is a faithful saying', with Mr Nyborg in the pulpit with him. He returned via Laugharne, Llandeilo and Llangadog, where he preached in the open air to a crowd of many thousands, Rhayader, Tyddyn, and Builth Wells. He noted that the journey lasted seventeen days; that he preached eighteen times; travelled over three hundred miles on bad roads; and that if all his congregations were amalgamated their number would be over fifty thousand.

9 May 1764. Harris set out for the Woodstock Association, passing through Trecastle, Carmarthen, St. Clears and Haverforwest and preaching at each venue, arriving at Woodstock on the 15th. At the Association Harris pressed Daniel Rowland to take the lead, and the latter refused more than once. Williams, Pantycelyn, stated that it was Harris that had the gifts for which they stood in need; that the main strength of Rowland, Howell Davies and himself, was in appealing to the feelings, and that God blessed them in this; but that since Harris had left them no one had been able to fill his place; that he preached excellently, exalting Christ above all things and laying great emphasis on bearing fruit; but that he was yet a man, hot of temper, and that the exhorters believed that he was ambitious to be head, and that it would be good if he spoke less of attending the

Church. Harris replied that he wished the work to proceed in the same spirit as that with which it commenced; that he believed the opposition (on the part of the bishops) would soon cease, and that evangelical bishops would be established. He complained that the people were not attending communion at Church but receiving it in their homes, and that because of this a distancing was taking place.

After this, Popkin read a paper, condemning the images of Christ to be found in some churches. Harris was deeply hurt and threatened to take hold of his hat and leave. Rowland and Williams managed to quieten him down. Williams and Howell Davies condemned Popkin fiercely. Davies said of him that he was as fickle as the wind; some time ago Elisha Cole was his favourite author, after that Erskine, then Hervey, but presently, Robert Sandeman was everything to him. The Association proceeded happily from then on. Rowland preached in the open air, on Mary washing the Saviour's feet, and Harris after him, with great authority. Harris returned, happy in spirit, through Haverfordwest, St Clears, Cross Inn, Llansawel, Llanfihangel-fach and Llangadog. Never before had he had more numerous congregations, nor greater authority when speaking.

## FIRST THOUGHTS OF A COLLEGE AT TREFECA

20 July 1764. Harris went to Brecon to bring the Countess of Huntingdon to Trefeca. He there heard Rowland preaching in the street, on every good and perfect gift coming from the Lord; and Peter Williams after him, preaching in English. The Lord was evidently with them both. The Countess stayed many days at Trefeca, greatly approving of the place and of the discipline kept, and informing Harris that she had a desire to establish a college for her preachers there, so that they might go out to preach Christ in the spirit of Trefeca; that they could preach amongst the Methodists and Nonconformists, living in Harris's house and being under his discipline. As he bade farewell to the Countess at Bristol she again questioned him on Lower Trefeca and its suitableness as a college, which she called 'a School of Prophets', with Mr Jordan, who at the time kept a grammar school at Abergavenny, being principal. The idea of a school of prophets at Trefeca greatly commended itself to Harris.

He stayed in the Bath and Bristol area until 14 August. On the 21st, he proceeded to the Llangeitho Association. There he encountered some feeling from the exhorters, because he spoke against the tendency of forsaking the Church of England. Williams, Pantycelyn, preached on Christ as the fulfilment of all the shadows; and after him, Peter Williams. Strong breezes affected the crowd; many of them sang and rejoiced, particularly when the sacrifice of the cross was referred to. After dinner Harris addressed the private society, showing them their great privilege that they were out of hell and in a gospel land, and that God had, in whatever degree, touched their hearts. He emphasized also the necessity for them to come under discipline. He was given much freedom. Popkin disturbed him slightly again with his comment that he could not pray with anyone who made a picture of Christ; but Harris was enabled to pray for him. It was agreed to meet at Carmarthen in September to examine the exhorters, and to hold the next Association at Newcastle Emlyn. Harris returned through Abermeurig, Lampeter, Llandovery and Brecon.

12 September 1764. Harris met with Williams, Pantycelyn, Daniel Rowland, Howell Davies and John Sparks, at Carmarthen, in order to examine the exhorters and to discover their qualifications. He told them of the intention of the Countess of Huntingdon to establish a college at Trefeca; he exhorted John Sparks to free himself from his trade in order to devote himself fully to the gospel. Harris was in a distressed condition, not knowing whether God was calling him to go amongst the people, and to be a father to the exhorters; he saw his unfitness because of his sins, both private and public; at last, the Lord gave him peace to accept. He saw that he differed to a degree from his brethren as far as the Church was concerned, and with respect to taking communion; he did not wish to form any church or sect, but to reform the Church of England. He saw them also as more popular than himself, and more successful; and he felt able to respect them on this account. He examined the counsellors throughout the day; and cried out:

O, my children, how strongly I feel that you are placed upon my heart! How rich I am, and how happy, that I have possession of you again!

He added:

Whoever was at fault in the Disruption; that is over. O, such bowels of compassion I feel towards them. I felt that I was theirs to serve. Our Saviour has brought things about beyond the expectations of any. I found them all to be one with me in the light.

Harris felt that this was a great day; he told the exhorters that he has been amongst them for a year and a half, but that only now was he beginning to accomplish a work. He preached at Castle Green before a great crowd and received much liberty; he returned through Cross Inn and Llandovery, preaching to large congregations in both places.

19 October 1764. Harris departed for London. He returned to Trefeca on 16 November. Two days later he sets out for the Association at

Newcastle Emlyn. He there met Daniel Rowland, Enoch, Benjamin Thomas, William John, Popkin and Howell Davies. He discovered that there was a degree of prejudice in the minds of the brethren against the proposed establishment at Trefeca. He was hurt also by the arrangement for Rowland to be preaching at the same time that he, Harris, was to examine the exhorters; he heard a rumour also that the exhorters perceived him as being too authoritarian over them. Daniel Rowland, after preaching, hurried to him, and Harris complained that they had no need of his (Harris's) gifts and that they must take him as they find him. In a little while, Thomas Davies, Haverfordwest, and John Harry approached him, in loving spirit, inviting him to Pembrokeshire. He met the exhorters, about a hundred of them altogether, and discussed with them their prejudice against Trefeca. They suggested that the matter be presented for consideration to Humphrey Edwards and John Evans, both of Bala. He refused. He heard himself being called 'Esquire Harris', and, later, 'Captain Harris'; he objected to the first name, but accepted being called 'Captain' if that should be to the advantage of the gospel. He spoke privately with Humphrey Edwards and John Evans and promised to visit Bala to help them. He preached at eleven in the morning, with much liberty and power. Rowland told him at the end of the service that he still possessed the same voice and same force that were his thirty years before; he answered that he wished for nothing different from Rowland than he heard from him that first time, when they met at Defynnog Church. Harris itinerated through Pembrokeshire, visiting Eglwyswrw, Dinas, Woodstock, Wolf's Castle, St David's, Narberth, Haverfordwest, Laugharne and Carmarthen. After preaching also at Llangadog and Trecastle he arrived at Trefeca on the first day of December.

11 December 1764. Harris set out on a journey to Montgomeryshire. He preached first at Builth Wells to great effect. He preached at Rhayader in the market-place to a large crowd, on God being manifest in the flesh, and received much power. He crossed the mountain to Llanidloes, descending near The Red Lion but was not allowed to preach. At last, the inn-keeper permitted him the use of his house but such a multitude had gathered, and with excise officers present amongst them, that all order in the place was lost. The town hall was refused him. He tried to speak in a small outhouse but failed, because the place was too confined. He departed for Tyddyn; the same mob, with the same leader, followed him. Nobody laid a hand upon him, nor on the carriage; they contented themselves with shouting, 'Whoever heard of our Saviour riding in a chaise?' He preached at Tyddyn from the words, 'And with his stripes we are healed',

and received considerable strength to explain the nature of the suffer-ings of our Lord. At Newtown the text was, 'This is a faithful saying.' He visited Welshpool, Shrewsbury, Wenlock, Madeley, Ludlow, Leominster and Hay-on-Wye, returning to Trefeca on 22 December.

1 January 1765. He left for the Llansawel Association. William Richard began the Association with prayer, and Harris delivered a penetrating ad-dress to the exhorters, referring with great commendation to the hymns of Williams, Pantycelyn. He examined twelve exhorters. In the Association he pressed for union with the Wesleyans and Moravians, stating that John and Charles Wesley had met for this purpose with Mr Nydberg, the Moravian minister at Haverfordwest. Daniel Rowland showed a degree of opposition. Harris received a blessing while hearing Popkin preach on, 'How then can I do this great wickedness?' He returned to Trefeca on 5 January.

20 January, 1765. He set out for parts of Glamorgan that he had not visited for fourteen years. He preached at Glascoed to a small gathering, on the depths of man's misery. He visited Bassaleg, near Newport, and Cardiff. At the latter place the chapel was completely full and Harris received particular power when preaching. He dined with Mrs Jones, Fonmon, and then visited Llantrisant, where he received great liberty to excite and thunder from the words, 'They that be whole need not a physi-cian.' He then preached at Portvane, Pyle, Neath, Swansea, Gower, Llanelli and Carmarthen, returning to Trefeca by 2 February.

## HARRIS DECIDES NOT TO RETURN TO THE POSITION OF GENERAL SUPERINTENDENT OF THE SOCIETIES

The journal for the rest of 1765 is lost. By the beginning of the next year, Harris had become completely convinced that to return to his old position as general superintendent of the Methodist Connexion in Wales was impossible for him. Many factors had combined to produce this decision. Let us review these briefly:

1. Harris's separation and absence from amongst his brethren for thirteen years was such that its effects could not be erased. Although Daniel Rowland was ready, eager indeed, to pass the rule over to him, and although Williams, Pantycelyn, and Peter Williams shared this desire, a class of exhorters had arisen in the intervening years who knew not Harris, and were not willing to submit to him. We have reason to believe that there were a considerable number of them, and Popkin was their spokesman. They swore by Daniel Rowland, and would not have anyone take the sceptre from his hand.

2. Harris's rule tended to be restrictive. We find him, time and again, stressing the need for discipline amongst the exhorters. By this he meant a detailed examination as to each individual's qualification; an allotting to each man his appropriate area of work, according to his gift and ability; and a forbidding of him to proceed out of that area, whatever his motivation, on pain of public rebuke. We remember, at the very beginning, John Richard and others writhing under this detailed mechanical planning, and it was only with considerable difficulty that such opposition was overcome at that time. Presently, with Harris having been a military officer for some years, it is easy to imagine that his sense of discipline and submission was so much stronger again. He expected the obedience due to a superintendent from the exhorters, just as that of soldiers to a captain; and that obedience the exhorters were not prepared to give. On the other hand, it is probable that Rowland's discipline had been slack to some degree. The exhorters had been allowed to preach wherever they wished, or at least, wherever they had received some kind of invitation, without anyone placing any barriers in their way. The probability is that there was considerable disorder amongst them at this time, their liberty possibly even being used for an occasion to the flesh. Harris's whole nature would rise up against such licence, but the exhorters, after having their liberty for so long, would not allow themselves to be subjected to that which they considered a yoke of captivity.

3. During the time of his separation at Trefeca, Harris had drawn much closer to the Church of England. He had made his peace with Price Davies, the old vicar of Talgarth; he had succeeded in obtaining a monthly communion service at that church, and in having the gallery set aside for the Trefeca singers; Mr Morgan, the curate, was a close friend who visited him regularly. When the clergy and bishops began persecuting the Methodists and refusing the sacraments to them, Harris had said that he would cleave to the people, and he expected to see them being turned away as a proof that God was leading them to form a new connexion. Now, he was determined to remain in the Church, even if it meant turning his back on his old friends. When he saw the churches closing their doors to Daniel Rowland, his great anxiety was that no one should speak out harshly against the bishop, and he continued to dream of the appointment of evangelical bishops who would replace the evangelical curates and ordain many of the leading lay preachers. The Methodists' feelings for the Established Church, on the other hand, had weakened considerably during Harris's absence. Many years of persecution, scorn and threatening had had their effect, and their spirits were now bitter on

seeing Daniel Rowland, whom they considered a prince of God amongst them, thrown out of the churches. As a result they did not now attend the parish church even for communion but received the elements in various appointed chapels. Harris stated that they administered the Lord's Supper in their homes, a practice which he very much opposed. The only thread that connected the Methodists with the Church at this time was that it was still only from the hands of the clergymen that the majority of them received the sacraments, and that they had not generally begun to ordain amongst themselves. There were some indications that even this was about to take place. Already, Morgan John Lewis had been ordained as minister at New Inn; David Williams as minister at Aberthin; and Thomas William and William Edward as ministers at Groes-wen; and Harris believed that a more general move towards ordaining would soon arise. With such a move he would have no part whatsoever.

4. The Methodists, for the most part, had not taken to the establishment at Trefeca at all. While they acknowledged that Harris was sincere of purpose, and was acting under the influence of unselfish motives, they believed that both the building and the family were grave mistakes. Even as true a friend to Harris as Williams, Pantycelyn, blamed him in this respect, as is seen from the following quotations from his elegy to him:

| | |
|---|---|
| Why retreat into a grotto, | Pam y llechaist mewn rhyw ogof, |
| To a castle built by man? | Castell a ddyfeisiodd dyn? |
| And forget the lambs' entreaties, | Ac anghofiaist dy ddeadell, |
| Whose new life your words began? | Argyhoeddaist ti dy hun? |
| Many of your spiritual children, | Y mae plant it ar hyd Cymru, |
| Some now thirty-five years old, | Yn bymtheg-mlwydd-ar-hugain oed, |
| Long have yearned to hear you preaching | A ddymunasai gennyt glywed |
| Those first fiery sermons bold. | Y pregethau cynta erioed. |
| Wanting honour? Wanting profit? | Eisiau parch, neu eisiau elw? |
| Or some blessing from on high? | Neu ryw fendith is y ne? |
| You departed from your children, | Rhoist ffarwel i'r fyntai ddefaid, |
| No more now they hear your cry. | Ac arosaist yn dy le? |
| Hundreds would be found in mourning, | Yr oedd cannoedd gynnau'n gruddfan, |
| Asking what had now become | Ac yn gofyn beth yw hynt |
| Of the trumpet from Trefeca | Yr hen utgorn fu'n Nhrefeca, |
| That in their ears, of old, had rung. | Ac yn uchel seiniodd gynt. |
| | |
| Can a flock of scarce one hundred | Ai bugeilio cant o ddefaid, |
| Barren followers, cold and dry, | O rai oerion, hesbion, sych, |
| And the care of a vast palace, | Ac adeilo iddynt balas, |
| With its rooms and chimneys high, | A chorlanau trefnus gwych, |

E'er compare with glorious preaching
Of salvation, far and wide,
From Caerleon fair to Pembroke,
From Holyhead to Swansea side?

Etyb seinio pur efengyl,
Bloeddio'r iachawdwriaeth rydd,
O Gaerlleon bell i Benfro,
O Gaergybi i Gaerdydd?

Why spend so much time and money
Building a great monastery,
When King Henry in his wisdom,
Pulled them down so eagerly?
Surely you'd have seen more summers,
Sweeter still would be my song,
If you'd stayed amongst your children,
Watched the flock, your whole life long.

Pam y treuliaist dy holl ddyddiau
I wneud ryw fynachlog fawr,
Pan y tynnodd Harri frenin
Fwy na mil o'r rhain i lawr?
Diau buaset hwy dy ddyddiau,
A melusach fuasai nghân,
Pe treuliasit dy holl amser
Yng nghwmpeini'r defaid mân.

\* \* \* \* \*

Sad the circumstances following
Your withdrawal from your peers;
Greater still your praise and glory
Had you laboured through the years.

Trist yw'r ffrwythau a ddigwyddodd
O it beidio rowndio'r byd;
Mwy fuasai dy ogoniant
Hyn pe buasai'th waith o hyd.

If this is how such a close and affectionate friend as Williams felt on the matter, then clearly many others felt similarly. At the same time, like the poet again, they surely forgave him his mistake:

But today, all is forgiven;
There's a purpose wise, above,
Well determines all the currents
That on earth below we prove.

Ond mae pawb yn maddau heddiw;
Mae rhyw arfaeth faith uwchben,
Ag sy'n trefnu pob materion
A ddychmygo dyn is nen.

But Harris would not have it that he required any forgiveness on the matter, and to see his brethren and friends eyeing the establishment at Trefeca with suspicion wounded him greatly.

5. The concept of a general union amongst all who possessed a religious spirituality had possessed him. He dreamt of bringing together all the followers of Whitefield, the Wesleys, the Moravians and the Welsh Methodists, in one great union. He once thought of placing John Wesley, towards whom he felt immeasurable affection, as head over this union, and it may well be that this was in his mind at this time also. This dream speaks highly of Howell Harris's catholicity of spirit, but it was only a dream; it would have been hopelessly impractical. The first to declare against it was Howell Davies. Perhaps he felt injured by the establishment of the Moravian work in Pembrokeshire, as Harris did himself at first. Not one of the Methodists looked favourably upon the idea; they saw it as a

bringing in of strangers to reap the fruit of their labours. Harris would react by calling them narrow; reminding them that these souls were the possession of Jesus Christ, and not theirs.

Because of these reasons, and perhaps others also, at the beginning of 1766 Harris was convinced that he could not act as the general superintendent of the Methodists. On 19 February 1766, an Association was held at Carmarthen and there he announced his decision not to undertake the superintendency but that he would come amongst them as friend and family, and would preach in their chapels and Associations whenever convenient and invited, although he could not consider himself as completely one with them. It is worth noting that his relationship with the chief men among the Methodists was excellent at this time, particularly so with Daniel Rowland and Williams, Pantycelyn; a close brotherly love was maintained between them until the day of his death. At the Association, John Harry preached on the words of Christ to the woman of Samaria; after him was Mr Grey, the successor to Mr Phillip Pugh at Llwynypiod and Abermeurig. His matter was Christ ascending on high, leading captivity captive and receiving gifts for men. At three, Daniel Rowland preached. His text was, 'My beloved is mine.' It was a service forever to be remembered. Harris wrote:

> I saw such incomparable glory upon him, far above myself; I was enabled to respect him and to pray that the Lord might extend his life and usefulness. O, how he showed the mystery of the union between Christ and his church! He showed that heaven begins here in love; that death introduces no change for the believer except an increase of grace. He cried out: 'Every kind of creature has its song; and the church has its song; and this is it, "My beloved is mine!" Sing on, I tell you!'

Such was Howell Harris's description of his friend's sermon, and it is clear that its effect upon him was overpowering. There is no record that he himself preached during the Association, but he addressed the exhorters with great solemnity. He arranged also a journey of three weeks through parts of Pembrokeshire and Carmarthenshire. We find him therefore visiting Narberth, Pembroke, Redford, Haverfordwest, Tenant, Llandegege, Fishguard, Woodstock, Machendre, Newchapel, Felindre, Gwaunifor, Glanrhyd, and Carmarthen – where many thousands heard him on Castle Green, Llanddarog, Llandeilo and Llangadog. He arrived at Trefeca on 12 March. He noted that this particular journey had involved preaching only, together with exhorting the societies and preachers on spiritual matters; he had not participated further in any arrangement as he felt he had no right to do so.

On 3 April 1766, he was to be found at a place called Petty France, not far from Bristol, in a Moravian meeting. On being asked, he spoke forcefully against Sandemanianism; he also told the Moravian preachers of the danger existing amongst them of the Bible losing its position as the rule by which all things were to be proved. Here also he read John Wesley's sermon on imputed righteousness. He much appreciated it, and as he read, his hope with a view to a union increased. On the Sunday he was at Bath. He went to the church in the morning and received the sacrament. In the afternoon he preached at the Wesleyan chapel, and in the evening he went to the Countess of Huntingdon's chapel where Howell Davies was ministering. Mr Davies' subject was, 'Blessed is the people that know the joyful sound.' Harris and he shared fellowship until ten o'clock.

Within three weeks of returning home, Harris set out for Glamorganshire and parts of Carmarthenshire. He preached first at Llanbradach, a farmhouse about five miles from Caerphilly. The next day he was at Watford, preaching at the Nonconformist chapel, but he passed by Groeswen without a visit. He had a powerful service at Cardiff, speaking on God being manifest in the flesh, and he preached with great influence also at St Nicholas. He does not appear to have taken a text but his themes were: believing, loving and repenting. At Llantrisant he thundered forth against self-righteousness. His text at Cowbridge was, 'O Israel, thou hast destroyed thyself.' He was next at Bridgend, where he preached in the Methodist chapel and was given great freedom in dealing with the doctrine of the person of our Lord. At Margam he preached from the doorway of the inn; his listeners numbered many hundreds. His text was, 'It is a faithful saying', and he earnestly pleaded with self-condemned sinners to come to the Saviour. At the old Abbey in Neath many thousands heard him. He had a good congregation also at Swansea. Having travelled through Gower and visited Llanelli, Llanedi, Llan-non, Golden Grove and Llangadog, he returned to Trefeca by 18 May.

Most of July and August were spent in the north of England, amongst the Wesleyans. He made Huddersfield his main centre and travelled to preach through the surrounding country. He was present at the Wesleyan Conference at Leeds in mid-August. In September we find him visiting various places in Carmarthenshire. He had an enormous congregation at Llandovery of many thousands. He preached on the feeding of God's flock; he spoke both in Welsh and in English as so many were present, and the ministry was accompanied by considerable influence. He experienced a powerful service at Llangadog also, but nearly took offence at the innkeeper, at whose house he stayed, because he was not allowed to pay for his room and for stabling. The Methodists had a new chapel at Trecastle. Harris met there with some twenty members of the society and gave them much profitable advice. He was at home for two days before setting out again for the west of England. In November, he undertook a long journey through Glamorganshire, and at the end of the year he was in London. We refer to this constant travelling in order to disprove the general impression that Howell Harris shut himself up at Trefeca during the last years of his life, with the exception of an occasional visit to those places where he was invited. On the contrary, we find that his journeys were long and often, and his commitment to the proclamation of the gospel unflagging.

Howell Harris spent the first two months of 1767 in Brighton, preaching amongst the Moravians and the Wesleyans and visiting London now and again. His journal from that time up to the end of the year is lost, but we find that he was present at the Wesleyan conference held in London in mid-August. The first information we have of him in 1768 is of his visit to the Methodist Association held at Caeo on 17 February. On the way there, he felt the need of some degree of faith to attend as a visitor where he had once ruled. He met with Rowland and asked him if all were happy with his attendance. Having received a positive response he went to the private meeting and, at the request of Williams, Pantycelyn, addressed the exhorters. He was given much liberty in this. The Association extended to him an unanimous invitation to be present amongst them, and he answered that he would be glad to be with them whenever they required his help. He referred to the college that the Countess of Huntingdon intended to establish at Trefeca, but found considerable prejudice against it. He then proceeded to speak on faith, self-examination and the reading of the Bible. When he had finished, Williams stood up to add his support to the message. At the public meeting, Rowland preached from the words, 'Purge me with hyssop, and I shall be clean: wash me, and I shall be whiter than snow.' Harris comments:

> On hearing him preach so effectively on the blood of Christ and the necessity for it to be poured out upon the conscience, and his opposition to the views of Sandeman, earnestly inviting everyone to come to Christ, and in such a way that I never heard from him before, I felt great love for him and for the people. Having been asked, I myself spoke on looking to our Saviour and his sufferings. As Rowland had expounded upon the blood of Christ, that it sanctifies and glorifies, so I confirmed his words. I was given remarkable freedom to preach Christ.

It is clear that Harris had a good service, and he departed from his old friends with a warm heart towards them, as did they from him. That night he preached at Llandovery, Williams returned with him. The meeting was disturbed by a drunken clergyman and Harris was extremely severe with him.

## THE COUNTESS OF HUNTINGDON'S COLLEGE

Although the Countess of Huntingdon had long cultivated the thought of a college at Trefeca, the plan was not fulfilled until 24 August 1768, the Countess's birthday. The college, which was built on Harris's land at Lower Trefeca, was opened by a sermon from Whitefield on Exodus 20:24, 'In all places where I record my name I will come unto thee, and I will bless thee.' Whitefield again preached on the following Sunday, in the open air before the college building, to a congregation of many thousands. It appears that the event which finally persuaded the Countess to realize her intentions was the eviction by Oxford University of six young men because of their Methodist tendency. This occasioned much excitement, and was painful to the feelings of many who loved the evangelical faith. These six, it may be supposed, became the first-fruits of Trefeca students, and their numbers were augmented by others from every part of England and Wales, until the total reached about thirty.

Having been diligent in their studies during the week, the students departed to all directions on Saturdays in order to preach the gospel; and for those who would have long distances before them, the Countess provided horses. They preached to all denominations indiscriminately, but mainly amongst the Methodists. It is worth noting that this was a college for preachers. No one could enlist who had not provided satisfactory proof that he had been converted, and had declared his determination to devote his life fully to the service of Jesus. The institution's first principal was the Rev. John Fletcher, the vicar of Madeley, Shropshire, a man who deserves more attention than we are able to give him. He was a native of Switzerland, and it appears he was a descendant of one of the noblest of families. It can almost be said that he was godly from birth, and his greatest desire when young was to serve Christ in the gospel. In 1752, when he was twenty-four years old, he came to England to learn English. There he met with John Wesley and became a member of the Methodist society in London. In 1757, he was ordained as deacon by the Bishop of Hereford, and shortly afterwards, on the basis of recommendatory letters by the Bishop of Bangor, he was ordained priest by the Bishop of London. On the day of his ordination he assisted John Wesley at his chapel in London to administer the sacrament of the Lord's Supper. In 1760, he was appointed to be vicar of Madeley. It seems he was a brilliant scholar and a sound theologian, and John Wesley's trust in him was such that he intended him to be his successor as head of the Wesleyan connexion. This plan, however, was prevented by death. It does not appear that Fletcher fulfilled many duties as principal at Trefeca other than to visit the institution occasionally as he had leisure.

Who the first tutor of the college was is a matter of some uncertainty. Undoubtedly, a man called John Jones, an itinerant preacher amongst the Wesleyans and of Welsh descent, applied for the post. John Jones was a brilliant Classics scholar and the author of a well-known Latin grammar. Charles Wesley said of him that of all his acquaintance, he was the most qualified to teach young men. But because of some eccentricities which he possessed, and particularly because he had been ordained by a bishop of the Greek Church, it does not appear that he was appointed. In the Life of the Countess of Huntingdon it is said that the college tutor was Joseph Easterbrook, the son of a Bristol town crier, brought up in the Wesleyan school at Kingswood. Tyerman, however, does not agree. He states that Easterbrook was appointed schoolmaster in the parish of Madeley, so that although he was under Fletcher, he had no connection with Trefeca.

On the basis of a funeral sermon by the Rev. W. Agutter, Tyerman claims that the only tutor for Trefeca's first year was a twelve-year-old child called John Henderson. This is how Mr Agutter writes of Henderson: 'When he was only a boy he was employed to provide an education in the classic languages. When only twelve years old, he taught Greek and Latin at Trefeca College. The principal of the College at the time was Mr Fletcher, the vicar of Madeley.' It is true that the youth John Henderson was almost a miracle of knowledge, and the above reference proves that he was a tutor at Trefeca at an extraordinarily young age, but it does not prove that he was the only tutor. We strongly believe that Tyerman is mistaken. Apart from the incongruity of placing a child as the sole teacher over an institution that contained grown men, there are many references in Howell Harris's journal to Easterbrook at Trefeca, although it is not stated definitely that he was there in the position of a tutor. Whoever the tutor was, it is certain that much of the responsibility fell upon Harris's shoulders.[3] However, at the beginning of 1770, Joseph Benson, the great-grandfather of the present Archbishop of Canterbury, was appointed principal. The college was at Lower Trefeca until 1792. That year, because Howell Harris had been dead some years, and because the lease of Lower Trefeca had expired, the College moved to Cheshunt. From its formation there was a close connection between Howell Harris and the College; the students were considered to be under his discipline; he would often address them and preach in the College chapel. His influence must have been great.

## HARRIS'S FINAL YEARS

On 22 November 1768, Harris set out on a long journey through Carmarthenshire and Pembrokeshire. He visited Trecastle, Llandovery, Llangadog, Llandeilo, Carmarthen, Narberth, Haverfordwest, Woodstock, Eglwyswrw and Newchapel. On his return he preached again at Carmarthen and Llandovery, and was back at Trefeca on 4 December. In the last week of the year he was at a Methodist Monthly Meeting at Llanfrynach, Breconshire. He received the warmest of welcomes. He spoke at length on the beginnings of the work. He promised to attend the Monthly Meetings whenever he was called for, and he encouraged them to emphasize the blood and death of the Saviour. He preached powerfully from the words, 'And no man is able to pluck them out of my Father's hand.' His subsequent comments are worth recording in that they contain much information on the state of the cause in Wales. He wrote:

I heard from Benjamin Thomas that twenty-four exhorters in north Wales meet monthly and quarterly to arrange their journeys; that there are 140 members at Bala; that the work succeeds remarkably in Cardiganshire. At Llangeitho about 140 of the children of the revival meet every week to pray, to sing, and to open their hearts one to another; and many carnal are convicted on hearing and seeing them. They meet also at Llanddewibrefi and other places. At Llanddewibrefi, where the people were once all carnal, they have built themselves a chapel where Benjamin Thomas was preaching a fortnight ago and after he had finished they sang and prayed until twelve o'clock at night. I see clearly that the Lord is amongst them and is honouring them. We rejoice greatly in this, and I was given strength to cry to the Lord for Rowland, that he might be kept from pride at his success and popularity, and that the success might be in the Spirit.

This quotation shows that powerful revivals were shaking Wales at this time, and that the work was progressing mightily. It shows also that Harris's spirit was in complete sympathy with his Methodist brethren, and that their success rejoiced his own heart.

About the beginning of the year 1769 Harris was often troubled by weariness and he travelled little from Trefeca. In the March of that year, he suffered the severe tribulation of the death of his dear wife. She was a notably godly woman, possessing in addition much strength of character. She could even withstand her husband when he tended to go to extremes. Her health deteriorated slowly. She realized that her end was approaching and she told Harris not to weep when her spirit escaped the body, in that she would then be with her Saviour. But in the event, the end came suddenly. At evening, when Harris was at a religious meeting with the family, and a Mr Cook was addressing them, a shout from Miss Harris, out of her mother's room, echoed through the building. He raced up immediately, but was hardly in time to see her breathe her last breath. The blow stunned him for some time, for his love for her was great. He said:

It was a blow such as I had never experienced before; the floods engulfed my soul; I was completely under the waters; they reached the very core of my life. For a time I was so overcome that I could not perceive anything, but only call upon the Lord; and the first thought that struck me was whether his work in taking her away and in not hearing my prayer for her recovery, was a loving stroke.

He experienced great agonies of soul at this time. He says that he passed from one time of wrestling to another, and that he could witness to the existence of the devil. However, eventually, he had the victory over the flesh and the devil. On 13 March he wrote, 'Here is a day ever to be remembered by me, in which the body of my dearest wife, whom the Lord gave to me, was laid to rest at Talgarth Church.' The day of Mrs Harris's funeral was wet and stormy. At the house, Mr White preached first, followed by Harris himself, who, in Welsh, gave a history of her life and an account of the strength of her religion. The body was carried by members of the Trefeca family. As well as many others, all the students of the Countess of Huntingdon's College were at the funeral and they sang at the house, and almost throughout the journey to Talgarth, ignoring the rain. At the church, the curate, the Rev. John Morgan, officiated, and Harris returned to the empty house – empty to him, though many were present – feeling that he had laid a part of himself in the ground. He noted that he gave black gloves to all the students, and mourning clothes to all the women and girls of the family, fifty-three in number in all.

On the last day of March, he departed for London and Brighton, primarily for a visit to the Countess of Huntingdon, and he returned to Trefeca on the day before Whitsun. On 8 July, he set out on a journey through Glamorganshire and Monmouthshire. The first place he visited was Llanbradach where he had a large congregation of at least a thousand, and great power accompanied his words as he warned the crowd to flee for their lives. By the time he arrived at Caerphilly the gathering there was even greater. He preached in Welsh and in English, and after thundering forth for some time he was led to preach the gospel with great sweetness. After preaching at Lisvane, he arrived at Cardiff complaining of feeling ill, of being in much pain, and of frequently losing his voice. At Baduchaf, the congregation was great but the preacher was hoarse, nevertheless, in his weakness, he was strengthened to speak of Jesus recovering the sight of the blind and delivering the captives. The water given by our Lord, which springs up into everlasting life, was his theme at Llantrisant, where a large crowd had gathered to hear him, and where he, in considerable weakness, was given strength to preach. After speaking again at Cowbridge, he dined at Fonmon Castle, and preached that night with greater freedom than usual, at Aberthaw. His next entry is of preaching at Llan-gan, 'Mr Jones's parish', and when it is remembered that this Mr Jones was the venerable Jones of Llan-gan, the reference is full of interest. It does not appear that Mr Jones was present. After visiting Bridgend he went to Pyle, where he complained of the heat and again of his weakness, but, as usual, when he proceeded to preach he was strengthened remarkably. At Llanilltyd Church, near Neath, he heard an excellent sermon on the person of Christ from a priest called Jones. Was this possibly Mr Jones, Llan-gan? Harris then preached in the court of the old Abbey to ten thousand people, at least. His congregation at Swansea, where he preached from the turnpike gate, was just as numerous.

He did not preach again until he reached Llandeilo. He was here greatly strengthened to expound the work of God in taking away the heart of stone. In the new chapel near Pontargothi, his text was, 'I am black, but comely.' He was extremely severe in this sermon. He was next at Carmarthen, by the castle wall. His theme was God humbling the lofty looks of man. After visiting Llansawel he came to Cil-y-cwm. He preached in the village square because of the numbers that had gathered, and his text was, 'If we suffer, we shall also reign with him.' He marvelled at how he was being sustained in the work, and at the reception being given to him, and the love shown to him by Rowland's people. He referred also to the fire amongst them. After preaching to another large multitude at Trecastle he reached Trefeca on 22 July. He wrote:

> I arrived here last night about nine. I heard God's praise being sung, and I told my people the great things that I had seen, that the whole country is ripe for harvest; that never before had I such congregations, nor such liberty in preaching, nor such a hearing. I said further that I had returned in order to raise their spirits, to set them on fire, and to witness of the Saviour to them.

It is easy to see that the journey had been of great blessing to him. On 16 August 1769, the Countess of Huntingdon came to Trefeca to celebrate the first anniversary of her college. She brought with her the Countess Buchan, the Lady Anne Erskine and Miss Orton, together with the Rev. Walter Shirley, the brother of Earl Ferrers. Fletcher, the college principal, Daniel Rowland, Williams, Pantycelyn, Howell Davies, Peter Williams and John Wesley all came to meet her, together with a host of lesser luminaries. In honour of their gathering, a week of preaching services was held. On Saturday morning, 19 August, Rowland preached in the College chapel to a large congregation and from the words, 'Are there few that be saved?' In the afternoon the sacrament of the Lord's Supper was administered, with Fletcher addressing the communicants, Williams giving out the hymns, and the singing of the congregation near to raise the roof with praise. By the evening the crowd was too great for the chapel, and Harris preached outside from the words, 'For the time is come that judgment must begin at the house of God.' On Sunday, Fletcher read the service in the courtyard outside, and Shirley preached. At one, the sacrament was again administered, with Rowland, Fletcher and Williams taking part. In the afternoon Fletcher preached first before an enormous crowd, from the text, 'For I am not ashamed of the gospel of Christ,' and Rowland, in Welsh, after him from, 'And as it is appointed unto men once to die.' It seems that John Wesley, Howell Davies, and Peter Williams arrived on the Monday, and on that day and the days following they took their part in the work. John Wesley wrote, on the last Thursday of the celebrations:

> I administered the Lord's Supper to the family. At ten, the public service began. Mr Fletcher preached an exceeding lively sermon in the court, the chapel being far too small. After him, Mr William Williams preached in Welsh, till between one and two o'clock. At two we dined. Meantime, a large number of people had baskets of bread and meat carried to them in the court. At three, I took my turn there, then Mr Fletcher, and, about five, the congregation was dismissed. Between seven and eight the love-feast began, at which I believe many were comforted.

He added that Howell Harris's house, 'with the gardens, orchards, walks, and pieces of water that surround it . . . is a kind of little paradise.' Assuredly, the festival was a success, and on reading the names of the men gathered there together it is hard not to think of those words from Scripture, 'Behold how good and how pleasant it is for brethren to dwell together in unity!'

Soon after, Howell Harris was taken ill and hardly left Trefeca until October, when he set out for a visit to Pembrokeshire. We find him preaching first at Haverfordwest Chapel. He then went to Woodstock. After this, he visited Fishguard, Solva, St. David's and Gwaunifor. On returning he preached at Carmarthen, Llandeilo and Llangadog. He greatly enjoyed this journey. 'I feel as if the country is being given to me anew,' he wrote. This was his last journey of 1769.

On the first Sunday of February 1770, he was at Carmarthen, on his way to Pembrokeshire again. After preaching at Narberth, he went to Haverfordwest where a Monthly Meeting was being held, the first after the death of Howell Davies. A large number of preachers, exhorters and stewards had gathered there. On being pressed by John Harry, he addressed the crowd for nearly three hours. He told them that he had come in answer to a letter from Mr Thomas Davies; he emphasized the necessity for them all to know Christ. 'We have nothing to say for ourselves, if we go about to preach without being ordained,' he said, 'unless we are sent by the Holy Spirit.' He conversed privately with John Harry, who told him of his son who intended to come to Trefeca College. This son was, no doubt, the Rev. Evan Harris, who was ordained at the first Ordination of 1811 in Llandeilo. In the chapel, Harris preached for nearly two hours from no particular text. He preached there also on the following night, with much liberty, on the divinity of the Saviour. After visiting many places in Pembrokeshire, mainly in the English part, he went to Woodstock to meet Daniel Rowland, and his thoughts during the journey are worth recording:

I am going to hear Mr Rowland about asking him and the Association to come to Trefeca, leaving all the consequences to the Lord. Finding amazing flames and success with him. People coming to Llangeitho Sacrament on Saturday above two thousand, and from forty Welsh miles around. O! What am I? Yet I do not understand these outward frames of jumping.[4]

He wrote further:

I had much love today for Rowland, on seeing that he is much more loved than I ever was, and that he has had more grace than I to keep him humble, and to be faithful to the Lord. He is greater in ability and authority, and his success has been greater. With all my heart I long for his success to continue, and for him to have long life, and heaven at last.

It is delightful to consider how these two old friends, after having been apart for a time, had come to understand one another, and had found their hearts cleaving together once more. Rowland's text was, 'Take heed, brethren, lest there be in any of you an evil heart of unbelief, in departing from the living God.' He had a remarkable service, and Harris prayed for him that he might continually receive such an abundant unction. After the sermon was the sacrament. 'The Lord drew near to me,' wrote Harris, 'bearing witness to his body and sacred blood.'

The next day, 14 February 1770, a Quarterly Association was held at Fishguard. It does not seem that Harris had intended to be there, but on the unanimous request of Pembrokeshire friends he consented to go. He did not attend the private meeting immediately, but said he would do so if asked. The invitation soon came. The question under consideration when he arrived was the recommendation to appoint William Davies, Neath, as superintendent of the Pembrokeshire societies instead of Howell Davies. Harris implored them to act with restraint and to hear Davies first so as to judge whether the Holy Spirit had qualified him to be a father. He charged them also to continue to communicate as often as they were able at their parish church. Harris's invitation for the next Quarterly Association to be held at Trefeca was then raised. John Evans of Bala, who had asked that it come to Bala, opposed the suggestion. Harris noted that this was the first request that he had made for twenty years, and that by refusing they would not be showing much love towards him. John Evans replied that Harris was putting a personal favour to himself before the spiritual good of the north. How the matter was decided is not stated but it appears that John Evans won the day. At eleven, Mr Grey prayed, and Mr Rowland preached from the words, 'Set me as a seal upon thine heart.' He was very brief and no general rejoicing broke out. After him Howell Harris preached. His text is not mentioned but he was given much power.

After arranging his journey at Fishguard, Harris proceeded to Bontfaen. He then visited Eglwyswrw, where he bade farewell to John Harry and Thomas Davies; Newchapel; Machendref; Carmarthen; Llanddarog; Llandeilo and Llandovery; and arrived at Trefeca on 24 February. In May of the same year he was back in Pembrokeshire, preaching at the same places. In June, he visited various societies in Radnorshire, such as Clyro, Caebach, Dolswydd and Pen-y-gorig.

He was severe with them at Dolswydd because they were forsaking the Welsh language, and he attributed that to English pride. At Caebach, near Llandrindod, a clergyman came up to him at the end of the service to thank him for the sermon, and desiring him to go through the whole county with that doctrine. Although at Fishguard he had failed to get the Association to Trefeca, and Bala had won the day becuse of the impassioned intercession of John Evans, Howell Harris took no offence and set out for the Llangeitho Association, 20 August, believing that this was the Lord's will. No doubt he had been invited to attend by Daniel Rowland. On the way he preached at Builth Wells, Cribat and Llanwrtyd Wells, where by now a chapel had been built. On the night before the Association, he arrived at Tregaron. It seems that he did not take a text here, but preached on marriage to Christ. He reached Llangeitho by twelve the next day.

There were some hundreds of preachers and stewards in the new chapel. He recorded nothing on the discussions of the private meeting but in the public meeting, on the first afternoon, a brother from the Wrexham area, whose name is not given, preached, from the words, 'For God hath not appointed us unto wrath, but to obtain salvation by our Lord Jesus Christ.' He spoke on election, on the satisfying of justice by the death of our Lord, and on the redemption of the sinner in that our Saviour has paid all that the law could ask. It appears that it was a fine service. Afterwards Davies, Neath, stood up, taking as a text, 'For Christ also hath once suffered for sins, the just for the unjust, that he might bring us to God.' It seemed to Harris that this preacher's ability was greater, his light stronger, and his knowledge of the Scriptures more extensive than the first, and that there was more unction upon his ministry. The crowd broke out in rejoicing time and again, while God's ambassador cried out that Christ had taken our place, that our sins had become his, and that his righteousness had become ours. The influence was so great that Harris was almost amazed. 'I stood in silence,' he wrote, 'as I thought how the Lord had prospered them; I saw that Jerusalem was here, and that there was such life, power and remarkable glory here, and that it was spreading far and wide.' Harris was given the most privileged position, the sermon at ten o'clock on the second day. He does not record his text, but God was with him. He returned that night to Tregaron and preached to a large crowd. The next day he travelled directly to Trefeca, across the hills. This was his last visit to Llangeitho; indeed, this was his last journey from Trefeca.

On his return he found that the meetings commemorating the second anniversary of the establishing of the Countess of Huntingdon's College were under way. The report of those present and of those who took part in the meetings, given in *The Life and Times of Selina, Countess of Huntingdon*, is far from being consistent with the details in Harris's journal; and in all probability it is the journal that is correct. The meetings began with the administering of communion in the College chapel at eight in the morning; the Lord drew near during this service. In the afternoon, Mr Fletcher preached on the mystery of Christ. After him, Peter Williams spoke, in English and in Welsh, on the vanity of the world. When he began to mention the glory of Christ, and the heaven of his love, a mighty stirring arose amongst the people and the whole place became full of life and glory. That night a love-feast was held.

The next day, Harris preached on Daniel sorrowing for the wickedness of his people, and he noted that the Rev. J. Walters, the clergyman, author of the *English and Welsh Dictionary*, was present. That night, Mr Walters preached an important sermon. We find, in addition, that Simon Lloyd of Bala was present, together with a Mr Hammer who also took part in some of the public proceedings. A number of strangers had also arrived and Harris noted that twenty beds in his house were occupied.

But a storm was about to break over the Countess's College at Trefeca. At the beginning of August, about a fortnight before the College's anniversary, the Wesleyan Conference was held at London. There, John Wesley declared that as a body they had inclined too far towards Calvinism, and he gave expression to views that were much more Arminian. Amongst other things, he said that Wesleyans should be taught to aim for, and to expect, sanctification, not gradually through a life of effort, but directly. When the minutes of this conference reached the Countess she was greatly distressed. She could not refrain from copious tears, and felt that an impassable rift had opened up between her and Wesley's followers. She had fully resolved upon taking him with her to Trefeca again that year, but now she could not consider such a step. As Benson, the Classics tutor at the College, was a zealous Wesleyan he was given warning that he must leave, which he did at the end of the year. As the Countess had announced publicly that no Arminian would be allowed to maintain any connection with the college, Fletcher resigned the principalship. The controversy must have produced considerable agitation within the college, and, as can be imagined, the sympathies of the students lay strongly with the Countess, by whose bread they were fed. Some of them went to opposite extremes, preaching Hyper-Calvinism, if not something verging on Antinomianism. Harris, however, although a strong Calvinist, thought that the Countess had acted too hastily, and he felt deeply for Benson. John Wesley had ever a warm place in his heart, and as his friend held firmly to the evangelical doctrine of justification by faith, Harris did not want to condemn him for his other views. Because of this a degree of coldness arose between Harris and the Countess for a while. It seems that Mr Shirley took Benson's place for a short period.

The Countess, at this point, was spending much of her time at Trefeca, and many Welsh preachers visited the place as a consequence. At the beginning of September, Daniel Rowland visited, and preached to the college from the words, 'For it pleased the Father that in him should all fulness dwell.' Harris noted that he received much light, and that the congregation was enormous. 'While Rowland preached,' he says, 'my spirit loved him; I felt that he was bone of my bone and flesh of my flesh.' In the same week came a Mr Owen from Meidrim, who preached excellently, both in Welsh and in English, from the text, 'I am the Rose of Sharon, and the lily of the valleys.' At the end of September, Peter Williams and

Williams, Pantycelyn, were at Trefeca. The first preached in the college chapel on, 'I am the way', and after him William Williams preached on the house on a rock. Next day, Peter Williams preached again, on the Lord making a new covenant with the house of Israel. He showed that the covenant was unconditional, that a new heart was part of it, and he stood firmly for perseverance in grace. The influence was great, his gifts and ability were such that Harris felt ashamed to open his mouth.

In the journal for 22 October is noted:

> Today, about four o'clock, Edmund Jones arrived here, in the carriage which we sent to obtain him. He preached to the students at six, on the ram caught in the thicket.

It is good to see those who at one time could not bring themselves to understand one another, being reconciled again. Edmund Jones stayed for some days at Trefeca and preached again, on the words, 'Neither pray I for these alone.'

On 10 December, Harris heard of the death of Mr Whitefield in America, and his grief, together with that of the Countess, for this famous servant of Christ, was great. Although a degree of separation had arisen between himself and Whitefield, they were bosom friends at heart, and when Harris heard the news of his death the blow was as hard as when he lost his wife. At the Countess's request he preached that evening.

> I showed that a pillar had been removed; that I had known him for thirty-two years; I referred to the large place he filled, the great emptiness left behind him in the three kingdoms, the vast numbers that are grieving because of his loss, and that over a thousand souls would be acknowledging him that day as their father. I reminded them of his zeal, his labours, his faithfulness and his courage in carrying the truth of free grace far and wide. I longed that his mantle might fall on those remaining behind, and I showed the majesty of God's grace in keeping him in the midst of such praise and popularity.

We can be certain that the preacher delivered his sermon under the effects of strong emotions, and it would be hard not to believe that the tears were flowing down the cheeks of his hearers.

The journal for part of 1771 is lost, but it is almost certain that Harris did not leave his home to preach during the rest of the year, nor indeed for the rest of his life. Weakness had overtaken him. His constitution, once so strong, was rapidly breaking up. When we consider the extent of his labours, the wonder is that it lasted as long as it did. He says that he finished the building at Trefeca that summer, and he took that as an indication that he was shortly to finish his work. Yet, he still preached daily, if not more often, to the family at Trefeca, and usually he would also address the students at the college. He was also responsible for the day-to-day management of the house at Trefeca, though he had able assistants in Evan Moses and Evan Roberts. In August, the yearly College celebrations were held as usual, but neither Daniel Rowland nor Williams, Pantycelyn, were among the visitors. Those who were present were John Harry and Benjamin Thomas, and the first of these preached from the words, 'Create in me a clean heart, O Lord.' The journal ends in February 1772, and for Harris's history after this date we depend on the testimony of the members of the family which he had gathered about him.

## THE DAMAGE DONE BY THE DISRUPTION

Perhaps this is the most appropriate point at which to discuss the damage suffered by religion in Wales, and particularly by the Methodists in Wales, because of the unfortunate Disruption between Harris and his brethren. It is certainly the case that the damage was great. The loss of the Reformer's service and the directing of that energy, that once had been let loose throughout Wales, inwards towards the confined area of the Trefeca family, was not the greatest loss. We confess that this was considerable, but it must be remembered that Howell Harris had already, through his previous labours, weakened his constitution considerably, and that he would not have been able to continue long with his journeying at the same level of commitment and self-sacrifice. The more important damage caused by the disruption was the devastating influence it had upon the societies, so many of which had only recently been formed and which were composed of relatively young believers. When we consider that Harris's preachers after the Disruption had travelled throughout Wales, proclaiming fiercely that the clergy had lost God; and then that those preachers who followed Rowland, hard on their heels, had been calling Harris a Sabellian, a Patripassian, and a host of other names, it is no wonder that the societies were stunned, with their members in extreme perplexity. Many were split up as a consequence, and some were never re-established.

Furthermore, after Harris's settlement at Trefeca, some of his followers tried to found smaller parties with themselves at the head. Amongst these we could refer particularly to Thomas Meredith and Thomas Sheen, the former from the Builth Wells area, and the latter from Montgomeryshire. They were both present at Harris's early Associations, but succumbed gradually to a mixture of Antinomianism and Sandemanianism which no one understood. They both had a number of followers for a time, but their groups soon dwindled and disappeared.

Gwynedd did not experience anything like such a storm because of its geographical distance from the heart of the struggle, though it did not fully escape the ravages of the tempest. In the south, Cardiganshire suffered least. Rowland's influence extended throughout the county. The society at Hen Fynachlog, near Pontrhydfendigaid, is the only society of which there is a record that they invited members of Harris's party. Nor was the damage in Carmarthenshire great, in that Williams, Pantycelyn, in the north, and Rowland in the south, through his monthly preaching in Abergorlech Chapel, wielded considerable influence throughout the societies. The split was greater in Pembrokeshire. Howell Davies was respected as a father by hundreds, but John Sparks and John Harris, St Kennox, were of great influence, and were strong supporters of Harris, and when the latter retired to Trefeca these two went over to the Moravians. They must have had a powerful effect on a great many. There is no doubt that the Glamorganshire societies were fearfully shaken, and many of them disappeared. After the Disruption, there is no more mention or record of Gelli-gaer, Lisvane, Cymmer, Dol-y-gaer or many other societies. As for Monmouthshire, the vast majority of the societies were shattered, and of all those established by Harris the only one remaining to Methodism was the society at Goetre, near Pontypool. All those other causes within the Connexion in Monmouthshire are the fruits of later efforts. It is true that New Inn and Mynyddislwyn continued to consider themselves Methodist for some tens of years, but as they were so far from the centre of the revival, and as no preacher of real influence rose up from among them, they gradually drew closer to the Independents and were lost to the Connexion.

The most distressing results of all occurred in Radnorshire. All the societies of the county were lost. Many reasons can be given for this. For one thing, no chapels had been built there. The only one in the county of which there is any record is Maesgwyn chapel. The societies met in houses and so were the more easily dispersed. For another, at about the time of the disruption the English language descended as a flood over the county and it does not appear that the Methodists had the English preachers to visit the congregations regularly so that many of the converted remained with the Established Church, and others joined the Independents and Baptists. And lastly, many of the more prominent believers went to Trefeca, joining with the family there, so that those remaining were left without leaders, without men of maturity and experience to be life and strength in their midst. The net result was that all of Radnorshire was lost to the Methodists. It seems that nearly all the societies had dissipated in Harris's lifetime. The only ones we find him visiting after his reconciliation with his brethren are Penybont, Claerwy and Llandrindod. If there were others, half-alive, and if they received a measure of reviving through the establishment of the Countess's College at Trefeca, in that they could find there those who could minister to them in English, they disappeared completely when the College was moved from Trefeca to Cheshunt. The present Methodist causes found in Radnorshire arise from much more recent [nineteenth-century] labours. Yet it must not be supposed that all the converts, nor indeed the majority of them, were lost to religion. Hundreds of them united themselves to other denominations. There are very many relatively strong Baptist and Independent causes in Glamorganshire, Monmouthshire and Radnorshire whose foundation can be traced back to the labours of Howell Harris or those of some of the other Methodist Reformers.

## HOWELL HARRIS'S DEATH AND AN
## ASSESSMENT OF HIS CHARACTER

Throughout 1772, Howell Harris's health declined, his constitution was rapidly breaking down. As long as he could, he visited the College to address the students. But soon, even this was too much for him. According to the Countess of Huntingdon:

> The last time he preached there, there was as great a crowd as usual, and his preaching was as searching and rousing as ever. He spake with a mighty sense of God, eternity, the immortality and preciousness of the souls of his hearers; and of their original corruption, and of the extreme danger the unregenerate were in, with the nature and absolute necessity of regeneration by the Holy Ghost, and of believing in Christ in order to our pardon and justification, yielding acceptable obedience, and obtaining salvation from hell and an entrance into heaven. He spake as became the oracles of God in demonstration of the Spirit and power; and especially when he came to his application, he addressed himself to the audience in such a tender, earnest, and moving manner, exciting us to come and be acquainted with the dear Redeemer, as melted the assembly to tears.

Towards the end, though he could not leave the house, he would drag himself down to the ground floor to speak to the numerous family gathered at Trefeca. His addresses at these occasions left an indelible impression on the minds of those who heard him, and in the strength of their love for him they recorded many of his words. We can only provide some of them:

> I love all that come and feed on his flesh and blood. I feel that he and not anything here is my rest and happiness. I love eternity because he is there; I speak with and cry to him. O the thickness of this flesh which hides him from

me; it is indeed lawful to be weary of it; for it is a thick veil of darkness, and I feel clearly it is this that makes me weary of everything here and longing to go home to my dear Saviour. O thou who didst bleed to death and who art alive, come and take me home; and as for the passage, I have committed that to thee to take care of me. I am thine here and forever; I am one of thy redeemed, the fruit of the blood and sweat, and thy will is my heaven.

He became confined to his bed and was unable to write, but he continued to worship God:

Blessed be God, my work is done, and I know that I am going to my dear God and Father, for he hath my heart, yea, my whole heart.

On 21 July 1773, when in his sixtieth year, his pure soul took its flight to his God and Father. Great mourning for him resulted, not only within the Trefeca family but throughout Wales. Thousands attended his funeral. The Countess of Huntingdon numbered them as twenty thousand, including fifteen of the clergy. The enormous crowd was addressed, from three separate platforms, by six clergymen. The minister officiating at the grave was the Rev. John Morgan, the curate of Talgarth, with whom the deceased had been on terms of friendship for many years. The assumption that the Rev. Price Davies, the vicar, had died and that his position had been given to a man called William Davies, is incorrect. Price Davies was granted a long life. He lived for some years after the death of the Reformer from Trefeca, but he was too weak to take part in the funeral service and indeed it does not appear that he was present. There is a tradition, similar to that of Howell Davies's funeral, that John Morgan broke down as he read at the graveside and had to hand the book to another. He too, and others after him, failed to read, being choked by tears, and that it was in the midst of groaning and loud weeping that the mortal remains of Howell Harris were laid to rest in the earth. This is easy to believe for he was loved beyond any other man by hundreds. His grave is at Talgarth Church, close to the altar.

The Reformer had no interest in amassing wealth. Whilst he travelled throughout the land, shaking Wales by his ministry, his own records reveal that he received little in terms of remuneration. It was only with difficulty that he was enabled to keep his head above the waters, as far as his own affairs were concerned. But in his latter years, because of his diligence and the efforts of those gathered about him, and because of his great administrative skills whenever he applied himself to anything, the free-hold of the house at Trefeca, together with the lands and houses around it, were in his possession. In his will he left it all, not to any relative, but to the Community, under the oversight of Trustees. He had only one child, a daughter, to whom had passed his wife's money, and by the time of his death she had married a doctor from Brecon and was in no need. He was therefore at liberty to do as he wished with his possessions. With the Founder's death, the family at Trefeca dwindled. There was no one of sufficient vision to continue the work, and by the beginning of the nineteenth century the community had shrunk to nothing more than a small rural shop. About 1840, the remaining members of the family presented the estate to the Breconshire Monthly Meeting, on condition that they might receive some amount of annuity while they lived. The Monthly Meeting passed all on to the South Wales Association, and from the year 1842 a Theological College of the Connexion has had its home there.

Howell Harris possessed a remarkable character. In sheer commitment to his labours; in courage in the face of dangers and obstacles; and in disregard for physical comforts, not one of the Methodist Fathers can compare with him. The only ones that can bear comparison are Whitefield and Wesley in England, but when the condition of Wales at the time, is considered; the state of the roads, many of which were just tracks; the poverty of most food and shelter; the ferocity of the wrath of the clergy and populace; the scales turn, and turn significantly, in favour of the Reformer of Trefeca.

It is almost impossible to convey to present-day readers any true idea of his energy and commitment. He travelled over rugged hills with hardly a suggestion of a path; he was often caught out in wild tempests; he would have to struggle through surging streams that had burst their banks, and not infrequently would his life and that of his horse be in considerable danger of being carried away by the flood. He would often preach to great congregations while wet to the skin, and starving from lack of food. No obstacle could hinder him. We often read of Rowland and the others being kept from attending an Association because of the inclement weather; we do not find this, even once, of Harris. Having swum across rivers, and been up to his chin in snowdrifts, he would preach as an ambassador from eternity, his spirit flaming within him.

He might spend the following evening lying in his wet clothes on chairs before the fire, in order to set out with the dawn the next morning. It is no surprise that he would sometimes, half-teasing, half in earnest, accuse his brethren of laziness and of caring too much for their physical comforts. He was the pioneer for Wales; he it was who faced the fiercest opposition. The labours of Rowland, Williams and Howell Davies were great, and their suffering not small, but their journeyings and tribulations could not be compared with his.

It was Harris's genius also that was the most versatile. Rowland was at his best in the pulpit; there, no one could compete with him. Williams excelled at leading the society and, particularly, at writing and as a hymn-writer. But as for Howell Harris, he excelled in all that he undertook. As far as the thrilling power of his oratory is concerned, he was only a little behind Rowland; and as a theologian, particularly in his deep discernment of the doctrine of the Person of Christ we believe, for all the degree of confusion in his thought, that he was greater than all his brethren. And not one of them could hold a candle to him as an organizer. He had the creative imagination for devising plans, and for all the attraction which the mystical held for him, his plans were always eminently practical. The combination in him of the mystical and the practical is reminiscent of Oliver Cromwell. There is no doubt that Harris is the father of the ecclesiology of the Calvinistic Methodists in Wales. He was the main architect of the present structures with respect to the Associations and Monthly Meetings. And had he been enabled to maintain his connection with the Methodists, as General Superintendent, throughout his life, it is certain that the order of the Connexion would be that much more definite and detailed, with greater central authority abiding with the Association. The question as to whether this would have been to the advantage or to the disadvantage of the Connexion, we do not propose to address. But there were other facets again to the Reformer's genius. A man who could not only rule over a family of a hundred-and-twenty adults of every kind of temperament collected together from every part of the country, but could provide for their sustenance by planning their various spheres of work, must possess intellectual energies of the first degree, even if he had no other tasks to fulfil. In order to offer work for those under his roof and to meet their needs, Harris undertook all kinds of activity. He farmed the land; he laid out roads; he had woollen and wood mills; in a word, hardly anything lay outside the circle of his genius. When considering, in addition, that he was for years the mainstay of the Breconshire Agricultural Society, and that he proved himself an effective military officer, it must be acknowledged that very few men could be compared to him for versatility of mind.

He was not without his weaknesses and these, as is usually the case with men of strong feelings, lay on the surface and were very evident. It can be said of all of them that they inclined in the direction of virtues. If he was hot of temper, with a tendency to tyrannize, this arose from the depth of his convictions and his great zeal for what he considered to be truth. He was as open as the day and completely free from any form of cunning. Because of this he would sometimes fall into the net laid for him by unprincipled men. Nor do we know to what extent bodily weakness, brought about by overwork, was responsible for the triggering of his temper. But alongside this, he possessed a full heart of affection; he could love passionately; and his hold upon his friends was as unshakeable as death. If someone had given him offence, a kind word from the offender would be sufficient for immediate reconciliation. He would insist that he himself was most responsible for any coldness. He could at times be found in such a state of mind that no rebuke or advice would be in any way acceptable, and opposition to himself would be equated to opposition to God. It is difficult to account for these periods other than that a condition of derangement had taken hold of him.

At the same time, we believe that his brethren could have shown more sympathy towards him on taking into consideration his immense labours and commitment. When the Methodists eventually extended their hands in reconciliation, he, in an instant, stretched forth his own in response. We found it a pure joy to discover from his journal that the last ten years of his life was so much brighter than any had imagined, and that he had spent them in close fellowship with his old friends. He and Daniel Rowland came to understand each other thoroughly and, after their reconciliation, no cloud even of the size of a man's hand ever came between them again while they lived. During these years, and up to the grave, Howell Harris was one of the Methodists in all things but name. He journeyed amongst them; he preached in their chapels; he was present at their Monthly Meetings and their Associations; and he received from them the highest station that they could give. It is worth remembering that a journey to a Llangeitho Association was the last he ever made before weakness confined him to Trefeca, and that what he heard and saw there thrilled his soul to such an extent that he declared his conviction that God was evidently among them and that Llangeitho was the Jerusalem of Wales. He returned, over the hills, to Trefeca as one that had found great spoil, and though he could no longer journey afield, Rowland, Williams and Peter Williams would often visit him.

Howell Harris died a relatively young man. He was not sixty years old when called from his labours to his reward. But in this short time he achieved an amazing quantity of work – work which will be remembered even when time shall be no more. And he lived long enough to witness a moral and social revolution take place in Wales. If on his first breaking out the world viewed him with suspicion, considering him a hot-headed dreamer, yet, before his death, he was surrounded with honours, and today

is esteemed as one of the mightiest men of Wales. Our historical firmament contains no greater star than he. Whenever we shall be blessed as a
country with a history which shall to some degree be worthy of us, there
must be an honourable place for Howell Harris, the unflagging traveller;
the courageous pioneer; the fluent preacher; the fiery seraph; and the
pure-hearted patriot, in that history. We find great difficulty in bidding
him farewell, such is his spell over us. William Williams, Pantycelyn, in his
fine elegy to Harris, has displayed his character and attributes so clearly
that we cannot refrain from quoting more of his verses:

How he strengthens the weak-hearted,
Bears the faltering on his arm;
By his doctrine they are nurtured,
There the wounded find a balm;
Solemn words, substantial, glowing,
Tempered in the holy flame,
A clear light to lead Christ's children,
A lantern for the blind and lame.

Mae'n cryfhau y breichiau gweinion,
Ac yn dala'r llesg i'r lan;
Yn ei athrawiaeth y mae ymborth,
Bwyd i'r ofnus, bwyd i'r gwan;
Geiriau dwys, sylweddol, gloew,
Wedi eu tempru yn y tân,
Lamp i arwain pererinion
Trwy'r anialwch mawr ymlaen.

Now salvation's gracious story
Is proclaimed both far and wide,
Thousands find their hearts drawn to it,
Through their faith are justified;
Hear him tell how Christ's atonement
Makes a sinner right with God,
And how sinners vile and filthy
Can be washed in Jesu's blood.

Y mae'r iachawdwriaeth rasol
Yn cael ei rhoddi maes ar led,
Ac sy'n cymell mil i'w charu,
Ac i rhoddi ynddi eu cred;
Haeddiant Iesu yw ei araith,
Cysur enaid a'i iachad,
Ac euogrwydd dua pechod
Wedi ei gannu yn y gwaed.

Let no man speak of his failings,
Do not linger o'er his fall,
All the books of heaven are blotted,
Why should men his flaws recall?
Let not tongue, nor pen, nor writing,
I forbid them from this day,
Mention ought but the Revival,
That through Wales pursued its way.

Byth na chofier am ei bechod,
Na 'sgrifener dim o'i fai,
Blotiwyd llyfrau'r nef yn hollol,
Pam gaiff rhagfarn dyn barhau?
Ni chaiff pen, nac inc, na thafod,
Rwy'n eu gwa'rdd o hyn i maes,
Sôn am ddim ond y Diwygiad
Trwyddo lanwodd Gymru las.

Now he rests beneath his tombstone
In a dark and silent place,
Harris, who of old awakened
Many ministers to grace;
For a deep sleep from th' Almighty
As a flood had filled the realm,
Until Harris loudly thundered,
'God will Nineveh o'erwhelm!'

Nawr mae'n gorwedd yn y graean
Mewn lle tywyll, distaw iawn,
Harris, gynt, a'i waedd ddihunodd
Weinidogion lawer iawn;
Can's trwm gwsg oddiwrth yr Arglwydd
Oedd fel diluw'n llanw'n lân,
Yn y dydd cyhoeddodd Howell
I fod Nini'n mynd ar dân.

| | |
|---|---|
| Griffith Jones, by then, was quickened, | Griffith Jones, pryd hyn, oedd ddeffro, |
| Preaching mercy all around, | Yn cyhoeddi efengyl gras, |
| Loud he cried from many a pulpit, | Hyd cyrhaeddai'r swn o'r pwlpud, |
| Sometimes from the burial-ground; | Neu, os rhaid, o'r fynwent las; |
| But because his days were clouded, | Ond am fod ei fore'n dywyll, |
| And his faith was small and bound, | Ac nad oedd ei ffydd ond gwan, |
| He would not agree with preaching | Fe arswydodd fynd i'r meusydd, |
| Save on consecrated ground. | Ac i'r lleoedd nad oedd llan. |

| | |
|---|---|
| Howell was not called to labour | Yntau Harris, heb arddodiad |
| By the laying on of hands, | Dwylaw dynion o un rhyw, |
| Nor ordained by any bishop, | Na chael cenad gan un esgob |
| Or other power in the land; | Ag sy'n llawer llai na Duw, |
| He proclaimed the glorious gospel, | Fe gyhoeddodd yr efengyl, |
| God's abundant treasure-store, | Anfeidroldeb dwyfol stôr, |
| From the banks of quiet Severn | O derfynau'r Hafren dawel |
| Westward to the ocean shore. | Obry i'r gorllewin fôr. |

\* \* \* \* \*

| | |
|---|---|
| If a faithful friend was wanted, | Os oedd eisiau ffrind ffyddlonaf, |
| Howell Harris would be he, | Harris unig oedd efe, |
| Better than the dearest kindred, | Gwell na'r ceraint goreu anwyd |
| True as ever friend could be; | Mewn un ardal is y ne'; |
| Pardoning faults and keeping counsel, | Maddeu bai, a chadw cwnsel, |
| Quick to comfort every groan, | Ysbryd cydymdeimlo yn un, |
| Bearing a companion's burdens | A gwneud holl ofidiau ei gyfaill, |
| As if they were all his own. | Megis ei ofidiau ei hun. |

\* \* \* \* \*

| | |
|---|---|
| Sleep at last by Talgarth's altar, | Cwsg i lawr yn eglwys Talgarth, |
| Where no pain or woe can come, | Lle nad oes na phoen na gwae, |
| You will soon be raised and quickened, | Ti gai godi i'r lan i fywyd |
| Called to your eternal home; | Sy'n dragwyddol yn parhau; |
| Better to be resting meanwhile, | Gwell i ti gael gorffwys yna |
| Mingled with the worms and soil, | Blith dra phlith a'r pryfed mân, |
| Than to gather further troubles, | Na chael mil o demtasiynau |
| And 'gainst new temptations toil. | At y dengmil ge'st o'r blaen. |

\* \* \* \* \*

| | |
|---|---|
| Farewell, Harris, now has ended | Ffarwel, Harris, darfu heddiw |
| All the striving to be head, | A chwenychu bod yn ben, |
| You've been called to greater glory, | Ce'st ddyrchafiad mwy godidog, |
| And to heaven in triumph led; | Canu yn y nefoedd wen; |

As for us, not far behind you,
We are following on our way,
Soon our hour will be striking,
Very soon will dawn our day.

Ac 'rym ninnau yn dy ganlyn
'R hyd y grisiau yma lawr,
Ac nid oes ond rhyw funudau
Rhwng y gloch a tharo ei hawr.

---

[1] HHRS, p. 175–6.

[2] Ibid., p. 196.

[3] The first tutor was in fact a Welshman called John Williams. He was converted under Harris's preaching and taught Welsh, Latin and English. He was dismissed by the Countess in 1769 for courting Betty, Harris's daughter, and distressing Hannah Bowen, the College's matron, who had developed strong affections for him. He had however some connection still with the College in 1771. See Faith Cook, *Selina, Countess of Huntingdon*, pp. 241, 252, 261, 264–6; and STL, vol. 2, pp. 122–3, 137.

[4] CH, 29, p. 47.

TOP: LLANDDEWIBREFI CHURCH, CARDIGANSHIRE, AS IT WAS IN ROWLAND'S TIME
MIDDLE: PETER WILLIAMS
BOTTOM: LAUGHARNE, CARMARTHENSHIRE

Top: Laugharne
Middle: David Jones, Llan-gan
Bottom: Water Street Chapel, Carmarthen

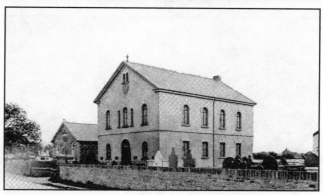

Top: Llandyfaelog Church and Cemetery
Middle: Llan-gan Church, near Cowbridge
Bottom: Salem Chapel, Pencoed. The first chapel on this site was built
in 1775 by David Jones, Llan-gan

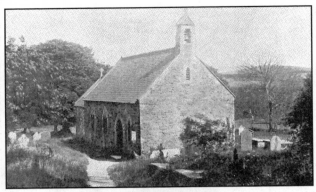

Top: Manorowen Church and Cemetery, Pembrokeshire
Middle: The gravestone at Llan-gan of David Jones's first wife
Bottom: Stangrach, near Llanfynydd, Carmarthenshire

PLACES ASSOCIATED WITH WILLIAM DAVIES, NEATH:
1. THE RUINS OF THE OLD GYFYLCHI CHAPEL, BUILT 1776   2. THE EXTERIOR
OF THE RUINS   3. THE PULPIT OF THE OLD CHAPEL   4. NEATH CHURCH
5. LLANILLTYD CHURCH, NEAR NEATH

Places associated with Dafydd Morris, Twrgwyn:
Top: Twrgwyn Chapel, Cardiganshire
Bottom: Penffos, near Twrgwyn. Dafydd Morris lived in the cottage
in the foreground

PLACES ASSOCIATED WITH WILLIAM LLOYD OF CAEO:
1. BLAENCLAWDD FARM 2. HENLLAN FARM 3. CAEO CHAPEL 4.CAEO
CHURCH AND CEMETERY
TWO OF THE OLDEST CALVINISTIC METHODIST CHAPELS IN
CARMARTHENSHIRE:
5. CEFNBERRACH, 1747 6. LLANLLUAN, 1745

# 18

# PETER WILLIAMS

## HIS BIRTH AND UPBRINGING

*T*here is no more familiar and respected name in Wales than that of Peter Williams, the evangelical preacher, and godly commentator. It may be that he can hardly be called one of the founders of the Methodist Connexion. About eight years of the Revival had passed and numerous Quarterly and Monthly Associations held, before the time of his conversion. And some further years again were to pass before Providence led him to throw in his lot amongst the Methodists. But because of the brilliance of his talents, the godliness of his spirit, the breadth of his knowledge, and the completeness of his commitment, it was not long after he had joined before he was recognized as belonging to the foremost amongst them and accounted as a leader. 'Peter Williams, Carmarthen', was the usual designation for him, but it appears that he only lived a very short while in that town, so that 'Carmarthen' must be considered as referring to the county rather than the town.

He was born on 7 January 1722, in a farmhouse called Morfa, near Laugharne. As its name suggests the farm was near the sea. The natives of Laugharne spoke English, as they still do. The reason for this, it is said, is that a colony of English settled here in a past age. The language has survived up to the present day, even though it is Welsh that is spoken in all the surrounding districts. For this reason, when he was a child Peter Williams was more of an Englishman than a Welshman. His parents were respectable people, well off in the things of the world, and descended from very worthy families. His mother, particularly, was a very religious woman. She used to travel on horseback on Sundays to Llanddowror to hear the famous clergyman, Griffith Jones, and often she would take her child, Peter, with her. Although she had other children, a son and a daughter, it seems that Peter was her favourite. She saw in him unmistakeable signs of abilities. His lively mind and excellent memory convinced her to expect great things from him, and she determined to provide all possible educational advantages for him. Her wish was to consecrate him for the ministry, and no doubt she expressed her hopes many times to the young Peter as they travelled on the road from Laugharne to Llanddowror and at other times.

But when Peter was only eleven years old, his mother died suddenly from a fever. The following year, his father died. The three orphan children were left at a very young age to face the storms of life. Providence interposed on their behalf, and in an evident way; the Lord showed himself to be a father of the fatherless. A nobleman from Bristol took care of the girl; an uncle from the father's side took responsibility for the younger son; and an uncle from the mother's side received Peter to his home. It appears that the daughter died when young. As for Dafydd, the younger son, he was sent to a good school by the uncle and lived in the vicinity of Bristol until the day of his death. Whether he married and had children is not known. Peter was kept at school while his parents lived, and made great progress in learning. His uncle continued in the same way, placing him immediately in a school and maintaining his education until he was sixteen years old. His lust for knowledge was immense. When the other children in the school would be outside playing, he would be at his books. He could not sit at the table to eat without a book being open before him. Once he had begun to familiarize himself with the Greek and Latin languages his progress became more evident, and his own commitment more thorough. He took no rest during the holidays, as would the other boys, but continued to ponder and study diligently. From what he relates of himself, we can infer that at this time he tended to be much on his own, disinterested in games, careless of the company of other boys of his age, and fully taken up with his studies.

His behaviour was moral, almost from the start. For this he was indebted in part to his natural temperament, and in part to the care and counsels of his mother. He mentions that once during his childhood he heard someone cursing and swearing, and he learnt some of the phrases. But when his mother heard him she rebuked him sternly, and he was never guilty of that sin again. And after she had been laid to earth, her counsels clung to his mind so that he was never tempted to licentiousness. He said that God kept him free, in the days of his youth and in his unbelieving years, from presumptuous sins and from those sins that men consider shameful. Nor was he lacking in religious impressions. His conscience was often filled with a fear of dying and a terror of judgment. He said:

> The greatest question for me was, 'How should I appear before God? How could I expect pardon and forgiveness from that pure and holy God, from whose presence, at his appearing, the earth and all that is in it will flee away?'

He tried to comfort himself that he was no worse than other men and that there were thousands of sinners as bad as himself, some of whom, he knew, having died with a hope of the resurrection to eternal life. But these empty excuses were not enough to quieten his conscience. He began to examine himself regularly; inspecting the chambers of his heart; discovering there the seeds of every corruption. But for all this, he did not know the Lord, and knew hardly anything of the gospel way of forgiveness.

When he was about sixteen years old, Peter Williams's uncle pressed him to decide on an occupation. He found this very difficult to do or, rather, he found great difficulty expressing his decision. In his own mind he had set his heart on becoming a clergyman. As we noted, this longing had been planted in him by his mother. And about a year before her death, the young Peter had received a strange dream in which, amongst other things, he saw two strange men, as beautiful as angels, coming to him and conversing with him. His mother interpreted the dream as an omen that she would soon die but that Jesus Christ would come to take her place, and that Jesus would make her dear child a famous minister in the land. It is certain that this dream and its interpretation made a deep impression on Peter's mind, and probably it was a significant factor in his thoughts of the ministry. Certainly it was not because he had found grace, or that his soul within him was aflame with the desire for the salvation of souls, that he sought the office. According to his own description of himself, he had not yet experienced conversion, but because of the impression made by his mother, together with his own love of books and learning, nothing would satisfy him but the priesthood. It does not seem that he was afraid to speak to his uncle, but that he feared that the expense involved in his choice would be too great. But eventually he had to explain himself, and matters did not turn out as badly as he feared. The uncle saw that his nephew would never make a farmer and he was glad to have him engaged in work that suited his temperament. The scholarly boy was sent to a good grammar school maintained in Carmarthen by Mr Thomas Einion. Peter was there for a diligent and studious three years, during which he made such progress in the classical languages that he was able, when departing, to compose a Latin letter of appreciation to his tutor. This letter, as we shall see, became the means of bringing about his ordination.

## HE IS CONVICTED WHILE HEARING
## WHITEFIELD PREACH

We have every reason to believe that his life while at the academy was moral and his behaviour courteous. His tutor probably considered him a model scholar. But he had not yet been brought to an appreciation of the way of salvation in Christ. Throughout this period his conscience was uneasy. The terrors of judgment and of having to give an account to God had not left him. He made many vows which, subsequently, he found he could not keep. But in the April of 1743 an event occurred which changed completely the direction of his life and made him a new man. That event was the visit of George Whitefield to Carmarthen to preach. The preacher's fame preceded his arrival. The fluency of his oratory together with the fact that, although an ordained clergyman, he preached in the open air and at unconsecrated sites, produced much talk. But the greatest wonder of all associated with him was that he taught original sin, the necessity of the rebirth, and justification by faith without works. The majority of the Church of England clergy considered such things rank heresy, and so also did they appear to Mr Thomas Einion, the grammar school tutor. The tutor's usual practice was to release the children at eleven o'clock, except for the more able – those with their eyes upon the ministry – whom he would detain for a while longer in order to guide them in their choice of reading or study. But on the day of Mr Whitefield's visit, Mr Einion's message to his best scholars concerned the dangerous preacher visiting the town. He warned the young men most solemnly not to attend the sermon. In spite of his warning, four of them, one of whom was Peter Williams, determined secretly to go, in order to see and hear for themselves.

At about twelve noon, Mr Whitefield stood up at the head of Lammas Street. His text was Isaiah 54:5, 'For thy Maker is thine husband; the Lord of hosts is his name; and thy Redeemer the Holy One of Israel; the God of the whole earth shall he be called.' He began by describing the excellencies of Jesus Christ as a husband, and he exhorted the whole congregation to accept him:

> Does anyone wish for a wise husband? Christ is such a one. Does anyone wish for a rich husband; one who will pay all their debts, as is so necessary for us sinners? Jesus is that husband; he owns all the treasures of heaven and earth, he owns everything that is in the possession of the eternal Father. O, my poor fellow-sinners, we are all debtors to the law of God; we are in danger every hour of being apprehended by his justice, of being cut down in our sins and finding ourselves in that place where there is no hope. It is no wonder that Felix trembled when Paul reasoned of righteousness, temperance, and judgment to come. Yet, for all this, there are men to be found who are pleased with their virtues and their own righteousnesses, and who protest their innocence before the law and the gospel. If they are innocent, then Christ has died in vain, which is a foolish and blasphemous thought. The best of us can only declare like the Apostle, 'In me, that is, in my flesh, dwelleth no good

thing.' If the best of us were called to judgment and dealt with according to our deserts, we would be thrown into hell eternally.

Peter Williams was deeply convicted under the sermon. Yet, it seems that he still sought to make a refuge out of his own righteousnesses, hiding in their shadow from the awful arrows shot at him from the preacher's bow. He said of himself, 'I was wounded, but not converted; I felt as it were the edge of the sword but I did not fall to the ground.' But Whitefield was not yet finished, nor had the Spirit of the Lord finished with Peter Williams. The preacher raised his voice like a trumpet, and with a remarkably effective shout, which reached the furthest edges of the crowd, he proclaimed:

My dear people! I was for many years as diligent and careful as any here present. I prayed seven times a day; I fasted twice a week; I attended church every day and received Communion every Sabbath; and yet, the whole time, I was not a Christian.

With this blow Peter Williams's refuge of self-righteousness was broken in pieces; he no longer had any hiding place. He said:

The above words, spoken with such authority, sped as an arrow into my heart; I was smitten to such an extent that my every joint trembled. My old self had gone; I was as clay in the potter's hand.

The only subject that the youth now longed to understand was, what it meant to be a Christian. On this matter, the preacher did not leave him in the dark:

To be a Christian is to receive the Holy Spirit. 'If any man have not the Spirit of Christ, he is none of his.' To be a Christian is to have experienced your wretchedness by nature; to have seen your need of a Saviour; to believe that the man Christ Jesus is the Son of God who has come into the world to save sinners and that he is able to perform that work which he came into the world to do. Furthermore, to be a Christian is to recognize the voice of Christ, to take up your cross and follow him; to be one with him, bone of his bone, and flesh of his flesh; to dwell in him; to be his temple; to commune with him; to know his will, and live to his glory.

We cannot follow the preacher further in his sermon but Peter Williams was saved during its delivery. As they departed, his friends praised the preacher; they greatly admired his fluency, his solemnity, and his gifts; 'They little knew,' said Williams, 'of the building he had raised within me, or the new creature which he had formed within me, all in the course of an hour.' For all this, he does not seem to have entered into the liberty of the gospel. Sinai's ministry filled his soul; he dwelt amongst the thunder and lightning; Calvary was not yet clearly in view, nor the lightning extinguished in the blood. He said:

> The angels visited me from on high; the time of my reformation had come; and all my sins, in thought, word, and deed, came to my mind, as if floodgates had been opened and the waters poured over me so that my soul was sinking in fear and fright.

All things had now changed for the young man. The classical works, the books of the pagan authors, Homer, Horace, Virgil and Ovid, now became of no interest to him; he could not concentrate his mind upon them at all. He tried to hide his turmoil, but his tutor understood clearly that Whitefield's sermon had affected him though he did not say a word. His friends deserted him; they would pretend not to see him in the street. Others complained of him that there were once signs that he would make a good scholar as well as a good friend but that he had now gone over to the Methodists. 'Friend and family have left me,' he said. He knew of no one to whom he could pour out his soul and ask for a word of counsel, except for one young woman, a member of the family with which he lodged, who had been convicted under the same sermon as himself. How long it was before he found relief to his soul, and what the instrument was by which his burden was removed, is not known. What is certain is that his snare was broken and he escaped as a bird from the hands of the fowler. Peter Williams was now a new creature, and everything was new to him. Before his conversion he, with some of his young friends, had arranged to hold concerts for singing and dancing during the Easter and Whitsun holidays. They had employed a harpist for this purpose. Now, such meetings held no interest for him. We do not know whether they ever took place, but if they did, he was certainly not present. Nor does it seem, however, that he joined the Methodist society at Carmarthen.

## ORDAINED CURATE OF EGLWYS GYMYN AND EVICTED BECAUSE OF HIS METHODISM

Soon after this time he left the academy and went as a schoolteacher to Cynwyl Elfed, a rural parish, about five miles from Carmarthen. He does not appear to have sought episcopal ordination directly. He wished for some leisure to study theology, and perhaps also his conversion had confused his thoughts for a while so that he was unclear as to his future. He was most diligent at Cynwil Elfed, not only as a schoolteacher and in his studies, but also in his efforts against immorality and in encouraging his neighbours to think of religion. To do something for Jesus had become a powerful desire within him. The longing in his soul to dedicate his life to the ministry was reawakened in him. He felt, like Paul, that woe would be to him if he preached not the gospel. But his old motives, of sympathy for education, and a love of books, now had no influence upon him. He wished rather to proclaim abroad the treasures of grace so that all might receive them as he had done himself. He applied to the bishop for ordination, and he received the recommendation of Mr Einion, his old tutor, who was kind enough not to mention a word of his Methodist tendencies. It appears also that Mr Einion passed on to the bishop the Latin letter of thanks that the young man had sent to him. This proved an effective key for opening to him the door to the ministry, and he was ordained to the curacy of Eglwys Gymyn, a parish on the borders of Carmarthenshire and Pembrokeshire. We do not have the date of the ordination, but it was almost certainly towards the end of 1743, or the beginning of 1744.

At Eglwys Gymyn he was responsible for the care of the whole parish. The vicar lived in England, where he held a high position and received a good salary. He had no care at all for his poor Welsh parishioners, other than to visit them once a year to receive their tithes. Peter Williams's salary was very small, for the vicar ensured that any abundance came in his direction, but this did not concern the young curate for he required little, and the day-school which he kept saved him from any fear of starvation. He immediately threw himself into the work. He preached with power, though he read his sermons. He soon established a prayer meeting in the parish, circulating it around various homes. In these meetings he not only prayed but gave also a word of exhortation to those present, encouraging them to live a virtuous and godly life. It is impossible to read of his life without noticing that his beginnings were almost identical to those of Howell Harris. The only significant difference was that Peter Williams was ordained whereas Harris had failed to obtain that advantage. It seems that there was something of the wisdom of the serpent in the young curate. At the time the country was filled with the fear that the Pretender would gain the English crown. London trembled at the thought. The result was that many who were not generally in the habit of praying, called to God for the protection of the king. Peter Williams took advantage of the turmoil to conceal that which would normally be considered irregular, namely, his prayer meetings. But, for all his care, he was suspected of favouring the Methodists. His purity of life, the warmth of his prayers, the fact that he did not read his prayers, the tone of his addresses, these all strengthened his people's suspicions that he was a Methodist. And to be of such a tendency was considered a mortal sin among Church people at the time. Their doubts were amplified by another habit of his also. Whenever any of his parishioners died, he would utterly refuse the usual Popish rites that were practised in the locality at such a time, but would rather encourage the people to be sober, to read the Bible, pray, and sing Psalms.

But soon an occurrence took place that decided the matter beyond all argument. One Sabbath morning the curate arrived at the church as usual. He had his sermon carefully written on paper. Having proceeded through the prayers he began to read, with much seriousness, what he had written. On raising his head and casting a hurried look over his congregation, he saw some careless young people, not listening to his words, but joking, and playing with a posy of flowers, throwing it back and forth between them. The spirit of Christ's minister was roused. He paused for a while, to see if his silence would shame them. When this proved not to be the case he began to speak to them of the sanctity of God's house and the respect due to God's ordinations. He told them that their behaviour was such that would not be tolerated in a playhouse let alone in the sanctuary of God and that they were guilty of perpetrating the greatest insult to the majesty of Jehovah. After having spoken sufficiently to satisfy his conscience he tried to continue his reading, but failed to find his place. He was thrown on to his own resources, as the Lord gave him utterance, for the remainder of the sermon. He felt at the time that this was a considerable offence, and he appealed publicly for the congregation's forgiveness. But to forgive such an atrocious sin was completely beyond the ability of those gentlefolk present. The horseplay and laughing of the young people during divine service was a matter of indifference to them. It was a little thing to them that the common people were dying for want of education. But to speak from the pulpit under the influence of holy zeal for the glory of God, without having written out such comments previously, this was such a shameful sin that they considered it beyond the boundaries of forgiveness. As he departed, Peter Williams heard the leading men whispering to one another. 'We suspected before,' they said, 'that he was a Methodist. But now the matter is quite clear. He has thrown aside his disguise.'

The vicar's wife happened to be present and she reported all to her husband. By the return of the post, the curate received a letter informing him of his dismissal. The reasons for so doing, according to the letter, were: 'Peter Williams, the curate of Eglwys Gymyn, is accused of preaching original sin, justification by faith, and the absolute necessity of the rebirth.' Odious sins indeed in a minister!

Peter Williams answered that those doctrines, for preaching which he was being condemned, were in his judgment the basis of the Articles of the Church of England, and he requested the vicar to explain his criticisms in the light of those Articles. He promised that if the vicar could do so with a clear conscience, he would follow any instruction of that nature given to him. The vicar did not reply to this letter but arrived himself in August, intending to serve the church himself until the curate's year came to an end. The young man visited him and asked if he might preach in the vicar's hearing so that his suitability for the ministry might be judged. The only answer that the vicar gave him was that he believed him to be a Methodist and would have nothing further to do with him. The curate argued that he was licensed to preach by the Bishop of St David's. The vicar answered that he would bring him to the Bishop's Court so that his licence might be soon taken from him.

By now Peter Williams realized that the clouds were gathering about him from all directions. He hurried to the Bishop to forestall the complaints that he knew would soon arise. But he received a very cold reception. Others had been busy carrying tales about him to the Bishop. 'I have heard about you,' said he, 'that you have been preaching at Llanlluan and at Capel Ifan.' These two were chapels of rest which had been allowed to fall into ruin by the Church authorities, but had been taken over by the Methodists, renovated to some extent, and used for preaching the gospel. The Bishop's accusation suggests that there was already considerable contact between Peter Williams and the Methodists, although he had not formally joined them. Williams tried to refute the charge by arguing that the chapels were consecrated sites belonging to the Church of England. The only response from his lordship was that he must cease from preaching for three years, must behave himself in a seemly fashion, namely, no doubt, that he must not associate with the Methodists, and that at the end of this time the Bishop would receive him into full orders. 'How can I live for such a long period without work or wages?' asked the curate. 'Do what you can', was the answer. Thus the interview ended, and Peter Williams was dismissed from the episcopal palace without even having received any offer of food or drink.

## HIS EVICTION FROM TWO OTHER CURACIES

Here was poor Peter Williams without work or any prospect of it, because of preaching what he considered to be the truth of God. But he had a true friend in the Rev. Griffith Jones of Llanddowror. When the latter heard of his predicament he sent for him and told him of a vacancy for a curate at Swansea. Williams hurried there and secured the post. But he was to be there for only a month. The occasion for his dismissal was as follows. The Sunday arrived at which the Mayor, the Corporation of Swansea and the

Member of Parliament for the borough, attended the church. After Peter Williams had read through the service, the gentlemen rose to leave; they did not usually receive a sermon on such occasions. He, however, gave out a further psalm to sing, and after they had resumed their seats he preached to them an effective sermon on 2 Chronicles 14:6–7, 'For ye judge not for man, but for the LORD, etc.' He thundered against the receiving of bribes by judges and told them that if they did not act conscientiously according to God's law they would be accountable for all the sins of the people. Some of the gentry were much disturbed, the Mayor amongst them. They considered that the curate had been much too bold with them and they repaid him by not extending to him the usual invitation to the banquet. Within a month, Peter Williams arrived at his church and found a man occupying his place in the pulpit. On conversing with him, he discovered that he had been sent to take his place. The excuse that this man gave to the curate was that his parishioners had become dissatisfied with him. Although he was only a short time in Swansea, yet it appears that Peter Williams's labours had been greatly blessed. Many of those who loved the Lord Jesus testified that he had been instrumental in strengthening them in the truth as it is in Jesus.

After returning to Carmarthen he heard of a need for a curate in Llan-grannog and Llandysilio, Cardiganshire, and having applied, he obtained the place. The position was definitely agreed for a period of three months, but he was retained for two months only. He was very acceptable to the parishioners but his Methodism offended his patron, and he had to go. With this, his association with the Established Church came to an end. He was a loyal member of the Church. Had he been allowed to do so he would have remained in its communion and served at its altar to the end of his days. But godliness, and a desire to preach the gospel in its purity to sinners, were unacceptable attributes within the confines of the Church in those days, and Peter Williams had to look elsewhere. He went out as Abram of old, not knowing whither he went. He had heard of some famous exhorter in Pembrokeshire, most probably that well-known servant of Christ, the Rev. Howell Davies, that he was preaching the gospel with power and great blessing. He decided to go to hear him. This occurred at a place called Castell-y-gwair, in 1740, when Peter Williams was about twenty-four years old. He was so impressed by the preaching of Howell Davies that he broke out in public prayer at the close. He did so with such warmth and heavenly unction that all were moved, and the whole congregation was taken up in general glorying. He decided to throw in his lot amongst the Methodists immediately. The preacher conducted him to the Monthly Meeting that was held in Pembrokeshire. He presented him to the fraternity for consideration, and his name was included amongst the brethren.

## HIS FIRST JOURNEY TO NORTH WALES

From this time forward Peter Williams was an itinerating preacher, and it seems that he commenced upon his labours immediately. Soon, he attended the chapel at Abergorlech in order to hear Daniel Rowland, but Rowland pressed him to preach instead. He was granted a powerful service. Under God's blessing the sermon was the means for the conversion of many. Rowland took him to Llangeitho where he again preached with much influence. He confessed that he knew nothing at this time of the various viewpoints of the different parties. No doubt he had heard of Arminians, Baxterians and Moravians, but he knew little more about them than their names; their different opinions upon points of religious doctrine were unknown to him. But he preached Jesus Christ and him crucified, as the all-sufficient Saviour for sinners, and the Lord blessed his simple message.

From Llangeitho he departed on a journey to north Wales. The first place he visited was Llanidloes, where he had been instructed to call at the house of the cobbler, Evan Morgan, who lived on the north road. There was a strong spirit of persecution in Llanidloes at this time. It was always dangerous for a Methodist to enter the town and Peter Williams encountered considerable difficulty before finding his way to the cobbler's home, but having succeeded he received much kindness. He does not seem to have preached in the town other than to exhort a few poor people who gathered at Evan Morgan's house.

From there he travelled towards Newtown, preaching wherever he found opportunity, and sometimes he would be accompanied by a believing brother, who would escort him from one place to the next. He had much trouble at Newtown. He had called upon a blacksmith to shoe his horse but soon heard the people whispering that he was a Cradockian, and they began to throw stones at him. He said that the stones were thrown with such force that they drew sparks from the paving. He fled for his life in the direction of Llanfair Caereinion. In that neighbourhood he found a hospitable gentleman whom he had met previously at Llandrindod. He received much kindness from him and was also invited to preach on the following day at the home of one of his ploughmen. He commented that this was the first time he had felt something of the sun's warmth since the beginning of his afflictions.

Williams's next stop was Bala where he had heard that a few friends of the gospel used to meet. He stayed in the house of a godly Scotsman, at which it seems he also preached. His visit was not made public but a few friends and neighbours were invited to hear him. More came than were invited and in order to remove prejudice the preacher wore a neckband as he addressed them. Some listened seriously, others were careless and even discourteous. In order to gain their attention he took as a text, not a verse from the Bible, but a section of a Confession from the Book of Common Prayer: 'We have erred, and strayed from thy ways like lost sheep.' It was still only some who were willing to listen, others were full of persecution, and later that evening they threw large stones, some up to three pounds weight, at the place where they believed him to be sleeping. But the Lord kept him from any injury.

He heard that a few were willing to give a hearing to the gospel in Lleyn, and so he journeyed there but does not mention the places visited. He had large congregations, not because the majority gave any respect to the Word of the Lord but because they were interested in experiencing an open-air religious service conducted by a clergyman of the Established Church. Many however were convicted. Among them was a young gentlewoman who testified that she would acknowledge him as spiritual father for as long as she lived.

From here, Peter Williams turned his face to Anglesey. He had heard frightening things concerning Anglesey men and their hatred of itinerant preaching, their cruel attacks upon the preachers and their followers. He had heard particularly of one recent service where the congregation was of two parts, one party wishing to hear what the blasphemer (as they called the preacher) had to say, the other wishing to drive him out of the county. The occasion terminated in violence and bloodshed, with the preacher having to flee for his life. Peter Williams did not allow himself to be frightened by these stories; he confronted the island in God's strength. To begin with he kept away from the towns and areas of large population, travelling around the more hilly parts of the county where the inhabitants were fewer. He knew that a large congregation would never allow him to speak. He would preach wherever he could gather together five or six hearers, but if the news had spread abroad that one of the 'Roundheads' had arrived to preach so that a multitude collected, he would make his escape. In this way he was enabled slowly to gain the ears, and then the hearts, of a large number, so that he was able to become more public. He met also the son of a gentleman, who had been convicted under the preaching of Howell Harris. This man conducted him about for some time, taking him to areas where there were others who sympathized with his work. He was not allowed to leave Anglesey however without experiencing something of the fury of the enemy. In a town, which he does not name, the persecutors had collected at one spot, mocking and heckling, and attempting to frighten the horses of Peter Williams and his friend by shaking a large bag of stones fixed on top of a long staff, but they did not go as far as to throw stones. At a time when the preachers thought that they would get past with nothing worse than scorn and mocking, some cobbler emerged from his workshop, scooped up a handful of the mire of the road and threw it into Peter Williams's face so that for a while he was blinded in both eyes. However after washing his face he found that he had escaped without injury. 'Then I rejoiced,' he said, 'and I was glad that I had been accounted worthy to suffer for Christ and his pure gospel.'

From Anglesey he went to Trefriw. His arrival there was announced too publicly and his persecutors enabled to welcome him in their typical way. A furious mob had gathered, paid by two gentlemen who were drunk at the time. They do not appear to have beaten the preacher but they placed him under lock and key at the inn and kept him there from six at night until two in the morning, seeking to make of him an object of amusement, as the Philistines did with Samson of old. According to Peter Williams:

> They made me drink; they loosened my clothes by unbuttoning me from top to bottom; thay placed a girl on my knee, and asked me many questions as to my teaching, my doctrine and my followers, and as to my text that morning. I answered, 'If you wish, gentlemen, I will recite the text and the sermon also.' At that, one of them called out for silence, 'He is going to preach in order to reform us.' This produced more general mirth and mocking. I asked for food and a bed and they laughed again, saying scornfully that I would have food and sleep later. I expected to be turned out and stoned to death, and that my end would come there in the dark. I gave myself to the Lord, continuing to pray for my blasphemous scoffers. I was not allowed to pray or preach in a loud voice, and I groaned for having to listen to their obscenities, their oaths, and their filthy expressions.

Throughout this distressing experience in the midst of such an ungodly rabble, he was comforted by reminding himself that he was receiving better treatment than had been extended to his Lord. He was released before cockcrow. What circumstances brought about this release we do not know. Before letting him go, the two gentlemen told the innkeeper to give him food and drink and paid all his costs, but they warned him never to preach in the village. By now, however, he was in such a state that he could not eat or drink. He went to his bed and slept, which was more than his friend could do. His letters of ordination had been stolen from him by deception but, during the day, the daughter of the man who had stolen them returned them, fearing a lawsuit. He and his friend felt as if they had experienced a deliverance as great as that of Daniel from the lions' den. Such events were certainly a fiery trial for a young man, not yet twenty-five years old, to experience.

It is not known where Peter Williams lived when he first joined the Methodists, but before many years were past he settled at Llandyfaelog, near the main road from Kidwelly to Carmarthen. The name of his farmhouse was Gellilednais; it is about five miles from Carmarthen. He lived there for the rest of his life and is buried in Llandyfaelog cemetery nearby. He married and had many children. His wife was called Mary Jenkins, the daughter of a gentleman from the neighbourhood of Llanlluan. Little is known of her but that she was a quiet, virtuous woman, notable for her godliness. She outlived her husband by twenty-six years and was nearly a hundred when she died. She continued to attend worship until the end and is said to have ridden to the chapel within a fortnight of her death. As all loyal wives, her faith in her husband was limitless. In her old age, when her eyes had failed, she often had her grandchildren read a chapter of the Bible to her, and they had to read her husband's explanatory notes for her as well. She considered the notes to be almost as inspired as the chapter itself. They raised six children; three boys and three girls. Two of the sons – Ebenezer and Peter Bayley – became fairly well-known as learned and hard-working priests within the Established Church, but the third son, John, died when relatively young. The three daughters were called Deborah, Margaret and Beti. All three married and raised families. One was the mother of the Rev. David Humphreys, Llandyfaelog, a well-known minister amongst the Methodists, who is often compared by many of the older people to Ebenezer Morris. His daughter, and therefore the great granddaughter of Peter Williams, is Mrs Davies, the widow of R. J. Davies, Esq., Cwrtmawr. Many of Peter Williams's descendants, through his daughters, may be found today throughout Carmarthenshire and other counties, and the majority are still in fellowship with the Methodist Connexion.

## A LEADER AMONGST THE METHODISTS

We must return to Peter Williams's story. It is known that he was prominent amongst the Methodists from the very first. One reason was because he was an ordained minister, which was considered such an advantage at the time. But his many abilities and the extent of his learning were also crucial. In May, 1747, that is, within a year or so of joining the Methodists, we read of him preaching before Daniel Rowland, at the Quarterly Association at Cil-y-cwm. His text was, 'O how I love thy law,' and Howell Harris praised the sermon greatly for its scriptural nature. From this time we find him taking a leading part amongst them. Though not perhaps considered the equal of Rowland, Harris, Williams of Pantycelyn, and Howell Davies, he was yet very close to them and much more able than any other. The great feature of his sermons was their strong scriptural emphasis. He would never presume to ascend to the pulpit without preparation and so, while others often depended on the inspiration of the occasion, he was always consistent, biblical, and doctrinal, and always had something to say. This is why Williams, Pantycelyn, teased him, saying, 'You, Peter, can preach when the Holy Spirit is in France; but I cannot do a thing unless He is at my elbow.' John Evans of Bala said of him, 'Peter Williams was strong in mind and body. He laboured diligently and faithfully. His ministry was greatly blessed and was the means for the conversion of many.' One comment about him is that he was: 'A man with two themes,' which the following couplet describing his preaching explains:

| Two topics were ever present – | Y ddau iawn bwnc ganddo'n bod, |
| Man's evil and Christ's atonement. | Y camwedd a threfn y cymod. |

A man of Peter Williams's abilities would hardly confine himself to these 'two topics', yet they no doubt received special attention in his ministry in that all the great truths of God's salvation are necessarily linked with one or other of them. If it was the case that his theological knowledge was small at first, he soon made much progress and before long there were few of the Methodists who excelled him in the understanding of the principles of religion.

Peter Williams joined the Methodists at a crucial time, namely, at the very outbreak of the quarrel between Howell Harris and the other leaders. He was present at many Associations at which there were fierce arguments and strong feelings engendered. He was present, and preached, at the Llanidloes Association, which was the last, before the Disruption, where both Rowland and Harris were present. He does not seem to have taken part in the controversy. Perhaps he considered himself too much of a novice in the faith to contribute on the one side or the other. It might be conjectured, from the views that he afterwards expressed, that he would have taken Harris's side of the argument. His views of the Trinity would appear to have been very similar to those of Harris. Yet he cleaved to Daniel Rowland. Was he, perhaps, that fourth priest, present in the company of Rowland, Williams and Howell Davies at the Llantrisant Association of 1750, when it was decided to sever all connections with Harris? On the one hand, we do not know of any other priest, living at the time, who was likely to have been invited to such a meeting. But on the other, this would hardly be compatible with Peter Williams's presence at the first Association of Harris's people at St Nicholas. And what his purpose was at St Nicholas is a complete mystery. It is clear that he did not attend in order to join with them; he firmly refused to do so. We might conclude that his intention was to attempt to repair any break before it had gone too far, for when Harris made a speech detailing the evils of the behaviour of Rowland and of his followers and of the impossibility of uniting with them again except that they repented in sackcloth and ashes, Peter Williams left and, as far as we know, had no further connections with Harris's people for as long as they remained a separate party. When Harris was reconciled to the Methodists, thirteen years later, Peter Williams was one of the main leaders of the Connexion, second only to Rowland himself. We find that, together with the other leaders, he received the Reformer from Trefeca back with open arms. But it does not appear that there was any great friendship between them. Harris's two great friends throughout his life, despite all the clouds that had arisen between them, were Daniel Rowland and Williams, Pantycelyn. His soul was bound up with these two just as that of Jonathan with David.

## HE ENDURES MUCH PERSECUTION

The *Autobiography* written by Peter Williams concludes with the history of his first journey to north Wales. We have very little detailed knowledge of him after this. It is clear however that he spent his life as an itinerating preacher, and that he travelled across Wales, from Holyhead to Cardiff, dozens of times. Physically he was strong and hardy, able to withstand all kinds of weather. His spirit was courageous and bold, and he had no fear of the wrath of the persecutors. His ministerial gifts were appealing, he would often charm his hearers without their realizing it, and his commitment and perseverance were unending. It must also be remembered that, at least in his early years, he did not visit places according to some detailed, pre-announced itinerary, with kind friends waiting to welcome him at every stop. He had to work his way forward as best as he could, sending messages before him if at all possible to give notice of his arrival. At times the only welcome awaiting him would be a mob of persecutors, with stones and staves in their hands and their hearts full of anger. We cannot imagine the extent of his sufferings. In a letter which he wrote on 3 January 1747, he describes how he and others were arrested in their beds at Rhosllannerchrugog under a warrant signed by Sir Watkin Williams

Wynn; how they were examined by Sir Watkin at his home until evening, being given nothing to eat or drink, and how the trial ended by his being fined twenty pounds, and every one of his congregation five shillings each. After announcing the sentence they were all released. But about ten o'clock, the church-warden together with some constables arrived at Peter Williams's lodging demanding the payment of the fine. He was asked to pay. The senior constable then held his arms and the churchwarden searched his pockets, taking all the money that he had at the time, namely, a pound and two pence.

His main enemies were the priests of the Established Church. Some of these often came to his meetings in order to disrupt them, and when they were not present they were careful to engage ruffians to do the work. He was preaching once at Garnedd Fawr in Anglesey, when a clergyman came forward who had been a fellow student of his at Carmarthen Academy. 'Fie, Peter,' he said, 'how dare you preach in an unconsecrated place?' He answered, 'Forgive my ignorance. I was under the impression that the whole earth was consecrated to the gospel of Christ, ever since the days that he himself walked upon it.'

At another time when he was in Anglesey, he stood up to preach near an inn at Rhosllugwy. A crowd of unruly people had gathered, determined not to allow him to speak. They had not let him enter the inn nor allowed him to stable his horse. He, with no lack of courtesy but strong in faith, gave out the following hymn to sing:

| | |
|---|---|
| The earth belongs unto the Lord, | Yr Arglwydd biau'r ddaear lawr, |
| And all that it contains; | A'i llawnder mawr sydd eiddo; |
| The world that is inhabited, | Yr Arglwydd bia yr holl fyd, |
| And all that there remains. | A'r bobl i gyd sydd ynddo. |

Such an influence accompanied the announcing of the hymn that the rioters dropped their cudgels, horns and their other equipment for disrupting. The preacher was given complete freedom to deliver God's message, and many who were saved during that service were later to become strong pillars of the Saviour's cause in Anglesey.

Peter Williams was not only persecuted in the north, he was mistreated also in the south, even, indeed, in his own county. He was preaching one Sunday afternoon at a place called Cwmbach, near the parish church. He stood on a mounting-block and a crowd gathered to hear him. As he stood, the huntsman of Mr Pryse, Plasnewydd, the local magistrate, arrived. His intention, clearly, was to cause trouble, and just as clear was the fact that he had prepared himself for the task by much drinking. He approached the preacher with oaths and threats, full of bluster against the holding of such meetings. Mr Williams desisted for a while, asking if there were any present who could persuade the disrupter to leave. Two gentlemen attempted, one of them a certain Henry Pugh. They stopped the huntsman from attacking Mr Williams and succeeded in leading him away. As they were leaving, Peter Williams drew the attention of the crowd and in the most solemn tones declared, 'If I am a true ambassador for God as I speak to you today, you will find that that man will not die as do other men.' His words were true. Nine days later, the huntsman fell into a deep coal shaft and died from the fall. 'Surely there is a God who judges on earth.'

At Kidwelly, a town not far from his home, he once received as violent a reception as anything he had experienced elsewhere. It appears that this area was particularly godless. There is a tradition that Howell Harris was very badly treated there when he attempted to preach the gospel. Peter Williams arrived on Sunday afternoon and stood on a horse-block outside the house of a man called John Rees. A crowd of wastrels gathered, intent on disturbing matters. They were led by a giant of a man, of rough appearance, known as *Deio Goch* (*Red David*). Mr Williams had read a chapter of the Bible and had begun to pray, when *Deio Goch* jumped upon him, tore the Bible from his hand, and threw him down from the horse-block. It is said that these ruffians had been instructed what to do by the parish priest and had been drinking heavily beforehand to prepare themselves for the work. The preacher was now in their hands. They beat him mercilessly with their clubs, then placed him on his horse and drove him along the salt marsh, forcing him to jump over large ditches. It was a wonder that the horse did not break its legs, nor the rider his neck. They next took the preacher to the inn intending to make him drunk and so to present him an object of derision. 'Will you drink?' they asked. 'Yes, like an ox,' he replied. The ale was passed to him, but he secretly poured it, not down his throat, but into his top-boots until these were full. His wife, realizing that he was by now very late, sent the servants to look for him, and by their timely intervention he was rescued from the ruffians' clutches.

It would be pointless to attempt to describe all the privations endured by Peter Williams during his labours on behalf of the gospel in Wales. It is said that in 1766 he visited Llanrwst with the intention of preaching near the town hall. As he began, a young maidservant came out of a nearby house and attacked him, throwing rotten eggs at him so that his clothes were in an awful state. She then saw that a near relation of hers, a man called Gabriel Jones, was standing next to the preacher and was being hit by some of the eggs. She therefore stopped her throwing but a group of wastrels immediately took hold of him and dragged him down to the river. There, some of them held up his arms while the others gathered up water and poured it over him. As the temperature was freezing he was in grave danger of his life. The consequences might have been tragic had not a responsible man of good character, and of particularly strong physique, Richard Roberts of Tymawr, passed by. He was outraged by what he saw and rushed upon the scoundrels scattering them to all sides and saving the hapless victim from their grasp. Roberts then carried the preacher to his own home, provided all necessary treatment for him, and on the next day he accompanied him for three miles along the road, in case he again fell into the hands of his attackers. This Richard Roberts was not in any way a Methodist. He was a Churchman and remained so all his life, but his character displayed many Christian virtues and he could not bear to see a minister of the gospel mistreated.

Peter Williams would generally endure suffering without any attempt to defend himself. This was also the general Methodist response at first, but occasionally their patience wore thin and they appealed to the law of the land. Mr Williams was once abused dreadfully in Denbighshire; it was not sufficient for his persecutors to beat him but they also stole all that was in his possession. Having returned to the south he told his friends all that happened. They were indignant on his behalf and collected enough money to instigate a law suit. The case was placed in the hands of a lawyer from Brecon. As a result, eight of the main ringleaders were summoned to London to stand trial, amongst them a young man from a most respectable family. This youth was sufficiently wealthy to hire the best advocates to argue his case, but for all their efforts the defence failed and all eight were found guilty. The sentence passed upon them was that they were outlawed, that is they were deprived of all protection by the law. Feelings now turned against them and all declared their sentence to be just. They were therefore considered *personae non gratae* and could not remain in their localities. Some soon died. Others of them disappeared and were not heard of again. As for the rich young man, he went into hiding in exile until his parents were able to redeem his liberty and buy back for him again full legal rights. It is said that this legal judgment brought great relief to the Methodists – the gentry now becoming fearful of proceeding with further persecution.

As mentioned before, Peter Williams was predominantly a doctrinal preacher. He generally addressed the understanding and the conscience and did not often appeal to the feelings. There is room to believe that he had no great sympathy for the breaking out of rejoicing seen in many congregations during times of revival. Yet his own congregation not infrequently erupted in praise and worship under his own preaching. On one occasion, after his reconciliation to his brethren, Howell Harris was visiting Llangeitho and Peter Williams was preaching. The congregation as a whole was aflame with praises so that the heart of the Reformer of Trefeca rejoiced. There is another reference to Peter Williams found in the diary of one of the members of the Trefeca 'family'. The preacher was on a journey through Breconshire, after the death of Harris, and did not wish to return home without having preached at Trefeca. Evan Moses was the leader at Trefeca at the time, and it seems that he was no supporter of any over-indulgence of feelings in religious services. The following is the record:

Wednesday, 6 July, 1774. Peter Williams preached here. Gwen Vaughan began to jump. Evan Moses was most unwilling and demanded that she be still. But the students [those of the Countess of Huntingdon's College] took her side. But he [Evan Moses] testified strongly against her performance and told Mr Williams that he would have to give an account for encouraging such inappropriate behaviour. He argued that it resulted only from natural feelings, and that there was a great difference between a broken spirit and contrite heart and the proud, unbroken spirit which pertained to Gwen Vaughan. Mr Williams descended from the pulpit immediately Evan Moses told him he would have to give an account, responding that yes, most certainly, he would have to give an account.

This is the record, and it suggests that Peter Williams was of the same mind as Evan Moses as far as jumping and rejoicing were concerned.

## PETER WILLIAMS'S BIBLE, AND HIS OTHER LITERARY WORKS

It is fairly certain that as well as travelling the length and breadth of Wales Peter Williams was instrumental also in forming religious causes in his own county. It was he, as will be seen later, who built the Methodist chapel in Water Street, Carmarthen, mainly, if not completely, at his own cost. If it were only for his work as an evangelist, he would deserve a place of the highest standing amongst the Methodists fathers, yet it is no exaggeration to state that it was in another area completely that he fulfilled his greatest work and placed his nation under the greatest obligation. We are referring to his work as a commentator. His achievement in 1770 of publishing an edition of the Bible with notes on every chapter was the commencement of a new era in the history of religious literature in Wales. Very little of this nature had been done before. It seems that the Rev. Evan Evans (better known in Wales by his bardic *nom de plume, Ieuan Brydydd Hir*) had begun to write comments on the Bible on a not dissimilar plan to that of Peter Williams. But he had only completed a few books of the Old Testament and the work was never published. The only Welsh commentary published before Peter Williams's Bible was *The Harmony of the Four Gospels*, with a short introduction and doctrinal notes on passages considered most dark and difficult,[1] by the Rev. John Evans. John Evans had been raised at Meini Gwynion near Llanarth but had ministered at Plymouth and was therefore known in his native country as the 'Plymouth Priest'. Though the *Harmony* appeared in 1765, about five years before Peter Williams' Bible, yet Mr Williams must have begun his work at least as early as, if not earlier than, John Evans, so much greater was the scope of his work. It is not too much to say therefore that to Peter Williams belongs the honour of being the father of Welsh expositional commentary.

It is impossible to comprehend the influence wielded by '*Peter Williams's Bible*' upon the spiritual life of the nation. It was eagerly bought; no religious family within the Principality would be without it if they could somehow procure the money to buy it. Labourers put aside a little of their meagre earnings, and would almost go without food in order to possess a copy. During family worship, not only the appropriate Scripture chapter would be read but Peter Williams's comments also, and even good and godly men would almost consider that the comments were as inspired as the Bible. In vain would any dare to criticize them. Peter Williams's explanation on any matter would put an end to argument. It was viewed with the greatest respect, being considered an indispensable ingredient of the worship of God within the family. His comments would be remembered and discussed in the societies and they have proved to be food and nurture for Zion's travellers from the day they were first printed up to the present. Some today belittle his work, declaring that it does not bear comparison with many of the commentaries that are now available in Welsh. We would answer that it ought not to be compared with these. A true appreciation of the value of his comments is not to be gained without first remembering the state of education in Wales at the time they were written. There were very few books in the land, and most of these were out of the reach of the common people. The Sunday Schools had not been founded. The evangelist of Carmarthen was nearing the end of his career by the time Mr Charles, at the height of his powers, was striving to establish them. Very few in reality could read, although Griffith Jones's Circulating Schools were rapidly improving matters in this area. The only means within the reach of the common people for increasing in religious knowledge lay, therefore, in the ministry of the gospel or in the societies. For the peasant population of the time nothing could have been better than the expositions of Peter Williams. After taking all factors into consideration, the wonder of his achievement is that his comments are still today so substantial, valuable, and complete in nature.

He followed his own plan and his own image is clear in every comment. He was not however without the use of reference books, of which the most important perhaps was the commentary of the Swiss author, Sternward, which had recently been translated. Mr Williams had two main principles in mind when producing his commentary: in the first place, that it should contain sufficient matter to be a substantial spiritual help to his fellow Welshmen; and secondly, that he should not write above the level of the common people and his labours thus prove to be unprofitable. In both these areas he was eminently successful.

Immense labour was required for the preparation of such a work and it is amazing that he accomplished it when we consider his constant travelling to preach the gospel. The financial risk of printing 8,600 copies was also great, particularly when we remember that the population of the country was little more than a third of what it is today. Many of the brethren whom he consulted for advice believed it would be folly to proceed and advised him to give up the idea. But so great was his zeal and so strong his faith that he set his face as a flint. The consequences proved that his was the correct judgment, and the venture was crowned with success. The first edition was sold out within a few years and a second printing was soon necessary.

As well as his *Bible Commentary*, Peter Williams published a *Scriptural Concordance*, which, although not completely original, proved of great value to the nation. Mr Charles spoke very highly of it, and it gained a wide circulation. To Peter Williams also goes the honour of being the first to produce a Welsh periodical, to which he gave the name *Trysorfa Gwybodaeth*, or *Yr Eurgrawn Cymraeg* (*A Treasury of Knowledge*, or *The Welsh Treasury*). This was a fortnightly magazine, costing three pence. Only fifteen issues appeared. By today there are a great many Welsh periodicals, but Peter Williams's *Treasury of Knowledge* was the first sheaf of that harvest. As well as the *Family Bible*, the *Concordance*, and the *John Canne Bible*, to which we shall refer later, he published many small booklets on various topics, some original and some translations from English, but all tending to improve his fellow Welshmen morally and spiritually. He wrote a good deal of excellent poetry from time to time but as a contemporary of such a brilliant star as Williams, Pantycelyn, he was never very prominent.

These facts show clearly however the unremitting nature of his labours and his indefatigable energies.

## HIS EXCOMMUNICATION FROM THE METHODISTS

We have mentioned that his *Bible*, with its comments on every chapter, was Peter Williams's main achievement but it proved also to be the beginning of his sorrows and, eventually, the cause of his excommunication from the Methodist Connexion. We would be glad to be able to bypass this matter but it is so well-known that it cannot be ignored. In his first edition of the Bible, in the notes on John, chapter 1, is found the following comment:

> The mind of God is equivalent to his will, and his will is equivalent to his word (because there in no change in him), and he willed, before the existence of any world or angel, to place Christ as head over the world; therefore God is Father, Son, and Holy Spirit, from eternity, in his own eternal will; not 'in a necessary mode of existence, even if no man was to be saved nor one soul to be sanctified', as some in their ignorance state; but because he willed to save and sanctify; for Christ (in whom the wisdom of God chiefly appears) was the delight of the Father in the beginning of his way; and the Alpha and Omega of all his works; in agreement with the which will, the Word (in the fullness of time) was made flesh and dwelt among us – and some beheld his glory, and believed that Jesus was God! Not 'God by ordination' as some foolishly speak, but that he is the only true and living God – for the Scriptures witness that the Man Jesus is the eternal Father; and what Christian would endure the blasphemy of those who deny the Deity of Christ?

His meaning is not entirely clear in this paragraph. The words are not perhaps completely inconsistent with the view that the Godhead has always existed essentially as Three Persons, but of this essential existence we have no certain knowledge in that it has not been revealed; what we do know is that the relationships between the Divine Persons in the plan of salvation for sinners are denoted by the names Father, Son and Holy Spirit. If this is what he meant he was most unfortunate in his choice of words, to say the least. How soon it was before the leaders of the Methodists noted the comment and brought the author's case before the Association, accusing him of Sabellianism, is not known. The probability is that this did not occur before the publication of the second edition of *Peter Williams's Bible* in 1781, containing the identical comments. Soon after this date the topic was the cause of heated and painful controversy in many Associations. The history of the debate is not known but Peter Williams referred to it in one of his letters written towards the close of his life. He wrote:

I suspect that some were stirring up strife by resurrecting the old controversy concerning the Sonship of our Saviour Jesus Christ; namely, whether he was begotten by eternal generation from the essence of the Father, as some say, or whether, as I humbly think, he was termed the Son because of his human nature generated by the Holy Spirit. Psalm 2:7.

This quotation proves that a distressing disagreement on the topic had occurred in their midst. The Association generally would surely have disapproved his comment. It would have been impossible for Daniel Rowland not to have done so after the stance he took in his argument with Howell Harris, and no doubt William Williams would be in agreement with him. On the other hand, though there was a party that called for Peter Williams's excommunication, Rowland and Williams were strongly against such extreme measures. Very possibly they were both sorry that they had been so hasty with Harris, and the unfortunate results of that disruption weighed heavily upon them. The maturity of years and the beginning of old age had taught them to be tolerant. Neither therefore would hear anything of excommunication but were satisfied with a declaration of disapproval of Peter Williams's comments and an administering of a rebuke. Quite probably the rebuke from Rowland was severe, but the Commentator knew that it arose out of love and he was able therefore to bear it. He could write, later, in his elegy to Rowland:

| | |
|---|---|
| Rowland, I will ne'er forget thee, | O, mrawd Rowland, ni'th anghofiaf, |
| Nor thy frequent reprimands; | Ti roddaist i mi lawer sen; |
| Yet in every storm and trouble, | Ymhob tywydd, ymhob dirmyg, |
| Who but thee would heal my wounds. | Pwy ond ti orchuddiai 'mhen. |

The storm passed for a while and Peter Williams was free to itinerate as usual, to preach the gospel and sell his books. But about the year 1790, the storm clouds gathered again with much greater ferocity. The cause was as follows. During the year noted Peter Williams brought out a small-sized edition of the Bible with the marginal references of John Canne and his own comments at the bottom of each page. Most probably he undertook this task after receiving the approbation of his brethren and their promise of helping with the distribution. The edition carried explanatory notes on the Trinity and on the Sonship of Christ which were not dissimilar to those that had appeared in the *Family Bible*. Indeed, if anything, the Commentator had used even stronger language in putting forth his own particular views.

Inevitably, this served to rekindle the flames. In order to arrive at clearer knowledge of Peter Williams's views on the Trinity we will quote a few phrases from an essay he wrote soon after he was excommunicated and entitled, *Dirgelwch Duwioldeb* (*The Mystery of Godliness*). He stated:

> It is essential to believe that there is in the unity of the Godhead a Trinity, namely Three Persons in one God, and called in the Scriptures, the Father, the Son, and the Holy Spirit. But the reader must not understand this as involving three different essences, for this would be contrary to the unity of God. No, they are rather Three Persons of one essence.

What could be more orthodox? Later, he wrote:

> The Father is the fountainhead of Deity, for God through the Spirit begot the Son of the virgin Mary. And, as stated in the Creed, the Spirit proceeds from the Father and the Son.

But a degree of confusion soon enters; a confusion of ideas as well as a lack of clarity of expression:

> They who are taught of God to see the blessed Trinity in the flesh of the man Christ Jesus (however deficient they may be in human understanding) may testify from experience that this view of him quickens their souls.

Again:

> I do not dare to say that a Trinity is essentially necessary in God, as some blasphemously claim, but I will say, and believe, that a Trinity is completely necessary in order to reveal God to the heirs of eternal life.

And again:

> God is One, and the Son is in him as the mistletoe is in the tree, living by the life of the tree, not having any other root.

A further example:

> 'A Second Person,' they say [that is, Peter Williams' detractors], 'generated by God'! It is impossible for God to generate another God. If God generated God, it must be that the one who was generated is less than the one who generated. Is not such an unfounded doctrine a disgrace to Christianity?

And again:

> A Second Person generated by the Father in eternity, out of himself, and in his own image, is but an imaginary person, with no mention of him in the Bible.

And finally:

> . . . so have the Three Persons prepared themselves for the work of salvation, or, as can be said, God has adapted himself under the names of Father, Son, and Holy Spirit.

Clearly many of these references contain inappropriate statements, to say the least, concerning the Trinity and the Person of our Lord, and unless it is supposed that they are due to confusion of thought and phrasing, and an inability to express arguments clearly, it is very difficult not to agree with the accusation that Peter Williams was strongly inclined towards Sabellianism.

Another factor involved in the publication of *John Canne's Bible* that contributed to the bitterness felt against Peter Williams, was his willingness to change the translation in many places. For many of the Methodists the Welsh translation of the Bible was almost as inspired as the Scriptures themselves. For anybody, however well educated, to attempt to change a phrase, or even a word, would be considered an awful presumption. If anyone attempted it he would be sure of receiving the weight of the Methodists' disapproval. When it was understood that Peter Williams had presumed to include changes a general protest arose. He was accused of doing so in order to shape verses to fit his own system. It does not appear that the majority of his changes in reality were very important and we tend to believe that he had no such motive in mind. On the other hand, it must be acknowledged that it is easy to understand how some of the changes could give rise to suspicion. For the verse, Proverbs 8:25, where it is understood that Christ declares: 'Before the mountains were settled, before the hills was I brought forth,' Peter Williams has the translation, 'Before the hills was I born.' And as he denied that Christ was generated from eternity, other than in the abstract, this change produced suspicion in the minds of many good men. His explanation was that the word in the original carried the meaning that he gave it. In Isaiah 53:10, instead of, 'When he gave his soul an offering for sin,' [according to the 1588 Welsh translation], he had, 'When he gave himself an offering for sin.' He gave two reasons for this: that the word in the original signified the whole man; and that he wished to forestall the error of those who believed that it is only the soul of man that sins and that therefore only the soul of the Saviour needed to suffer.

No translator, however, has the right to decide on a particular reading merely to forestall error. In the twelfth verse of the same chapter, for 'He shall divide the spoil with the strong,' he has, 'He shall possess the spoil of the strong.' In Hebrews 5:9, instead of, 'He was made the author of eternal salvation' [1588], he has, 'He became the author of eternal salvation.' Many of his changes produced no difference in meaning whatsoever, but because of the crime, in the eyes of many, of tampering in any way with the Welsh translation, on top of the very mixed wording (if not worse) of his comments on the doctrine of the Trinity, a very strong tide arose against the Carmarthenshire commentator.

Before pursuing the controversy to its close, it is worth noting that throughout this period in which he was preparing an edition of the *Canne Bible* for the press, Peter Williams was labouring as diligently as ever in the preaching of the Word. A notable proof of this is found in a letter in his own handwriting which has not been published before and which is preserved at Trefeca.[2] We reproduce as it was written because of its intrinsic interest:

> Carmarthen, 22 August, 1789. My friends, I hope you are well, even as I am, by grace. Please find enclosed Gig 4X; please note, have you received every sheet which you should have? Mr Wosencroft told me that his friend left the one entrusted to him either with Longfellow at Brecon, or at the post-house. If you have not received it I will make further enquiries. I have presumed throughout to change the occasional word in the translation; and I trust that, in the Lord, you will judge impartially; and if you see me straying, follow the old paths! I believe that you are in my debt for one proof copy, but do not fear that I will escape too far from you! I find Mr Canne's Bible to be more and more profitable the more I work on it, and if it does not suffer injury in the press it will be excellent. You sent me two proof sheets the last time. Whether deliberately or accidentally I do not know; but one of them was too dark! And I threw it away. Next Sunday I am going to Capel Colby, or the new chapel, near to Cardigan, and intend to return on Tuesday in order to proceed with the work. May the gospel prosper more and more, for all the strength of the enemy. And may God's blessing be upon every godly purpose and benefit to Zion, and to the building of the new Jerusalem! is the wish of your fellow-pilgrim and your friend in that love which has no end – Peter Williams.

It would appear that this letter was sent to the manager of the press at Trefeca, where the Bible was being printed. It is evident that Peter Williams, although approaching his 69th birthday, was full of the work of preaching the gospel, and continuing with his itinerating over considerable distances. It needs also to be pointed out that the Rev. David Jones, a minister with the Baptists, was associated with him in publishing Canne's Bible, but it is said that the bulk of the work fell upon Mr Williams' shoulders.

The tempest fell upon Peter Williams in its full force in the year 1790, at which time his views were the topic of bitter argument in many of the Associations, in the north and the south. His main opponent, according to tradition, was the Rev. Nathaniel Rowland, the son of the old evangelist of Llangeitho. He was a very ambitious man, full of pride, and desirous of ruling the Association, and he no doubt considered that if he could remove Peter Williams his path to the throne would be clear. Daniel Rowland was failing and could not travel from home, and died, as we have seen, in October 1790. The weaknesses of old age were getting the better of Williams, Pantycelyn, also, who died the following January. There was no one therefore from amongst the old companions of the Commentator able to be present at the Association to defend him. It is said that Rowland, whilst strongly disagreeing with his friend's views, did not wish to discipline him severely, and when his son returned home from some meeting, boasting that he had succeeded in obtaining a vote of censure against Peter Williams, he cried out, saying, 'Nat, Nat, you have condemned your better!' Supporting Nathaniel Rowland was Griffiths of Nevern, another clergyman, and there was no one in the Association with the strength to withstand these two acting together. It must be said also that Peter Williams himself was stubborn and uncompromising. His tone when defending himself was bitter. He refused to moderate his phrases or to revise his forms of expression, in order to conform to the views of his brethren. How true the saying that the strength and weakness of a man arise from the same source! Now, the strong, inflexible will of the old minister of Carmarthen, which enabled him to withstand the wrath and persecution of his enemies, moved him to stubbornness when friends were seeking to persuade him.

His biographer, Owen Williams, states that the argument began at the Bala Association when Daniel Rowland was present, and that Peter Williams defended himself so strongly and reasonably from the Scriptures that his accusers were struck dumb; and that when Rowland was asked to rebut him he refused, saying that the matter was too important, and that he did not have sufficient understanding to know whether Peter Williams was erring or not. It is said that the only one who dared to speak against Williams at that Association was Richard Tibbott who, although he had joined the Independents, attended the Methodists' assemblies and took part in their debates. It is to be regretted that the Commentator had no better biographer. Owen Williams, quite apart from other disqualifications, was deeply prejudiced against the Methodists. The matter was under discussion again at the Aberystwyth Association, when Daniel Rowland was not present, and it was here, it is supposed, that Nathaniel Rowland took a leading part in the discussion. At the Llanidloes Association of 1791, after a lengthy investigation, the fraternity decided that Peter Williams had to be thrown out unless he rejected all the views that he had propagated and promised not to publicize them again. He himself was not present so a letter was sent to him informing him of the decision. He writes of this in a letter to a friend:

I received an unloving letter from my brethren at Llanidloes; this caused me much grief of heart.

But he would not withdraw his words, nor promise not to repeat them in print. On this, he would not be moved, and the result was that he was eventually excommunicated at the Llandeilo Association of 1791. We do not have the account of the debate and do not therefore know who took part. There is no doubt that Peter Williams's main opponent was Nathaniel Rowland, who was held in great respect on account of his famous father. Traditionally, he alone bears the responsibility for the action, the main body of the Connexion being considered passive. It is true that the Rev. Thomas Charles of Bala, together with his brother, Mr David Charles of Carmarthen, were present but it does not appear that they contributed to the discussion. The Rev. Thomas Charles bore no ill-will to the old Commentator. He was of the same age as his son, Mr Eliezer Williams, with whom he had been a student, and it was said that he was on friendly terms, if not more, with one of his daughters. It is known of him also that he was one of the peacemakers of Israel. But he was relatively young and had not been with the Methodists many years, so it was hardly appropriate for him to intervene in such an important matter, he could hardly dare to oppose two clergymen of such stature. As for David Charles, he also was a young man and it is hard to imagine him saying a word in the circumstances.

We know that there was a tradition in the Williams family, and it remains to this present day, that the brothers Charles proved unfaithful to Peter at the Association, and that they bore some of the responsibility for his excommunication. Because of this, relations between the two families were not the best for some time. If there was any foundation for the tradition it is probably due to the silence of the Charleses when, according to Peter Williams's friends, they should have spoken.

There has been much criticism of the Methodists for their treatment of Peter Williams. It is suggested that jealousy was involved, and that they were narrow, uncharitable, and acted as if they were infallible. As far as Nathaniel Rowland and other specific opponents were concerned, there might well have been personal antipathies at work, but it is impossible to believe so for the main body of the Association. If personal feelings had come into play, the probability is that the Commentator would not have been thrown out, because of his age, his high standing, and his great usefulness. It is necessary also to underline again the fact that the majority of the body were neutral in the matter. The great emphasis placed on orthodoxy in those days must also be remembered; that a lapse in judgment on the main topics of the gospel was considered worse even than a lapse in morals. Our fathers paid great homage to the truth; they believed that the faith once delivered to the saints was worth suffering for, and merited the sacrifice of friendship and personal feelings when necessary. Who would presume to say that they were wrong in this? Is not much of the liberality and tolerance manifested when dubious doctrines are being aired – a liberality and tolerance so praised in this present age – nothing more than indifference and lack of heartfelt faithfulness to the truth? It is hard not to sympathize with Peter Williams when we see him, in his old age, exiled from amongst his brethren and friends, because of his defence of that which he considered true doctrine. The Assembly itself was also the object of pity in that many had eyes full of tears as they witnessed his departure. John Hughes commented in *Methodistiaeth Cymru*:

> If any injustice was done to him, it was done mistakenly and not deliberately; if he was thrown out in too much haste and discourtesy, it was done in the heat of argument and the shock of controversy.

We are quite certain, from our knowledge of the chief men of the Methodists at the time, that they were generally undecided in their view of the injustice – if it was indeed an injustice – and they would not have been so undecided had not the incautious expressions of the Commentator caused them much uncertainty.

His excommunication by the Methodists proved a tragedy to Peter Williams for not only were the Methodist chapels now closed to him, and the Methodist members warned not to attend his ministry, but because of these steps the sale of the small Bible he had produced, the *John Canne Bible*, was greatly hindered. His biographer, Owen Williams, Waunfawr, berates the Methodists furiously because of this, accusing them of breaking their word to him. On this point again it is quite evident that he does them an injustice. They had made no promise to support the sale of a book that, in their view, contained comments that were erroneous and dangerous. If there was any breaking of promises in the matter, it was done by Peter Williams when he included in his Bible notes for which the Methodists had already expressed their total rejection. As a result, Peter Williams and David Jones were left with thousands of Bibles on their hands, and the venture proved very costly to them. After being thrown out, the old Commentator continued with his itinerating as before but his old friends kept away from him. The other denominations opened their doors to him, but there is room to believe that they did not do so in every case out of compassion for his situation, or out of sympathy for his views, but because they enjoyed the opportunity of welcoming one whom the

Methodists had refused. But if any group anticipated that he would join with them they were disappointed. He never showed any indication of wishing to become a member of any other religious party; indeed, it does not appear that any such idea ever entered his head. He rather appealed again and again to his brethren in the Association that they would reconsider his case. His letters of appeal have been preserved and they reveal his learning, his thorough knowledge of the Scriptures, and a high degree of reasoning ability; they reveal also much of a very bitter spirit. But in that they did not reveal the least indication that he was willing to withdraw a thing, nor to stop defending his particular views, the Association would not receive his appeal. His cleaving on the one side, and the Association on the other, to that which they each considered to be the truth, however strong the pressures for a compromise, are clear indications of the thorough conscientiousness of both parties.

But we cannot but grieve that he gave way to the temptation to attend the Bala Association and so place himself and his old friends in such a bitter tribulation. His biographer states that he was refused leave to preach from the platform. We doubt whether he would have sought this; if he did, it was with the certain knowledge that his request would be refused. There was not the slightest justification for allowing someone who had been excommunicated for error to preach in a most public position, and on behalf of the denomination that had excommunicated him. Instead, between services, when the streets were full of people, Peter Williams stood up at a street corner to preach. He must have been motivated by a longing to receive sympathy and to shame the Methodists. It must be acknowledged however that he never expressed one word of disrespect towards any, and that often during the sermon he referred with praise to the earlier sermons of the day. But those who saw him were saddened that he had placed himself in such a situation.

## HIS FINAL YEARS, AND TRIBUTES TO HIS CHARACTER

Peter Williams did not depend on his itinerating for opportunities to preach or to obtain hearers. It was he, as has been noted, who had built the chapel at Water Street, Carmarthen, at his own expense. It does not appear that the chapel had been placed in the hands of trustees nor transferred to the Methodists.

Legally, therefore, it was his personal property. And it was mainly here, during the last years of his life, that he preached the gospel, without being a member of any party. He lived for some five years after the Llandeilo Association. His health weakened gradually and his strong constitution gave way, but he continued to preach and to study for as long as possible. In order to illustrate his spiritual state we include parts of a letter which was written by his son, the Rev. Peter Bailey Williams of Llanrug, on 5 August, 1796; three days before his death:

My dear brother,

From every indication, my next letter to you will bear the news of the death of my dear father ... He preached at Carmarthen a fortnight last Sunday, and at Llanlluan the following Sunday. On the first Sunday he preached powerfully and effectively to a large congregation, and on the second, it proved impossible even for the most careless to resist his solemn appeals. But what added to the seriousness of the occasion was that he spoke and looked like a dying man, and the whole congregation wept at the prospect of not seeing him ever again. He continues to rise each morning, or at least he did so until a few days ago, and follows his usual studies. He is remarkably godly in spirit and completely content for all his weariness. He maintained family worship for as long as he could speak. Last Sunday, he asked Bowen, who was present, to pray, explaining that he was unable because of his breathlessness. 'While I could,' he said, 'it was my sweetest duty to draw near to the throne of grace.'

Yesterday, when my mother brought him a little flummery and wine, he stood up to ask a blessing, though unsteady through weakness and not able to express himself understandably just before. He said the following as clearly as I ever heard him, 'Dear Lord, may I have the privilege of coming before thee one more time and speaking to thee to ask thy blessing. What shall I say? Thou art wondrous in all ways, this side of destruction and hell. Teach us to bow to thy will, and to say with old Eli, "It is the Lord; let him do as he sees best."' My mother is deeply afflicted and far from being well; I fear that she will not be long after him. I have arranged to sell the chapel in Water Street in order to pay his debts. Have you any objection? The Methodists have offered £250 for it. The profit from the large Bible will be sufficient to meet the costs of the little Bible, and another £200 or so will cover the rest. He has made his will, leaving all to my mother, of course, and after her death anything remaining will go to David Humphreys and his children. I have watched over my father, night and day, since I came home, and I have never before encountered such a heavenly attitude. 'I went on my knees to pray to my dear Saviour,' he said one day, 'but I was so weak I could scarcely rise from my knees.' A day or two ago a local clergyman visited him and his only serious contribution was to counsel my father not to become sad, or in his own words, 'not to let your heart get down'. 'It cannot go far, sir,' was my father's ready reply, 'for it is on the rock.' My paper forces me to end; my next letter, I fear, will bring bad news.

We can only consider one or two things from this very interesting letter. The 'David Humphreys' referred to was Peter Williams's son-in-law, and the father of the Rev. David Humphreys, Llandyfaelog. We may suppose, as the chapel at Llanlluan where Peter Williams preached his last sermon on earth was owned by the Methodists, that during his last years he was being allowed to preach in some of the Connexion's chapels. We do not know how to reconcile what is said concerning the Water Street chapel with the report given to the late Rev. J. Wyndham Lewis by one of the elders of the place that Peter Williams set out in his will that the Methodists were to have the chapel provided they gave three hundred pounds to his trustees. Nevertheless, whether by his will or by agreement with his sons, the chapel was sold to the Methodists for three hundred pounds in the year 1797. The first trustees included three clergymen, namely, the Revs. David Jones, Llan-gan; Griffiths, Nevern; Davies, Abernant; and three laymen, Messrs. David Charles; W. Lloyd, Henllan; and J. Bowen, Tygwyn, Llangunnor.

On Monday, 8 August 1796, Peter Williams died, aged 76 years old. He was buried in Llandyfaelog cemetery. On his gravestone is seen:

> Here lie the remains of the Reverend Peter Williams, late of Gellilednais in this parish. He consecrated his whole life to the uplifting of his fellow-countrymen both temporally and spiritually. To this end he published three editions of the quarto Bible in Welsh with comments on each chapter. He published also an edition of an octavo Bible, a Welsh Concordance, together with many small essays, mainly in Welsh. For all these, it may accurately be said, he received nothing but ingratitude and persecution. He continued to labour faithfully and diligently as a minister of the gospel for 53 years; and died, rejoicing in God his Saviour, 8 August 1796, when 76 years old. 'For it was not an enemy that reproached me; then I could have borne it: neither was it he that hated me that did magnify himself against me. But it was you, with whom I took sweet counsel together and walked to the house of God in company.'

No doubt it was his sons who were responsible for the epitaph, and it was only natural for them to sympathize with their father; but it was a shame that they should make a cemetery and a gravestone the opportunity for the expression of their bitterness.

In *Methodistiaeth Cymru* it is said that the excommunication of Peter Williams did not affect the Connexion as much as might have been expected; that there were hardly any departures from the body because of it, though there was much sympathy towards him, and great respect, in the minds of all who knew him. On the whole this is certainly true. Yet, as far as we can make out, the common people though unable to follow the details of the discussion, still felt that the old Commentator had been hard done by. Large numbers of Methodists felt the same, though they did not go so far as to leave the Connexion because of it. One important secession that did take place occured in the Vale of Glamorgan, under the leadership of Thomas William, afterwards, the Rev. Thomas William of Bethesda'r Fro.

This man deserves some attention. He was born in a farmhouse called Trerhedin in the parish of Pendeulwyn, not far from Cowbridge, Glamorgan. His father was a farmer of some substance. He was thoughtful and serious even as a child, and when he was ten years old he joined the Methodist society at Tre-hill. He nearly despaired when joining them when, on his failing to answer a question put to him by the leader of the meeting, it was suggested he be refused entry until he had better learnt his lesson. But Thomas William soon showed his progress. He started attending the prayer meeting and the societies and soon no such meetings throughout the Vale were considered complete without his presence. It is very likely that he was considered something of an exhorter, although there is no evidence of him being acknowledged as such in the Monthly Meeting.

In 1790, as a result of his marriage, he went to live at Fonmon in Penmarc parish; he was probably a member at Aberthaw. He was very much in agreement with Peter Williams's views. Whether there were many others of the same views at Aberthaw is not known, but, from the beginning, a strong party at Aberthin nearby tended towards Sabellianism. When Peter Williams was excommunicated, Thomas William together with those of similar views from the societies of the Vale turned their backs upon the Methodists and formed a group on their own. They met for worship at three different locations: Thomas William's home at Pen-marc; a rented house in Aberthin; and another house in Burton. For some years they had no one to administer the sacraments to them, but in 1789 they chose Thomas William as minister, ordaining him by the laying on of the hands of the elders, together with prayer and fasting. The secretary of the churches was John Williams, St Athan, a very able poet, author of the well-known hymn:

Who is this from Edom coming?    Pwy welaf o Edom yn dod?

As already mentioned, Thomas William was a great admirer of the old Commentator; his heart burned within him as he saw the injustice, as he judged it, that he received at the hands of the Methodists. When Peter Williams died he wrote an elegy for him in which he scourged his opponents severely. The following stanzas give an indication of the poem's tone:

Behold an ox, of mighty labour,
From the threshing floor has gone;
Long and hard his day of service,
Peace at last he now has won;
Oft a target for men's arrows,
Now he need not fear them more,
Prejudice and jealous hatred,
Never reach that further shore.

Peter, when your name is mentioned,
Longing rises in my heart,
You, I loved, and you who loved me,
It was hard with you to part;
We were dear to one another,
How I loved your company,
And beyond the love of women,
Was your sympathy to me.

Many men spoke out against you,
Some of them, men of renown,
Others of much lower station
Sought to trample your name down;
You were mocked by all and sundry,
You were mocked by small and great,
E'en your mother's children viewed you
As an object of their hate.

Not in love they reprimanded,
They, the righteous and the good,
For their sweetest oils appointed
Left him sore in wounds and blood;
In the house of friends he suffered,
In the even of his days,
Now at last, in heaven, unblemished,
Hear him sing his Saviour's praise.

Why a harrow to thrash lentils?
(How your brethren wandered so)
Used a wagon wheel on cummin,
When the least of rods would do;
Sharp-edged words that cut like daggers,
Without mercy at you thrown,
Fiery arrows and mortal weapons
Were their choice to bring you down.

Dacw ych o lawr y dyrnu,
Wedi myned eto i'r lan;
Hir ddydd gwresog iawn y gweithiodd,
Heddiw safodd yn ei ran;
Fe fu'n nod i saethau lawer,
Darfu hynny, fe aeth trwy,
Ni ddaw rhagfarn nac anghariad
Byth i'r lle mae'n aros mwy.

Peter, mae llythrennau d'enw
Yn creu hiraeth dan fy mron;
Dyn a gerais, dyn a'm carodd,
Meddwl dy fod dan y don;
Annwyl oeddem yn ein bywyd,
Cu iawn gennyf oeddit ti,
A thu hwnt i gariad gwragedd
Oedd dy gariad ataf fi.

Fe chwedleuodd yn dy erbyn
Ddynion rai o ddoniau mawr,
Dynion eraill isel raddau
Geisiodd dynnu d'enw lawr;
Ti ge'st wawd oddiwrth bob enw,
Ti ge'st wawd oddiwrth bob dawn,
Plant dy fam edrychent arnat
Megis estron dieithr iawn.

Ca'dd ei guro, nid mewn cariad,
Gan y cyfiawn is y nen;
Waith eu holew pennaf dorodd
Glwyfau dyfnion ar ei ben;
Ond mae'r clwyfau dyfnion hynny,
Heddiw'n holliach yn y nef,
Ga'dd e'n nhy ei garedigion,
Ym mhrynhawn ei fywyd ef.

Cymryd og i ddyrnu ffacbys
Wnaeth dy frodyr (gwyro 'mhell),
Troisant olwyn men ar gwmin,
Pan oedd gwiail lawer gwell;
Geiriau llym fel brath cleddyfau,
Leflwyd atat heb un rhi',
Saethau tan ac arfau marwol
Gym'rwyd i'th geryddu di.

For refusing Athanasius,
As have many men before,
Old Sabellius was thrown at you,
Often his reproach you bore;
Creeds, confessions, catechisms,
Articles to fence the fold,
Only strife and broken churches
Were the effects of these of old.

Am wrthod credo Athanasius,
Fel gwnaeth gwyr o ddoniau maith:
Fe siglwyd urn yr hen Sabellius
Yn dy wyneb lawer gwaith;
Cyffes ffydd, a llunio credo,
Gwneud articlau mawr eu clod,
Magu 'mryson, rhannu eglwysi,
Fu effeithiau rhain erioed.

Far from all their noise and hatred,
On the wings of doves you flew,
From the storm and roaring tempest,
To those regions ever new;
Where the myriads of the weary,
Once in prison, once in shame,
Now are resting from enduring
All reproaches for his Name.

Tithau gym'raist aden c'lomen,
Est o'u swn yn ddigon pell,
Draw o'r dymhestl a'r gwynt stormus,
I ardaloedd llawer gwell;
Lle mae myrdd o rai lluddedig,
Fu mewn carchar, fu mewn tan,
Yno'n gorffwys wedi gorffen
Eu cystuddiau mawr yn lan.

Affection is evident in every line of this elegy, and for a season it was very popular. It is not known whether Thomas William and those associated with him intended to begin a new denomination. If they did, the attempt proved a failure. In time, he made the acquaintance of the Independents, and in 1814 he was received, together with those who still cleaved to him, into the Independent fold. Whether they were examined on their doctrinal beliefs is not known. By this time they had left Burton and had settled at Bethesda'r Fro. Thomas William was the sweetest of preachers; his sermons were always about twenty minutes in length, and during the last five minutes the whole congregation would be on their feet, like a grove of trees, so great would be the influence upon them. But he was never very successful at all, as is proved by the following verses written by him after more than thirty years of ministerial labour:

Now, for thirty years I've laboured,
Thirty years the seed have borne,
But that seed has fallen mainly
On the road, the rock, the thorn;
Very little found the good soil,
Little indeed, yet there was some,
May the dew of heaven refresh it,
That some fruit one day might come.

Deg-ar-hugain o flynyddau,
Bum yn hau trwy hyd y rhain,
Syrthio wnaeth yr had gan fwyaf,
Wrth y ffordd, y graig, a'r drain;
Mewn tir da ni syrthiodd nemawr,
Nemawr iawn – fe syrthiodd peth,
Gwlith y nef aroso arno,
Fel nad elo byth ar feth.

O Bethesda, how ungrateful!
And forgetful of your God;
Having sown and sown aplenty,
Nothing rises from the sod;

O Bethesda anniolchgar,
Ac anghofus iawn o Dduw,
Wedi hau, a hau drachefn,
Braidd eginyn sydd yn fyw;

Nearly all the older brethren
Have departed, rich in grace,
With no signs of others rising,
Others who will take their place.

Mae'r hen frodyr, ond rhyw 'chydig,
Wedi myned draw i dre,
Ac nid oes arwyddion nemawr
Am rai eraill yn eu lle.

O that from the south, a preacher
Might arise, or from the north,
East or west, it does not matter,
Only that the Word go forth;
Let him be by heaven appointed,
(If not so, he'll toil in vain)
And Bethesda hear the gospel,
And rejoice in Christ again.

O na ddoi rhyw un o'r Gogledd,
Neu o'r Dwyrain, ynte'r De,
O'r Gorllewin, neu o rywle,
Ni waeth gennyf ddim o ble;
Ond i'r nefoedd fawr ei anfon,
Heb ei anfon, thal ef ddim,
I Bethesda i bregethu
Gair y bywyd yn ei rym.

It is an interesting question – how could the ministry of a man of such brilliant talents prove so unsuccessful? Dr Thomas Rees attributes the lack of success to the fact that Thomas William ministered to his people without remuneration. He considers a church that does not pay as much an obstacle to its own success as a church that does not pray. No doubt there is an element of truth in this, but there must have been other reasons that are not now known. Whatever the reason, Thomas William was an unsuccessful minister. He had a long life, and died on 23 November, 1844, at 84 years of age.

We have stayed with Thomas William for some time because he is the only well-known name (apart from his friend, the secretary of his church, John Williams of St Athan) who left the Methodists because of Peter Williams's excommunication and tried to establish separate churches. But to return to Peter Williams: It is said that he was of gentlemanlike and dignified appearance, fairly tall, with rather a long, pale face. He was always neat and tidy in his dress and person. He had a strong physique and a determined and courageous spirit, and was as if exactly adapted in mind and body for the situation in Wales at the time. There is no doubting his godliness and integrity. Whatever mistakes he made, his motivation was pure and his single purpose was the glory of God and the good of souls. The remembrance of him is still fragrant today. And though the Methodists felt it necessary to break all connection with him, they maintained a deep respect for him while he lived, and for his memory after his death. In the first issue of *Y Drysorfa Ysbrydol* [*The Spiritual Treasury*] there is a memoir of him, by the Rev. Thomas Charles most probably, in which there is not one word of criticism; he is held up, rather, as a man who was most useful in his time. Says Mr Charles:

Mr Peter Williams possessed the strongest endowments of mind and body; a brave spirit but yet gentle and affectionate to his friends and family; and committing all his energies, determination and zeal continuously to the work of the Lord. There is reason to believe that he proved a blessing to many, being instrumental in turning them from darkness to light and from the power of Satan to the Lord.

The Rev. John Elias, when addressing the students at Bala, said once that he had been preaching for years without possessing any commentary on the Bible other than that of Peter Williams. And he added:

It is a good and concise commentary; and he himself was a good and useful man throughout his life.

And it is well-known that Mr Elias had little sympathy for those who departed from true doctrine. It is a very significant fact that more of Peter Williams's descendants remained as members amongst the Methodists than those of any of the other Fathers. This suggests that they were sufficiently convinced that the majority of the Connexion was neutral in the controversy. There is no better way to conclude this memoir of the old Commentator than by quoting another stanza from Thomas William's elegy:

| | |
|---|---|
| Now in Llandyfaelog's churchyard, | Nawr ym mynwent Llandyfaelog, |
| After all his journeys long, | 'Nol ei flin siwrneion pell; |
| Rests his flesh, in patience waiting | Gorffwys mae ei gnawd mewn gobaith |
| For the resurrection song; | Am yr atgyfodiad gwell; |
| This poor body, Adam's image, | Y corff gwael ar ddelw Adda, |
| The first Adam of the Fall, | 'R Adda cyntaf aeth i lawr, |
| Will awaken in Christ's image, | A ddihun ar ddelw ei Arglwydd, |
| At the final trumpet's call. | Gyda rhyw ogoniant mawr. |

---

[1] *Cysondeb y Pedair Efengyl, gydag agoriad byr a nodau athrawus, ar yr hyn a dybid yn dywyll ac anhawsaf ynddynt.*

[2] Now at the National Library of Wales, Aberystwyth.

# 19

# DAVID JONES, LLAN-GAN

## DAVID JONES'S PLACE AMONGST THE
## METHODIST FATHERS

*T*he first leaders of the Methodists in Wales were Daniel Rowland, Howell Harris, Howell Davies, William Williams and Peter
Williams. These form a group on their own. It is true that the honour of
setting down the foundation belongs to the first three only, but the two
Williamses joined them so early that they are hardly considered apart
from the founders. The hymn writer joined them within five years of their
beginnings, and the commentator followed within another five years. Furthermore, these two possessed such gifts, their commitment to the work
of the revival was so complete, and their partnership with the founders so
close, that the unnecessary work of distinguishing between them is just
too difficult. We need not hesitate in considering these five famous men
as the first leaders of Welsh Methodism. They were all filled with the same
hard-working, self-sacrificing spirit and each possessed such talents and
abilities as to establish their pre-eminence up to the present day.

David Jones of Llan-gan was not a member of this sacred elite, nor was
it possible for him to be so. The year in which Welsh Methodism began,
1735, was the year of his birth. His labours in the Welsh revival did not
commence until he arrived in Llan-gan in 1768, when 33 years old.
The revival had spread over the whole country and had rooted in the
land long before he appeared on the field. A whole generation had passed
and the days of three of the founders were approaching their close when
his ministerial work amongst the ranks of the Methodists began. Howell
Davies died within two years of David Jones's appointment at Llan-gan,
and within another three years Howell Harris had also crossed the Jordan.
David Jones is seen therefore as belonging to the second class of preachers
and leaders in the revival – a second class as far as time is concerned, that
is – he is of the second generation of our ministers. He had the privilege
of working together with Daniel Rowland and the two Williamses for
many years but he was not their contemporary. When old age overtook

them, he was still comparatively young, and he laboured in the vineyard for another twenty years after the last of them had entered into his reward. David Jones's contemporaries were John Evans of Bala; William Davies of Neath; David Griffiths of Nevern; David Morris of Twr-gwyn; and William Lloyd of Caeo, though there was considerable difference in age between the oldest and youngest of these. The first two mentioned were older than David Jones, and the others younger. He can be considered as the link between Daniel Rowland of Llangeitho and Thomas Charles of Bala, being twenty years younger than the first and twenty years older than the other.

It would be very convenient for us to have a neat division of the history of the Connexion, so that the chronological position of the lives of the various ministers could be seen at a glance, together with that of the various movements within Methodism. Our history extends presently over one hundred and fifty years – too long a time to analyse without dividing it up into periods. But it would be very difficult to do this. It may be that the celebration in 1893 of the Connexion's Jubilee has already contributed to laying down a chronological plan. Our history was then divided up into three periods of fifty years, beginning with the establishing of the Connexion at the Watford Association of 1743. The eight years previously was considered a time of beginnings and preparation although, admittedly, these were years of the right hand of the Most High and a great work was performed during them. We are led to make these comments at this point by the fact that more mistakes are made over the chronology of the ministry of Jones of Llan-gan than of any other of our main preachers. There is another reason for this apart from the lack of convenient historical division. Almost without exception, when authors write of the notable preachers of the Welsh pulpit they associate the name of David Jones with those of Daniel Rowland and Howell Harris. Very often, if not always, he is the first to be named after these two. This is what Dr Owen Thomas does, for example, when he writes of them in his excellent biography of John Jones, Talsarn. But it must be remembered that this honoured position is given to him because of his fame as a preacher and not from any chronological considerations. Having noted these erroneous views let us proceed to the main facts of his life.

The early history of David Jones is not known. Unlike Howell Harris and Peter Williams he never wrote anything of an autobiographical nature and unfortunately there was a delay of 31 years after his death before anyone attempted a biography. By that time much of what might have been known of him was lost. This biography appeared in 1841 and was written by the

Rev. Edward Morgan of Syston, the author of many such biographies of Methodist notables. Mr Morgan was born at Pyle, not far from Llan-gan, and he knew David Jones; he was also in complete sympathy with him in his doctrine and was perfectly qualified to write such a work.

## HIS BIRTH AND UPBRINGING

David Jones was born in a farmhouse called Aberceiliog in the parish of Llanllwni, Carmarthenshire, on the banks of the river Teifi. This was in 1735. His parents' names are not known but it is clear that they were of comfortable circumstances in that they intended to raise up one of their sons as a priest in the Church of England. They had two sons and a daughter. The father wished to settle the eldest son as a clergyman, with David becoming a farmer like his father. But heaven's arrangements were different, and this was made manifest in a very remarkable and painful manner. When David was a very young boy he fell into a cauldron full of boiling milk and was nearly scalded to death. He was a long time recovering and was for many years weak and in poor health. In time, the father realized that his plans were thwarted and that David would never now make a farmer, but perhaps he might still become a clergyman. He decided to do the best he could under the circumstances. David was therefore sent to the Church and the elder brother kept on the farm. In later years, referring to this providence, David Jones would say: 'I carry the marks and causes of my calling upon my back', for he carried the scars of his accident to the grave.

A saying of his when young suggests that some degree of religious education was provided at home, sufficient at least for David to make striking use of the Scriptures. One day, long after the accident but not before he had recovered completely from its effects he cuddled up to his mother. She pushed him away, saying, perhaps laughingly, 'Poor thing, I am quite tired out with nursing you.' He looked up into her face and replied, 'When my father and my mother forsake me, then the LORD will take me up.' His mother immediately picked him up in her arms saying, 'After such an answer, I'll happily nurse you for as long as you live.' He was noted as an adult for the readiness, the wit, and the appropriateness of his replies and in this story we have a glimpse of this talent in the bud.

He received all his academic education at Carmarthen College. He himself affirmed that he never spent any time at one of the main schools. He was ordained to the curacy of Llanafan Fawr in Breconshire about the year 1758, but moved fairly soon to Tudweiliog on the Lleyn peninsula, Caernarvonshire. His stay here again was short, for we find him serving the parishes of Trefethin and Caldicot, Monmouthshire, in 1760. What the cause was of these many changes is not known, but we can safely say that it was not his religion. Up until then he was sufficiently careless of his spiritual condition and of the responsibilities of his office to satisfy any of the vain and empty parsons of that period. It is said that at this time he was an appealing and popular preacher, and no doubt this in itself was sufficient sin in the eyes of those parsons whom he served. Whatever the reasons, he arrived at Trefethin, a village near Pontypool. At that time, a doctor, well-known in his profession and well-known also for his virtues and godliness, lived in another nearby village, Pontymoel. This man's name was Dr William Read. His fame was such that patients sought him from all over Wales. He was connected with the Methodists and was a warm friend of the hymn writer of Pantycelyn. When the doctor died, in 1769, Williams composed an elegy for him, one of the best that he wrote. It is found in his published works. There is a suggestion in the poem that Williams was present at his funeral.

Dr Read was still alive and at the height of his popularity and usefulness when the young curate came to Trefethin. They lived close to one another and became very friendly. It is not known whether it was the religion of the doctor that was the cause of the conversion of the curate, or whether the conversion of the curate brought him to friendship with the doctor. Mr Morgan, Syston, states that it was through reading a book by the famous Puritan, John Flavel, that he was converted at this time. He says further that the young man, having had his life turned upside down, received much unkindness and cruelty from the clergyman whom he served, and that David Jones had no friend or relative to whom he could pour out his complaints and from whom he could receive counsel, except for Dr Read. It may be that the friendship with the godly doctor of Pontymoel began after the great change, through the reading of Flavel's books, had occurred, but it is just as possible that it was the doctor who brought Flavel's works to his attention. Whatever the circumstances, it was at Trefethin that David Jones made the acquaintance of the Methodists, and his friendship with Dr Read lasted until the latter's death. Indeed, it was not the fault of David Jones that he was not married to one of the doctor's daughters some years later.

## HIS SETTLEMENT AT LLAN-GAN THROUGH THE INFLUENCE OF THE COUNTESS OF HUNTINGDON

How long the vicar of Trefethin remained content with his curate after the misfortune of the latter being converted, is not known. No doubt, in the vicar's mind, the event greatly disqualified him for the services of the Church. One of the consequences, however, was that the locality was stirred up by the curate's preaching. Large crowds came to hear him; there was an unction and an edge upon his ministry; he catechized and taught the young people in the truths of religion, and he led them in singing the praises of God. He was himself a great lover of music. There was nothing to be done with such a disorderly young man but to send him away. His next stop was Bristol but he was hardly any time there before moving to Wiltshire.

By now he was like Noah's dove, finding no rest for the sole of his foot; for there was nowhere in the Established Church in the England or Wales of that day where a curate of his spirit could find a welcome. His ministry was a flame, burning within him, but the possessors of livings had no need of such a service. He unsettled the country and agitated his hearers' consciences. Such underhand activities were unacceptable failings. It seems that while he was in Wiltshire he came into contact with some of the English Methodists, and in particular came to know the Countess of Huntingdon, of noble memory. She was in the habit of seeking out the faithful ministers of Jesus, sponsoring and helping them in their religious service. The Countess had been instrumental in bringing another noble-woman to the feet of the Saviour, namely, Lady Charlotte Edwin, the owner of a large estate in Glamorganshire. Soon, the living of Llan-gan, that was in that Lady's possession, became vacant, and on the request of the Countess it was offered to David Jones. This occurred, as we have mentioned previously, in 1768, when he was 33 years old.

Llan-gan is a small parish lying between Cowbridge and Bridgend in Glamorganshire. There is a small scattered village of the same name. The church is a very old building, though not very large. It was renovated throughout in 1856. There is a notable cross in the graveyard – one of the old remains of the Roman Catholic period. It dates from the twelfth century.

It is often thought that David Jones's connection with the Methodists dates from his coming to Llan-gan. From what has already been said, it can be seen that this was not the case. But if there is some uncertainty as to when he became a Methodist, his early commitment to the work is proved from the following words of his found in the memoir he wrote of Christopher Basset:

> My excellent brother (Basset) was called a Methodist; an important name, undoubtedly, for it arose at the first from a very learned place, no less a place than Oxford itself, and as the place, so also the fruits. I was never there for any

term of time, yet for all that, my qualifications were judged to be such that I was awarded with this degree also, though I am quite devoid of any other. My own thoughts of the name are these: that it is a glorious charter that slipped unknowingly from amongst the doctors there to every clergyman who stands conscientiously for the purity of the articles of the Church of England. It is valued at such a price by those that bear it that I am ready to desire that it should be placed on my coffin, and if it rots there, let it be, for the devil will ensure that God's people are honoured by some new name again, just as the name *Methodist* now is taking the place of *Roundheads* and *Cradockians*.

This is an unambiguous recommendation of Methodism in David Jones's own words, and it is in complete agreement with the life that he lived.

Nevertheless, his arrival at Llan-gan was the beginning of a new period in his life, for here, for the first time, he was a free man. He had escaped from the tyranny of parsons and been given ecclesiastical authority over a small parish in a densely populated county. Now, particularly, his labours outside his own parish prospered.

## THE MORAL AND SPIRITUAL CONDITION OF LLAN-GAN PARISH

It might be useful at this point to provide an overview of the state of religion amongst the Glamorganshire Methodists at the point when David Jones came to Llan-gan. In previous chapters, especially those involving Howell Harris, we have shown that much early labour had been expended in evangelizing the county, and that much success had resulted. We only wish to add to this sufficient to provide a clear understanding of the links of the history. Societies had been formed in Glamorganshire within the first eight years of the revival and by the time of the Watford Association, the church at Groes-wen had begun the work of building a chapel, the first in the county. The numbers of societies increased greatly during the next years, but the people were reluctant to raise chapels. A second was built within six years of the first, namely Aberthin Chapel. These were the only places of worship in the possession of the Methodists when David Jones arrived. Aberthin is within two miles of Llan-gan, and Groes-wen within twenty miles. There were strong churches, with settled, ordained men as ministers, in these two places. Williams Edwards, the builder, at Groes-wen and Dafydd Williams, Llysfronydd, at Aberthin. Both were mature men, over fifty years of age at this time, and men of ability and much influence. There were also many exhorters serving in the county, the most notable being William Thomas of Pyle and Jenkin Thomas, better known as *Siencyn Pen-hydd*. The first was 45 years old and the second 31

696 THE CALVINISTIC METHODIST FATHERS OF WALES

years old. At the time, Christopher Basset and Howell Howells, Tre-hill, were but youths, but they became Methodist clergy of great fame and usefulness in due course. In addition to these, another clergyman arrived in the county at the same time as David Jones, namely, the well-known and much loved William Davies, Neath. The two men were soon acquainted, even if they were not so before, and were co-labourers and fellow-travellers throughout Wales in the service of the gospel for the next twenty years, that is until the death of William Davies. He had been a curate at Neath under Mr Pinkey (who had the care of two livings, Neath and Llanilltyd) and he never rose above the position of curate throughout his life. The arrival of these two faithful ministers of Christ proved an immeasurable blessing to religion in Glamorganshire.

Up until now, not one of the stars of the pulpit had arisen from Glamorgan, whether native or immigrant. The people of the county looked chiefly to Howell Harris as their father, and when he seceded and stopped his regular visits, he left no one that could be in any way compared to him. The disruption had occurred eighteen years before the advent of these two famous men, so that their arrival was as the rising of the sun upon the county, and indeed upon the whole of Wales.

Those disruption years had proved years of tribulation for God's people; a time of stubborn controversy and of the decline of religion. They were followed by better days, days of awakening and recovery, and it is acknowledged generally that it was through the instrumentality of David Jones and William Davies in Glamorganshire; the two Williamses, together with William Lloyd, Caeo, in Carmarthenshire; and Daniel Rowland and Dafydd Morris, together with Dafydd Jones of Derlwyn, in Cardiganshire, that the south was regained for Methodism.

David Jones's history at Llan-gan is very similar to that of Daniel Rowland at Llangeitho, but on a smaller scale. The place became a great gathering-point, the centre of the religious activities of a large and important part of the land. When he arrived, the spiritual condition of the parish was deplorable. Even Mr Morgan, Syston, acknowledges that Jones's predecessor had been careless of his duties, and no doubt could have added that he had misled his people by word and by example. Quite likely he resembled the parson in charge of the parish next to Llan-gan of whom Shanco Shon sang:

| | |
|---|---|
| The foolish, hellish parson, | Y 'ffeiriad ffol uffernol, |
| How can he preach salvation? | Shwd achub hwn ei bobl, |
| Who can't refrain one day in seven | Sy'n methu cadw dydd o saith, |
| From being the leaven of Satan. | Heb ddilyn gwaith y diafol. |

The clergy, with a few exceptions, continued to be careless and indifferent; many of them being pre-eminent in ungodliness and intemperance. They were not even respected by the good-for-nothings with whom they spent their time. They were despised by all men of integrity and were the main objects of the scorn of poets and bards. Even Iolo Morgannwg was tempted to satirize them. He composed a song called *The Priests' Triads*, a long poem of twenty-four stanzas. The following, the first and last stanzas, are given as examples of the contempt felt by that most circumspect of bards for men whose lives were so inconsistent with their office and work:

| | |
|---|---|
| Three things are hateful to me, | Tri pheth sydd gas gan brydydd, |
| The boasting of a ninny, | Bost uchel gwr annghelfydd, |
| A muse that fails to fire or kick, | Awen ddiflas, heb ddim hwyl, |
| A cleric who is silly. | A 'ffeiriad plwyf di'menydd. |
| | |
| Three things I vow are lovely, | Tri pheth a gâr fy nghalon, |
| To reconcile two parties, | Heddychu rhwng cymdogion, |
| To keep the law with ready will, | Cadw'r iawn heb fynd ar goll, |
| And killing all the clergy. | A chrogi'r holl 'ffeiriadon. |

It is clear that the majority of the clergymen of the country at that time were not better in the slightest, in morals and behaviour, than those of a hundred years earlier, and the children of the revival had also backslidden and not progressed, during these twenty years. As we mentioned, controversies had entered the Methodist churches, together with divisions of every kind, and these had turned the garden of the Lord into a desert. It is not easy to describe the decline that had taken place amongst believers in as short a time as twenty years. To read the history of the Methodist church at Aberthin over this period is to be reminded of the history of the Independent churches of Cefnarthen and Cwm-y-glo, near Merthyr, in an earlier age. The arrival of a man of Mr Jones's spirit and talents was therefore as life from the dead to such a locality. Llan-gan was granted the honour, and it was not long before its effects were evident. David Jones's soul flamed with love for his Saviour and with compassion towards his parishioners, bound for death. Soon the people were awakened and the church full. The news spread of the power of the ministry and crowds would gather from neighbouring parishes. Llan-gan became like Llangeitho – a centre of attraction for people far and wide.

## A COMMUNION SUNDAY AT LLAN-GAN

To give some indication of the work done at Llan-gan, we include an excellent description by the Rev. William Williams, Swansea, of a communion at Llan-gan during the times of David Jones:

Come with us, and let us sit down on this large stone on the ridge of Eglw-ysfair Mountain. It is a beautiful Sabbath morning. Do you see on your left hand, towards the south-east, a majestic old building, hardly visible behind the trees that surround it? That is Pen-llin Castle. Look again to your right, about four miles to the west, and you will see a small town on a pleasant plain. That is Bridgend. Now look before you. Directly to the south, at the bottom of the valley below us, you will see a small, scattered village. And almost directly between us, just a little to the west, a small church, rather unprepossessing, having no bell tower but only something rather like a chimney containing a bell, whose toll we would not hear even at its loudest. That is Llan-gan. That is where Mr Jones will preach and administer the sacraments today, and where a large congregation will meet with him. Wait a bit; you will see them gather. Look! There are some already appearing. Down to your side you will see that steep road to Llan-gan from the top of the Golden Mile, full of people – many of them on horseback. They are natives of Wick, Lampha, Ty'rcroes and Colwinston, all heading for Llan-gan. Look again between us and Pen-llin Castle, there is another crowd pouring from the various cross-roads towards Llan-gan. On your right is that narrow, level road from Tyle-y-rhôd, past Coychurch and Melin-y-mur, to Tre-os, full of travellers. That is the road for the people from Bridgend, Laleston, Pyle, Llangynwyd, Margam and Aberavon. Some of them are from Neath and the Neath valley, and even from Llangyfelach, Gopa and Swansea. But let us now descend to the plain and towards Llan-gan. An exhorter will address the gathering from the vicarage barn at nine o'clock. Mr Jones will not be in the church until half past ten. Before us is a thin, keen-eyed man, with an aquiline nose, standing on a stool. One look at him is enough to convince you that the man has never attended any academy and his manner of speaking shows that he has never studied oratory or grammar. But there is a power in his words – an originality in his expressions – a melody in his voice – which prove that he is someone out of the ordinary. This is Edward Coslett, a blacksmith by occupation, but a preacher by vocation, and the best Methodist preacher in Monmouthshire, as he himself would attest. His reason for doing so is that as yet there is no other Methodist preacher in the county but himself. Mr Jones had asked him, after hearing him preach in some place, where it was he had studied his sermon. 'A place where you have never once studied, Sir,' was the answer. 'Where is that then, Ned?' 'Between the fire and the anvil,' was the answer. Some men judged that this is why Edward Coslett's sermons were so warm, or so fiery, as they said. But, after all, he is but exhorting a little. It is Mr Jones who is to preach in the church. Let us therefore enter the church. There is Mr Jones ascending the pulpit. Look at him for a moment. Not often does one see such a handsome man. He is too tall to be called short and too short to be called tall; broad-shouldered, strong of arm, fair of hair, and full of face. His arched brows; large, shining, black eyes; large broken nose; and gracious lips, reveal one who abounds in the realms of common sense and good nature. Now he begins to read: 'When the wicked man turneth away from his wickedness that he hath committed, etc.' He seems as if he is in a hurry to finish. The words, prayers and lessons flow one after another from his lips in a torrent. Before we are aware the 'Amen' of the appointed service is reached. Now for the extempore prayer, the singing, and the sermon. The first shows the speaker's familiarity with the realm within the veil. It is clear that he had visited heaven the previous evening, so easily does he enter there today. The singing is as the sound of many waters. There is no great control to it, but its spirit and vigour is excellent, and its effect indescribable. We would give anything to hear its like again.

The singing ends and the sermon begins. A silence like that of the grave rules throughout the church. Every man seems to forget all his other faculties save those of his eyes, ears, and heart. The preacher begins as if he means to provide sufficient work for all three. The burden of his heart flows in such a constant stream, so quickly and effortlessly, that it makes you imagine that the source of all his thoughts and expressions must reside in his mouth and lips. His words are choice, his voice melodious; the people consider him a preacher without equal. All these factors contribute to the feelings that you see and hear spreading throughout the congregation. But this is not all; the secret of his strength is not in these things. There is life in every word; power in every sentence; he shouts, but it is the eternal Spirit who has already told him what to shout. The preacher believes that every word he proclaims is eternal truth. He feels the inexpressible weight of every sentence that proceeds from his lips; an inexpressible weight for himself, and an inexpressible weight for every living soul before him! He is a man just recently rescued from the flood, only just now delivered from drowning, having only just found the lifeboat himself, he shouts, 'Rescue! Rescue!', to those sinking around him. In declaring his sermon he is declaring his heart. He speaks of the tears, sweat and blood; of the cross and death of our Saviour, with his infinite love stirring up his soul. He talks of the resurrection of the dead and the eternal judgment; and as he speaks he feels as if he himself stands at the boundary of the invisible world, and his hearers feel so also. The sweat and tears flow down his cheeks, and the floor of the old church is showered with tears. But the sermon ends. Surprisingly short, but wondrously sweet. The preacher sits, bathed in sweat. The hearers, for the first time since he began speaking, look at one another, noticing the rivers of tears.

But all is not yet over. The table is spread; the congregation, before departing, intend to commemorate the death of their great Saviour. Stay to see the end. The minister reads the usual lesson but he does not rest there. There is no sign that he thinks of sparing himself; the powers of the sacrifice fill his soul. The usual words, 'The body of our Lord Jesus Christ, etc.,' do not in any way lose their potency by being repeated over and over; their strength increase; their effect upon the preacher himself deepen the oftener he repeats them. He pushes through the crowds; he quickens them with his tears; he stirs up their innermost beings with his sweet words – now a part of a hymn; now a point of doctrine; now an inimitable cry concerning the death of the cross. On the one side:

Jones, the angel of Llanganna,          Jones fel angel yn Llanganna,
Sounds aloud the gospel cry.            Yn udganu'r udgorn mawr.

And on the other:

Myriad hordes, in warmest feelings,     Dorf, mewn twym serchiadau,
Lifted up above the sky.                Yn dyrchafu uwch y llawr.

The sparks from the sermon have become a fierce flame. You must now look after yourself, friend. I cannot continue my description. My pen falls from my fingers. The crowd have turned to rejoicing, and we rejoice with them. Who could refrain from doing so? Glorious! Glorious evermore!

But, in the end, we are not at Llan-gan, but here, at this spot; fifty years too late to see that place in its glory; we saw only an imperfect image of the reality. O, that we might see the thing itself! Failing that, it may be that this present description might provide as good a picture as can be obtained in the meantime.

## PREACHING, BUILDING CHAPELS, AND SUFFERING PERSECUTION

David Jones did not confine himself in any way to his own church and parish. To do so would have been to him a bowing down to mere human arrangements. He would rather conform to the heavenly commandment: 'Go ye into all the world, and preach the gospel to every creature.' He preached in season and out of season, and in every kind of place – sometimes in a barn or on the side of the highway; in a home; under the shelter of a tree; or on a hillside – anywhere, in fact, where he found opportunity to preach Christ and his cross. No doubt he was an inconsistent and irregular Churchman but he was, nevertheless, a shining and determined Christian, valuing the acknowledgment of God more than the smiles of the nobility, and preferring to retrieve sinners from their wicked ways than to confine himself to any religious sect or party.

In the year 1775, seven years after coming to Llan-gan, Mr Jones and the Methodists built Salem Chapel, Pen-coed, at a convenient spot near the main road between Bridgend and Llantrisant. Two acres of land were obtained and made over by deed to the Connexion. At the time, Salem was considered to be a large building for worship. Mr Jones particularly liked the place and superintended the construction work himself. A chapel house was built at one side of the building and a cemetery for the graves of members at the other. It is notable that the first to be buried there was the faithful old minister, Dafydd Williams of Llysworney. Soon afterwards, Mr Jones's wife died, and he desired that his beloved 'Sina' be buried next to the old preacher. He often said that he wished his own remains to rest here, but this was not to be because of his second marriage and his move to Pembrokeshire.

It is a strange fact that David Jones, the priest of Llan-gan Church, should wish to bury his dear wife in the unconsecrated ground alongside Salem, the chapel of the Methodists at Pen-coed, rather than at the convenient cemetery of Llan-gan, where he himself ministered. It demonstrates the liberality of his views as to the consecration of land, and the loyalty of his heart to the Methodists.

Salem Chapel was only three miles or so from Llan-gan Church. Mr Jones used to preach at his own church at half past ten on a Sunday morning and at Salem at two o'clock in the afternoon. No society meetings were ever held at Llan-gan but only at Salem. They were held there every week, together with a preparatory meeting once a month, at one o'clock, on the Saturday before the Communion Sunday at Llan-gan. Mr Jones would always be present if he was at home, and his amiable and godly wife was ever present.

Salem Chapel was the first chapel to be built by Mr Jones but not the last. He was, perhaps, instrumental in building more Methodist chapels than any other of his contemporaries. He was a trustee of most of the chapels of south Wales built in his day, and very active also in raising monies for their costs. He built some also in north Wales; the first chapel at Dolgelley, for example.

It is said that few of the parishioners of Llan-gan were converted through the ministry of Mr Jones. His labours were more blessed in other places than in his own parish. The scriptural proverb was borne out in his history. His hearers were mainly the Methodists of surrounding localities, those who thirsted for the living God and longed for the courts of the Lord.

For all the labours of the Reformers in the county before David Jones's day, they had not succeeded in putting a complete stop to the dissolute pastimes of the peasantry of Llan-gan. The parish feast days were still being observed. One example was the yearly festival at Peterston-super-montem, a village about five miles north of Llan-gan. This was the main festival of the locality. Hundreds of the young people of Glamorgan gathered there to drink, to get drunk, to dance, fight, and indulge in every kind of ungodliness. And the Lord's Day was the high day of the feast. Mr Jones resolved to put an end to the sinful assembly. He had been preaching against it in Llan-gan but this was not sufficient. He went one Sunday to the village and preached Christ and him crucified to the villagers. He succeeded in his goal, and for the next thirty years visited the place on the festival day to hold preaching services. The Lord compelled the enemy to retreat before the preacher at his first attempt, and he determined ever afterwards to maintain his conquest.

It is reported of him that when once returning after having been preaching, he met a group of wastrels who had gathered together for cock-fighting. He turned towards them and greeted them kindly, saying, 'I have some remarkable good news for you, dear people, if you would be so good as to listen. You can continue with your work afterwards if you wish.' Having been won over by his kindness, they told him that he could do as he wished. At that he started telling them of the state of their souls and of the love of the Saviour, and God's power fell on them as he spoke. The men were struck with amazement and returned to their homes having forgotten their previous intentions.

David Jones was always gentlemanly in conduct, tender of spirit, and remarkably gentle in all his dealings with others, yet he suffered his portion of persecution. On one occasion a man knocked the Bible from his hand when he was preaching in north Wales. The only comment he made at such unruly behaviour was, 'O poor man! You have struck your judge!' When preaching at Machynlleth, a large crowd of enemies gathered about him, pulled the Word from his hands and began to abuse it. They told him they would do him no harm if he would promise never to come there to preach again. 'O no,' he said, 'I could not do that; you have no right to a single promise, and neither does your father.' He was persecuted often by the nobility and clergy of his own locality. Complaints were sent to the bishop that he preached without a book, that he drew hearers from outside the parish to Llan-gan and other places, and that he was guilty of every kind of irregularity. The bishop closed his ears to as much of these complaints as he could, but he was forced at last to call him to account. He greeted him by saying, 'I am very sorry, Mr Jones, that there are complaints against you. You are accused of preaching at unconsecrated sites.' 'No, never, my lord,' said he. 'When the Son of Mary placed his feet on this earth he consecrated every inch of it. If that were not so, I fear that no amount of consecrating on your lordship's part would do any good at all.' After a few friendly words they parted, and Mr Jones continued as before. The bishop at the time was

Dr Barrington, and he was supportive of, or at least he was not opposed to, the irregular activities of the Llan-gan parson.

The complaints were renewed when Dr Watson became Bishop of Llandaff. The new bishop decided to compel him to remain within his own parish. He called him aside during an episcopal visit to Cowbridge and told him that he was not at liberty to go to other parishes until every soul within his own parish had been saved. Mr Jones replied respectfully that he felt himself under obligation to comply with the requests of those living in parishes where the incumbents were careless of their duties. 'If that is the case,' said the bishop, 'then I must take steps to stop you.' 'You may do that, my lord,' answered Mr Jones, 'but I cannot change my decision.' The bishop, amazed at such unconcerned courage associated with such courteous gentility, asked him if he had any family. 'Yes, my lord,' was the answer. 'I have a wife and three children.' 'Well,' said his lordship, overcome by his feelings, 'dear Mr Jones, I would not wish in any way to harm you, but the priests of the parishes of P— and F— are very opposed to you. Will you do this as a favour to me, that you will not visit their parishes?' 'I will do what you want,' was his reply, and he kept to his word.

## HIS LABOURS IN ENGLAND

It would be an impossible task to record all the labours of David Jones during the forty years from his arrival at Llan-gan to his death at Manorowen. It is clear however that he was wholly taken up with the work, and that the Lord blessed that work with success in a notable way. As well as his efforts in Wales, he ministered regularly throughout his life to the Countess of Huntingdon's Connexion in England, and his ministry was as acceptable with the English as with his own people.

| | |
|---|---|
| Proud, chaotic, crowded London, | Llundain boblog, falch, derfysglyd, |
| Heard the music of his voice; | Glyw[odd] lais ei bibell ef; |
| Learnt that far away in Gwalia | Cafodd wybod fod yng Nghymru |
| Could be found a preacher choice. | Ddyn oedd lawn o ddoniau'r Nef. |

No man of common abilities would suffice at that time to preach for the Countess's congregations. Many of them were from the cream of society, people of education and taste. They had been gathered together by the incomparable oratory of Whitefield and were accustomed to the highest of pulpit talents. Mr Jones often visited the main churches of various cities and more often yet those of the capital. The English gathered in their thousands to hear him, and followed him from chapel to chapel. He possessed such abundance of talent, such eloquence of expression, and such warmth of spirit, that all kinds of people were overcome under his ministry. He was certainly one of the most popular preachers in the country in his time. He often visited Bristol, and when he was there Mr Rylands would always ensure that he obtained his services for one or more meetings. Almost invariably these would prove most successful. The reverend Doctor would tell him at the end of each service, 'Here you are, Jones of Llan-gan, having again stolen the hearts of my people and spoiled my listeners for a whole month. I will not get them to listen to anybody else now for a long time.' He ministered for a period of some weeks at Spa Fields Chapel, London, one of the largest churches of the capital at that time, and was enormously popular. He was often asked to preach amongst the English for their high feasts and special anniversaries, invariably satisfying the expectations of the crowds that would gather to hear him. To him was afforded the honour of preaching the funeral sermon for the Countess of Huntingdon, and it appears that he was the only clergyman to minister to the Countess during her last illness.

It was David Jones also who was asked to preach at the second anniversary of the founding of the London Missionary Society. This took place in one of the largest of London's churches on 13 May 1796, two months before the first party of missionaries were to be sent to the South Sea Islands. The following reference to his address is found in the anniversary's report:

> On Friday, our public services were terminated by an excellent sermon from the Rev. David Jones of Llan-gan. His method and spirit is too well-known to make any commendation from ourselves necessary.

This sermon was published in the first volume of *Missionary Sermons,* and it provides a typical example of his preaching. Mr T. Chapman of Fleet Street, London, published the sermon separately, and Mr E. Griffiths, Swansea, brought out a Welsh translation in 1797.

If the English were eager to hear him, David Jones was just as ready to visit them, for he ensured that these connections with the wealthy in England brought some advantage in return to Wales. He would generally be pressing the case of some chapel or schoolroom that needed to be built or paid for, and he brought many substantial sums of English money back home with him. His gentlemanly appearance, attractive style and ready eloquence, produced such an effect upon his hearers that they could not keep their gifts from him. Some of the old believers used to recount many stories of his fund gathering. The following are one or two examples. A Welshman on a visit to London went to hear him preaching in one of the English chapels. When appealing for the collection at the end of the service, the preacher released the full force of his eloquence upon the congregation in order to persuade them to contribute. The Welshman felt the ties between himself and his money being rapidly loosened, and was forced to cry out in his native tongue, 'Dear Mr Jones, please stop! Do not press further or I will have to give all that I possess, without leaving me a farthing to get home.' Another tale also has him in London and making effective use of the story of Peter casting his hook into the sea and catching the fish with the piece of money in its mouth. The next morning, the servant of a noblewoman knocked at the door of his lodging and left a basket with the note, 'To the Rev. Mr Jones, Wales.' On opening the basket, behold a fish with a letter in its jaws containing a bill for ten pounds. Mr Jones saw the Lord's hand in this as surely as in Peter's case.

But for all his many journeys into England, Wales remained the chief field of his labours. The Welsh spirit burned in his veins and he consecrated his life to serve his nation. We cannot list the many and long itineraries that he took throughout Wales anymore than we could those of Williams, Pantycelyn. Nearly all of the history of Mr Jones that we possess is made up of short anecdotes of his associations with the early days of our churches: something done by him or to him, or some striking comment from him. It may be that these recollections are as much an indication of his character as anything.

## HIS COURTESY, KINDNESS, AND HUMILITY

We have already shown how he overcame the resentment of the clergy by his courteous behaviour before the bishop, and we have other examples that prove that this was his usual way of dealing with such troubles. He was once preaching at Dolgelley when, in the middle of the service, a man trundled a wheelbarrow back and forth through the congregation, causing much distraction. The next time Mr Jones came to that town this man, because of some offence, had been placed in a jail near to where the preacher lodged. As a consequence, his family had fallen into poverty and disgrace. This was told to Mr Jones who, always ready to help those in distress, explained the circumstances to the congregation, appealed earnestly on behalf of the impoverished family, and asked some of the friends to circulate with a hat in order to collect the people's contributions. This kind behaviour helped greatly to reduce the persecution of that town against the Methodists.

A story in *Methodistiaeth Cymru* relates how he pre-empted persecution in Caernarvon. The earlier Reformers had received brutal treatment in this town and there was no certainty that the evangelist from Llan-gan would be welcomed any differently. However, he and a few friends ventured on to the street and walked towards the castle gates. Mr Jones climbed up on to a nearby cart and a crowd gathered. Some were present with the intention of disrupting proceedings, some were there out of curiosity, and others, perhaps, with the best of intentions. The preacher removed his outer coat and the people saw more of the gentleman in him than they had expected to see in any roundhead. The black gown, white cravat, and square lapels that hung over his breast, had now come into view. Such a thing amazed the people: to see a churchman in his clerical robes addressing them at the side of the road! They had expected some peasant exhorter in very plain clothes and with no attractiveness or distinction about him, but instead here was one before them who, in both dress and appearance, was evidently a gentleman. There was at least one man present among the crowd with stones in his pockets, ready to injure, if not kill, the speaker, but he became afraid when he saw that he was a clergyman, and dropped the stones, one by one, in his shame. It was gently raining at the time.

Mr Jones began by addressing the crowd with warm words and with an air of confidence as if he were a man standing amongst his friends. Soon he asked if someone would be kind enough to lend him a blanket to shelter his head from the shower. This was a courageous request from someone who knew himself to be in danger of receiving harm rather than favours from those before him. But he made the appeal in his own gracious way, and immediately a Mr Howard, a lawyer of much influence in the town, departed to find him a blanket and on his return, handed it to the preacher. He received it from his hand with a respectful gesture and with the warmest of smiles and began his sermon by stating that he felt as comfortable under the blanket as if he were in St Paul's in London. He was given perfect liberty to preach, the first time this had happened at Caernarvon. This is the manner by which he overcame evil with good, and by which he heaped coals of fire upon the heads of his enemy.

Unquestionably, he was a preacher of amazing appeal and popularity. His delivery was faultless: every emphasis of the voice; every gesture of the hand; every movement of the body; all contributed to his hold over his congregation so that the most careless of hearers were obliged to listen. He would be at his most majestic when the bright tears would roll down his cheeks as the thoughts flowed forth from a compassionate heart. No offence was ever given by anything in his person or his words; nothing to spoil the effect of the gracious words that fell from his lips. He was a natural orator. Every word would fall into its place as if by instinct. His phrases were choice and his taste pure. He touched the hearts of all kinds:

the sophisticated and learned would be as overcome as the untaught and uncultivated. All felt the power of his ministry. We find that men like Jack Jones, the butcher, would understand more of Mr Jones, Llan-gan, than he would of a common exhorter. Mr Jones was preaching once at Rhuthun from the words: 'Never man spake like this man.' He read his text as usual in his strong voice, his face revealing the warmth of his intentions. There was something immediately striking in his opening words. 'This man spoke eyes to the blind,' he said. 'He spoke ears to the deaf, feet to the lame and health to the sick; he spoke demons out of the possessed, yea, even life into the dead. He can do the same again', etc. Jack Jones, the butcher, was the ringleader of the troublemakers at the meeting but he was so taken by the power of the sermon that he cried out: 'And no man spoke like you either. By the old Nick! I'll make sure you get fair play to speak and anybody who does anything to you will have me to deal with.'

The zeal of a godly old woman from Newborough, Anglesey, was so great as to be almost unbelievable. He had been speaking at a preaching meeting there and was about to begin the journey home when the old lady, whose name was Annas, came up to him to obtain a promise that he would return. 'When, Mr Jones, will you come back again to us?' 'When you, Annas, will come to Llan-gan to ask me back,' was his reply, thinking, no doubt, that he was laying down an impossible condition. But the old lady kept hold of the promise and determined to visit Llan-gan. She had a hundred and fifty miles to walk with nothing but clogs on her feet, nothing to maintain her but what she could obtain by begging and no food but what would be given her on the way. Yet, before long, she began the journey. It would be interesting to learn the details of this walk – where she lodged on the way; what obstacles she met with; what ungraciousness she received from some and what kindness from others; but all this we can only imagine. To the great astonishment of Mr Jones however, she duly arrived at Llan-gan. One day, he was looking through his window and spotted the old lady, her staff in one hand and a bag in the other, approaching the house. He went to meet her, exclaiming, 'Oh no, Annas! Have you come already?' The result was that she obtained a full reward for her labour, in that she was given a promise that three of the chief evangelists of the day would come to Anglesey: Jones, Llan-gan; Rowland, Llangeitho; and Lloyd of Henllan. These three were faithful to their promises and before long Anglesey was able to harvest the fruit of that field so well sown by one poor woman.

It may be noted at this point that it was under David Jones's ministry that the seraph preacher, Robert Roberts, Clynnog, was brought to faith.

This again shows his ability to overcome so many different hearts and minds. It occurred during a meeting held at Brynyrodyn, near Caernarvon. His text was, 'Turn you to the strongholds, ye prisoners of hope', etc. It is well-known that Mr Roberts subsequently became one of the foremost ornaments of the Welsh pulpit, one for whom it was difficult to get anyone to preach with in an Association. Soon after Robert Roberts had begun preaching, he was appointed to preach with Mr Jones at an Association held somewhere in south Wales. Robert Roberts preached with extraordinary power, completely overcoming the congregation. After him, Mr Jones arose and, as is so often the case when the first sermon is so very effective, the second was rather heavy and lifeless. The following morning was a private meeting for the preachers. The topic for discussion was the 'Self'. While many were contributing on the evil and danger of being ruled by a selfish spirit in the service of the Lord, it was noticed that Mr Jones was restless, rising and sitting, and sometimes walking back and forth along the aisle. Eventually the chairman asked him, 'Now, Mr Jones, will you tell us something of this "Self"?' He replied in some agitation, 'No. No! I'll say nothing now. But you go on, dear brothers. You go on. Keep at it, attack it, don't spare it, for it nearly killed me last night, on seeing that little Robin from the North was so far ahead of me.'

A similar story is told in *Methodistiaeth Cymru* of Mr Jones preaching together with Hugh Pritchard, the sexton of Llanhir-yn-rhos, Radnorshire. The latter was a sexton in the Established Church and an exhorter with the Methodists. On this occasion also, Hugh Pritchard, preaching first at an Association in the south, was more successful with his sermon than Mr Jones after him. Mr Jones could not help but be struck by this and wrote later to a friend, 'Do you know with whom they partnered the old white-haired clergyman, in the Association? The Llanhir sexton, if you please! And if all is said, it must be acknowledged that the sexton beat the parson hollow!'

We do not find that David Jones exerted such an influence within the conferences of the Connexion as might have been expected. His service to the Connexion was immeasurable, but it was in the pulpit that it was accomplished, rather than in the committees of the Associations and Monthly Meetings. He was chairman of the Association many times, particularly after the death of Daniel Rowland, but it can hardly be said that he proved himself a skilful leader in times of crisis and controversy. He was a son of peace and was too tender-hearted to be a safe leader during troubled and dangerous times. Yet he possessed many of the requisites of a leader. He was patient and prudent; of mature judgment; full of common sense and kind to all; perhaps he was a little deficient in courage. If he had been of a more ambitious nature and of a more determined mind, he could easily have become the leader of the Connexion after the death of Rowlands and Williams, Pantycelyn, because it cannot be doubted that he, at that time, was the most respected and best loved of the Welsh Methodists. But he was too timid of spirit and too sensitive of feeling to lead. He does not appear to have contributed to the discussions concerning Peter Williams's theological views, and both the circumstances of the excommunication of Nathaniel Rowland and of the argument over ordaining ministers towards the end of his life, revealed the weaknesses in his character. Most certainly he was not a man of war but a son of peace.

## HIS GIFTS AS A PREACHER

Above everything, David Jones, Llan-gan, was a preacher; we would almost say that he was nothing but a preacher, so great were his preaching skills. His ability in proclaiming Christ put all his other skills in the shade and totally hid his other weaknesses and strengths. If he hardly contributed to the theological arguments of the Methodists in his day, he did immeasurably more service to the religion of the country through his leading role in the powerful revivals that visited the land. As many as five mighty revivals occurred in Wales during the years of his public ministry. The first of these was in 1773, about five years after he had settled at Llan-gan; and the last was in 1805, five years before his death. Who could measure his contribution with respect to these revivals? The Evangelist of Llan-gan preferred to preach Christ to warm-hearted souls in times of revival than to argue stubbornly over the doctrines of religion.

It is a cause for regret that no elegy was written for David Jones, Llangan, by our chief elegist. That was impossible in that Williams preceded him to the eternal world by twenty years. But the poet of Pantycelyn has one or two references to him worth noting in the elegies he wrote to others. In his memorial to Mrs Grace Price of Watford, he says:

| | |
|---|---|
| In Llan-gan, beneath the pulpit, | Yn Llan-gan, o dan y pwlpud, |
| Was her heaven, was her home, | Roedd ei hyspryd, roedd ei thre', |
| While the harpstrings, plucked by David, | Tra f'ai Dafydd yno'n chwarae |
| Sang the song of life to come; | 'N beraidd ar delynau'r ne'; |
| Christ the Text, and Christ the Sermon, | Iesu'r Text, a Iesu'r Bregeth, |
| Christ the Law, and Christ the Key, | Iesu'r ddeddf, a Iesu'r Ffydd, |
| So preached Jones, and so she answered – | Meddai Jones, a hithau'n ateb – |
| 'Thus forever it shall be.' | Felly mae, a Felly bydd. |

Similarly, in his elegy to Daniel Rowland, he salutes the son, Nathaniel Rowland, in this way:

| | |
|---|---|
| Be a father to the 'Sasiwn, | Bydd yn dad i'r Assosiasiwn, |
| And if wanting help from man, | Ac os teimli'th fod yn wan, |
| Turn to one of faithful service, | Ti gei help gwir efengylwr, |
| Honest David of Llan-gan, | Dafydd onest o Langan; |
| He who melts the stones with sweetness, | Dodd y cerrig a'i ireidd-dra, |
| As he sows the gospel seed, | A thrwy rym ei 'fengyl fwyn, |
| Makes the sturdiest oak before him, | Wna i'r derw mwyaf caled |
| Bend as pliant as the reed. | Blygu'n ystwyth fel y brwyn. |

All the references to him by his contemporaries are consistent. Robert Jones of Rhoslan in his *Drych yr Amseroedd* [*A Mirror of the Times*] writes of him: 'He would ply the strings of the golden harp of the gospel so that many a fearing believer would be ready to jump for joy.' And Christmas Evans's testimony is: 'Listening to Dafydd Morris, Jones of Llan-gan, Davies of Neath, and Peter Williams, was of great benefit to me to lead me to understand the grace of God through a Mediator, without any human merit.' A worthy tribute to him is given by the late Dr Owen Thomas in his *Life of John Jones, Talsarn*:

Without question, he was a remarkable preacher. He was considered the most melting of all the early fathers. Nobody could compare with him in this respect, with the exception of Evan Richardson, Caernarvon. He was, in particular, an evangelist. There was nothing of the 'rushing mighty wind' about his ministry, but rather a gentle 'south wind', 'blowing upon the garden' and causing 'the spices thereof to flow out.' We remember hearing our dear mother describing him as being exactly like that verse, 'My doctrine shall drop as the rain, my speech shall distil as the dew, as the small rain upon the tender herb, and as the showers upon the grass.' We recall the late Mr Michael Roberts of Pwllheli describing how he went for the first time, as a fourteen-year old boy, to the Bala Association, in 1794. Mr Jones was preaching there with such unction and effect that the whole congregation was bathed in tears, and many, not able to withhold, had broken out in great rejoicing. 'I looked at him,' he said, 'as if he were an angel from God. He was leaving the Association that morning and I had gone to Mr Charles's house to see him depart. I well remember how Mr Charles, shaking hands with him at the door and with tears running down his cheeks, said, 'Hasten back to us again, Mr Jones, for us to be baptized again by your ministry.'

## HIS FINAL YEARS

David Jones spent the last sixteen years of his life at Manorowen, a village about two miles from Fishguard, Pembrokeshire. This move was occasioned by his marriage to a Mrs Parry, a respectable widow, who lived there. This lady was the sister of Mr Gwynne of Kilkifeth, a rich man, who was a member of a well-known local family. He owned many farms and husbanded the land on which he lived. His sister, Mrs Parry, was also considered to be in comfortable circumstances. The Kilkifeth family had been kind and sympathetic towards the Methodists throughout the years, and had kept a pew in Fishguard chapel for many years. After the death of her husband, Mrs Parry lived at Manorowen mansion with Miss Gwynne, her brother's daughter, as a companion. It was this young lady who later became the wife of the Rev. Thomas Richards, Fishguard. There is every reason to believe that this union between Mr Jones and Mrs Parry proved of great advantage to him in his latter days and greatly added to his comforts.

Mr Morgan of Syston relates an interesting story about him soon after he had remarried. When setting out on a preaching tour Mr Jones found a very handsome horse awaiting him. He mounted the horse and rode forth for a while when, on looking round, he found that a servant in fine clothes was riding behind him, as was the custom with the nobility. He returned home immediately, telling the servant to wait for him. When he arrived at the house he dismounted and asked Mrs Jones, 'Mary, why did you send that boy after me?' 'Because it looks more respectable, Mr Jones,' was the reply. 'Oh!' he said, 'You had better leave that with me. I have travelled thousands of miles in the service of my Heavenly Father without having anyone behind me.' Then he asked her, with a warm smile, 'What would my friends say of this? They would surely believe that old Jones of Llan-gan has become proud. No, it is better not to be ostentatious. I will send the boy back to work on the farm.'

He continued to hold the living of Llan-gan for the rest of his life, although he lived at Manorowen. He used to spend the three months of the summer at Llan-gan, and be present also at the church on the Communion Sunday of each month, until old age and weakness prevented him. And Llan-gan was close to his heart to the last. He wrote on the 19 May 1808, two years before his death, 'At last I have arrived back in this county, in which is my chief pleasure. O Llan-gan! Blessed of the Lord! My soul so often feasted within thee! My friends continue in their usual generosity towards me and I am perfectly happy in their company. I have now been here for five weeks, after a winter of much affliction at Manorowen.'

Mr Jones's move to Pembrokeshire proved a great blessing to the county. Nathaniel Rowland had, by now, taken control of the churches planted by Howell Davies; and he ruled them with a rod of iron. He would not preach in the chapels of Fishguard, but only in the church, and he would administer the sacraments in homes. He felt happier in his conscience doing so rather than administering the Holy Communion in a chapel. When asked to preach in a chapel rather than in the church, he would steadfastly reply that he would never do so; and he kept his word. But, after a while, Mr Jones brought about a transformation. He obtained permission from the Association at Llangeitho in 1802 to administer communion at Fishguard Chapel, as had been done previously at other chapels. He was instrumental in obtaining the same privilege for the Carmarthen chapel under extraordinary and exciting circumstances. Mr David Charles, in an Assembly in Carmarthen, ventured to ask for the privilege of celebrating the Lord's Supper at that chapel.

'The church at this place,' he said, 'has placed the responsibility upon me to ask on their behalf whether they may obtain the privilege of remembering the death of their Redeemer.' At that, Nathaniel Rowland replied, in some indignation, 'No, you may not. Llanlluan Church is close enough.' It was about ten miles away. But David Charles would not take this brusque, dictatorial reply as a final answer. 'Once again,' said he, 'I ask if we might receive this honour? We are allowed to preach Christ, to profess him, and to believe in him. May we not also remember his death for us?' 'No! Not in this place!' replied Nathaniel Rowland a second time. 'I was not charged to ask you,' persevered David Charles, 'but to ask the Assembly.' At this, Mr Jones could not restrain himself, and he shouted out, 'Of course you may!' He then addressed Mr Charles in the warmest of tones, 'When do you want it, Deio bach? I'll come to help you remember him.' And so it transpired.

It cannot be denied that Mr Jones proved eminently faithful to the Methodists up to his dying day. He remained a clergyman of the Established Church to the end, it is true, but he was more of a Methodist than he was a Churchman, judging by the whole tenor of his life. When he moved to Manorowen he came within the area of influence of clergymen who were much more committed to the Church than he. David Griffiths of Nevern and Nathaniel Rowland were much narrower than himself. While they sought to place the Methodists under disadvantages, he had been operating on the opposite principle throughout his long life. But the Methodist priests of Pembrokeshire were men of inflexible determination and strong will and it is quite possible that their influence affected Mr Jones's thought in one respect at least. We do not intend to discuss here the part that he played in opposing the ordination of ministers, we will refer to this later.

It cannot be said that Mr Jones contributed much to the literature of his country. He did not consider himself a writer, other than in the sense that every preacher who composes his own sermons is so. In 1784, he published a memoir of Mr Christopher Basset under the title, *A Letter from Dafydd ab Ioan, the Pilgrim, to Ioan ab Gwilym, the Poet, giving a short account of the Life and Death of the Reverend Mr Christopher Basset, Master in the Arts, from Aberthaw, Glamorganshire. Printed in Trefeca.* There is no doubt that Jones, Llan-gan, was the 'Dafydd ab Ioan, the Pilgrim', and that Mr John Williams, St. Athan, the author of the well-known hymn, 'Pwy welaf o Edom yn dod,' etc. was 'Ioan ab Gwilym, the Poet'. His funeral sermon for the Countess of Huntingdon was published in 1791, and the sermon he delivered in the Spa Fields Chapel for the London Missionary Society, in 1797. Many skeletons of his sermons have been published in periodicals at later times.

We have now come to the final years of this faithful minister. He could make use of the apostle's words, 'I have fought a good fight, I have finished my course, I have kept the faith.' In his last years his health greatly deteriorated, the earthen tabernacle was dissolving, but he continued to go about preaching as long as he could. He visited London within two years of his death. During his last illness, he wished to spend a few weeks in the neighbourhood of Llan-gan, his old home. He wrote from there, three months before his death:

> I hope to stay here till Whitsun, and if there is anything I can do for you, I will do it, to the utmost of my ability. I have many things I would love to say to you, if I had time to write, but I am always hurrying from place to place. I wish greatly to see you but, dear friend, you would be amazed how much I am broken up. The last winter was a great tribulation to me. I was wearied by the gout, almost to the grave. I had awful attacks of stomach complaints, but here I am, a trophy of the mercy of the Almighty, able to lift my head yet again! I am such a debtor to heaven's grace. I am now trying to compress my religion into one point – Christ is all. In this way, I am proceeding to end my course on earth, which is short and evil. Belief in Christ is the marrow of faith. He can save to the uttermost. Dear Jesus! Make us yours forever!

David Jones preached in Llan-gan on that Whitsun, and administered the communion for the last time.

It was from Llan-gan that he departed on his last journey. He left the place, as he had intended, on the Tuesday after Whitsun, and travelled in a straight line to Llangeitho, where an Association was to be held, a journey of seventy miles, preaching at various stops on the way according to his custom. He reached Llangeitho at the beginning of August. He preached gloriously before the Association, from the words, 'For my flesh is meat indeed, and my blood is drink indeed.' When the assembly was over, Mr Jones, and the servant looking after him, departed for Manorowen but he broke the journey at Newchapel, Pembrokeshire, and preached again, on the words, 'Come now, and let us reason together, saith the LORD: though your sins be as scarlet, they shall be as white as snow; though they be red like crimson, they shall be as wool.' This was his last sermon. He reached home, tired out, on the Friday, 10 August.

He was visited on Saturday by the Rev. Thomas Harris, Wotton-under-Edge, who was originally from Pembrokeshire. While conversing with him, Jones drew out his journal and read Isaiah 45:24, 'Surely, shall one say, in the LORD have I righteousness and strength.' He had written this sweet verse in his book the previous Thursday. 'This I have, dear Harris,' he said, 'and it is sufficient to strengthen me to face the world to come with ease.' In the afternoon he was told that the friends had announced him to preach at Woodstock the following day. 'They are very forward with me,' he said, 'but no more than they are welcome; if I am here, I will try to go there.' On Saturday night he said to one of the maids, 'Little Lettice, the house is full of servants dressed in heaven's livery who have come to take my soul home. If you brush against some of their wings, don't be frightened, my good girl.' Before dawn on the Sunday morning, 12 August 1810, he had fallen asleep in Jesus, aged seventy-five, and was buried in Manorowen cemetery. He was succeeded in the living of Llangan by a man of completely different spirit, one who had no sympathy for Methodism whatsoever. This put an immediate end to all the great concourses that used to gather at the church.

## 20

# WILLIAM DAVIES OF NEATH; DAFYDD MORRIS OF TWR-GWYN; AND WILLIAM LLOYD OF CAEO

## WILLIAM DAVIES OF NEATH

*W*e can but express our regret that so little is known of many of the leading preachers of the early Methodist period, men of remarkable abilities and of great popularity. They laboured diligently, suffered greatly, and their works no doubt have been carefully recorded in heaven, but very few of their activities were noted in books on earth. Amongst such men, amongst perhaps the greatest of them, must be placed William Davies of Neath. According to the elegy written of him by William Williams, Pantycelyn, he was born about 1727 and was therefore only some ten years younger than the hymn writer, thirteen years younger than Howell Harris, and fourteen years younger than Daniel Rowland. He was therefore in the vanguard of the second generation of preachers. It seems that he was a native of Carmarthenshire. His parents were respectable farmers, living in a house called Stangrach, about half a mile from the Methodist chapel at Llanfynydd. The Methodists used to hold services at Stangrach, so that it is probable that the parents were members of the Connexion. We may presume that they were of comfortable circumstances in that they raised their son to be a priest.

We would be glad to know something of William Davies's youth, particularly the circumstances by which he was awakened to realize his state, and converted to God. But all these have been hopelessly lost to us and we know nothing of him until he appears as an evident Christian, an energetic and popular preacher, and a zealous Methodist, serving as a curate in Neath to a Mr Pinkney, about the year 1757. Williams is again our authority here for he notes, above his elegy, that Davies died, 'in the year 1787, in his sixtieth years of age, having spent over thirty years preaching Christ amongst the Methodists.' At the same time it must be admitted that there is considerable doubt over this date. We have searched the church registers of Neath and Llanilltyd carefully, and the first entry within them signed by William Davies is dated 24 December 1762. It is most improbable that he served there for five years before taking a baptismal or wedding service, particularly as Mr Pinkney did not live in either of his parishes. Perhaps Mr Davies served as curate in some place, or places, before arriving at Neath. It is clear, however, that he came to Glamorganshire some five years before David Jones arrived at Llan-gan.

Mr Pinkney held the livings of Neath and Llanilltyd, but did not live in either place, so that the care and responsibilities of the parishes fell upon the curate. When Mr Davies arrived the state of religion was very low. The Established Church did not have one congregation in attendance anywhere. The services were read to empty walls, while the people spent their lives in frivolities. The Methodist societies in the area were also very meagre; some of them may well have ceased to function. The disruption between Rowland and Harris had taken place some ten years before, the awakening associated with the first publication of William Williams's hymns had not yet taken place, and the religious condition of the whole country was paralysed. But the young curate was ready for work and the love of Jesus was burning in his soul.

As the people would not come to him in the church, he decided that he would go to them in their homes. There he exhorted them seriously and sometimes, standing on a large chair, would preach to them and to any neighbours gathered with them. He ventured also to the open air, to the middle of their games, preaching Christ crucified to the worst of characters. Very soon, there was some commotion amongst the dry bones. The people realized that there was power and life in the church's new curate and they began to gather there to him. Soon, the building could not contain them all.

Neath and Llanilltyd became a kind of Llangeitho but on a smaller scale; the crowds collected there from all directions. The men of Llansamlet in their rustic clothing, their women in their red shawls, would be seen dappling the approach roads on a Sunday morning. Large groups would come from the Swansea Valley, from Creunant and the Vale of Neath, even from Hirwaun, Wrgant and Aberdare. It was said of the Neath and Llanilltyd parishes themselves that half the population, at least, were regular hearers. Hundreds were saved to eternal life. It is thought that it was under William Davies's preaching that the remarkable Jenkin Thomas – 'Siencyn Penhydd'– obtained a view of the way of grace as sufficient for the chief of sinners, when he was almost despairing after hearing a fiery sermon from Iefan Tyclai.

## POPULARITY AND OPPOSITION

According to the unanimous testimony of our fathers, Davies, Neath, was a sweet preacher. He was not often to be found standing on Mount Ebal, proclaiming curses. He rejoiced rather to be on the summit of Gerizim, pouring forth descriptions of the blessings of the gospel. Wounding was not his favourite occupation, but rather, healing – applying the balm of Gilead to the deep wounds of sinners. Howell Harris, towards the end of his life, bore ample testimony to the sweetness of his talents and his ability to explain the comforting doctrines of the gospel. Williams, Pantycelyn, suggests the same in his elegy. In one stanza he depicts the Lord Jesus welcoming Davies to heaven, with the words:

| | |
|---|---|
| All your fare was love and mercy, | Cariad oedd dy fwyd a'th ddiod, |
| Sweetness dropped from every word, | Serchog oedd dy eiriau i gyd, |
| Warmth and kindness worked together | Dy addfwynder sugnodd yspryd |
| To draw many from the world; | Rhai o oerion blant y byd; |
| All your days were spent in labour, | Treuliaist d'amser mewn ffyddlondeb, |
| While you lived on earth below, | Trwy dy yrfa is y nen, |
| I've your crown reserved in heaven, | Mae dy goron geny'n nghadw, |
| Today I'll place it on your brow. | Heddiw gwisg hi ar dy ben. |

While the people gathered to hear Mr Davies and to receive food for their souls from his gospel ministry, there was another class, full of the gall of bitterness, eager to drive him from the parish. This group was made up mainly of the petty gentry of the town and its environs, being excited, no doubt, by the ungodly and untalented clergy of the surrounding parishes. They could find nothing to complain of in his conduct and behaviour, but the sanctity of his life, his passionate zeal for God's glory and the evangelistic ardour of his sermons, were unbearable to them. And above all, he was a Methodist. They therefore sent a memorandum to Mr Pinkney containing a full account of his curate's sins and pleading with him to send the latter away. Whether Mr Pinkney sympathized to any extent with the gospel, we do not know, but he believed in Mr Davies, and saw his worth; and while the Rector was alive, no one was allowed to disturb him. But Mr Pinkney died in 1768 and within two years of this date, the curate was evicted. His last entry in the church books was dated 5 April 1770.

The living of Llan-giwg, a parish about eight miles from Neath, was vacant at the time and an importunate request that William Davies be given it was made. But the great men of the parish were no friends to the gospel and they stood determinedly against him. Promotion in the Established Church at that time, other than by accident, was not a possibility to those who preached God's truth faithfully, particularly so if they tended towards the Methodists. As he was not acceptable to the Church, Mr Davies decided to do what he could outside her walls. He established in a society those who were faithful to him; he went out to the highways and fields; he travelled throughout Wales, north and south, many times and was the means of turning many from the error of their ways.

## GYFYLCHI CHAPEL

It seems that Mr Davies would hold his church services in Neath in the home of Edward Morgan of Penbwchlyd, near the spot where Daniel Rowland preached under a sycamore tree. The success of his ministry meant that this venue became much too small and a meeting-house was made out of two houses on the east side of the town. For a time after he left the Church he found it difficult to make ends meet. For a while he kept a day school, and some of the wealthier Methodists contributed to support him. It is said that a responsible farmer from Llan-giwg, after being disappointed when Davies was refused the living there, continued to support him financially until the day of his death. About the year 1776, the old chapel of Gyfylchi was built, or rather was renovated, for him.

This chapel is quite unique. It stands on a high hill between two deep valleys in St Michael's parish, a little to the east of Neath. In its architecture it is Anglican, and as the Methodist clergy used to administer the sacraments here, it was probably consecrated. It seems therefore to have been an old Anglican chapel that had fallen into ruin and that the Methodists had taken possession of, much as they did with Llanlluan Chapel. The building is formed as if it held two sanctuaries: the holy of holies and the common court. To the holiest would go only the clergymen; from the other, the Connexion ministers would preach. As a rule, an exhorter would address the congregation from the common pulpit at nine in the morning, then, when he had finished, the clergyman would appear at his station and the congregation would turn their heads towards him. This was the arrangement for many years, without any of the unordained preachers venturing to pass through the veil. But at last the spell was broken and the poor preachers were emboldened to enter the holiest place. Even if the building was not originally consecrated formally by a bishop, it was effectively consecrated dozens of times by the visitations of the Chief Bishop, the Lord Jesus. There were services held at Gyfylchi that were never to be forgotten. As well as William Davies, many others of the Methodist clergy ministered there: Jones, Llan-gan; Howells, Tre-hill; Howells, Llwynhelyg (better known as 'Howells, Longacre'); and Phillips, Coychurch. Of the exhorters who preached at the chapel, the most notable was Siencyn Penhydd, to whom we will refer later. He never spoke from the holiest place, but he was certainly within the tabernacle, and he had many remarkable services here. The old believers that used to gather at Gyfylchi were noted for the warmth of their spirit and the fervour of their feelings. Very little unction accompanying a service was needed for them to break out in rejoicing; on hundreds of occasions they danced in sacred delight on the floor of the old chapel, and caused its walls to echo with the sound of their praising. The memories of those glorious meetings still remain warm in the hearts of many of the local inhabitants to the present day. The Methodists worshipped here until 1827, when the chapel at Pontrhydyfen was built. Richard James, also, was connected with the Gyfylchi church when he began preaching, and it was here that he ended his days.

A proof of the extent of the Methodists' esteem for William Davies's ministerial abilities and his skill at applying the Word of life to the converted is seen in the circumstances of the Fishguard Association of 14 February 1770.[1] He was there nominated as superintendent of all the Pembrokeshire societies, as a successor to the Rev. Howell Davies who had just been taken to glory. When we remember the seraphic nature of Howell Davies's ministry and the great respect in which his brethren held him, his successor would have to have been judged as possessing the highest abilities. That Davies was not appointed was due only to the strength of Howell Harris's objections and to his appeal that the brethren be less hasty. Not that Harris either had anything against William Davies, but he wished for more time to judge him, to discern whether the Holy Spirit had fitted him to be a father. It was during Harris's withdrawal that Davies had come to prominence. Harris therefore did not know him so well, and argued for a delay before appointing him to such an important post.

But in his report of the Llangeitho Association held in the August of the same year, we find Harris himself bearing testimony to the excellence of the evangelist from Neath. On that day, Davies had preached after a brother from the Wrexham area. It appears that the latter had had a good service, a strong influence having accompanied his message in which he had described Jesus meeting all the demands of the law and redeeming the sinner's liberty. Christ's Passion was Davies's theme also. His text was 'For Christ also has once suffered for sins, the just for the unjust, that he might bring us to God.' Harris wrote: 'The preacher's ability seemed greater, his light stronger, and his knowledge of the Scriptures more extensive than the first, and there was more unction upon his ministry.' In fact, the evangelist from Neath had completely overcome the vast crowd before him.

When he shouted forth, causing the hills either side of the Aeron valley to echo and re-echo his words, that Christ had taken our place, that all our sins had become his, and that his righteousness had been made ours, the crowd burst into rejoicing, time and time again. The influence was so great that Harris was amazed. 'I stood in silence,' he wrote, 'as I thought how the Lord had prospered them; I saw that Jerusalem was here, and that there was such life, power and remarkable glory here.' This was the last Association on earth that Howell Harris attended. Soon afterwards Davies preached at Trefeca, and Harris received considerable blessing from the service. In his journal he praises the preacher greatly, referring with admiration to his understanding of the doctrines of the gospel, the brilliance of his abilities, his serenity of spirit, and the solemnity that accompanied his appeals to sinners to come to the Son of God.

## ANECDOTES RELATED OF HIM

As we have noted, there is no detailed history of William Davies, so we must be satisfied with relating some of the anecdotes that survive concerning him. He was once announced to preach at Cenarth church. When Captain Lewis, who lived nearby at Gellidywyll, heard this, he sent his servant there with a gun, with the orders that he shoot the preacher. Mr Davies was told of his intention. 'Let me go to the pulpit,' he said, 'and then I will be happy for him to shoot me.' To the pulpit he went, and preached with such sweetness and influence that the whole congregation, the captain's servant included, was one sea of tears. When the servant returned to his master he had only the same excuse to give as was given to the Sanhedrin by the officers sent to arrest Jesus: 'Never man spake like this man.' Some years afterwards, this captain died in circumstances that indicated God's disfavour. His state was so pitiful and his conscience so painful, that even the ungodliest of his friends found it impossible to remain in the same room as him.

But the sweet preacher of Neath did not succeed in every case to overcome the obstacles placed in his way. Once, when journeying in the north, he preached at Betws near Abergele, where a pulpit had been raised for him next to a high stack of firewood and sticks belonging to an old man and his wife, who were confirmed enemies of religion. As he spoke, these two, together with some other irresponsible creatures, who wishing to avenge themselves upon believers, tried to push over the stack with pitchforks from behind so that it would fall upon the preacher's head. He heard the branches rustling and understood what was afoot, but this so confused his thoughts that he could not proceed any further.

A very interesting story about him is given in *Methodistiaeth Cymru;* one which illustrates the self-sacrificing nature necessary at that time even in the most eminent of preachers. It had been arranged that he preach in a mountainous area, somewhere in the south, where the cause was in decline and the people very poor. As he was travelling along the way, and finding the journey long and difficult, he argued with himself in the following way, 'Why have they dealt with me like this? Why arrange to send me to such an obscure spot, along such rough roads?' Having arrived, the view of the place, the houses and the people, served only to increase his discontent. All that could be seen were a few poor houses in the middle of wild and barren mountain slopes. And the chapel where he was to preach was as abject as the surrounding poverty. On his arrival he was led to a miserable cottage where three sisters lived – three old spinsters. One of these took his horse to the stable, another was leading him to the cottage, and the third was preparing the chapel for the service.

By now the preacher's feelings were even more agitated. The circumstances were sufficient to tempt him to conclude that it was too much humiliation for a man of his position to be sent to such a place. This was his frame of mind when the time came to begin the service. A small number gathered, but the preacher was in no mood to appreciate the opportunity to address them. But as he proceeded with the service he became aware of the atmosphere; the reading of the chapter gave him considerable pleasure; there was a heavenly touch in the singing; in the prayer he felt as if his soul had been given an abundant access to God. While preaching, he was in his element; speaking was as easy as breathing. He had a glorious service and at the end he thought not of the poverty of the old sisters, but of their complete commitment to religion. After returning to the cottage, one of the sisters placed before him a small table, about as high as his knee. On it was placed a coarse cloth, but as white as a piece of cambric. She then took up a few potatoes from the peat ash on the hearth, which had been placed there to roast, and after drying them clean and removing their skins, she placed them on the table, asking the gentleman if he would ask God's blessing on their meal. It seems that there was no more to the meal except for a little bread and butter. Mr Davies was amazed. He was experiencing the joint operations of great kindness and great poverty. He felt by now that it was a privilege to visit the place, and he asked the sister who served him what the membership of their society was.

'There is only the three of us,' she answered.

'How is it possible, then, for you keep up the cause?' he asked.

'Each of us has her duties,' she replied. 'One sister looks after the meeting-house, the other the room and horse of the preacher, and I have the privilege of serving him at the table. The three of us meet for a society once a week, leaving the door open for anyone who might wish to join with us.'

As he departed, Mr Davies was offered six pence in recognition of his labours; he demurred, but they would not be refused. They said that the coins were set aside for the Lord's work and that they would not dare use it for anything else. By now, his heart was overflowing. As he journeyed homewards, he rebuked himself, 'You proud devil', for sneering at God's work purely for its low outward appearance. Some years later, he visited them a second time. By this time the church numbered 180 members.

As mentioned, the Rev. William Davies travelled the length and breadth of Wales many times. In his elegy to him, Williams, Pantycelyn, refers to many of his friends, from all parts of the Principality, who having preceded him to heaven were now giving him a welcome. About the year 1780, a notable Association was held at his home town, Neath. Daniel Rowland, his son Nathaniel, Peter Williams, William Williams, and many others were present. They experienced much of the unction of heaven; the dews of grace descended in abundance, and the season was long remembered. William Davies lived for about seven years after this Association. In 1787 he fell asleep in Jesus, when sixty years of age, and was buried in Neath cemetery. Mr Jones, Llan-gan, preached at the funeral and as he ministered at the graveside his feelings overcame him: 'Oh! Dear brother Davies!' he cried out. 'Oh! Davies, Servant of the Lord! You have died! You have descended into the grave with the crown upon your head.' We will close this account with a few stanzas of William's elegy:

Why did death remove so swiftly
Gentle Davies from the field?
Who'll continue in the harvest,
And the reaping sickle wield?
Who will labour as he laboured,
Without murmur or complaint,
Gathering golden sheaves together,
Garnering for heaven the saints?

In his prime, and at his strongest,
Heaven's friend was called away,
Sixty years the time appointed
Here on earth for him to stay;
Then his time to change forever
Friends, relations, earthly gains,

Pam y tynnodd angau diried
Ddavies fwyn oddiwrth ei waith?
Pwy sy i gario ymlaen ei ystod
Aeddfed ar y meysydd maith?
Pwy heb flino, megis yntau,
Ac heb orffwys, gasgla 'nghyd,
Yn ddiachwyn, yn ddiduchan
Feichiau mawrion, trymion yd?

Yn ei rym ac yn ei hoywder,
Galwyd ffrind y nef i'r lan,
Tru'gain mlynedd ar y ddaear
Drefnodd arfaeth idd ei ran;
Yna rhaid oedd iddo newid
Ei berth'nasau, ei ffrins, a'i le,

Leave his body in the churchyard,
Soon to rise, cleansed from all stains.

A rhoi ei gorff i'r ddae'r i gadw
Nes glanhau'i fudreddi e'.

\* \* \* \* \*

There are nearly forty preachers
Home to heaven gathered now,
Who with him proclaimed the gospel
During his career below;
They are singing the same measure,
The same song, with harps of gold,
That the heavenly chorus carolled
To the shepherd boys of old.

Deugain agos o bregethwyr
Oedd e'n nabod yn y nef,
Ac fu'n seinio'r jiwbil hyfryd
Yn ei ddyddiau byrion ef,
Oll a'u t'lynau aur yn canu
Yr un mesur, a'r un gân,
Ag a ganodd y cor nefol
A'r bugeiliaid gwych o'r blaen.

Weep no more for gentle Davies,
Time to turn again to work,
Still the harvest fields are whitening,
God's true heralds must not shirk;
Each one to his field of duty,
Countless others must be told,
He who's faithful with one talent
Will be paid a hundredfold.

Na alerwch mwy am Davies,
Ond dihatrwch at eich gwaith;
Y mae'r meysydd mawr yn wynion,
Mae llafurwaith Duw yn faith;
Pob un bellach at ei arfau
Aml yw talentau'r nef;
Sawl sy'n ffyddlon gaiff ei dalu
Ar ei ganfed ganddo ef.

# DAFYDD MORRIS OF TWR-GWYN

The second name in the title of this chapter is Dafydd Morris, one of the most powerful preachers ever known in Wales. He is generally known as 'Dafydd Morris, Twr-gwyn', but of old he was called 'Dafydd Morris, Lledrod', because it was at Lledrod, Cardiganshire, that he was born, raised, started to preach, and made a name for himself as a preacher. Lledrod is a rural, rather hilly, area in the upper part of Cardiganshire and some eight miles from Llangeitho. Dafydd Morris appears to have been born about 1742. Some nine years before, Daniel Rowland had begun his fiery ministry in Llangeitho. It is very possible that Dafydd Morris, when a young man, had gone to Llangeitho with others from the neighbourhood to hear the *'Ffeirad crac'* ['*mad* or *angry Priest*'] and that it was some arrow from Rowland's bow that wounded him. Whatever the circumstances, he came very early to religion and began to preach when twenty-one years old. His early education was extremely limited, his parents probably were poor, but he worked hard at gaining knowledge and learning, succeeding to a considerable extent. He became a good writer; he had an excellent knowledge of the works of many of the most important theologians; and he could make appropriate use of other English authors. As was the case

724 THE CALVINISTIC METHODIST FATHERS OF WALES

for most of the Methodist preachers of that period, he was a diligent student throughout his life. The itinerating nature of their ministry required that they spend much of their time on horseback, but he ensured that this time was not wasted; he would be continually employed either in reading or in composing sermons.

Dafydd Morris was popular as a preacher from the outset of his ministry. Daniel Rowland, in particular, regarded him highly. He invited him to Llangeitho, to the 'end-of-the-month Sunday', as it was called, to address the thousands that would gather there from all parts of Wales. In his youth he was strikingly handsome – smooth of face, light brown hair, large and lively eyes, and a strong, melodious voice. While still comparatively young, he became unnaturally corpulent. This tendency increased with age, so that, in later years, it was impossible for him to ride on horseback and he had to travel by carriage. We have seen examples in many a Cardiganshire chapel of a wide, old-fashioned chair, capable of holding two people comfortably. This was called a 'Dafydd Morris chair', and it is said that they were made particularly for his use. This obesity was the inspiration of the following verse from the poet Dafydd Ddu of Eryri, written when he was a young, mischievous boy:

By Dafydd Morris I'm perplexed,
There's not, amazing notion,
A better Christian anywhere
Who carries more corruption.
Soon now his righteous soul will fly
To heaven and all its glories,
His body in the grave will lie,
A feast for creepy-crawlies.

Am Dafydd Morris, 'rwyf fi'n syn,
Nid oes, mae hyn yn rhyfedd,
Berffeithiach cristion mewn un plwy',
Yn cario mwy o lygredd.
Ar fyr eheda'i enaid ef,
Yn iach i'r nef fendigaid;
A'i gorff a fydd, yng ngwaelod bedd,
Ddanteithiol wledd i bryfed.

As a preacher he had a profound understanding of the main doctrines of the *ordo salutis*; every sermon of his would contain examples of discerning comment and thought. But his pre-eminent attribute was depth of feeling. The truths he preached would fire his own soul and kindle similar flames in the souls of his hearers. Christmas Evans said of him: 'Dafydd Morris was most influential in the way in which he addressed the consciences and feelings of his hearers. It is difficult to describe the effects which his sermons produced in those exciting days.' A visit by him to a particular locality would be described as the breaking of a storm of thunder and lightning. Listening to him, utterly indifferent and careless men would be dumbstruck, stricken by terrors, as if the Judge himself had appeared. And as the storm passed it would be followed by plentiful showers of gracious rains. As a means for conveying the ardour of his ministry, he had been given a strong, musical voice which was both penetrative and melodious. His son, Ebenezer Morris, had a very similar voice. *Gwilym Hiraethog* once asked Dr Owen Thomas, 'Do you remember Eben Morris?' He replied that he did not. 'Well,' said *Hiraethog*, 'you have never therefore heard a voice.' But the people of old who were familiar with both father and son, insisted that Dafydd's voice excelled even that of his son.

## HE SETTLES AT TWR-GWYN

In the year 1774, he moved from Lledrod to Twr-gwyn. He did so in response to the request of the churches of the Troed-yr-aur valley for him to put aside all secular work and devote himself entirely to the work of the ministry. He would lead their church services and preach also in the week, and they would promise to maintain him. In today's parlance, they were calling him to be a pastor, and he obeyed the call. Religion was in decline in the lower regions of Cardiganshire at this time, though it had once been flourishing. The disruption with Harris had spread its poison over the societies and all aspects of the cause were wilting. But his arrival soon changed things for the better. Powerful impressions accompanied the ministry and many were added to the different churches. The prejudice that existed towards the Methodists in the minds of many was removed, and the numbers attending increased greatly; to such an extent that, within four years, namely in 1778, the meeting-house at Twr-gwyn was much too small and a larger building had to be built.

Some four years after opening the new building a powerful revival broke out. It began on a Sunday morning when Dafydd Morris was preaching, and it spread over the whole region, bringing hundreds to a profession of religion. Though some of these fell away, the vast majority remained faithful, manifesting unmistakeable signs of having been returned to God. It is said that this revival continued for a long period.

We cannot give a complete account of the life of Dafydd Morris – the material is not available. We are dependent on various anecdotes that have survived in different places, but these all confirm the truth that he was a remarkable preacher. Dr Owen Thomas, in order to illustrate his philosophical way of thinking, recites the following story:

> On a Sunday in 1834, Dr Thomas was travelling from Llanllyfni, after the morning service, towards Talsarn. Accompanying him was one of the older brethren of Llanllyfni. To shorten their journey, they crossed a field, at which the older man said:
>
> 'Do you see that stone? Do you know, I saw Dafydd Morris preach here, and he was standing on that stone?'

Dr Thomas was considerably interested.

'Indeed?' he said. 'Do you remember the text?'

'Oh, yes, perfectly well; those words in the Psalm, "The earth is full of the goodness [margin, and in Welsh: 'mercy'] of the Lord"'

'Do you remember anything of the sermon?'

'Yes. I remember that he spoke of mercy in creation; mercy in providence; and mercy in salvation. And when speaking of mercy in creation, I remember that he referred to those who would raise objections in that so much of the earth is barren desert, or unfruitful seas or wild mountains.'

'How did he answer these objections?'

'I don't remember how he replied to the objection as regards the sea,' said the old man, 'but as for the mountains, he said that they were God's chests: "They are God's treasure chests, dear people," he said; " and when he sees his children in need he throws someone the keys so that they may open them."'

It would be difficult to find a stronger proof of astuteness, particularly when we remember that science at the time was in its infancy, and the wealth concealed in the rocks of the mountains was hardly recognized.

## NOTABLE SERVICES

At times, such an incomparable power would accompany his ministry that not even the hardest could stand before it. An account of a remarkable sermon called 'The Sermon on the Great Loss' that he delivered in Pontrhypont, some four miles from Holyhead, can still be heard today in Anglesey. The text was, 'For what is a man profited, if he shall gain the whole world, and lose his own soul? Or what shall a man give in exchange for his soul?' As he considered a soul that was lost, Dafydd Morris was moved to the depths, and cried out to the assembly before him, 'Oh! Oh! Children of the great loss!' He then described the immensity of the loss, and as a refrain at the end of each comment would come the heart-rending cry, 'The great loss!' Because of the strength and penetration of his voice, and the effectiveness with which it was delivered, the people ran towards him from all directions, and as soon as they reached the spot the unearthly solemnity of the preacher, and the power of the shout of 'The great loss!' sobered them immediately, and disturbed them to the point of madness. It is judged that everyone who heard that sermon was saved.

In Owen Thomas's *Life of John Jones, Talsarn*, there is a very interesting anecdote relating to this service. One Sunday night, the late Rev. David Roberts, Bangor, was preaching at Llannerch-y-medd. After the service a society was held, and the preacher went round some of the members

asking them for their experiences. He came to one old sister and thinking he might receive a word from her, asked her how long had she been
in the faith. The old lady could not say. 'But,' she said, 'as a small girl, I
lived close to Pontrhypont, and one day, while on the way somewhere, I
lost my apron. I had gone to look for it and was very upset, on the point
of crying, if not actually crying, because of its loss. While I was searching, I heard a loud powerful voice sounding in my ears, "The great loss!
The great loss!" I thought it was referring to my apron. But I followed
the noise until I arrived at the place. There were many people there, and a
man preaching on the verse, "For what is a man profited, if he shall gain
the whole world, and lose his own soul?" And soon I came to realize that
I was in danger of losing something unspeakably more precious than my
apron. That was the time that I began with religion. And that preacher
was Dafydd Morris.' A sermon that produced such an impression on a
young girl's mind, as well as upon the adults present, that she and they
forgot every other loss when confronted with '*The* great loss', must surely
have been powerful indeed.

Another, equally remarkable, sermon was preached by him at Llanarmon
Dyffrynceiriog. He was preaching under a large tree in the farmyard of
Sarphle, on the text, 'Give an account of thy stewardship; for thou mayest
be no longer steward.' Under the effects of this sermon it is said that all
were either rejoicing or weeping, either praising or praying. The preacher
cried out, with all the authority of eternity in his voice, 'Give an account
of thy stewardship!' and, with the sense of the final accounting upon
them, the hardest of men trembled and their knees quaked; the stoniest
of hearts melted as wax before the fire. Such a scene had never before
been witnessed in that locality and the pagans of the place could give no
account for it, other than that some attack of lunacy had fallen abruptly
upon the hearers.

We have already noted that he was a great traveller. For years, he would
take four journeys a year to Anglesey, Caernarvonshire and other counties in the north. He was as well-known in the north as in the south, and
the expectancy for his coming, and the hunger to hear him, would be
great. Very rarely would an Association be held without a sermon from
him. On his travels, he encountered all kinds of difficulties and received
varying kinds of welcome at different places. When journeying once in
Denbighshire, travelling from Pont Uchel to Adwy'r-clawdd, he found
that the announcement of his coming had not been delivered at Adwy.
As this was his first visit to this area, nobody there knew him. However,
he came across a number of women who professed religion and told them

that he was a preacher from south Wales. He asked if it was possible to send round a message in the locality and collect a congregation. At this point an elder arrived who asked him rather scornfully, 'Who are you? Is it worth collecting the people for you?' The man appeared to be of doubtful temper and rather bitter spirit. But a congregation was eventually gathered. Dafydd Morris began to preach and immediately it was recognized that no ordinary man was amongst them. Soon, an irresistible power was felt; the people were swept by his words like a forest before a tempest; the deepest feelings of the heart were poured forth in loud groans and rivers of tears. The sour old elder was as overcome as everyone else. At the close of the service, he went up to the preacher and apologized, saying, 'Dafydd Morris *bach*, I hope you will forgive my treatment of you before the meeting.' He replied, 'I can see that you are a dog. Before the meeting you were showing your teeth; now you are wagging your tail.' In this, his discernment was evident, because the man was soon to turn his back on the society and would end his days in open immorality and an opposer of the gospel.

He suffered many persecutions and, on many occasions, was remarkably delivered by the Lord. He was once preaching at Berthengron and a large crowd had gathered. At the beginning of the meeting a number of rough-looking men were seen approaching. They were clearly prepared to disrupt the worship and to injure any who attempted to stop them. But as they neared the house, their leader, though on firm, level ground, suddenly fell and broke his leg. The mob had sufficient work to do to tend to the injured man, and Dafydd Morris was able to proceed with the proclamation of the gospel. Another time he was in Caernarvonshire and visited Gwastadnant, where preaching services were occasionally held. Unfortunately, the man of the house was away and his wife was opposed to the gospel. When the preacher knocked at the door and asked if they were expecting a stranger, she answered bad-temperedly, 'No; all that there is here is a collection of poor people trying desperately to raise their children.' Her tone was so bitter that Dafydd Morris judged it wiser to leave. He therefore had no lodging for himself or his horse, and spent the whole night out on the mountainside between Llanberis and Llanrug.

It is thought that he was the preacher of whom a story is related in Llangynog, Montgomeryshire. He stood to declare the Word near an inn door. Opposite him, on the other side of the road, were three trees growing at the side of a river. Soon after he had started preaching, a drunken man passed by who started shouting out at the end of every sentence from the preacher, 'He's lying!' Dafydd Morris suffered this for a while, but as the man continued with his shouting and threatenings, his spirit was aroused, and he said to the crowd around him, 'Listen! Those three trees will bear testimony against that man on Judgment Day, unless retribution overtakes him before then.' The people noted his remark, and it was soon brought to their notice again when the drunkard fell over a wall in his drunkenness one dark night, and was drowned. And this took place only a few paces away from the spot where the preacher had stood. As the Bible says, 'Be not over much wicked, neither be thou foolish: why shouldest thou die before thy time?'

He is described as preaching in Amlwch, Anglesey, before the first chapel there was built. He was ministering in the open air because the concourse that had gathered was too much for any house. He stood before the gable-end of the house of the old preacher, William Roberts, the cobbler. There was a rather large and dirty lake near the house. At the time, a farmer living in the neighbourhood was full of wrath against the Methodists. On hearing of the meeting to be held in the town, this man decided to attend in order to mock the preacher and disturb the meeting. He came to town on his horse, intending to ride through the congregation, scattering and confusing them. He thought it would be amusing to see the disorder amongst the poor people who had gathered. But when he approached them, his horse, for all the rider's efforts, insisted on turning towards the lake and when he had got there he threw his rider off his back and into the water. He then lay over on him so that he could not move. The onlookers thought that he would be drowned and cried out for someone to rescue him. 'Oh, no,' said one old woman, more from anger than grace, most probably, 'Leave him alone; if the Lord has seen fit to take him there, that is probably his place.' Some imagine that she had that verse in mind, 'A man that doeth violence to the blood of any person shall flee to the pit; let no man stay him' (*Prov.* 29:17). However, others rushed into the water and dragged the poor man out, not much the worse for wear except that he was considerably dirtier. The persecutor was disappointed; instead of amusement he had received pain; instead of disturbing the means of grace the people had ample opportunity to listen without anyone daring to interfere further.

Dafydd Morris was the first of the Methodists to preach in Beaumaris. He stood on the highway, but had little peace there. Stones and dung were thrown at him, and such a disturbance arose that he was forced to stop. Dafydd Morris's voice was loud and as clear as a bell and he was brave of heart, but it seems that there was amongst the Methodists in the town a man, William Lewis, of even louder voice. When the disturbers had overcome the preacher from the south, he stood up bravely in his place and rebuked the people for their behaviour towards a stranger who had travelled far in the hope of doing good. This quietened the mob to some extent, and opportunity was given to complete the service. If Dafydd Morris had written a detailed journal of all that happened to him, the persecutions he suffered and the deliverances he experienced, as did Howell Harris, it would read like a chapter of a romance rather than a piece of history.

*Methodistiaeth Cymru* provides an interesting timetable of his engagements in Caernarvonshire during one journey in 1771:

> 23 November, 1771: 12 pm – Waunfawr; evening – Llwyncelyn.
>
> Tuesday: 2 pm – Llanllyfni, and a private society.
>
> Wednesday: 10 am – Tynewydd; evening – Bryn-y-gadfa.
>
> Thursday: 12 pm – Nefyn; evening – Tudweiliog.
>
> Friday: 10 am – Tymawr; afternoon at 3 – Lon-fudr.
>
> Saturday: 12 pm – Saethonbach.
>
> Sunday: morning – Pwllheli; 2 pm – Cricieth;.
>
> Monday: 10 am – Brynengan; 5 pm – private society at Y Garn.

These, probably, are all the preaching stations maintained by the Methodists in Caernarvonshire at the time, and if so, the progress of the work there must have been very slow.

In the same book is found the summary of an itinerary made in Cardiganshire about the year 1789, that is, about two years before his death. The summary also contains the texts from which he preached at each venue.

| *18 July 1789* | Twr-gwyn Chapel | Isaiah 4:3. |
| | Glynyrhedyn | Luke 1:74. |
| | Cardigan | Canticles 7:1. |
| | St Dogmaels | Luke. |
| | Llechryd | 1 Corinthians 3:21–22. |
| | Tre-main | Luke 1:47. |
| | Morfa Uchaf | 1 Corinthians 3:21–22, in a funeral. |

| *To the Llangeitho Association* | | |
| | At the Association | Canticles 7:1. |
| | Llanddewibrefi | 1 Corinthians 3:21–22. |
| | Tregaron | Acts 16:30–31. |

| | |
|---|---|
| Swyddffynnon | Hebrews 6:7–8. |
| Lledrod | 1 Corinthians 3:21–22. |
| Llangwyryfon | Luke 1:74. |
| Llanbadarn Fawr | Hebrews 4:3. |
| Aberystwyth | Acts 16:30–31. |
| Rhydyfelin | Zechariah 12:10. |
| Llanrhystyd | Phillipians 3:20–21. |
| Llan-non | Hebrews 2:3. |
| Pennant | Acts 16:30–31. |
| Llannarth | Hebrews 2:3. |
| Geuffos | Zechariah 12:10. |

One interesting fact disclosed in this list is that Dafydd Morris was preaching in an Association held in his own home county. This was a year before Daniel Rowland died, and no doubt the latter was involved in the arrangement. It is said that he had as many as seven different sermons on Acts 16, verses 30–31. He continued to compose new sermons throughout his life; this was, it seems, an easy task for him. The author of *Methodistiaeth Cymru* says that in 1789, two years before Dafydd Morris died, he saw seven sermons of his, written within six weeks. There is nothing to suggest that this was in any way unusual. Mr John Jones, Newcastle Emlyn, states that he heard him on twenty-seven occasions in one year, and that each time he had a new sermon. The skeletons of his sermons that survive do not reveal anything remarkable in form or content, their main feature is their scripturalness. No doubt many of his most brilliant thoughts would strike him as he preached, when his spirit was at its most fervent as he handled divine truths.

We have already shown examples of Dafydd Morris as a wise discerner of men. An occasion in Llansamlet provides another example and demonstrates also his particular authority to rule and discipline when it was necessary. At Llansamlet lived Llewellyn John, a bright Christian of exemplary character. He was gifted in public prayer and would often accompany ministers in order to lead the devotions before a service. He once travelled through north Wales with Jones, Llan-gan. In his old age, Llewellyn Jones had become very poor. The society had decided to support him with weekly contributions, but the decision had engendered jealousy and strife. The chief troublemaker was Beni the cobbler. Because of the bad feeling, it was decided to send delegates to them to re-establish order. In the meantime, Dafydd Morris had visited the area. After the service, in the church meeting, the brethren lay the matter before him. Right at the beginning of the discussion, Beni gestured to Dafydd Morris to read the third chapter of 2 Thessalonians that contains the words, 'If a man will not work, let him not eat.' 'No, I will not,' was the reply, 'You read it yourself, if you insist.' Beni did so, and referred to it again during the discussion as providing a complete adjudication on the matter. By now, Mr Morris's spirit was up, he could not hold back, and poor Beni's fate was sealed. 'Listen, you devil,' he said, 'Are you applying that verse to this godly old man? You are a schismatic, and those are schismatics who are in league with you. Out you go! You and them!' The Rev. Hopkin Bevan was at the meeting and he used to say that he had never, before or since, been in such an awe-filled meeting. It felt as if the very floor of the chapel shook with the authority accompanying Dafydd Morris's words. The trouble-maker soon joined up as a soldier, and peace was restored to the society.

As well as being a noble preacher, Dafydd Morris was an eminent hymn writer, and many of his verses are included in the present hymnal of the Methodists. He published a small collection of his hymns before leaving Lledrod, and the title-page notes that it was printed in Carmarthen in 1773. The author was therefore only twenty-nine years old. The book's title was *Can y Pererin Cystuddiedig* [*The Song of the Afflicted Pilgrim*]. In the Introduction is written:

Let him into whose possession these hymns should come, know that I never intended that they should be printed, and that I have no desire for making my name known by publishing them. But as I remembered those rich men who cast into the treasury of their abundance, I felt some obligation that I should contribute my two mites. Furthermore, in giving out one or two verses in Christian services and finding some hungry children being awakened by this poor food, the Lord shining upon them through the means, I thought it a sin in me to keep the barley bread from hungry souls. This is my only purpose in placing them before you in this form. If you receive a blessing through reading or singing them, give the praise to God, and pray for me, who am your companion in affliction.

DAFYDD MORRIS

The words in italics suggest that the author was in ill health at the time. Certainly, there was no need for him to apologize for publishing the book, nor any need to call his hymns 'poor food' or 'barley bread'. The 'spirit of the living creature' is in many of them and they will continue to be sung while Welshmen praise their God. Amongst others, Dafydd Morris wrote the hymns:

'Brethren who have gone before me'      'Mae brodyr i mi aeth ymlaen,'

| | |
|---|---|
| 'If Mara's waters we must drink.' | 'Os rhaid yfed dyfroedd Mara,' |
| 'Gracious Sovereign, will you aid us,' | 'Arglwydd grasol, dyro gymorth,' |
| 'After midnight, comes the dawning?' | 'A ddaw gwawr ar ol y plygain?' |

If his muse is not as lofty as that of Williams, his hymns are notable for their scriptural nature and their solemnity.

## HIS WIFE AND FAMILY

Dafydd Morris was an exceptionably loving-hearted man and of tender affections. He exercised hospitality on a large scale, as there was opportunity to do in those days. His wife, Mary, one of the kindest women on earth, if anything, excelled him in this respect. No week would pass without some 'speaker' visiting Twr-gwyn, and on some weeks there might be four or five, for this was the age of the itinerant. They all usually lodged at Dafydd Morris's house and Mrs Morris would be in her element serving them. She would respect them all, those of lesser ability as well as the brightest stars; the ignorant and the learned. She respected the least talented as an ambassador of God. She died in 1788 at a comparatively young age, and William Williams, Pantycelyn, composed an elegy on the occasion. It suggests that she possessed no great shining gifts, but that she excelled in godliness and kindness. The following are a few of its stanzas:

| | |
|---|---|
| Now the mighty congregation | O galared y gyn'lleidfa |
| Weeps at news that grieves them all, | Fawr, luosog, faith, am hyn, |
| All who meet to share communion | Sydd yn bwyta bara'r bywyd |
| Within Twr-gwyn Chapel's walls; | O fewn capel y Twr-gwyn; |
| Lost – a mother, sister, matriarch, | Collwyd mam, a chwaer, a mamaeth, |
| Lost – a wife and partner true, | Collwyd gwraig garuaidd wiw; |
| Making up for such privation | Ac nid oes all lanw'r golled, |
| Only God himself could do. | Ond yr Hollalluog Dduw. |
| | |
| If by Providence's pathway – | Os rhagluniaeth drefna i mi – |
| Though it might not ever be – | F'allai fyth fydd hyny'n bod – |
| In my journeys with the gospel, | Wrth gyhoeddi'r 'fengyl olau, |
| I should Dafydd's cottage see, | I dy Dafydd Morris ddod; |
| And there Mary's absence strike me, | A gweld Mary'n eisiau yno, |
| Then I know that bitter tears | Gwn y tyn afonydd hallt |
| From my eyes would flow as rivers, | O fy llygaid, fel o greigydd, |
| Though I'm old and full of years. | Er mor wynned yw fy ngwallt. |

Dafydd was greater far than Mary,
Greater to a vast degree,
Greater in talents, greater in knowledge,
Greater in office than was she;
But for loving, and for caring,
For a welcome from the cold,
There was no one quite like Mary,
Not one wife throughout the world.

Mwy yw Dafydd ym mhob ystyr,
Uwch na Mary raddau heb ri',
Mwy talentau, mwy arddeliad,
Godidocach swydd na hi;
Ond am garu, ymgeleddu,
Gwneud y rheidus oer yn glyd,
Yr oedd Mary'n abl ateb,
Neb rhyw wraig o fewn y byd.

When a preacher on his travels,
From the north or south or east,
Came to Twr-gwyn with his message,
Came to spread the gospel feast;
Then no matter what his talent,
Whether glorious, poor, or fair,
He'd receive from Mary Morris
Warmest welcome, love, and care.

Doed pregethwyr fan y deuant,
Gogledd, de, neu ddwyrain bell,
I'r Twr-gwyn, gyhoeddi allan
Bur newyddion Juwbil well;
O ba ddwg, o ba dalentau,
O ba raddau, o ba ddawn,
Hwy gaen' ffeindio Mary Morris,
O garueiddiwch pur yn llawn.

Dafydd and Mary Morris had three children, Theophilus, Eleazar and Ebenezer. Death carried away the first two while still in their youth, but the third, Ebenezer, became one of the brightest stars of the pulpit and the name 'Eben Morris' is still dear to the nation today. His life will be dealt with later. Dafydd Morris's life was a short one; he was a candle burning brightly, quickly burning to the socket. On 17 September 1791, he was called away from his work to his reward when only forty-seven years old, and having been preaching for some twenty-six years. His remains were laid, with many tears, in Troed-yr-aur cemetery. We should remember that though he lived at the same time as the first Methodist Fathers – Daniel Rowland died about a year before him; Williams, Pantycelyn, about eight months before him; Peter Williams survived him; he was a fellow-labourer of Howell Harris and Howell Davies – yet, in the midst of these mighties, he still won for himself a name as a preacher of the greatest magnitude, a name which was familiar throughout Wales, north and south. And as he turned many to righteousness, he must be today, as the Scripture says, one of the brightest stars in heaven's firmament.

## WILLIAM LLOYD OF CAEO

The third name in the title of this chapter is that of William Lloyd of Caeo, Carmarthenshire. As with many of the early Methodist preachers, Mr Lloyd came from a respectable family of free-holders. They were related to the Llwyd, or Lloyd, family of Briwnant, who still live at

Briwnant, between Caeo and Pumsaint, and are considered amongst the nobility of Carmarthenshire. His father was Dafydd Lloyd who lived at Blaenclawdd, near Caeo. William was born in 1741, that is, about six years after the beginning of the Methodist revival, and two years before the first Association at Watford. When he was a small boy, playing around his mother's feet, Rowland and Harris were setting Wales aflame and, under God's blessing effecting a revolution in the moral condition of the times. It would seem that some of the sparks of their ministry must have landed on William as a boy, because he states that he was under some measure of conviction and anxious over his spiritual condition, when only seven years old. This must have been due to some influence arising more or less directly from the early ministry of the Reformers. Of the circumstances of his boyhood we know very little, except that he had a better education than most and spent some time in the school of the Rev. Owen Davies, a minister with the Dissenters. When he was eighteen, he heard Peter Williams preach and under that ministry his convictions deepened to such an extent that the things of the soul took precedence over all other matters in his thoughts. Thomas Charles describes him:

Before this, his convictions in comparison were dead and ineffective, revealing and sentencing him as guilty, but without bringing him to flee from the wrath to come nor placing that cry in his soul, 'What must I do to be saved?' But the preaching of that laborious minister, the Rev. P. Williams, affected him to the quick, revealing to him all the depths of his sinfulness and his consequent misery, and convicting him that to save one's soul is the most important matter in the whole world.

The young man suffered the weight of soul-conviction for some time; he dwelt under Sinai and the sound of its thunders. For a year the terrors of law filled his soul and he could find no peace anywhere. The instrument for his deliverance was Evan Jones, an exhorter from Lledrod, Cardiganshire. We know nothing of this man except for finding his name in a list of Rowland's exhorters. Whether he was naturally gifted as a speaker, or whether he was of very little ability, we do not know, but he was blessed to pour the balm of the gospel on to the deep wounds of William Lloyd, and the young man was Christ's servant from then onwards.

He hastened to join Christ's church. According to Mr Charles, he threw in his lot with the Dissenters in the locality, which would almost certainly mean the congregation at Crug-y-bar. Mr Charles further suggests that the reason why he did so was that there was no Methodist society within reach, and that the Caeo society was not formed until 1760. This can hardly be correct for the Trefeca records show that there was a strong society of forty-four members in Caeo as early as 1743, under the leadership of James Williams. Mr Hughes, the author of *Methodistiaeth Cymru*, suggests that this society died out, or was considerably weakened, during the period of Harris's defection and of the resultant strife. 'During this time,' he says, 'many of the early exhorters stayed their hands; the momentum of the organizational structure set up by the Reformers was confused, and many of the small church groups collected together during the previous years were scattered.' Very probably, this is what happened at Caeo, with the cause being restarted about the year 1760.

William Lloyd was not long with the Independents at Crug-y-bar. It was by means of the Methodists that he was brought to know the Saviour, and it was with them that he wished to settle. Therefore, when the cause began again at Caeo, although they were only about eighteen in number, he joined the fellowship immediately. Not that there was any ill-feeling at all between him and the Independent church; he was on friendly terms with them and their pastor throughout his life. Since being made a new man, he had a thirst for spiritual nourishment and found it, so it appears, mainly through the ministry of Daniel Rowland. For the rest of his days he journeyed monthly to Llangeitho, unless circumstances forbade him; and together with so many like him he profited abundantly from the spiritual delights that were poured out for them. When he was twenty-two years old he decided to give himself fully to the work of the gospel, and very quickly he became popular. His main characteristic as a preacher was fire, together with a strong and melodious voice. He was himself of quick emotions and notably fiery, and the tendency of his ministry was to fire others. Nothing could stand before him once the wind was behind him. He would spread his sails before the breezes, and his vessel would be carried away gloriously. His intentions were not so much to enlighten the mind as to touch the heart. He could not be compared to Rowland and Harris as far as the discernment of the deep things of God was concerned, and he was far below them in terms of content and thought, but he had his own special gift, a gift completely different from that of anyone else, and he was blessed to the recovery of hundreds to Christ. Said Mr Charles:

> There was a nobility and every kind of excellence in the preaching of Mr Daniel Rowland: a depth of content; a power and sweetness of voice; a clarity and liveliness in declaring the deep things of God; all of which would amaze and produce the greatest effect in his hearers. Mr Lloyd was more superficial, but evangelical, reviving, delightful and very melting, and what is more – the crown on all his other strengths – God gave him unction and much success in all his labours.

He married the daughter of John Jones of the Black Lion, Llansawel, and they went to live at Henllan, a farm near Caeo. Mrs Lloyd was a woman of evident godliness, and of a fiery spirit. In her own way she was just as notable as her husband. Mr Lloyd would travel much; he often visited every part of Wales. And generally Mrs Lloyd would travel with him as a companion. It is said that she would begin services for him. In the warmth of his feelings, Mr Lloyd would often break out into praise for Jesus in the middle of his sermon, and his wife would participate in the heavenly joy, jumping and praising in the body of the church. We heard of him that he once retired to the chapel house leaving the congregation rejoicing gloriously, and in their midst, his wife. In a little while a deacon came to him, saying, 'Mrs Lloyd is praising gloriously in the meeting-house.' 'Let her be,' was the answer, 'She is a very clever one. She never launches her vessel on to the waves, nor raises sail, except when the wind is with her, but as for me, I often have to sail against the winds and waves.' Some time after this, if we are not mistaken, the Association recorded a degree of unwillingness for preachers to take their wives with them on their itineraries, in that it was often awkward to arrange appropriate lodging for them.

Clearly, 'Lloyd of Caeo' possessed very appropriate gifts for the age in which he lived. He soon became one of the most popular preachers. Mr Charles provides this further comment, 'He was in every way winning: his person was handsome; his gestures seemly; his voice melodious; and his oratory, lively, sonorous and appropriate.'

He must have been a natural orator; and when this is combined with such a liveliness of spirit, it is no surprise that he became so popular as a preacher and that the country flocked to hear him. Although he could at times preach a convicting sermon, his main themes were Christ and his salvation, the riches of grace, the extent of the promises, the willingness of divine mercy to embrace the vilest and most wretched of sinners.

| | |
|---|---|
| Lover of peace, conciliator, | Tangnefeddwr, carwr heddwch, |
| Kind healer of the flock was he; | Meddyg mwyn at glwyfau'r gwan; |
| But a heavy leaded bludgeon | Ond dwrn o blwm ar ben rhagrithiwr, |
| To beat down all hypocrisy. | I'w guro i lawr, i'w gael i'r lan. |

In his days, Wales was blessed with many powerful revivals. We have already referred, when giving the history of Howell Harris, to the awakening that swept the country in 1763, when William Williams's hymns were first published. William Lloyd was witness to six other similar revivals. These occurred in 1773, 1780, 1789, 1790, 1794, and 1805. In all of these

Mr Lloyd took an active part. He fed the young with the sincere milk of the word; as a faithful shepherd he cared for them; and he maintained a steady discipline over them. According to Mr Charles:

> His discretion, carefulness, wisdom and, particularly, his faithfulness, when dealing with people's conditions, were immensely valuable. No one was more acceptable than he in his own county, and the fact that he was asked to preach William Williams's funeral sermon is a proof of the regard that his brethren had for him.

He continued to minister for about forty-five years, preaching much in his own neighbourhood and throughout Wales. He remained popular to the end and without a stain on his character. In his last years, he was considered one of the Fathers of the Connexion, and rightly so. On the last Sunday of his life, he preached in Llanddeusant and Llansadwrn. He came home unwell, and after five days of illness finished his race on 17 April 1808, when 67 years of age. The Lord granted him his request of being allowed to die without long illness. Throughout his short confinement his mind was perfectly calm, resting entirely on the merits and faithfulness of Jesus Christ. When one of the brethren asked him his opinion of the doctrine that he had preached for so many years, he replied, 'I am venturing my life upon it to all eternity.' His mortal remains were taken from Henllan, where he had lived for most of his life, to the cemetery at Caeo, and there he was laid to rest until the sounding of the trumpet.

The same comment made of Dafydd Morris would be true also of William Lloyd, namely, that he gained a name as a popular preacher in the days of Daniel Rowland, Williams, Pantycelyn, and Jones, Llan-gan, and that this is proof enough that his abilities were far above the usual and that he had an extraordinary gift for communicating the gospel.

---

[1] See pp. 637–8.

# A RELATED TITLE FROM THE
# BANNER OF TRUTH TRUST

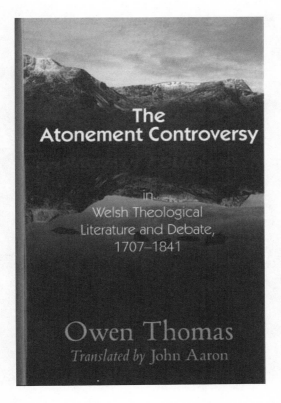

The
Atonement Controversy

in
Welsh Theological
Literature and Debate,
1707–1841

Owen Thomas
*Translated by* John Aaron

'Wales stands out as an example of high theological culture. Though small, and with very limited wealth, this land produced a host of sound preachers and theologians, and a plentiful literature. The learning and theological acumen of the Welsh preachers led to vigorous literary debates on the Atonement and its bearing on the content of evangelism. Because the highly-polished and prolific literature of Wales was produced in Welsh, English-speakers have remained ignorant of much valuable writing. The ministry of Dr Martyn Lloyd-Jones wakened many to some realization of the richness of the Welsh tradition; perhaps this book will help increase interest in Welsh theological writing . . . As usual, this Banner of Truth book is beautifully printed and designed, giving the reader a warm encouragement to delve into its pages. That the contents demand careful, even laborious, reading and thought, only increases its value. It is well worth the cost.'

ENGLISH CHURCHMAN

ISBN-13: 978 0 85151 816 9, 432 pp., clothbound

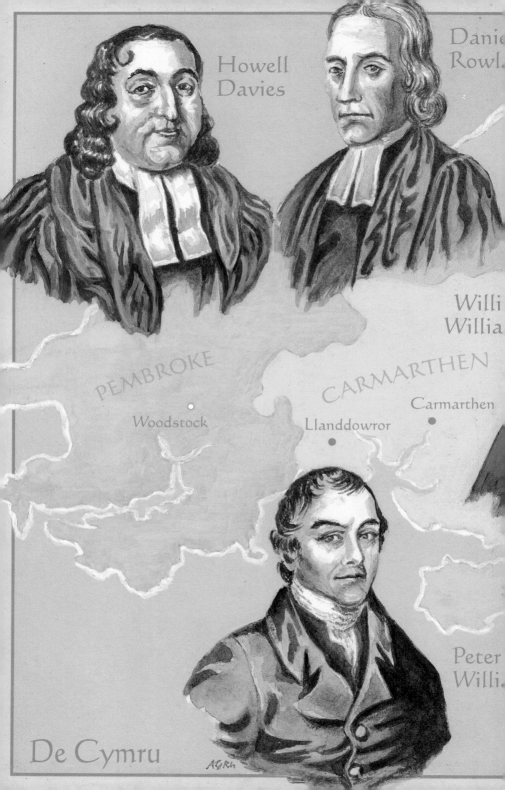

Howell
Davies

Danie
Rowl.

Willi
Willia

PEMBROKE

CARMARTHEN

Carmarthen

Woodstock

Llanddowror

Peter
Willi.

De Cymru